HISTORY OF THE MILITIA AND THE NATIONAL GUARD

HISTORY OF THE MILITIA AND THE NATIONAL GUARD

John K. Mahon

THE MACMILLAN WARS OF THE
UNITED STATES

Louis Morton, *General Editor*

Macmillan Publishing Company
A Division of Macmillan, Inc.
NEW YORK
Collier Macmillan Publishers
LONDON

Macmillan Publishing Company
A Division of Macmillan, Inc.
866 Third Avenue, New York, N. Y. 10022

Collier Macmillan Canada, Inc.

Library of Congress Catalog Card Number: 82-24902

Printed in the United States of America

printing number
1   2   3   4   5   6   7   8   9   10

Library of Congress Cataloging in Publication Data

Mahon, John K.
    History of the militia and the National Guard.

    (The Macmillan wars of the United States)
    Bibliography: p.
    Includes index.
    1. United States—Militia—History. 2. United States
—National Guard—History. I. Title. II. Series.
UA42.M33 1983   355.3'7'0973   82-24902
ISBN 0-02-919750-3

Contents

	ACKNOWLEDGMENTS	vii
	INTRODUCTION	1
Chapter One	The English Background	6
Chapter Two	Militia in the Colonies	14
Chapter Three	The American Revolution	35
Chapter Four	Militia in the Early National Period	46
Chapter Five	Jeffersonian Militia and The War of 1812	63
Chapter Six	Decline of the Militia; Rise of the Volunteers	78
Chapter Seven	Civil War	97
Chapter Eight	Reconstruction; Birth of the National Guard	108
Chapter Nine	The War with Spain	125
Chapter Ten	Reorganization, 1900-1916	138
Chapter Eleven	The National Guard in World War I	154
Chapter Twelve	The National Guard Between World Wars	169
Chapter Thirteen	World War II	184
Chapter Fourteen	The Immediate Postwar Period	198
Chapter Fifteen	The Eisenhower Administrations	214
Chapter Sixteen	The Turbulent 1960s	228
Chapter Seventeen	The Guard in the 1970s	248
Chapter Eighteen	Conclusion	260
	APPENDIX	268
	ABBREVIATIONS	270
	NOTES	272
	BIBLIOGRAPHY	323
	INDEX	357

Acknowledgments

I am indebted to the Center of Military History, Department of the Army, for the opportunity to learn more about the American military institution in the three-and-one-half years I worked for it (it was then known as the Office of the Chief of Military History) than I could have learned elsewhere in twice that time. It was a great opportunity for me to serve one year as visiting professor at the United States Army Military History Institute, where I had access to one of the finest collections of material on U.S. military history in this country, or any country. There I also had the help of a staff that worked tirelessly to be of service. I am grateful to the National Guard Association for permitting me to select from its picture files many of the illustrations appearing herein.

I owe a great obligation to the late Frederick Porter Todd, who was fascinated by the citizen soldier, was a fine scholar of him, and who encouraged me to work in this vast and, to a great degree, unexplored area. I am also grateful to the late Victor Gondos for encouragement. I have never met Jim Dan Hill or Elbridge Colby, or Martha Derthick or William H. Riker, but their pioneer work has been indispensable to my own efforts. I did long ago meet R. Ernest Dupuy, now deceased, and owe him a debt too. For the most part, I appear to owe people I do not know personally. I have studied all the doctoral dissertations on the militia and the National Guard that I could learn about, and all of those writers, cited in the Notes and Bibliography, have helped along the study of the citizen soldier.

John K. Mahon
Gainesville, Florida
June 1980

Introduction

This study deals with the ways in which the United States has turned citizens into temporary soldiers to supplement its professional military forces in time of war. Such a focus requires consideration of the following modes of procuring men for active duty: (1) calling reserves into federal service; (2) drawing volunteers from the eligible population; and (3) drafting men from the same source. However, the only reserve systems considered here are those that have always had a dual political connection; with the states on the one hand, and with the national government on the other. Throughout, the term *militia* applies to these systems, and during the last one hundred years, *National Guard* has been the term applied to the organized portion of the militia.

Militia was a form of universal military training (UMT) for men of suitable age and health, shaped and operated first by colonies and then by states, or by locales within them. By the turn of the twentieth century, compulsion to back up UMT had been factored out of the system in practice, but in law the militia was still defined as the able-bodied portion of the population, aged 17-45, with a few specific exceptions.[1] There have been several organized efforts in this century to enforce UMT in practice, but they have all failed.

The militia—usable only for limited tours of active duty within limited geographical boundaries—was a defense system only. It was supposed to have the advantage of putting into service units composed of men who had developed some esprit de corps by training together in time of peace. Actually, however, militia companies, battalions, and regiments rarely entered active service intact. Instead, they became the pools from which authorities could obtain volunteers or draftees.

1

The individuals thus drawn from their units then formed into new units, under officers with whom they were not familiar. If they learned any unit cohesion, it had to be after the formation of the new companies, battalions, and regiments.

During the colonial era, a volunteer segment of the militia developed, consisting of the arms too expensive for the ordinary citizen: cavalry, artillery, and elite types of infantry. If the volunteer units offered themselves for active duty intact, they could escape the limitations of the compulsory militia and thus could engage in offensive operations. It is the volunteer militia from which the National Guard sprang, and that is why for generations Guardsmen were all volunteers. This ceased to be so in the two World Wars. Guard divisions, it is true, entered both wars intact, but, being below strength, they had to be diluted with thousands of draftees. Later, in the era of the Cold War, dilution came in a different form: individual rotation. At the end of one year's service in Korea or Vietnam, a Guardsman could return home, and his place at the front would be taken, most probably, by a draftee. When the draft ended in 1973 and the All-Volunteer Force was substituted (AVF), it seemed that the Guard was on the road back to the volunteer principle. In the early 1980s, numbers fell off so much that Guard leadership began to demand a return to some level of conscription.

If every volunteer unit in the militia/National Guard had entered federal service in the mass wars—the Civil War and World Wars I and II—there would still have been a need for much more manpower. Volunteers were welcomed into the armies of the Civil War, but both sides had to inaugurate a draft. Expansion by volunteers reached its peak during the War with Spain, in part because the conflict was very popular. It remained popular because it was quickly over.

Even when volunteer militia units entered federal service intact, they seldom were permitted to stay intact. First, to reach required strength they had to suffer dilution with drafted men in large numbers; second, in the two World Wars they were required to transfer many of their officers and technicians to outside units and to discharge some of their skilled people due to age or physical unfitness. Whole battalions were transferred out to fill gaps in drafted divisions or to serve as units independent of divisions. What was left in the end was no more than the unit designation and such esprit de corps as a few officers, who had not been transferred, might have been able to salvage.

The National Guard never ceased to insist on induction not of its individuals but of its units, and on maintenance of the integrity of those units once in service. Otherwise, the leaders argued, all the cohesion developed through training together was lost and wasted. Finally, in the 1970s, they appeared to receive some guarantees that this would be the federal policy; still, the doubts in their minds did not dissipate. Their skepticism sprang from awareness that the major pool of trained personnel existed in the units of the reserves, especially the National Guard. In crises the need for pretrained individuals would, as in the past, become very great, and the federal commanders would be likely to do what they had done before, that is, lift the men they wanted out of their organizations, and let the reduced units limp along the best way they could.

The fear of standing forces—brought to America from England with the earliest settlers—looms large in the history of the militia. Behind it, to be sure, was the greater fear of arbitrary, highly centralized government, but such a government was not dangerous without a force arm to compel obedience. These fears are part of the history of the militia because the dual control under which it functioned impressed Americans as the best security against what they feared.

An additional reason why the militia and the National Guard have always received strong support was that they seemed the cheapest vehicle for protecting the nation. It went with the American grain to have an establishment capable of delivering a large number of citizen soldiers, presumably with some training, in a reasonably short time, but an establishment that, when the crisis was past, could disband its men and let them slip back into the population, leaving no trace of a military caste.

In spite of steady sentiment in favor of decentralization, the trend has been to draw the reserves closer under the control of the national government. Intermittently, the regular army, and some other agencies, have offered plans to cut the states away from the reserves altogether and substitute a system free of dual loyalties and a dual chain of command. The Army, Navy, Marine, Air Force, and Coast Guard Reserves resulted. Guardsmen, however, have always opposed such projects and in opposing have been able to preserve the Guard's state connection. They have believed, more often than not, that the federal form of government, indeed, the liberties of individual Americans would deteriorate if state-oriented reserves were wiped out. These views insured support from states' rights men, both in and out of government.

William Riker published a very useful book in 1957 about the National Guard. Entitled *Soldiers of the States*, it does not emphasize enough the federal connection of the Guard. By stressing the states, it does suggest—there being fifty states—how difficult it will be to write a definitive history of the militia and the National Guard. I have read as widely as I could and still tried to retain the ability to shape the mass of material gathered into a coherent narrative. Although I have used thousands of manuscripts, I have relied mainly on printed material. The method followed has been to draw samples from the evidence, and in some cases generalize from it. For example, information gleaned from a competent dissertation about the militia or the Guard, of one state has frequently been treated as if it had general application unless there was overpowering reason to do otherwise.

Because there is no Navy National Guard, I have not included the history of naval militia.

DEFINITIONS

Following are selected definitions that will enable the reader, I hope, to follow the narrative with minimum hindrance.

Citizen Soldier: A person who is primarily a civilian, acting, in war or peace, as a soldier. He may be a militiaman, a National Guardsman, or a member of Army, Navy, Marine, or Air Force Reserves. He may have been brought into military service via volunteering or conscription.

Elite Militia Units: Cavalry, artillery, riflemen, grenadiers, and light infantry units manned by persons liable for militia service who volunteered to enter these units. Usually, such men came from higher-income levels than the standing militiamen. Usually, too, they provided themselves with uniforms. Although subject to militia regulations, they had more cohesion than the average standing unit.

Militia in Federal Service: The Constitution provides that militia may be called into federal service for three purposes only: to enforce the laws of the United States, to suppress insurrection, and to repel invasion. Militiamen were not legally in United States service until mustered by an officer of the United States Army or by some other designated federal official. Once mustered they were not required to serve beyond the traditional short term unless they consented to do so.

National Guard: The inheritor of the militia tradition, the crucial part of which is the dual connection, state and national. Traditionally, the National Guard has been manned by volunteers.

Regular Military Forces: Forces maintained both in war and in peace by the national government. The members are military first and citizens second. They are also referred to as Standing Military Forces.

Reserves: Individuals or units available to fill out national forces when needed. Reservists are presumed to have skills which the military needs and to have at least rudimentary military training. The Army and the Air Force Reserves differ from the National Guard in that their chain of command starts with the federal military departments and does not run through the state military hierarchy.

Standing Militia: Universal military training for men of military age. First the colonies and then the states required eligible, able-bodied men to muster and to be associated in companies and larger units to drill. State laws specified the frequency of training. Most states restricted the standing militia to white men only. Enforcement of laws and regulations was a state not a national responsibility.

Volunteer Militia: Individual militiamen often volunteered for particular duty, usually for the limited duration characteristic of the militia. If they volunteered for a longer tour, or for service beyond the boundaries of state or colony, they entered into a different legal category, that of war volunteer. Elite militia units often volunteered in toto.

War Volunteers: Individuals or units, more often than not from the militia, who volunteered to serve for an extended period, perhaps for the duration of an emergency. They became subject to laws different from those for the militia.

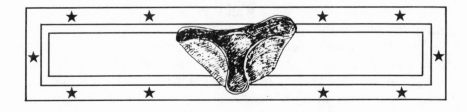

ONE

The English Background

One major theme in the history of citizen soldiery in the United States begins in the Germanic area of Europe during the Middle Ages. That theme is the obligation of every able-bodied man to defend his society. As this obligation reached England through the Angles and Saxons, it was embodied in what C. Warren Hollister calls "The Great Fyrd," consisting of the entire free male population of military age.[1] It bound the males for defense only and traditionally only for service close to home. At first, the legitimate sovereign could call out the Great Fyrd if the men might return to their homes by nightfall. Five calls occurred during the Danish invasion of 1016 A.D. There is no evidence of attempts to train the whole unwieldy body, but individuals were expected to turn out when called with whatever weapons they could acquire. Probably some sort of periodic muster of manpower was held to determine liability for service. In any event, the obligation on which the Great Fyrd was based made its way into United States history via colonization. Once transplanted it never ceased to apply, although it has done so in diverse, almost unrelated ways. First it was expressed in the colonial militia system and later in that of the states. In this form it lasted, in theory at least, until the Dick Act of 1903. It reappeared actively during the Civil War in the form of conscription and in that configuration again during both World Wars and the peacetime drafts from 1940 to 1973. It lay behind the three or four efforts in the twentieth century to install UMT.

The pre-Norman governments of Britain, in need of a less unwieldy reserve than the Great Fyrd, employed what Hollister calls "The Select Fyrd." The American tradition of select units of citizen soldiers may stem in some way from this institution, but the lineage cannot be traced directly because the Select Fyrd was based on ownership of land. The possessor of five hides of land was required, when called upon by his suzerain, to provide and equip one soldier and also to pay four shillings for each hide of land.[2] The sum of twenty shillings was expected to see the soldier through two months' service, the customary limit of his duty. The assumption was that the same person would, if possible, turn out for any particular five-hide area at each call. He would thus become a relatively practiced warrior. There is some evidence, too, that he was required, when not on active service, to train in arms with comrades and so gain practice in cohesive action. The ownership of land as a basis for membership in the militia never reached the English colonies in North America, but it is true that the American militia was more often than not controlled by officers who were landowners.

Another prototype of a later institution, which can be traced to pre-Norman England, is found in the guardsmen whose duty was to defend the Saxon kings. Canute the Dane, who ruled from 1016 to 1035, enlarged this force. These Houseguards became professionals by reason of continuous service and may be considered forebears of later regular armies. It was with a mixed force of Houseguards and Select Fyrdmen that King Harold tried to expel William the Norman from England in 1066 A.D. He failed. William took over the rule and superimposed a continental type of feudal military service on the Anglo-Saxon system. What he did obscured but did not eliminate the universal military obligation of the fyrds.

One hundred and fifteen years after William the Conqueror's successful invasion, Henry II (1154-1189) reemphasized and amplified the universal military obligation. His Assize of Arms (1181) required able-bodied men to keep arms, the nature of the weapons depending on what they could afford, and to use them only in the service of the king. Because the practices mandated by the Assize grew lax, Edward I felt obliged to reaffirm them in the Statute of Winchester (1285). In so doing he confirmed two roles for what, by this time, may be called the militia: (1) to be a keystone in the defense of the island; and (2) to maintain law and order within it.[3] The framers of the militia laws in some of the early English colonies drew specifically upon both the Assize of Arms and the Statute of Winchester, as did the American militia tradition of requiring men who owe a military obligation to supply themselves with arms.[4]

The Assize of Arms and the Statute of Winchester had laid duties on men, but in the fourteenth century, due to the instability of the throne and the increased power of Parliament, the laws also began to speak about the rights of individuals. Thus, a statute of 1327 in the reign of

Edward III stipulated that the king might not order militia to serve outside the county of its origin, unless England itself was invaded.[5] He could extend their range only if they agreed and if he paid them to do so. This geographical limitation, coupled with the limitation of time of service, which depended on ancient custom, were built into the militia of the English colonies.

It is true that in times of danger English monarchs, relying on royal prerogative, overrode the stipulated geographical limitation. Edward III invaded Scotland with militiamen, but the results of overstretching the system did not justify the costs.[6] Later, Elizabeth I moved militiamen beyond bounds without their consent, but her Council was so sensitive about the constitutionality of her action that they felt it necessary to arrest and detain those persons who challenged the process. In general, it was considered better to develop some sort of contractual method to procure men for overseas excursions.[7]

As the time-and-place limitations reached America, they hardened and became more inviolate than in England. No one on the American side of the Atlantic had the power to send militiamen across borders that they did not agree to cross; but on both sides of the Atlantic it was usual to employ the militia mechanism to secure volunteers for foreign service. In addition, the British resorted to impressment, by which they captured and sent on expeditionary forces the poor, the unprotected, the unemployable, the wanderers, all drawn from the very bottom level of society.[8]

One way or another, Edward III sent at least 20,000 soldiers across the English Channel into the Crecy campaign in 1346. Carrying a secret weapon, the longbow, they decimated the opposing French army.[9] Although this had few implications for the military institutions that developed in the English part of the New World, it revealed the growing power of the citizen when he served as a soldier. The same trend was confirmed during that century in other battles in which the Swiss and German polearm wielders defeated the mounted knights of the feudal array and unwittingly opened a new era in warfare. What they did gave strength to the idea of relying upon citizen soldiers.

A large share of the history that shaped the use of citizen soldiers in British North America took place under the Tudor monarchs (1485-1603). True professional forces, the instruments of kings, had been taking form on the continent of Europe since the middle of the fifteenth century, but the economy of Tudor England could not support so expensive an establishment. By this time, too, the feudal military system had virtually disappeared, so the Tudors had to turn to the able-bodied male population for their military manpower.[10] Accordingly, in the last year of the reign of Mary Tudor (1557-1558), the Crown attempted to make some sort of army out of the mass of potential citizen soldiers. The new regulations specifically repealed the Statute of Winchester. As far as they could, considering the diversity of English society, they sought to make the county the basis of militia organization. To that end, the office of lord lieutenant was created; it was filled in each county by an important member of the local gentry. Under the lord lieutenant was a hierarchy of deputies, who worked without pay, among them sheriffs, who from the time of the fyrd had dealt with citizens as soldiers, constables of the hundreds, justices of the peace, and commissioners of musters. The government was careful to see that no one along this chain of command accumulated enough power to become a menace to it.[11]

The attempt to build a citizen army rested on the muster—a mandatory gathering of able-bodied free males, aged 16 to 60, in order to examine the individuals, their weapons and horses, and such armament as it was the responsibility of the towns and counties to maintain. Mustering was a very ancient but sporadic and unsystematic practice. Training as a regular adjunct of peacetime musters was virtually unknown before Elizabeth's statute of 1573. That statute required musters four times a year and authorized payment for the attenders. The commissioners of musters were employed by the Crown, but except for them the gatherings were carried out by local officials, most of them without any pay. The musters were held at traditional gathering places, and they were social as much as military events. People looked forward to and took part in them as a break from the monotony of their lives. They ate heavily, often drank heavily, and engaged in fights, some of them mock battles, which gave pleasure to all.[12]

Militia musters were brought into the English colonies without much modification from the Elizabethan practice. The carnival mood and the escape from monotony became as much a part of the American muster as of the English; so too did flamboyant uniforms and martial swagger bordering on burlesque. What did not migrate across the ocean was the practice of paying militiamen for appearing at musters, an Elizabethan practice, or the office of commissioner of musters.

In any case, for the first time in English history, there began in the 1570s systematic attempts to train citizens as soldiers. From that decade forward, militiamen gathered together to train in units. Men who failed to appear at musters or training days, or who turned out without the equipment required by law, were subject to fine. In times of stress, officials collected the fines; at other times, they grew careless.[13] Because of a general disinclination to military exercise, tension existed between the government and the people over training, especially during peacetime.[14] Crises sometimes dissolved this tension; for example, when invasion threatened England in the years from 1585 to 1599, the mass of the militia more than once swarmed to protect the queen. In one of these episodes, in 1599, 25,000 armed citizens, more a horde than an army, milled about London.[15]

Laws requiring training days and the use of fines to insure attendance were among the earliest enacted in the English colonies in North America. But these laws did not overcome the reluctance, anymore than similar laws had in England, to train when there was no conspicuous danger to the colonies.

Elizabeth's government sent professional soldiers into the counties of England to assist in making citizens into soldiers.[16] With similar intent, the organizers of every colony sent one or two professional soldiers whose main task was to instruct the male citizens in the use of arms and military formations, and in some cases to lead their trainees.

It is estimated that there were between 200,000 and 250,000 free, able-bodied male Englishmen, aged 16 to 60, around 1570.[17] Of course the government could not afford to train and arm such a horde. Accordingly, by means of statutes in 1572 and 1573, Elizabeth created a select corps and insured that it be well trained and supplied. The resulting units were designated train bands, and they are the forebears of such elite units in American history as the Minutemen.[18]

One thread that runs through the military history of England is a demand for low-cost protection. Indeed, much of the time cheap security was all that the ruler could afford. Therefore the central government tried to shift the costs of supply, muster, and training to the local authorities. Owners of land bore those costs for the most part, but the lowest strata of society paid their share if they were impressed into service for extensive overseas duty. In England, the complaints of the landholders over the costs of the militia on the one hand and the pressures exerted by the Crown to make them pay those costs on the other hand shaped military policy.[19] Demand for low-cost military security reappeared in the British North American colonies.

A final powerful heritage to come to North America from Tudor England was a belief in the invincibility of citizen soldiers when fighting for home and family. At least one responsible historian claims that this conviction stemmed from the desperate era, 1585-1599, when England, for the first time since 1066, was once again threatened with invasion. The militia swarmed to defend the island. They manned a chain of beacon lights along the coast to warn of imminent landings, while the train bands drilled with unaccustomed fervor. But their efforts did not impress so seasoned a warrior as the Earl of Essex, who wrote:[20]

Ther numbers do for the most part consist of artificers and clownes who know nothing of the warres and little of the armes they carry. . . . Wee must have as many officers as wee have soldiers: ther leaders of quality dwelling neere, butt as insufficient commonly as the soldiers. . . .

The earl's derogatory estimate of citizen-soldier quality has innumerable counterparts in American annals. Such opinions notwithstanding, the mass of the people viewed the militia differently. They were convinced that it could drive any invader back into the sea. Since, due to weather and the British Navy, the system did not undergo a severe test in the era of the Spanish Armada, no evidence appeared to change the prevalent opinion of the militia as an efficient bulwark against invasion.[21] That opinion traveled with the settlers into the North American colonies.

The second of the Stuart kings, Charles I, continued to impress men from the lowest social strata to fight foreign wars. Because he lacked the popularity of his Tudor predecessors, the practice created some resistance. Charles assumed, as monarchs before him had, that he commanded the militia, but Parliament, as it gathered power and thus confidence, challenged him. In 1642, Parliament presumed to appoint the lords lieutenant of the counties and to assert that only they could direct forces sent overseas. Naturally, the king refused to agree to these usurpations—for in the light of the past that is what they were—so he resorted to arms. What he commanded was virtually a feudal array.[22]

To oppose him, the antiroyalist leaders, headed by Oliver Cromwell, gradually forged the New Model Army. In this, as never before, common men who had shown courage and talent in battle could earn commissions as officers. In this way they affected the future of citizen soldiers. The New Model did indeed temporarily overthrow the monarchy and make possible the beheading of the king. But in so doing it injected into thoughtful Englishmen a haunting fear of standing armies, which became one of the sturdiest props of the militia system. Englishmen at home and abroad saw military forces under Cromwell's command interfere at least six times in the processes of civil government. They viewed these as naked displays of might, without regard to right, and the subsequent rule of the major generals further increased their fear. All in all, abhorrence of such an engine as the New Model Army contributed to English willingness to restore the Stuarts to the throne.[23]

With the Restoration, the principle of Parliamentary control over the armed forces, except in appropriations, ended without public outcry. The issue of whether to rely on a standing army or upon militia, however, persisted. The militia acts of the first years of the Restoration, which conceded control of the militia to the king but established the gentry as his agents, set the pattern for the next hundred years. The gentry had to assume most of the cost of island defense. A gentleman with an estate of £500 was obliged to field and maintain a cavalryman; one with £50 must produce and sustain an infantryman. The king, of course, could appoint the lords lieutenant, but he could not summon the militia except to drill, suppress insurrection, or repel invasion. He could use the militia anywhere in England but not beyond its borders. His government would pay for active service, but not by this time for drill. As before, the result was that the citizen soldiery was dominated by the gentry. The militia was not a very efficient instrument, but its shortcomings did not concern Charles II or James II, who feared possible uprisings from a people too well armed and trained.[24]

Some writers openly found fault with the military policy of Charles II and James II. They wanted the citizen soldiery to be strengthened. James Harrington (1611-1677) argues that the militia had to be officered by the gentry to afford security against possible military dictatorship. Harrington and other critics viewed the growing trend toward professionalization in the military as evidence of corruption seeping through society. In contrast, they opined that an active militia constantly injected the martial spirit into the whole people, a spirit necessary for national survival.[25]

In spite of these critics, Charles II maintained a small standing force of approximately 6,000 men, organized around the duke of Albemarle's old regiment, which was all that remained of the New Model Army. Charles was able to support this unconstitutional establishment without any aid or even approval from Parliament because of a secret subsidy which his uncle Louis XIV paid him. When James became king in 1685, he openly defied the public mood more than Charles had ever been willing to do by enlarging the standing army to 53,000. As he was an avowed Roman Catholic, this as well as many of his other actions irritated the militant Protestants of the country.[26]

By the 1670s, the military instrument had become a party question. The Court Party supported a sizable standing army, whereas its opponent, the Country Party, asserted that such a military force dislocated the necessary balance among the Crown, the aristocracy, and the common people, a balance required by the English constitution. A standing army made the power of the king dangerous to a free society. Drawing upon Renaissance thought, the Country Party asserted that a free people could be safely defended only by citizen soldiers. This military issue, coupled with many others, resulted in the unseating of James II in 1688, followed by the accession of his daughter, Mary, and her husband and his nephew, William III of the Netherlands.[27]

The settlement of William and Mary on the throne required difficult compromises. One was the recognition for the first time of a standing army as sanctioned by the Constitution. Only Parliament could appropriate funds for the army, and even Parliament lacked the power to make long-term appropriations for it. Rules concerning army discipline also had to be renewed periodically or they would cease to be applicable. Limitations similar to these could be found later in slightly altered form in the Constitution of the United States.[28]

The acts of settlement did not quiet opponents of a standing army. As late as 1697, John Trenchard wrote a pamphlet, entitled *A Standing Army Is Inconsistent with a Free Government and Absolutely Destructive of the English Monarchy*. Trenchard's views were not those of the underprivileged and unrepresented elements of the society. Trenchard, indeed, was in sound enough circumstances to lend William III £60,000. This may have protected him when he made statements that must have irritated the king. He and other pamphleteers supported the militia with as much vehemence as they opposed the standing army. All of them had classical educations which enabled them to draw historical illustrations from ancient history: the Greek militia had destroyed Xerxes' huge Persian army; Xenophon led the militia on his celebrated march through Persia; and the Roman militia had been invincible, while Roman regulars were eventually defeated by the barbarians.[29]

Roughly half a century after the Glorious Revolution, the English legal scholar William Blackstone stated well the basic faith in a system that moved citizens in and out of military service as required by the needs of the state.[30]

> In free states . . . no man should take up arms but with a view to defend his country and its laws; he puts not off the citizen when he enters the camp; but it is because he is a citizen, and would wish to continue so, that he makes himself for a while a soldier.

Blackstone's views were well known in the American colonies. Many American lawyers knew little more of the law than what they read in Blackstone's *Commentaries*. But beyond Blackstone, most of the history of the struggle over a standing army and the debate concerning the role of citizen soldiery, which had taken place in England, was known to a majority of educated colonists. The tension between the existence of a standing army and the necessary function of the citizen soldiery crossed the Atlantic intact and influenced events in the United States both before and after the Revolution.

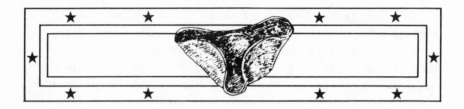

TWO

Militia in the Colonies

However different the agencies that founded the various English colonies in North America may have been, all of them, as well as the colonists themselves, believed that a military obligation rested on every free, white male settler. Accordingly, the charters issued by the king to the colonizing agencies gave their representatives the right "to assemble Marshal Array and put in Warlike posture the inhabitants of said colony." This clause referred specifically to able-bodied males, aged 16 to 60. These, led by constituted authority, were authorized to "expulse repell and resist by force of Arms . . . and also to kill slay destroy by all fitting ways . . . all and every Person or Persons as shall attempt the destruction invasion detriment or annoyance of the . . . Inhabitants. . . ."[1] These words, taken from Charles II's charter to the colony of Connecticut, are not found verbatim in other charters, but the same idea and powers are present. The charter granted to the last of the original colonies, Georgia, speaks specifically of the militia as the "backbone of colonial defense."[2]

Thus, very early in their existence, the several colonies began progressively to enact laws that created militia systems. Pennsylvania, because of its Quaker spirit, was slower than the others, but even it, seventy-five years after being chartered, under the threat created by the French and Indians during the Great War for Empire, enacted a militia law in 1755.[3] Once the militia obligation was defined, it became necessary for each colony to see that its citizen soldiers had arms and received training.

The obligations imposed by the enlarging tangle of militia laws were a nuisance to individual colonists, but the people generally accepted them because of their lofty purpose. That purpose was well

14

stated in a training manual printed in Boston in 1758 (like the Pennsylvania law a consequence of the Great War for Empire): "On no other soldiery but its own Citizens," could a free government depend, "So every man therefore that wishes to secure his own freedom . . . should . . . think it his truest honor to be a citizen soldier."[4]

The French, the Dutch, and the Spanish established similar systems also based on acceptance of the idea of a universal military obligation for free able-bodied males. The French and Spanish did not confine their militias to white men as did the English and the Dutch. Although rivalry among the colonizing powers also resulted in military efforts and measures, it was the Indian presence that encouraged the development of militia systems in the New World.[5]

The keystone of the system in the English colonies was the company. Formed within a township, a county, or perhaps a city, the company had a geographical rather than a numerical basis. Numbers depended upon the male population within any given geographical base. The vitality of the company depended upon its officers. Initially, when the colonies were mere beachheads, officers were professional soldiers who had been hired by the colonizing agencies and sent to America to instruct settlers in military matters. Neither the Crown nor any colonizing agency provided a significant body of soldiers, for they assumed that the citizens would function as soldiers when the need existed. During the beachhead stage, the hired captains had authority to enforce discipline and training, if necessary by the most draconian means. Later when settlement had expanded into plantations and towns, company officers were designated in ways that varied from colony to colony. In New England, a full company could usually elect its officers. Elsewhere, the choice was sometimes made by election, sometimes by appointment from higher officials of the government. Whatever the method of choice, the positions carried with them social prestige.[6]

At first, except for the governor and his council, companies were the sole level of militia organization. Then, as numbers increased, the several colonies began to establish regiments. Massachusetts in 1643 reached that plane first, Virginia in 1651, Connecticut in 1653, Maryland in 1658, and South Carolina in 1685. The county was the common base, but, where the population grew dense, the area could be even more restricted. In a county, the companies could be widely dispersed and the regimental control would necessarily be loose. However loose the organization, both company and regiment provided rosters of officers and men that became the essential starting documents in any sort of mobilization of manpower for military purposes. Here, at least on paper, was a roster of names and a chain of command.

Governor and legislature in all colonies had a hand in the selection of regimental officers.[7] In royal and proprietary colonies, the governor and council selected the colonels and their subordinates, in some cases with the consent of the legislature. In the other colonies, the general assemblies nominated these officers, and the governor commissioned them. Whatever the type of colony, the commission issued from the office of the governor. It was rare for a governor to appoint an officer whose duty it was to take care of logistics in peacetime. Commissaries and quartermasters appeared only when troops actually took the field.[8]

Even though there were at least thirteen separate militia systems, certain generalizations apply to all: (1) a substantial citizen could not decline a commission except for drastic reasons; (2) a commissioned officer could not resign at his pleasure but had to be released by the governor; and (3) the officers were drawn from elites. In early New England, for example, they had to be members of that self-limiting minority, the congregation. Indeed, during the Pequot War, several key officers were decommissioned and banished because of heresy. In the South, officers had to own specific quantities of land; in South Carolina, for example, even a captain had to be the owner of at least forty acres. Thus, in all the colonies, the officers occupied a fairly high station in a deferential society.[9]

The colonizers in England sent armaments with the settlers. In the first two settlements, Jamestown and Plymouth, however, these proved inadequate both in kind and in number. Polearms and steel armor were not useful against the Indians. In contrast, Massachusetts Bay, with past examples to learn from and with more adequate funding, spent £22,000—that is, one-ninth of its original colonizing capital—on twenty cannon and enough infantry gear for one hundred men. Most colonies decreed that every household should provide its own arms, but if the householders lacked the means for this, diverse methods came into use to supply them. Those who could not own might rent in New England, while in South Carolina a man who could not afford a weapon was required to work six months for someone who would supply him. Men were expected to arm their servants, and in Connecticut a person who had an estate worth at least £350 was required to arm himself and one other man. Connecticut towns also assessed special taxes to provide arms for the poor. Eighty-seven percent of Virginia settlers were armed, at whatever sacrifice, because of their determination to live widely scattered in isolated farms to produce tobacco.[10]

Supplies of armament became especially critical during open conflict with the Indians or with the Dutch, the Spanish, or the French. In such emergencies some colonies possessed the power to impress weapons and redistribute them equitably. But this did not increase the total supply of arms which constantly needed enlargement. Grants to colonial proprietors originally included a monopoly of the sale of arms within their territory, but this monopoly was soon rescinded. In Maryland, a 1639 law curbed sales of arms in which the profit exceeded 100 percent. So critical was the shortage of gunpowder in 1617 that anyone wasting it could be sentenced to one year of involuntary servitude. Since no substantial quantity was produced in the colonies before the 1670s, colonial ports charged every entering vessel a tonnage fee, payable in gunpowder. In addition to shortages of weapons and gunpowder, there was also an insufficient number of gunsmiths. Those who were present were so essential to the public weal during the seventeenth century that their activities were carefully regulated.[11]

All the colonies kept public arms, but only in New England were the stocks anywhere near adequate. The tight-knit township system in that region created effective local responsibility, enforced by periodic inspection of the mandated stores. Naturally, the use of public arms always created problems. Weapons loaned to the poor for drill were often not returned; weapons in private hands were not always kept in good repair. The town system in New England was more effective in enforcing the maintenance of these stocks than were counties and other larger jurisdictions. Cannon, of course, required heavy investment. It was usually made by governments, but sometimes by artillery companies. In return, these companies received special privileges, such as freedom from any draft. The established churches usually stood foursquare behind military strength; in Massachusetts, for example, Cotton Mather used church funds to purchase cannon. Men who served in the artillery were volunteers.[12]

Similar problems existed with the horsemen who acted as scouts for foot units. As their numbers increased they formed themselves into troops. Citizens who could equip themselves with horses and appropriate accouterments volunteered for service in these troops in return for exemption from the draft and for certain tax advantages. Even though the early horse soldiers rode their work animals, the mounted service was expensive. In addition, Massachusetts, for example, required a cavalryman to possess at least £100 worth of property.[13]

If not in the cavalry or artillery, some men with a special interest in martial exercise volunteered to join elite foot companies, such as grenadiers, light infantrymen, or riflemen. Volunteer units of all sorts usually flourished in the cities where short distances made it easy for the members to assemble. These volunteers uniformed themselves and paid dues to maintain meeting places. The oldest volunteer group was the Ancient and Honorable Artillery Company, chartered in Boston in 1638.[14] Throughout the colonial period, others came into being. Some were independent of the militia and had legislative permission to be separate. Most, however, were part of the system but were accorded special privileges. These volunteers were the true forebears of the National Guard, which was based, at least until the 1950s, exclusively on volunteers.[15]

Frequency of training fluctuated with the degree of danger. When Massachusetts Bay was no more than a beachhead, company drill took place once a week. Thirty years later, in quiet times, they dropped to four meetings a year. Regimental assemblies were of course less frequent, varying from one per year to one every three years. Volunteer units, especially those in the towns, met regularly. Some of their meeting time went to fraternal matters, but some of it was always reserved for military exercises.[16]

From the earliest times, the colonies allowed certain exemptions to the militia obligation. Quakers, although required to serve in the militia, could often provide a substitute or, as in North Carolina, pay a fine if called into active service. In Connecticut, they were excused from service but not from keeping arms. No colony forced Quakers, or other religious objectors, to bear arms if they were willing to pay for exemption. There were also exemptions for nonreligious reasons. South Carolina exempted any newcomer from the arms requirement for one year. The slave states increasingly exempted overseers of four or more slaves. In Virginia, free blacks were expected to march along if called into service to be used for labor not for fighting.[17]

Methods of enforcement of militia regulations varied from colony to colony and from one period to another. If there was a clear and present danger, most colonies permitted officers, captain and above, to inflict corporal punishment. Sentences included being trussed neck and heels, riding the wooden horse, wearing irons, serving time in the stocks, and running the gauntlet. For blasphemy, the penalty in war or peace was boring the tongue.

In peacetime a system of fines replaced corporal punishment, stipulating sums for failing to appear at a muster, or to be armed properly, and so on. When punishments were limited to fines, people of means preferred to pay rather than to serve. In this way much of the upper crust of society disassociated itself from the standing militia and either entered volunteer units or avoided service altogether.[18]

Limitations on the use of militia similar to those developed in England appeared in America. The militia was for defense and could be used only close to the area it was supposed to defend. Just as the English had stopped at county lines, the several colonies stopped at their own boundaries. It is true that the charter of South Carolina gave the proprietors permission to lead their citizens, in their capacity as soldiers, outside these limits, but in 1690 the assembly forbade it. Later the legislature of North Carolina gave express permission to use its militia in South Carolina and Georgia.[19] George Washington's disastrous campaign which opened the Great War for Empire in 1754 affords an example of the problem created by the special limitations on the use of militia. Washington could not employ the Virginia militia in Ohio County because that area possibly lay outside the boundaries of the Old Dominion[20] (i.e., as the boundaries were not clear, the militia men did not have to cross them; they were not required to enter Ohio County).

The second major limitation was on length of service. Since most citizen soldiers were farmers, they relied on their labor for subsistence. Thus, colonial custom provided that the standard period of active duty was three months. This time limitation, coupled with that on space, made the militia a defensive instrument only. For continuous or distant operations, a different method of procuring manpower must be employed.

Although organized local units might turn out to meet a specific emergency, such as a sudden Indian attack, the system worked differently when the governor or a regimental commander issued a call for men. It then became a mechanism for compelling men who had a military obligation to assemble. Orders went down through the chain of command to the captain, who was required in one way or another to notify his men to assemble. Once they were before him he explained that the company had a quota to fill, and then asked for volunteers. If the number who came forward filled the quota, he dismissed his unit. A popular officer had a good chance of securing the necessary number of volunteers, but if there was a shortage, for whatever reason, the captain was obliged to resort to a draft. He could not impose it at the muster because drafting required legal action. In Massachusetts, he had to obtain a warrant and give it to a constable to serve on each draftee. Even then the impressed man could avoid service by paying a fine or finding a substitute. When the duty extended beyond the legal term of service, officials had the power to impress replacements for the men who had a right to return home. If a danger became pressing, or the determination to annihilate some Indians was particularly strong, legislatures sometimes permitted a draft of men to serve outside the colony. At such times the power to requisition horses and necessary supplies was also granted to surrogates whom the governor appointed to handle logistics, but this was not done without issuing receipts which promised future compensation.[21]

Men were not paid for training, nor in the early days sometimes even for active service. Officials assumed that it was not necessary to pay a man to carry out an obligation he owed as a citizen. In some cases, to alleviate this burden, a man might serve ten days, then be relieved by someone with the same tour of duty and the same obligation. Soon it became the practice to pay for active service, with the pay of servants and minors going to master or parent.

In addition, the colonies had to provide compensation for injury. They dealt with this risk in different ways. Virginia's General Assembly ruled that the injured be "Mayntained by the County, and in case any shall be slayne, all possible Care shall bee taken of their estates and their widowes and children."[22] North Carolina paid the costs of any necessary cure, and awarded one male slave to any maimed veteran or to the widow of a veteran. During the Great War for Empire, the colony withdrew these generous benefits. In New England there was no blanket provision for compensation to injured militiamen. An injured or aggrieved citizen soldier had to petition the General Court for relief, and that body dealt with each case separately. Colonies with unoccupied lands offered land bounties to men who gave extended service. Thus, Massachusetts designated twelve townships in New Hampshire, before that colony became separate, for her citizen soldiers.[23]

Because people were geographically mobile and land was available, colonial governments had to consider the possibility that families might simply relocate if their militia burdens became too heavy. Passage between the two Carolinas and Virginia was especially easy. Such fluidity tended to confound authorities who were trying to construct a reliable system of defense on a known supply of manpower. Accordingly, South Carolina required a man eligible for militia service to give three weeks notice of his intention to leave the colony. Of course such a law was basically unenforceable.[24]

Other conditions besides geographical mobility enabled the militia system to meet its quotas without dislocating people or curbing the growing spirit of individualism. The most important of these was the presence of men who could be recruited to enter combat with a minimum of economic loss to the community. In 1645, to cope with a major Indian confrontation, the General Assembly of Virginia ordained that every fifteen tithable persons produce and maintain a soldier for an extended tour of duty. Behind this lay the power of the authorities to press men into service, and, if necessary, to employ the militia draft. In any case, the military force that took form consisted of indentured servants, unemployed men, vagabonds, and prisoners released for this service. Here was no cross-section of the citizenry, serving as soldiers, but a slice cut off of the bottom level of Virginia society. A quasi-standing army, it remained on duty for two years and eight months. In 1698, Governor Francis Webb used indentured servants—mostly Irish Roman Catholics—to create a similar army. Other examples can be found in almost all the colonies.[25]

Simultaneously, there was a tendency to turn to small mounted units, denominated rangers, to patrol boundary lines vulnerable to Indian attack. Some rangers served under militia terms and conditions, but most of them were retained on a contract basis. Conflict with the Indians produced many instances of quasi-standing forces. In 1671, South Carolina used contract troops instead of the militia against the Kussoe tribe. Later, during the so-called Yamassee War in 1715, the same colony fielded one of the largest quasi-standing armies. Because the militia of North Carolina had failed to repel the Indians and because the Indian border was critical to South Carolina, this colony drew together a mercenary army consisting of 600 white men, considered of scant social importance, 400 black slaves, including 100 from Virginia, and 100 friendly Indians. Commanded by Colonel John Barnwell, this force saved North Carolina from being overrun by the Indians. The following year, the governor literally bought the service of thirty indentured Scotsmen (who had sold their labor for seven years) to man several frontier forts.[26]

Thus, an informal and unacknowledged alternative to the militia system had come into use. The alternative troops were not raised through the militia organization but through special officers who were given "beating orders" to recruit volunteers and, if necessary, to impress men who were not protected from such arbitrary action. to expedite enlistment, the several colonies offered various inducements to volunteers. In 1745, Connecticut gave men who volunteered to join the expedition against Louisbourg one month's pay in advance, freedom from impressment for two years, and above all a share in the plunder. Even though Massachusetts offered less than Connecticut, more than 4,000 Massachusetts men presented themselves for this same foray. These men and others like them were a new type of soldier in the colonies. They were probably on the militia rolls but had not been called up from them. They were young, single, landless, poor, and in need of the money offered for military service. Most of them volunteered, but some had been impressed. Like the enlisted soldier of Europe, this new type came from the lowest social stratum, but unlike the European they were freer to enter or to stay out of service, and they were rarely in it for a large portion of their lives.[27]

The promise of plunder drew men into Indian campaigns, for Indians did have valuable property. There was also the scalp bounty. Connecticut raised this to its highest level during King George's War in the 1740s: £400 for the scalp of a male Indian (£25 more than a live male captive would bring), and £200 for a female scalp. If the level of hatred was high enough, no bounty was necessary to turn out soldiery. That was the case at Jamestown after the near total massacre of 1622. Once the colony had stopped reeling from this blow it set out to annihilate its Indian enemies.[28]

In spite of the alternative system for raising men, the militia system remained the mechanism for large-scale mobilization in case of an attack serious enough to threaten the life of the colonies. The system remained useful for defense but not for aggressive military action.[29]

Since military manpower was always a problem, colonial governments had to consider whether or not to modify the rules against the use of blacks. South Carolina, which contained more black slaves than white men, was most inclined to use the slaves as soldiers. As noted, 400 of them served with John Barnwell in 1715 against the Yamassees. This was a special force, but slaves in South Carolina could also constitute up to one-third of the militia. Should the militia, however, enter active service, one-quarter of its white members would be required to stay home to guard against slave insurrection. Every substantial slave owner was obliged to maintain one slave in a separate black company, commanded, of course, by white officers. Although the Stono Rebellion in 1740 lessened the willingness in South Carolina to arm blacks, it did not end the practice altogether.

In 1690, South Carolina enacted its first law to create a slave patrol. This law required each area to establish a detachment, made up of slave owners or their surrogates, to patrol every day to keep slaves within bounds. Even women who owned more than ten blacks were required to participate in the patrol, either personally or through a representative. At first a separate organization, the patrol system was eventually absorbed into the militia. The primary mission of the slave states' militias increasingly became the slave patrol.[30]

In slave states other than South Carolina, blacks were used in the militia, but with more restrictions than in South Carolina. North of the principal slave-holding region, blacks were expected to respond to a call for the militia, but only to do the necessary labor and not to carry arms.

During the first three-quarters of the seventeenth century, no central authority attempted to unify the militias of the several colonies.

If intercolonial military cooperation occurred, it was unsystematic. Plymouth sent fifty men to aid Massachusetts against the Pequot Indians in 1636, principally because the larger colony pressured the smaller one into it. When Massachusetts had destroyed the Pequots, its government tried unsuccessfully to secure help from neighboring colonies to force the other Indian tribes to move west. Massachusetts' request went largely unheeded because the other New England settlements, especially Connecticut, were repelled by what they considered to be the arrogance of Massachusetts. Connecticut preferred to reserve its manpower for its own possible use.[31]

In spite of early lack of cooperation, Massachusetts, Plymouth, Connecticut, and New Haven successfully organized themselves into the United Colonies of New England when the Civil War broke out in England in 1642. With England preoccupied, they felt the need for more self-protection. Sometimes this confederation fielded minuscule coalition armies against the Indians. It was still in existence thirty years later when King Philip's War erupted, but it could then achieve limited cooperation. This time, Connecticut, directly threatened by the Indians, made a much greater effort than formerly, even resorting to impressment.[32]

During the 1670s, the government of Charles II began to strengthen ties between the colonies and the mother island. Royal governors assumed control of militias not heretofore commanded by crown officers. Governor Edmund Andros of New York, for example, attempted to take command of the militias of Connecticut and Rhode Island. Both colonies obstructed his effort; Connecticut even summoned its militia to prevent his landing on its soil. Andros had to abandon his attempt. After Massachusetts became a royal colony following the loss of the original charter in 1684, the governor was also supposed to command the Rhode Island militia, but in fact he was never able to do so.[33]

Before Charles II died in 1685, he ordered the creation of a regional royal polity named the Dominion of New England. At first composed of Massachusetts, including Maine, and New Hampshire, it grew under James II with the addition of Plymouth, Rhode Island, and Connecticut in 1686, and New York and New Jersey in 1688. A prime purpose was to oppose the growing power of New France in America; therefore, the militias of the consolidated colonies were to come under the command of the royal governor of the Dominion. In every way that they could the colonies impeded the organization of the Dominion. As a result, although in Massachusetts many good congregational military officers were replaced by Anglicans, the militias were scarcely affected. The Glorious Revolution of 1688,

which toppled James II from the throne and replaced him with
William and Mary, probably prevented a desperate confrontation with
the Crown. There were ripples of the regime-shaking event in America
with militia on both sides of the cause.[34] Soon, however, the militia
systems resumed their pre-Dominion posture with one towering
variation. Now it was more apparent than ever before that a citizenry
could oust a sovereign who had flouted the social contract and that
citizens, functioning temporarily as soldiers, were an essential
ingredient in such an upheaval.

That alternative to the citizen soldier, the regular, first appeared in
the colonies during the Dutch War in 1664.[35] Thereafter, he was never
altogether absent from the colonies, although always few in numbers
until the Great War for Empire. In general, colonials did not get along
well with the redcoats; provincial officers resented the precedence
that British officers assumed regardless of rank. Still the colonies
requested additional regulars from the Crown when confronted by the
Indians, the French, or the Spanish. They likewise requested that
regulars garrison the frontier forts. That was a duty citizen soldiers
hated and performed badly. It was also deadly. One independent
company of regulars, stationed on the Carolina frontier with an initial
strength of 94 men, lost 130 men and five officers to disease in four
years.[36]

The presence of British regulars awakened in some colonists the
fear of a standing military force, but only in Massachusetts did this fear
generate any substantial dialogue until the era of the Great War for
Empire. In addition, the presence of quasi-regular forces, in place of
the militia, occasioned concern among a few thoughtful British
Americans.[37]

Oblivious to this particular colonial concern, the government in
England more often than not sent military officers as administrators to
the colonies. Sixty percent of the royal governors came from a military
career. In order to carry out the British policy of increased
centralization, they felt it essential that they themselves command the
militia or at least appoint those officers who did. Even though they
disliked the use of military officers, the colonists in some cases abetted
the process of royalization. The two Carolinas, for example, not
satisfied with the military protection provided by the proprietors,
petitioned the Crown to take over the colony. Early in the eighteenth
century this was done.[38]

Under William III (1688-1703), the North American colonies
were drawn for the first time into direct involvement in the struggle to
curb the expanding power of France. New France seemed to be
snaking its way up the St. Lawrence, across the Great Lakes, and down

the Mississippi River and its tributaries. This amounted to an encirclement of the British colonies. The first declared strife for hegemony in Europe and empire in America was King William's War (1689-1702). One major expeditionary force led by William Phips, himself a provincial, conquered Port Royal in French Acadia without help from the metropolis. But the men who made up the conquering army were not drawn into service by the militia mechanism. Militia could not be called out for such an expedition or for the subsequent abortive attempt to take Quebec. The men had volunteered for this service in the hope of plunder and adventure. There were, however, many border raids against small settlements, carried out by Indians led by French officers, which the militia had to try to parry directly.[39]

Unquestionably, Massachusetts carried the weight of King William's War on this side of the Atlantic. The English were too preoccupied with the armies of Louis XIV to detach significant forces to aid the Americans. As for the other colonies, Connecticut contributed one-ninth of the manpower of Massachusetts, sending no one at all on the forays against Port Royal and Quebec; close to home, it advanced men only into parts of New York through which Connecticut itself could be attacked. New Hampshire, on the inflamed border, needed assistance because she had no more than 1,000 men of military age for defense, but when the governor called for help in 1694 he discovered that the citizen soldiers from Massachusetts were not willing to risk their lives in the New Hampshire wilderness. At the rare times when troops from the several colonies were actually assembled to act together, there was invariably a squabble over whether officers from one colony could be obliged to take orders from those of another. An added altercation never failed to develop when an officer of the Crown was placed over the citizen soldiers. This was resolved by a compromise; during peacetime the several militias remained subordinate to their own governors, but, in time of declared war, the British government might name a supreme commander. No such officer was appointed during King William's War, but the sharp debate over the matter signaled the growing awareness of a military connection between the metropolis and the colonies.[40]

The Peace of Ryswick ended King William's War in 1697, but only five years later Queen Anne's War (1702-1713) began. To the south, small armies composed of white South Carolinians and friendly Indians, neither of which had been procured by the militia mechanism, marched into Spanish Florida. In 1703, that quasi-standing force destroyed the chain of Spanish missions in Florida and wiped out certain of the aboriginal Florida Indians. At the northern borders, intercolonial cooperation improved after King William's War. Quasi-standing forces—made up of soldiers from New Hampshire, Connecticut, Rhode Island, and Massachusetts, serving under a common commander—moved against Montreal and Quebec. Now Connecticut kept 400 men ready at all times; now there was grumbling in the intercolonial force because New York persisted in carrying on a profitable trade with Canada. As for the government in England, it devised two grand schemes for the invasion of Canada, using an ocean-borne wing from Britain and an overland wing from the colonies. Accordingly, in 1709 an expeditionary force containing men from New England, New York, New Jersey, and Pennsylvania, marched up the Hudson River-Lake Champlain route to intersect the naval wing coming up the St. Lawrence River from England. Unfortunately, the naval wing was diverted to Europe and never reached America, but the colonial army was not so informed, and it waited in vain while disease killed off many of its men. In 1711, another coalition army marched northward. In this case, the British wing reached the St. Lawrence, but it was battered by such heavy storms that the commander, Sir Hovenden Walker, who was supposed to assume supreme command of the joint metropolis-colonial force, withdrew his fleet and transports and returned to England. As before, the provincials struggled forward to the headwaters of Lake Champlain and waited in vain. Once again disease ravaged them. This fiasco created so unfavorable an impression of British cooperation that the colonies became permanently wary.[41]

The mode of assembling quasi-standing forces for extended, distant fighting continued. Plunder and other inducements were supposed to lure men into the service. If volunteering failed, impressment took over, and the bottom layer of society was once again scraped. Thus it was not the "substantial" people who sickened and died waiting for the British who never arrived, but rather the most expendable males.[42]

The militia did perform certain services. As in King William's War, it parried the numerous and savage raids made by the Indians under French leadership at the frontiers. Typical was the attack on Deerfield, Massachusetts, on February 28, 1704. The attackers, striking at 2 A.M. in bitter cold, achieved complete surprise. They penetrated the town and inflicted many casualties before they met stubborn resistance. The survivors made their way to blockhouses, where the militiamen successfully defended them.[43]

The globe-altering Treaty of Utrecht ended Queen Anne's War in 1713 but did not stop the border forays. When Massachusetts asked Connecticut for aid in these, Connecticut refused because its authorities said Massachusetts had wronged the Indians.[44] South Carolina's appeals for help during the Yamassee War in 1715 brought no more than 100 white men and 60 Indians from North Carolina. Virginia sent some muskets and 120 volunteers, but attached an exorbitant price to them: 22s 6d plus one female slave to be sent to Virginia for each Virginian serving in South Carolina. This price was later lowered.[45]

The first major expeditionary force mounted after Queen Anne's War took place in 1740 against Cartagena, a keystone of the Spanish empire in America. Command fell to Admiral Edward Vernon of the British Navy, who sailed from the British Isles with 5,500 soldiers and sailors. The colonies, for their part, recruited and delivered to the rendezvous in Jamaica 3,500 men who either had responded to the lure of plunder or had been impressed. Virginia impressed men whom the authorities chose to designate as vagabonds. Once the colonial force reached Jamaica, the cost of its maintenance shifted to the mother country, but the cost in life continued to rest on the colonies. Disease took such a toll that no more than 600 of the colonials lived to return home.[46]

Major General James Oglethorpe aimed a lesser expeditionary force, also in 1740, at St. Augustine in Spanish Florida. He commanded 500 friendly Indians, 400 South Carolinians, some of them volunteers and the others impressed, 500 redcoats from a British regiment, and 400 rangers and Scots highlanders. This army, following what was now an established pattern, was not raised directly from the militia system. It was able to capture St. Augustine, but not the stone Castillo de San Marcos, and in the end Oglethorpe had to abandon his forward position and return to Georgia.[47]

The major enemy for a short interlude had been Spain, but in May 1744 the conflict between France and England erupted again in a declared war, known in the colonies as King George's War. Governor William Shirley of Massachusetts, using only colonial troops, but with aid from the Royal Navy, planned to capture Louisbourg on Cape Breton Island, guarding the mouth of the St. Lawrence River. Pennsylvania would contribute nothing, but Connecticut supplied 500 men; New Hampshire, 450; and of course Massachusetts the major share of 3,000 men. Because the chance of plunder was great, more men poured into the port than could be accepted into the expeditionary force. Cooperation from the British Navy proved effective, and the citizen army, commanded by a Maine militia officer, Colonel William Pepperrell, was successful in 1745 in the capture of Louisbourg. Intercolonial cooperation had been noteworthy, as had been the means of procuring men for the conquest.[48]

Louisbourg was the high point of King George's War which came to an end in 1748. Six years later, skirmishes in the Ohio Valley resulted in the last and greatest of the colonial wars. Known in Europe as the Seven Years' War and in the colonies as the French and Indian War (1754-1763), this was the Great War for Empire. The skirmishes in the Ohio Valley began when the Crown gave Governor Dinwiddie of Virginia permission to expel the French from the area west of Virginia. Dinwiddie knew that the House of Burgesses would not agree to draft the militia, so he attempted to induce men to volunteer. Since the promise of loot was negligible, even Lord Thomas Fairfax, a very powerful landlord, could not oblige his tenants to enlist. In six weeks only 300 men had enlisted, and 100 of them were Indian traders who had a special interest to protect. The other 200 came from the dregs of society. Command over this fragile column settled upon George Washington because of his status as a substantial planter with rising prospects. A detachment of North Carolina recruits actually started toward the rendezvous, but it mutinied and turned back. Other colonies refused to contribute men. In time, a company of regulars that had been stationed in Virginia joined the force, but its use was limited because the captain would not accept a lieutenant colonel in the Virginia service as his superior. All in all, the column was inadequate to the task, the circumstances of the campaign were unlucky, and logistical support was virtually nonexistent. Washington was obliged to surrender at Ft. Necessity on 4 July 1754.[49]

Slightly more than a year later, in August 1755, the English cause suffered a far worse disaster in the notorious defeat of the force led by Major General Edward Braddock. The citizen soldiers with Braddock did not come directly from the militia system but had been enlisted or impressed for this specific mission. Braddock spoke of them as slothful. Whatever he said, they performed better than his regulars, primarily because they were to some degree familiar with the conditions under which they had to fight. George Washington, who was present, said they behaved like men and died like soldiers. Farther to the north, the irregular soldiery contributed to a victory. These were men whom William Johnson raised and led. Johnson's citizen army of about 2,000 men met the opposition army under Baron Dieskau near Lake George on 8 September 1755 and defeated it. Dieskau used his regulars about the same way as Braddock had done and with the same results.[50]

Throughout 1756 and 1757, the British suffered defeats in America. Poor manpower was one of the main reasons. The earl of Loudoun complained that the colonies sent to him "fellows hired by other men who should have gone themselves."[51] Provincial officers also complained. Washington, now a colonel of the Virginia militia, spoke bitterly of the "obstinate, self-willed, perverse" men he received, "of no service to the people and very burthensome to the country."[52] Many were draftees from the militia, which meant that they were probably substitutes for the men who had actually been picked. Washington continued, "No man was ever worse plagued with drafts sent from several counties. Out of 400 recently received 114 have deserted. . . . I am determined to hang two or three."[53] Later, he did hang a few. Beyond Virginia to the south, North Carolina contained nearly 9,000 men of military age, but it could not produce enough volunteers. North Carolina's major contribution in manpower was in regiments made up largely of indentured Germans paid for by the British government. As for Maryland, it supplied neither men nor money. The best men continued to evade service, and as late as March 1758, General Abercrombie still demanded that the governors send him men "fairly drafted out of (the) best militia."[54]

Late in 1757, William Pitt became prime minister for the second time and began to shake up the war-waging machinery in England and in the colonies. He reached down below the top of the seniority list to select officers for the command in America. More important for the colonies, he promised to pay them for any costs incurred if they would truly throw their weight into the fight. In addition, he removed a long-standing grievance by making a provincial officer equal in rank to a Britisher of the same grade. Having offered these inducements, Pitt asked for 20,000 American citizen soldiers. This time, the militia system procured men directly. Results at first reflected enthusiasm but hardly efficiency. The Governor of Connecticut ordered out one-quarter of the colony's militia to go to the aid of Ft. William Henry, but no more than 1,200 men appeared. As this was not enough to reinforce the garrison adequately, the commandant was obliged to surrender.[55]

Soon, however, the system improved. One out of every four eligible men in Massachusetts and one out of every three in Connecticut at some time entered service. Thus, partly through the militia system and partly through alternative methods, the colonies during the next two years raised 18,000 men. They helped turn the military tide. In August 1758, Colonel John Bradstreet, with provincials from New York, New Jersey, Rhode Island, and Massachusetts, captured the strategically vital Ft. Frontenac at the head of the St. Lawrence River. General John Forbes relentlessly advanced a column to achieve what Braddock had failed to do three years earlier. Upon capturing Ft. Duquesne, he renamed it for Pitt. Along with his regulars marched an entire regiment from Virginia, commanded by William Byrd II, a grandee of the Old Dominion, together with contingents from Maryland, North Carolina, and Delaware. The militia system had worked effectively, but it was far from being the decisive agency in turning defeat into victory. When General Wolfe captured Quebec in the final campaign, he had only six companies of American irregulars with him,[56] whom he regarded as "the dirtiest, most contemptible cowardly dog[s] you can conceive."[57] Wolfe, with his rigid European training, could hardly have evaluated American citizen soldiers fairly. Those he saw were probably impressed men and substitutes.

The Great War for Empire had forced the colonials to cooperate with each other on an unprecedented scale. It also had crowded them into a new intimacy with the military of the metropolis. Unimpressed by what they saw, they claimed that their citizen soldiery had been the prime mover in driving the French from North America. Englishmen, on the other hand, believed that their regulars had been the decisive agents, indeed, that the colonials had often been delinquent in their duty. They were convinced that colonial cooperation had been bought and that without the British effort North America would have become French. As they saw it, the American citizen soldier had been ineffective. This dispute exacerbated antagonisms during the twelve years following 1763 and contributed to the coming of the American Revolution.

The Great War for Empire did not alter the militia system of the colonies. The system had supplied manpower, but so had the alternative method of producing short-term standing forces, manned in part by volunteers and in part by impressed men. More often than not the provincial commanders came from the roster of militia officers. Adam Stephen, Moses Hazen, David Wooster, Seth Pomeroy, Israel Putnam, John Stuart, Philip John Schuyler, and George Washington, all generals in the American Revolution, learned what they knew about warfare from service as militia officers during the Great War. They also learned that the British military system was flawed and perfectly capable of defeat.[58]

Trained companies, known as trained bands, did not provide quick manpower during the Great War. They seldom turned out as companies but rather were the source of detachments that joined with similar detachments from other companies to make new ad hoc units. In New England, where the trained bands were generally more efficient than elsewhere, detachments from them were constantly defending new settlements before those settlements could defend themselves. Mobilization would have been faster if the trained bands had been inducted intact.[59]

At both Jamestown and Plymouth, the first two permanent beachheads, it became apparent that the settlers had not had enough militia training in England to prepare them to survive in the wilderness. The men seemed to be too inexperienced with firearms to kill the game they needed. Nevertheless, they were in the end able to overpower their Indian neighbors. Jamestown, however, was nearly wiped out in 1622 by the redmen, whereas Plymouth joined with Massachusetts Bay to exterminate their tribal neighbors, the Pequots, in 1636.[60]

By the middle of the eighteenth century, there were at least thirteen different militia systems. Each of them sprang from and reflected a different culture and operated under different laws. The units of the several colonies were in no way interchangeable, making it difficult for them to amalgamate into large units if there was a need. The New England militia was the best because the political township provided a compact base upon which military organization could rest. In addition, the Puritan congregation provided strong spiritual support. The clergy in Massachusetts considered the militia the true bulwark of their bible commonwealth. They fully supported the principle of universal military obligation in peacetime as well as in wartime. To them war was inevitable because it sprang from the corrupt nature of man, a nature which would never change. The density of population, too, made it easier for men to gather for training in parts of New England. On that account Boston developed the best units. In contrast, Rhode Island's militia was inferior to the general New England standard.[61]

Neither the militia of New York nor that of Pennsylvania was strong in the middle of the eighteenth century. It is difficult to account for New York, but Pennsylvania was restrained by its Quaker tradition. As for the two Chesapeake Bay colonies, Virginia and Maryland, their militia traditions were deep-rooted, and the quality of their systems was about equal. Their counties were larger than the New England townships and offered a less compact base for military organization. Moreover, their Anglican and Roman Catholic parishes did not provide a spiritual support equal to that of the Puritan congregations.[62]

South of Virginia, militia quality varied widely. Charleston, South Carolina, was the home of some of the best units to be found anywhere, but out in the country the Charleston level of excellence was not maintained.

In all the colonies there were at least four types of citizen soldiers:

1. *The Standing Militia.* It was made up of individuals who under colonial law had a military obligation. The men were organized into companies and higher units, and were obliged to arm themselves and to train periodically.

2. *The Volunteer Militia.* It was composed of volunteers from the militia system and organized into units of cavalry, artillery, and various types of

elite infantry units. Although an integral part of the militia, this category enjoyed special privileges because the men provided for themselves expensive equipment and horses and also uniformed themselves.

3. *War Volunteers.* Volunteers who offered to serve in quasi-standing armies formed for specific expeditions or purposes. These men served longer than the traditional militia term of three months and might be used beyond the colony's borders.

4. *Involuntary Servers.* They might have been swept up in an impressment ordered by the governing elite to catch the socially and economically undesirable, or they might have been drafted from the militia.

The latter sort were not required by law and custom to serve longer than the traditional militia term nor to march beyond the colony, but occasionally some colonial authority forced them to do so. Categories 3 and 4 were the troops to be employed in offensive operations.

When immediate danger threatened an area, the senior militia officer there had authority to call out the units of the standing militia. This type of mobilization was especially successful during the Dutch Wars of the seventeenth century. During the second of those wars in the 1660s, militia companies called en masse prevented the landing of parties from Dutch warships that had penetrated Chesapeake Bay. During the third war, in the next decade, the New York militia fended off hostile landings. In 1706, Charleston, South Carolina, companies foiled a Spanish attempt to capture their city.[63]

Colonials did not want their militia too closely associated with British regulars. Ezra Stiles, president of Yale College, judged the redcoats to be without any religion unless it was to gratify their own appetites.[64] He worried lest such godlessness and hedonism spread in America through contact via the militia during the Great War for Empire. But colonial troops had scant desire to press close to regulars, for the independent companies, which they most often observed, were frequently ragged, ill-fed, and badly sheltered. Moreover, they were controlled by a discipline so brutal that it even repelled the colonial spectators, who themselves were capable of much brutality.[65]

A majority of thoughtful colonials cherished an idealized image of the citizen soldier. He was the civilian who served when needed as a soldier because it was his civic responsibility to do so. He was indeed the bulwark of defense of the colonies. The alternate system, which gradually developed in all the colonies, did little to alter this image. It did not matter that the militia system conceded the offensive to any foe, because it had what has become known in the twentieth century as second-strike capability—it could absorb the first shock of an enemy and still proceed to develop an efficient fighting force.[66]

On the eve of the American Revolution, Timothy Pickering of Massachusetts suggested that if the colonies reformed their militias they would never need standing forces. To achieve this desirable and low-cost position, it was necessary to involve the social elites once more in the standing militia. Because it was so simple to avoid service by paying a fine, the upper levels of society had stepped aside and allowed the standing militia to be operated by less competent persons. Simply require participation and close the avenues of evasion, Pickering insisted, and the citizen soldiery would become the best and the sole bulwark of the colonies. This was the way a free people ought to defend itself.[67]

Contemporary observers of the wars for empire rated the Canadian militia as better suited to its mission than those of the British colonies. The man of military age in Canada accepted service in arms as an inevitable obligation. Their acceptance did not rest on belief in the duty of a free citizen but rather on their conditioning to an arbitrary form of government. That government required every man to be armed and ready for rapid mobilization. One British observer during the Great War for Empire characterized the resultant militia thus: "These are troops that fight without pay—maintaining themselves in the woods without charges, march without baggage, and support themselves without stores and magazines—we are at immense charges for those purposes." He could have added that the Canadians were well disciplined and trained, and more skillful at Indian-style fighting than their English counterparts.[68]

Modern students of the English colonies concede the value of the militia system. It provided a necessary pool of manpower from which men could be drawn by volunteering, by calling up units, even by draft if need be. This pool performed a useful function even though the men drawn from it were insufficiently trained. One scholar of the Virginia militia writes that the colony took a medieval and communal institution and adapted it to new conditions.[69] The adaptation made it possible for a loose society of acquisitive individuals to carry out military actions with a minimum dislocation of the economy. A student of the New England militia, Donald E. Leach, said about the same thing: "Much credit must be given to the system of compulsory military training that provided the colonies with an ever available reservoir of manpower. The fundamental soundness of the old militia system, one of England's important legacies to America, was tested and proved in the Indian wars of the seventeenth century."[70] If one tacks on the alternative system of securing manpower for extended expeditions and inserts a caveat concerning militia efficiency during the Indian wars, Leach's evaluation rings true.

No scholars deny that the militia system was flawed. Citizen soldiers on active duty often showed slack discipline, poor camp sanitation, chronic shortage of weapons, and a propensity to opt out at the most critical moments. Also, their training did not equip them to fight Indians. Benjamin Franklin spoke of them as "of little or no use in our woods." All in all, then, it is not possible to draw up a balance on the colonial militia that will show either profit or loss. The best that can be said is that the system contained characteristics brought from the Old World and were modified in the New World, and that its existence and performance left an indelible impression on the future history of the United States.[71]

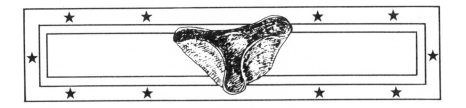

THREE

The American Revolution

When General Thomas Gage reached Boston in May 1774 to become commander-in-chief of the British forces in North America, the royal governor of Massachusetts ordered out two elite companies of the Boston militia and some standing militia companies to honor the new official.[1] But in the following months the power of the commander-in-chief, of the royal governor, and indeed of all the royal officials waned.

The militia officers generally were affluent and influential. Many of them, holding commissions from the Crown, were reluctant to sever ties with England. The major general commanding the Massachusetts militia and half the colonels of regiments were Tories. The same proportion existed throughout New England. As the power of the royal officers waned, that of colonial institutions waxed, and local governments soon stripped the Tories of their commands. In addition, they restructured the militia system. Their purging and restructuring were revolutionary acts. The emerging patriot leadership—according to John Shy an outgrowth of the militia—enforced the boycott of British goods and identified and isolated loyalists.[2]

The First Continental Congress, in existence only from September 5 to October 25, 1774, exhorted the colonial governments to bolster their militias. The Second Congress constructed a uniform table of organization, recommended that companies elect their own officers, that companies group themselves into regiments, and that the legislatures designate officers for the regiments. Power by this time resided largely with elected governors and legislatures and not with the Crown agents. Unfortunately, the militias directed by the governors and legislatures were too different from each other to be interchangeable.[3]

Nevertheless, the colonies/states quickened militia preparations. Most of the governments attempted to enlarge their stocks of munitions. Colonials who continued to correspond with Englishmen inflated the war preparations in their letters.[4] "All the towns of the Province, Boston excepted," wrote one, "are at the desire of Congress exercising their militia every fair day, and are also chusing their own militia officers; another act of treason."[5] A second correspondent, asserting that there would be no shortage of arms for the Americans, described the prevailing mood as "The Rage Militaire."[6]

The revolutionary government in Massachusetts directed all company officers to prepare one-third of their command to respond instantly to calls. Thus were created the Minute Man units, copied then by other colonies/states. Minute Men first came under fire at Lexington when Captain John Parker's company stood in the way of the British march toward Concord to confiscate military stores.[7] Although Parker's Minute Men fired the shots "heard round the world," they scarcely halted the march of the foe. At Concord, however, militia units—some of them with ancient lineages—lined the rise overlooking the British line of march. Behind them stood a company made up of old men and boys. Still farther behind were citizens who removed the stores the redcoats had come to confiscate. Foiled in their mission, the British began the return march to Boston, only to be hit by fusillades from behind every stone fence. This fire came not from organized militia but from clusters of enraged citizens. Had the marksmen been better organized, they might have destroyed the invading column.[8] As it was, a relief force had to come from Boston to rescue them. Lord Percy, commanding the relief, was impressed by the Americans in arms: "Many of them concealed themselves in houses and advanced within ten yards to fire at me and other officers, tho they were mortally certain of being put to death themselves. . . . I never believed . . . that they would have attacked the King's troops, or have the perseverance I found in them."[9]

After Bunker Hill, General Thomas Gage wrote to Lord Dartmouth, secretary of state for the colonies, "Americans are not the despicable rabble too many supposed them to be. . . . There is a military spirit . . . joined with common zeal and enthusiams. . . . The conquest of the country is not easy."[10] Unfortunately for the British cause, the earl of Dartmouth and others in high position continued to view the Americans as merely rabble in arms. They could not believe that an army in which a bookseller (Knox), a blacksmith (Greene), and a tavern keeper (Putnam) were generals needed to be taken seriously.[11]

After Lexington, at least 20,000 men from Rhode Island, New Hampshire, and Connecticut swiftly converged on Boston. Israel Putnam traveled one hundred miles in eighteen hours using the same horse and pausing to summon additional men along the way. But when the military situation at Boston settled into stalemate, this crowd dispersed as fast as it had formed. The General Court of Massachusetts called for the formation of a New England army, 30,000 strong, to serve through the balance of 1775. No such number actually appeared, but those who did were placed under the orders of Artemus Ward, a veteran of the Great War and commander of the Massachusetts contingent. The length of their service, longer than the traditional militia tour, was stipulated. Governor Trumbull of Connecticut wrote that the citizen thought of his service as "purely voluntary; therefore when the time of enlistment is out, he thinks himself not holden without further engagement. . . . This is the genius and spirit of our people."[12]

Even though Americans generally expected a short war, Congress felt the need for a semiregular force, free of the limitations of state armies and militia. Accordingly, it constituted twenty-six regiments to serve during 1776, subject to Congress and to the commanders appointed by Congress. Since much of the time Congress could not sustain its regiments, it promised to pay the costs ultimately if the states would meanwhile take care of them. To broaden support for the war effort, George Washington of Virginia was asked to take command of the total force.[13]

Washington counted on the citizen soldiers present around Boston to enlist in these new Continental Regiments, but few did. These men viewed their connection as a contractual one, and having fulfilled one contract, they did not feel morally bound to enter into another one. But Washington ascribed to them a "dirty, mercenary spirit." How could they abandon the Cause when it needed them most?[14] Abandon it they did, and he was obliged to call for 7,000 militiamen to serve only until January 15, 1776. For him such troops were a last resort, "They come in," he wrote, "you cannot tell how, go you cannot tell when, and act you cannot tell where, consume your provisions, exhaust your stores, and leave you at last at a critical moment."[15] Yet it was the militia, however unreliable, that saw his army through 1775.

Massachusetts began to draft men in 1776, and the other states did so later. As in colonial times, men in favored social circumstances could escape the draft by paying a fine or by finding a substitute. Masters of indentured servants and owners of slaves could send their laborers as substitutes, and fathers could send their minor sons. In Northampton County, Pennsylvania, 54 percent of the enlisted men were substitutes for actual draftees. Thus, in the colonies as now in the states the burden of compulsory military service fell most heavily on men at low social levels.[16]

The laws and customs on which the power to draft rested, supported a militia system that was purely defensive and permitted only short tours of duty within the boundaries of the state. Yet militiamen did receive notices such as this one placing them involuntarily in Continental service: "This is to inform you [that you] are drafted as one of the Continental men to go to George Washington."[17] Such conscription was illegal and could be practiced only because the men drafted were too poor or too ignorant of the law to contest being selected.

Some of the states impressed men who were not part of the militia, sweeping in free blacks, vagrants, and in some cases imprisoned felons. In South Carolina, a militiaman who mutinied could be sentenced to serve in the Carolina Continental Line Regiment for as long as one year. In general, persons with genuine religious scruples were not forced into service; they could pay a fine or secure a substitute. They could not, however, escape harsh criticism and sometimes violence, especially if the enemy was at the gate.[18] Not all Quakers avoided service; Nathanael Greene was "put from under the care of the Meeting," when he accepted a commission; while other Friends banded into their own companies where they responded to such commands as "Shoulder thy firelock!"[19]

In every quarter the use of militia was essential to the continuation of the conflict. Major General Charles Lee defended Charleston, South Carolina, in 1776 with a mixed force of 2,000 state troops, 2,700 local militia, and about 900 Continentals.[20] At around the same time, Congress resolved to call upon Massachusetts, Connecticut, New York, and New Jersey for 13,800 militiamen to serve alongside the regulars, and upon Pennsylvania, Delaware, and Maryland for a highly mobile force of 10,000.[21] Accordingly, when the British finally appeared from Halifax in June 1776 to attack New York, Washington was able to assemble 28,000 men, 19,000 of them were either short-term militiamen or recruits with less experience than the militia had. Washington was defeated on Long Island on 27 August 1776, whereupon some three-quarters of the militia dribbled away, "dismayed," in Washington's words, "intractable, and impatient" to return to their homes.[22]

Throughout 1776 there was an American army only because there was a militia system. To be sure, the commander-in-chief could never be certain what quality of performance he could expect from the citizen soldiers the system produced. When Washington was forced out of New York and into New Jersey, the men once more began to sidle away, some of them because their terms had expired, others because they deserted. In the northern American army, five-month men completed their tours and went home, leaving Newport, Rhode Island, dangerously undermanned. All in all, as 1776 ended, the American cause seemed to be in nearly fatal decline: Newport and New York were enemy-occupied, Philadelphia was undefended, and New Jersey was overrun. General Greene blamed the loss of Jersey, the breadbasket of the Cause, on shortcomings of the Jersey militia.[23]

The heady battles of Trenton and Princeton bolstered faltering American resolve. For a time afterward, militia flocked to Washington's army, then as quickly began to drift off home. With whatever force he could hold together, Washington had to wait to find out where the British might strike in the central area. While he waited, the largest British army fielded so far, commanded by Major General John Burgoyne, commenced a ponderous advance southward from Canada. The local militia might have failed altogether had not an atrocity committed by Indians in British pay stimulated them. Washington wrote to New England governors asking for help against a foe who used savages to do his fighting.

When the New England militia responded en masse, New Yorkers also began to stir. Seriously weakened, Burgoyne's column halted, foiled by the wilderness and the swarming of the militia. "The civilian population," Don Higgenbotham wrote, "gradually [changed] into a loosely arrayed body of irregulars of the sort unknown in the Old World."[24] As seen by British Sergeant Lamb, "Numerous parties of American militia swarmed around the little adverse army like birds of prey."[25] That little adverse army surrendered on October 17, 1777, and one of the mercenaries among the surrendered forces wrote of the conquerors: "Not one of them was properly uniformed, but each man had on the clothes in which he goes into the field. . . but they all stood like soldiers, erect . . . so still that we were amazed . . . and we were all surprised at the sight of such finely build people. . . . Most of the colonels and other officers were in their ordinary clothes."[26]

While the northern army struggled against Burgoyne, Washington faced General Sir William Howe in the vicinity of Philadelphia. Howe settled himself for a comfortable winter in that city, with 9,000 troops as an outpost at Germantown. Washington attacked Germantown on October 4, 1977, using four columns in an elaborate converging tactic, too elaborate, indeed, for the two columns that were made up of militia. Although unable to expel the British from Germantown, the American force came close enough to a signal victory to shake the enemy's confidence.[27] Nevertheless, Howe remained cozy in the city while the American army suffered at Valley Forge close by. Most of the militiamen went home and did not receive the instruction given by Baron von Steuben during that bitter winter.

Burgoyne's surrender had convinced the French government of the value of an open alliance with the United States, entered into in February 1778. When this took place, the British shifted their strategic focus southward. Late in 1778, they captured Savannah and brought Georgia back under their domination. For the second time during the war they made Charleston their target and were able after a six-week siege to enter it on May 12, 1780. Half the surrendered American force of 5,000 was militia, most of whom took the oath of loyalty to the king.[28]

During the southern campaigns, the British high command relied too much on Tories, individual and banded together in militia units. Tories were cheaper than regulars or mercenaries. Drawn by the enthusiasm of southern loyalists, Tories from New York and New Jersey traveled south to join the British forces there. From the southernmost of the erstwhile colonies, Florida, raiders for the British cause marauded into Georgia and South Carolina.[29] At the Battle of King's Mountain, October 7, 1780, one thousand Tories constituted the bulk of the British defenders. They were surrounded by patriot citizen soldiers, swarming as they had done around Burgoyne's army in 1777, and were overwhelmed.

Brigadier General Daniel Morgan, a veteran handler of citizen soldiers, returned to active duty when the enemy came south. Morgan achieved almost the perfect use of militia at the Battle of Cowpens on January 17, 1781. In an open area, with the French Broad River at his rear, he formed his 1,040 men into two lines with the irregulars in the front line where they had to receive the initial shock. The reasons he gave for the field he chose and the formation he took were that with the river behind them the militiamen had no avenue of retreat, and he needed his regulars as a steady reserve in the rear rank. He had a way with citizen soldiers, and moving among them man to man, he exhorted them to stand firm for two volleys and then run for safety behind the Continental line. As the 400 militiamen believed in Morgan, they did as he requested; but they did more. Once secure behind the second line, they reformed and at a critical moment swept around the protective line to attack the right flank of the enemy. At the same time a small detachment of dragoons hit the left flank, resulting in a nearly perfect double envelopment. Of the 1,100 men in the foe's detachment, 110 died and 702 were made prisoners, at a cost of twelve American killed and sixty wounded.[30]

Daniel Morgan had risen to command at Cowpens from the lowest ranks. As a wagoner in the British service during the Great War for Empire, he had had his back bloodied for the violation of orders. Not motivated to stand and die for the British cause in the midst of the American wilderness, he had, on the fatal ground of General Braddock's disaster, cut the traces of his team and ridden the horses at full gallop to safety. Standing well over six feet and weighing about 200 pounds, all of it bone and muscle, he derived some authority from his size. He was also skillful with a rifle, and when Congress constituted ten rifle companies to make up the first Continental regiment, he was made captain of one company, whereupon he marched his men the 600 miles to Boston in three weeks. He distinguished himself, above everyone else, before Quebec in December 1775. Captured there, he was exchanged in time to give indispensable aid in the final battles that forced General Burgoyne to surrender in the fall of 1777. By now he was colonel, but he was forced to drop out due to crippling arthritis. When the British moved southward, Morgan reentered active duty, this time as a brigadier general of Continentals. He had had so little schooling that he read with difficulty, wrote nearly illiterately, and could hardly add and subtract, but he had common sense, untutored intelligence, and experience in what citizens turned soldiers were capable of in combat. In other than American circumstances, he might never have had a chance to reach star rank.

Morgan's tactics were so successful that Nathanael Greene, Continental commander in the south, tried to use the same at Guilford Court House two months later, with much less success; still, he inflicted casualties which the invaders, unable to secure replacements, could not afford. Numbers of citizen soldiers associated themselves with the partisan leaders Thomas Sumter, Andrew Pickens, Francis Marion, and William Moultrie. These, and Greene's main army, operating in a wary coalition, gradually nudged Cornwallis out of the deep south into Virginia where he could combine with other British troops and gain the aid of the British navy. But at Yorktown, a mixed force of 5,700 Continentals, 7,800 French soldiers, and 3,200 militiamen encircled Cornwallis's force by land while the French fleet closed his access to the sea. Unable to escape, the cornered force surrendered on October 19, 1781.[31]

In warfare with the Indians, at this time a biproduct of the Revolution, the citizens soldiers were not generally successful. As early as 1774, major combats in western Virginia revealed too little cohesion among the irregular troops at a heavy cost in white casualties.[32] Maximum success for the Indians came during the summer and fall of 1778, when British-led redmen laid waste the Wyoming area in northern Pennsylvania and the Cherry Valley in New

York. Since the militia seemed paralyzed, General Washington was obliged to make a substantial detachment from the Continental Army and sent it, under the command of Major General John Sullivan, to break the fighting power of the Iroquois. Sullivan achieved that objective in 1779.[33]

Conflict with the Indians did not stop after Yorktown. Full of hatred, Pennsylvania militiamen in 1782 massacred ninety defenseless Christian Indians encamped at Gnadenhutten. During the following summer when Colonel William Crawford led a militia column into the same area, the Indians, seeking revenge, saw their chance, and encircled the white formation. Crawford pleaded with his men to stick together or face certain doom, but individualists first and soldiers second, most of them banded into small detachments and tried to escape. A majority of them were captured and tortured to death. Crawford himself was broiled alive on a slow fire in revenge for Gnadenhutten. Even Daniel Boone was unsuccessful. At Blue Licks in mid-September 1783, he placed a sizeable force of Kentucky militia in a strong defense position. They were attacked by 200 Indians directed by some British rangers and were routed in five minutes, suffering heavy casualties.[34]

Although almost all combatants started as citizen soldiers, those who served long terms in the Continental Army developed the skills of regulars. When in 1777 Continentals enlisted for three years, certain of the civilian revolutionaries thought they saw developing an instrument the British experience had taught them to hate: a standing army. Samuel Adams expressed their fear:

> A standing army, however necessary it may be at some time, is always dangerous to the Liberties of the People. Soldiers are apt to consider themselves as a Body, distinct from the rest of the citizens. They have their arms always in their hands. Their rules and their discipline are severe. They soon become attached to their officers and disposed to yield implicit obedience to their commands. Such a power should be watched with a jealous eye.[35]

Samuel Adams and other revolutionaries like him did not want any sort of power, least of all military, concentrated in whatever central government was to replace the British, whose centralized authority they had struggled to throw off. Sovereignty, they were sure, rested in the individual states. Thus, Governor John Houstoun considered the Continentals to be intruders into his state of Georgia. All four of the great partisan leaders in the southern campaigns worked reluctantly with central military authority. Sumter resigned rather than accept subordination to a Continental officer. To the north, John Stark, who had dropped out because of the intrusion of central authority, took leadership again to oppose Burgoyne's advance, but after the surrender at Saratoga he marched his men back to New Hampshire rather than take orders from a Continental officer. In all the states, militia officers resisted being subordinated to Continentals and endlessly bickered over relative rank.[36]

Most of the states, jealous of their sovereignty, created small armies strictly for state defense. Although the Continental commanders could never be sure of the cooperation of these state forces, they did have the use of parts of them in certain critical movements. Washington had detachments from New York and Connecticut with him at Yorktown, and George Rogers Clark counted 200 men from the Virginia army as a necessary part of his force used to conquer the French settlements in the far-off Mississippi Valley.[37]

Of all types of soldiers, the militiamen most nearly conformed to the image of the citizen soldier. Moreover, the militia system was the source of the other soldier types. Most of the Continental officers came out of it; examples are John Sullivan, sometime major in New Hampshire; Benedict Arnold, captain in the Connecticut Governor's Guards; and Benjamin Lincoln, colonel of a Massachusetts regiment, commanded by his father before him.[38]

In the fall of 1776 George Washington wrote privately about the militia: "The dependence which Congress have placed upon (them)... I fear will totally ruin our cause. Being subject to no control themselves, they introduce disorder among the troops . . . while change in living brings on sickness; this makes them impatient to get home . . . and introduces abominable desertions."[39] Nathanael Greene expressed much the same view but stressed different reasons why militiamen could not be relied on: "People coming from home with all the tender feelings of domestic life are not sufficiently fortified with natural courage to stand the shocking scenes of war. To march over dead men, to hear without concern the groans of the wounded, I say few men can stand such scenes unless steeled by habit and fortified by military pride."[40] Greene felt that militia and Continentals did not operate well together, and when possible, he used militiamen in small detachments in which he considered them to be most effective.

Both Washington and Greene knew they had to depend on militia and did so, but they were less tolerant of it than some officers of foreign extraction. Charles Lee, who had been a British officer before becoming a Continental, wrote a pamphlet to show the superiority of American militiamen over British regulars. Unlike Greene, he thought the irregulars worked best when associated with Continentals.[41] Horatio Gates, also commissioned in the British army, had confidence in militia and skill in using it. At the Battle of Camden on August 16, 1780, he entrusted the entire left side of his line to militiamen from Virginia and North Carolina, who unfortunately collapsed when attacked with bayonets.[42] LaFayette spoke for the American militia at every opportunity, and his countryman Rochambeau directed his men to share with them.[43]

The militia was, obviously, unpredictable. A call for it might produce more men than could be supported, or a mere trickle, or no men at all. This being so, commanders found it difficult to plan their moves in advance. Once the troops assembled, the uncertainty was by no means dispelled, for there was a constant ebb and flow as men came and went. It can be said that the American commanders, in trying to use efficiently a wildly fluctuating number of men, faced at least as difficult a problem as did their opponents, who had to try to conquer rebel armies, then overrun and occupy a vast hostile terrain with an insufficient force.

John Shy has identified three missions carried out by the militia without which independence could not have been won:

1. Militia controlled communities, holding them to the patriot cause, either through indoctrination or if necessary by intimidation.

2. Militia provided "on short notice, large numbers of armed men for brief periods of emergency service."

3. Using the militia system, authorities bribed or drafted enough men each year to keep the Continental Army alive.[44]

Men from the lowest layers of society made up part of the revolutionary military force, but they were by no means a majority. Washington and Congress accepted the recruitment of Negroes—the layer farthest down of all—because of the never-ending need for men in the ranks. Low-status whites came in, but yeomen and artisans also entered the ranks. By and large, the enlisted men of the Revolutionary Army were not the castoffs and conscripts characteristic of European forces. What the Americans fielded was unique for the end of the eighteenth century: it was a citizen army. This new institution was the product of a culture that rejected the idea that the soldier was in a caste different from his countrymen. Later in the life of the nation, the enlisted soldier in peacetime sometimes resembled his low-caste counterpart in Europe; but in wartime the forces always filled up with substantial citizens turned soldiers for a time.[45]

George Washington emerged from the Revolution with a world-wide reputation. Like his fellow Virginian Daniel Morgan, he had served in the Great War for Empire but, unlike Morgan, always in positions of command, at least of Virginia militia. Douglas Southall Freeman describes Washington at the time of his resignation from the Virginia militia in 1758 as humorless, ambitious, obstinant, acquisitive, suspicious and too sensitive, not qualities one would look for to make a man a general. But by the time the Congress offered him the Continental command eighteen years later, he had mastered the least attractive of these characteristics simply by the thorough performance of common daily duties. Although never close to his men in spirit, and more often than not critical of the militia, he never left them physically. During eight and one-half years of grueling service, he was with the troops constantly, except for ten days at Mount Vernon. His unfailing presence, his imposing bearing, coupled with unflagging good manners and endurance, seemed to inspire both Continentals and militia to do their best.[46]

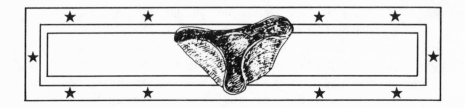

FOUR

Militia in the Early National Period

The Continental Congress established a committee to work out a charter of government in 1776, but the document that committee produced was not ratified until 1781 because other issues demanded prior treatment. The delayed document was the Articles of Confederation. It created a decentralized government with sovereignty vested in the states. It was a "firm league of friendship," in which the individual states pledged to defend each other. The bulk of the armed forces of the Revolution had already percolated back into the population; the term "army" appeared only once in the articles.[1] But the document did declare that "Every state shall always keep up a well regulated and disciplined militia, sufficiently armed and accoutered, and shall provide, and constantly have ready for use, in public stores, a due number of field pieces and tents, and a proper quantity of arms, ammunition, and camp equipage."[2] All officers called to active duty by the Congress of the Confederation below the rank of colonel were to be appointed by the states, but colonels and generals were to be appointed by the United States "in Congress Assembled." Congress had the power to declare war. No state was to maintain an army or a navy in time of peace without the consent of Congress. Yet the Articles authorized no sanctions to enforce these war powers, leaving the situation as it had been in pre-Revolutionary days between the colonies and Great Britain. The central government could requisition men and money from the states, but it could not compel their delivery. The same limitation applied to the responsibility of the states to keep a well-regulated and disciplined militia.

Congress presided over the liquidation of the fast-shrinking Continental Army and in 1784 constituted a small replacement consisting of 720 men drawn from the militias of Connecticut, New York, New Jersey, and Pennsylvania, to serve for one year unless discharged sooner. It placed Lieutenant Colonel Josiah Harmar, from the Pennsylvania militia, in command. At the end of the first year, Congress voted to sustain the unit for three additional years. Thus, without drawing substantial contemporary notice, a militia force became in 1785 the nucleus of the original regiment of the United States regular army.[3]

At the frontiers, fighting with the Indians continued virtually unaffected by the creation of the new government under the Articles.[4] In 1786, Virginia persuaded the Revolutionary hero George Rogers Clark to lead a state force against the Indians in and beyond the Wabash area. Even so notable a leader found it necessary to draft militiamen, with violence and riots resulting. At last he secured some men but found them of such doubtful quality that he took charge only reluctantly. His instincts about them were correct; they refused to carry the campaign through to a decision, and he was forced, in spite of his pleading to the contrary, to turn back with them.[5] Frontiersmen generally felt the need for more aid than they were getting from the central government and were accordingly skeptical of the value of the Confederation.

In 1786, a body of men under Daniel Shays, who had been the efficient captain of a company during the Revolution, rebelled against the foreclosure of their land in Masachusetts. As many as 1,100 of them threatened the Supreme Court, while 800 militiamen, called to defend the court but sympathetic to the rebels, looked on. The mortgage holders resided in eastern Massachusetts, the rebels in the west. Because there was ill-feeling between the two sections of the state, the creditors were able, using influence and money, to gather enough militiamen from eastern Massachusetts to march against the insurrectionists. The eastern force broke the rebellion six months after it had begun. The use of citizen soldiers to suppress rioters became the pattern for dealing with insurrections in the last decade of the eighteenth century. The difficulty in suppressing Shays' Rebellion was only one episode that convinced former leaders of the Revolution that the Articles of Confederation were too weak to preserve the structure they had fought to bring into being. Pressure from these men led to the calling of the Constitutional Convention which assembled in May 1787 in Philadelphia.[6]

A crucial division separating the fifty-five delegates to that Convention appeared between those who favored a strong central government and those who wanted sovereignty to reside with the states. The advocates of state sovereignty expected the new nation to rely principally on militia, whereas their opponents stressed the need for effective standing forces. Military affairs received little attention in the debate, conducted in secret sessions from May until September, because centralizers were in the majority. The delegates approved the principal military articles of what became the Constitution on August 27, 1787.[7]

Military issues comprised a major concern of the conventions called in the states to consider ratifying the new charter. One argument presented by anticentralist delegates—also expressed at the Constitutional Convention—was the pressing need of the states for a military instrument to check the potentially arbitrary power of the central government. Another argument was that the framers had assigned far too much power over the state militias to the center. Patrick Henry concluded, or at least for public effect said, that the framers must have intended to rob the states of their only security.[8] Other critics pointed out that the states would lose their vitality and become political nonentities if they did not retain full control over their own militias. If state power deteriorated, the proposed government of the United States might systematically destroy the personal liberty of men who were liable to militia duty and eventually the liberty of other persons as well.[9] A proposal to soften this objection by creating a select corps within the larger militia—to be composed of the ablest men—died because anticentralizers feared an elite corps in the militia as the seedbed of a standing army.[10]

Fear of a standing army was one of the principal weapons used by debaters who favored decentralized government and hence militia. Luther Martin referred to a standing army as an "Engine of arbitrary power, which has so often and so successfully been used for the subversion of freedom."[11] Samuel Nason labeled standing armies "the bane of Republican governments. By this have seven-eighths of the once free nations of the globe been brought into bondage."[12] The second portion of this argument was that the United States had no need of a standing force. Without one, reliance upon the militia would be complete, encouraging its development to the point where it could serve all national needs. Elbridge Gerry said: "If a regular army is admitted will not the militia be neglected and gradually dwindle into contempt? and where then are we to look for defense of our rights and liberties?"[13] Governor Randolph told the Virginia convention: "With respect to a standing army, I believe there was not a member in the Federal convention who did not feel indignation at such an institution."[14]

Both the framers of the Constitution and a majority of the delegates to state ratifying conventions were more concerned with foreign aggression than with internal subversion. As a result, the ratified Constitution contained adequate legal basis for a standing army if Congress chose to create one. On this matter the anticentralists were defeated. But in the clauses pertaining to the militia they came close to achieving their objectives. Here, as in the entire Constitution, the object was to prevent the accumulation of overwhelming power in any person or agency. The method used was to split power into fragments, and in no part of the document was this done in more detail than in the militia clauses. Congress received authority to organize, arm, and discipline the militia; the states, the power to appoint officers and to train the citizen soldiers according to the discipline prescribed by Congress. Not the president but Congress acquired the authority to summon state militias into federal service, for three specific tasks only: to execute the laws of the Union, to suppress insurrections, and to repel invasion.

Because the militia clauses, like the rest of the Constitution, were written in general terms, they had to be interpreted to have meaning in specific cases. Only case-by-case interpretation could make it clear what exactly was meant by the power to appoint the officers and to train the militias. Likewise, some agency would have to decide in every case whether a federal call for militia to enter national service was for one of the three purposes stipulated. One observer might see an invasion where another saw only a maneuver; an insurrection to one man might be nothing but a harmless gathering to another. In any given situation there could be disagreement over whether or not troops were needed to enforce the laws. The framers did not designate an agency to interpret the Constitution. Over a long period of time, the courts assumed that indispensable task, but not without challenge.

Another clause gives Congress power to govern such part of the militia as may be employed in the service of the United States. A second says that the president shall be commander-in-chief of the militia when it is called into the actual service of the nation. A third clause, added to the Constitution as the Second Amendment, states that "A well regulated Militia being necessary to the security of a free State, the right of the people to keep and bear arms shall not be infringed." In the twentieth century, the Second Amendment has become the center of a controversy between those citizens who want to see gun carrying restricted and those who insist that free Americans must have the right to be armed. The authors of the Amendment left no clues as to their intentions; but it seems likely that they felt scant concern about firearms in the hands of people and that they had the militia in view when they wrote the clause.

In the central issue—centralization in government versus the reverse—which side prevailed in military matters? During the pre-Civil War period, the decentralizers seem to have gained the most. The standing forces were small, and when expanded for short wars were supplemented by drawing citizen soldiers of one sort or another into federal service, using state mechanisms. Control of the militia rested almost totally with the states. Indeed, the emphasis did not shift until the twentieth century. In the two World Wars and in the intervals of peace, the federal government steadily assumed power over the successor of the militia, the National Guard. The lean wording of the Constitution, of course, made it possible for the generations succeeding the framers to adopt any interpretation that seemed at the time to satisfy the competing interests and assure national security. Even though the historical process forced the United States to move toward centralization, the existence of the militia, and later the National Guard, insured retention in military affairs of involvement of the states, as mandated in the Constitution.

Government under the new charter went into operation in April 1789. Its problems were legion, one of the first being relations with the Indians of the Old Northwest. The hostility of these Indians was causing the loyalty of the frontiersmen to the central government to waver. Those citizens appeared to be willing to turn toward other attachments if they could obtain security. Accordingly, late in the summer of 1790, President Washington ordered a column commanded by Lieutenant Colonel Josiah Harmar to advance against the Northwest Indians and punish them. Its nucleus was his First American Regiment, carried over from Confederation days. Harmer led approximately 1,775 men, three-quarters of them militia from the frontier. In October this federal force was roughly handled by the red foe and was forced to return to Fort Washington. The Indians were encouraged, the local settlers disgusted. Harmar ascribed the outcome to the miserable quality of the citizen soldiers with him. Kentucky, for example, had sent him only old men and young boys. He reported to his government about the "shameful, cowardly conduct of the militia, who ran away and threw down their guns without firing scarcely a single gun."[15] The militia commanders, of course, disputed this assessment.

Wherever the truth lay, it was plain to the president and his advisers that the United States must make a better showing or risk secession of the Northwestern frontier. Accordingly, it prepared a second expedition under the command of Major General Arthur St. Clair, governor of the Northwest Territory. Very late in the season for campaigning in 1791, St. Clair moved north from Fort Washington with 2,700 men, of which only 625 were regulars. A large proportion of the rest were known as "levies," similar to militia because of their short (six months) tour of service and similar to regulars because they had no relationship to any state government.[16] In spite of Washington's express warning of the danger, St. Clair led his men into an ambush on November 4, 1791, losing one-third of his men. In proportion to numbers involved, this was the severest disaster to American arms up to the Battle of the Little Big Horn in 1876. St. Clair defended his loss by emphasizing the lack of experience and the insubordination of the militia and the levies.[17] Congress, not satisfied with this explanation and horrified by the result of the campaign, conducted its first investigation into the operations of the commander-in-chief. Washington turned over all related papers, and on the basis of these the investigators found some errors in judgment, but they did not heavily censure anyone. The precedent set for thousands of subsequent hearings was of far more importance than the findings. Two defeats and an investigation, coupled with indignation on the frontier, caused the Washington administration to prepare more carefully than before to send out a third punitive expedition. The result was a reorganization in which the United States Army was reshaped into the Legion of the United States; and the Legion, commanded by Major General Anthony Wayne, defeated the Northwest Indians in 1794, with little support from the citizen soldiery.

When George Washington became president he had had at least thirty-five years' experience with citizen soldiers. He knew, and often voiced concern, about their faults, but he also appreciated the new nation's commitment to reliance on them. Even before he became president, he had requested from several general officers of the Revolutionary conflict their opinions on the future role of the militia. All of them considered the prevalent fear of a standing army to be unwarranted, but they recognized that the country would support at most only very small army in peacetime and would continue to place ultimate reliance upon militia. They agreed, too, that the only way to establish an efficient militia force, available for national use, was by classifying eligible men by age. Young and active men, intensively trained, would be called first. Training for the rest would be scaled down with their increasing age; the oldest would be called only in the gravest sort of national crisis. All of Washington's respondents recognized the need to use the several militias somehow as an efficient national reserve.[18]

During his first term as president, Washington relied on Henry Knox to prepare a comprehensive proposal for the national use of the militia. In spite of the fact that Knox spoke in his treatise of the need for "a strong Corrective arm," certain to be unpopular, Washington approved the Knox plan and submitted it to Congress on January 21, 1790. He and the secretary of war both felt the need for urgent action on the militia, but the Congress repeatedly set the Knox Plan aside to address other pressing issues.[19] Despite intermittent and sometimes sharp debate, two years and four months elapsed before Congress passed *An Act more effectually to provide for the National Defense by establishing an Uniform Militia throughout the United States* on May 8, 1792. This law gave the militia whatever slight central direction it was to have for 111 years. It stated that all free, able-bodied white men, aged 18-45, owed military service to both state and nation. It further directed the eligible males to furnish themselves with proper firearms and accouterments. Certain categories of men were exempt from service and the law authorized the states to expand further their own lists of exemptions.[20]

If there was to be a truly uniform militia, the units of the several states would have to be interchangeable. To this end the law stipulated that the militias must be divided into brigades and regiments, but it added the unfortunate phrase, "if the same be convenient." If such subdivision was inconvenient for the states, as it often was in the future, then the units would not be interchangeable, and the several militias would not function effectively as a federal reserve.

The act acknowledged the existence of specialized infantry, including riflemen, light infantry, and grenadiers, and stipulated that there should be one elite company for each standard line battalion. Cavalry and artillery units were to be filled by volunteers within brigades, not less than one company of each per division, but the size of a division was not established. The ratio of all noninfantry troops to infantry was established at a maximum of one to eleven.[21]

Each state was to have an adjutant general, the key person to maintain uniformity among the several militias. He was to report the condition of his militia once a year to the governor and to the president of the United States. For every brigade there was to be a brigade major, who, in conjunction with the adjutant general, was to insure the interchangeability of the troops. The act did not create the select corps recommended by the planners but provided instead for the organizing, arming, and training of all men aged 18-45. Since they numbered in the vicinity of half a million, this provision was unrealistic, made more so because there were no penalties for failure to comply. The act included no sanctions against either states or individuals. The Uniform Militia Act had the weight not of law but of a recommendation to the several states.[22]

In passing this act, Congress made a choice that was to shape American military affairs for a century. President Washington presented Knox's plan to Congress to create from the diverse militias a workable national reserve. This reserve might be called to active service for any of the three missions stipulated in the Constitution. Congress rejected this objective and in effect remanded control of the militias to the states. Future application of the law to supplement the regular army proved it to be haphazard and uncertain in its results.[23]

On May 2, 1792, Congress passed another statute vital to the future of the militia. Entitled *An Act to Provide for Calling Forth the Militia to Execute the Laws of the Union, Suppress Insurrections and Repel Invasions,*[24] it delegated to the president some of Congress's power to call the militia into federal service. Upon invasion or the threat of it, it empowered the president to summon as many troops from areas adjacent to the danger as he deemed necessary and to issue orders to any officer so summoned, bypassing the governor. In addition, the law transferred part of the power in cases of insurrection or for execution of the laws from Congress to the president. Here, however, the chief executive might not act alone; he could summon militia for internal disorders only if a federal judge notified him that civil authority was insufficient. When insurgents were involved, the president was required to order them to disperse and allow adequate time for compliance before resorting to militia force. Clearly, the anti-Federalists in Congress feared interference by the federal government in their internal affairs more than its help to repulse an invasion. Unlike the Uniform Militia Act, this one provided sanctions for failure to answer summons from the president. Why, then, did Congress make this law enforceable and the other one unenforceable? The answer is probably that the legislators felt no strong objection to the president's involvement in affairs too difficult for the states to handle (repelling invasion), but were, on the contrary, most unwilling to create a national militia capable of being turned against the states and thus leaving the states a prey to possible federal despotism. The act confirmed long-standing custom in limiting the compulsory term of any militiaman in federal service to three months in a year.

All fifteen states enacted laws in response to the Uniform Militia Act. They confirmed the right of the people to keep and bear arms; made the governor commander-in-chief of the militia; and uniformly exempted conscientious objectors from service although some states required them to pay a commutation fee. All states reaffirmed the power to draft but without exception permitted a drafted man to procure a substitute. This affirmed the power of the state to put a militia force in the field, yet at the same time deprived it of any control over the quality of that force.[25]

State laws differed on many vital points. Some permitted people of color to serve in secondary capacities, usually not to bear arms. Most provided for the election of company officers, but they varied on the ways in which higher officers were selected. Also diverse were provisions requiring the frequency of training. The Uniform Militia Act had left that entirely to the states. In states where there was clear and present danger as well as in those which had long-established systems, training days were frequent. In other cases, training might not be required more than once a year. All states affirmed the duty of the individual to arm himself, but some made provision to supply those persons who could not do so. The New England states in particular had maintained arsenals since colonial times. The slave states continued to require militiamen to do patrol duty to discourage slave insurrections.[26]

State laws triggered by the Uniform Militia Act were often quite thorough. If enforced these laws would create vigorous state militias; but neither they nor the federal statutes were capable of integrating the several militias into a reliable force for federal purposes.[27]

The method to subdue Shays' Rebellion in 1786 was repeated during the Whiskey Rebellion of 1794. Western Pennsylvanians, considering the whiskey tax to be discriminatory, resisted it. The Washington administration, for its part, determined to force their compliance. The militia of the rebellious area was sympathetic to the rebels, and militia from the eastern seaboard was drawn together to do the work. The administration deliberately chose militia rather than regulars to act against the insurrectionists because it recognized the feeling among its political opponents that the regular army was a menace to them. Accordingly, Pennsylvania, New Jersey, Virginia, and Maryland produced 12,950 men for the excursion. But even in eastern Pennsylvania it was necessary to draft men to raise the quota of 5,200. In spite of riots in Philadelphia over the draft, the Pennsylvania detachment was finally raised and marched off toward the disaffected area. The governors of Pennsylvania, New Jersey, and Virginia personally led their contingents. With a minimum of looting and the accidental deaths of only two civilians, this army of newly organized citizen soldiers carried out its mission in a responsible way.[28]

A variation of the Shays pattern occurred in the Fries Rebellion of 1798, in which insurrectionists in Bucks County, Pennsylvania, rebelled against the federal assessors, who were evaluating their properties for one of the two direct taxes ever levied by the United States government on real property. The purpose of this tax was to raise money for war with France which seemed imminent. Both England and France were violating the rights of neutral shippers—at least as the United States interpreted those rights—but in 1798 France appeared to be the most serious threat.[29] The militia of Bucks County gathered, not to enforce the law but to hunt down the assessors. A mob, the nucleus of which was militia, marched toward Bethlehem to free prisoners taken by a federal marshal. John Adams, unlike Washington, reacted to this threat by sending a small detachment of regulars and volunteers to subdue the rebels. William Duane denounced these soldiers for their brutality, whereupon some of them dragged him into the street and flogged him.[30]

The French Revolution was unsettling the world at this time, and both Federalist and Republican leaders in the infant republic were sensitive to its influence. As long as France seemed to present the principal menace, Congress gave the president power to alert detachments of militia, as large as 80,000 men, to be in a state of readiness. More important to the Federalist administration was the enlargement of the regular forces. Most of the leaders of the Federalist Party had been officers in the Continental Army, whereas the Republican leaders, if they had had any military connection at all, had more often been officers in the militia. The Federalists were centralizers, the Republicans the opposite. Each party came to regard the other not as loyal opposition but as traitorous. Alexander Hamilton went so far as to assert that the Republicans intended to make the United States a dependency of France. As the Federalists slowly built up the army and navy, the Republicans became convinced that they intended to use it in the long run to displace the militia and to destroy the opposition party.[31]

By 1798, the regular army had grown from 700 men to an authorized strength of 12,696. It was no fault of the Federalists that this strength was largely on paper. Military expenditures were twice as much as they had ever been before, consuming close to 50 percent of the federal receipts. The following year, Congress authorized up to 41,000 men, a provisional army to be raised if France invaded. No more than 5,100 of these were ever enrolled.[32] To the Republicans it seemed that this was an army without an enemy, since a French invasion could never bypass the British navy. They suspected that its true purpose was to reduce them, the Republicans, and they became more convinced of this when Congress passed the Alien and Sedition Acts in 1798, probably aimed at destroying the political opposition.[33]

The right wing of the Federalist Party, known as the High Federalists, considered war with France indispensable to national survival. Initially, President John Adams sided with them, even though he saw no need for the Provisional Army. Gradually, his position changed until in 1799 he sent a peace mission to France without consulting influential members of his party; the commission secured a peaceful convention with the French Directorate, which ended the threat from France. The convention with France split Adams's party and in effect sustained the Republican position. George Cabot, a High Federalist, said ruefully: "The whole world is becoming military, and if we are wholly otherwise we shall be as sheep among wolves."[34] Adams did not agree that the United States was otherwise. He believed that four institutions had made his own New England great: militia, towns, schools, and churches.[35] Although a member of the right wing of the Republican Party, John Randolph of Roanoke agreed with the president about the militia:

> It is by cultivation of your militia alone that you can always be prepared for every species of attack. When citizen and soldier shall be synonymous terms, then you will be safe. . . . The military parade which meets the eye in almost every direction, excites the gall of our citizens; they feel a just indignation at the sight of loungers who live upon the public. . . . They put no confidence in the protection of a handfull of ragamuffins. . . . I could wish to see the whole of the regular army abandoned and the defense of the country placed in the proper hands—those of the people.[36]

●　　　●　　　●

Despite the policy of the Federalists to enlarge the regular services, the era following the American Revolution stands out as a high point in the history of the militia, a time when it was performing particularly well. The Uniform Militia Act amounted to virtual abdication by the federal government of all authority over the state militias. As a consequence, the states acted upon the recommendations of Congress according to their diverse needs. An effective militia was easiest to develop in areas of dense population. Though the frontiersman did more fighting than his urban brothers, he did it most often in ad hoc groups that were short on military characteristics. Like his chief adversary, the Indian, he was usually an individual fighter. When necessity caused him to join others, the resulting combined action was unsystematic. If his operations happened to have true military cohesion, it was because of dynamic leadership. Even such leadership seldom overcame the pervasive lack of organization for supply. This lack was most likely to be overcome in densely populated areas where men were more used to cohesive action.[37]

Everywhere men sought avidly to become generals in the militia because there was genuine prestige in it. The move from general to governor or senator was not uncommon.[38] In addition, a general had patronage to dispense, especially if the state activated some sort of military expedition.

Since federal law ignored the rank of colonel, lieutenant colonels commanded regiments. Majors therefore filled the role of lieutenant colonels in the regular service, that is as second in command, while captains commanded companies. If there were brigades in the state organization, the brigade major, appointed by the brigadier general, was required to inspect and instruct his brigade and to report to the adjutant general the condition of the unit. A few states allowed this officer some compensation.[39]

As in the colonial militia, the captain of a company was the lynchpin of the system. When a company failed to elect a captain, more often than not it deteriorated. Sometimes men purposely left the office vacant in order to avoid having to train.[40] In such cases the states made various laws for filling the captaincy. At the end of the eighteenth century, there were about 28,000 militia officers in the system. No scholar has yet compiled figures showing the proportion of these who were attentive to their duties. Court martial records reveal extreme cases only, such as the captain in South Carolina who was cashiered for gouging out of its socket the eye of one of his men at a muster.[41]

The laws of all the states required that a captain give adequate notice of a muster or a training day, either by leaving summons at houses or by running a newspaper notice a prescribed number of times. Once the men were properly notified, it was their responsibility to be there with firearms. City men had scant difficulty in assembling; elsewhere the process could be laborious. Frequently, drills took place on greens around courthouses, but they were forbidden there when the courts were in session and when there was an election.[42]

Company training consisted of practice in the manual of arms and in performing the simplest company evolutions. The quality of training varied widely; in the cities there were expert units that maneuvered with precision, a rare thing in the country. Training days for battalions and regiments were less frequent, but when they did occur they were like festivals. Entire families traveled long distances to reach them, and peddlers and roving entertainers appeared. Local folk sold cold drinks and sweets; gingerbread was a muster-day specialty. The men were apt to get quite drunk, disorderly and pugnacious.[43]

Men of the standing companies seldom had uniforms, but their officers did. In contrast, the volunteer companies turned out as splendid as peacocks. The Salem Light Infantry, for example, sported a blue uniform coat with scarlet facings, brass buttons and gold lace, a waistcoat and breeches of pure white, and a shiny brass helmet with horsehair plumes falling to the right.

The training day started with drill, first company, and then, if numbers warranted it, battalion exercises. Officers inspected all firearms, but were lenient since many a yokel had only a shotgun. Toward noon the general or even the governor might arrive, and then all units would combine for regimental maneuvers. At the appropriate break, local folk often served a heavy repast accompanied by much imbibing. After a rest period, there would be more drill, and finally, the day's climax, a sham battle. The cavalry charged; the infantry rattled away with blank cartridges; even the artillery, wadding their guns with rags, blasted until their pieces were hot. With the noise and smoke, ladies screamed and children yelled. When all was over at sunset, the crowd, desperately tired, straggled home.

Except in New York and New England, militiamen were generally short of arms for training purposes. One reason was that some men who owned guns would not bring them to drills because there was no regular channel for compensation if a weapon was broken. This meant a replacement cost to the owner of about $13.00. Only the legislature, by special enactment, could give him relief.[44]

Several seaboard states abandoned the principle that every militia-man must arm himself. By the end of the eighteenth century, a few states were systematically acquiring small arms. In some cases they sent agents abroad to buy weapons; in others they found in-state manufacturers to patronize. But as states were forced into this expenditure, they began to complain that the federal government was not adequately providing for the common defense. Under pressure, Congress gradually modified the stipulation in the Uniform Militia Act that every man must arm himself. It authorized the loan of some arms to the militia in 1798. Later it directed the president to sell or loan arms to volunteer companies and sell, if he deemed it expedient, 30,000 firearms to the states.[45]

Militia cavalrymen usually provided their own horses and horse furniture, but artillerymen could scarcely afford cannon. Some artillery pieces from the Revolution lay here and there rusting. Certain states collected, rebored, refitted, and then issued these old pieces to their units.[46] During the French scare, the federal government itself authorized the loan of up to two guns to any accredited militia artillery outfit. Only Massachusetts and Virginia undertook to supply every bona fide artillery company with guns.[47] Even when the guns were provided, another heavy expense remained: horses. To own the necessary teams was expensive; so was horse hire. Companies urged the states to pay this cost, but only Massachusetts complied.[48]

Supply was the weakest point in the militia system. One reason was that the federal government left it up to the states except when the militia was in national service. The states for their part usually did not concern themselves with supply problems until an expedition was in the field and was short of needed items. Once again, Massachusetts and Connecticut were exceptions to this general indifference. They required each town to keep on hand specified quantities of powder, flints, lead, and camp equipment. Selectmen were responsible for meeting these requirements and could be fined individually if their towns were delinquent.[49] In other states the governor and the adjutant general had only themselves to rely on in supply matters until the governor appointed an officer for some special excursion.

When the United States summoned militia into United States service, either the state or the federal government entered into contracts with private suppliers for food. Such contracts stipulated the price per ration, that is food per man per day. Suppliers entered the agreements for profit, but they were often frustrated. To avoid loss or increase profit, some of them cheated on quantity and quality.[50] All in all, the contract system for food supply was unsatisfactory to everyone involved. It demonstrated the fallacy of habitually waiting until a crisis arose, then trying to improvise a food supply.

Only Massachusetts had a quartermaster in peacetime. Elsewhere, even in time of conflict, a unit in the field supplied itself as well as it could and let the bills trickle back to the state authorities. The following receipt is an example: "I acknowledge the recept of a good Dinner and liquor for my party consisting of 50 men . . ."[51] The tavern keeper forwarded this to the governor, praying that he would be reimbursed.

A citizen's failure to discharge militia duty made him liable to be fined. There were scores of offenses that produced a fine: striking an officer, failing to enroll in the local unit, failure to turn out for drills, appearing improperly uniformed and armed, refusing to accept an appointment as a noncom, failing to answer any call to active duty, careless firing, and many others. Size of the fine varied with the nature of the deficiency; it could be 75¢ for missing company training, $2.00 for failure to arm, and $10.00 for refusing to become a noncommissioned officer. Fines against officers were a great deal higher. If the fines are compared with the cost of living, they appear punitive enough to have obtained results. In Virginia, for example, beef brought 5¢, mutton and pork 7¢, and butter 20¢ to 25¢ per pound; a dozen eggs cost 8¢, and a chicken 8¢. The authorities could seize and sell all of a man's goods to satisfy a militia fine; but in such cases the property owner had a right to a hearing before special boards. These boards, composed of militia officers, met soon after training days to hear excuses and assess fines.[52]

The fine system clearly favored the well-to-do. Since they could pay without hardship, they often avoided the nuisance of militia duty. The poor objected to this discrimination, and the thoughtful rich objected to it because it meant entrusting their property to men who had no property.[53] But in spite of complaints, the laws, modified by experience, remained in effect. In practice, however, fines were carelessly collected and failed to achieve their purpose.

State or federal ability to make full use of the militias depended on knowledge of their strength and organization. Yet in at least half of the states, this information was not available. Distance and bad roads handicapped reporting. These and other factors made reporting from state to nation worst of all. In spite of the provisions of the Uniform Militia Act, states were careless about their annual reports, and the Federalist administrations did not press them. In 1801, President Jefferson could find figures for only six states and one territory. He thought it was clear that the Federalists did not count on the militia as a national resource.[54]

The real test of the militia system occurred when detachments were called for state or federal use. Within a state it was the governor who had the power to call out the militiamen, but in some cases he could delegate his power to division or brigade commanders. Local officers could bypass the hierarchy and call out their own men in case of sudden invasion or imminent danger of invasion. Rarely, though, did any exigency require the summons of the entire militia of an area.[55]

If the call passed down the chain of command, the governor set the numbers assigned to each area and stipulated how the detachments were to be organized once assembled. He usually appointed the officers as far down as the field grades, that is, major and lieutenant colonel. The governor's order went first to the adjutant general, who probably had joined the commander-in-chief in allotting numbers to areas. Then the adjutant general sent the orders on to the next level of commanders beneath him. It was up to the recipients, whether generals or colonels, to split the quota up among the units under them. Finally, the mobilization order reached the company commanders, who were required to give their men advance notice of a special muster. At this muster the captain explained the situation, revealed his company's quota, and asked for volunteers. If more men were needed than volunteered, compulsory mechanisms went into operation. Certain states divided their companies into classes, calling the first class first, and so on down the line. All states exempted a militiaman from serving twice, as long as there were eligibles who had not served once. If a company was not classified, the men drew lots to see who had to serve. Any drafted man had the right to hire a substitute. As with the system of fines, the right of substitution favored people of means and placed a burden on the less well-to-do.

A company's quota was, as a rule, only a small fraction of the whole. When it was completed, one of the company officers would have to lead the selectees to the point of rendez-vous. There they would join detachments from other companies to form a new company under an officer they did not know and had not worked with previously. That ad hoc company would in turn be associated with other new companies to form a new regiment. Through this mechanism, detachments from all parts of a state ultimately formed into regiments and higher units to serve for the duration of a particular mission, to be dissolved afterward.

The new units either trained together or, more probably, marched off at once to carry out their mission. If, as was rare, they had time to train for an extended period, the men might overcome some of the strangeness they felt at serving with persons they had not known under officers with whom they had never worked. In any case, they left behind whatever esprit de corps they might have generated in their conventional units. Certain elite corps volunteered en masse, thus preserving their cohesion and spirit, but companies from the standing militia seldom did.

When large detachments were alerted—80,000 in 1794 and the same number in 1797—simply to be ready, a different sort of erosion undermined efficiency.[56] New units formed as described above and were directed to train together. But the men detached from the standing companies found it nearly impossible to gather to train in the new units. Distance alone made their presence at battalion exercises almost impossible. Since the detached men were excused from training with their old companies in order to train with the new ones, they in fact stopped drilling altogether. They were thus less rather than more ready. This manipulation appeared to give the nation at low cost a substantial ready force, but in reality it did no more than produce an ill-organized body of men, not as well trained as the mass of the militia.

Militiamen served their states far more than they ever did the United States; indeed, the states could not have carried on government without them. They were an indispensable part of ceremonies and parades; they turned out when the police could no longer keep order; they manned coastal forts, for example, during the pseudo-war with France; they guarded criminals; and enforced quarantines against infectious diseases. In slave-holding areas they also functioned as patrols. Sometimes, however, the states found it necessary to hire "state troops" to serve longer than militiamen could. Massachusetts employed some for three years in 1795; so did South Carolina.[57] Even though the Constitution forbade any state to keep troops other than militia in time of peace, such soldiery did from time to time appear. One reason for it was that the federal government simply could not carry out its Constitutional obligation at all times to protect the several states from invasion. But the states, in protecting their own borders during the 1790s, sought to pass the costs on to the federal government. After long delays and much bickering, Congress usually authorized payment,[58] and in this indirect manner, at least, fulfilled its obligation to defend the states. The method was expensive, but at the same time it magnified the role of the citizen soldier and minimized that of the army.

If state interests clashed with those of the United States, the militia system underwent severe strain. This occurred in 1794 when Georgia disagreed with the federal government over the treatment of the Indians inside Georgia. In that year, regulars and Georgia militiamen faced each other with firearms loaded and cocked. In the end, local commanders kept cool, the United States yielded its position, and the issue was resolved without conflict between state and nation.[59] In 1798, the Old Dominion was so deeply opposed to the Alien and Sedition Acts that it began to prepare its militia for action.[60] This tension, like that in Georgia, passed. The eighteenth century ended and the nineteenth began without open conflict between militiamen of the states and regulars of the U. S. Army.

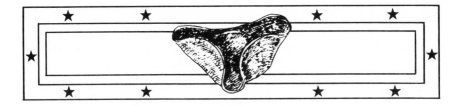

FIVE

Jeffersonian Militia and the War of 1812

So great was the ideological difference between the Federalists and the Republicans revealed during the election of 1800 that insurrection loomed large. But the peaceful inauguration of Thomas Jefferson demonstrated that the young Republic had staying power. Much of the Federalist heritage was too firmly hardened into place for the new administration to attempt to dislodge it; one feature cemented in was a standing military establishment. Although Jefferson said, "None but an armed nation can dispense with a standing army,"[1] he did not eliminate the Federalist army. All he did was to scale it down drastically. At his behest, Congress cut the army appropriation down from $2,093,000, where it stood in 1801 to $680,000 in 1803, and the navy from $3,000,000 to $1,000,000.[2]

In Jefferson's view, the only force competent to defend the nation against attack was the militia, since there were innumerable points at which an enemy might strike from overseas or across the borders of Canada or New Spain.[3] If the militia was properly organized and disciplined every able-bodied man of military age would have some training and weapons. Since Jefferson was determined to rely heavily on this system, he must know its size. Accordingly, the administration jogged the adjutants general of the states, through the governors, to turn in the reports mandated to be sent in annually to the president. So little had this stipulation of the Act of 1792 been heeded that it was 1804 before the secretary of war could even approximate a comprehensive report. The figures were not encouraging: there were 525,000 men enrolled in the militia, most of them in the infantry and only one in

63

ten reporting possession of a firearm.[4] The states' arms were badly out of balance—Massachusetts had 40 percent of the artillery—but more serious than this imbalance was the glaring discrepancy between the strengths mandated by the Uniform Militia Act and those actually existing. Whereas the Act called for 770 men per regiment of infantry, Rhode Island had only 400 while South Carolina had 850.[5] Plainly, the state units could not serve as interchangeable parts of a federal reserve.

The Jeffersonians never ceased to believe that the militia could be shaped up. Jefferson himself had no personal experience as a member of any militia unit, but it was plain to him that the system was in theory the best of all for a free people. His experience as governor of Virginia for two years during the Revolution did little to change his viewpoint. Providentially, the Peace of Amiens, which went into effect in the spring of 1802, gave him time to work on the militia as a national instrument. During this breather in the struggle between Napoleon and the various coalitions formed to fight him, Jefferson kept the army small, drydocked most of the ocean-going navy, and secured authority to build 263 gunboats, which, manned by naval militia, were to protect the coasts. He also agreed to put the United States Military Academy into operation, in part to be the center from which military knowledge could radiate out to the militia, and in part to train a corps of officers who were not unbending Federalists. The High Federalist slant of the officers of the army seemed to the president to be a threat to the future of America as a republican society.[6] Finally, his administration, and his Republican successors, supported in the private sector of the economy the ability to supply the nation with war materials when necessary. Jefferson never questioned the need to be prepared to use war as an instrument of national policy; but this posture did not require maintaining large standing forces.

When Louisiana was acquired during the Peace of Amiens, Jefferson called on the militias of the adjacent states to stand by to suppress insurrection if the French, Spanish, and Indian peoples who had been annexed without their consent rebelled; but there was no insurrection.

Jefferson's dream of an America lightly burdened with military expenses evaporated when war broke out again in Europe in 1803. Almost at once United States shipping began to be squeezed between the giant belligerents, and national sovereignty with it. Congress's response was to authorize 30,000 volunteers, who would be liable during two years to be called up and who would serve one year if so called.[7] Jefferson referred to this new type as those militiamen "to whose habits and enterprise active and distant service was most congenial."[8]

In March, the president asked Congress for the power to use the regular forces to suppress insurrections and enforce the laws of the

United States. This was radical action for one of Jefferson's convictions, since the Constitution seemed to imply that only the militia would be used for internal discipline.[9] It is certain that if the Federalist administrations had asked for such power, the Jeffersonians would have regarded it as primarily a menace to them.

On June 22, 1807, the British Frigate *Leopard* fired a shot across the bow of the U. S. Frigate *Chesapeake*, and Captain Humphreys of the *Leopard* demanded that his officers be allowed to remove from the American crew British deserters whom he knew to be aboard. Captain James Barron of course refused, since the demand was a gross infraction of American sovereignty, whereupon the British ship opened fire, killing three and wounding twenty Americans. Since the *Chesapeake* was unable to return the fire, because she had put to sea with her guns unmounted, the British officers boarded and removed four men. American newspapers spread the knowledge of this humiliation widely and rapidly. Americans became fighting mad, but not the president. Determined to avoid war if possible, he pushed an embargo through Congress designed to keep United States ships out of the way of trouble with British warships, and at the same time to deny indispensable goods to England, which American ships had been carrying as a neutral power. Put into operation early in 1808, the embargo imposed the herculean task of trying to prevent movement of ships from more than 2,000 ports and inlets, and interdicting the passage of goods for England across the Canadian border. Both regular service and the militia were not enough to achieve complete enforcement, but they tried. The government designated a reliable militia officer near each port or navigable inlet and ordered him to respond rapidly whenever the port collector called for help.[10] When Vermont militia would not enforce the embargo along the Canadian border, Jefferson sent regular artillery there.[11]

Reluctantly, the administration urged Congress to enlarge the army and thereby precipitated a sharp debate which continued off and on for the next three years. Dissident Republicans, now known as Democrats, opposed enlargement because, as John Randolph put it, the administration had never defined the role either of the army or of the militia clearly enough.[12] Peter Buel Porter, a successful commander of New York militia, offered a definition: the militia, he said, was the shield of the Republic, and the regular force, its sword. Randolph and some of his followers doubtless agreed with Porter's definition, but they opposed Jefferson's plan because they saw no need for the sword.[13] So great was the political power of the president that before the debate came to an end Congress had agreed to enlarge the army to six times its previous size.

Various aspects of the militia received examination. Porter

demonstrated that it penalized the poor. Many a man was incapable of spending $15.00 to equip himself with a firearm, but he was subject to fine if he did not. In contrast, well-to-do persons escaped service by paying the fines, which deprived them of very little. Thus it happened that men who served owned less than 1 percent of the property they helped to protect.[14]

Some debaters argued that the traditional restriction on the use of militia outside the United States was invalid. Might not a preemptive invasion by an American force sometime be necessary to repel an imminent invasion? Also, these men argued, was not a declaration of war by Congress a law whereby under the Constitution, militia could be used without restrictions to enforce?[15]

In 1808, Congress appropriated $200,000 per year to arm the militia. This sum was to be divided among the states according to the number of militiamen shown in their annual return to the secretary of war.[16] It would hardly buy arms for the men who became eighteen each year—to arm the militia fully would have required $50,000,000—but it was important because the act committed the federal government to the principle of providing arms to the citizen soldiers.

Jefferson's alternative for war did not work; the embargo proved to be a heavier burden in costs, at least, than war itself. It was repealed in March 1809 after fifteen months of operation. British naval captains continued to impress sailors from American ships, until by 1812 they had forcibly removed about 6,000. Except for expressions of indignation and the enlargement of the army, America presented no martial reaction to this outrage. As new territories came into the Union through the Louisiana Purchase and turned into states, the need for effective militia increased, but the territorial militias did not measure up to it. Until the very eve of the War of 1812, the system as a whole actually declined. The average number of training days dropped from six to four per year. In some states the militia became more a money game than a training program. These states commenced to charge fees against many persons whom state laws exempted from duty, and to collect fines with more vigor. Where there was need for prolonged service to garrison sensitive places, the states maintained small state armies. Massachusetts, Virginia, and Georgia had such forces at various times. In the larger cities, militia units bigger than battalions formed. These were useful for ceremonial purposes, except that party politics permeated some of them: there were Federalist brigades and Democratic brigades. When John Adams became president, partisan feeling ran so high that some of the Republican units in Philadelphia would not be part of his escort through the city. Conversely, the three firmly Federalist troops of the Philadelphia City Cavalry would not parade in honor of the acquisition of Louisiana.[17]

By 1812, the debate in Congress focused on volunteers. This was because they could be used for longer terms and farther afield than militia. Nevertheless, Senator William Branch Giles of Virginia argued that they had no standing under the Constitution. Other debaters considered volunteers to be subject to militia limitations.[18] Supporters of volunteers denied both arguments and insisted that these troops were to be preferred to hastily raised, raw regulars, who invariably were riffraff.[19] The supporters in the end won out, and Congress authorized up to 50,000 volunteers. One provision of the new law awarded 160 acres of land to the family of any volunteer killed in the line of duty. It prompted one Ohio man to write thus to his senator: "Who the devil would turn out to get himself killed for 160 acres of land? Many wished every member of Congress had 160 acres . . . stuffed up his ———."[20]

By the time the United States declared war on Great Britain on April 18, 1812, Congress had authorized a formidable land force: 35,925 regular army; 50,000 volunteers and 100,000 alerted militiamen.[21] Neither the regular army nor the volunteers ever reached such large numbers, but the militiamen who came and went for short tours of duty exceeded 100,000. Not all the states accepted the war declaration, however. The governor of Connecticut, John Cotton Smith, with the concurrence of his council, said that the cruising of a hostile fleet did not constitute invasion or prove that invasion was imminent; nor was there an insurrection to suppress or any unusual need warranting militia help to enforce the laws. He added that he could not legally place Connecticut officers under United States officers. For all these reasons, he concluded, the president's call was unconstitutional.[22] Governor Strong of Massachusetts refused his state's militia, too. He could not, he said, detach the portion of the militia required by the president without dangerously weakening the whole state system. He did call out three companies, simply to cope with lawless people on the Massachusetts border. He gave no orders to his militia but exhorted them "duly to notice the solemn and interesting crisis . , . and to meet it with constancy and firmness." Later, in 1813, both Connecticut and Massachusetts consented to place men in federal service, but only to guard their own coasts.[23] In the end the United States paid for other coast guarding detachments.

At the start of the war, the governor of Vermont was sympathetic to the Madison administration, and he filled the state's quota. Then, in 1813, Federalist Martin Chittenden became governor by a plurality of one vote; he reversed the previous posture, ordering the Vermont brigade serving in New York to come home at once. The officers of the brigade, being war sympathizers, flatly refused to obey. Some of the enlisted men, however, started home to bring in the harvest, whereupon the officers sent out detachments to round them up. In the resulting confrontation, at least one man was killed. By September 1814, the governor was urging cooperation with the United States.[24]

The attitude of Connecticut and Massachusetts deprived the nation of its best militia; more important, it precluded cutting the British jugular vein, the St. Lawrence River. It forced the government to operate far to the west in an area nowhere near as critical to British control as the river itself. The reaction of these two states to the president's call underscored a problem created by the Constitution. Each militia had two commanders-in-chief, a governor and the president, and if those two disagreed on policy, the several militias could not function as a national reserve.

At the start of the year 1812, the regular army had a few less than 7,000 enlisted men in it. If, as Peter Buel Porter had said, the standing army was the sword of the Republic and the militia its shield, the sword was little more than a dagger, totally inadequate to invade Canada. For this reason, the Madison administration made the mistake of trying to use the shield for cutting and thrusting, a function it could not perform, since it was a defense mechanism only. For its first thrust, the strategy makers sent Brigadier General William Hull to invade Canada from Detroit with a small army of mixed components. The Ohio militia with Hull refused, on statutory grounds, to cross into Canada. Hull had developed a deep distrust of militia during his service as an officer in the American Revolution, and militia action once again shook his confidence. For this and other reasons he surrendered his force to an inferior one on August 17, 1812. When tried many months later for cowardice and other military crimes, he testified that his failure had been due in large part to the rawness, lack of discipline, and insubordination of the militia.[25]

That militia was completely unsuitable for invasion was illustrated also at the other (eastern) end of the Ontario Peninsula. There, Major General Stephen Van Rensselaer, New York militia, led 350 regulars and 250 volunteers across the Niagara River on October 12, 1812, making a defendable lodgment on high ground at Queenstown, Canada. He had three men to the British one, but most of his force was still on the United States side of the river. It only remained to bring them into the fight to win the action, but the militia refused to cross into foreign territory. No more regulars were available to cross because their commander was unwilling to be subordinate to a militia officer. The senior militia officer over the men who had crossed, General Wadsworth, turned the command over to Colonel Winfield Scott, U. S. Army, but nothing could rescue that detachment from surrender save reinforcements, which did not come.[26]

After this fiasco, Brigadier General Alexander Smyth, who had refused to serve as second in command to Van Rensselaer, took charge. He planned to cross again on December 1, and issued a bombastic proclamation to stir the citizen soldiers to make the crossing. He needed 3,000 men, but got less than half that number, since the militiamen continued to refuse to invade. Soon Smyth lost the command, left the area, threatened by the citizen soldiers, and thereafter was dropped from the rolls of the army. Like Hull, he blamed his failure on the militia.[27]

Such American strategy as there was called for coordinated penetrations of Canada along a front 600 miles long, most of it trackless wilderness. The expected coordination did not occur. Hull surrendered in August before the offensives to the east had got under way. Van Rensselaer surrendered his invasionary detachment in October, when Major General Henry Dearborn was just arriving at the Canadian border in the Lake Champlain region. Once Dearborn at last was ready to invade, two-thirds of his militiamen announced that they were not required to cross an international boundary and would not do so. Thereupon Dearborn canceled the invasion and put his army into winter quarters.[28]

Brigadier General Zebulon Pike, operating in the same area as Dearborn, although a regular, was a more charismatic leader of citizen soldiers than Dearborn; he was able to lead 400 New York militiamen with some regulars into Canada. His regulars were in one column, his irregulars in another, and in the gloom of early morning, they fired a volley or two at each other. Later in 1813, New York militia refused to cross with Major General Wade Hampton.[29] The early months of the war demonstrated that militia could not be used as an offensive force.

William Henry Harrison was the type of officer who could get the most out of irregulars. When very young, he had served in the regular army, but he became a general officer during the War of 1812 through the Kentucky militia. He commanded in 1813 in the theater where Hull had failed. Loyal to Kentucky, he turned to that state for men at a time when 10,000 Ohio militiamen were already on the march to join him. One of his great skills was persuasion, and he used it in this case to halt the Ohio column and turn it around. The column was led by the governor himself, Return Jonathan Meigs, who of course resented the preference shown for Kentucky troops. One of Meigs's officers lamented: "The militia of Ohio have been made pack horses and merely served as convenience for others to receive the honor and glory."[30]

Honor and glory had to be postponed while Harrison's army was detained for many months until the navy could secure control of Lake

Erie. The troops lived in mud and cold, but Harrison was able to hold them together and at the same time establish depots of supplies for the future advance. Clad in common hunting garb, he rode through his sprawling theater talking with the citizen soldiers. A master of harangue, with a superb voice, he persuaded men to his will "as a father would his children." Moreover, if his men endured the rain all night without tents, so did he, sitting on his saddle, wrapped in his cloak, propped against a tree.[31]

Even Harrison could not keep militiamen beyond the tour for which they had contracted. Pennsylvania and Virginia militia, their terms up, marched away from Ft. Meigs on the Maumee River in February 1813, leaving only 400 men to man works built for 2,000. There followed a race between the British, to capture the fort while it was weak, and Harrison, to get more troops into it. Finally, on May 5, 1813, 800 Kentucky militiamen dashed in, quickly overran the British batteries that were harassing the place, and then, without bothering to spike the guns, loped off in undisciplined pursuit. The British rallied and killed or captured all their pursuers. Harrison ascribed the disaster to the overconfidence which he said always attended militia. However, in the same report he praised a militia company that had held its ground against four times its number.[32]

Once the navy had secured control of Lake Erie in September 1813, Harrison led his army into Upper Canada and virtually wiped out British control there. His campaign displayed almost the perfect use of citizen soldiers. Due to the depots he had established while immobilized the previous winter, his column kept moving, thus avoiding boredom among the men. Also, the morale of his troops was high because Isaac Shelby himself, governor of Kentucky and popular hero of the Revolutionary War, led them. In addition, although horse costs were usually considered prohibitive, Harrison allowed the Kentuckians to ride from home to the point of embarkation. Finally, because the men were away only three months, their crops and businesses suffered a minimum of loss.[33] Viewed as part of a planned, coordinated war effort, the campaign was far from perfect. Instead of 7,000 regulars, as the administration had intended, Harrison commanded only 2,500 regulars plus a horde of citizen soldiers; and the latter served under conditions set not by the administration but by the governor of Kentucky. Harrison's army was good for one campaign only.

Along the northern border of New York there was no such triumph as Harrison enjoyed in the west. Quite the contrary! On July 20, 1813, 1,900 British troops landed close to Plattsburgh on Lake Champlain and advanced toward the town. Brigadier General Benjamin Mooers called out the local militia en masse but brought forth only 300 men and one small cannon. The British brushed aside this token resistance and plundered the town. Westward in the Niagara region, the defense collapsed utterly. American troops still held Ft. George on the Canadian side of the Niagara River, but in November the tour of the volunteers ended and they marched out, leaving sixty regulars and forty volunteers to try to save the place. Brigadier General George McClure, New York militia, issued a call for the militia to turn out en masse, but only 400 men responded, and none of them for service in Canada. McClure talked so bitterly over this showing that he became dangerously unpopular with the militia and was replaced by Major General Amos Hall, also New York militia.[34] Hall, too, sent out a frantic summons for local soldiers, but the militiamen had stood too many drafts and been away from home too much to care. The small force Hall was able to assemble faded away before the invaders. Consternation replaced order, and the Niagara frontier lay naked before the enemy. The British, with Indian allies, arrived, burned Black Rock and Buffalo, looted as much as was profitable, and, having met almost no resistance, departed. This fiasco shook faith in the belief that men would fight to the last to defend hearth and home, and the secretary of war announced that the New York militia had shamefully failed to do their duty.[35]

Not all citizen soldiers on the New York frontier, however, were supine. When the British attacked Sackett's Harbor, the principal United States naval base on Lake Ontario May 20, 1813, Major General Jacob Brown emerged as a towering leader of the militiamen. Brown held his force of irregulars together on the beach to oppose the landing as long as he could, but at last it began to give way and the men abandoned the field. Now Brown sent runners out on all roads to announce an American victory. The men, not wishing to lose out on the honor, returned. Brown was able to get them into cohesive formations and drove the British back to their ships.[36]

In the months that followed this success, Brown shifted to western New York and engaged the main British force in two of the bloodiest battles of the war. He restored some order on the distracted Niagara region with the aid of Brigadier General Peter Buel Porter, an able commander of citizen soldiers. Porter was as delighted to serve with Brown as Brown was to have his services, for Porter found the regulars difficult to work with. "It is certain," he said, "that no militia general is to gain any military fame while united to a regular force and commanded by their officers."[37]

During September 1814, the British encircled Ft. Erie, the last installation that Americans held on the Canada side of the Niagara River (General McClure had abandoned Ft. George in November

1813). British siege batteries cruelly punished the defenders. At this juncture, Peter Buel Porter persuaded 1,500 New York militiamen to cross into Canada. This remarkable development made General Brown decide to attempt a sortie from the beleaguered fort, even though half of his men were Porter's militia. At the zero hour, the American force poured out of the security of the fort and overran the punishing batteries, causing the British to lift the siege. Everyone who had worked with militia knew that this was an astonishing feat, and Brown retracted his earlier derogation of the New York militia, who, he said, had redeemed their character.[38]

Later in 1814, for some unaccountable reason, the Secretary of War, John Armstrong, ordered Major General George Izard to leave the Lake Champlain zone, where invasion was imminent, and to go to the Niagara area to take command. Izard was finely trained in European warfare, but he did not adapt well to the unpredictable conduct of irregular soldiers. Accordingly, late in November he acknowledged to the secretary that Brown was better qualified than he to handle the northern army, and requested to be relieved. Brown once more assumed the command.[39]

The threat in the Champlain area resulted from the transfer of an army of seasoned British troops from Europe. Napoleon's abdication in April 1814 and subsequent exile enabled the British government to address the American problem. It sent one army under Lieutenant General Sir George Prevost to advance into the United States via the Richelieu River and Lake Champlain. A second army, under Major General Robert Ross, was to operate in the Chesapeake Bay region in order to provide a diversion for the northern column. Ross landed 4,500 men at Benedict, thirty miles from Washington, D.C., and moved inland to feel out the resistance. Since almost none developed, he and Admiral Sir George Cockburn, who was marching with him, could choose whether to aim toward the capital or toward Baltimore and Philadelphia. They picked Washington in order to disrupt American morale. Neither United States regulars nor militia obstructed the roads, no surprise to Admiral Cockburn who after marauding in the area earlier with a minuscule force had developed scorn for the American spirit.[40]

On the American side, the government as early as July 4, 1814, had alerted 93,500 militiamen from the Middle Atlantic States. In response, Pennsylvania authorities informed the United States commander that their state could not compel any man to serve because of a new militia law which temporarily deprived the officers of their authority. The state's militia system was undergoing reorganization when it was most needed in the field.[41]

Brigadier General William Winder was the United States commander, but he could not actually call any of the 93,500 supposedly alerted men into federal service until the Secretary of War, John Armstrong, gave him permission. Armstrong's permission arrived even as the British column was moving across the undefended countryside, and Winder at once summoned the men of Maryland, Virginia, Pennsylvania, and the District of Columbia en masse. His frantic call brought out only 6,000 men, some of whom arrived at Bladensburg, where Winder had determined to take a stand behind the eastern branch of the Potomac River, at the moment when the British were preparing to force a crossing of the stream. In the resulting battle, certain militia units and some regulars stood stoutly until overrun, but a majority of the citizen soldiers fled with such speed that the action became known as the Bladensburg Races.[42] One member of the invading force who observed the conflict wrote that had the Americans "conducted themselves with coolness and resolution, it is not conceivable how the battle could have been won."[43] Ross's column brushed aside the few resolute resisters, marched into the District of Columbia, burned some of the public buildings, and then, having no further mission there, returned to their ships. The militia in this instance, as on the Niagara front less than a year before, had seemed to make a myth of the general belief that they would fight to the death to protect their homes and their hallowed monuments.

Very soon, however, the militia of the Chesapeake region performed as a majority of believers expected them to. Ross and Cockburn turned their army toward Baltimore whereupon that community responded with an energy that Washington had not shown. Command fell to Major General Samuel Smith of the Maryland militia, who let it be known that he would not take orders from the federal commander. He was backed in this stand by the governor of Maryland, a relative of William Winder. Smith put the civilian population, free and slave, to work digging defensive works and summoned the entire militia of Baltimore and of two Maryland counties. They responded in such numbers that when the British landed and marched toward the city, Baltimore's defenses bristled. Two young citizen snipers shot General Ross dead off his white horse, and his successor found the defending earthworks so formidable and the position so unfavorable for help from the British navy that he gave up the attempt and returned to the shipping.[44]

While the British diversionary army in the Chesapeake area scattered the United States government, how did the main British army fare moving southward from Canada? Its prospects seemed good, since the American command before it was constantly shifting from one officer to another. The invading column, this time containing nearly 20,000 seasoned veterans of the Napoleonic Wars, once more approached Plattsburgh. The federal commander there, a young brigadier, Alexander Macomb, having only a scant force to work with, asked for militia help. General Mooers called out his entire command but received just 700 men. He reported to Governor Daniel D. Tompkins that "a portion of the militia have entailed eternal disgrace upon themselves."[45] Macomb handled his tiny force with skill, but he could not stem the British advance by land. It was the United States Navy that halted it with a stunning victory on the Lake. Lieutenant Thomas Macdonough's four small warships and ten gunboats wrecked the smaller British lake squadron, thereby exposing the flank of the invading column on its water side. Lieutenant General Sir George Prevost was not willing to advance under such conditions and marched his powerful force back to Canada.

President Madison had removed John Armstrong after the Washington fiasco and had appointed James Monroe as Secretary of War. The new secretary was an unswerving optimist, and the withdrawal of the British army into Canada meant to him a real resurgence of American prospects. Looking northward from Washington, Monroe saw Daniel D. Tompkins, governor of New York, as the man of the hour, and accordingly he appointed him to be commander of the United States Third Military District. Since the District included New Jersey, Jersey's governor immediately protested that the governor of New York could not legally command New Jersey militia within the boundaries of New Jersey. Monroe wrote off ten pages in his own hand to demonstrate to the dissident that Tompkins's attributes as governor were phased out when he functioned as federal commander. The result was that Tompkins retained the command, but without any military rank whatever.[46]

Partly due to Monroe's unflagging spirit, the Madison administration kept up its courage, even when manpower for the war effort seemed out of reach. From South Carolina came word that the courts of the state had made the militia dependent on the willingness of individuals to serve in it.[47] From several states came protests about attempts to place regular officers over their militias. No less a figure than Samuel Smith, savior of Baltimore, resigned as major general rather than continue under the command of Winfield Scott, who was one of the finest of the regular officers. With Smith went John Stricker, commandant of the militia of Baltimore.[48] In New England, a convention at Hartford, Connecticut, resolved that it was unconstitutional to put regular officers over militia, and while at it resolved also that it was unconstitutional for the federal government to try to classify a state's militia.[49]

Monroe, apparently convinced that the militia system had failed, proposed the formation of a national reserve of 100,000 men independent of the states. Although he did not say so, his plan required conscription. Daniel Webster in Congress recognized this and denounced it with his usual eloquence. "Not one half of the conscripts," he said, "will ever return to tell the tale of their sufferings. They will perish of disease or pestilence, or they will leave their bones to whiten in fields beyond the frontier. [Such a law] cannot be executed."[50] The bill was not enacted.

If the militia system had often failed up to this point, there was one area in which it had been highly successful. It had pushed upward outstanding leaders of citizen soldiers, among them William Henry Harrison, Jacob Brown, Peter Buel Porter, Richard Mentor Johnson, and Samuel Smith. Its most conspicuous graduate was Andrew Jackson, who owed much of his rise in prominence to the militia. His mother had urged her sons, when boys, to involve themselves with the local units, and Andrew had done so. The system operated democratically, indeed, was an important adjunct of politics, and in 1796 Jackson presented himself to the officer corps of the new state of Tennessee as a candidate for major general. All he had for credentials were experience as a boy-orderly for a Carolina dragoon outfit during the Revolution and a charismatic presence. This did not win for him the office he coveted, but he commenced then to build for a future chance. The time seemed to have come in 1802 when he presented himself against John Sevier, a man of long experience in frontier style fighting. The vote was a tie, and the governor of Tennessee, allied with Jackson politically, broke the tie in his favor. Sevier and Jackson fought a bloodless duel and were never reconciled. Jackson's success split the politics of Tennessee; Jackson became the dominant political figure in the western segment of the state, Sevier in the east. Lack of military experience did not result in any lack of confidence; the general kept close in spirit to his troops. "My pride," he said, "is that my soldiers has (*sic*) confidence in me, and in the event of war I will lead them on, to victory and conquest."[51]

No sooner had the second war with Britain begun than Andrew Jackson wrote Madison offering himself and his Tennessee troops to go anywhere to "repel hur (*sic*) [the United States'] enemies without Constitutional scruples of any boundaries."[52] Politically tainted by some relationship with Aaron Burr, Jackson was not acceptable to the commander-in-chief, who ignored his offer. Jackson had to wait until 1813, every day of the wait frustrating to him, for his chance. The administration directed the governor of Tennessee to raise a force of volunteers and move southward to engage the Creek Indians, allies of the English foe. As Jackson at all times considered Indians to be in the way of progress, the assignment was a welcome one; but he had to assert himself to get it. He was seriously crippled and ill from a brawl of some months earlier, and the governor considered him too unwell to take command. Jackson, whose will always overcame pain and physical debility, dragged himself out of bed and demanded the command as his right, being major general. Since the federal government authorized only the grade of brigadier general for this excursion, he accepted that rank and proceeded to lead the Tennesseans deep into Indian territory. There, short of supplies and, so they claimed, at the end of their tour of duty, the men became determined to go home. Jackson denied their right to leave service, cajoled them at first, then screamed oaths at them, and, when these methods failed, threatened them with the cannon of a regular artillery outfit. Having imposed his will on the soldiers, Jackson turned to stiffening the backbone of Willie Blount, Governor of Tennessee. "Arouse from yr lethargy; despise fawning smiles and snarling frowns—with energy exercise yr functions—the campaign must rapidly progress or . . . yr country ruined."[53] Blount could have removed his general for insubordination, but he and Jackson were political allies, and he understood the man. He found supplies and recruits to keep Jackson's army in the field. At the Horseshoe Bend of the Tallapoosa River on March 27, 1814, that army broke the fighting power of the Creeks in one of the major battles of the War of 1812, although not a Britisher was present. This victory, conspicuous among so many American defeats, made Jackson known all over the United States and brought to him a commission as major general in the U. S. Army.

The main British strategic focus was by this time upon New Orleans, and Jackson received orders to go there and defend this, the finest city of the South. As usual, the general turned to his Tennesseans for troops as well as to Kentucky. To his dismay, Kentucky forwarded to him unarmed militia in disreputable condition, but his long-time friend, business partner, and personal defender, John Coffee, marched Tennessee horsemen to the scene without sleep to arrive in record time. Speed was essential, for Jackson's intelligence service had failed and the invaders were already within eight miles of the city on a good road running beside the Mississippi River. Here was a crisis, the best possible environment to bring out the highest form of leadership in Andrew Jackson. Too ill from chronic dysentery to stand, Jackson radiated energy from a couch. Citizens working alongside slaves dug earthworks, patrols scoured the area for any firearm that would shoot;

Jean Lafitte and his pirates offered themselves as skilled gunners, and Jackson accepted them to get not only their skills but also the stores of ammunition they controlled. The general reviewed the militia, including the black units of New Orleans, and keyed them to fighting pitch. Drawn finally together in less than ten hours, his mongrel army struck the British at night in their camp beside the river on December 23, 1814. Thereafter, in a series of battles, culminating on January 8, 1815, the ragtag American army stopped the advance of British regulars who had been part of the force that defeated Napoleon, inflicting 2,444 casualties to 336 suffered, a ratio of seven to one.[54]

It did not matter that the Battle of New Orleans took place two weeks after a peace document had been signed far off in Ghent, Belgium. This victory shaped American military policy for decades to come by fostering the conviction that every American citizen soldier could, even with scant training, whip at least seven of the finest soldiers. Moreover, it confirmed what Americans wanted to believe, namely, that the nation could draw together a fighting force at the moment of need, not before, without elaborate and expensive pre-planning.

Neither did it matter that an inordinate number of men were used to achieve the scant results flowing from the War of 1812. There were 398,000 individual enlistments of men who served less than six months, and 60,000 more who served only a little more than six months. Volunteers for twelve months or longer, with no restrictions on where they could serve, totaled only 10,000 of the 50,000 authorized at the beginning. These 10,000 were the best type of citizen soldiers in the action. Claimants of some sort continued to receive pensions for this war as late as 1946, and the total of pensions paid from 1872, when they began, to 1946 totaled $65,000,000.[55] (Pensions for military service do not go only to soldiers who served, but to their wives and sometimes other dependents. Older veterans not infrequently married very young women, and these wives in some cases were quite long-lived).

As in the Revolution, militia was indispensable in the War of 1812. What is striking is that its performance was less efficient than in the Revolution even though the United States had had a quarter of a century under the Constitution to tighten up a loose union. More than any other, this war revealed the weaknesses of the militia system, but at the same time it included a few of the most inspiring examples of superior fighting of citizens turned soldiers when commanded by officers who understood how much and how little they could expect from irregulars.

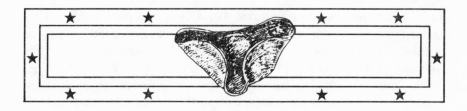

SIX

Decline of the Militia;
Rise of the Volunteers

A committee of the House of Representatives in 1827 effectively stated what statesmen thought the military policy of the United States ought to be:

> Removed as we are from every powerful nation, we may rely . . . under the benign dispensations of a protecting Providence on an inconsiderable regular army; a few durable fortifications; a considerable navy; a well organized and disciplined militia; good roads and other channels of communication to facilitate their marches, and the republic will stand erect among the nations for ages unlimited.[1]

The Congress did nothing about the protecting Providence except to assume that it would always be on the side of the United States, but, acting on the premise of an inconsiderable army, it cut the authorized number of enlisted men from 10,000 to 5,642 in March 1821. To supply the few durable fortifications, Congress appropriated about $1,000,000 per year, but when it cut the army in 1821 it also halved this figure, so that the system of forts never equaled the level intended nor ever received the guns necessary to make it effective. In contrast, the considerable navy seemed well on the way when Congress in 1816 authorized nine new ships of the line and twelve frigates. By 1823, the navy included eleven ships of the line, fourteen frigates, twenty-three sloops, eight brigs, eight schooners, and eight steamers. Roads and railroads proliferated sufficiently in the decades after the Treaty of Ghent to carry all the men and materiel the army might require, but not necessarily where the army needed them, for the transportation net grew in response to the requirements of trade.[2]

The militia system became in fact less well organized and disciplined, but this did not shake the faith in it as the bulwark of national defense. Between 1816 and 1835, the several presidents recommended to Congress thirty-one times that the legislators attend to the militia, but the Congress did not act. The New England states, however, did. The adjutant general of Massachusetts insisted that his militia was sound and that it helped elevate the moral tone of the people. His counterpart in New Hampshire was so proud of the showing of the militia in 1833 in his state that he suggested the possible elimination of the regular army.[3]

Congressmen not infrequently took the same position as the adjutant of New Hampshire. Gideon Tomlinson of Connecticut said that when the homeland was attacked the citizen soldier would "present a front of steel to an invading foe; a protection much to be preferred to the 'iron front' of a standing army." A couple of decades later, Edward Black, congressman from Georgia, told his colleagues, "The best army we can have is the armed people—the citizens of this country who will fight for a great stake—for their wives and children, their homesteads and their honor."[4]

A considerable number of commentators regarded the militia as the keystone on which individual liberties rested. Their line of reasoning ran thus: if there were no militia the states would cease to be politically effective, and when that moment arrived, civil liberties would soon be denied by a too highly centralized government. Indeed, in 1831, a group of militia officers from Massachusetts expressed their belief that the states were already at the mercy of the United States.[5]

The dreaded engine that grew out of and sustained a hypertrophied central authority was the standing army. Again and again, speechmakers pointed to this instrument as being hostile to civil liberty and as a potential destructer of free government. Monarchy had always depended on this, "the right arm of tyranny." They drew on history to prove their fears well founded. Virtue and liberty died in Greece, Carthage, and Rome when mercenary troops replaced citizen soldiers. During the Age of Jackson, this fear and other causes led to attacks on West Point as the training place for possible future tyrants. The money going into the Military Academy ought to be taken from it, the place shut down, and the funds invested in the militia system.[6]

Speakers drew proof for the effectiveness of militia also from history. They cited the power of the citizenry in arms during the French Revolution. In the American Revolution they found proof in the battles of Lexington and Concord, Bunker Hill, Bennington, King's Mountain, and other actions, and from the War of 1812 the battles at the River Thames, Plattsburgh, and above all at New Orleans. Successes such as these proved that the nation could rely on its irregulars, who were doubly attractive because they dissolved into the general population when the need for them was over, leaving no residue resembling a standing military force.[7]

Militia supporters argued that citizen soldiery was so much cheaper than regulars that the militias of the several states could all be kept in good condition for the price of 2,000 regulars. Since pensions for war service were not common at this time, they did not seem likely to enlarge the cost of using militia, and the cessation of costs when use ended appeared a real saving.[8] Moreover, the existence of the militia saved the expense of any but a cadre-sized regular force.

One piece of evidence that became available in the 1830s convinced persons who believed in the militia system that it was perfectly capable of defending the nation against attack from any overseas aggressors. The report showed the number of militiamen, who, if the data were accurate, could be concentrated at each of the principal ports on the Atlantic and the Gulf of Mexico.[9]

	First Day	Eleventh Day
Boston	5,422	144,076
Newport, R.I.	1,397	130,824
New York	20,218	191,353
Philadelphia	26,132	221,603
Norfolk, Va.	1,864	45,549
Baltimore	10,046	101,970
Charleston	2,513	59,701
Savannah	1,173	60,422
New Orleans	3,032	31,647
	69,497	987,145

Most reflective observers of the scene thought it right that in a free society men should rely on citizen soldiers for their protection. To be thus self-reliant developed the moral fiber of the doers. There ran in the public philosophy a belief that the martial spirit might counteract what was seen as an excessive desire for wealth among the people. Aside from the moral value of discharging military duty, there was a peace-keeping value. An armed and trained citizenry could not but be a deterrent to foreign aggressors in search of easy conquests.[10]

Even its sturdiest supporters knew that the militia system badly needed improvement. Since there were 1,500,000 to 2,000,000 men who owed service under existing law, the institution was clogged with numbers it could not possibly arm and train. Several thoughtful reformers recommended classifying this unwieldy crowd into age groups, giving the youngest fairly intensive training for about two years and then releasing them into an intermediate reserve. Such a system would provide the nation with an effective citizen force, subject to call, of about 400,000 men. Each man would attend a training camp for ten days every year at the expense of the federal government.[11] Sound though it was, this proposal was not acceptable and was never in whole or in part put into practice.

James Barbour, Secretary of War in John Quincy Adams's administration, created a board of officers in 1826 to study the condition of the militia. The Barbour Board gathered testimony far and wide, then submitted to the secretary the following list of changes to improve the militia.

1. Cut the active militia down to 400,000 and seriously train that number.

2. Divide the 400,000 among the states according to population, and let the states raise their quotas in their own ways.

3. Appoint an adjutant general for militia affairs in the War Department.

4. Make the units of the several states truly interchangeable by enforcing common tables of organization.

5. Distribute drill manuals to all militias at federal expense.

6. Run a training camp each year in every state for at least ten days at federal expense.[12]

Not one of the proposed reforms ever went into effect. During the mid-1830s when a substantial surplus built up in the United States Treasury, the government spent no part of it to improve the condition of the militia. A few states made weak reform efforts, but the Congress did not act, and the militia, in spite of the faith voiced in it year after year, decayed.

After the War of 1812, the State of New York sought to collect fines from militiamen who had dodged war service. State tribunals assessed fines of $200,000 against 4,000 militiamen, but so indifferent was the public that collection costs exceeded income by $25,000. A few units elected unqualified persons to be colonels purposely to ridicule the system. Ridicule was so widespread that the New York legislature enacted a penalty of one day in jail for any militiaman who in anyway mocked the training.[13]

Cornstalks and brooms appeared with greater frequency in place of firearms on training days. The First Regiment, Iowa Territorial Militia, listed 950 men but only 63 muskets. Attendance fell off and frequency of training diminished. Officers failed to carry out their duties, and some of them bothered to keep rosters only in order to qualify for the issue of federal arms under the law of 1808. In California, when the statutory militia failed to respond, as in riots in San Francisco in 1856, vigilante groups cropped up to maintain law and order.[14]

Substantial elements in the society were glad to see the militia decline, indeed, wanted it to disappear. The American Peace Society, whose aim was to end the use of war as an instrument of national policy, contended that the militia was weaker than before because public sentiment was repudiating war. William Jay, a member of that society and the son of John Jay, stressed the wastefulness of the system. "What comforts, what benefits," he asked, "are derived from the numerous and onerous trainings of the New York militia, and the vice and drunkenness and idleness which attend them?" The charge of vice and drunkenness was a common one, which of course temperance reformers picked up and used as a reason for discontinuing the militia system.[15]

The organized labor unions of the 1830s and 1840s attacked the militia with all their might because it severely penalized working people and the poor. Men who depended on wages, the argument went, could not afford to lose a day's pay to attend a drill or muster and could not expect pay, under the economic practices of those decades, for time off to perform a public service. Even the secretary of war spoke in 1826 of the need to release all but an elite corps from "the unprofitable pageantry of military parade for five or six days in the year, constituting so injurious a draft on their industry."[16] Some person estimated that one muster day for the entire unclassified militia took $1,000,000 away from laboring people. Equally hard for the poor to bear was the cost of the military equipment for which they were responsible. In the 1830s, for example, the cost of a suitable shoulder weapon was $14.00. Finally, there were fines, which, though of no consequence to people of means, were more than poor persons could afford, and legal authorities had the power to distrain property of all sorts to collect those fines. The unions therefore strove to abolish the militia altogether.

John C. Calhoun, able Secretary of War during both of President James Monroe's terms (1817-1825), thought it a delusion to rely on the militia to oppose the trained regular forces of Europe. Although he knew that the American force had to be small in peacetime, he did not recommend reliance on any sort of citizen reserve. Instead he proposed a regular army with a high ratio of officers to enlisted men. In wartime, the number of enlisted men would be increased to combat strength, and the officer corps with limited expansion could train and shape the full-sized units. This was Calhoun's expansible army plan. A later able secretary, Joel R. Poinsett, agreed with Calhoun but stressed the role of the militia to offset any danger that might arise from the standing army. To both these remarkable secretaries, the danger from standing military forces in the United States seemed small indeed.[17]

As new territories entered the Union, they invariably established the full militia mechanism. Mississippi, in her first constitution of 1817, stipulated that only white men of military age who were enrolled in the militia could vote. But neither in Mississippi nor in any of the other new territories did the paper structure translate into a strong organization de facto. In 1827, the highest ratio of militiamen to population was one to five in Ohio, the lowest one to nineteen in South Carolina. The War Department continued to issue weapons to the states on the basis of enrollment figures, but in 1830 the appropriation could equip only 12,500 men out of an eligible military population ranging between one and two million.[18]

The governor of Massachusetts insisted that there was nothing wrong with the militia system that improved laws could not correct, but most of the states made laws in the opposite direction. In 1831, Delaware abolished its system altogether. Massachusetts eliminated compulsory service in 1840, followed by Maine, Ohio, and Vermont in 1844, Connecticut and New York in 1846, Missouri in 1847, and New Hampshire in 1851. Indiana classified its militia according to age in 1840, and exempted all but the young men from service. New Jersey withdrew the right to imprison a man for failure to pay a militia fine in 1844; Iowa did the same in 1846, Michigan in 1850, and California in 1856.[19]

As the compulsory system, a form of UMT, waned, volunteering waxed. During the early decades of the nineteenth century, volunteer units satisfied the sort of public demand that sports were to fulfill later on. In some of the people, the martial spirit combined with a love of colorful uniforms, military ceremonials, and martial music was ever present. Such props appealed to the vanity of many persons and to the noble instinct of others, and through them citizens of all sorts sought to escape being ordinary. Most of the volunteers were men of substance who saw in volunteer units instruments by means of which they could help defend what they owned. The wealthier among them tended to join the cavalry, which was exclusive because it was expensive, while clerks and shopkeepers enrolled in grenadier, light, and other elite infantry companies. All volunteers had to be able to afford their affiliation: as much as $72.00 for the uniform, an initial investment in armament, and various levels of dues. A mere private in Massachusetts in 1824 incurred annual costs of $9.00, plus $21.00 for his uniform. There were fines for missing drills and ceremonial occasions; for example, the Salem Light Infantry charged each member who missed the Fourth of July annual muster and banquet $3.00. Dues, running from 50¢ to $6.00 per month, went into the rent for a place to drill, or in the case of the more affluent units, into the building of an armory. Entrance fees ranged from $50.00 for the First California Guards of San Francisco to $2.00 for the Charleston Independent Greens. Finally, volunteer units had the power to levy special assessments.[20]

Despite costs, volunteer units proliferated. Three hundred of them sprang up in California between 1849 and 1856. Relative to population they were most numerous in the District of Columbia where one out of every twenty-nine persons was a member of a unit. Volunteer units virtually took the place of a police force there.[21]

As the volunteers became the only reliable part of the militia system, the states began to offer them more support. California levied a 25¢ tax on all men who were not affiliated with a unit and used the proceeds for the existing organizations. In 1844, Massachusetts began to pay each volunteer $1.00 for every muster or drill, but it limited the number of sessions for which a man might collect, and the total number of collectors could not exceed 5,000. Connecticut allowed members of volunteer units to deduct $4.00 from their taxes. Pennsylvania made its contributions to the units themselves: $300 to each regiment that trained for three consecutive days and $100 to each battalion.[22]

The opportunity to wear a uniform attracted some men, the gaudier the uniform the better. It is true that a few outfits affected studied simplicity; the Crooked Creek Rangers of Armstrong County, Pennsylvania, wore a homemade linen hunting shirt, dyed with tanbark juice, buckskin breeches, and a cap with the tail of a fox, coon, or deer dangling from it. Much commoner were flamboyant uniforms such as those of the Swatara Guards, Middletown, Pennsylvania: a blue swallowtail coat, faced with yellow and trimmed with yellow cord, and rows of bullet buttons. Huge yellow epaulets covered both shoulders. Trousers were blue with wide yellow stripes. Topping off this show of blue and yellow was a high, stiff cap with a large brass plate in front and a plume of scarlet feathers, a foot high, on one side.[23]

The Wallace Guards in California dressed in highland tartans, while the Black Hussars of San Francisco adopted an all-black uniform, heavily trimmed with silver cord. Of course, the members rode only black horses. Bearskin was in common use for shakos and trimmings, but the Washington Light Artillery of Charleston, South Carolina, used instead a scrap of leopard skin to commemorate the *Chesapeake Leopard* affair which had brought them into being in 1808. As uniforms enlarged the self-respect of the wearers, so also did they stir those persons who saw them. After witnessing a parade of volunteers in Salem, Massachusetts, the local reporter could only say, "We cannot do justice to their appearance."[24]

Festivals would have been drab without the volunteer militia, the units of which were easy to involve in public appearances. For examples, they paraded for LaFayette wherever he passed in 1824 and 1825; they marched at the grand opening of the Erie Canal in every village along the route; and especially they turned out for the fiftieth anniversary of independence. For that occasion the 7th New York Volunteer Infantry was willing to spend $1,136. They also conducted target shoots, and marched with much ceremony to visit neighboring units. The encampments occasioned by these visits involved themselves and the host communities in gargantuan feasts, much fancy drill, and sham battles.[25]

The volunteer militia were useful to state and local officials in maintaining law and order. They guarded prisoners to prevent lynchings and prisons where unpopular executions were being carried out. They enforced quarantines. Riot duty was an integral part of their service, for riots were endemic to the cities. After 1831, the abolitionist movement increased incidence; there was a race riot in Philadelphia in 1833, another against the abolitionists in New York in 1834, yet another in Alexandria and Georgetown in 1835. Later, the Fugitive Slave Law of 1850 brought work to the units. In Boston, it required twenty-two militia companies, a battalion of regulars, and a company of marines to restore one slave to his owner. In Milwaukee, certain units flatly refused to help enforce the Act, whereupon the governor of Wisconsin revoked their charters.[26]

The famous 7th New York Regiment served again and again in the cause of law and order. During the troubled election of 1834, the regiment stood under a hail of bricks and stones, but managed to withhold its fire. The following year, the city suffered a great fire, and the regiment policed the streets to stem looting. When stevedores rampaged in 1836, the 7th helped to put them down, and at the height of the Panic of 1837, with the streets full of hungry people demanding food, the 7th took up its arms to protect property.[27]

In the 1840s, Irish Roman Catholics began to migrate to the United States in large numbers, crowding into the seaboard cities, where, wretchedly poor and uprooted from their past as peasants, they often took to the streets. In 1844 in Philadelphia, they clashed with the older residents, who considered them ignorant, degraded, and virtually subhuman. Local sailors joined with the volunteer militia to put down this riot in which thirty persons were killed and 130 more injured. On May 24, 1849, a mob of Irishmen attacked the New York Opera House because a famous English actor was playing there. The 7th New York subdued them, but the cost was twenty-two persons killed, thirty-six injured, and the opera house gutted.[28]

Substantial numbers of the Irish enrolled in volunteer units. Indeed, in New York in 1848, they organized an entire regiment, the 69th, which the State of New York accepted as part of the official system on December 21, 1849. The Irish founders of the 69th intended to use it one way or another to fight England for the liberation of Ireland, but the state authorities were not aware of this objective. In 1850, a second regiment, the 9th, made up of Irish rebels, was constituted. Both regiments insisted on a green dress coat instead of the regulation blue, and so attired 3,000 of them paraded on St. Patrick's Day in 1853. The two regiments combined into an Irish brigade which began to loom too large to the Native American Party, then at its strongest in New York. Accordingly, the 69th was excluded from the St. Patrick's Day Parade in 1855, but it defiantly marched by itself down different streets. The next move to weaken the Irish strain in the New York Organized Militia was to merge the 9th Regiment with the 69th. This consolidation might have induced violence, were it not that times were hard and the Irish were preoccupied with survival.[29]

Just as the 69th New York seemed to be gaining a measure of native American support, Edward, Prince of Wales, came to the city on an official tour in 1860, and the authorities ordered the organized militia to parade in honor of the visitor. The colonel commanding the 69th requested permission to keep his regiment out of the march. The city authorities denied permission, but the regiment chose not to march anyway. The New York officials preferred charges against the colonel and considered disbanding the 69th. Just at that time President Lincoln's call for 75,000 militia to save the Union reached the states. The 69th volunteered, was accepted as part of New York's quota, and the issue of the missed parade died.

The Know Nothing Movement, that is the Native American Party, affected militias other than that of New York. The State of Massachusetts disbanded its Irish units in 1855, and Connecticut followed suit the next year.[30]

Indians became the active enemy of the militia, both standing and volunteer, during the decades following the War of 1812. A major project of the administrations of Andrew Jackson was the removal of the eastern Indians to areas west of the Mississippi River which the white man would not want. The Sauk and Fox Indians of Iowa, Illinois, and Wisconsin opposed removal in 1831 and 1832. The resultant Black Hawk War showed the citizen soldiery at its worst. Many of the short-term irregulars considered these redmen to be animals, much lower on the life scale than man. They wanted this animal out of the way and welcomed the chance to kill it, especially since they could do so and prosper, for the United States took 10,000 citizen soldiers onto its payroll, 7,787 of them from Illinois.[31]

This untrained horde never became an army. The units elected their own officers, and in doing so chose many ill-qualified men. For this reason and for others, there was scant discipline. Lieutenant Philip St. George Cooke, a conscientious regular officer, looked with disgust on the irregular scene: "A whole brigade was regularly paraded and firing in the air as regularly as they knew how, while their general, mounted on a tall stump, was endeavoring to argue them out of it. . . . [Unsuccessful] their general finally damned them to all posterity and resigned his commission in violent disgust."[32] This gathering of armed men had no single head. Although the United States government designated Brigadier General Henry Atkinson, United States Army, to command. But Governor John Reynolds of Illinois, wont to take the field himself, often bypassed Atkinson and issued orders directly to his Illinois commanders. The resultant lack of coordination brought a defeat on the Illinois militia on May 15, 1832, and a retreat so swift that it became known as Stillman's Run. Colonel Zachary Taylor, a regular who witnessed it, described it as unutterably shameful.[33]

It was not shame, however, that grew among the citizen soldiery but hatred of the Sauks and Foxes. The Illinoisians now intended to hunt down and exterminate their foe. Some of them, finding a few Indian women burrowing in the river bank to hide, shot them and especially relished watching them jerk as they died.[34]

This Black Hawk War uncovered at least one highly effective leader of citizen soldiers: James D. Henry, Brigadier General of Illinois militia. Henry kept clear of the regular officers, took orders from Reynolds when he had to, but in the main followed his own sound intuitions. Like all successful militia commanders, he knew how to coax his men and was able to hold them together and move them rapidly. He and Henry Dodge, working far ahead of Atkinson and the regulars, found the trail of Chief Black Hawk's main band and followed it relentlessly to the Bad Axe River. Atkinson with 1,500 regulars caught up just in time to take over the battle and send Henry and his men to the rear to guard the baggage. He may have done this out of pique or he may have done it to avoid the brutality characteristic of the irregulars in this conflict.[35] After Bad Axe, the Sauk and Fox, unable to fight more, entered reservations.

Three years later, a conflict over removal broke out in Florida Territory. Known as the Second Seminole War, it lasted seven years,

1835-1842, involving every unit of the United States Army, at one time or another, about 1,000 sailors, some Marines, and 30,000 irregulars. But in this grueling conflict, the regular officers kept better control and thus reduced the level of cruelty.[36]

At the start of the Second Seminole War, Brigadier General Duncan L. Clinch, a regular, was in command. He counted on cornering the warriors in a thick hammock, the Cove of the Withlacoochee River, and breaking their fighting power at once. The Seminoles did not come out and fight so as to present themselves for annihilation; instead, they caught Clinch's force astraddle the river and hurt it so badly that the general marched back the way he had come. He would not have been vulnerable as he was, astride the river, he said, if the militiamen had crossed as they were ordered to do. The militia officers involved challenged Clinch's official report as face-saving, arguing instead that the general did not know how to fight Florida Indians.[37]

The old Indian fighter Andrew Jackson, now commander-in-chief, could see no excuse for suffering humiliation from a band of Indians. He removed Clinch and replaced him with one of the young heroes of the War of 1812, Brevet Major General Winfield Scott. Scott made the same assumption as Clinch, namely that he could trap the warrior force in the Cove and wipe them out, but his strategy was far more complicated than his predecessor's. He sent three columns snaking through virtually unknown Florida terrain to converge at the Cove and crush the foe. The problem with this was that the Indians knew every minute of every day where each column was, harassed them when they could, and slipped out of the Cove when Scott's army finally was ready to bring them to battle there. Bitter over the failure of his too elaborate plan, Scott charged the white Floridians with shying from every bush for fear of a redman, or even a redwoman, behind it. For his failure and for alienation of the Floridians, Scott was recalled and replaced by the governor of Florida and long-time supporter of Andrew Jackson, Richard Keith Call. This arrangement conformed more to the wishes of the white population, but it did not meet the expectations of the president. Call could not find and eliminate the warriors, and he in turn was removed.[38]

The government looked once more to a professional soldier to finish the war, Brevet Major General Thomas S. Jesup. But national attention turned to his subordinate, Colonel Zachary Taylor, because it fell to Taylor to direct the one action of the war that resembled a traditional white-style battle. The red foe prepared a strong position naturally protected by a wet prairie and a dense hammock. Indians seldom assumed such a posture unless they thought the odds were strongly in their favor, and they cut firelanes through the brush and notched the trees for rifle rests to increase the advantage. Taylor formed his command in two lines with the regulars in the second line and 132 men of the First Missouri Mounted Volunteers—all that were fit for duty out of 600—to receive the initial shock in the front line. It was Christmas Day 1837. The Missouri Volunteers were severely shot up, and the folks back home were outraged. Thomas Hart Benton, senator from Missouri, charged Taylor with sacrificing the citizen soldiers in order to save his precious regulars. The Missouri legislature voted censure upon the colonel. Taylor, for his part, stated only that he had put the regulars in the second line because he must have a reliable reserve to fall back on. Although the Missourians never accepted this logic, Taylor came through the altercation with an enhanced reputation, received a promotion to brigadier general, and gained a national reputation.[39]

Congress authorized three- and six-month volunteers to receive the same pay as regulars and to share some fringe benefits. For example, the widow of a volunteer killed in action could draw half pay for five years. Volunteering made sense to certain senators, who contended that regulars were useless as Indian fighters and that the war ought to be conducted altogether by irregulars who understood how to overpower Indians.[40]

Volunteer enthusiasm brought into Florida more citizen soldiers than Jesup could support. Late in 1837, he controlled 9,000 men, 4,100 of them volunteers. Battalions came from Florida itself, from Louisiana, Georgia, Tennessee, and Missouri; two companies appeared from Pennsylvania, and one each from the District of Columbia and New York. So many of these took most of their contracted time getting to Florida that they had to be used at once or not at all.[41]

The most articulate volunteers were romantics who came to save the white people of Florida from "the dark demons of ruin." One of the Charleston officers wrote, "Never did Rome or Greece in days of yore—nor France nor England in modern times—pour forth a nobler soldiery than the volunteers from Georgia, Alabama, Louisiana, and South Carolina."[42]

Of course, the regulars saw things through different eyes. Lieutenant John T. Sprague described a column of Florida volunteers as "a long string . . . dirty, ragged and dusty, seated upon long tailed and short eared horses with the deadly rifle resting in front and a short jacket, long beard and hair and a broad brimmed white hat."[43] His choice of words revealed that he had little confidence in this string as a military force. General Jesup wryly commented, but not for public hearing, that he would gladly have done without the volunteers if he had had any alternative.[44]

Horses made the volunteers more expensive than regulars, yet the volunteers would not walk. The regular officers, who controlled the nature of the manpower in the end, reduced the number of irregulars bit by bit until by the time Brevet Brigadier General Walker K. Armistead assumed command in the spring of 1840, the volunteers were set in a purely defensive role. Armistead drew an imaginary line eastward from Tampa and turned the territory north of it over to the citizen soldiers. For the most part the Indians had been driven out of that area. South of the line, small detachments of regulars searched out scattered bands of Indians to destroy them and their crops and dwellings.[45]

Within the Territory of Florida, the statutory militia, because of its UMT character, was so unpopular that the territorial legislature met in secret to discuss it. Floridians of military age were divided; many were determined to remain close to home in case of Indian attack, while about an equal number sought above all to get onto the federal payroll. Enough of them were accepted into federal employment that it cost about $1,000,000 finally to pay them. But the statutory militia of the Territory ended the war as it had entered it in a disorganized condition.[46]

While the Florida War was slowly winding down, certain imbroglios, which have been called wars, took place elsewhere in the country. One occurred in Pennsylvania in 1838 when two rival political factions each elected a speaker of the Pennsylvania House of Representatives and neither would give way. The governor called out some of the militia and stipulated that the ammunition they carried be ball and buckshot. Thus this bloodless controversy became known as the Buckshot War. At about the same time, a dispute arose between Maine and Canada over the location of the international border. Maine concentrated several thousand militiamen along the Aroostook River, and Canada placed as many on the other river bank, but no military action occurred when the matter was settled diplomatically.[47]

Meanwhile, war in the classic pattern was developing. Late in 1845, President James K. Polk ordered Zachary Taylor, now a major general, to occupy disputed territory along the Texas-Mexico border. The Mexican government reacted militarily and the United States declared war in April 1846. Polk authorized Taylor to call upon the governors of the Gulf states for militiamen to serve for six months. The president assured the governors that their militia would be used only defensively but did not promise that they would remain within the United States. This did not matter; enthusiasm ran high and so many militiamen and war volunteers reached Taylor that he had to leave 6,000 of them behind when he moved into the offensive.[48]

Before long, Taylor's army turned into an expeditionary force, leaving the militia to guard sensitive places in the United States near the combat zone. But even though the use of militia was limited, the militia system was the standard means of procuring volunteers. In states where the system had atrophied too far to be useful, sheriffs and other peace officers somehow had to assemble men to ask for volunteers. All in all, the government mustered 12,500 statutory militiamen into federal service during the war, which amounted to 12 percent of the total manpower employed.[49]

The first call for volunteers gave men the choice between one year or the duration of the conflict. In May 1846, the one-year alternative was deleted. Final results were 27,000 men for one year, and 33,500 for the duration. All but 2,000 of these saw active duty and amounted to 58 percent of the combat force. The other 30 percent of the American force was regular. The war placed no strain on the population; one man served for every thirty-one of military age, which was light compared to one for each 1.28 men during the Revolution and one for each 2.4 in the War of 1812. Nineteen out of the twenty-nine states sent troops, as did some cities: St. Louis (the St. Louis Legion), Louisville (The Louisville Legion), and Washington, with some members from Baltimore. States that sent no troops were close to the sensitive Canadian border, where, it was feared, trouble might erupt. The War Department alerted 25,000 New England militiamen to enter active duty if called, but never called them.[50]

Major General Winfield Scott, now Commanding General of the U.S. Army, determined to train the war volunteers before they crossed the southern border, and proposed postponing entrance into Mexico until September 1846. As was common in American wars, the impulse to close with the enemy and subdue him took precedence over training. The controlling political word was "On to Mexico," and Scott's sensible policy was overruled. Observers generally agreed that the war volunteers could be relied on to fight effectively, but a significant number of regular officers disagreed even with this. At the start of the war, some Mexican officers and many foreign observers believed the soldiers of Mexico to be superior, but as action followed action, they abandoned this appraisal. Santa Anna, the most successful Mexican commander said, "If we were to plant our batteries in Hell, the damned Yankees would take them from us."[51]

The volunteers were less successful in the noncombat aspects of an expeditionary force. For one thing, they stood on their right to serve only the amount of time for which they had originally contracted and no more. As a result, the one-year tour of seven regiments with General Scott ran out when Scott's army was half-way between Vera Cruz and

Mexico City. The general had no choice but to allow them to return to the coast and take ship for the United States. This left him in the heart of a hostile country with only 7,113 men. He then did a daring thing. He cut his line of communications to the coast and hedgehogged his troops to await reinforcements. He waited from May until August when volunteers who had enlisted for the duration of the war arrived. They built the army back up to 14,000 men, but about 2,500 of them were continually unfit for duty.[52] Twelve percent left the service for health reasons, compared to eight for the regulars. General Scott accounted for the difference.

> A regiment of regulars in 15 minutes from the evening halt will have tents pitched and trenched around, besides straw, leaves or bushes for dry sleeping; arms and ammunition will be secured and in order for any night attack; fires made kettles boiling . . . all the men dried or warmed, merry as crickets before the end of the first hour. . . . Volunteers neglect all these points; eat their salt meat raw . . . or fried . . . worse than raw— death to any christian man the fifth day; lose or waste their clothing, lie down wet or on wet ground—fatal to health, and in a short time of life; leave the arms and ammunition exposed to rain and dews; hence both are generally useless and soon lost.[53]

The regulars never ceased to believe that an expanded regular army could have defeated Mexico much more cheaply and more humanely than a force made up of 70 percent citizen soldiers. They complained that the volunteers consumed twice as much equipment and supplies as the professionals but performed far less well in combat. The proof lay in the casualty statistics: three regulars per hundred died as a result of combat, compared to one per hundred of the volunteers.[54] Whenever the army halted and was idle for a time, the volunteers got out of hand. Georgia troops rioted in July 1846, and suppressing them cost three lives and several persons wounded. The colonel of a North Carolina regiment singlehanded put down a mutiny, but he had to kill one man and wound several others to do it.[55]

Raphael Semmes, serving in the navy during the war, observed chronic jealousy between regular and volunteer officers. Certainly, the regulars resented the meteoric rise of some irregulars, who knew little of warfare. Most conspicuous of these was Gideon Pillow, law partner of President Polk, who became a general officer at 35. A regular more often than not would still be a lieutenant at that age. Lieutenant Colonel Ethan Allen Hitchcock referred to Pillow and others like him as "mushroom generals—political appointments usually." The volunteers, Hitchcock wrote, would have been no better than a loose mob except for the discipline, organization, and tactics imposed on them by the Old Army.[56]

Finally, the regular officers felt that the United States war volunteers were the wrong kind of troops to carry out the national purpose in a foreign land. Too many of the them considered the Roman Catholic Mexican peasants as being on a low rung of the life ladder, no higher than the North American Indians. General Taylor himself said that the Mounted Texans seldom went out without committing a murder. The testimony of Samuel Chamberlain, far below Taylor in rank, was in the same vein. Chamberlain had started out as a war volunteer from Illinois, then transferred to the First U. S. Dragoons. More than once, the First Dragoons saved native Mexicans from rape, pillage, and death at the hands of the volunteers. An irregular unit, he wrote, was "fighting over their poor victims like dogs, and the place resounded with horrid oaths and the groans and shrieks of the raped," until the First Dragoons arrived.[57]

Only a small segment of the war volunteers were guilty of atrocities. Most of them in fact had been wafted off to Mexico on gusts of patriotic romanticism. Jacob Oswandel, an enlisted volunteer, conveyed the romantic mood well in a letter to his brother. "I shall go into this battle with a firm heart and contented mind, and should it be my lot to fall, or death be my fate, I say 'Let it go!' with a will, and then my name and those of other gallant patriots will be recorded on the bright pages of history of this glorious war."[58] Such a mood filled up fourteen regiments in Illinois when four had been called for, and 30,000 men from Tennessee where 3,000 were wanted. So eager were these men to go that they drew straws to see which one out of every ten might make up the quota.[59]

The citizen soldiers who reached Mexico for the most part quickly lost the romantic dynamic that had sent them there in the first place. A new set of drives helped to hold them there: the same pay as the regulars received, and added to that a quarter section of land for twelve months' service. "I have been thinking of home today," wrote one of them from central Mexico, "here knee deep in dust in the boiling sun—beef and crackers to eat and nasty water to drink—and no chance to buy anything—this heat is killing . . . but if these blame Regulars can stand it, so can I."[60]

Two generals, both regulars, who could hardly have been more unlike, emerged from the Mexican War as candidates for the presidency. Their nicknames reveal how opposite they were; Winfield Scott was known to the troops as "Old Fuss and Feathers," Zachary Taylor as "Old Rough and Ready." Scott, six feet four inches tall, seldom appeared out of uniform, which was embellished with braid and feathers. Taylor, in contrast, of average height and not at all prepossessing, seldom in uniform, and often without insignia of rank, was so easily mistaken for any old soldier that a newly arrived lieutenant offered him fifty cents to polish his sword. Both generals served in the War of 1812 and in the wars of Indian removal, and both had had extensive experience with volunteers. The irregulars were not popular with either general, but Taylor held them in higher respect than Scott. At the Battle of Buena Vista, when Taylor's aide, Major Bliss, suggested to the general that the troops were whipped, Taylor replied, "I know it, but the volunteers don't know it. Let them alone, we'll see what they do." It is fair to say that Taylor and Scott could get about equal performance from irregular troops in combat; but it is equally fair to add that Scott could control the volunteers when not in battle much more efficiently than Taylor. The atrocities which came from Taylor's columns did not appear under Scott.[61]

From declaration of war to signing of a peace treaty, the War with Mexico lasted twenty-one months. The overwhelming reaction of Americans to the experience was pride in the magnificent conquest the nation had made. A princely domain had been added to the country without either significantly enlarging the public debt or bringing into being a permanently enlarged regular military establishment. The militia and volunteers, who made up 70 percent of the wartime force, simply slipped back into the population. The war had shown that the martial spirit was very much alive in the nation, a spirit essential to the mood of Manifest Destiny abroad in the land. President Polk told Congress what he thought the war proved about the citizen soldier: "The events of these few months afford a gratifying proof that our country can under an emergency, confidently rely for the maintenance of her honor and the defense of her rights on an effective force ready at all times voluntarily to relinquish the comforts of home for the perils and privations of the camp."[62]

The consensus was that the military instrument, especially the war volunteers, had vindicated the national honor. Thus the war volunteer became more accepted than ever before as the efficient agent by means of which to carry out national objectives. This acceptance did not wane with the passing of time. On February 25, 1858, Senator Albert Gallatin Brown of Mississippi reaffirmed it before his colleagues. War volunteers are the best of soldiers, he said, because "they will pitch in and fight it out more valorously, more daringly. . . . They fight by the job; they fight quick, with a design to end the contest as soon as possible."[63] Congress, acting on the supposition that war volunteers would always be available when the nation was endangered, cut the regular army from 29,512 enlisted men authorized in 1847 to 11,685 in 1855.[64]

The Mormons, when driven out of New York where they had originated, settled for a time in Iowa, Illinois, and Missouri. Because hostility toward them always developed, they constituted their own militia, calling it a legion. But numbers of Mormon men joined the 53rd Regiment of Missouri Militia, enough indeed to give rise to an anti-Mormon revulsion. When the anti-Mormon faction of the regiment seized the Prophet, Joseph Smith, the commander of the state militia ordered Smith's execution. Brigadier General Alexander Doniphan, however, refused to carry out the order.[65] For the time being, Smith's life was spared, but he was later martyred by a mob in Illinois. Under Brigham Young, the majority of the Mormons soon began their heroic trek to get out of the United States. Although Utah was not a part of the nation in 1846, the Mormon church nevertheless organized a battalion to serve with the American forces in Mexico. Young did this primarily due to the need of money; the church collected the pay of the Mormon soldiers. These, under stern discipline, marched with Alexander Doniphan, who had earlier saved their prophet.

Brought into the United States reluctantly because of the Mexican Cession, the Mormons accepted their bad fortune, except that they would not receive "gentile" officials to preside over Utah Territory. The United States thereupon assembled a small army of 5,000 men, put it under the command of Albert Sidney Johnston, and dispatched it to Utah to escort the gentile officials. For a time, the Mormon Legion harassed the column, but seeing that the odds were too great, they came to terms, thus ending what is known as the Mormon War.[66]

Back to the Indians in the 1850s. Some 2,000 militiamen served in 1853 in Utah in an action known as the Walker War. Twenty of them and an unknown number of Indians lost their lives. In Washington Territory in 1856, Governor Isaac Stevens summoned volunteers to fight the Indians, but the federal commander, Major General John E. Wool, an officer in both the War of 1812 and the War with Mexico, canceled Stevens' call, contending that only he as federal military representative had the power to call out citizen soldiers. He added that the white settlers were cruel and unjust to the redmen. Stevens, ignoring Wool's intervention, raised his volunteers, and with them all but annihilated the Indians. In addition, he had the presumption to bill the United States for the costs incurred, and in spite of all Wool could do, was able to persuade Congress to appropriate the money, albeit three years later.[67]

In 1855, war broke out once more between the remnants of the Florida Indians and the United States. The War Department rushed regulars to the peninsula, expecting to prosecute the conflict with them. As in the Second Seminole War, so now in the Third, small units had to penetrate the remotest Indian keeps and there destroy the subsistence of the redmen and kill or capture the resisters. This time, the composition of those small units was different; whereas in the Second War it had been the regulars, in this one it was the citizen soldiers of Florida. When the Third War ended in May 1858, less than one hundred Indians remained in Florida.[68]

Irregulars in the 1850s were militarily engaged against foes other than Indians. The doctrine of Popular Sovereignty put into practice flared into intrastate war in the Territory of Kansas where citizens who favored the institution of slavery fought citizens who did not. The forces were too fluid to be called militia, but they certainly were volunteers on opposite sides of a burning issue. At last, President Buchanan sent the regular army to restore peace, a peace that favored the slavery faction.

Elsewhere in the country an uneasy peace hung on; but conflict was so close to the surface that people paid more attention to the nearly defunct statutory militia than they had done in many decades. More important, new volunteer units sprang up, organized by men who expected to lead them in war. One way or another, the loose-knit society evinced a firmer discipline following the War with Mexico.

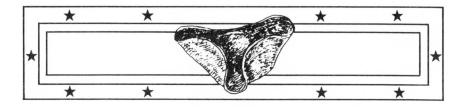

SEVEN

Civil War

Just before the Civil War began, the army of the United States consisted of no more than 1,108 officers and 15,259 enlisted men. Hardly anyone realized that mass war had come for the first time to the United States and that the Union Army alone would expand at least to 2,500,000 men, and the Confederate Army to somewhere around 1,000,000. The conflict would enroll one man out of every 1.66 men of military age on the Union side, and one of every 1.2 in the Confederacy.[1] Procurement of so much manpower was a central problem of the Civil War.

At first, of course, the belligerents had to look to the militia. Militia rolls in the North showed 2,471,377 men, but some of the reports on which these figures were based dated as far back as 1827.[2] No one supposed that these statistics could be converted into a flesh and blood army; even on the remote possibility that the numbers were correct, they gave scant indication of quality. Random sampling of the Union states reveals poor quality. Iowa officials flatly admitted that their militia was in bad condition. Maine, with around 63,000 men enrolled, could field at most 1,200. Michigan, with 109,000 on the muster rolls, could assemble in a short time no more than 1,241 men in twenty-eight companies. The total militia force of New Hampshire consisted of the adjutant general alone. Except for the old volunteer companies, the New York militia had become so decadent that the legislature did not want to waste funds on it. There were 19,000 men in the organized militia of New York, but only 8,000 muskets for them. Similarly, Ohio could find only 1,984 shoulder weapons for an alleged twenty-three regiments. Delaware had scrapped its system and could not raise even 780 men called for by President Lincoln, but loyal citizens unofficially raised and equipped that regiment.[3] Connecticut, Massachusetts, and Rhode Island were exceptions to this shabby story, as they had throughout the years attended to their militias.[4]

There were 692,334 men on the militia rolls of the Confederate states, but as in the North these figures were of uncertain value. In Arkansas the militia was acknowledged to be in a lamentable condition. It was ineffective in Florida due to sparse population and poor communications. Militia performance in defense of the coast in North Carolina was poor.[5] Perhaps with the exception of the units around Charleston, South Carolina, conditions similar to those in Arkansas, Florida, and North Carolina were characteristic.

Since Congress was not in session when the Confederates fired on Ft. Sumter, the president had no legal way to enlarge the fighting force except to call the state militias into federal service. Accordingly, on April 15, 1861, he summoned 75,000 militiamen apportioned among the states according to the size of their militias. They were to serve for three months under officers appointed by their governors. Even though Maryland, Kentucky, Tennessee, Arkansas, and North Carolina, assigned quotas, sent no men, 93,000 militiamen answered the call. Looking back, even the oversubscribed number seems far too small for the task ahead, but few contemporary observers realized that a long war had begun. One who did was Winfield Scott, Lieutenant General by brevet and commanding general of the U. S. Army, but he did not foresee a mass war, and that is why he expected to get along with 75,000 militiamen used as a defense force and a striking force behind them of no more than 35,000 regulars plus 60,000 volunteers enlisted for the duration of the war. He intended to keep the regulars intact to function as his ultimate reserve, since he had scant faith in irregular soldiers.[6]

Old volunteer units made up 40 percent of the 93,000 militiamen who answered the president's call. New Jersey was able to send the first fully organized brigade to Washington because the constituent companies of its four regiments were old volunteer units. Soon, four Massachusetts regiments arrived to try to keep the Confederate forces out of the nation's capital. One of these, the 5th Massachusetts, had one company that had been constituted in 1804, as well as one that was brand-new. The 7th New York was able to mobilize and reach Washington promptly because it had experience stretching back to 1824. The Irish 69th, arriving early, had had experience since 1849. The few Irishmen who refused to be mustered into federal service were humiliated by their fellows and drummed out of the camp. New York sent 8,634 of the citizen soldiers who came to the defense of Washington, most of them as parts of old units which had volunteered intact. The early defenders of the capital remained to take part in the First Battle of Bull Run in July 1861, after which their ninety days were up and they went home.[7]

Ohio delivered 12,357 men for Lincoln's first call, raising its initial two regiments in one day. These regiments, though new, were built around old established companies: the Cleveland Grays, Rover Guards, Columbus Videttes, State Fencibles, Governor's Guards, Dayton Light Guards, and Guthrie Grays. Pennsylvania troops were on the way to Washington just three days after receiving the call. Their mobilization, too, was expedited by the existence of old volunteer companies that volunteered intact. For example, the 1st Regiment contained the Ringgold Light Artillery of Reading, the Logan Guards of Lewistown, two seasoned companies from Pottstown, and the Allen Infantry from Allentown. The 2nd Troop of Philadelphia City Cavalry answered Lincoln's first call, went home at the end of three months, volunteered two more times during the war, but was accepted only for a short tour during the Gettysburg Campaign.[8]

Wisconsin's quota was one regiment of 780 men which the governor expected to be made up of old volunteer units, but they did not come forward as he had hoped; of the fifty-one in being when the war broke out, only twenty-six volunteered for duty intact. The governor took the weapons of those who declined federal service and issued them to brand-new units.[9]

Lincoln's initial call went out as far as the West Coast and the Southwest. There was a division of loyalty in California, and the volunteer units there were retained largely within the state. Washington Territory, however, found six companies to answer the call with eighteen officers and 336 enlisted men. Like the other far western states and territories, New Mexico had no quota, but it raised and sent eastward 1,510 men.[10]

Although the critical border states were asked to send militia, they all declined. But when the governor of Missouri officially refused the state's troops, Francis Preston Blair, loyal to the Union and to Lincoln, acting on his own, raised four regiments. The governor of Kentucky informed the president that his state would not furnish soldiers for "the wicked purpose of subduing her sister Southern States," and no private citizen stepped forward, Blair-like, to raise troops unofficially. With equal emphasis the governor of Tennessee refused the call, and the following month he transferred all state troops into the Confederate Service. But the people of east Tennessee provided 25,000 men in volunteer units to the Union cause.[11]

Aside from their response to the April call for militia, the old volunteer units contributed only a tiny percent of the total Union force during the war. Out of more than 1,780 volunteer regiments that served, just fifteen of them had had continuous existence before the war. A few, it is true, turned out intact more than once; the 5th Massachusetts volunteered during the summer of 1862 when General Lee threatened to invade the North. This time, the government sent it, with twelve other Massachusetts regiments and one from New Jersey, to the Pamlico Sound area of North Carolina. During a nine-month tour there, its principal function was to release longer-term outfits to oppose Lee in Maryland.[12] The 7th New York served intact again for three months beginning in May 1862, and once more, for one month only, when Lee advanced toward Gettysburg in 1863. More significant than their service as units was the contribution made to the Union officer corps by the old units. The 7th New York alone sent 600 officers into the Union Army, while one established company, the Peoria National Blues, furnished thirty-five officers, three of whom became brigadier generals by brevet.[13]

The activities of the Union Congress in July 1862 indicate the seriousness of the manpower problem in the second year of the war. The legislators seemed to have learned the need for long-term soldiers; on July 2, they authorized the president to call for 300,000 men for a three-year tour to be raised by the states on a quota basis. But only fifteen days later, Congress authorized Lincoln to accept as many volunteers as would come forward to serve for only one year. The reason for the change toward a shorter term is not clear, nor is it clear how Congress expected to get men for three years if they could opt for one instead. The next manpower move is even more remarkable: an added 300,000 men were to be drafted from the state militias for nine months. Now the legislators began to have second thoughts about the 300,000 men for three years, so they did an unprecedented thing. Where the states failed to raise their quotas under the Act of July 2, they were directed to draft to make up the shortfalls. This meant that militiamen, who historically could be called out for no more than ninety consecutive days, might be drafted for three years. Historically, when the United States had wanted citizen soldiers from the states, it had merely set quotas according to population or the size of the militia forces and then had left the states to procure the men in their own ways. Up to that moment, the power to draft had belonged not to the nation but to the states.[14]

Most states, jealous of their powers, did not bother to conduct these drafts, and those that did swept in too few men. Wisconsin, for example, conscripted 4,537 men, but exempted 988 of them on one account or another, lost 19 through desertion, had to furlough 129 at the start, while 1,662 never bothered to report. This left only 1,739 to enter service. Conscription of the militia from all the states garnered only 87,588 men plus an unknown number of volunteers who would have counted being drafted a humiliation.[15]

The militia systems of the states, loose though they were, did render significant service to both belligerents. Ohio volunteers, for example, procured from the militia, cleared western Virginia of Confederate forces in July 1861 and prepared the way for West Virginia to enter the Union two years later.[16] The commander, a major general of Ohio volunteers and one-time regular officer, George B. McClellan, there began his climb to the top of the command structure. Farther east, as Stonewall Jackson dominated the Shenandoah Valley and threatened Washington in 1862, 15,000 men responded to urgent calls upon the militia to turn out; half of them were from New York, 5,000 from Ohio, and one regiment came from Rhode Island. At about the same time in the western theater, Major General Henry Wager Halleck was moving deliberately toward the critical rail junction at Corinth, Mississippi. Confederate General Beauregard, recognizing the importance of Corinth, summoned militia from Alabama and Mississippi, and as far away as Louisiana. During the fall of 1862, when the Confederate Army advanced northward through Kentucky, the governor of Ohio declared a levee of the entire militia from the southern counties of his state. To the east, as Lee marched toward Maryland, the governor of Pennsylvania also resorted to a total levee of the militia close by for two weeks of service.

When General Lee attempted his second invasion of Union territory during the summer of 1863 and President Lincoln called for 100,000 men for a six-month term, only 16,361 responded. But the invaded state, Pennsylvania, cried out to its neighbors for help and summoned 20,000 of its own militiamen. The response to the state call was good, primarily because it was for a far shorter tour than six months. The Pennsylvanians once again served only a few weeks, New York found 13,391 men to send, Rhode Island one regiment and one battery of artillery. Ohio was too much preoccupied with the invasion of its own soil by John Hunt Morgan's marauders to aid Pennsylvania; indeed, Governor Todd again declared a total levee of the militia of the southern counties. The bill for the Ohio service alone ran to $212,318.97, a sum paid by the United States, along with the militia costs of the activities in Pennsylvania.[17]

What the militia of certain of the border states, for example, Missouri, did was of pressing importance to both sides. As early as May 1861, the Missouri legislature put its militia on a war footing, and within three months it was involved in internecine war. Engaged on both sides, it took part in the bloody but indecisive battle of Wilson's

Creek on August 10, 1861; thereafter, the pattern was brother against brother. Before the year was over, there arose out of the confusion an identifiable body known as the Missouri State Militia, supported by United States funds for the defense of the state against the Confederacy. Under the command of the Union generals in the West, this militia was used mainly to combat guerrillas. It had orders to subsist on rebel property, which gave rise to excessive pillage. By February 1863, it had broken the fighting power of the guerrilla bands, but its role was so tangled that the U. S. government did not make final payment for its services until the 1890s.[18]

Another of the precarious states, Kentucky, tried to remain neutral officially, but the militia was not sympathetic. Simon Bolivar Buckner, later of Confederate fame, began at once to develop and drill companies with Confederate sympathy, known as the State Guards. To counteract this, the Unionist legislature authorized the formation of the Home Guards but stipulated that neither of the Guards be used by the belligerents. In September 1861, it abolished the State Guards, whereupon most of the State Guardsmen joined the Confederate Army. As in Missouri, the United States agreed to support the organization that would defend the Union cause within the state. Bit by bit, however, all identifiable units entered the service on one side or the other, and Kentucky's quasi-neutrality came to an end.[19]

Without the militia system neither belligerent could have mobilized as it did. Russell Weigley, a distinguished American military historian, said, "Merely by giving the Union a stop-gap army and a breathing spell, the country's militia institutions amply justified themselves."[20] They did so in the Confederacy as well.

Nevertheless, the combination of militia and spontaneous volunteering did not produce the numbers and the regular flow of manpower required in mass war. It was especially essential that the Confederacy involve more of its 1,064,193 males of military age than had come forward. Accordingly, on May 16, 1862, the Confederate Congress enacted a conscription law. But since the several Confederate states, grounded as they were in the doctrine of state sovereignty, never agreed that the central government needed to draft, they opposed the system. Florida did not conduct a draft, and several of the other states did so only perfunctorily, but in all states the draft coralled some volunteers.[21]

Even though the Union could draw from 4,559,872 men of military age, it too saw the need for a draft, and Congress enacted a conscription law on March 3, 1863. This first conscription at the national level, not confined to the militia and administered by the army, was a milestone in the nation's history. Some of the methods used to gather in draftees smacked of impressment of times past. But men who were drafted could escape service either by paying a commutation fee of $300 or by finding a substitute. Both of these escape routes obviously favored people of means, and on July 4, 1864, commutation was ruled out but not substitution.[22]

There were four different draft calls in the Union with the following meager total results: 46,347 draftees who served in person, 116,188 substitutes, and 87,724 exemptions due to commutation. All in all, conscription swept in only 6 percent of the total Union force. On the other hand, like the Confederate draft, it did drive men, who would have considered it a disgrace to be drafted, to volunteer. This category of involuntary volunteers usually carried the calls for three-year service over the top. More important than the immediate impact on manpower was the precedent set by Civil War conscription: that the United States government had the right to draft as one of the ways to raise an army, delegated to it in the Constitution. Thenceforward, this mode of raising armies would be available to the nation when it became involved in mass war or was threatened by it.[23]

Conscription brought about massive riots in some of the major cities. New York was a center of opposition to the war and the city in which the most violent riots occurred. Mob hatred turned irrationally upon the blacks; many were killed and thousands were terrorized. William Jones, a Negro and the first man in the city to be drafted, was killed by rioters, not by the enemy. On the third day of disorder the governor called out the 7th New York, and later the 74th Regiment, badly battered from Gettysburg. In Boston, the 5th Regiment had to perform similar duty.[24]

Critical as manpower was, officials began to look at black men, generally excluded from the prewar militia. Even though the Lincoln administration at first refused them as soldiers, some white officers raised black units on their own authority. Such units were cheaper; the pay for a black private being $10.00 per month, and for a white one, $13.00. Nevertheless, on November 1, 1863, the secretary of war informed the governor of Ohio, who had sanctioned the raising of a black regiment, that his new unit could not carry a state designation. The War Department created a special category to contain black troops when they were at length accepted, the United States Colored Troops, directly under the jurisdiction of the national government. Later, certain black units began to carry state designations. All in all, 186,017 blacks entered Union service, 35,699 of them from northern states, 44,034 from border states, and 93,346 from the seceded states, more than twice as many as the other two areas combined. But it was 1864 before blacks were allowed to do soldier's work, and even then they were not permitted to capture white women. As for the Confederacy, scarce as manpower was there, only at the end of the war when the cause was lost did the officials enroll blacks as soldiers.[25]

A continuing problem on both sides was to keep seasoned regiments up to strength. Early in the war, authorities allowed volunteer regiments to place two officers and four enlisted men on recruiting service to procure replacements. General McClellan considered one replacement put into an old regiment to be worth two in an untried unit, while Grant put the advantage at three to one. Even so, detachment for recruiting was discontinued, and the old regiments commenced to shrink. The 7th Iowa Volunteer Infantry entered the Battle of Corinth, October 3-4, 1862, with only 327 men and 26 officers out of 1,000 authorized.[26] Beginning early in 1863, the draft was expected to build up the veteran units, but it failed to do so in part because state officials bickered with the War Department over draft quotas, while their veteran units in the field continued to dwindle. After the first flush of enthusiasm for a fight began to fade, it became necessary to offer higher and higher bounties. States and cities, competing with each other, paid out $750,000,000 in bounties during the war. Their largess created a new livelihood, bounty jumping, whereby a man accepted a bounty, deserted as soon as he could, traveled beyond reach of his payors and collected another bounty, and perhaps another and another. Aside from bounty jumpers, the desertion rate was high. Including all volunteer desertions, the figure reached 182,680 men from the Union Army.[27]

In April 1864, when Grant's relentless drive southward was consuming manpower faster than it could be replaced, the governors of Ohio, Indiana, Illinois, and Iowa offered to raise 85,000 men to serve 100 days. The men actually delivered totaled 83,652, but Kansas, Wisconsin, Massachusetts, New York, and New Jersey had to chip in to reach that figure. These troops were sent to hold the line in Missouri and Kentucky so that long-term soldiers could leave the border states and join Grant's offensive.[28]

In both armies, the historical tension between regulars and irregulars reappeared. As an example, Major General James G. Blunt of the Kansas Volunteers scoffed at what he called the textbook warfare being carried on by his superior, John C. Fremont. He questioned General Halleck's loyalty to the Union when Halleck took a month to move from Shiloh to Corinth, Mississippi, and he accused Major General John M. Schofield of abandoning the Kansas troops under his command, leaving them in a desperate position without even notifying Blunt.[29]

Major General John A. Logan, of the Illinois Volunteers, was the irregular with the most power after the war to injure the regular service. Logan never forgave General Sherman and the regular coterie for their treatment of him. He was a successful corps commander, and when Major General James B. McPherson was killed before Atlanta, Logan succeeded to the command of the Army of the Tennessee. Sherman very quickly removed him, replacing him with Major General Oliver Otis Howard. Howard was a West Pointer and a career soldier, and Logan remained convinced that Sherman did not trust citizen soldiers in high command, even one who had commanded as effectively as Logan had. Thus, as a congressman in the postwar era, Logan spoke out against the West Point clique. He preached that the military academies promoted a spirit of aristocracy in a land where such a spirit was alien. The military elite, he said, set apart by uniform and by place of residence and legally vested with control of weapons and power over the lives of other men, was a danger to the Republic.[30]

Tension between state governments and the central power was at high levels, especially in the Confederacy. The Confederate government placed Major General T. C. Hindman, a West Pointer, in command in Arkansas where the state had a small army. When the state refused to place its force under him, Hindman threatened to draft the members of the Arkansas army into the Confederate service, and for a time in that way secured command of it. But the authorities in Arkansas, affronted by such high-handedness and by a regular soldier at that, protested to Jefferson Davis, who, for political reasons, subordinated Hindman to a less assertive, less effective officer.[31]

Like Arkansas, Georgia had a small state army, as well as a navy. Governor Joseph Brown of Georgia invariably put the defense of Georgia ahead of the Confederacy. He insisted that the War Department accept skeletal regiments, not full companies, so that he could appoint the field officers. He never seemed to be aware of the degree to which service in the state troops satisfied patriotism, frittered away enthusiasm, and dampened ardor for the Confederate cause. When Sherman moved upon Atlanta, Brown called for a levee of all men aged 16-55. He gave command of the resultant force to General John B. Hood but only until such time as he might choose to assume command himself. When the scourge had passed through and beyond Atlanta, he furloughed the Georgia troops until the state—not the Confederacy— might need them once again. Brown's actions, even though the most extreme of all the Confederate governors, were characteristic.[32]

Although obstructionist in many cases, the states were still the active agents in procuring men for the armies. With the exception of the United States Colored Troops, the Invalid Corps, and the United States Sharpshooters, the regiments and brigades on the Union side proudly bore state designations throughout the war. A Wisconsin soldier wrote that he "felt about him the care, not of a socialized impersonal state, but of a big, generous hearted community of neighbors."[33] The states classified most of their recruits as volunteers, disregarding the pressure of the draft to force men to volunteer. During the first year of the war, the Union Congress authorized 500,000 volunteers, but the War Department accepted 700,680.[34] Most of these were for short terms, and at year's end an acute shortage of manpower developed. During the balance of the war, however, through training and experience, the corps of men who began as volunteers and stuck it out had by 1865 become as fine troops as there were anywhere in the world.

Frederick Porter Todd, one of the most perceptive early students of the militia institution wrote of procurement of men during the Civil War, "The common militia was an impractical political concept, the Volunteer an inescapable reality."[35]

Of the thousands of scenes of the war volunteer and his officers at their best, none excels the performance of the 20th Maine Volunteer Regiment at Gettysburg. Colonel Joshua Lawrence Chamberlain, a Bowdoin graduate who in civilian life taught rhetoric and literature to young ladies, was in command. On July 2, 1863, the second day of the Battle, the 20th Maine found itself dangling on the left flank of the Union line, with no support whatever beyond its own left. It was positioned on the shoulders of Little Round Top and under orders to hold there at all cost, lest the entire Union position be rolled up. Well placed among the rocks of the steep hill, the Maine men fought off heroic charges of two fine Confederate regiments, the 15th and 47th Alabama. Under Chamberlain's steady direction, the regiment refused its own left flank and pivoted on its connection with the 83rd Pennsylvania until it no longer formed a straight line but a right angle, capable of firing in two directions. At the start each man had sixty rounds of ammunition, but soon these were blown away. Chamberlain, reasoning that he must not withdraw, that he could rely on his men to carry out orders, however desperate, and that unable to fight with bullets he must now rely on bayonets, ordered the 200 survivors to fix bayonets and charge down the hill into far larger forces than their own. This they did, and the Alabamians, who by sensible standards could assume that they had taken Little Round Top, could not cope with this unorthodox reversal, and collapsed. Afterward, with no more than 150 of his men able to fight, Chamberlain occupied Big Round Top. That is where they were when the third day of the battle dawned. The 20th Maine had saved the dangling Union flank. It took thirty years to evaluate this feat, but at length on August 11, 1893, Chamberlain received the Congressional Medal of Honor.[36]

One of the great virtues of the war volunteers was that, skilled soldiers that they had become, they merged back into the population when the war ended. They had a powerful effect upon the population; they never forgot their war experience and never let the country forget it. Major General John A. Logan, described them as they saw themselves and pretty much as the American public have since viewed them:

> Away off in the wilds of America a soldier had been found totally different from any that had ever walked a battlefield. Upon one day he was a citizen, quietly following the plow; upon the next he became a soldier, knowing no fear and carrying a whole destroying battery in his trusted rifle. He was a soldier from conviction to principle, from loyalty to his country, from duty to his family. He moved with the discipline of an educated soldier but he fought with the desperation of a lion at bay.[37]

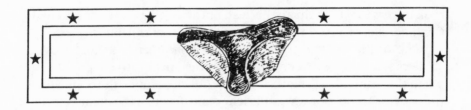

EIGHT

Reconstruction;
Birth of the National Guard

Following the Civil War, the militia was dead in spite of statutes to the contrary. Indeed, during most of the Reconstruction era the volunteer militia was dormant, except in the ex-Confederate states. There, the provisional governors had permission to constitute militia units even though Carl Schurz and General Grant advised against them. What Grant and Schurz feared happened. The militia was virtually the old Confederate Army down to the worn gray uniforms left over from the Civil War. A Confederate militia was intolerable to the Radical Republicans; so when they gained control of Congress they attached a rider to the Army Appropriations Act of March 2, 1867, that finally prohibited the formation of military units in the once Confederate states. President Johnson, rather than see the soldiers go without pay, signed the bill but attached to it a sharp dissent that it was unconstitutional to deny a state the right to have militia.[1]

It soon became obvious that the state governments, forming under the radical regime, had to have more support than the scattered units of the regular army could provide. Accordingly, two years and one day after prohibiting militia in the rebel states, Congress on March 2, 1869, reallowed it. As far back as March 1862, Congress had stricken "white" from the basic militia statute, so the Radical Republicans intended to make the southern militia predominantly black. The law expressly denied the militia privilege to Virginia, Texas, Mississippi, and Georgia because if militias formed in those four states they would in no time return political control to the ex-Confederates. Not until July 15, 1870, were those states authorized to constitute militias.

The southern militia units, usually referred to as Negro militia, were not all black.[2] There were some white units, but the two colors did not mingle. Since the new units were above all expected to protect the Radical administrations, there was a flurry of activity to obtain weapons for them. The protected governments canvassed the north for guns to buy and importuned the federal government for help. Congress passed a law on March 3, 1873, to arm the militia, but the War Department did very little to procure the weapons.

Because armed blacks were intolerable to the southern whites, they obstructed the black militia as much as they could. They could not, however, prevent the units from being on hand to see that safe candidates got elected. At the polls and elsewhere, black militiamen were often obnoxious. For this and other reasons, racial hatred reached a peak in 1874 and 1875, and violence became characteristic of public affairs. Certain clashes were even referred to as wars, as, for example, the Brooks-Baxter War in Arkansas which started in 1874 for racial reasons and became a fight for political power. The bloodiest encounter took place in New Orleans on September 14, 1874. Here, ironically, the conflict was between government forces of about 500 under the command of no less a person than General James Longstreet and opponents drawn together by a white league. Casualties came to 27 killed and 105 wounded. Longstreet found himself in this alignment because he was adjutant general of Louisiana, with a salary of $3,000 per year, the appointee of a Radical governor. On this account and because he commanded black troops, he was ostracized by the "best" society.[3]

To the white people of the South and to the Dunning school of historians of Reconstruction, the Negro militia was made up only of swaggering bullies. The whites opted, therefore, to use unbridled violence if necessary to eliminate it. Two hundred and ninety white rifle companies sprang up at one time in South Carolina alone. From one place or another, they found weapons. Although they lacked official sanction, these companies had behind them the determination of the society to establish white supremacy at all cost. Actual clashes between black and white units were rare, but bloodshed was not. White riflemen ambushed and killed black officers and white supporters of the Negro militia. These assassinations often took place in broad daylight with witnesses, but prosecutions were nonexistent. This way, in the end, the leadership that supported the black militia was either killed or intimidated. When the Democrats returned to power in state after state of the ex-Confederacy, they terminated the black militia, disarmed the blacks, and excluded them from any role in the militia.[4]

The black militia might have survived if the Radical governors had trusted it enough to use it fully and if the national Republican administrations had stood behind it. As it was, all the costs fell on the unwilling southern states. The demise of the Negro militia was just one aspect of returning the problem of race relations in the mid-1870s back to the white people of the South.[5]

In all the states of the Union, not just the ex-Confederate states, shortage of funds required cutbacks in militia programs, and the first units to be reduced or deleted were black ones. Some Negro units, however, hung on tenaciously, as in Chicago and elsewhere in Illinois, and in New York. In the District of Columbia, blacks made up 33.6 percent of the population but 42 percent of the organized militia. In 1887, the District raised $50,000 to finance a showy drill competition among volunteer outfits from all over the country, but companies from Memphis and Vicksburg dropped out of the grand parade rather than march behind the District's black companies.[6]

Ohio omitted the term "white" from the militia statute in 1878, and black units flourished. Among them, however, racism existed. The officers were all mulattoes, determined to maintain a wide distance between themselves and the enlisted men, who were blacker. Nevertheless, the Ohio black militiamen presented a united front to the white people. They were proud of their organizations and sensitive to any slights to it. The black community stood behind them and went so far as to threaten to quit the Republican Party if their units were left out of ceremonies. This gained them a presence at such events as the funeral of President McKinley, and brought Theodore Roosevelt himself to review them.[7]

More and more, the term National Guard was being used. By 1896, only three states were not using it for their organized militia.[8] The nucleus of the Guard was formed by the old volunteer companies, some of which had been in existence, side by side with the statutory militia, for generations. In spite of the word National, the Guard units were primarily instrumentalities of the states. Governors summoned their troops 481 times from the Civil War to 1906. Fifty-nine of these calls were to intervene in lynchings, while thirty more of them resulted from racial tensions between blacks and whites. Twice, the governor of California called detachments to suppress anti-Chinese riots. There were seventy-five calls to put down disorders of various kinds, and twenty-three to enforce state laws. Political disputes brought out Guard detachments thirty-one times; the transportation or safeguarding of prisoners produced forty-one calls. Disputes over the location of a county seat occasioned three militia calls, religious disputes three, and three were to prevent prize fights from taking place. Governors made twenty-six calls for detachments to give aid in fires and floods, and two to enforce quarantines.[9]

In all the states the drift was in the direction of volunteering, but the drift was interrupted. The new constitution of Florida, 1868, reaffirmed the principle of universal military obligation for all men aged 18-45 but not UMT; not all men of that age had to train. Stress was on volunteer units, and by 1870 ninety-six of these were active. Four years later the state listed 25,000 organized militiamen, of whom half were still black. The social activities of many small towns centered on their organized militia units.[10]

Florida laid the foundation for its modern Guard organization with a new militia law in 1887. It excluded the Negroes. The legislature provided $5,000 annually to send active units to summer camp and required the county commissioners to provide a suitable armory for drill during the rest of each year. By 1891, the federal government was providing $4.00 per enrolled Florida soldier, and the state, $2.00. Private capital stood behind the Florida Guard as a security for property. For example, the railroads furnished free passes to get the men to summer camp.[11]

Massachusetts during the Civil War had returned to the concept of universal military obligation for all young men. But in May 1865, it reverted to the volunteer system, limiting the organized militia to 100 companies of infantry, six troops of cavalry, five batteries of artillery, and one company of engineers. These units were required to drill during the year and to go to summer camp for four days; in both exercises their men earned $2.50 a day. In addition, the state made substantial appropriations for uniforms and equipment.[12]

In Missouri in 1871, only seven volunteer units remained active. In 1887, the legislature disbanded the entire Missouri National Guard except the Third Regiment in Kansas City and a few scattered companies. Why this apparent dismantling of the institution? One cause was the hatred developed during the Civil War; another was the opposition of the farmers who fought the railroads which subsidized the Missouri Guard. Not until 1891 did the legislature appropriate $25,000 to support the system. Since this was not enough, various units attempted to raise funds through entertainment or outright solicitation of businessmen. Encampments close to cities were not necessarily best for training, but there, through lively drills, lilting music, and sham battles, they could raise money.[13]

As governor of Ohio, William McKinley did much for the Guard. He had the appointment of the adjutant general, the quartermaster general, and the state staff, which he used to select qualified men. The citizen soldiers elected the other officers. In the 1890s, state support ran between $30,000 and $120,000 per year. In return, the state made more than average use of its Guard; in the decade 1886-1896, the governor called out six detachments to prevent lynchings, during one of which Guardsmen killed five persons and wounded twelve. Someone charged the commanding colonel with manslaughter, but the legislature voted $17,500 for his defense, and after a trial which ran for four months he was acquitted.[14]

With increasing frequency Guard units became involved in industrial strife because that strife was verging on small-scale internecine warfare. The key year was 1877 when a railroad strike in West Virginia rapidly spread through most of the industrial states. It became most violent around Pittsburgh, Pennsylvania, and severely strained the National Guard of the state. Major General Alfred Pearson said, "Meeting an enemy on the field of battle, you go there to kill. . . . But here you had men with fathers and brothers and relatives mingled in the crowd of rioters. The sympathy of the people, the sympathy of the troops, my own sympathy was with the strikers. We all felt that these men were not receiving enough wages."[15] Pearson's sensitivity disqualified him from strike duty at Pittsburgh, so the governor ordered 600 men to come from Philadelphia, commanded by Major General Robert M. Brinton. Most of Brinton's officers—indeed most Guard officers—came from people of means and considered the protection of private property to be a high order of civic duty. Brinton's 600, even under a barrage of bricks, held their cohesion and remained responsive to commands. When they were at last surrounded by a menacing mob, they formed square and wheeled Gatling guns into firing position. The general gave the order to fire, whereupon the Gatlings mowed down an unknown number of demonstrators and spectators. Fifteen Guardsmen suffered injury but none was killed.[16]

In the course of the strike, the entire Pennsylvania National Guard entered state service—870 officers and 9,000 enlisted men. Serving with them to break the strike were regulars, a few marines, police, greatly augmented in numbers for this duty, and private armies formed and paid by the coal operators. The latter, later known as the Coal and Iron Police, gradually displaced the Pennsylvania Guard as the force arm in industrial warfare.[17]

At the height of the 1877 strife, eleven states called 45,000 Guardsmen into state service. The War Department committed 2,100 regulars. Usually strikers stood more resolutely before Guard detachments than before regulars, even though it was more dangerous to do so because the Guard at that time had no training in crowd control, and its weapon was the deadly rifle. Guard officers had few qualms about ordering rifle fire when it seemed to them that their detachments were in danger. In general, the Guardsmen on duty in 1877 carried out their orders even when their sympathies lay with the strikers. Lives lost that year—not all of them due to the Guard—totaled one hundred, with scores crippled. The railroads estimated their property losses at $26,500,000.[18]

The railroad strike of 1877, and the industrial warfare it induced, was the stimulant that set off the development of the modern National Guard. At that time, business moved into a tacit alliance with the Guard as an important agency in protecting private property and thereafter provided it with financial aid, beyond what the state and national governments gave.[19] The main support of the Pennsylvania Guard between 1879 and 1900 came from private funds. Private funds built armories and purchased weapons, and the Pennsylvania Railroad shipped the entire Pennsylvania division free of charge to the inauguration of James A. Garfield as president. Funds came from the state, too; Pennsylvania financed a summer camp for the first time in 1880 at which officers of the regular army helped with the training, a thing they had never done before. Attendance was large enough to make possible even some exercises by entire brigades.[20]

Ironically, West Virginia, where the fateful railroad strike began in 1877, seemed indifferent to the stirring of the Guard. It had at the time only four companies of volunteers and an adjutant general whose primary function was to be state librarian. Since the businessmen of the state showed little interest, the few volunteers had to provide their own uniforms and even help pay for rented armory space. In 1887, Congress made $5,000 available to the organized militia of West Virginia. This moved the state legislature to pass a comprehensive militia statute in 1889, which created two infantry regiments of ten companies each. Blacks could serve as long as they were in all-Negro companies. In 1894, the organized militia of the state assumed the name of National Guard. One of its first duties was to stop the train bearing Jacob Coxey's so-called army from crossing West Virginia. By 1897, the two infantry regiments became a brigade, supported by one battery of artillery.[21]

Wisconsin entered the Civil War with an organized militia of fifty-two companies, containing 1,993 men and 33 generals. But when the war was over it took the state until 1870 to reform its first regiment. The pace quickened when the legislature in 1873 provided $100 to each active unit to help with armory rent. This amount tripled in 1875, but was available only to twenty-four units. The Organized Militia of Wisconsin became the National Guard in 1879. During the 1880s, $5.00 per man was available to the members of companies that held their strength between fifty-five and seventy-five. Throughout the

1890s, regular officers inspected the units and helped instruct them at summer camps. Influential citizens of the state no longer viewed their Guard as primarily a counterforce to the accumulating power of the federal government, but they did see it as a reason why the nation could get along with a small standing army. To them, the National Guard kept alive the skills necessary to use in mass war and remained the bulwark of national defense.[22]

The Wisconsin experience at equipping and training its citizen soldiery was probably typical. The state was slow to spend money on training, therefore the regiments had to pay for the fuel, straw, floor boards, bedding, and cooking gear used at camp. As in Missouri, commanders more often than not picked summer camp sites close to cities and towns. The cities welcomed this because it helped business, and the Guard profited because the camps drew public attention and financial assistance. Often the officers' tents were furnished like the sitting room of a house; entire families vacationed by camping next to the Guard's training grounds. Criticism of training exercises could become public affairs. In one such case a Civil War veteran shouted, "I have fought in sixteen pitched battles. I ain't any damned play soldier. Me and half a dozen of the old boys could clean out this whole outfit."[23]

Reviews, parades, and sham battles kept the local folk closely involved. One sham battle was staged outside Milwaukee to raise money to build an armory. When the attack began, the spectators moved in so close that the planned retreat could not take place. Now and then a team of horses would run away with wagon or carriage and open an unplanned gap in the military lines. Regulars took part to gain some visibility, while Indians were useful in attracting funds. In one case, however, the redmen enjoyed the sham battle so much that they refused to give up and continued the fight after they were supposed to have been wiped out.

In the Territory of Washington, a permanent militia organization came into being in 1884 and 1885 because of strong anti-Chinese sentiment. One element of the white population wanted to drive all Chinese out of the Territory, but the people of property valued the cheap labor; consequently, they supported the militia, since the Territory did not, and even organized private companies to protect the Chinese. Tension reached crisis proportions in Seattle in 1886. Bands of white men entered the Chinese quarter and ordered the people to remove at once to a steamer in the harbor. About half of the Chinese population got aboard the vessel before militia units, sent by the governor, arrived to prevent forcible removal. These units next escorted the enforced emigrants from the ship back to their habitations, and in doing so killed two white persons and wounded three. The governor found it necessary to declare martial law and to request federal aid, which came in the form of 350 regulars.[24]

In 1886, the Territorial legislature first referred to the organized militia as the National Guard and levied a tax to support it. Little changed when the Territory became the State of Washington on November 11, 1889. Miners struck in 1891, whereupon mine owners imported 600 blacks to dig and hired mercenaries to protect their premises. In response, the Knights of Labor began to organize and drill military companies. Dark as the prospect seemed, the trouble subsided without bloodshed when the Guard was called out. Behaving in a friendly way, the Guardsmen served as a buffer among the armed strikers, the company's hired gunmen, and the blacks.

In the light of this performance, it is surprising that in subsequent years the State of Washington cut back its Guard until in 1896 there were only sixteen companies, containing 1,306 men. The state cut its financial support from $40,000 per year to $6,000. The most plausible explanation for the reduction is that the Washington National Guard during the 1890s became a permanent, professional police force which had no need to be very large. The adjutant general recognized the new role.

> In these times of contention between capital and labor, and strife between races . . . where the turbulent elements are so easily excited to deeds of violence by unscrupulous demagogues; the better classes of society . . . naturally turn to a stronger force than can be put forward by individual effort, and this force is the military arm of the state, which by its unity of action and through discipline becomes the peacemaker upholding the law and destroying anarchy.[25]

The Utah militia experience was not typical because of the Nauvoo Legion which had been created by the Mormons to defend themselves before their migration westward. For thirty-eight years (1849-1887), Lieutenant General Daniel Wells commanded it. When it was 6,000 strong, a gentile governor drove it out of the militia and forbade any further meetings. The legion defied this order, whereupon the governor brought criminal charges against the officers. He could never bring them to trial since grand juries would not indict them. What the governor tried unsuccessfully to do, the legislature achieved. In 1887, it dissolved the legion but made no provision for any militia whatever. Unofficial marching clubs sprang up, and from them came the officers who organized the new militia when the legislature provided for it in 1894. As in Missouri and West Virginia, one of the earliest missions of the Utah militia was to free the area of Coxey's Army as fast as possible.[26]

During the post-Civil War decades, swarms of immigrants entered
the United States from southeastern Europe. Native white Americans
regarded the newcomers, whom they called wops, hunkies, Polacks,
and other derogatory names, as lower on the human scale even than
Negroes and Indians. Most of these immigrants crowded into
industrial cities where they seemed to the propertied classes to be
forming into a Marxian proletariet. Church, press, colleges, and other
elements of the respectable society spoke harshly of them. One of the
spokesmen of respectability, Henry Ward Beecher, the most popular
preacher of his day, told his affluent congregation that the man was not
fit to live who could not survive on bread and water. Beer and tobacco
and other vices, he said, kept the families of laborers in poverty. Many
native Americans would have added that innate inferiority had a great
deal to do with it. More than one church journal accepted Napoleon's
maxim that the best way to deal with mobs was to blow them away
with cannon. The concept of a living wage hardly existed anywhere in
American thought, so the comfortable elements of the society, when
they happened to notice the misery of some of the recent immigrants,
accepted it as the inevitable result of the working of the immutable
laws of life, such as natural selection and supply and demand.[27]

The rulers of the American establishment were adamantly set
against organized labor. Their antilabor feeling merged with their
dislike of the new immigrants into a conviction that the tools of organized labor, that is, strikes, were un-American. During the 1880s and
1890s, strikes increased in number and in violence. This convinced the
proprietary class that the strike leaders were "vile demagogues who
[preach] to the people that property is plutocracy." The National
Guard was an instrument in combating what it agreed was un-
American. One Guard leader stated that physical force was the only
way to keep down the "savage elements of the society," and the editor
of the *National Guard* wrote that the laws the Guard upheld with its
weapons were "enacted by the people before this fair country was
overrun by the outcasts of Europe . . . villains from all parts of the Old
World."[28]

In 1886, a strike began in Milwaukee to obtain an eight-hour
workday. In the past, the mere arrival of a Guard unit had been enough
to restore order in Wisconsin, but not this time. Governor Jeremiah
Rusk shared the belief that the strikers were foreigners infected with
anarchistic propaganda, and he ordered the Guardsmen to open fire if
industrial property was invaded. The result was seven strikers dead and
scores wounded. The citizen soldiers dispersed the remnant of the
crowd with their bayonets. On three subsequent occasions, in 1889,

1894, and 1898, when Guard detachments appeared in labor disputes, strikers offered no resistance. The Wisconsin legislature, dominated by men of property, cherished the National Guard more than ever before.[29]

The eight-hour day agitation of 1886 culminated in the Haymarket Riots in Chicago. The Guard had scant part in this; the law-and-order agency in it was the Chicago police, supplemented by scores of deputies. The next strike on a grand scale in which the Guard was involved took place in 1892 at the Homestead works of the Carnegie Steel Corporation in Pennsylvania. Almost as soon as the strike began, the governor called out the entire Guard, 8,000 men. Though the numbers involved were smaller than in 1877, military efficiency was much higher. Full mobilization took only thirty-two hours, but it continued in effect for seventeen days. In fact, selected units remained on duty for three months. With almost no bloodshed and a cost of $1,000,000 to the state, the troops broke the strike. Laborers hated the Guard for the role it had played.[30]

The year 1894 involved the National Guard deeper than before in the conflict between capital and labor. Workers struck the Pullman Sleeping Car Company in Pullman, Illinois. In order to force the company into negotiations, they drew the railroad unions into a boycott of Pullman cars. Disorder and property damage spread, causing the management of the company, the city government, and other agencies to appeal for help directly to President Grover Cleveland. They did not even ask Governor John Peter Altgeld to use the National Guard because they did not trust him to protect their interests. Altgeld was notorious among conservative elements for having pardoned three persons accused of throwing a bomb during the Haymarket Affair. From Altgeld's point of view, the three had been convicted on insufficient evidence, convicted really because they were anarchists.[31]

Altgeld protested the use of regular troops, since he, the governor had not asked for them, but companies of the 15th U. S. Infantry reached Chicago on July 3, 1894. Two days later, the mayor of Chicago finally requested help from the governor. Altgeld speedily summoned the five Chicago regiments into active state service and called other units from as far away as 150 miles. Within thirty-four hours he placed 4,000 Guardsmen in Chicago. Soon after, the 2nd Illinois Regiment fired into a crowd—in self-defense, its commanders insisted—killing twenty or thirty people and wounding many more. Violence then subsided, General Nelson Miles, commanding the regulars in Chicago, took credit for the pacification, but Altgeld said that Miles's troops had done nothing but intensify bitterness while the general issued reports that he had the situation under control.[32] Neither agency felt it necessary to deny its part in killing insurrectionists; rather, they attempted to take credit for it.

In the end, 14,186 armed men were employed to suppress the Pullman strike. Of these, 1,936 were regulars and 4,000 Guardsmen; the rest were sheriffs, policemen, and around 5,000 special marshals. The latter were hired, paid, as well as directed by the General Managers Association, but they functioned as federal officers without federal supervision.

The boycott of Pullman cars had spread across the country and, until it was broken by an injunction—the first use of this instrument against labor—it paralyzed the railroad system. State troops entered into active duty in California, Iowa, and Michigan. The California Guardsmen stayed on duty for a month, but having no training in crowd control, they accomplished little. As elsewhere, their weapons were too lethal for the mission.[33]

President Cleveland appointed a special commission to investigate the strike. The commissioners found that the state forces were largely recruited from laboring people and that their sympathy lay with the strikers. This may have offset to some degree the excessive deadliness of the rifles they carried. Not especially concerned with the suitability or unsuitability of the weapons, the commissioners recommended for future strike wars—their term—that it might be necessary to draw volunteers from other social strata. The evidence shows that the Guardsmen, whatever their origins and wherever their sympathies lay, obeyed their orders.[34]

Of the 481 calls of detachments from the National Guard to keep the peace between the Civil War and 1906, 156, or almost one-third, stemmed from labor trouble. Although industrial strife had much to do with stimulating the Guard, leaders of the Guard did not accept internal police work as the only or the true mission of the National Guard. They considered their system to be an integral part of the United States military establishment, but at the same time they considered the state connection of the Guard to be indispensable to the ultimate security not only of the states but also of the nation. Accordingly, some of them formed the National Guard Association (NGA) in 1879. The key figures in this momentous action were Dabney Maury, West Point graduate and sometime Confederate general officer, Brigadier General John W. Denver of Ohio, and Brigadier General George W. Wingate of New York. Wingate occupied the presidency until 1890; the other first officers were General P. G. T. Beauregard, vice president; William L. Alexander of Iowa, secretary; and A. H. Berry of Massachusetts, treasurer. When Wingate stepped down, there was a slump in activity, followed by ups and downs, but at all times the association remained influential.[35]

The NGA never stopped insisting that the National Guard was a natural component of the nation's military force; nor did it cease fighting the development of a monolithic military establishment under the control of regular officers. The first major legislation it pushed successfully was an act of 1887 that raised the annual federal appropriation to arm the Guard to $400,000 and authorized grants-in-aid to states that had at least one hundred active Guardsmen for every senator and congressman. The association also successfully resisted the creation of a veterans' reserve which would have had no connection at all with the states.[36]

Among the officers in the Middle West there grew a feeling that the NGA was too much dominated by easterners. They formed a new organization in 1897 known as the Interstate National Guard Association (INGA). The two groups ran parallel for some time, but the INGA became more aggressive than the NGA and bit by bit absorbed the older organization. The last year of separate meetings was 1899, but the name that persisted was the National Guard Association.[37]

The role of the citizen soldiery in Indian warfare was diminishing, but it did not disappear. In Minnesota in August 1862, 644 white people lost their lives in a Sioux uprising before Minnesota Volunteers, directed by a regular officer, terminated the conflict. On November 29, 1864, the 2nd Colorado Volunteer Infantry perpetrated what has become known as the Sand Creek Massacre. In slaughtering 300 Indians, of whom only seventy-five were warriors, the Colorado Volunteers showed the citizen soldier at his most bloodthirsty. In New Mexico, Colonel Kit Carson, commanding mostly irregulars, carried out a strategy of annihilation against the Apaches. More creditable and beyond doubt heroic was the stand of fifty-one irregulars, who happened to be seasoned scouts, at Beecher's Island in the Arkansas River on September 17, 1868, in which they held off several hundred mounted warriors, with a loss to themselves of twenty-three killed and wounded. In the main, the regular army was taking over Indian fighting.[38]

Eight years before the founding of the NGA, a group of New York Guard officers organized the National Rifle Association (1871). One of the founders was George W. Wingate, first president of the NGA. Besides improving marksmanship, the need of which had appeared during the Civil War, Wingate set out to draw the National Guard and the regular army closer together. He achieved this by establishing a series of rifle competitions in which the Guard and the army competed vigorously against each other.[39]

In shoulder weapons provided, though, the Guard never kept up with the regular service. When the latter was using the Springfield Model 1873, breech-loading, single-shot, 45 caliber rifle, the Guard still had a medley of Civil War pieces. In 1892, the army adopted the Krag-Jorgensen, 30 caliber, five-shot repeater. Still, the Guard did not graduate to the Springfield '73 even though the chief of ordnance often spoke of the high quality of the weapon and of the large stock of them still on hand. The main drawback of this rifle was that it used black powder which revealed the position of the marksman to his opponents. Ordnance, weighing the pros and cons, finally in 1897 began to issue the '73 to Guardsmen, and by 1898 it had distributed 33,898 of them.[40]

What had some of the articulate regular officers to say about the role of the National Guard? General McClellan forsaw the possibility of wars ahead, perhaps with England over trade, with Spain over Cuba, or with Mexico about the border. In any of these contingencies, the primary mission of the Guard would be to protect the coasts of the United States; therefore, government should see that the Guards of coastal states received intensive training in forts with big guns. As for internal enemies, McClellan believed that pacification of the Indians should be assigned to the regulars, but that states close to troublesome Indians must be prepared to assist. In contrast, his recommendation was that state troops ought to fight the battles of industrial war. And, in apparent indifference to the consequences, he recommended that Guardsmen have abundant chance to train for crowd control with Gatlings and other types of machine guns.[41]

General James B. Fry, Provost Marshal General during the Civil War, unlike McClellan, conceded no significant mission to the National Guard. For national missions, the instrument was the army; nor did this instrument, whatever the public prejudice, threaten civil control of the government. There was no danger from the army, Fry insisted, unless the people had first become corrupted. Fry denied that opposition to the regular service really rested on fear; it rested instead on stinginess, on the determination to secure protection cheaply, too cheaply from his point of view.[42]

Emory Upton, brilliant young general of the Civil War, would have factored the states out of national defense if he could. What the United States needed was a Calhoun-type service (see p. 000), just big enough in peacetime to train the legions of volunteers who would have to serve in wartime. Those volunteers should have had some pretraining through UMT, directed by the professionals altogether. He was impressed by the Prussian military which included UMT and a reserve into which the trainees could graduate; yet he never presented any plan for a pool to contain and exercise the men who went through his proposed American UMT. He agreed with Fry that fear of the standing army was silly in the United States, but he disagreed with General McClellan about the proper component to wage strike wars. His choice was the regular army.[43]

Among influential writers on American military affairs, Emory Upton, the army's most conspicuous intellectual, stands out as the principal opponent of reliance upon militia and upon the use of state-controlled troops, and of states rights. State power to arm and equip troops, as in the Civil War, weakened the military strength of the Union and increased the costs of the war. War resources, he said, must be controlled by the general government to whom the people owe their paramount allegiance. If there were to be volunteers involved at all, they must be maintained, trained, and controlled not by individual states but by the central government. Actually, regulars were the only safe reliance in a prolonged war. How did Upton arrive at a point of view so opposite from the popular American way? To begin with, he was graduated from West Point in May 1861, then plunged two months later into major warfare. From second lieutenant he climbed the ladder of rank until by war's end he was brevet major general at age 25. During the conflict, he had devised tactics for his troops that enabled them to survive the withering fire that mowed down standard formations. In 1875, General Sherman sent him off for eighteen months to study the armies of Asia, and his report became a book, which he paid for himself, that emphasized the need for centralized control of military matters, China's weakness being ascribed to the lack of it. Upton began to write in favor of professional military and against citizen soldiery during the army's so-called Dark Ages, 1865-1880, when Americans were not interested in his message but were concentrating on economic enrichment. Upton took his own life at the age of forty-two in 1881; his message did not become widely known until Secretary of War Elihu Root published in 1904 Upton's unfinished *The Military Policy of the United States*.[44]

Some writers, less well known than McClellan, Fry, and Upton, claimed a central role for the Guard in national defense. One cited the speed with which the Pennsylvania Guard had been mobilized for the Homestead strike in 1892; it could come equally fast to defend the nation. Others pointed out that the geographical limitation that had disqualified the statutory militia as an instrument of national security did not handicap the Guard. A declaration of war was a law, and even if the Guard was considered only militia, it could be used anywhere to

TABLE 8.1.
Statement of Appropriations for the Militia by the States and by the United States

STATES	NUMBER OF ORGANIZED MILITIA	ANNUAL APPROPRIATION BY STATES	ANNUAL APPORTIONMENT U. S. APPROPRIATION	AMOUNT APPROPRIATED BY STATE FOR EACH MAN	AMOUNT PER MAN UNDER U. S. ALLOTMENT	AMOUNT STATE WOULD RECEIVE BASED ON NO. OF TROOPS
Alabama	2,954	$29,300	$9,214.30	9.96	3.12	$11,047.96
Arkansas	•	†	6,450.01			
California	4,340	156,573	7,371.44	36.07	1.69	16,331.60
Colorado	780	40,000	2,764.29	5.10	3.54	3,917.20
Connecticut	2,627	117,000	5,528.58	4.44	2.10	9,825.08
Delaware	564	3,900	2,764.29	6.91	4.90	2,109.36
Florida	996	7,500	3,685.72	7.51	3.71	3,725.04
Georgia	4,041	25,000	11,057.16	6.18	2.73	15,113.34
Idaho	308	†	2,764.29		8.97	851.92
Illinois	3,722	132,500	20,271.46	35.60	5.45	13,920.28
Indiana	2,166	37,000	13,821.45	17.08	6.38	8,100.84
Iowa	2,521	35,000	11,978.59	13.88	4.07	9,428.54
Kansas	1,859	22,350	8,292.87	12.00	4.46	6,952.66
Kentucky	1,316	10,000	11,978.59	7.59	9.10	4,911.84
Louisiana	1,665	12,600	7,371.44	7.50	4.43	6,227.10
Maine	1,094	20,000	5,528.58	18.30	5.05	4,064.56
Maryland	2,036	40,000	7,371.44	19.60	3.17	7,614.64
Massachusetts	5,289	244,630	12,900.02	46.25	2.44	19,780.86
Michigan	2,491	73,286	11,978.59	29.42	4.81	9,176.34
Minnesota	1,907	40,000	6,450.01	20.92	3.37	7,132.18
Mississippi	1,525	†	8,292.87		5.43	5,703.50

State					
Missouri	2,161	†	14,742.88		6.82	7,982.14
Montana	677	6,500	2,764.99	9.60	4.07	2,531.98
Nebraska	1,344	12,500	4,607.15	9.30	3.43	5,026.56
Nevada	565	8,200	2,764.28	14.51	4.89	2,113.10
New Hampshire	1,110	30,000	3,685.72	27.03	3.32	4,151.40
New Jersey	4,301	148,516	8,292.87	34.53	1.92	16,085.74
New York	13,710	400,000	33,171.48	29.18	2.41	51,275.40
North Carolina	1,478	13,000	10,135.73	8.81	6.85	5,527.72
North Dakota	513	11,000	2,764.29	21.44	5.38	1,918.62
Ohio	5,110	87,400	21,192.89	17.10	4.14	19,111.40
Oregon	1,701	20,000	2,764.29	11.96	1.62	6,361.74
Pennsylvania	8,444	300,000	27,642.90	35.53	3.27	31,580.56
Rhode Island	1,332	24,000	3,685.72	18.01	2.78	4,981.68
South Carolina	5,213	10,000	8,292.87	1.92	1.58	19,496.62
South Dakota	493	4,000	3,685.72	8.11	7.47	1,843.82
Tennessee	•	2,900	11,057.16			
Texas	2,691	15,000	11,978.59	5.57	4.45	10,064.34
Vermont	784	30,000	3,685.72	38.25	4.70	2,933.16
Virginia	2,808	10,000	11,057.16	3.56	3.94	10,501.92
Washington	1,145	80,000	2,764.29	69.85	2.41	4,282.30
West Virginia	848	10,000	5,528.58	11.78	6.52	3,171.52
Wisconsin	2,659	69,431	10,135.73	26.22	3.81	9,944.66
Wyoming	243	†	2,764.29		11.40	908.82
Total	103,531	$2,339,086	$387,000.60			

• No return received.
† Not reported.

Source: *The National Guard* II, no. 17 (Dec. 19, 1891), p. 559; compiled September 19, 1891, from information furnished by the Adjutants General of the several states.

enforce the laws. Moreover, a legitimate constitutional use of militia was to repel invasion, which could include pursuing an invader beyond the national borders.[45]

The NGA insisted that the Guard was an integral component of the national military force. To exclude it from that role was to weaken the federal system and endanger national security. Support for the NGA position could always be found in Congress. There were devoted states' rights legislators who would not agree to anything that might tend to obliterate state lines and state authority.[46]

Whatever the reasons for it, the condition of the National Guard slowly improved. As Table 8.1 shows, the rolls contained 103,531 men in 1891. That year, the states spent $2,339,086 on their Guards. The federal government contributed $387,000, but the federal sum rose steadily until at the turn of the century it amounted to $1,000,000. Only eight states lacked a summer camp; those with camps used regular officers to aid in the training.[47]

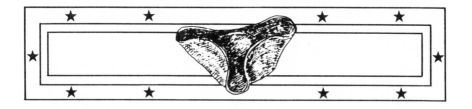

NINE

The War with Spain

Congress, in the fifteen years from 1885 to 1900, appropriated $60,000,000 for coastal forts, slightly more than 1 percent of the total expense of the federal government during the same period. Estimates set 100,000 as the number of men needed to garrison the coastal defenses, and regular army commanders expected them to come from the National Guard. Since the total enrollment of the Guard at that time averaged 114,000, thousands of them in landlocked states, the Guard alone could not supply the garrisons. Revolt in Cuba, begining in 1895, made coastal defense especially pressing. Cubans sought to throw off Spanish rule, while Spain, determined to retain one of its last New World possessions, resorted to very harsh methods to suppress the rebellion. Sympathy for the rebels ran very high in the United States.[1]

What of the National Guard if war sprang from this sympathy? Of the 114,000 Guardsmen, 100,000 were infantry, 4,800 cavalry, and 5,900 artillery; the balance consisted of small units of support troops. Five states were able to maintain divisions, three brigades per division, three regiments per brigade. Twenty-five other states supported brigades, but the rest had no organization higher than regiment. All levels were short of quartermaster, commissary, and other auxiliary troops.[2] If the state forces were coordinated at all by the federal government, the Military Information Division of the adjutant general's office did it. That division, established in 1889, had almost accidentally begun to correspond with state officials and with regulars assigned to duty with the Guard. The regular officers so assigned totaled forty in 1898. The division also prepared such mobilization plans as existed, for all components, but it was handicapped relative to the Guard because of uncertainty about Guard service outside national boundaries.[3]

Thus the division assigned certain defensive roles to the Guard if war came: to serve as short-term local defense forces in case of invasion; to provide a cadre of experienced officers to train volunteers; and to guard the coasts to prevent invasion. These roles satisfied Guard leaders on the eastern seaboard and along the Canadian border, but not, remarkably enough, the officers from the interior who had no intention of being confined to a purely defensive role.[4]

One of their own number, Representative John A. T. Hull from Iowa, introduced a bill on March 13, 1898 that proposed to enlarge the wartime army to 104,000 men without including the Guard in any way as a source of this manpower. Hull's bill provided for constituting regiments of national volunteers with just enough state connection to have local appeal and to provide a recruiting base, but not enough to permit significant control by state governments. The McKinley administration supported the Hull bill, but the inland Guard officers, aligned with southern Democrats and western populists, so strongly fought it that it was defeated on April 7, 1898.[5]

President McKinley then backed a new bill which became law on April 22, 1898. It gave more authority to the states and stipulated that volunteers should be drawn from the states in proportion to population and that the governors would have the appointment of all officers through the regimental level. It reaffirmed the concept of universal military obligation—all men aged 18-45 made up the national force. It also constituted the Army of the United States to consist of two components: regulars and volunteers. National Guard units that volunteered intact could retain their prewar organization and officers, but each man had to volunteer as an individual, since the War Department lacked legal authority to accept Guard units into federal service. All the unit had to do to regroup as it was before was to elect the same persons as officers. Customarily, however, the members of a unit took the oath en masse, thus at least partially bringing into federal service the esprit of the prewar unit. Many Guard units entered war service via this indirect route, but one of the finest prewar regiments, the 7th New York Infantry, chose to stay out lest it lose its identity. Almost all the Guard units entering via the indirect route were below strength and had to recruit, some up to 50 percent in order to meet army standards. They did it, even though they rejected one half of the men who came forward because of physical disabilities.[6]

Since Americans continued to be excited by the plight of the Cuban rebels, on March 9, 1898, Congress, without a single dissenting vote, appropriated $50,000,000 for the president to spend at his discretion to prepare for war. When the battleship *Maine* sank in Havana harbor on April 15, 1898, carrying down with it 260 United States sailors, people back in the states assumed (although it was far from certain) that the Spanish had sunk the ship. The leaders of the Republican Party forced President McKinley, unwillingly, to send a war message to Congress, and that body on April 25, 1898, declared war on Spain.[7]

The administration originally intended to raise 60,000 men under the new Volunteer Act, but enthusiasm—much of it created by the National Guard—ran so high that on April 23, 1898, the president called instead for 125,000. After war was declared by both sides there was a tidal wave of volunteering. To Americans their newly declared war was a crusade for humanity, perfectly free of selfish motives. Senator George F. Hoar of Massachusetts spoke of it as the "most honorable single war in all history," while his colleague from Utah, Frank J. Cannon, called it a stroke to emancipate "an enslaved and suffering humanity."[8]

Unabated war fever, fanned by the Press, produced heavy political pressure to admit more volunteers. In response, on May 26, 1898, McKinley called for another 75,000 men. Within six weeks, 200,000 had volunteered; thousands more were turned away. The rally to the colors surpassed by ten times the first six weeks of the Civil War, even with a tour of duty that was eight times longer.[9] The average white volunteer was in his mid-twenties, unmarried, native born, and of working class background. As there was no draft, the citizen soldiery did not present the cross-section of society seen in the mass wars of the twentieth century.[10]

The usual fracas developed over enrolling black volunteers. Alabama, North Carolina, and Virginia, lately of the Confederacy, accepted Negro regiments with white officers, as did Illinois, Kansas, Indiana, and Ohio, lately on the Union side. Few of the black volunteers, however, reached Cuba; one exception was the 8th Illinois, trained not to fight but to promote good relations among Cubans of different races. Only Company L of the 6th Massachusetts, ever got into the fight.[11]

The Civil War experience showed that volunteer outfits almost invariably included too many colonels and generals. The Volunteer Act, therefore, gave the president the appointment of all general officers and their staffs. Moreover, the call of April 23 and May 26 stipulated the number of units called and the officers to come with them. The April call was for five regiments and seventeen troops of cavalry, sixteen batteries of light artillery and twenty-two regiments, ten battalions, and forty-six companies of infantry. It designated what state would provide each of these units. The May call was different: 40,000 volunteers were to fill up the units already in being.[12]

All told, the president appointed 441 regular officers to posts with volunteers. The Volunteer Act had permitted the colonel of a volunteer regiment to request one regular officer for his unit. McKinley shifted 481 volunteer officers into regular commissions. He appointed twenty-six major generals for duty with volunteers, nineteen of them from the regular army and six others who were West Point graduates. He commissioned 102 brigadier generals, sixty-six of whom came from the regulars. Some political considerations were evident; one was John Jacob Astor, one of the nation's richest men, who had raised a battery of artillery with the understanding that he could command it. Another was the grandson of General Grant; a third the son of Civil War General John A. Logan, who, after the war was an influential politician. Also included was William J. Sewell, senator from New Jersey, who continued as senator while he was a major general, and a couple of ex-Confederate general officers, Fitzhugh Lee and Joseph Wheeler, to show that the nation was once again unified.[13]

The volunteer National Guard units usually had deep-rooted local ties, and so did other volunteer outfits. Both soldiers and civilians regarded their unit as an extension of their community, a community that accepted a large measure of responsibility for its boys. If a local newspaper could afford to do so, it sent a reporter to tag along, but if this was too expensive the editor arranged for some literate soldier to report. The government made no attempt to interfere with the news that flowed back, however inaccurate and heavily biased it was.[14]

Previous training fell far short of the willingness to serve. Forty percent of volunteers had had no drill and a surprising number had never fired a gun. The War Department pulled them together into several large collection points and tried to train them, but the army lacked sufficient cadre to handle so large a job. At the start, accommodations were primitive; men slept on plank or cement floors with newspapers for covers. Much of the Tampa camp was flooded, and it was not long before disease took hold there and in other camps. There had been an ingredient of politics in the appointments of surgeons in the states, but even without that few doctors drawn from private practice had adequate knowledge of public sanitation. Typhoid was the real killer in this war.[15]

Almost every sort of equipment was in short supply; the men wore their civilian clothes for awhile. Rifles were too few to permit target practice; and when enough were issued they were the old Springfield, single-shot, 45 calibre weapons, using black powder which set up a wisp of smoke that gave enemy marksmen an aiming point. The chief of ordnance claimed that a rifleman could fire the Springfield fourteen times a minute, but the inspector general referred to it as a "suicidal blunderbuss."[16] The regulars had the more versatile Krag-Jorgensen. The inspector general found that regiments coming from states where the National Guard was strong were better prepared to cope than others.[17]

In the far-off Pacific, the decisive Battle of Manila Bay took place on May 1, 1898, six weeks before any troops pulled away from the United States to bring relief to the oppressed insurrectionists in Cuba. Admiral George Dewey had military control of Manila Bay, but he could not project his power ashore for lack of soldiers. Meanwhile, men for the invasion of Cuba were being concentrated in Tampa as the V Corps. In command there was Major General William H. Shafter. Shafter had enlisted in 1861 in a Michigan regiment and had attained the rank of brevet brigadier general by war's end for effective service. He was in the South at the time of the buildup of tension over Cuba and slipped into the command partly on that account and perhaps partly because Russell Alger, the secretary of war, was a loyal Michigan man. Shafter is conspicuous in American military history as the heaviest general officer to serve in the field, weighing close to 300 pounds.[18]

V Corps had five volunteer units in it: the 1st U. S. Volunteer Cavalry (made famous because of its lieutenant colonel, Theodore Roosevelt, but not considered here because it was not state-connected), the 2nd Massachusetts Infantry, the 71st New York, and the 31st and 34th Michigan. All these had to scramble amidst the confusion to keep from being left behind. The first obstacle to be overcome was the nine miles of single-track railroad which led from Tampa to the port of embarkation. Theodore Roosevelt got his Rough Riders to the port by stopping a train of coal cars coming to Tampa, and forcing the engineer to back it, with his men on board, to the port. Next came the problem of boarding transports. Roosevelt solved this by double-timing his men to the gangplank of one, loading them on and then holding off the 2nd U. S. Infantry and the 71st New York. The 71st found its way aboard some other vessel and reached Cuba. Russell Alger made sure that the two Michigan regiments would reach the fields where glory could be earned. But for weeks no one moved toward Cuba. Even after men were loaded on the transports, there was a delay because the navy had purportedly sited a Spanish squadron in the Caribbean. Volunteers and regulars aboard were virtually parboiled from confinement in the transports. Finally, when it was ascertained that the "phantom fleet" was not there, the transports actually headed out on June 14, 1898.[19]

Shafter had in his initial expeditionary force 819 officers and

16,058 enlisted men; of the latter, 2,465 were volunteers. The debarkation on the beaches east of Santiago, Cuba, was deliberate and vulnerable, but it was not interrupted by the defenders of the island. Regulars and volunteers began their tours in tropical Cuba in woolen uniforms, as lighter weights were not immediately available. General Shafter elected to try to take the hills overlooking the city of Santiago. The 2nd Massachusetts took part in the attack up El Caney, which in retrospect seems to have had no military value, and so did the Rough Riders. New York's 71st was assigned to work along the base of San Juan, the major hill, but when it encountered heavy fire, it recoiled and never got started again. The men found that the smoke from their black-powder Springfields attracted the fire of Spanish marksmen, who were using superior Mauser rifles. Lieutenant John H. Parker—known as Gatling Gun Parker because of his devotion to the early rapid fire weapon—in command of a battery of Gatlings, was supposed to find the 71st and go up the hill with them. When he found them they were strung along beside the road at the foot of the slope, not moving and not about to move, and he went on without them.[20]

The 2nd Massachusetts and the 71st New York, because they were brigaded with regulars, were at least brought into action. The 33rd and 34th Michigan Regiments were brigaded together. The 33rd and one battalion of the 34th took part in the Santiago campaign; the balance of the 34th arrived too late and could only join in the mop-up. Reinforcements, arriving in increments from the United States, finally raised Shafter's volunteers to 7,443, but the newcomers saw no action. About 600 prisoners were confined on the U. S. ship *Harvard* under guard of the 4th Massachusetts. Jittery and eager for action, a guard detachment from the 4th overreacted to a minor incident by firing into the prisoners, killing six and wounding thirteen. American casualty figures for the Cuban campaign reveal how light volunteer participation was: 18 volunteers out of 243 Americans killed, and 121 of 1,545 wounded.[21]

In their letters home, Guardsmen made it plain that they did not accept the caste system which the regulars tried to impose. They continued to view their officers as home-town boys, whom no amount of military courtesy could transform into anything more lofty. Moreover, they were sure that they and their officers, without resorting to caste distinctions, could fight as well as the professionals. These views annoyed the regular officers, but the war was too short and the enemy too weak to overcome this deep-seated conviction of the citizen soldiers. "The nation for the last time," historian Gerald Linderman wrote, "could afford volunteer informality."[22]

Shortages and faulty equipment occasioned numerous complaints. The surgeon general had to ask the state governors for their stocks of medicines, but even then he never had enough. Major General Nelson Miles charged the War Department with supplying canned beef that was rotten and flour that was wormy; whether the charges were justified or not, the food was indeed unpalatable. Sickness spread more from contaminated water than from the victuals, but where the food was the agent it was largely because it was poorly prepared by soldiers untrained in food preparation. To solve the problem, Congress on July 7, 1898, authorized a cook for every company. Typhoid caused 80 percent of the deaths, but malaria and yellow fever neutralized the troops. When the fever season arrived, officers and men wrote back to persons of influence pleading with them to bring about the removal of the army from Cuba, lest all in it die. In the fall of 1898, most of them were pulled out and sent home, obviously in bad health. When the 2nd Massachusetts returned, the community wanted to have a grand parade and welcome, but the leaders could see that the veterans could not stand it and needed instead to get home as fast as they could and rest.[23]

Major General Nelson A. Miles, Commanding General of the U. S. Army, did not direct the Cuban campaign, which turned out to be the principal one in the Caribbean, in part because he argued from the beginning that Puerto Rico was the proper place to start. He did command a campaign in Puerto Rico, where his army made a landing on July 25, 1898. His army, unlike that of General Shafter, consisted primarily of state volunteers. Nine states contributed to it, which at its peak contained about 17,000 men.[24] This force took part in six recognized engagements and saw eighteen days of action at a cost of three enlisted volunteers killed, and four officers and thirty-six men wounded.[25] Major General James H. Wilson, a distinguished cavalryman during the Civil War, was impressed by the volunteers serving in Puerto Rico. "It is evident," he said, "that the Republic has lost nothing in the quality of its manhood during the thirty-five years of peace."[26]

Forty days before V Corps embarked for Cuba, the president ordered 5,000 troops to the Philippines, four-fifths of them volunteers, and by August 4 there were 10,907 American soldiers in those islands, most of them volunteers from the western states. California, Oregon, Nebraska, Colorado, Wyoming, Idaho, Utah, and Minnesota sent men in this first wave, and Pennsylvania placed one regiment in it. Colonel William Jennings Bryan, lacking the political status of Republican Theodore Roosevelt, could not get his Nebraska unit overseas because he was too conspicuous a Democrat. In the second increment, volunteers came from middle America: Kansas, South Dakota, North Dakota, Montana, Washington, and Iowa, with the east represented by one regiment from Tennessee and the Astor Battery from New York.[27]

All the volunteers carried the black-powder burning, single-shot Springfield rifle, and they fought in the Philippines under as trying conditions as the army has ever had to endure. In the attack on Manila on August 13, 1898, they battled from street to street and house to house without having ever been taught the special tactics for such action. Out in the jungle, they sometimes had to form two ranks, back to back, to hold off assailants, unseen until they rose up from the bamboo thickets, swinging their deadly machetes. At other times they found themselves operating against hostile parties in deserts where they could be seen for miles.[28]

Until the summer of 1899, state volunteers made up 75 percent of the American force in the Philippine Islands. Bit by bit they acquired the skills of the regulars but never their military courtesy or discipline. When they wrote home they more often than not disparaged the regulars over them, but they did not spare their own officers either. Concerning the enemy, they were in general harsher on the natives than the regulars. It was common to refer to the Filipinos as "niggers" or "missing links," or brainless monkeys "on whom no cruelty was too severe." [29]

Like their predecessors in earlier American wars, the volunteers grew eager to go home. By the end of the first year of their two-year term, they began to badger the authorities to get them shipped back to the United States. Unfortunately, Filipino patriots got in their way. The natives had been under the impression that the United States was aiding them to win independence, so when they learned of their annexation, they attacked the American lines around Manila on February 4, 1899, beginning what is known in American history as the Philippine Insurrection. Regiments from California, Idaho, Washington, North and South Dakota, Wyoming, Nebraska, Colorado, and Montana (all numbered 1st regiment) played honorable roles in repulsing the attack. So did the 10th Pennsylvania, 20th Kansas, some units from Tennessee, and two batteries from Utah.[30]

Combat losses, but especially war fatigue and sickness, began to deplete the state volunteers in the Philippines. Before June 30, 1899, volunteers bore the heaviest casualties from enemy action: 12 of 16 officers, and 134 out of 209 enlisted men killed; 61 of 82 officers and 859 of 1,275 enlisted men wounded.[31] Accidents, drowning, suicide, and murder took 233 lives. Greater by far was the toll from disease. Typhoid killed 1,900 state volunteers; others died of malaria, diarrhea, yellow fever, and measles.[32]

During the summer of 1899, the clamor to go home bcame so strident that Major General Elwell Otis, commanding in the islands, realized that he must either use the volunteers at once or lose them. He lost them. By June, only half of the 120,151 soldiers in the Philippines were state volunteers, and that proportion was diminished when shipments to the United States began on June 14. Last to leave were the 20th Kansas, 1st Washington, 51st Iowa, a troop of Nevada Cavalry, and the 1st Tennessee. Back home, the returning soldiers received heroes' welcomes. The governor of Utah proclaimed an arrival day with triumphal arches, speeches by notable persons, and heavy feasting.

The returning citizen soldiers had earned a reputation for steadiness under the harshest conditions. They were sure, as were the home folks, that they had taken part in a very noble cause.[33]

To maintain an army in the Philippines, Congress authorized twenty-five new regiments in July 1899, recruited from the nation at large. Although three of the regiments, two infantry and one cavalry, were to be recruited if possible from state volunteers already in the islands, these regiments did not have a sufficiently intimate connection with the states to make them a part of the history of the militia or of the National Guard.[34]

Table 9.1 shows the importance of the state volunteers and the nature of their employment. Early in the war, the regular army contained 38,816 men, up 10,000 from prewar levels. At the same time, there were 124,776 state volunteers in the federal service, that is, 3.2 volunteers per one regular. When state volunteer manpower reached its peak in August 1898, there were 3.8 state volunteers for every one of the 56,362 regulars. After that the number of volunteers dropped rapidly, while the regulars rose slowly. By June 1899, the balance had shifted; there were then 64,729 regulars and only 55,422 state volunteers.[35]

In round figures, 233,000 state volunteers entered federal service up to July 1899 when United States volunteers began to take over the job. Most of the 233,000 came from the National Guard; only Kansas spurned the Guard as a recruiting base. Indeed, so strong was the bias of the governor that he disbanded all the units of the Kansas National Guard. His purpose in part was to obtain the political advantage which accrued from appointing a new set of officers. Congress, however, frustrated this objective by refusing to recognize new Kansas units as long as old ones were not filled up.[36]

Every state in the Union, plus the two territories of Oklahoma and New Mexico, and the District of Columbia, contributed volunteers, ranging from one battalion of infantry from Nevada to fifteen regiments of infantry, three troops of cavalry, and three batteries of artillery from

TABLE 9.1

Statement showing the monthly strength and losses, from all causes, in the armies of the United States between May 1, 1898, and June 30, 1899 (H.C. Corbin, Adjutant General, U.S.A., Adjutant General's Office, Washington, D.C., October 1, 1899)

	STRENGTH			LOSSES — OFFICERS											LOSSES — ENLISTED MEN														WOUNDED	
					Resigned or,		Died								Discharged				Died												
Regular Army	Officers	Enlisted Men	Total	Retired	Discharged	Dismissed	Killed in Action	Of Wounds	Disease	Accident	Drowned	Suicide	Murdered	Total	Expiration of Service	Disability	Sentence of General Court-Martial	By Order	Killed in Action	Of Wounds	Disease	Accident	Drowned	Suicide	Murdered or Homicide	Retired	Deserted	Total	Officers	Enlisted Men
May, 1898	2,191	36,625	38,816	3					3					6	615	36	23	58			6	1	2	1		13	4	758		15
June, 1898	2,198	45,669	47,867	6										8	637	34	24	75	8		21		6			10	39	856	3	
July, 1898	2,327	51,721	51,048	7			18	6	6					37	689	71	31	71	175	73	134	7	3	8	3	14	84	1,354	83	1,111
August, 1898	2,323	54,039	56,362	5	2				12		1			20	886	105	16	120	8	8	401	2	4	4	3	6	90	1,657	3	40
September, 1898	2,325	57,325	59,650	6	3				9					19	663	114	20	334	5	1	321	7	1	1	7	6	272	1,746		
October, 1898	2,326	58,310	60,636	6	2				4	1				13	667	152	28	1,348			145	12	3	2	7	7	393	2,768		10
November, 1898	2,324	61,444	63,768	5	1				3					9	612	185	50	1,243		1	83	11	1	3	1	10	310	2,501		
December, 1898	2,311	63,370	65,681	5	2				2					13	595	277	110	2,233			59	5	1	4		10	365	3,666		
January, 1899	2,308	63,223	65,531	4	2				2					8	523	248	124	4,749			61	5		3	1	9	233	5,955		
February, 1899	2,373	57,684	60,057	4			1	1	2					8	535	161	118	9,106	18	2	48	8	3	2	2	6	144	10,147	3	80
March, 1899	2,357	61,110	63,467	13	1		3		4					21	533	172	119	3,495	26	5	44	8	2	2	3	15	162	4,585	7	180
April, 1899	2,435	60,804	63,239	4		1	1							6	623	167	101	5,288	7	7	72	4	8	3	1	10	320	6,611	3	22
May, 1899	2,433	60,766	63,199	9	1				3					13	624	169	60	3,741	2	2	67	6	8	3		8	308	4,997	1	29
June, 1899	2,471	62,258	64,729	8	2				1				1	12	685	211	100	1,651	21	15	62	4	6	1	1	9	312	3,079	6	99
Total				91	15	1	a24	7	51	1	2	1	1	193	8,887	2,102	924	33,512	270	114	1,524	72	48	32	26	133	3,036	50,680	109	1,586

134

Volunteers

Month	Officers	Enlisted	Aggregate																								
May, 1898	6,221	118,555	124,776	6				2				8	5		5	62			39	5	2			19	132		28
June, 1898	7,160	153,210	160,370	56	1			3				60	68		33	253	7	1	75	9	4			109	534	3	190
July, 1898	8,640	202,841	211,481	110				11	1			124	447		54	443	32	10	288	10	2			309	1,576	12	95
August, 1898	8,895	207,361	216,256	124	2			29				155	850		39	459	14	4	908	27	10			575	2,907	11	
September, 1898	8,726	199,805	208,531	187		1		33	2			222	673		42	1,426		2	1,148	21	6			534	3,854		
October, 1898	7,127	157,612	164,739	189		1		19				209	577		41	1,957			631	25	3			537	3,779		
November, 1898	5,216	110,202	115,418	143				3			1	147	379		70	1,705			270	8	3			326	2,736		
December, 1898	4,775	98,481	103,256	147				2	1			151	281		74	1,606			124	12	3			195	2,295		
January, 1899	4,303	85,938	90,241	90	1			5				96	395		62	1,331			103	12	3			68	1,992		
February, 1899	3,515	66,181	69,696	73	1	4		4	4	1		84	237		46	1,057	44	19	94	1	1			56	1,576	17	259
March, 1899	2,740	47,586	50,326	81		6	1	1	1			90	106		25	1,094	46	14	68	6	4				1,386	21	354
April, 1899	1,849	28,277	30,126	102		2		1				105	35		14	579	29	20	35	1	2				726	17	160
May, 1899	1,108	15,825	16,933	149		2						152	20			430	11	6	25					5	512	6	58
June, 1899	933	14,499	15,422	122	1			1				123	31		3	278	5	2	12					3	336	1	34
Total			91	1,579	6	17	3	114	5	1	1	1,726	4,104		508	12,683	188	78	3,820	137	40	20	26	2,736	24,341	88	1,178
Aggregate				1,594	7	a38	10	165	6	3	2	1,919	8,888	6,206	1,432	46,195	458	192	5,344	209	88	52	133	5,772	75,021	197	2,764

a Three officers of the Regular Army who were killed also held commissions in the volunteer forces, in which they are included, and are, to avoid counting twice, deducted from the aggregate.

Source: Report of the Major General Commanding the Army, ARSW, 1899, vol. 1, part 3, p. 384.

135

Pennsylvania. Among the heaviest contributors were New York with fourteen regiments of infantry, two troops of cavalry, and four batteries of artillery; Indiana, with eight regiments of infantry; Michigan, with the equivalent of six regiments of infantry; and Ohio, with ten regiments of infantry, two squadrons of cavalry, and a battalion of artillery.[37]

As far back as 1887, a proposal to create a naval reserve had been introduced into the Senate but had failed; thereafter, states with extensive shorelines took the initiative. The result was that during the last two decades of the nineteenth century ten states on the Atlantic Ocean established naval militias: Massachusetts, New York, Rhode Island, Maryland, South Carolina, North Carolina, Georgia, Connecticut, Virginia, and New Jersey. Florida and Louisiana, on the Gulf of Mexico, also created water-borne militias, as did California on the Pacific coast. In addition, five states around the Great Lakes followed the pattern: Pennsylvania, Vermont, Michigan, Illinois, and Ohio— Vermont's waterfront being Lake Champlain. The naval units of these states contributed 4,224 citizen sailors to the United States Navy during the War with Spain. The Navy Department used these state volunteers as individual replacements aboard ships of the United States Navy, and as such every one of them saw some action.[38]

In summary, the United States enlarged its peacetime force for the Spanish-American War primarily with volunteers. The traditions of the militia and the legal strictures on induction into the Army of the United States made it impossible for entire units of the National Guard to volunteer. Some of them, it is true, got into federal service because their members volunteered as individuals and, once inducted, drew together again into their prewar organizations. But the Guard's principal contribution was to provide men who had some military training and who were motivated to volunteer by their experience in the Guard.

The mechanism for volunteering was similar to that of the Civil War, except that it was not supported by a draft which in the earlier war had stimulated men to volunteer. There was no need for conscription because the war was so popular that far more men were willing to sign up than could be used. Besides, the necessary ground force was less than one-tenth the size of the armies of the two belligerents in the Civil War. As an effective instrument for enlarging the armed forces, volunteering reached its peak during this conflict. The states raised their quotas faster and easier than during the Civil War. Since the war in the Caribbean theater lasted only 113 days, the state volunteers did not have the time to become as professional as their forebears had done. Even though conflict lasted longer in the Philippines—it was taken over during the second half of the year 1899 by the regular army and by United States volunteers with scant state relationship—in that theater too there was not time to attain the professionalism of the Civil War volunteers. Throughout the war, the states kept in touch with the volunteers they sent and were proud of them. The state volunteers and their families, for their part, often doubted the competence of the regulars who commanded operations, but they never questioned their own ability to defeat what to them was a tyrannical foe.

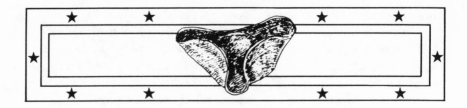

TEN

Reorganization, 1900-1916

After the War with Spain, Congress held extended hearings, filling volumes of testimony, to try to identify the causes of failures that had occurred in the military machine. While the congressional committees were at work, President McKinley appointed a distinguished corporation lawyer, Elihu Root, to serve as secretary of war. Root had no military experience, but without any special mandate to do it, he undertook to bring the United States Army into the twentieth century. Immersed in the literature, ancient and modern, Root came under the influence of the ideas of Emory Upton, and through him of the Great German General Staff. In the end, the reforms Root instituted scrapped the old army command structure with a commanding general at the top. During eighty-five years it had never been clear precisely what it was that the commanding general commanded. His place was taken by a chief of staff whose authority would be worked out during the first two decades of the twentieth century.

One of the new institutions to come out of the Root reforms was the Army War College. Within it, the framers placed a Planning Division, the first agency the United States had ever had to scan the world for menaces to the national security and to devise strategies to foil them. Root's designers had purposely hidden this new brain of the army in the War College for fear that legislators, if they saw it in the open, might regard it as a mechanism that would lead the nation into war.[1]

Elihu Root saw clearly that the United States needed a workable reserve system. What it had was the militia, resting still on the obsolete Uniform Militia Act of 1792. The secretary called in Colonel William Sanger, Inspector General of the New York National Guard, to study what advanced nations were doing about citizen reserves. Sanger traveled to Europe, and late in 1900 submitted a report on the English and Swiss systems. He wrote, "We always have been and always shall be largely dependent on our citizen soldiery to fight our battles . . . an effective militia is a force of the greatest value."[2] Back in the United States, Sanger developed a close working relationship with Charles Dick, a major general commanding the Ohio National Guard, president of the National Guard Association (NGA), congressman from Ohio, and chairman of the House Committee on the Militia. Dick immediately appointed a panel to draw up a bill to present to the annual meeting of the NGA on January 23 and 24, 1902.[3]

The War Department submitted to Congress a bill of its own. Although that bill was based largely on the NGA draft, it contained one section which the association could not support. Section 24 provided for a national reserve having no relationship to any state and made up of 100,000 men with prior military service. Secretary Root insisted that the purpose was simply to keep 100,000 veterans allied with the military establishment, but Guard leaders saw it as an entering wedge for a national reserve of the sort long sought by the regular army, which in the end would crowd the National Guard out of the effective military force. In spite of NGA opposition, important members of the House pushed the bill through to passage, with Section 24 in it.

The case was different in the Senate: Republicans favored the bill, Democrats opposed it. At this time, the legislation to reform the army's command structure was also before the Senate. Democratic senators labeled the Republican administration as at once antistate and militaristic. Labor unions opposed the bill. Finally, seeing the political set, Root withdrew Section 24, whereupon the Senate, with only one day's delay, passed the bill; the president signed it on January 21, 1903. The new act repealed the hoary statute of 1792 which had stood on the books for 111 years, honored in the breach.[4]

The new law, generally known as the Dick Act for the part which Major General Charles Dick had had in initiating and moving it, started the volunteer militia—by this time known as the National Guard in most of the states—along the irreversible path toward federalization.[5] In the beginning, however, that path could be opened only by action of the governors: a governor had to request added arms before the War Department could issue them; he had to ask for joint maneuvers with the regulars during summer training, or it could not take place. Even then it could not occur until federal inspectors had certified that the Guard was ready for it. With such certification it became legal to use funds, traditionally marked to supply arms to the states, to help finance summer training, and to pay the militiamen at the same rate as regulars.

Only if a governor asked for regular support could professional officers be assigned to help train a state guard the year around.[6] Once a governor took the fateful step of accepting federal aid, his state was required to see that its organized militia drilled twenty-four times a year with two-thirds of its strength present, and to turn out in the summer for five days of encampment every year. In addition, all units must stand an annual inspection by federal officers and must correct the shortcomings noted by the inspectors.[7]

The Dick Act contained a provision for which the NGA had never ceased to work. When it was necessary to use military force to suppress insurrection, repel invasion, or enforce the laws of the United States—the Constitutional grounds for summoning the militia into federal service—and the regular forces proved inadequate, the president was directed to call the organized militia "in advance of any volunteer force." He could then set the term of service, not exceeding nine months.[8] An act of 1908 enlarged on this stipulation by declaring that all branches of the organized militia had to be called before any volunteers could be used. This meant that although the need might be for infantry, Guard cavalry and artillery would have to be summoned ahead of infantry volunteers. Congress corrected this awkward priority to some extent on April 25, 1914. Still, if three-quarters of an organized militia unit voted to enter federal service, the War Department had to induct the members of that unit, whatever its branch, and had to commission the officers who came with the outfit.[9]

No portion of the Dick Act guaranteed the integrity of National Guard units when in federal service. On the contrary, General Orders in 1907 stated categorically that an organized militia unit which enlisted en bloc lost its identity as militia and became part of the volunteer army.[10] The Dick Act then rested on the premise that America's future wars would be fought not by units of the organized militia (National Guard) but by volunteers who might or might not have come out of the militia.

Elihu Root considered the Guard's primary mission to be the peacetime training of men who in wartime would become volunteers.[11] The regular army had failed to perform that vital task; indeed, the Military Academy at West Point seemed to train its graduates to handle a small professional force rather than a large mass of partly trained volunteers of the Civil War variety. The secretary's intention was to open the army's schools for officers to the officers of the organized militia to prepare them for the training of future volunteers. It would not then be necessary to assign excessive numbers of regular officers to the state organizations. Root, when addressing the NGA, took care to say the right things. War, he said, was inevitable from time to time, and the martial spirit, necessary to wage it, could not be fostered from the center but only in the states. He rebutted the charges of militarism leveled at him and the administration, arguing that what had been done by way of reform insured not war in the future but peace. Strength was essential since the United States grew richer with every passing year, and "undefended wealth but invites aggression." To oppose such aggression, the secretary concluded, the three components of the Army of the United States—regulars, volunteers, and militia—would "stand together in unity, strength and efficiency to fight the battles of our beloved country."[12]

Meanwhile, Congress made appropriations to carry the Dick Act into effect. It invested about $4,000,000 annually in the Guard, while the states together spent from $5,800,000 to $9,000,000 each year. In 1906, Congress raised the sum to arm the militia up to $2,000,000, five times the $400,000 authorized in 1887 and ten times the $200,000 of 1808. From 1903 to 1916, the central government spent $53,000,000 on the Guard, exceeding all peacetime expenditures before 1903 for that purpose.[13]

From 1903 to World War I, the strength of the National Guard fluctuated within rather narrow limits. Its high, achieved in 1916, was 129,000 officers and men, its low 112,000 in 1912. The 1912 figure was disturbingly low, since the eligible male population totaled 13,000,000. Equally disturbing was the rapid turnover of personnel; 40 percent had been members for less than one year. A few commanders had to go into the streets to gather in enough men to stand inspection, and some kept names on their rosters to stay above minimum figures, which they knew did not represent living persons. Many units were often only at 42 percent of war strength. An added concern was the extreme imbalance of the Guard: 95,296 infantry in 1905, but only 4,551 cavalry, 6,268 artillery, 933 engineers, 964 signal corps, and 1,594 hospital corps.[14]

New York maintained the largest state establishment with 963 officers and 13,688 enlisted men; Nevada, the smallest, with no enrollment whatever, and, close to Nevada, Utah with only 39 officers and 328 enlisted men. Hawaii made the fullest use of its eligible manpower, enrolling 71.8 out of every 1,000 men. At the bottom of this scale stood Indiana with 3.5 and Tennessee with 3.6 men per 1,000 eligibles.[15]

Professional officers persistently tried to establish a national reserve free of all relationship with the states. Two reasons were the small size and the imbalance of the organized militia. Another was the firm belief that national security could not safely depend on reserves that had two commanders-in-chief and two chains of command. Governors could veto national policy as they had done during the War of 1812 and during the Civil War.[16] Still another reason was the question of where Guardsmen could be required to serve and for how long. On May 27, 1908, Congress removed the nine-month limitation on service and gave the president the power to set the length of a tour of duty. At the same time, it reaffirmed the right of the United States to use the Guardsmen within or without the country for Constitutional purposes. A simple call from the president would accomplish the transition from state to federal control. Moreover, the act made the commander-in-chief the exclusive judge of the need to call militia into federal service, leaving a governor no grounds to withhold his troops. Organized militia had, of course, first call, but the War Department did not have to accept any unit that did not conform to regular army tables of organization.[17]

Unfortunately for the Guard, the Act of 1908 was not the final word. In February 1912, George W. Wickersham, U. S. Attorney General, with the concurrence of Enoch H. Crowder, Judge Advocate General of the Army, decided that the Act of 1908 was unconstitutional and that the National Guard, which was the militia of the Constitution, could not be used outside the country, since it was a defense force only. In August of the same year, the War Department published an influential pamphlet, *Organization of the Land Forces of the United States*, which adopted as doctrine what Wickersham and Crowder had said.[18]

That pamphlet contained much of the thinking of Major General Leonard Wood, one of the most influential proponents of a national versus an organized militia reserve. Wood, who served as chief of staff from 1910 to 1914, spoke of the National Guard as "an uncoordinated army of fifty allies."[19] In addition, he mistrusted the Guard because in all but two of the states the men elected the company officers, and the latter in turn elected the field officers. Besides, Wood was convinced that he could take raw recruits with no military training at all and turn them into good soldiers within six months. If Wood was right, there was less need for a peacetime reserve since the United States would always have at least six months to prepare for war.[20]

Wood and other proponents of a national reserve persuaded Congress to add a rider to the Army Appropriations Act of 1912, creating a reserve free of all state ties. Men would enlist for seven years, serve the first three on active duty, then enter the reserve for the last four. The reserve would be nothing more than a pool of individuals with prior experience, required neither to belong to a unit or to train. In practice, enlistees after three years' service left without bothering to enter the reserves. Since the Act contained no sanctions, the reserve failed for lack of members.[21]

When the 1912 reserve failed, Chief of Staff Wood put his weight behind the "Plattsburgh Idea," a project to create a trained reserve through Citizen's Military Training Camps (CMTC) held each summer. These camps attracted well-to-do business executives, who took pride in spending a virile week or two with the regulars and brought into being a strong supporting association, sustained by such believers in the strenuous life as Theodore Roosevelt. The CMTC leaders insisted that their camps were not intended to compete with or to undermine the organized militia, but privately, Granville Clark, a principal founder, wrote to a friend, "Everybody interested in getting a sound system is preparing to knife the National Guard at the first opportunity." Woodrow Wilson would never permit the War Department to endorse the CMTC; indeed, he deplored the movement which seemed to him a devise to draw the United States into the war in Europe.[22]

The Dick Act had established a Division of Militia Affairs in the War Department and had mandated that a regular officer must head it. There were to be no Guard officers in the office staff. Whereas before, militia affairs had meandered among the assistant secretary of war, the chief of staff of the army, the adjutant general, and other bureau chiefs, they now had a focus. Nevertheless, this organizational reform did not help the Guard to become an integral part of the efficient national military force because the first three chiefs of the Division were national reserve men. The first, Colonel Erasmus M. Weaver, stated in his annual reports that only a reserve controlled exclusively by the War Department could assure the national security. Such a reserve, Weaver said, would operate not under the militia clauses of the Constitution but under the Army clause.[23] The second chief, Brigadier General Robert K. Evans, concurred with Weaver, while the third, Major General Albert L. Mills, referred to the National Guard in testimony before congressional committees as forty-eight little state armies, energized by a love of states' rights.[24]

The NGA opposed each attempt to create a national reserve, insisting that the National Guard was the proper one. *The National Guardsman*, a semiofficial journal from 1896 to 1905, and the *National Guard Magazine* (1907-1917), privately owned but recognized by the NGA, regularly played down the role of the Guard as internal constabulary and regularly stressed the Guard as part of the efficient national military force.[25] Militia leaders believed that the general staff of the army did what it could to obstruct the Guard's ambition. They believed, probably correctly, that the chief of staff and his associates did not wish to see the organized militia strengthened unless the control of the regulars over it was also enlarged. The War Department, they said, released a steady stream of insidious propaganda in favor of a national reserve and against the organized militia. Naturally, they looked less than before to the executive branch to realize their ambitions and more to Congress where there was a strong sympathy for the concept of the citizen soldier together with a fierce loyalty to states' rights.[26]

A basic question with which all interested persons had to cope was who, among the large number of males of military age, would make up a reserve. When President Woodrow Wilson considered the problem, which was not often, he spoke in Jeffersonian terms of "a citizenry trained and accustomed to arms."[27] Jefferson had meant by this a compulsory militia system, but what Wilson meant is not clear as he swung from one position to another. Colonel John McAuley Palmer, respected as a military thinker and friend of the citizen soldier, supported a national reserve made up of volunteers. As a friendly gesture to the organized militia, Palmer said that the founders of the national force would have to be from the Guard.[28] John H. "Gatling Gun" Parker agreed with Palmer on the need for a national reserve, but he scorned the idea of filling it by volunteering. It was the birthright of every able-bodied American male, he said, to discharge military service as part of his obligation as a citizen. The National Guard could play no role in the efficient national military force but, he wrote, ought to be sustained as "a constitutional check against the over-development of the regular army and against possible militarism."[29] Leonard Wood and Theodore Roosevelt favored UMT as the source for a national reserve, but Roosevelt, at least, believed it to be unattainable at the time.

While the debate over military posture and the role of reserves in it went on, the regular army and the National Guard did more training together than ever before. In September 1904, 5,000 regulars and 21,000 Guardsmen simulated the Second Battle of Bull Run on the original battlefield. During 1906, the two components worked together in eight camps, but the peak of joint exercise came in 1908. That year 45,000 men from the organized militia took part in joint maneuvers, while another 10,000 exercised in the coastal forts with the regular coast artillerymen. Since the regular service could provide only 741 officers and 19,000 enlisted men for coast defense, the National Guard had an important role in it. Joint maneuvers were scheduled every two years, and in between them companies of Guardsmen were linked with regular companies. During the four years from

1912 to 1916, National Guard artillery units rose from 7,700 men to 11,555.[30]

Certain common themes run through the reports that regular officers, assigned to the Guard to aid in training, sent to the War Department. One was the problem of employers who penalized employees for service with the Guard. Men who went to summer camp sometimes lost their jobs. One major asked that protection be extended to victims of "unpatriotic and unsympathetic people in mercantile life." Another theme was the politics resulting from the election of officers, and the consequent loss of efficiency. Certain of the attached officers recommended a program to brighten up the armories to overcome part of the apathy which they observed. Above all, they recommended some compensation for drill time and for summer camp.[31]

In 1911, the House Committee on Military Affairs considered federal pay for drill. This issue, like every other issue relating to the organized militia, brought out recommendations that were the exact opposite of each other. One was that as little as $1.00 per drill could attract more men, and a better class, into Guard units. The opposite was that every man owed a military obligation and ought to be paying it instead of being paid. "While serving as a soldier [a patriot] achieves the highest form of his existence as a citizen."[32] No federal pay was forthcoming.

Absence from training concerned both regular and militia officers. The national absentee average was 21.02 percent in 1904, which included a range from 100 percent for Nevada, with no organized units, to 1.05 percent for Rhode Island. One obvious explanation for some of this was the turbulence caused by the excessive reorganization mandated by the War Department. During the decade 1903-1913, 792 units were disbanded and 902 new ones constituted.[33] Many Guard officers earned praise from their regular advisers for their steadfastness. One regular referred to the Missouri officers as "martyrs to duty, anxious to learn, and patriotic to the core." He recognized that the Guard was going through a difficult transition from being a club, emphasizing fellowship and recreation, to becoming a public institution, turning citizens into real soldiers.[34]

In 1910, tables of organization were prepared for seventeen mixed divisions, each to consist of two-thirds organized militia and one-third regular army. Since these divisions were never manned, they were replaced in 1912 by sixteen unmixed divisions, four of them regular army, the other twelve National Guard. Both New York and Pennsylvania supported a full division, but other states had to supply units to ten interstate divisions.[35]

There was a sharp controversy over the way in which soldiers, regular and irregular, should use their shoulder weapons. The National Rifle Association championed aimed fire and held national competitions in marksmanship. Gradually, the soldiers of the U. S. Army turned into the world's deadliest marksmen, with sharpshooters of the National Guard close behind. Most Guardsmen supported individual aimed fire, but several high-ranking regulars opposed it due to waste of ammunition and the loss of unit cohesion. Finally, General Pershing resolved the issue in favor of aimed fire during World War I.[36]

An Act of March 2, 1907, required the War Department, whenever it adopted a new shoulder weapon, to establish a reserve stock for issue to Guardsmen when called into federal service. Meanwhile, although the regulars adopted a more advanced weapon, the Springfield '03, the Guard continued to use the Krag. At the same time, however, the organized militia was drawing ahead of the regulars in machine guns. In 1915, thirty-four National Guard infantry regiments contained machine gun companies, whereas the regulars had none at all, even at a time when the war in Europe was beginning to demonstrate that machine guns could dominate a battlefield.[37]

On May 30, 1908, the Guard began to go vertical. About twenty-five men of the New York Guard volunteered to learn ballooning and formed into the 1st Aero Company, Signal Corps. In 1911, Glenn Curtiss Aviation loaned the company an airplane and a pilot, Beckwith Havens. The year 1916 was pivotal for air service in New York; the Aero Club of America equipped the unit with five planes, valued at $29,500. At the same time, a second New York air detachment came into being in Buffalo. Even before the Buffalo outfit was operating, the air trend had spread to California. There, in February 1911, an Aero detachment of the 7th Company, California Coast Artillery, appeared. Eugene Ely, celebrated in the history of flying, was the air detachment's first private, the first Guardsman to be sent to the Curtiss aviation school in San Diego, the first Guardsman to receive a pilot's commission in California, the first pilot ever to fly a plane from the deck of a ship, and one of the first early fliers to die in an air accident—killed at Macon, Georgia, during an air show on October 19, 1911. In the middle of the country, Missouri entered the air game with a Aero detachment in its signal corps in 1911.[38]

When Leonard Wood stepped down as army chief of staff in 1914, official doctrine on the training of citizen soldiers changed. The Army War College published a booklet, entitled *A Proper Military Policy for the United States*, which said that for war service troops had to have no less than twelve months' training at 150 hours per month. The Guard could not measure up to such a standard with its twenty-four drill periods and five-day summer camp.[39]

In 1915, the issue of a national reserve versus the National Guard came to a head. Wilson's Secretary of War, Lindley Garrison, presented a bill to Congress to create what he called the "Continental Army," to consist of 100,000 regulars and 400,000 national reservists devoid of state connections. At the time, the president supported Garrison's bill.

The NGA was unalterably opposed to the plan, and it took political steps to thwart it. The politician with the most leverage who would not tolerate the Continental Army was James Hay, veteran congressman from Virginia, and chairman of the House Committee on Military Affairs. Recently, he had argued that the United States had nothing to fear from the war in Europe, which had turned all the preparedness people against him, but he had heavy political clout without them. Although not especially in tune with the NGA leadership, he, like they, would not stand for a monolithic army. To frame a bill to counter Garrison's he found an ally in Major General Fred C. Ainsworth who as adjutant general had battled with Chief of Staff Leonard Wood for control of the army hierarchy, lost the battle, and been forced to retire from the service in 1912. Ainsworth was bitter toward a highly centralized military system, at least one in which he was not top man.[40]

During 1916, the Committees on Military Affairs in both houses of Congress were holding hearings on military posture, including reserves. Before them, ex-Secretary Root spoke against the Guard as a reliable reserve. "The idea . . . that forty-eight different governors," he said, "can be the basis for developing an efficient, mobile national army is quite absurd."[41] Garrison, when his time came, testified that the 129,000 men of the Guard were inadequate; the reserve should contain 400,000 men. Leonard Wood lectured the legislators on the need for UMT not only for security reasons but also for the mental health of the nation. Nations softened by affluence had been swept away throughout history; UMT would save the United States from that fate.[42]

Congress had before it three bills to raise military manpower. One was Hay's bill, backed by the NGA; another was Garrison's. The third, introduced by Senator George E. Chamberlain of Oregon, incorporated a reserve free of state influence and fed by UMT. In the end, National Guard and states' rights supporters swung Wilson away from the Continental Army and behind a modified version of Hay's bill. Lindley Garrison then resigned. Thereafter, Hay's measure, broadened to deal with defense problems in general, passed the House by a vote of 402 to 2, and after some appeasement of Senator Chamberlain, also passed the Senate. President Wilson signed the new law on June 3, 1916.[43]

From this milestone legislation, called the National Defense Act, the proponents of a national reserve gained both an Officer's and an Enlisted Reserve Corps, free of state entanglements. Officers, after a tour of active duty, could enroll in the reserve and be available in times of crisis. The Enlisted Reserve Corps included only men who had served either as engineers, in the signal corps, as quartermaster, or in ordnance and medicine. Both reserve corps contained no units, only individuals.[44]

The National Defense Act brought into being another reserve element, the Reserve Officer's Training Corps (ROTC), to operate in the land-grant colleges throughout the nation. Its purpose was to provide a source other than the regular army from which to draw officers to command the reserves. To qualify for a detachment a college had to employ regular officers to instruct the cadets, but the professionals who could be so detailed were limited to three hundred.[45]

The act categorically stated that the National Guard was an integral part of the Army of the United States when in federal service. But as long as the president called out the Guard through the governors, the Guardsmen remained within the organized militia. On the other hand, when Congress authorized the use of military forces, the president was empowered to draft individual Guardsmen into federal service for the duration of the emergency. Guardsmen so drafted ceased to be in the organized militia. The power to appoint officers for the drafted men belonged to the president, except that the Senate had to consent to those of general grade. It was up to the states to replace those Guard units eliminated by this sort of summons to federal duty. The power to draft individuals of the organized militia was the sole drafting authority possessed by the federal government at that time, and the only national conscription authorized since the Civil War.[46]

The National Defense Act greatly enlarged the power of the federal government over the National Guard. It doubled the required training periods to forty-eight and tripled the summer camp sessions to fifteen days. But at last some federal pay would be available for drill and camp. No state could disband a unit without the consent of the War Department. The president received the authority to assign regular officers and noncommissioned officers to states without a request from the governors, as well as the power to place professional officers in command of Guard divisions and brigades, except where those units were contained within one state. Individual Guardsmen now had to take an oath of loyalty not only to the state but also to the United States. Should any state refuse to comply with the mandates of the act, the War Department had authority to cut off all federal aid.[47]

What had been the Division of Militia Affairs was redesignated the Militia Bureau. Although the entire organized militia was referred to in the act as the National Guard, the unorganized militia continued in being, made up of all able-bodied men between the ages of 18 and 45. In this way, the act confirmed the existence of a universal military obligation, but it did not attempt to translate this into UMT. Reaffirmation of the amorphous grouping known as the unorganized militia as well as the existence of some naval militia made it necessary to name the agency the Militia Bureau rather than the National Guard Bureau. This bureau was shifted from the office of the chief of staff of the army to the direct control of the secretary of war, a transfer which the Guard leaders welcomed since they had come to think of the chief of staff as an enemy. The chief of the Militia Bureau still had to be a regular officer, but for the first time he could employ two Guard officers in his office. The first acting chief, Colonel G. W. McIver saw no way for the reserve system to work unless fed by UMT.[48]

The unorganized militia included all able-bodied males without regard to color, but the role of blacks in the organized militia was second class. A white regular captain on duty with the Kansas Guard protested the use as servants of all Negroes who came to summer camp. This practice, he said, defrauded the taxpayers, who were paying to train soldiers not servants. But the prejudice throughout the nation was too great to overcome in the Guard. In fact, the regular army did all it could to discourage blacks from attending summer camps. Even the CMTC felt obliged to plan for a separate camp for well-to-do blacks in the summer of 1917, a plan which American entry into the war canceled.[49]

While the place of the National Guard in the efficient military force continued to develop, the Guard went ahead doing what it had always done at the state level. The disasters in which Guardsmen were called to help were legion, but the one that compelled international attention was the San Francisco earthquake in 1906. Authorities divided the stricken city into districts and assigned one of them to the National Guard. The mayor charged it with highhanded arrests; a local paper accused the men of looting. The governor of California, however, upon investigation branded these accusations as "absurd and cowardly." The citizens of the district assigned to the Guard wrote, "We have been able to retire to our houses at night with a feeling of perfect security" and requested continued Guard protection.[50]

Florida, from 1898 to 1916, called out part of its Guard twenty-one times, all but six of them to prevent lynching of black men. Missouri was unique in making the cadet corps of the state university a part of its organized militia. It also permitted the regular officer, detailed to service at the university to organize a company of coeds. Enoch Crowder, the regular involved, on his own authority permitted the women to drill without their corsets. Rates paid by the states for drill varied from nothing in some to ten cents per drill in West Virginia and $1.25 per day for summer camp, while an officer at camp received two-thirds of the pay of a regular officer of the same grade.[51]

Industrial strife brought about calls for the organized militia. In 1902, the coal miners struck in West Virginia, whereupon the mine operators brought pressure on the governor to use the Guard to break the strike. The governor called out the troops not to break the strike but to keep the peace. Results were good; the relationship between the strikers and the Guardsmen was virtually cordial. Indeed, the strikers requested that the Guard continue on duty to protect them from the Mine Guards, hired by the operators who, the miners said, were little better than thugs. Public esteem dropped, however, when the Guard carried out orders to evict the miners from the cabins owned by the operators. The entire state Guard, 1,000 enlisted men and their officers, were on active duty at a cost in the end of about $400,000.[52]

Across the border in Pennsylvania, the situation was close to open warfare. The operators at first tried to rely on their own Coal and Iron Police, but when violence increased the governor called out the entire state division of 8,750 men on October 6, 1902. The commanding general ordered his men to arrest anyone who obstructed troop movements and to fire upon persons who used weapons, even bricks and stones thrown by hand. In spite of this, Guard-miner friction remained low. When the operators requested President Theodore Roosevelt to send regulars to break the strike, he refused and instead used his power to enforce bargaining. The Guard meanwhile did a great deal to keep the level of violence low.[53]

All 290 men of the Utah National Guard remained on state duty for sixty-two days in 1903 in Carbon County. In Colorado, organized militia and striking miners fought a fifteen-hour battle. When the Guardsmen burned the strikers' tent city, violence escalated, and after ten days, the president sent a detachment of regulars. In Seattle, Washington, the greatest strike ever to occur in the city took place in 1916, but the governor handled it so skillfully that the Guard was neither needed nor used.[54]

In general, organized labor considered the National Guard to be an enemy. The leaders of the Guard, recognizing that this antagonism hurt their chances to be part of the efficient national military force, wanted to see special constabularies formed to deal with industrial strife, thus relieving the Guard of the onus.[55] Over a long period of time the industrial states moved in the direction the Guard leaders recommended. The editors of the *National Guardsman* saw honor in the Guard's role in industrial warfare. The duty of the Guard, they wrote, was to stamp out anarchy and to reinstate civil processes. To carry this out Guardsmen need not be reluctant to use their firearms because the life of one of them was worth the lives of hundreds of those miscreants "engaged in destroying and trampling underfoot the rights, liberties, and laws of the people." To the editors the labor agitators were not true American laborers but the "scum of foreign countries."[56]

In March 1916, Francisco (Pancho) Villa shot up the town of Columbus, New Mexico, killing seventeen citizens of the United States and wounding many more. Villa gave the National Guard its first opportunity in the twentieth century to function as part of the national military force against an enemy. Two months after the Columbus affair, President Wilson called the Guards of Texas (3,381 men), New Mexico (972 men), and Arizona (907 men) into federal service. On June 16, he called the entire National Guard—123,605 enlisted men and 8,589 officers—through the governors to duty on the border but attempted to limit the participation of black Guardsmen. Many units had to travel long distances to reach the border, and some of them had to increase their strength by 50 percent before they could even start. Apparently, the president issued his call primarily to test the capability of the Guard to mobilize as part of the national military force. The Guard he summoned was, after all, 97,350 men short of war strength and 4,083 short of peace strength. Recognizing the pressure put on the Guard system, the War Department advised the states' adjutants general not to try to conform to the requirements of the National Defense Act which had become law only fifteen days earlier.[57]

While the Guardsmen gathered in their rendez-vous areas, about 60 percent of the regular army was concentrating near the Mexican border. President Wilson directed Brigadier General John J. Pershing to take a provisional division of regulars and pursue Villa into Mexico. Pershing entered Mexico with about 12,000 men, none of them National Guard. Since Wilson had made the call for the Guard under the militia clause of the Constitution, the units of the Guard remained intact. By July 1, 1916, only two weeks after being summoned, 110,957 Guardsmen had reached the Mexican border, while 40,149 were mobilized but held in state camps. In these two weeks, the Guard had enlarged itself by roughly 20,000 men. Because it lacked essential equipment and certainly much discipline, its performance was spotty. Floyd Gibbons, writing for the *Chicago Tribune*, dealt harshly with the

Guard's performance. In contrast, Newton D. Baker, who had replaced Lindley Garrison as secretary of war, expressed admiration for the Guard's spirit and the speed of its response. Major General Hugh L. Scott, Army Chief of Staff, simply stated that it would have taken six more months of training to make the Guard ready for combat.[58]

About one-quarter of the Guardsmen mobilized for the Mexican border proved to be physically unfit for service. Another 10 percent never bothered to answer the call, while 17 percent were excused from duty because of dependents. For those in the latter group who elected to remain on duty, Congress appropriated $1,000,000 to be paid to their families at the rate of $50.00 per month if they had no other support.[59]

Turbulence resulting from the federal call was universal. The entire Utah National Guard consisted of five companies of infantry, one troop of cavalry, and one battery of field artillery. The War Department directed Utah to convert the infantry to cavalry and combine it with the one existing troop into a squadron. In addition, Utah was ordered to provide a field hospital and a sanitary detachment. The state somehow accomplished all this and sent its men off with a rousing patriotic demonstration.[60]

Many Guardsmen went to the border hoping to get into a quick fight and go home covered with glory. Instead, they camped on the United States side of the national boundary, fighting nothing but heat, insects, and boredom. Most of them served an average of nine months during which, however reluctantly, they gained a great deal of valuable experience. The Mexican rehearsal was especially worthwhile for officers and for state staff who had to direct mobilization. Two major generals and twenty-four brigadiers from the Guard gained priceless experience in handling big units. Forty-four regular officers, assigned to the Guard, had a chance to command large numbers of men for the first time.[61]

Two historians who have dealt with the National Guard assert that in the period between the War with Spain and the Great War the Guard had to fight for its life. Other historians have suggested that the experience on the Mexican border saved the Guard.[62] The Guard was, in fact, saved because of the way in which a broader problem was resolved, namely, if the United States would either rely on a citizen army, summoned in times of need, or support at all times a middle-sized standing army dominated by professional officers. Emory Upton, although long dead, gave the definitive expression to the professional position, and he supplied the ideas which Elihu Root, as far as it was politically possible, embraced. The most influential spokesman on the other side was Major General Leonard Wood. Wood's insistence that

I am the Guard

Civilian in Peace, Soldier in War . . . of security and honor, for three centuries I have been the custodian, I am the Guard.

I was with Washington in the dim forests, fought the wily warrior, and watched the dark night bow to the morning. At Concord's bridge, I fired the fateful shot heard 'round the world. I bled on Bunker Hill. My footprints marked the snows at Valley Forge. I pulled a muffled oar on the barge that bridged the icy Delaware. I stood with Washington on the sun-drenched heights of Yorktown. I saw the sword surrendered . . . I am the Guard. I pulled the trigger that loosed the long rifle's havoc at New Orleans. These things I knew — I was there! I saw both sides of the War between the States — I was there! The hill at San Juan felt the fury of my charge. The far plains and mountains of the Philippines echoed to my shout . . . On the Mexican border I stood . . . I am the Guard. The dark forest of the Argonne blazed with my barrage. Chateau Thierry crumbled to my cannonade. Under the arches of victory I marched in legion — I was there! I am the Guard. I bowed briefly on the grim Corregidor, then saw the light of liberation shine on the faces of my comrades. Through the jungle and on the beaches, I fought the enemy, beat, battered and broke him. I raised our banner to the serene air on Okinawa — I scrambled over Normandy's beaches — I was there! . . . I am the Guard. Across the 38th Parallel I made my stand. I flew MIG Alley — I was there! . . . I am the Guard.

Soldier in war, civilian in peace . . . I am the Guard.

I was at Johnstown, where the raging waters boomed down the valley. I cradled the crying child in my arms and saw the terror leave her eyes. I moved through smoke and flame at Texas City. The stricken knew the comfort of my skill. I dropped the food that fed the starving beast on the frozen fields of the west and through the towering drifts I ploughed to rescue the marooned. I have faced forward to the tornado, the typhoon, and the horror of the hurricane and flood — these things I know — I was there! . . . I am the Guard. I have brought a more abundant, a fuller, a finer life to our youth. Wherever a strong arm and valiant spirit must defend the Nation, in peace or war, wherever a child cries, or a woman weeps in time of disaster, there I stand . . . I am the Guard. For three centuries a soldier in war, a civilian in peace — of security and honor, I am the custodian, now and forever . . . I am the Guard.

I am the Guard. (NATIONAL GUARD ASSOCIATION)

North Regiment, Massachusetts Bay Colony, 1636. Drawn by Hugh Charles
McBarron, this picture accurately shows the carry-over from the European
heritage of armor and polearms—of little use in North America. The 182d
Infantry, Massachusetts National Guard, is the official inheritor of the
lineage of this, the oldest English military unit in North America. (THE
COMPANY OF MILITARY HISTORIANS)

Bunker Hill, June 17, 1775. In this splendid rendition of citizen soldiers versus regulars, eighteenth-century style, the officer is passing down the line giving his men an order that has become a colloquial expression in the United States: "Don't fire until you see the whites of their eyes." (A NATIONAL GUARD HERITAGE PAINTING)

Battle of the Thames, October 5, 1813. The Regiment of Kentucky Mounted Riflemen riding down the attenuated British line, using unorthodox weapons for horse troops: long rifles and tomahawks. (A NATIONAL GUARD HERITAGE PAINTING)

Caricature of a militia muster in Boston, 1835. Ridicule of this sort accompanied the decline of the militia following the War of 1812, and was part of the pressure to do away with the institution. (ANNE S.K. BROWN MILITARY COLLECTION, BROWN UNIVERSITY LIBRARY)

Soldiers of the 4th Michigan Volunteer Infantry Regiment in the Civil War. A liberated black man crouching behind. (NATIONAL ARCHIVES)

5th Ohio Volunteer Regiment breaking camp during the War with Spain. (NATIONAL ARCHIVES)

6th Maryland Regiment firing on the rioters in Baltimore during the Great Railroad Strike of 1877. (J.H. McCabe, *History of the Great Riots*, 1877)

Strike Duty, Lawrence, Massachusetts, January 1912. By this time there was greater reluctance to fire into crowds than was evinced a quarter of a century earlier. (Library of Congress)

Battery A, 1st Field Artillery, California National Guard, 1915. Typical equipment and road conditions of that time; but this equipment was borrowed from a private supplier as the Guard had not yet acquired automotive vehicles. (NATIONAL GUARD ASSOCIATION)

Major General John F. O'Ryan inspecting his 27th Division with George V, King of England, during World War I. O'Ryan was the only National Guard division commander to start the war, go through it, and finish it with his Division. (NATIONAL ARCHIVES)

The 369th Infantry in action with the French during the Meuse-Argonne offensive. One-third of the men were casualties in this engagement on September 29, 1918. The 369th, formed from the 15th New York National Guard Regiment, a black regiment except for white officers, was attached to the French Army throughout World War I. (A NATIONAL GUARD HERITAGE painting originally done by Hugh Charles McBarron for the *Army in Action* series)

Major General Charles W.J. Dick, Ohio National Guard, and longtime Ohio representative and then senator in Congress. Dick introduced what became the Dick Act of 1903—the act that repealed the Uniform Militia Act of 1792 and opened the way for modernization of the militia/National Guard. (ADJUTANT GENERAL'S DEPARTMENT, STATE OF OHIO)

Major General George Collins Rickards, Pennsylvania National Guard, who in 1921 became the first Guardsman to become CNGB. (NATIONAL GUARD ASSOCIATION)

Major General Ellard A. Walsh, President, NGA, from 1943 to 1957, who worked tirelessly and effectively to maintain the Guard as an important part of the American military system. (NATIONAL GUARD ASSOCIATION)

MAJ. GEN. E. A. WALSH.
PRESIDENT

Major General Milton A. Reckord, regimental and division commander, and Adjutant General of Maryland for forty-five years. Powerful supporter of the Guard during eight decades. (NATIONAL GUARD ASSOCIATION)

Robert S. McNamara, eighth Secretary of Defense, 1961-1968. He undertook to concentrate all ground reserve units in the Army National Guard, leaving only individuals in the Army Reserve. This failed, but his impact on the National Guard was lasting. (OFFICIAL DEPARTMENT OF DEFENSE PHOTO)

Urgency of Guard duty. Guardsman has left a wedding party to report for active duty in 1961. (OFFICIAL PHOTO, VIRGINIA AIR NATIONAL GUARD)

Happiness is return from duty faithfully performed, 1962. (NATIONAL GUARD ASSOCIATION)

When a tornado destroyed more than 30 percent of Xenia, Ohio, in 1974, the Ohio National Guard took up its perennial task of rescue and relief. (NATIONAL GUARD ASSOCIATION)

Two-page ad, run in magazines with nation-wide circulation in 1974—part of the drive for recruits after the draft ended. (NATIONAL GUARD ASSOCIATION)

Rescue of a lost child. (NATIONAL GUARD ASSOCIATION)

What the National Guard had to fly in when it first took to the air. A
Gallaudet Military biplane of the 1st Battalion, Signal Corps, New York
National Guard, 1915. (NATIONAL GUARD ASSOCIATION)

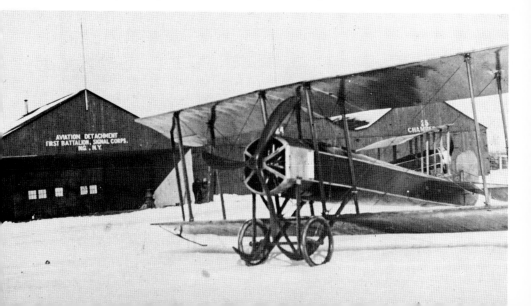

TAC fighter-bomber F-105D in the Air Guard inventory in the 1960s flies beside the P-47, the first fighter craft the Air National Guard flew after World War II. (National Guard Association)

Women break into the Guard. Flight nurses, Pennsylvania National Guard in 1964. (National Guard Association)

citizens could be trained in a few months to be good soldiers was unacceptable to the hard-core professionals. Wood himself was barely acceptable to them. He had, after all, started out as a medical doctor and had slipped into a military career because of problems encountered as an intern. He never championed the National Guard nor became acceptable to them as a spokesman, because he wanted a reserve made up of individuals who had been trained in UMT, whereas the Guard stood for a reserve consisting of units that trained together in peacetime.[63]

As the events that shaped America's military future succeeded one another—the Dick Act and its modifications, the defeat of the concept of the Continental Army, the preparedness movement—Wood pressed steadily to wake America up to its defense needs as he saw them. As a result, by the time war broke out in Europe, the United States had, without really knowing it, opted for a citizen army. The concession made to the Uptonians was that this army would be trained and led almost altogether by professional officers, who discovered that they could, when they had to, develop a respectable army of citizen soldiers in much less time than they had believed possible. Wood had been right. Among the men that stand out in this period—Charles Dick, James Hay, Claude Kitchin in the House of Representatives; George Chamberlain in the Senate; Major Generals Leonard Wood and Fred Ainsworth in the military; and Root and Theodore Roosevelt in the executive branch—the National Guard found enough champions to maintain its foothold and to see itself established as the principal part of such reserve as the nation had.[64]

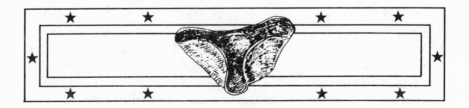

ELEVEN

The National Guard in World War I

In January 1917, President Woodrow Wilson, addressing the United States Senate, urged the belligerent powers in Europe to accept a peace without victory. As his own nation became more deeply ensnared in belligerence, Wilson continued to think of the American role as a lofty one. Finally, on April 2, 1917, he felt obliged to appear before Congress to ask for a declaration of war against Germany. "The right," he said, "is more precious than peace," and he contended for the rest of his life that in this conflict the United States was the disinterested champion of right.[1] He spoke of making the world safe for democracy and of waging war to end war once and for all as America's goals. Congress declared war by joint resolution on April 6.

Wilson recognized the importance of the citizen soldier. "It is not an army that we must shape and train," he said, "it is a nation."[2] The National Guard, based as it was on a citizenry trained for defense, found the president's rhetoric appealing, and its leaders set about rebuilding their units which in many cases had declined. Service on the Mexican border had cooled Guard enthusiasm. No less a person than Leonard Wood, recently Army Chief of Staff, had pronounced the Guard mobilization an utter failure. The chief of the Militia Bureau—expressing more a regular army view than a Guard one, as he himself was a regular officer—said that the Guard had proved on the border to be "an expensive system to the nation and to the individual." As for the Guardsmen who had participated, they had found camp life boring and had felt defrauded because they had not had a chance to fight.[3] Nevada and New Mexico now had no active units at all, and in California the companies had dropped to an average size of eleven men. But as American participation in the war loomed, interest in the Guard picked up. California improved its mode of officer selection and began to enlarge its units. In March 1917, there was everywhere a marked buildup of enrollment.[4]

Meanwhile in Washington, a fierce struggle went on over the best way to raise the huge army now obviously needed. The issue was between volunteering and drafting. Senator Robert La Follette of Wisconsin demanded a referendum if Congress chose the latter, on the grounds that a democracy ought not to fight a war it could not man with volunteers. In contrast, the National Guard generally favored a draft to stimulate voluntary enrollments in its units. President Wilson himself, as early as February 1917, seems to have turned to conscription but not as the sole means of gathering manpower. For the regular army and for the National Guard he would stick to volunteering, but for the balance of the army, which came to be referred to as the National Army, he wanted conscription as the exclusive means of enlargement.[5] A draft bill, formed along those lines, went to Congress on April 7, the day after the declaration of war. Then followed a heated debate which occupied the rest of April and half of May. Out of that emerged "An Act Authorizing the President to Increase Temporarily the Military Establishment of the United States," signed into law on May 18, 1917. It empowered the president to raise half a million men at once and another half million at his discretion. If the president judged that the regular army and the National Guard could not be filled by volunteering, he could apply the draft to those two components as well. The National Army was to be dependent on the draft altogether. One clause permitted the president to raise four divisions in the National Army by volunteering if he chose to do so. That clause was for the benefit of Theodore Roosevelt and other near-jingoists who wanted a chance personally to lead divisions in combat. Wilson refused to grant this desire, especially to Roosevelt, an old and bitter political rival. Through section 111 of the National Defense Act of 1916, the president had the power to draft all members of the National Guard, a power reconfirmed in the new conscription statute.[6]

The 1917 system, known as Selective Service, profiting from studies made of the Civil War draft avoided some egregious mistakes. It eliminated exemption by commutation and by substitute, and it forbade bounties. It provided for the registration of all men, first those aged 21 through 30, later 18 through 45. A total of 24,000,000 men registered. The next step was selection, which began with a lottery; the president himself drew the first numbers from a huge tank. The holders of those numbers in every draft district of the nation then became liable to be drafted. The 4,648 local boards took up the task of determining who must enter the service, who might be deferred, and who would be permanently exempted. These boards operated under the supervision of the judge advocate general of the army, Enoch Crowder, and the adjutants general of the several states. To the men picked to serve went out notification, opening with a clause that was perpetuated in later drafts, "Greetings, Your neighbors have selected you. . . ." Despite dire warnings based on the Civil War experience, Selective Service brought 2,810,296 men into the armed forces without riots, and turned up only 295,184 cases of draft delinquency.[7]

Before war was declared, the president had begun to call National Guard units into federal service on March 25, 1917, to guard bridges and other sensitive areas from possible sabotage. By July 15, 44 percent of the Guard was enrolled, and on that day Wilson called the entire Guards of eleven states. Three days later, the War Department published a list of sixteen divisions into which the Guard was to be formed and specified the units to go into each one. Finally, the president summoned the entire National Guard into federal service on July 25. He had made all the calls up to this point under the militia clauses of the Constitution; thus, the units retained their identity as part of the National Guard.[8]

When war was declared, the strength of the Guard stood at 177,000, but four months later it had risen to 377,000, partly because of the stimulation to volunteering which the draft act provided. The chief of the Militia Bureau announced that the Guard divisions were ready any time facilities were available for them. Whether this was true or not, the president on August 5, 1917, exercised his power to draft the Guardsmen into federal service as individuals. He did this because under the earlier calls, the units of the Guard remained more or less inviolate and their use subject to the traditional limitations of the militia.[9] Drafted, too, were the 4,443 individual members of the National Guard Reserve, a reserve created by the National Defense Act of 1916. The August 5 draft of the Guardsmen drew its justification from the acts of June 3, 1916, and May 18, 1917, which in turn rested not on the militia clauses but upon the army clause of the Constitution. That clause grants to Congress the power to raise and support armies and imposes no qualification whatever. Once drafted the men ceased to have any legal connection with the National Guard and became instead individual members of the United States Army. The draft act stipulated that the Guard units were to retain their identities "so far as practicable," but it did not turn out to be so, and the units were swallowed up in a mechanistic system devised for this war. All draftees, including Guardsmen, were to serve as long as the national emergency lasted.

The War Department laid a uniform numbering system upon the three components of the ground forces. It reserved the bloc of numbers from 26 through 75 for National Guard divisions, 51 through 150 for Guard brigades, and 101 through 300 for the infantry and artillery regiments of the Guard. These numbers were middle blocs, below which were the units of the regular army and above which was the National Army, that is, the units created altogether by the draft.[10]

The Guard divisions traveled to warm parts of the country for assembly and training: Camps Fremont and Kearny in California; Cody in New Mexico; Bowie, Logan, and MacArthur in Texas; Doniphan in Oklahoma; Beauregard in Louisiana; Shelby in Mississippi; Sheridan and McClellan in Alabama; Wheeler and Hancock in Georgia; Sevier and Wadsworth in South Carolina; and Green in North Carolina. The movement of around a third of a million men to these camps placed a severe strain on the railroad system. Nevertheless, the transfer was completed between August 15 and October 15, 1917. In their camps, the Guardsmen lived in tents, whereas the regulars and the National Army men, camping in colder areas, had to have heated barracks. For this and for other reasons, the average cost of a Guard cantonment was $4,500,000 compared to $12,500,000 for the regulars and for the National Army.[11]

With the entire National Guard in federal service, only the adjutants general and their headquarters staffs remained in the states. They were never considered a part of the Guard that could be taken into federal service. Since the states needed some sort of force available at home, State or Home Guards came into being. Because some states were slow to constitute these, the War Department took the lead, creating the United States Guard by General Orders 162 dated December 22, 1917. The chief of the Militia Bureau was made responsible for organizing it. At its peak strength, the United States Guard included forty-eight battalions with 1,194 officers and 25,068 enlisted men. Many of its members had been Guardsmen who on account of squaring the divisions or for other reasons had been sloughed from their original units. A fair share of the officers were businessmen who had a personal interest in preserving law and order. Much of their training was in riot control.[12]

President Wilson and Newton D. Baker, Secretary of War, chose Major General John J. Pershing over five senior general officers to command the American Expeditionary Force (AEF). Pershing decided that the United States must have a far heavier division than any of the

European belligerents, a division with enough weight to break through enemy lines and penetrate their rear positions. It was called a square division, made up of two brigades of infantry with two regiments in each, one brigade of artillery, containing three regiments, three machine gun battalions, plus a complement of supporting troops.[13] Pershing's division, with 991 officers and 27,114 enlisted men, was more than double the size of any division in use in the war. The Guard divisions were triangular at the time, that is, they consisted of three infantry regiments, no brigades, and a scaled-down representation of the other divisional elements. Conversion to the square configuration created great turbulence and much dislocation of people. The standard process was to dump surplus personnel into depot organizations. When the 26th Division was squared, it sent 217 officers and 3,674 enlisted men into the 51st Depot Brigade, a unit destined to function throughout in support only. While this transfer of men went on, draftees came into the Guard units with no training at all and devoid of unit loyalty.[14]

Guardsmen never doubted that the arithmetical manner of organizing the United States Army failed to utilize most of the esprit existing in National Guard units. It blotted out the identity of old units, rich in tradition; for example, the 69th New York, the Irish Regiment organized in 1849, became one battalion of the newly created 165th Infantry Regiment, a part of the 42nd Division. The old 6th Massachusetts sent men to three brand-new regiments, and its leftovers went to the 51st Depot Brigade. The same fate overtook the 1st New Hampshire, the 1st Vermont, and the 5th Massachusetts Infantry Regiments.[15] The famous 2nd Pennsylvania Infantry turned into the 108th Field Artillery Battalion, and the men of the First Troop of Philadelphia City Cavalry found themselves cadre for the 103rd Trench Mortar Battery. The 1st Illinois Infantry from Chicago, diluted with draftees became the anonymous 131st Infantry; the Richmond Light Infantry Blues from Richmond, Virginia, turned into artillery.[16]

Some of the loyalty was transferred to the newly created Guard divisions, but it vanished from many units because they became support outfits with no chance to earn military distinction. The 31st, 39th, 40th, and 41st turned into depot divisions, while the 34th and 38th became manpower pools through which men passed on their way to combat units. Table 11.1 shows the deployment of all National Guard divisions.[17]

Militant Guardsmen have maintained through the years that the army general staff set out purposely during this war to destroy the identity of the Guard units and in other ways to discredit the Guard. Even though most of the histories of the National Guard divisions are

Table 11.1
National Guard Divisions in World War I

#	States	Popular Name	Infantry Brigs.	Infantry Regts.	FA Brigs.	FA Regts.	Machine Gun Bns.	Hqs. in France	Killed	Wounded	Replacements	Days in line
26	Connecticut, Maine, Vermont, New Hampshire, Massachusetts, Rhode Island,	Yankee	51, 52	101, 102 103, 104	51	101, 102 103	101, 102 103	Oct. 28, 1917	2,281	11,383	14,411	205
27	New York	New York	53, 54	105, 106 107, 108	52	104, 105 106	104, 105 106	May 31, 1918	1,829	6,505	5,255	57
28	Pennsylvania	Keystone	55, 56	109, 110 111, 112	53	107, 108 109	107, 108 109	May 18, 1918	2,874	11,265	21,717	102
29	District of Columbia, Delaware, Maryland, New Jersey, Virginia	Blue & Gray	57, 58	113, 114 115, 116	54	110, 111 112	110, 111 112	June 28, 1918	1,653	4,517	4,977	82
30	North & South Carolina, Tennessee	Old Hickory	59, 60	117, 118 119, 120	55	113, 114 115	113, 114 115	May 24, 1918	1,641	6,774	2,384	69
31	Alabama, Georgia, Florida	Dixie	61, 62	121, 122 123, 124	56	116, 117 118	116, 117 118	Oct. 15, 1918	Became 7th Depot Division			
32	Michigan, Wisconsin	Iron Jaws	63, 64	125, 126 127, 128	57	119, 120 121	119, 120 121	Feb. 20, 1918	3,028	10,233	20,140	100
33	Illinois	Prairie	65, 66	129, 130 131, 132	58	122, 123 124	122, 123 124	May 24, 1918	993	5,871	5,415	98
34	Iowa, Minnesota, Nebraska	Sandstorm	67, 68	133, 134 135, 136	59	125, 126 127	125, 126 127	Oct. 3, 1918	Replacement Division			
35	Kansas, Missouri		69, 70	137, 138 139, 140	60	128, 129 130	128, 129 130	May 11, 1918	1,298	5,998	10,605	110

TABLE 11.1

National Guard Divisions in World War I

36	Texas, Oklahoma	Lone Star	71, 72	141, 142 143, 144	131, 132 133	July 30, 1918	591	1,993	3,397	19
37	Ohio	Buckeye	73, 74	145, 146 147, 148	134, 135 136	June 23, 1918	1,066	4,321	6,282	77
38	Indiana, Kentucky, West Virginia	Cyclone	75, 76	149, 150 151, 152	137, 138 139	Oct. 4, 1918	Replacement Division			
39	Arkansas, Louisiana, Mississippi	Delta	77, 78	153, 154 155, 156	140, 141 142	Aug. 27, 1918	Became 5th Depot Division			
40	California, Nevada, New Mexico, Arizona, Colorado, Utah	Sunshine	79, 80	157, 158 159, 160	143, 144 145	Aug. 24, 1918	Became 6th Depot Division			
41	Idaho, Montana, Washington, Wyoming	Sunset	81, 82	161, 162 163, 164	146, 147 148	Dec. 31, 1918	Became 1st Depot Division			
42	Alabama, California, Colorado, Georgia, Illinois, Indiana, Iowa, Kansas, Louisiana, Maryland, Michigan, Minnesota, Missouri, Nebraska, New Jersey, New York, North Carolina, Ohio, Oklahoma, Oregon, Pennsylvania, South Carolina, Tennessee, Texas, Virginia, Wisconsin, District of Columbia	Rainbow	83, 84	165, 166 167, 168	149, 150 151	Nov. 1, 1917	2,810	11,873	17,253	176

Source: *American Armies and Battlefields in Europe* (American Battle Monuments Commission, 1938), pp. 515–517.

written as straightforward narratives of combat with emphasis on the courage of the Guardsmen and the resourcefulness of their officers, some of the more candid ones let antagonism toward the professionals creep through. A historian of the 28th Division said that the soldiers in his division were the sort "before the war held in huge contempt by the average regular officer." Describing a valorous stand made by part of the division, he took pains to stress that it was made by "erstwhile despised National Guardsmen." Major General John F. O'Ryan, Commanding General of the 27th Division, New York National Guard, asserted after the war that regular officers had not kept in close enough touch with a changing America to realize, that they could not apply the old regular army methods to the citizen soldiers in this modern, mass war.[18]

It was not the shift from triangular to square divisions alone that produced turbulence for Guardsmen. By the time the United States entered the war it was plain that in the machine gun era cavalry would not play a large role. This brought about redesignation of almost all the Guard cavalry to artillery, which usually meant that it was separated from the other units of its parent state. The Utah cavalry was converted to field artillery, then shipped to California to become organic to the 40th Division. There it became the 145th Field Artillery, equipped with 4.7 inch guns instead of the 3 inch guns it had arrived with. Soon the 40th was made into the Sixth Depot Division, at which time the 389 members of the 145th were sent off as individuals as fillers for other units.[19] It was quite rare that the division artillery of one of the Guard divisions stayed with it. Usually, it was detached in whole or in pieces and was never returned to the parent division. A great deal of infantry underwent conversion to machine guns, mortars, or signal corps, and even engineering and other technical branches. If the officers in the converted units were slow in picking up the new skills, entirely alien to them, regular officers were quick to relieve them.[20]

The ultimate homogenization of the three components of the army came on July 31, 1918, when General Peyton C. March, Chief of Staff, issued General Orders 73 stating that "this country has but one army," the Army of the United States.[21] Thereafter, Guardsmen had to strip off any insignia they might have retained from the state affiliation and put on the simple lapel disc with U. S. on it. For this and for other reasons, partisans of the National Guard place March at the top of the list of regulars whom they considered to be hostile. None other than General Pershing himself sided with the Guard to the extent that he admitted in a postwar hearing that the army had never during the conflict given the Guard its wholehearted support.[22]

Resentment among disaffected Guardsmen centered on the way

the professionals handled Guard officers. Eleven Guard generals who had been considered fit enough for service on the Mexican border were immediately declared physically unfit for service in Europe. The War Department summoned 12,115 officers from the Guard at the start, but within a year it removed 501 of them for physical disability, permitted 638 others to resign, and through efficiency boards reclassified 341 others.[23] Although this left most of the original officers, that is, 10,602 of them, in place or at least in service, it seemed to observant Guardsmen that the replacements for the relieved ones, more often than not commissioned straight from civilian life, certainly had less experience than their predecessors and apparently also less aptitude.

Cases involving general officers were, of course, more conspicuous. Only one Guard general, called into service with his division, was still in command of the division at war's end; this was Major General John F. O'Ryan, 27th Division, New York National Guard. Certain of the regular generals, who earned the loyalty of their Guard subordinates, were relieved. A celebrated case was that of Major General Clarence E. Edwards, commanding the 26th New England Division. Edwards had retained most of the National Guard colonels and one brigadier when he took over the division from its National Guard general. He had won the confidence of the division by sending its units as soon as they were formed directly to ports of embarkation. Thus, before the army staff and the War Department realized it, the 26th was ready to be shipped to Europe, ahead of most regular divisions. As a result, it compiled the longest combat record of any of the Guard divisions. The high command, whatever its reasons, relieved Edwards on the eve of America's greatest battle up to that time, the Meuse-Argonne campaign, and replaced him with Brigadier General Frank E. Bamford. The new general at once removed two of the Guard colonels and the commander of the 52nd Infantry Brigade. All three had started as privates in the original Guard units and had worked their way up. They were popular with the men. The division historian wrote of this action, "Once more one witnessed the apparent blindness of those who, conducting the game of war, neglect to consider the psychology of the pawns on the chessboard."[24]

Brigadier General John A. Hulen of the 36th Division was one Guard general who lasted the entire war. Less fortunate was Brigadier General Charles I. Martin, commanding the 70th Infantry Brigade of the 35th Division. Martin had started his military career as an enlisted man in the Kansas National Guard many years before and was popular with the men. Command of the division was given to Major General Peter E. Traub, West Point, class of 1886. On the eve of the Meuse-Argonne campaign Traub relieved Martin. The division historian speaks bitterly of this action, "More of us," he wrote, "would have come out of the Argonne with [Martin] in command of the 70th Brigade." He continued that Traub's "dislike for anything National Guard overshadowed his desire for efficiency."[25]

The constant relieving of officers seemed to some observers to be more a device to bring in favored regular army replacements than to improve combat efficiency. To fill the vacancies, only one-third rose from promotions within the division, while two-thirds came in from outside, most of them regulars with no combat experience. The rate of flow may be judged from the 109th Infantry, 28th Division, which had eight commanding colonels in two months, six of whom were regulars.[26]

The *Salt Lake Tribune* even assailed the highest placed of all officers, General Pershing. Full of enthusiasm for the war, it described the departure of the Utah Guard artillery thus, "All the bouyancy of youth [was] in their step . . . [they] went forth with smiles on their faces to do their duty for liberty, justice and humanity." How bitter then was their disillusionment when the 40th Division, of which they became a part, was designated the Sixth Depot Division, certain to see no combat at all. The *Tribune* claimed that the degradation of the 40th into depot status was due to the personal antipathy which Pershing felt for its commander, Major General F. S. Strong.[27]

The suspicions of the Guardsmen do not necessarily reflect the truth, but they do indicate an ingredient in the armed forces that cannot be expunged. It is true that more Guard officers remained in responsible positions than otherwise; Jim Dan Hill, historian of the Guard and himself a major general in it, gives the typical pattern within a Guard division: the commanding general, one infantry brigade commander, and the division artillery brigade commander were regulars, but one brigade commander was National Guard. The commanding general would have a staff of a dozen officers who were regulars, but all the rest of the officers would have come from the Guard. In addition, Guard officers were assigned posts in the drafted divisions. The Massachusetts Military Academy, an adjunct of the State Guard, sent 600 officers out into the Army of the United States, and the New York system contributed 5,000.[28]

It was not discrimination against the National Guard that placed regulars in most of the general officer posts. The American military system was built on the premise that the military academies existed to provide the highest leadership in time of war. Thus, professionals were also placed in command of the divisions formed from drafted men. There were seventeen of these, and eleven of them were commanded by West Pointers who had been graduated during the 1880s, the same vintage as commanded the Guard divisions. The professionals expected to be inconspicuous during peacetime, but when the threat of war or war itself came, it was their right, as they saw it, to take command.[29]

The official lineages of the 26th through the 42nd Divisions belong to the National Guard. Division historians proudly narrate the exploits of these units and connect their courage and skill with their state heritages. But it must be recognized that the seventeen Guard divisions underwent severe dilution to reach war strength at the start and to stay full afterward. Numbers required to achieve table of organization strengths for the square division were as follows: 26th Division, 900 draftees, all from New England; 27th, 2,500, all from New York; 28th was able to enter federal service virtually 100 percent from Pennsylvania; 29th, 6,000 not from the five parent states but from New York; 31st, which soon became a depot division, required 10,000 draftees from the home states and afterward transferred men out constantly and received others in, most of them not from Alabama, Georgia, and Florida but from the Middle West; 35th, 3,000; 36th, 4,000; 38th, 9,800 not from the home states but from Arkansas, Louisiana, and Mississippi. Besides these initial increments, the Guard Divisions subsequently required around 112,000 replacements drawn from the draft (see Table 11.1). Thus, at any given time, the proportion of Guardsmen in Guard divisions varied. At the time of its embarkation, the 37th Division claimed that it was still three-quarters National Guard; at the time of the armistice, the 36th reported that most of its men were not from the Guard.[30]

It seems certain that the National Guard divisions retained a distinctive tone and that they strove to preserve it. In October 1918 the 26th Division adopted the YD (Yankee Division) shoulder patch, which harked back to its New England origin. The division historian asserted that the "spirit, skill, and discipline which made the artillery so valuable (this was one of the rare cases in which the division artillery remained with its parent division) were inherited intact from the original Massachusetts and Connecticut batteries."[31] The historian of the 28th Division wrote throughout as if his division was pure Pennsylvanian. Illinois clung to the 33rd Division as its own; the *Chicago Daily News* sent a respected reporter to follow the division as closely as he could and report its glorious achievements to the folks back home.[32]

The states did not cling tightly to the prewar black units of their Guards. The 8th Illinois Infantry Regiment, composed entirely of Negroes, was not permitted to become a part of the 33rd Division, nor was the 9th Ohio Infantry, all black, allowed to be part of the 37th

Division. The 15th New York Infantry shared the same exclusion. War Department policy was to keep the Negro units out of white divisions but to ship them overseas as fast as possible. One rationale for this was to avoid race riots. The Department constituted two black brigades in November 1917 and added to them the 15th New York, redesignated the 369th Infantry; the 8th Illinois, redesignated 370th; and a 372nd Regiment built up from the DC First Separate Battalion, the Connecticut First Separate Company, Maryland's First Separate Company, Massachusetts First Separate Company, and some small units from Tennessee, all black. Since there was need for a fourth regiment to fill out the two brigades, the 371st Regiment came into being, filled by black conscripts from the South. The other three Negro regiments protested being teamed with untrained and backward men of the sort making up the 371st, but the department made no change. The three were even built up to strength from the same southern source. For the most part, white officers relieved any black ones there might have been. The next step was to create a black division with white officers to accommodate the two brigades. Thus came into being the 93rd Provisional Division, but no supporting units were ever added to the four regiments.[33]

The new provisional division reached France early in 1918 and was at once attached to the French army. The divisional organization did not function, so the four black regiments, operating separately, fought beside the French throughout the war. Even when assigned to an American corps and to the United States First Army, these regiments remained under French control. The French government accorded them commendations, even though the American high command warned it now and then not to show excessive consideration to American Negroes. Since the initial units of the 369th, 370th, 371st, and 372nd came from State Guards, their lineages really belong in the National Guard, regardless of the numbers under which they served. Much later, the Guard welcomed them as part of its tradition.[34]

The 36th Division from Texas and Oklahoma contained more national and racial strains than any other division. Conspicuous in it were American Indians, who were placed in a company of their own so that they could communicate in native tongues. One of these languages had military significance: Choctaw soldiers were placed at both ends of communications, telephone or wire, speaking in their native mode, so that coding the messages was not necessary, since the Germans could not unravel Choctaw. Texas contributed to that division Mexicans, Germans, Irish, Italians, and Swedes, all from somewhere in the state.[35]

General Pershing assumed, incorrectly, that all American troops arriving in Europe had received six months' training in the United States. He intended them to undergo two more months of training overseas and one month in a quiet sector before engaging in active battle. Since all the National Guard divisions had been in federal service since July 25, 1917, and since most of them did not arrive in France for at least another year, they resented additional training. Their dissatisfaction increased when General Pershing insisted on mingling them with the British and French armies for final polish. Some of them, it turned out, developed a keen dislike for the British and especially for the French. A historian of the 35th Division wrote more candidly than was common at this point. "Lafayette," he said, "had been repaid, but the thanks of the French was expressed in increased prices to the soldiers."[36]

Since there was rivalry to get to France early, Lieutenant Colonel Douglas MacArthur suggested a way to prevent jealousy among the states. If some of the units, sloughed by the squaring of National Guard divisions, could be gathered together to form a composite Guard division, honor to many states would result. The War Department accepted this recommendation and on August 1, 1917, it constituted the 42nd Division and made it out of units from twenty-six different states. Thus was formed the Rainbow Division, probably the best known of the Guard divisions. Its headquarters reached France on November 1, 1917, only three days behind the 26th and four months later than the first regular army divisions, the 1st and 2nd.[37]

General Pershing's instructions were to maintain the integrity of the AEF as a separate fighting force. Pershing agreed entirely with this directive and was determined above all that his men and units not be swallowed up in the British and French armies as replacements. To that end, the general forbade the American troops from mingling with the Allies for doctrine or combat. But the Allies had exhausted their reserves, and their leaders subjected Pershing to heavy pressure to be less unbending. Although they failed to dent the general, the Germans succeeded in changing his mind by launching a last-ditch drive in March 1918 to reach the English channel and split the British and French armies apart. It was plainly a time of crisis; they gained more ground on the western front than they had done in years. Pershing therefore offered Marshal Foch, now supreme allied commander, the unrestricted use of his forces. These consisted of four divisions that were ready and five still training in France. The National Guard will always be proud that two of the ready ones were Guard divisions, the 26th and the 42nd. Parts of the 26th fought beside the French at Seicheprey late in April, and units of the 28th Division, ready enough to be used, stood with the French on May 28, 1918, at Cantigny.[38]

The 131st Infantry, 33rd Division, Illinois National Guard, was one of the units training with the British and not deemed ready for combat, certainly not to enter combat in small parcels as part of larger British units. This was the third summer for the Regiment in federal service, and it was tired of preparation and no action. Its British instructors, hard pressed at the Marne salient, begged for immediate help, and Major General George W. Read, Commanding General of the American II Corps, consented to the use of four American companies in an attack, backing up Australian units, upon the key town of Hamel.

General Pershing telephoned that the Americans ought not to take part, but somehow his wishes did not trickle down to E Company of the 131st, whose men were crouched ready to jump off at 3 A. M. on July 4. When the signal to advance came, Company E charged with the Aussies. Soon they were held up by the fire of a machine gun, but not for long. Sprinting zig-zag, Corporal Tom Pope flanked the machine gun position and dived into it before the gunners could turn their weapon upon him. He bayoneted all of them, then swung the gun to support the advance of Company E into Hamel.

When General Pershing heard of this violation of his policy, he ordered the 131st out from British and back under American control, but he never disciplined Read, who continued to command II Corps. He did, however, see to it that no unit smaller than a division would fight again under allied command. As for Corporal Pope, he received from the British the Distinguished Conduct Medal, from the French the Croix de Guerre, and from his own country the Congressional Medal of Honor.[39]

By July 1918, the enormous latent power of the United States was appearing as military might in Europe. From March 21 to July 18, seventeen U. S. divisions arrived in France. This raised the total to twenty-six divisions overseas: eight regular army, eight formed altogether of draftees, and eleven from the National Guard. Seven were fully combat ready and five more were holding quiet near the front lines, but these twelve divisions were each twice the size of the divisions of the other belligerent nations.[40]

Later, when the AEF attained its final strength, it consisted of eight regular, eighteen National Guard (counting the 93rd as National Guard), and seventeen draft divisions. The National Guard had demonstrated that it could ready divisions as fast as the regulars, and, because of prewar organization, could start training six to eight weeks ahead of the divisions composed of draftees. Two-fifths of the AEF soldiers were in Guard units, which sustained two-fifths of all casualties. Of the 1,400,000 men who entered combat, 440,000 came from what were originally National Guard units. Without the Guard mechanism, the

United States would not have been able to express its great power as fast or as effectively as it was able to do.

Combat service in World War I approached the limits of a man's endurance. The artillery barrages, hour after hour, drove some men mad. Burrowing like rodents in trenches and dugouts, more often than not they half-drowned there. Marching in the seemingly endless rain in the dark carrying seventy-eight pounds pushed those who did not lose their sanity close to despair. Swarms of cooties (body lice) took men's minds off larger terrors and gave them an occupation at every pause, taking off their clothes and running their finger nails down the seams. Before the war was over, the quartermaster had organized delousing units in which men were fumigated and their clothes boiled out. Humor saved the Guardsmen, whether serving in their parent units or somewhere else. The historian of the 35th Division affords a sample: "Rats and the troops at a later period developed as congenial bedmates."[41] Looking back on these hardships, a writer for the 29th Division saw a similarity to purification rites. He wrote, "God grant that someday, somehow, that spirit which possessed our fighting citizens . . . may be translated into the civic life of our country."[42]

European doubts of the fighting power of the Americans were dispelled once the troops began to take part. The 32nd Division became known as "Les Terribles." The German high command referred to the Americans as "inhuman foes." Capture, the directive said, "merely means being slowly tortured to death."[43] Of course this was propaganda issued for a purpose, but it showed that the Germans recognized a fighting spirit. The evidence was plain enough. Four companies of the 28th Division, in the front of the Marne line with the French, took the brunt of a German attack and continued to fight hand to hand even after the French had fallen back on both their flanks. The 28th's historian wrote, "The gates to glory and to death swung wide for many a Pennsylvania lad that night."[44]

Guardsmen proved their mettle to themselves as well to the Allies. The artillery of the 39th Division, made up almost entirely of men from Chicago, advanced in early October 1918 right through no-man's land, a standard performance except that every few minutes they would unhitch their horses, swing the guns around, and fire in the direction of the foe.[45] From among thousands of notable performances turned in by Guard units, one example will suffice. On February 28, 1918, the 102nd Infantry Regiment, 26th Division, advanced into forty German batteries that were laying down a barrage and captured them. The colonel commanding the 102nd wrote after this impressive performance that the American militia had reestablished its reputation. "The American militiaman, when he is properly led, is the finest soldier who ever wore shoe leather."[46]

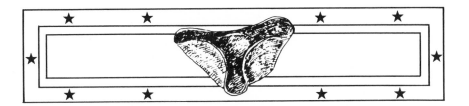

TWELVE

The National Guard between World Wars

The end of the Great War brought with it the usual impulse to reorganize the military establishment. This gave rise to a lively debate, in Congress and outside. Congress had before it three major bills based on UMT. The War Department introduced the Baker-March Bill—named for Secretary of War Newton D. Baker and Army Chief of Staff Peyton C. March—which authorized a regular army of 500,000 men, plus UMT for the 750,000 men who came of military age each year. Some people saw militarism in a force so large. What possible need existed for it?[1]

One answer was that the United States needed to be better prepared at all times for war than it had been at the outset of the Great War. Obvious military strength would deter aggression. Colonel John McAuley Palmer asserted that both the Civil War and the American participation in the Great War could have been prevented if a true citizen army had been in existence.[2] His plan included a national reserve, replenished by men who had passed through UMT. Other supporters of a large regular force backed by UMT suggested that these instruments might be needed to maintain internal order. Supporting organizations banded together into the National Association of Patriotic Societies, determined to see that all able-bodied men would fulfill their duty to help defend the nation. "A nation in arms," they concluded, "will not militarize democracy, but will democratize the military system."[3]

General Pershing was among the first persons called to testify before congressional committees. He was against the large army of the

Baker-March bill, but he was totally in favor of UMT. UMT could inject into the population qualities it badly needed: manliness, discipline, respect for authority, and patriotism; qualities, Pershing said, threatened by the large-scale immigration of ignorant foreigners, highly susceptible to "anarchistic and bolshevik thinking." UMT graduates, the general continued, ought to be placed in a national reserve, deriving its authority from the army clause of the Constitution rather than from the militia clauses. General Leonard Wood, with other persons recognized as authorities, opted, like Pershing, for a national reserve free of state connections.[4]

None of the three proposals left room in the national military establishment for the National Guard. General March, an Uptonian who had never rated the Guard very high, insisted that the Guard could not be used beyond national boundaries, hence had no role except home defense and constabulary duties. The National Guard Association (NGA), undaunted by the heavy brass lined up behind UMT and a national reserve, opposed both systems and set up a special committee to fight them.[5]

The NGA made its points where they counted, to senators and representatives, many of whom were conditioned to favor a state-connected reserve system. These legislators had nothing against a reserve made up of veterans if it was tied somehow to the states, but veterans were sick of the service and would not come forward.[6]

Supporters of a state-connected reserve deplored the way in which Guard units had been broken up during the Great War. Major General John F. O'Ryan, commander of the 27th Infantry Division in combat, testified that esprit de corps had died hard. New York Guardsmen, torn from their home units and shipped off to serve among strangers, had often deserted and made their way back to the 27th. O'Ryan's punishment for these offenders was to place them in confinement within the units they had rejoined.[7]

The NGA, cooperating closely with the Adjutant Generals' Association (comprising the states' adjutants general), worked tirelessly to keep the regular army small and to build up the Guard. Bennett Champ Clark, scion of a powerful family in Missouri politics and president of the NGA, said, "We are all absolutely united . . . to build up the Guard and smash the regular army."[8] This was too strong for most members of the NGA. Instead, they strove for four specific objectives: (1) National Guardsmen rather than regulars should in the future be chiefs of the Militia Bureau; here they were opposed by Major General Jessie McI. Carter, the regular officer who was current chief, and by General March; (2) the Bureau should be shifted from the control of the Army General Staff, considered by the NGA to be overall unfriendly to the

Guard; (3) the War Department must be required to bring units rather than individuals into federal service; and (4) whatever law came from Congress must designate the National Guard as an integral part of the efficient, national military force in peacetime and in war.[9]

Pershing's testimony and NGA lobbying in the end brought about a coalition of legislators from the Southwest and the rural Midwest that defeated both UMT and the Baker-March Bill.[10] The pleasure the NGA derived from this defeat stemmed from resentment of the way in which the Guard had been handled during the Great War. The memory of that experience lingered as late as 1942. That year, with the nation already into World War II, the top Guardsman cautioned his associates to be on the alert lest the regulars seek to eliminate the Guard, as, he seemed to believe, they had tried to do in the previous war.[11]

The act Congress at length passed on June 4, 1920, did not resemble any of the three bills previously considered. Known as an amendment to the National Defense Act of 1916, this legislation included a number of benefits for the National Guard. The most important was a simple statement that the Guard, when in federal service, was a component of the Army of the United States, along with the Organized Reserve and the regular army. Next, it mandated that the chief of the Militia Bureau must be at least a colonel in the National Guard with ten years or more of command experience. Whoever was appointed would be made a major general in the Army of the United States. The War Department must establish committees in the appropriate staff departments to consider matters affecting the National Guard, and half the members of these committees must be Guard officers. Finally, in line with NGA demands, the Militia Bureau was placed directly under one of the assistant secretaries of war. The only unachieved objective of the Guard lobbyists related to the integrity of units when the Guard was in federal service. The act said nothing on this point except that the lineages and honors of the Guard units in the Great War should, as far as possible, be perpetuated.[12]

A National Guard officer could now earn up to five days' pay per month if he attended all the drills, and if, at those drills, half the enlisted men were present together with 60 percent of the officers. Those who had been graduated from one of the high-level officer schools of the regular service or who had in other ways shown fitness, became, for the first time, eligible for general staff duty. Finally, if money was available, the president must assign up to 500 officers from the reserve components to active duty with the regular army for limited tours.[13]

The 1920 amendment to the National Defense Act of 1916 did not give the National Guard a monopoly of the reserve component of the army. Instead, it continued the Officer's Reserve Corps and the

Enlisted Reserve Corps created by the parent act. These two were made up of individual reservists, but if and when units might be created, they would be in the Organized Reserves. These three groups were, of course, national reserves with no connection to the chain of command of any state and were administered directly by the War Department. This time, the Officer's Reserve Corps contained a vitality it had never shown before. By 1926, there were 72,000 reserve officers, scattered in 2,738 towns and villages. Any one of these officers could serve in the National Guard without losing his reserve status. The Enlisted Reserve Corps, in contrast, contained only 5,116 men, but all of them were required to have had prior military experience.[14]

The Guard leadership kept to itself its thoughts about this second element with which the Guard had to share the reserve component. Guard strength was usually 70,000 to 80,000 men higher than the Reserves; if mission guidelines were followed, there need be little destructive competition between the two. As the missions developed over time, the Officer's Reserve Corps was to furnish noncombatant officers, and the Organized Reserve was to supply enough units to maintain the regular army and the National Guard during the first phase of a war. In addition, it was to provide junior officers for the expanding regular forces throughout a war. Last, it was to form more units to supplement the other components in the event of major mobilization. In any case, during the period between the two World Wars, the Guard and the Organized Reserve existed together peaceably.[15]

Following the Great War, the National Guard had to reconstitute itself, since units and men had been swallowed up into the Army of the United States. In 1920, Congress had appropriated enough money to support 106,000 Guardsmen, but the number actually enrolled was only 56,106.[16] The 1920 Amendment made recruiting easier by permitting companies with as few as fifty members to earn federal recognition, at least into 1921. Thus aided, the Guard pushed up to about one-quarter of its prewar strength.

There were some heavy handicaps in the way of reconstitution. The first was conflict between the State Guards, creatures of the war, and the old units which were trying to rebuild. State Guard units had possession of some of the armories and meant to retain them, indeed, to become part of the postwar National Guard. Second was the reluctance of prewar Guardsmen who had served during the war to become involved again. They had had enough of military service. Third, the states were slow to agree to new troop assignments, and fourth, labor unions were openly hostile to the Guard.[17] To try to help themselves over these handicaps, some states turned to the developing craft of advertising. Ohio used the following advertisement with success:

You don't know how good that recall sounds unless you've had a day of he-man work out in the open with the famous 37th Division, Ohio National Guard. It makes your muscles hard, fills out your chest, and gives you a steady eye. Makes you proud of yourself to hold your own with a bunch of buddies who went to France and back and won the old outfit a place in World History.[18]

Reconstitution of the Guard slowly progressed. Whereas in 1920 there were fourteen states with no units at all, the next year there were only four. By 1922, Nevada alone lacked Guard organization. Without UMT, the Army General Staff felt it necessary to include Guard divisions in the troop basis to be used in case of a national emergency. Accordingly, beginning in the 1920s the high command reshuffled the states in relationship to divisions as follows:

Georgia left the 31st Infantry Division and became part of the 30th.

The 31st gained Louisiana and Mississippi from the 39th.

The 34th lost Nebraska to the 35th.

The 36th became entirely a Texas division.

The 39th was discontinued since it lost Louisiana and Mississippi and Arkansas did not supply troops to any division.

The 43rd was created with Rhode Island, Connecticut and parts of Maine and Vermont.

The 44th came into being by drawing New Jersey away from the old 29th and adding parts of New York.

The 45th, new, gained Arizona, Colorado, and New Mexico from the old 40th, and Oklahoma from the 36th.[19]

Despite the swift decline of interest in military affairs after World War I, the General Staff constructed a grandiose organization chart to be fleshed out if large-scale war came again. In addition to its eighteen infantry divisions, the Guard was to organize four cavalry divisions, 21, 22, 23, and 24. Obviously, World War I had not convinced the planners that horse cavalry would have no place on future battlefields. Each of nine army corps areas was supposed to be able to produce one regular infantry division, two National Guard divisions, and three Organized Reserve divisions. Even though all components were funded far below needs, the regular divisions were supposed to be ready twenty days after a call, the Guard thirty days, and the Organized Reserve in sixty. In fact, the regular divisions existed only on paper, as did the reserve divisions, so that the principal resource of the plan was such strength as the Guard divisions happened to have. All divisions, corps, and non-divisional troops were grouped on paper under four continental armies.[20] The readiness timetable was based on the assumption that Congress would reinstate selective service, which, in turn, would begin to provide inductees within twenty-six days. In any event, the Guard would have to provide two-thirds of the American force during the first four months of any future war. Jim Dan Hill wrote of this period, "For all practical purposes the organized and equipped ground forces of the United States . . . were vested largely in eighteen National Guard infantry divisions plus four National Guard cavalry divisions."[21]

In 1921, Major General George C. Rickards became the first National Guard officer to be chief of the Militia Bureau. Since by law no more than four Guardsmen could serve in the Bureau office, the central staff by 1919 consisted of twenty-six regular officers and enlisted men, eighty-four civilians, and the four Guard officers including Rickards. It was the duty of the Bureau to mesh the Guard into the plans of the War Department and the ground forces in general. This was not an easy assignment, since the General Staff did not rate the potential of the National Guard highly.[22]

Nevertheless, the lot of Guard officers, especially below the grade of colonel, was improving. During the 1920s and 1930s, they could apply for a commission in the Officer's Reserve Corps once they had received federal recognition. Federal recognition was the systematic process by which the War Department determined which reserve officers and units were qualified to share in federal aid and become part of the Army of the United States. The advantage of the reserve commission was that the Guard officer, upon entering federal service, could begin to function at once without having to wait to be recommissioned. The number of officers who took this route climbed steadily from 9,675 in 1923 to 12,227 in 1932.[23] At the same time, more Guard officers were enrolling in the army's advanced schools and doing well in them, and more Guard enlisted men were given the chance to enter the Military Academy.[24]

The first administration of Franklin D. Roosevelt touched and changed almost every aspect of American life, including the National Guard. Spokesmen of the NGA originated and lobbied through Congress an innovative amendment to the National Defense Act of 1916, which became law on June 15, 1933. It constituted the National Guard of the United States as "a reserve component of the Army of the United States" consisting of federally recognized National Guard units which had been specifically admitted into it. The president had the power to order the individuals and units of this new part of the reserve component into federal service any time when Congress had declared a national emergency.[25] These clauses made it unnecessary ever again to bring the Guard into federal service by dissolving its units and drafting their members as individuals. The act stipulated that as far as possible the units of the Guard would remain intact while in federal service. Although nothing in the amendment said so, the National Guard of the United States must stand upon the army clause of the Constitution rather than the militia clauses.[26]

The amendment of 1933 defined another part of the National Guard in addition to the National Guard of the United States. The National Guard of the several states, it said, consists of "members of the militia voluntarily enlisting therein" aged 18 through 45, and is "that portion of the organized militia, active or inactive, federally recognized . . . and organized . . . in whole or in part at Federal expense and officered and trained under paragraph 16, section 8, Article I of the Constitution."[27] It can be called, not ordered, into federal service under the militia clauses.

The 1933 amendment listed the components of the Army of the United States as follows: the regular army, the National Guard of the United States, the National Guard while in the service of the United States, the Officer's Reserve Corps, the Organized Reserve, and the Enlisted Reserve Corps.[28] This clause placed the most active portion of the Guard where the NGA had striven to place it at least since 1879, that is, as part of the efficient, national military force at all times. Still, the members of the National Guard of the United States would not be "in the active service of the United States except when ordered thereto . . . and in time of peace they [are] administered . . . in their states as the National Guard of the several states."[29] The authority in the national government directing the Guard at last became officially the National Guard Bureau.

Recruitment in the Guard rose and fell with the business cycle. During the prosperous 1920s men opted out in such numbers that it was necessary to recruit 6,411 new men each month to maintain level strength. Officers resigned at the rate of 25.3 percent of total officer strength, compared to 2.6 percent for the regulars.[30] The Great Depression turned this around. In those lean times, a Guard private could earn on an average $54.15 a year if he regularly attended armory drills, plus $20.93 for summer camp. These were significant sums at the time. The strength of the Guard rose from 176,322 in 1924 to 185,915 in 1935 and the quality of the volunteers rose to new highs. Since during those eleven years federal appropriations for the Guard dropped from $31,104,642 to $29,527,575, a rare problem developed: to hold numbers within the limits for which there were funds. In its early economy-in-government phase, the New Deal in 1934 reduced drill pay by one-quarter, but the Guard continued to hold the same number of drills with the same number of men present at three-quarters of the previous pay.[31]

While the new National Guard of the United States tried to adjust to its role as part of the efficient, national military force, the National Guard of the several states continued carrying out the same sort of tasks which had traditionally involved it. The high point in coping with both natural and man-made disasters came in 1936 when detachments of the Guard were called out by state authority twenty-eight times.[32]

As in the past, the Guard served where there was industrial conflict. In West Virginia it was a strike of the miners in 1921 that revived the Guard. During earlier times, the West Virginia Guard had preserved neutrality between strikers and operators, but this time it was squarely on the strike-breaking side. Neither it nor the newly formed state police could stop violence, so federal troops took part.[33] In 1922, it was the coal miners of Carbon County, Utah, who brought out the Guard in Utah. Only after miners fired on a train bringing in strike-breakers was the governor willing to summon his military arm. Although he gave Guardsmen the distasteful job of entering miners' camps to search for weapons, he insisted on strict neutrality at all times—no favors for the operators. Since the miners appreciated this position, they submitted to search of the camps without violence and in the end thanked the Guard for reducing the chance of violence. There was no clash of miners with troops and no loss of life.[34]

On July 5, 1934, a strike of longshoremen in San Francisco developed into one of the most serious labor disputes of the twentieth century. In the first stages, nine policemen were injured, two civilians shot, and thirteen others hurt. When the city's food supply was threatened, the governor summoned detachments of the Guard into state service. Within four and one half hours, elements of the 159th Field Artillery had gathered from four communities around San Francisco. The commander of the strike detachment, needing mobility, organized fire units mounted on two trucks, one truck carrying a machine gun and a squad of infantry, the other truck transporting a squad of infantry only. Violence subsided, but not the strike; on July 16, it broadened into one of the few general strikes the United States has experienced. Now the usual American reaction set in: subversives must be responsible for the trouble. Guardsmen and police conducted raids to round up "communists and professional agitators." Some of these were located by Guardsmen circulating among the crowds in mufti. The adjutant general believed that the agitators would have turned the crowds into a revolutionary mob had it not been for the Guard. Informants told him that communists were spending $1,000,000 a day to destroy the American system. After four days, through the feverish work of arbitrators, the general strike came to an end. The performance of the California National Guard during this event was exemplary.[35]

Several Guardsmen lost their lives during severe industrial warfare in Ohio beginning in 1932. Units of the Ohio Air Guard became the first in history to drop tear gas onto rioters. There was some abatement of violence, but when the Congress of Industrial Organizations (CIO) attempted to unionize the big steel companies in 1936, it escalated once more. Governor Martin Luther Davey of Ohio used 4,000 Guardsmen to open up the closed steel plants. Guard costs soared and the popularity of the Guard plunged in Ohio.[36]

In a few instances, governors called parts of their Guards to block New Deal programs. Texas and Oklahoma did so to prevent federal officers from enforcing certain regulations pertaining to the oil industry. The governor of Arizona temporarily blocked a federal contractor from building a dam, while an Iowa Guard detachment halted a hearing of the National Labor Relations Board. In the end, these state-national controversies all became court cases in which judges denied the right of the states to interfere.[37]

Fear of internal subversion grew during the Great Depression, stimulating the National Guard to issue a new manual on riot control. Distributed in 1940, this manual was devoid of ideological exhortation but full of how-to-do-it information. Troops were not called out to punish rioters but to save property. The manual said to avoid gunfire and hand-to-hand fighting. "Troops must have their bayonets fixed whenever they are facing a mob. A unit of determined men slowly, steadily and silently advancing with bayonets fixed has a potent effect on any gathering." If this show of force did not stop the rioters, the manual added, gas should be used. If forced to close encounter, men should wield a night stick.[38]

The National Guard became one of the minor agencies through which the New Deal battled the Great Depression. Partial motorization of the Guard gave needed business to the automobile industry, but there were never enough vehicles for the Guard. By 1935, mobilization plans called for 12,000 motor vehicles in Guard units, while the actual supply stood at 7,182, many of which were obsolete leftovers from World War I. Still in mechanization, the Guard fared better than did the regular army. When the administration sought to give useful work to unemployed young men, it created the Civilian Conservation Corps and turned its operation over to the army. The latter then called upon the Guard and Reserves for 700 officers to help.[39]

Although pacifism dominated the nation's mood, the National Guard helped maintain the morale of many localities all over depressed America. Its armories became centers for community dances and other indoor festivals. Outside, Guard leaders placed heavy stress on athletic contests, parades, and target shoots. If the local unit had horses, towns people could make arrangements to ride them on Sundays.[40]

Armories became a way to provide jobs and stimulate building companies. Guard leadership pointed out to legislators that there were 1,740 active Guard units but only 866 armories. They argued that every unit deserved a decent place to train, and that the $150,000,000 of government property in Guard hands required to be securely housed. These arguments, blended with the recovery program, produced a 50 percent increase in appropriations for armories, camps, and equipment.[41]

The National Guard seemed to be weathering the Great Depression well, and the chief of the Bureau chose to project optimism. "The National Guard," he said in 1934, "has shown that it is possible to produce on the basis of an evening a week and a fortnight's field training at relatively small cost, a military organization capable of rendering useful services to the States and to the Nation." But to him the Guard was much more than just one part of the military establishment. "It is," he said, "a great school of citizenship which continually pours into the blood stream of the body politic wholesome corpuscles which help to purge it of dangerous infections." [42] Douglas MacArthur, Army Chief of Staff, saw another important contribution by the Guard. It stood shoulder to shoulder with him, he said, "to combat the wave of pacifism rising in the country." [43]

By 1937, the president himself began shifting his attention away from internal recovery and reform toward the menacing rise of militarism throughout the world. Against that background, American pacifism appeared grotesque. Accordingly, Roosevelt reversed his earlier economy stance and increased the number of annual armory drills for which there would be federal pay from forty-eight to sixty. He increased summer training time by seven days, and after the Nazis invaded Poland in 1939, he asked Congress to fund summer training for 280,000 Guardsmen, a substantial increase.[44]

Notwithstanding the president's concern, the army high command did not take essential steps to insure the readiness of the Guard. The professional soldiers at the top saw scant potential in the National Guard and did not recognize it for what it was in the 1930s: the principal military defense system of the nation. The regulars experimented with lighter and more mobile divisions than the World War I square type and finally converted to triangular divisions in 1939, but they did not apply the new divisional organization to the Guard. They did, however, apply almost every other sort of reorganization, redesignation, and conversion in the 1930s, in belated attempts to develop a balanced national force. At least 700 Guard units underwent wrenching changes of some sort. The army staff planners continued to assume that if American forces fought again, they would do so not as an expeditionary force but in defense of the homeland. This may have been one reason why the Guard divisions were left square; as such, though less mobile, they were judged to have greater defensive power.[45]

While Hitler overran most of western Europe and attempted to defeat Great Britain by aerial bombardment in 1940, the Congress of the United States debated what the national posture should be. It was a presidential election year with FDR pitted against his most formidable opponent Wendell Willkie, and running for an unprecedented third term; so he did little to influence the legislators. General George C. Marshall, Army Chief of Staff, however, testified in favor of declaring a national emergency and ordering the National Guard into federal service. He later admitted that he wanted Guard equipment as much as the Guardsmen. On August 27, 1940, Congress did declare a national emergency and authorized the president to federalize the National Guard. Its joint resolution set the tour of duty at one year and stipulated that Guardsmen might not be used outside of the Western Hemisphere except in United States possessions.[46]

Congress at the same time was debating peacetime conscription. Roosevelt would not support this until his opponent in the election neutralized the issue politically by declaring it non-partisan. Even after FDR endorsed the draft, opponents, of whom there were many, argued that the only truly American way was to rely on volunteers to fill out the armed forces. In rebuttal, supporters of the draft said that defense was the duty of all able-bodied males and that the nation could not afford to risk only the lives of the men patriotic enough to volunteer. In the end, Congress opted for Selective Service, World War I style, and the president signed the bill on September 16, 1940. The act required every male, ages 21 through 35, to register, and if selected through a lottery and certified by a local draft board, to enter military service for one year. Congress in this way authorized the first national draft to take place in peacetime in American history.[47]

Leaders of the Guard initially felt some misgivings about this act because of its possible effect on volunteering, the historic basis for Guard membership. However, they lobbied successfully for clauses that dispelled these misgivings. The most important clause read, "It is essential that the strength and organization of the National Guard as an integral part of the first line of defense of this nation be at all times maintained and assured."[48] That clause proved often to be a bulwark in the future. Other indispensible clauses required every man who had had training and seen service to enter one of the reserves at the conclusion of his active duty and remain in it for ten years or until he reached age 45.[49]

President Roosevelt ordered part of the National Guard into federal service on September 16, 1940. It was not coincidence that the date of reporting coincided with Selective Service, for it was known that the Guard units would have to take in inductees to fill up. Ordered in were the following four entire divisions: the 30th, South and North Carolina, Tennessee and Georgia; the 41st, Idaho, Montana, Oregon, Wyoming, and Washington; the 44th, New York and New Jersey; and the 45th, Oklahoma, Colorado, Arizona, and New Mexico. These rather than other divisions were selected because it was assumed that their induction would cause the least disruption to the nation's economy. The order summoned in addition seven coast artillery anti-aircraft units, three coast artillery 155 gun battalions, and eight coast artillery harbor defense units. It also included four observation squadrons: the 105th, 116th, 119th, and 254th.[50]

Soon the president ordered in all the rest of the National Guard. There were twenty-two increments, the last one entering federal service in June 1941. No Guard division was able to field more than two-thirds of the 22,000 men required by the tables of organization for square divisions, and the smallest had to find 57 percent new recruits. Manpower problems were heightened by the need to release about 96,000 men who had been inducted. Of these, 4,906 had to go because they were under age and had never secured parental consent; 3,727 had physical disabilities; 4,461 held jobs judged critical to the economy; and 5,340 had moved away from where their units were based. The largest number went out due to the ruling that men in the lowest three grades could be released if they had dependents. These totaled 51,126. Nor did this end the drain. Each Guard division provided cadre for at least one additional division, while three of the divisions, the 30th, 31st, and 32nd, became for a time merely manpower conduits through which personnel passed to other units. All in all, the initial twenty-five increments required 86,072 inductees to fill up.[51]

In spite of continual drains on it, the Guard in carrying out the president's order placed in federal service 20,298 officers, 221 warrant officers, and 278,526 enlisted Guardsmen. On the eve of Guard mobilization, the regular army stood at 264,118. Thus, the Guard, in supplying the largest organized force on which the nation could call in 1940, was doing exactly what its leaders had always wanted it to do: it was functioning as the principal reserve force in a national emergency.[52]

The mission which the leaders eagerly accepted brought hardship on themselves and on Guardsmen in general. Since General Marshall would never assure the Guard that their tour of duty was for just one year, it was hard for men to plan. Nevertheless, they went about the buildup cheerfully. "Join the Guard and go with the boys you know!" was the slogan. If this was a promise, it was broken, for units were almost ruthlessly reorganized or broken up. The 92nd Infantry Brigade, Minnesota National Guard, became coast artillery, even though its only coastlines were those of 10,000 mostly small lakes. In New Orleans, the Washington Artillery found itself part of the 73rd Field Artillery Brigade of Pennsylvania. During the fall of 1940, the entire Guard cavalry underwent conversion. Seven regiments retained some horses as they became mechanized horse regiments. Seven others became field artillery regiments, seven, coast artillery regiments, and one an antitank battalion.[53]

Black Guard units also faced severe alterations, but they were used to these. Following World War I, the War Department had created pioneer, that is, labor units, to contain most of the black Guardsmen. But even those regiments that had served effectively with the French army had had a hard time to retain their identity. It is true that the 369th Infantry fitted back into the New York National Guard, but it was excluded from becoming a part of either the 27th or the 44th divisions. It gained some distinction when Colonel Benjamin O. Davis took command—later the regular army's first black general—but upon mobilization it was redesignated the 369th Coast Artillery. The 370th Infantry returned to the Illinois National Guard as the 8th Illinois, excluded from the 33rd Division. In 1940, it lost its identity upon redesignation as the 184th Field Artillery. The 372nd was scattered among Ohio, Massachusetts, New Jersey, and the District of Columbia. At least, the units were no longer identified on paper as colored but were distinguished by an asterisk only.[54]

Mobilization of the Guard was to a great extent controlled by Lieutenant General Lesley J. McNair, a professional of the Uptonian school. McNair took charge first from his post as commander of GHQ when that was constituted and later as commander of Army Ground Forces. In the latter role, he wrote a memorandum to General Marshall containing the following indictment of the Guard: "One of the great lessons of the present war is that the National Guard, as organized before the war, contributed nothing to national defense. . . . The structure of the National Guard was pregnant with disaster for the entire nation."[55] Such statements seemed flagrantly unjust to Guard leaders, who believed that their organization had given the country the only starting cadre available.

Local arrangements for mobilization were perforce crude. Before unit mess facilities could be established, men were directed to eat breakfast at home; at noon they were marched to local cafés for lunch. When at last cooks and equipment were on hand, quartermasters bought food from the local groceries, rotating their purchases so as to pass the business around. At the national level, Guard officers resented the apparent fact that the professionals had not made adequate preparations to receive them. Units, directed to what they expected to be camps, found in some cases nothing but bare dirt with stakes where they had hoped to see latrines, mess halls, and barracks. As a result, the Guardsmen suffered acutely during the winter. Army supply personnel threw overcoats to them in bales, size immaterial, all shoes issued were mediums, so that many a citizen soldier wore his civilian footwear for months. In contrast, there was an oversupply of the wool wrap-around puttees, which had bedeviled earlier soldiers. Guardsmen had to use stove pipes to simulate mortars, sticks for shoulder weapons, and short pieces of thin pine logs on lawnmower wheels for machine guns.[56] Yet, having failed to anticipate the need for camp facilities, equipment, weapons, and professional instructors, GHQ was quick to send out hordes of inspectors to swarm over the raw training areas and report Guard deficiencies.[57]

Flaws, it is true, were obvious enough; they were inevitable. But Jim Dan Hill, as close to an official historian of the Guard as exists, asserts that the inspectors were told to find enough faults to justify officer removals. Regular officers, starved for promotion because of the promotion hump created by World War I, coveted the positions held by Guard officers. What developed among the regulars, according to Hill, was "a volcano of erupting military ambitions."[58] This pressure was eased somewhat by the new age-in-grade regulations. Whereas at least one-fifth of the Guard lieutenants were 40 or over, the new upper limit for second lieutenants became 30; 1,000 Guard captains were eliminated at age 45 because the new limit was 42. McNair asserted that the Guard generals were almost without exception incompetent to carry out the duties of star-bearing rank.[59]

According to Hill's interpretation, the professionals made the National Guard the scapegoat for their failure to make the necessary preparations. They told the public that they were achieving the all-but-impossible, "but being handicapped by the deadweight of the National Guard and its politicians disguised as officers, it was hardly possible to guarantee anything. . . ." Influenced by this sort of publicity, large numbers of Americans—not yet aware how close the United States was to participation in an overseas war—considered the prewar mobilization of the National Guard to be perhaps the most massive of New

Deal boondoggles. What hurt the Guard was that the entire command structure of the army uttered not one whisper to contradict this bias.[60]

One bald fact stands out no matter who interprets the record. Three months after the United States entered the war, the ground forces contained twenty-nine divisions, ten of them regular army, eighteen National Guard, and one (the 25th) the Army of the United States. During the war, the number of divisions rose to ninety-one, of which sixty-seven were infantry. This final figure makes the eighteen Guard divisions appear to be a small part of the force—no other Guard divisions were created—but at the start, that contribution loomed very large.[61]

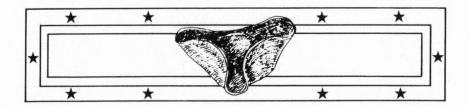

THIRTEEN

World War II

In June 1941, the War Department forwarded to the president a request that the one-year men, both Guardsmen and draftees, be retained longer than a year. The Senate held a lengthy hearing on the request, and General Marshall appeared to support the extension. Since it was a matter of military necessity, he said, he had not informed the president of his testimony because he "tried to keep as wide a separation as possible between military necessity . . . and political considerations."[1] Debate before the committee and in Congress was bitter, for opponents saw the extension as another sure step toward involvement in an overseas war. But in the end, Congress, urged by the president, approved the change by the narrowest of margins. Later, on December 31, 1941, it extended the obligation of the one-year men to the duration of the emergency plus six months.[2]

Under the new obligation, however, men 28 and over were to be released. As a result, 19,703 men in Guard units were separated in October 1941. Their departure left 25,084 officers still serving with the Guard divisions, 19,542 of whom had entered from the peacetime National Guard. Of enlisted men, 397,272 remained in units that had come in from the Guard, of whom 213,449 had started as Guardsmen. At least thirteen of the original Guard generals remained at that time, continuing to give tone to their divisions.[3]

Once the one-year men were locked in for the duration, General Marshall addressed the commanders of the Guard divisions very bluntly. The unwillingness of leaders "who knew their subordinates in civil life to hold them to strict compliance with military orders" jeopardized national security and would not be tolerated. He had created boards to reclassify officers who could not change their ways.

The boards, however, were to use sensible standards and were to contain adequate representation from the reserves.[4]

GHQ did not choose to change the Guard divisions from square to triangular until January and February 1942. By that time, four of the divisions had been in federal service for fifteen months. Part of the delay came from the need for the governors to approve the reorganization as it applied to their states. Since the triangular division contained around 8,000 fewer persons than the square type, all the divisions had to slough off not only individuals but also units. With some of the units went much history and accompanying morale; the 108th New York Infantry was shipped off to become part of the 40th Division on the west coast. The 121st Georgia Infantry, with a Civil War lineage, slipped for a time into the 8th, a regular army division, and then became a separate unit. The 129th Illinois Infantry, dating also from the Civil War, dangled between divisions for a time, then was placed in the 37th Division from Ohio.[5]

General McNair developed a strong conviction that tank destroyers (TDs) were the instrument with which to wreck German armor. Therefore, he ordered each Guard division to create one TD battalion from the elements it sloughed during triangularization. He ordered also that seven more battalions be formed from the National Guard corps artillery.[6]

During the 1920s and 1930s, the Guard had formed tank companies. By 1932, fifteen divisions had a tank company—26th, 27th, 28th, 29th, 30th, 31st, 32nd, 33rd, 35th, 37th, 38th, 40th, 41st, 43rd, and 45th—and each company had from six to eight tanks of the obsolete six-ton M-17 type. In 1935, partly as an economic recovery measure, Congress appropriated funds to provide each company with one modern light tank. But as soon as Roosevelt ordered the Guard into service, GHQ detached the tank companies and took them under its direct control. With those units went a good many officers who had developed an interest in armor. The companies from California, Minnesota, Kentucky, Ohio, Illinois, and Wisconsin shipped out to the Philippines where it became their misfortune to be part of the U. S. forces that surrendered at Corregidor. The twelve remaining tank units lost their identity.[7]

Air capability had grown faster than armor in the National Guard during the inter-war period, thanks to 8,500 surplus airplanes from World War I. By 1926, it consisted of sixteen observation squadrons, ten of them attached to corps, and twelve photo squadrons. Most of its 281 officers had had wartime experience. In 1927, Ohio had added an aero squadron to its 37th Division, followed by Illinois the next year, and by the 44th Division in 1930. By 1940, the service had built up twenty-one squadrons of twelve planes each. Some of the aircraft were obsolescent, but pilots, determined to fly, came forward anyway. One pilot remembered a neighbor telling his father, "Might as well let the boy learn to fly; he ain't any earthly use."[8]

As with the tanks, GHQ took the air units away from the Guard. In so doing, they discarded many Guard officers, most of whom, however, ended up in the Army Air Corps. General H. H. Arnold did not want to see their experience wasted. Most of the erstwhile Air Guard units were placed in the Pacific Theater.[9]

The absence of Guardsmen in Federal service increased the danger of sabotage at home. Congress, therefore, as in World War I, authorized the states to constitute new organizations known as State Guards. By June 30, 1941, nearly six months before war came to the nation, thirty-seven states had done so. Weapons for the roughly 89,000 State Guardsmen posed a problem. The main solution was to equip them with shotguns and other firearms borrowed from private owners. A unique mission fell to the State Guards of Utah when they were alerted to watch out for balloons launched by the Japanese to be carried in the upper air currents into the American Northwest, to explode when they came down. Only one arrived, but it was not discovered until after the war.[10]

Control of the State Guards became the principal mission of the National Guard Bureau (NGB) since it had no authority over the National Guard when in federal service. Indeed, the NGB became a war orphan; in the major reorganization of the army that produced the Ground Forces, Air Forces, and Service Forces (March 9, 1942), it ceased to be special staff and slipped into the jurisdiction of the adjutant general. Later, it was transferred to the Chief of Administration Services and later still to the Director of Personnel of the Army Service Forces. Not until the war was over could the Bureau once more find a secure place.[11]

Below general officer grades, National Guard officers survived rather well; less than 1 percent of them became the target of reclassification boards. At war's end, 19,542 of the original officers were on duty in some capacity; outnumbering the 15,000 who came from the regulars. To this must be added the 75,000 enlisted Guardsmen who became officers during the war. But most of the officer corps came from other sources: the Officer's Reserve Corps, 180,000; persons commissioned directly from civil life, 100,000; and Officers Candidate Schools (OCS), 300,000. The 15,000 regulars were outnumbered forty to one, but they controlled the highest posts. A typical infantry regiment was officered more or less as follows: the colonel, the executive officer, and one battalion commander were regular army; one battalion commander was a reserve officer, and one came from the National Guard. Probably two-thirds of the company commanders were OCS graduates; the other one-third consisted of Guardsmen with a few reservists.[12]

The Guard brought with it 273 colonels in the 1940-1941 mobilization, of whom 148 were still in service when the war ended. Fifty-four percent of them made it through, compared to 39 percent for regular colonels.[13]

The generals of the National Guard lasted well but not in command of the divisions they had brought into federal service. Only Major General Robert S. Beightler remained in command of the 37th Division, Ohio National Guard, from start to finish. Nevertheless, of the twenty-one Guard major generals on the permanent promotion list in 1940, nine, that is, 42 percent, were still active in some capacity on VE day. This compared with the same number of generals on the regular list in 1940, of whom only five, or 23 percent, were still on active duty in 1945. Percentages were about the same for brigadiers.[14]

Not enough Guard officers were promoted into the general grades during the war. When Guard leaders complained, General Marshall ordered a search of the roster of colonels for the most likely to receive one star. In any case, 84.5 percent of promotions at the general level went to regulars, only 2.4 percent to National Guardsmen, and 1.8 percent to the Officer's Reserve Corps. Only one general who originated from the Guard emerged from the war a lieutenant general; this was Raymond S. McLain, commander of the division artillery of the 45th Division.[15]

As in World War I, group loyalty seemed to focus on divisions. Table 13.1 gives some basic statistics on Guard divisions.[16] The time when a division entered combat seems to have been regulated less by the division's readiness than by the chance of the theater to which it was sent. The average time required to mobilize did not vary widely among the divisions of the several components; for Organized Reserve divisions it was twenty-two months, for regulars twenty-four, and for Guard divisions twenty-eight months.[17] Yet nine Guard divisions were in federal service from one year to nineteen months beyond the average mobilization time before becoming engaged. Observers thought this was too long; these divisions trained too much. The earliest involvement took place in the Pacific Theater when the 164th Infantry Regiment of the American Division (a part of the 34th Division while it was a square division) engaged the Japanese on Guadalcanal beginning on October 13, 1942. That same month, the 32nd Division entered combat, while four of the other Guard divisions were bloodied in the Pacific Theater sometime in 1943. In the European

TABLE 13.1

NUMBER OF DIVISION	FEDERAL SERVICE	THEATER	INITIAL COMBAT	TIME LAPSE FROM ENTRY TO COMBAT (IN MONTHS)
~ 26	16 Jan. 1941	ETO*	Sep. 29, 1944	44
27	15 Oct. 1940	Pacific	Nov. 21, 1943	37
28	17 Feb. 1941	ETO	July 22, 1944	41
29	3 Feb. 1941	ETO	June 6, 1944	40
30	16 Sep. 1940	ETO	June 15, 1944	44
31	25 Nov. 1940	Pacific	July 13, 1944	46
32	15 Oct. 1940	Pacific	Sep. 16, 1942	20
33	5 Mar. 1941	Pacific	Dec. 18, 1944	45
34	10 Feb. 1941	ETO	Nov. 8, 1942	20
35	23 Dec. 1940	ETO	July 11, 1944	42
36	25 Nov. 1940	ETO	Sep. 9, 1943	33
37	15 Oct. 1940	Pacific	July 22, 1943	32
38	17 Jan. 1941	Pacific	Dec. 1944	47
40	3 Mar. 1941	Pacific	Jan. 9, 1945	45
41	16 Sep. 1940	Pacific	Jan. 2, 1943	27
43	24 Feb. 1941	Pacific	July 1943	28
44	16 Sep. 1940	ETO	Oct. 10, 1944	36
45	16 Sep. 1940	ETO	June 1943	32

* European Theater of Operations.

Theater, it was necessary for seven of the nine Guard divisions to wait until the main assault on fortress Europe began across the English Channel. Before that the 34th Division landed in North Africa in November 1942; the 45th in Sicily in June 1943. The 29th Division was the only Guard Division to go ashore on D-Day, June 6, 1944, but most of the nondivisional units in that landing were originally from the Guard.[18]

Although the divisions in the Pacific Theater were in combat longer, those in Europe suffered higher casualties. Eight Guard divisions suffered losses expressed in five figures, all of them in Europe: the 45th, 29th, 36th, 30th, 28th, 34th, 35th, and 26th, in that order (see Table 13.2).[19]

When Major General Willard S. Paul, a regular, took command of the 26th Division in mid-1942, he spoke of its "hapless, unsettled fate." It had been in federal service since January 1941 and had suffered mainly mutilation: 3,000 of its men went to form a new truck unit, and the 182nd Infantry was chipped off to become part of the Americal Division. To fill the gaps it took in strangers who were not from New England. Partly because of these drafts on its vitality, the 26th remained in training status for four years.[20]

The 27th Division from New York regained the 69th Infantry Regiment, the Fighting Irish, which in World War I had been redesignated the 165th Infantry and assigned to the Rainbow Division. The 27th was in service three years before it got into combat in November 1943, but its real test came in 1944 in the Battle for Saipan in the Marianas. There, the Division was required to intern 10,000 hostile natives and care for them. Burdensome though this was it was mild beside the combat experience. The men carried thirty days' rations with them as they jogged along behind tanks in the dense growth and learned through heavy casualties the reverse-slope tactics of the Japanese.[21]

Marine units were associated with the 27th in the Saipan fight, and bad blood began to develop early between the two services. Two battalions of marines moved into the terrain assigned to the 27th without requesting permission, indeed, without even notifying them. There, they lit fires, pitched tents, and slept on cots as if the foe was beneath notice. Unbeknownst to the American forces, the Japanese emperor ordered a banzai attack, which only he had power to do and in which each Japanese soldier was to die and take seven of the foe with him. The brunt of this attack of July 7, 1944, fell upon the 105th Infantry, but Lieutenant General Holland M. Smith, the Marine general in command on Saipan, gave principal credit for stopping the drive to the marines. *Time* magazine, accepting the official report as the whole truth, published a derogatory account of the performance of the 27th Division which wrecked morale among the men. The general commanding the 27th, a regular himself, wrote a strong rebuttal of the official version of the action, but General Marshall refused to have it printed, lest it disrupt interservice harmony. On Saipan no such harmony had existed. Late in June, Holland Smith had relieved Major General Ralph C. Smith as the 27th's commander because Ralph Smith was not able to drive his men along fast enough. The men, totally absorbed in survival, hardly noticed the change, but Army Lieutenant General Robert C. Richardson did and engaged in some harsh words with the high command of the navy in the Pacific.[22] Wherever truth or justice lay, it is a fact that the 27th remained overseas longer than any other division.

Historians of the 28th Division stated that the regulars monopolized credit that should have been shared. The Guard's competence in the killing game, they pointed out, was confirmed by the German foe, who called the Division insignia the "Bloody Bucket." The 28th, its chroniclers wrote, deserved equal credit with the 101st Airborne Division for stopping the German drive in the Battle of the Bulge but did not receive it. Even though the 28th's personnel was now different

TABLE 13.2

NUMBER OF DIVISION	STATES	INFANTRY REGIMENTS	ARTILLERY BATTALIONS	KILLED	WOUNDED	POPULAR NAME
26	Massachusetts, New Hampshire, Maine, Vermont	101, 104, 328	101, 102, 180, 263	1,587	12,077	Yankee
27	New York	105, 106, 165	104, 105, 106, 249	1,844	4,689	Orion or New York
28	Pennsylvania	109, 110, 112	107, 108, 109, 229	2,683	14,079	Keystone
29	Maryland, Virginia, District of Columbia	115, 116, 175	110, 111, 224, 227	4,515	16,105	Blue Gray
30	North Carolina, Georgia, South Carolina, Tennessee	117, 119, 120	113, 118, 197, 230	3,516	14,930	Old Hickory
31	Alabama, Florida, Mississippi, Louisiana	124, 155, 167	114, 116, 117, 149	414	1,319	Dixie
32	Michigan, Wisconsin	126, 127, 128	120, 121, 126, 129	1,985	5,283	Red Arrow
33	Illinois	132, 130, 136	114, 116, 117, 149	524	1,902	Golden Cross or Prairie
34	Iowa, Minnesota, North Dakota, South Dakota	133, 135, 168	125, 151, 175, 185	3,350	13,051	Red Bull
35	Missouri, Kansas, Nebraska	134, 137, 320	127, 161, 216, 219	2,947	12,935	Santa Fe
36	Texas	141, 142, 143	131, 132, 133, 155	3,636	15,830	Texas
37	Ohio	129, 145, 148	6, 135, 136, 140	1,344	4,616	Buckeye
38	Kentucky, Indiana, West Virginia	149, 151, 152	138, 139, 150, 163	784	2,680	Cyclone
40	California, Utah	108, 160, 185	143, 164, 213, 222	748	2,277	Sunshine

41	Wyoming, Idaho, Oregon, Montana, Washington	162, 163, 186	146, 167, 205, 218	950	3,310	Sunset or Jungleers
43	Connecticut, Maine, Rhode Island, Vermont	103, 169, 172	103, 152, 169, 192	1,416	4,610	Winged Victory
44	New Jersey, New York	71, 114, 324	156, 157, 217, 220	1,206	4,449	
45	New Mexico, Oklahoma, Arizona, Colorado	157, 179, 180	158, 160, 171, 189	4,080	16,913	Thunderbird

NOTE: At first the 45th Division used as its shoulder patch a swastika, because it was an Indian symbol of good luck; then, because the emblem too closely resembled the Nazi swastika, the Division adopted another Indian symbol for its patch, the thunderbird.

SOURCE: *The National Guardsman*, vol. I (March 1947), p. 23; and R. Ernest Dupuy, *The National Guard: A Compact History* (Hawthorne, 1971), pp. 125–127.

from that at the time of entry into federal service, the Division still thought of itself as connected with Pennsylvania.[23]

While in the United States, the 29th Division was commanded by Major General Milton A. Reckord, who had joined the Maryland National Guard in 1901. He had commanded a regiment of the Division during World War I but now, being close to 60, was replaced by a younger man, a regular, for the trip overseas. The 29th was the second American division to reach the British Isles, and upon its arrival it was still about 40 percent National Guard and 60 percent selectees. Its mission was to decoy the Nazis into believing that an attack from England was imminent. Three years passed before the cross-Channel attack actually took place, but when it did the 29th contributed the 116th Regimental Combat Team (RCT) to the landing on D-Day at Omaha Beach. Each infantryman carried with him sixty rounds of M-1 ammunition, three bandoleers for machine guns, three fragmenting grenades, one smoke and one phosphorous grenade, and a quarter pound of TNT, one K ration, and three D-bars of concentrated chocolate. An American destroyer hammered the beach most of the day and could not be brought to stop; the members of the 116th who survived the landing always remembered Brigadier General Paul Cota working all the front areas on foot, carrying a cane and chewing a cigar and humming to himself queer toneless tunes. After D-Day, the 29th fought its way clear to the Elbe River, having spent 242 days in combat.[24]

At the start of the war, the 30th Division became merely a conduit through which men passed to other outfits. Combat teams were chipped from it, and one of these made the landing on D-Day. By the time the division ceased to be merely a replacement agency, most of its original members were gone. Like the 26th, it was in training and replacement status for four years before receiving a chance to get into the fight.[25]

When finally involved in the ETO, certain of the units were by accident heavily bombed by the U. S. Army Air Force. Lieutenant General Lesley McNair happened to be visiting and was killed in the bombardment, becoming the highest ranking American officer to lose his life during the war.[26]

The 32nd Division was ordered into federal service on October 15, 1940, twenty-three years to the day after being constituted as a new division in World War I. It was concentrated on the east coast for shipment to Europe, but, upon a change of plans at high strategic levels, was moved by rail across the entire country to go to the Pacific Theater. Its infantry was the first in the history of the United States to be moved by air, the destination being New Guinea. Once there, the

126th Infantry was obliged to snake its way on foot through the jungle over the Owen Stanley Range, a grueling journey of forty-nine days which more fortunate units accomplished in forty minutes by air. Before the war was over, the 32nd experienced 654 days of combat, the longest combat service of any American division.[27]

Table 13.1 shows that the 33rd Division waited forty-five months while in federal service before entering combat. Its major test did not come until the spring of 1945 in the Philippines. In April, the Division was stretched sixty-five miles from flank to flank. As it advanced along what the Americans called Skyline Drive, one company was cut off from the rest and surrounded. Supplies were dropped to them, but they were intercepted by their besiegers. Snipers killed the captain, and hand-to-hand fighting saved the company from annihilation until, under cover of night, it was able to rejoin the rest of the regiment. The Division used horses and native people, including women, as burden bearers.[28]

The 135th Infantry of the 34th Division claimed the 1st Minnesota of the Civil War as its forebear. At Gettysburg on July 2, 1863, General Hancock had ordered the 1st to charge to cover the rout of Daniel Sickles's division, placed by Sickles in an untenable position. There were only 262 men to make the charge, but they made it, incurring 215 casualties. Something of this fighting spirit lasted through a century and appeared again in active form when the 34th landed in North Africa on November 8, 1942, and later in the Italian campaigns. The 34th was one of the two Guard divisions to be first engaged with an enemy. During the summer of 1944, two Nisei units—the only two the United States allowed to fight—were attached to the 34th. Soon, sympathy for the Japanese-Americans ran high in the Division, coupled with some resentment of the way in which they had been treated. With 500 days in action, the 34th was third among the Guard divisions in combat time.[29]

Major General Fred L. Walker was a professional although not a West Pointer, whom GHQ sent to take over the 36th Division from the Texan who commanded it. Although not welcome at first, Walker came to value the Texas fighting spirit and tried to cherish it. Both Tom Connally, Senator from Texas, and Governor Coke Stevenson objected to the removal of the Texas high command, but the regular corps commander obliged Walker to relieve three Guard generals and one colonel. In spite of all this, Stevenson continued to regard the 36th as the Texas Division, and Walker abetted the connection by carrying the Texas Lone Star Flag ashore when the division landed in Italy. After General Clark had ordered a costly direct assault across the Rapido River, the 36th carried out a successful flanking movement which saved many lives. Walker later wrote, however, that Clark took the credit to himself and said little about the 36th. As soon as Walker turned 57, he was relieved and sent back to the United States to command the Infantry School. Walker's experience made him write, "No wonder the National Guard dislikes and mistrusts the Regular Army." Even though by 1933 the 36th was no more than 40 percent Texan, Walker still regarded it as a Guard Division, and the division had come to accept him as one of them.[30]

The 45th Division was one of four Guard divisions to enter federal service under the president's order of September 16, 1940. Created in 1924, it was the second of the nine Guard divisions assigned to the ETO to enter combat and second in number of days in contact with the enemy, logging 511 days. It suffered 27,207 casualties, more than any other Guard division, which obliged it to draw for replacements on every state and territory. It remained, nevertheless, basically National Guard. The 45th was peculiarly American in that it contained at the start 1,500 American Indians from twenty-eight tribes.[31]

Some of the units pushed out of the square Guard divisions when they were triangularized went to the Southwest Pacific Theater and were initially grouped into Task Force 6814. Among these were some old pedigrees: the 132nd Illinois, going back to the Civil War, the 164th, which had been part of the North Dakota National Guard since 1885 (the first American unit to be engaged in combat in any theater); the 182nd Massachusetts Infantry, with an official birthdate of 1636. These, with others, ceased to be Task Force 6814 when in May 1942 it became the nucleus of the Americal Division.[32]

Overall, what contribution did the National Guard make to victory during World War II? Most important, in the critical period before the United States entered the war, it provided the principal organized body of men for national defense. Jim Dan Hill wrote, "Pearl Harbor was one military disaster that could not be blamed on the Guard."[33] During the first fourteen months of the war in the Pacific, precipitated by Pearl Harbor, the Guard and the marines made up the bulk of the American fighting force. By 1942, the United States was able to place fourteen divisions overseas in all theaters, of which eight originated in the National Guard. Counting the Americal Division nineteen divisions started from the Guard. Although much diluted with out-of-state personnel, these nineteen retained to the end a distinctive Guard flavor. They performed as well as the best. Although regular divisions suffered an average of 14,541 casualties, and Guard divisions only 9,166, even critics never inferred that Guardsmen hung back in battle or were less effective than other types of soldiers. At the start of the war, when the need was critical, the Guard supplied to the common effort a body of officers with some training, and during the war it added 75,000 more, commissioned from enlisted Guardsmen. Because of the turbulence resulting from triangularization of the divisions, many Guard officers joined the armored force and helped develop it while the tank companies from the Guard provided a nucleus for this new arm.[34]

.   .   .

American participation in the war was just one month old when Major General George E. Leach, who had been chief of the NGB from 1931 to 1935 and who was currently vice-president of the NGA, requested General Marshall to establish a joint committee to study the postwar military posture of the nation. Guard representation on the General Staff had been suspended during the war, and Leach and other leaders began to dread the possibility of a fight for the very life of the Guard such as had followed World War I.[35]

In 1943, Major General Ellard A. Walsh became president of the NGA. His first action was to spend $11,000 of his own money to lease a suite in a Washington hotel more in keeping with the dignity of the NGA. The new president, 56 when he took office, had joined the Minnesota Guard in 1905 when he was 18. In World War I, he had entered service as a Guardsman and served overseas for thirteen months. Afterward, he had worked in Minnesota's War Bonus Office; later, he became chairman of the State Bonus Review Board, and in 1925 he was appointed adjutant general of his home state. In 1940, he took command of the 34th Infantry Division, Iowa, Minnesota and the two Dakotas, but he was relieved by a regular army general when the division shipped to the ETO. He then resumed being adjutant general of Minnesota, the post he held when called to the presidency of the NGA. Walsh's military record was not filled with combat honors, but the record he compiled as president of the NGA turned out to be dazzling. His presidential address, delivered in the midst of the war, must have been designed to shock listeners, for in it he used pejorative terms such as Brahmins, Bourbons, and Samurai to describe the army's professional high command.[36]

Once president, Walsh kept busy appearing before deliberative bodies concerned with postwar posture. After long delay, General Marshall had finally created a committee of three regular officers and three Guard officers to consider the postwar world and had recalled Brigadier General John McAuley Palmer from the ETO to be his personal adviser in this area. In the past, Palmer had argued for a federalized Guard but one in which units would train together in peacetime and fight together in war. Now, however, he concluded that it would not be feasible to bring reservists into active federal service in units; they must enter as individuals. Walsh, appearing before a House committee, disputed Palmer's contention and sought to strengthen the Guard as it stood with the nation-state connection. He began with a long history of the contributions made by the Guard in past wars and offered resolutions passed by the NGA on May 4, 1944, saying that the nonfederalized Guard must always be the top of the reserve component and that Guard leadership must be included in all future military planning. He counted heavily on the traditional willingness of Congress to support the Guard because of its local as well as national relationships.[37]

Meanwhile, Palmer wrote a position paper which Marshall approved and published as War Department Circular 347, dated August 25, 1944. It assumed, for planning purposes, that Congress would enact UMT legislation and that the resultant trained citizenry would render a large standing army unnecessary, thus avoiding a monopoly of the military by a special "class or caste of professional soldiers." Apparently, Walsh's testimony had influenced Palmer, for in the next section the circular said that in time of war the small professional army should be reinforced "by organized units drawn from the citizen army reserve, effectively organized for this purpose in time of peace." Palmer had returned to induction of units rather than individuals, but he did not designate the National Guard as the source of those units.[38]

All the while, the joint regular-Guard committee on postwar military posture continued to meet and study. Another committee met on the same issue, this one created by the Army Reserve. General Marshall merged the two and recalled Major General Milton Reckord, serving as provost marshal general in the ETO, to chair the consolidated committee. Finally, in October 1945, the policy this committee worked out was promulgated as official. It stated that the Guard was always to be "an integral part and first-line reserve component of the postwar military establishment." It added that the Guard strength, combined with the regulars, be kept sufficient to make up a balanced force capable of immediate deployment anywhere in the world. Finally, it provided that the Guard's position in the General Staff be expanded and that at least one member of the Guard be always on duty with that staff.[39]

With the publication of this policy, coupled with Circular 347, any threat to the position of the Guard similar to that which occurred after World War I faded away. The NGB naturally approved of the firm

position assigned to the Guard in the postwar world, but it acknowledged that the Guard would require very strong federal support to live
up to it. Only two elements were missing from the model used by the
planners: UMT did not go into effect nor was an effective reserve
requirement placed on the millions of soldiers who had served during
World War II.[40]

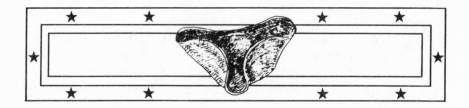

FOURTEEN

The Immediate Postwar Period

The National Security Act, which looms as the dominant feature of American military organization in the postwar period, was passed on July 26, 1947, to fill the need, revealed during the war, for one military instrument rather than several. It created as the agency to achieve this the Military Establishment with three military services in it — the new Air Force, the Army, and the Navy. Among other significant changes, it gave statutory basis to the Joint Chiefs of Staff and placed at the top of the whole system a secretary of defense. As the years passed, the power of the secretary grew and grew. The act implied, although it did not stipulate it in so many words, that the reserve components of the three services would have to become more and more integrated as smoothly functioning parts of a unified defense system.[1]

The Selective Service Act of 1940 had required all selectees who had received training or been in service to enroll in the reserves after the war for ten years or until age 45, whichever came first, but it did not force them to join a unit or even to train. The result was nothing more than a near endless list of persons with military experience. It did not help to populate the National Guard, which now had the difficult task of reconstituting itself from almost nothing, since the Guard had been absorbed into the Army of the United States. Nor did prewar Guardsmen come forward in large enough numbers to make reconstitution successful.[2]

Accordingly, Congress extended the wartime draft act and the president signed it on June 24, 1946. This extension started a significant flow into the Guard, enough to enable Major General Kenneth F. Cramer, chief of the National Guard Bureau (NGB), to report in mid-1947 that the Guard was once more "strong and vital." It contained 2,615 units and 97,527 men. The chief claimed that the public and the press were more strongly behind the National Guard than ever before. Congress went all out on paper, authorizing a Guard of 682,000 members in twenty-seven divisions, twenty-one Regimental Combat Teams (RCT), plus support units, but it voted funds for only a small fraction of this imposing array.[3]

When the extension of conscription ended in March 1947, the draft lapsed for fifteen months, and so did the flow of enlistees into the Guard. At that point, powerful public figures began to issue statements that they hoped would make the Guard independent of conscription. General Eisenhower said that the reserves were equal in importance to the regulars in the Army of the United States. The second secretary of defense, Louis Johnson, stressed War Department Circular 347 of August 1944 which said, "Our strength lies in the prepared citizen soldier . . . ."[4] Various framers of public opinion emphasized the benefits individuals derived from membership in the Guard, among them help in discovering the right occupation for them in civil life.[5] The chief of the NGB wrote that only because of the National Guard was it impossible for any nation to deal the United States a knockout blow. Even if the central government was destroyed, he said, the dispersed Guard would continue the fight.[6]

The NGA persuaded Congress to appropriate $1,000,000 a year for an intensive public relations campaign. The Guard turned to Madison Avenue and in mid-1947 began to place colorful, full-page ads in twenty-five of America's leading periodicals. In addition, it hired Paul Whiteman's big-name band to present a radio program each week called "The National Guard Assembly." It also sent out reams of copy for the state adjutants general to place with local news media. For three years, the Guard had the $1,000,000 to spend, plus much more from other sources. Donated radio time alone amounted to a gift of millions of dollars. In 1949, 640 business firms contributed time and money, and even two old enemies, the AFL and the CIO, expressed public support.[7]

It is difficult to determine how successful the publicity effort was because in 1948 more direct inducements went into effect, one of them of the carrot type, the other of the stick variety. In June, the so-called Vitalization and Retirement Equalization Act began to operate. Under it, for the first time, a Guardsman could earn credit toward retirement pay at age 60 by participating in peacetime training. If he accrued minimum retirement points each year for twenty years, he could qualify for pay. Five of the twenty had to be in active federal service. Unfortunately, the act had one grave fault: if a Guardsman who had served his twenty years died before reaching the age of 60, his dependents would receive nothing.[8]

The stick type of inducement, which also began to operate in June 1948, was a new Selective Service Act, to run for two years. It provided that after twenty-one months of active duty a selectee must enter the reserves for five more years. Men between the ages of 19 and 26 did not have to enroll in a unit or attend drill but could be recalled to active duty for one month during any year. Youths 17 to 18½ became exempt from the draft if they joined a National Guard unit and took regular part in its training for five years. As the act was extended, this provision maintained the strength of the National Guard for the next nine years.[9] Up to 161,000 18-year-olds could enroll for just one year of active duty instead of twenty-one months, thereby not only escaping the draft but also avoiding shipment outside the United States. At the end of their one year, like the others, they too had to enter the reserves.

Even though the draft was suspended during the presidential campaign of 1948, enrollment in the Guard rose sharply until by the end of 1948 it stood at 310,322 persons in 4,875 units, scattered through 4,000 different communities. Despite the fact that draft calls were light during 1949, the Army Guard reached a new high of 356,473 members. Although this was only 51 percent of the unrealistic troop basis set at 682,000, it was still too many for the funds Congress had appropriated. As a result, the army was ordered to cut the Guard back to 350,000, creating for the Guard a second time at which it was obliged to restrict enrollment.[10]

Whenever the NGB especially needed to influence Congress, it turned to the NGA.[11] NGA president Ellard Walsh was formidable and he had an able coadjutor in Major General Milton A. Reckord. Reckord had joined the Maryland Guard in 1901, primarily to play baseball, but had thereafter turned into an ardent Guardsman. In 1920, he became adjutant general of Maryland, a post he held for forty-five years. His age did not keep him in the United States during World War II; he was provost marshal for the ETO until recalled by General Marshall to chair the important regular-reserve committee on postwar military posture.[12]

Walsh and Reckord had influence with powerful people in Washington, and they used it to secure and expand the position of the National Guard. No congressional hearing having even the remotest bearing on the reserves went on without one or both of them there to testify. They were always fully informed, and Walsh usually brought with him a pride of adjutants general to bring pressure on the legislators of their several states. The Walsh-Reckord duo often spoke in harsh terms of the high command of the regular services; Lieutenant General Raymond S. McLain, himself a product of the Guard who had risen to command a corps in World War II, accused them of using Guard-Regular enmity for their own selfish purposes.[13] Few reasonable people agreed with McLain about the selfish interests, but all of them knew that Walsh and Reckord could sway votes in Congress, especially among the numerous states' rights supporters.

There is no doubt that enmity between Guard and regulars was there to exploit. Many Guard leaders firmly believed that high-ranking regulars exercised a long-standing but covert hostility and contempt toward the amateur soldiers to the detriment of the National Guard. They were convinced that the army General Staff still operated on the principle of the expansible army, formulated a century and a quarter earlier by Secretary of War John C. Calhoun, and on the primacy of the regulars given classic expression by Emory Upton in his *Military Policy of the United States*. Neither Calhoun's nor Upton's model included a meaningful role for the National Guard.[14]

Late in 1947, James Forrestal, the first secretary of defense, appointed a board, named for its chairman, Gordon Gray, Assistant Secretary of the Army, to examine the reserves and recommend their best use. In 1948, the Gray Board reported that reserves with a dual state-United States connection could not enhance national security. Accordingly, it recommended that the National Guard be merged into the Organized Reserve. Secretary Forrestal concurred.[15] Defenders of the Guard exploded. *The National Guardsman*, since 1947 the official publication of NGA, announced, "The Battle Is On!" Its editors charged the Board with marshaling evidence to discredit the Guard. Why, they demanded, submerge the Guard in the Reserve? The Guard, after all, had rebounded strongly after the war, while the Reserve barely held its own, and the Enlisted Reserve had, in fact, melted away. Next, the editors turned from the Gray Board to castigate the regular officer corps, which they believed lay behind a systematic effort to eliminate the Guard. National defense was endangered as long as the regular high command continued to try to "divide and destroy the National Guard. . . . Innuendos and falsehoods emanating from the Pentagon" must stop.[16]

General McLain, a member of the Gray Board, let it be known that neither he nor any other member of the Board had anything against the Guard except that it could not possibly be ready when needed. In three years, he pointed out, a Guardsman received 600 hours of training, at most only one-fifth of the time needed to make him ready for combat.[17] Ignoring this sort of testimony, the Guard leaders hurried with the matter to their ultimate protector, the Congress of the United

States. There, it was good politics to stress the power of the states. "So long as the Federal Constitution remains the Supreme Law of the Land," wrote the editors of *The National Guardsman*, "the states are sovereign." Congress quashed the merger proposed by the Gray Board.[18]

With one exception to be discussed later, the National Guard never sought to eliminate the Organized Reserve or to deflect funds away from it. It did, however, at all times insist on its priority as the first reserve component to be ordered into federal service in national emergencies. Only those combat units that could not exist either in the regular force or in the Guard were to be formed in the Reserve. The Reserve must consist, the Guard said, primarily of individuals who had a military obligation but did not belong to a unit.[19]

Major General Butler B. Miltonberger became chief of the NGB in 1946, but he fell ill and had to be hospitalized. Since the process of selecting a chief was complex and slow, he was followed by two acting chiefs, Colonel Dillon S. Myers and Colonel Edward S. Geesen. Meanwhile, the secretary of defense advised the governors of all the states that each might submit as many names for the post as he chose but each nominee must have had at least ten years' experience as an officer. After the governors had submitted their nominees, a board of six general officers screened the candidates and passed three names up to the secretary. He stated his preference and passed the dossier along to the president, who, with the consent of the Senate, made an appointment.[20]

The new chief was Kenneth F. Cramer, who, like his predecessors, did not command but rather advised, counseled, negotiated, supplied information, and persuaded. He had a staff consisting of sixty-nine officers, 40 percent of them from the Guard, and 207 civilians.[21] Cramer estimated that the United States spent about $600 to train each army Guardsman and the state another $300. The price of an Air Guardsman came higher, about $1,100 in total, but he was much cheaper than a regular. Cramer expressed pride in the low cost of Guard training.[22]

Because reserve matters continued to grow in importance, Secretary of Defense Johnson established in his office in May 1949 a Civilian Components Policy Board. Its chairman was a civilian presiding over six regular officers and eleven others selected from the following reserve components: the National Guard of the United States, the Organized Reserve, the United States Naval Reserve, the Marine Corps Reserve, the Air National Guard, and the Air Force Reserve. All matters relating to the reserves were supposed to come before this board, and it was expected to consult with other offices devoted to military affairs. When George C. Marshall succeeded Johnson as secretary, he renamed this body the Reserve Forces Policy Board.[23]

Although the aero units of the National Guard had been scattered during World War II, the Guard desired to reconstitute the air capability. Scant help came from the Army Air Corps which showed no interest in amateur air power, but General Marshall encouraged the movement in order to gain NGA support for UMT in peacetime. Accordingly, late in 1945 Marshall authorized the Air National Guard.[24]

The air force, separated from the army in 1947, felt no more need for the Air Guard than had the Army Air Corps. The chain of command had to run from the commanding general of the air force to the chief of the NGB, thence out to the adjutants general of the several states. Under this system, the air force could not compel the Guard to carry out any of its directives; indeed Chief Cramer instructed the Air Guard units not to comply with any air force order that had not first been cleared with NGB. Because of this faulty chain of command and for other reasons, air force leaders were convinced that the Air Guard would be of little use to the nation and not much more to the states. A governor, they said, would have as much use for his air units as a freight train has for a bomb sight.[25]

Air Force-Air National Guard relationships came to a head in 1948 and 1949. The NGA attacked the way in which the air force handled the Air Guard, and the air force counterattacked by stressing the ineffectiveness of the Guard under the existing chain of command. In October 1948, the NGB created within it two separate divisions, one for the army and the other for the air force. Still, the NGB remained under the Department of the Army, which meant that the Air National Guard was army-controlled. The merger of the Guard into the Reserves was in the forefront of the debate because it was recommended by the Gray Board, but President Truman did not choose to face the political rows with the states that would have resulted had he supported the merger. Since that route was closed, Secretary of the Air Force Stuart Symington persuaded Secretary of Defense Forrestal to send a bill to Congress to merge the Air Guard and the Air Force Reserve. The NGA was able to defeat this and managed to include in the Army and Air Force Authorization Act of that year clauses recognizing the state as well as the federal connection of the Air Guard of the United States. The price of this, however, was loss of power on the part of the chief of the NGB to interfere with the operations of the army and the air force through the divisions of the NGB.[26]

Tests in 1949 showed that Air National Guard units could not be ready fast enough. The air force estimated that they would require three months of intensive training to be in shape. When the Soviet

Union exploded its first atom bomb in 1949, the air force became even more concerned with the shortcomings of the reserve components, for now reaction time had to be shorter than before. Secretary Symington insisted that the Air National Guard was no longer reliable for first-line air defense, but he could not persuade the secretary of defense to agree to change the Air Guard's mission.[27]

In spite of the squabbling, the Air National Guard developed. The policy statement of 1945 had stipulated about 58,000 Air Guardsmen in 514 units. At the end of fiscal year 1947, 257 units had achieved federal recognition; a year later, 393 units containing 29,330 persons had reached that goal, and by mid-1949 all 514 units were federally recognized, with at least 75 percent full strength. There were 3,600 Air Guard pilots for all of whom funds had been appropriated—still 567 short of full mobilization needs. Lack of funds made it necessary to restrict admission into the Air Guard and to limit the pilots to 110 hours of flying per year.[28]

The Cold War began in 1947 with Soviet pressure on Greece and Turkey and with American retaliation against this pressure. It came close to combat when in 1948 and 1949 Russia closed off the land access to the city of Berlin. The United States responded by creating a massive airlift to keep West Berlin supplied, but in this successful effort the National Guard was not directly involved. However, new international tension increased interest in the reserves. As a result, the NGA lobbied for and received retirement pay for peacetime training, death and disability payments, equal pay with the regulars when on federal duty, uniforms like the regulars, and the right to attend the highest-level service schools if the Guard applicants were qualified.[29]

By 1950, the annual appropriation for the Guard had reached $206,000,000, up 6.8 times over 1947. Even this amount of money did not buy everything the Guard needed to become an efficient part of the national force. Equipment valued at $1,016,245,000 was only one-quarter of full war needs. There were only 2,209 armories whereas 3,000 of them would have been required to house 50 percent of the National Guard. Although $250,000,000 was spent on training facilities, they were still inadequate. The Reserve Forces Policy Board urged improvement in the following terms: "In order for the strong, clear thinking and patriotic youth of this nation to be attracted into and be retained as active participants, the reserve components facilities must lend dignity to the activity."[30]

In spite of handicaps, the Army National Guard vigorously reconstituted itself in the five years following World War II. By 1950, it consisted of twenty-five infantry divisions, two armored divisions, twenty RCTs, seven armored cavalry regiments, 570 antiaircraft units, and 701 other nondivisional units. The United States had given federal recognition to 4,436 units of the Army Guard, with 31,162 officers and 348,196 Army Guardsmen. By this time, Guard units were scattered in 2,200 communities, housed in 2,316 armories valued at $500,000,000. All this added up to only 56 percent of the full mobilization needs of the Army Guard but 100 percent of the force which Congress had funded.[31]

Enlargement of eighteen divisions—the number when the war ended—to twenty-five infantry divisions reshuffled the divisions among the states, preserving as far as possible historical continuity. The increase of population had made it possible that four states—California, Illinois, New York, and Texas—could support two divisions.[32]

26th Infantry Division	Massachusetts
27th Infantry Division	New York
28th Infantry Division	Pennsylvania
29th Infantry Division	Maryland and Virginia
30th Infantry Division	North Carolina and Tennessee
31st Infantry Division	Alabama and Mississippi
32nd Infantry Division	Wisconsin
33rd Infantry Division	Illinois
34th Infantry Division	Iowa and Nebraska
35th Infantry Division	Kansas and Missouri
36th Infantry Division	Texas
37th Infantry Division	Ohio
38th Infantry Division	Indiana
39th Infantry Division	Louisiana and Arkansas
40th Infantry Division	California
41st Infantry Division	Oregon and Washington
42nd Infantry Division	New York
43rd Infantry Division	Connecticut, Rhode Island, Vermont
44th Infantry Division	Illinois
45th Infantry Division	Oklahoma
46th Infantry Division	Michigan
47th Infantry Division	Minnesota and North Dakota

48th Infantry Division	Florida and Georgia
49th Infantry Division	California
49th Armored Division	Texas
50th Armored Division	New Jersey
51st Infantry Division	South Carolina and Florida

Before the Cold War began and even before World War II ended, UMT became a public issue. Bills to establish it reached Congress as early as 1943, and although neither Roosevelt nor Thomas Dewey made it a campaign issue in 1944, Roosevelt's two Republican cabinet members, Henry L. Stimson and Frank Knox, backed it. So did Lewis B. Hershey, Director of Selective Service, and most of the powerful eastern newspapers. The NGA, while opposing specific provisions, endorsed the principle. General Walsh asserted that the Guard did not need UMT and opposed any change that failed to support the clause in the Selective Service Act of 1940 which said, "The strength and organization of the National Guard is an integral part of the first line of defense." Moreover, any acceptable UMT enactment would have to channel trainees into the National Guard.[33]

Every peace organization and many educational associations opposed the proposed UMT legislation, as did organized labor. Hanson W. Baldwin, military specialist for the *New York Times*, saw scant use for large numbers of semitrained citizen soldiers in the cold war era. What was needed to impress the Soviet Union was industrial strength, technical skills, and air and sea power. But the most influential of all opponents was the Republican Party. Senator Robert A. Taft of Ohio declared UMT to be wasteful, obsolete, and un-American. He led a powerful group of western and midwestern legislators, teamed up with southern Democrats, in opposition.[34]

Undaunted, UMT supporters again used the arguments from the World War I era. The United States, they claimed, could have kept out of both world wars if it had had a citizen army. Besides being a strong deterrent to war, they argued, UMT was a character builder. The Reverend Daniel Poling, a popular minister of the gospel, said, "UMT will teach the rising generation that . . . patriotism . . . is something glorious, something divine." Harry Truman, first as senator, then as vice-president, and finally as president, never wavered from his support of UMT.[35]

Ironically, it was the Soviet Union that indirectly defeated the UMT legislation of 1948. That year, the Red Army overran Czechoslovakia and closed the land access to Berlin. In the United States, it no longer seemed necessary to give partial military training to a large body of citizens. Instead the need now seemed to be for fully trained troops, ready to go anywhere in the world where there was communist aggression. Congress lost interest in the UMT legislation and voted it down.[36]

No amount of opposition, however, killed the idea of UMT completely because it was, after all, one way to maintain a military capability in peacetime, used by half the nations of the world. When the need for manpower became pressing in 1950, the NGA, the Reserve Officer's Association, and the American Legion combined to bring it up again. The Reserve Forces Policy Board, drawing upon the thinking of both reservists and regulars, prepared a bill which the Department of Defense presented to Congress. Secretary of Defense Marshall, erstwhile general, wrote every senator, urging him to support the bill, and Anna Rosenberg, Assistant Secretary of Defense for Manpower, testified that if the bill passed, the Guard and the Reserves could be ready twice as fast as they then were.[37]

Action on UMT was delayed by President Truman's recall of General MacArthur, and Congress did not get around to passing the UMT bill until June 19, 1951. They called their enactment an amendment to the Selective Service Act of 1948 but later redesignated it the Universal Military Training and Service Act. For the first time in American history, the principle of UMT, administered at the national level, became law. The act also extended the draft. Under it, all males had to register when they became 18. Having registered, they then entered what was called the National Security Training Corps, incurring a total military obligation of eight years. If the president saw the need, he was authorized to induct through selective service as many men between the ages of 18 and 26 as seemed necessary. Inductees became obligated to two years of active service and six in the reserves.[38]

The Universal Military Training and Service Act stipulated that UMT could not go into effect until the National Security Training Commission had formulated a set of rules to govern it in the form of a bill for Congress to act upon. This commission, appointed by the president, consisted of three civilians and two regular officers. It met twenty-three times from July to September 1951 and formulated the draft bill. Opposition sprang up as soon as the content was made public. The NGA opposed it because it made no provision to bring either prior service men or inductees into the National Guard. The same organizations that had opposed UMT in 1948 did so again. Black congressmen obstructed it by proposing amendments to better integrate the National Guard racially. Also, costs, estimated at $4,187,983,600 for the first year, and half that much every year thereafter, alienated many legislators. Accordingly, the same coalition of western and midwestern Republicans and southern Democrats that had defeated UMT in 1948, now rejected the commission's rules for the National Security Training Corps. Without these rules, UMT could not go into effect.[39]

On June 25, 1950, the Soviet-trained and -equipped army of North Korea invaded South Korea. Swiftly, the Truman administration called on the United Nations to intervene and committed American military forces in South Korea. Now it appeared that the Cold War would surely involve the National Guard directly. The Guard leadership, expecting mobilization, sought to instill in its men "the will to kill a ruthless and savage enemy, who adheres to no established rules of land warfare." Every Guardsman must be "imbued with the combat esprit that calls for the utmost in stamina and guts, to include making the supreme sacrifice."[40]

The government, however, believed that Korea was a diversion to enable the Soviet Union to strike into western Europe. The Joint Chiefs of Staff thought the action would be too short to justify full-scale mobilization. Senior leaders in Congress did not favor mobilization. Thus, instead of procuring manpower by mobilizing reserves, the president decided to do it by means of a draft.[41]

As with other wars, the action in Korea went on much longer than the planners believed possible. Throughout its duration, Guard leaders attacked the policy of bypassing the reserves. Reliance on the draft, they stressed, brought into service hordes of people who were utterly untrained while excluding reservists whose training had already been paid for. Selective service operated unfairly, inducting one man in six of eligible age for two years of active duty, perhaps at the risk of his life, and, if he survived, for six more years in the reserves. In shocking contrast, the other five persons performed no service whatever for the country and incurred no reserve obligation.[42]

Major General Walsh indignantly rebutted the charge that the Guard was a haven for draft dodgers. Every man in the Guard, he said, knew he was subject to call and could not be labeled a draft dodger because the administration turned away from the reserves and toward the draft. Walsh also protested an act of June 30, 1955, which permitted the high command to pluck individuals out of Guard units for twenty-one months of federal service. Most of the men so chosen were veterans of World War II who protested that they had done their duty, that it was someone else's turn. General J. Lawton Collins, Army Chief of Staff, regretted the double jeopardy of individuals and the consequent weakening of units but stated bluntly that there was no other way to obtain men with the essential skills.[43]

Besides losing key specialists on which its units depended, the

Guard also had to give up 5,595 wheeled vehicles, 748 tanks, much artillery, 95 airplanes, and some of its best airfields. In addition, under the manpower policy, individual Guardsmen were gravely inconvenienced; they could not be sure whether their units would ever be called, so they could make no plans for their families and their jobs. General Walsh demanded some sort of call-up timetable, but he demanded in vain. General Reckord, in testifying before a congressional committee, lashed out at the high command of the regular services. "In some places in the Pentagon," he said, "they think they see just one more chance to destroy the National Guard." Later, if full-scale mobilization became necessary, he continued, they would say of the units they had crippled, "See, the National Guard is not ready, we told you it would not be."[44]

Before the Korean War was over, about one-third of the Army National Guard had been ordered into service. The one-third included eight infantry divisions: the 28th, 31st, 37th, 40th, 43rd, 44th, 45th, and 47th, called in two different increments. The 31st, 37th, 44th, and 47th never left the United States; the 28th and 43rd went to Europe; only the 40th and 45th became directly involved in the Far East. Besides the divisions, the army inducted three RCTs, forty-three antiaircraft battalions and many other nondivisional units, making a total—including the outfits within divisions—of 1,698 Army Guard units. Enrollment in these, plus individuals called separately, came to 138,600 Guardsmen, less than one half of 1 percent of the 2,834,000 ground soldiers who served.[45] As in the two world wars, the integrity of the Guard units was not maintained.[46]

Unlike the Army Guard, by the end of the first year of conflict, three-fourths of the Air Guard was in federal service. To achieve this level it had had to reorganize ninety-one units, activate eighty-eight new ones, and deactivate 170. Its total contribution came to sixty-six units with 45,594 men in them, providing support to the Tactical Air Command, the Strategic Air Command, and the Air Defense Command.[47]

In April 1951, the military services initiated a drastic new manpower policy, closely linked to reliance on draftees. They began to send individuals home after one year in the combat zone. No longer did the fate of a soldier depend upon his unit; if he survived the year, his war was over and he left his comrades with scarcely a backward look. Guard leaders denounced this system. Far better, they said, to have ordered Guard units into service, and after a reasonable tour in combat to have rotated them back home. This way a soldier would sustain his unit, since he could not go home unless it did. General Reckord expressed fear that individual rotation, if continued as policy after the

Korean War, would destroy unit loyalty, the essence of the National Guard.[48]

The 45th Division makes a good case study of the effects of individual rotation. By the time that division might normally have been rotated back to Oklahoma, there were no more than 2,000 Oklahomans left in it. There was no sense in shipping the rest of the division, 12,000 strangers, back to the home state of the 45th; besides, no other division was ready to replace this one. Here was a dilemma: the State had a claim on the honors of the 45th, as well as a need for militia, but at the same time the army had great need for the unit in Korea. The army escaped the horns of its dilemma in a way that was at least ingenious; there would be two 45th Infantry Divisions, one in Korea, the other in Oklahoma, but the stateside twin would be limited to 50 percent of wartime officer strength and 25 percent of enlisted personnel. Euphemists likened this duality to the British system which maintained part of each honored old regiment overseas and the rest at a home station. Really, however, there was no similarity, for the British system was built on unit loyalty, whereas the American system virtually excluded such loyalty. After the Korean War, the twins were merged and the colors and trophies came together in Oklahoma.[49]

In spite of protests, the services increased their reliance on selective service, as shown in the following table.[50]

	Regular Army	Selective Service	Reserves
June 1951	45%	40%	15%
June 1953	41%	57.5%	1.5%

In the midst of the Korean conflict, and after UMT failed to go into operation, congressional committees began to hold hearings on a new bill originated in the House in July 1951. General Reckord said that there was very little in the bill that would benefit the Guard; if left alone, the Guard could carry out its functions, established in the Constitution and existing statutes, without added legislation. Reluctantly, the NGA agreed to support the House version. After extensive committee hearings, the House passed the bill on October 15, 1951, and sent it to the Senate, touting it as a new Magna Carta for the reserve components.[51]

The Senate was not sufficiently impressed with the Magna Carta concept to hold hearings until May 1952. By this time, the NGA had changed its support to opposition because the bill clearly favored the reserves and did nothing for the Guard. Generals Walsh and Reckord pleaded with the senators to scrap the proposal and instead direct the president to order the Guard to duty in Korea. General Reckord referred to the Standby Reserve as no more than an unwieldy list of names with wrong addresses. *The National Guardsman* asserted that the NGA could never support a system that placed veterans in double jeopardy, while permitting other able-bodied men to avoid service altogether. This legislation had to have UMT to be effective, but UMT was not included; moreover, the Ready Reserve already existed in the National Guard. Guard spokesmen then offered ninety-seven amendments.[52]

NGA's shift touched off the sharpest interchange ever up to that time between Guard and Reserve. Brigadier General E. A. Evans, Executive Director of the Reserve Officer's Association, said he was stunned by the Guard's new position. Reserve officers, he added, would neither forgive nor forget. He felt too bitter to express all that was on his mind, but some of it escaped. Could it be, he suggested, that the National Guard was afraid to have a strong reserve built up, lest the reserves replace the Guard altogether as a federal force? Brigadier General Melvin Maas, speaking for Marine Reserve Officers, permitted his comments to be more ironical than Evans's: "I had never realized," he said, "that the main purpose of the federal government . . . was for the maintenance of the National Guard, and today was the first time I learned that the army was only an auxiliary of the National Guard." *The National Guardsman* noted that Evans and Maas had spoken in anger and said what would have better been left unsaid.[53]

After Congress had evaluated this altercation and other testimony and had adopted most of the amendments to the bill offered by the NGA, it passed the Armed Forces Reserve Act (AFRA) on July 9, 1952. The following were its most important provisions:

1. It eliminated red tape and delay when officers changed from one reserve component to the other.

2. It reaffirmed priority for the National Guard to be ordered into federal service ahead of other reserves.

3. It directed the military services to order Guard units into service as far as possible, but established the right of the military secretaries to transfer personnel among units, once in federal service.

4. It created a Ready Reserve with an upper limit of 1,500,000 members, to be ordered into federal service for up to two years by the president if the president declared a national emergency. The Ready Reserve included all units and individuals of the Army and Air National Guards of the United States as well as every person who had an unfulfilled reserve obligation.

5. It created a Standby Reserve available to be ordered into federal service only when Congress declared a national emergency.

6. It created a Retired Reserve available only in crises of the gravest kind.

7. It directed the military services to give persons ordered into federal service the maximum possible notice, but in no case less than thirty days unless the very life of the nation was at stake.

8. It gave the military departments permission, with the consent of the governors, to order any person in the National Guards of the United States into federal service for as many as fifteen days in any year.[54]

President Truman ordered desegregation in the armed forces, but his order did not apply to the National Guard except when in federal service. As of July 1948, there were 6,988 blacks in the Guard, about one-fifth of 1 percent of the 310,322 Guardsmen. There were twenty-seven National Guard divisions, but only Connecticut and New Jersey permitted Negro units to be part of a division. Ohio admitted a black battalion into the 37th Division, but when the 37th entered federal service and went to Texas, the battalion was detached and converted into a receptacle for black inductees. Nevertheless, by the time the Korean Action was over, five states included one Negro unit each in their divisions.[55]

Whatever the situation in foreign affairs, domestic events continued to involve the National Guard. During the last half of the 1950s there were floods in Florida, Indiana, Illinois, Missouri, Ohio, Nebraska, Iowa, West Virginia, Minnesota, the two Dakotas, and Oklahoma requiring active state service from Guard units. The Louisiana Guard had to haul water to drought-stricken areas. Fires, out of control, brought out Guard detachments in Iowa, New Jersey, South Carolina, Oklahoma, Arizona, Colorado, New York, Montana, Washington, and Maine.[56]

In addition to responding to disasters, the Guard also was called upon to maintain law and order. The most conspicuous case was a nationalist uprising in Puerto Rico. The governor called out the entire Army and Air Guard of 4,300 persons. The detachments engaged in real fighting against insurgents in ten towns. They were not especially sensitive to bloodshed, killing thirty-one insurgents and wounding twelve, with a loss of one of their own. The rebellion collapsed.[57]

After his election in 1948, Governor Adlai Stevenson outlawed racial segregation in Illinois, but when a black World War II veteran attempted to move his family into an all-white apartment building in Cicero, a mob gathered to stop him. After this white mob had wrecked the veteran's furniture on its way into the building, a federal court enjoined all persons from "shooting, beating, or otherwise harassing" this family. Because the mob did not disperse, Governor Stevenson called out 500 Guardsmen. Not since 1933 had the Illinois Guard been involved in riot duty, so it lacked both the training and the weapons for the task. Teenagers showered the Guardsmen with abuse and with stones and other materials, but the 500, in spite of deficiencies in their training, kept together, and with the aid of fifty policemen held off a crowd of many thousands. After they erected a barbed-wire barricade and took position behind it, there was no further trouble. In a few days the Guardsmen went home, with a record of no deaths and no serious injuries, but they had not been able to prevent the wrecking of the apartment building and had not been able to establish the black family in the apartment they had rented.[58]

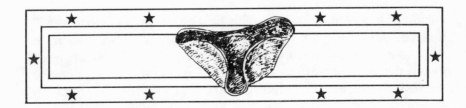

FIFTEEN

The Eisenhower
Administrations

The Eisenhower years are set apart not so much for what they did about the reserve components as for what they were supposed to accomplish in military policy. Secretary of State John Foster Dulles very early claimed to discard the strategy of containment of communism and substitute the liberation of areas under the Soviet yoke. The president himself insisted that all policies must be carried out at minimum cost because a healthy economy was essential to national survival. To that end the portion of the Gross National Product spent on the military declined during Eisenhower's terms from 12 to 8.5 percent. Eisenhower warned of the danger if big business and a highly centralized government drew together into a military-industrial complex that eventually might stifle free society.[1]

The Soviet Union, with its own atom bomb in 1949, hydrogen bomb in 1953, and Sputnik in 1957 was rapidly bringing to an end the American nuclear monopoly. It now seemed that a nuclear parity was essential to prevent large-scale war, a parity maintained only by spending huge sums on nuclear weapons. Since added expenditures for conventional armaments would have jeopardized the economy, the president's people developed a policy of relying on nuclear power to deter aggression at conventional as well as at total levels. That policy, known as Massive Retaliation, threatened to use strategic nuclear power against the homeland of the Soviet Union if the Soviets encroached on territory where they were not welcome. The show-down on this doctrine came when the Soviet forces in 1956 invaded Hungary to overthrow an unfriendly regime and establish a friendly one. They assumed that the United States would not really bomb their territory for this sort of aggression, and they were correct.

The revised American military posture after that was called the New Look. It was presumed to be made up of conventional forces which the economy could support and which at the same time would possess adequate power to cope with the Cold War. Army, National Guard, and Army Reserve must mesh smoothly and efficiently, for the New Look demanded greater reliance on the reserve components.[2] The president said that since half the American troops in Europe would have to be reserves, they must be brought to a high state of readiness. It was encouraging to Guard leaders that he spoke often of returning many governmental functions to the states, but they received a jolt when Dr. John D. Hanna, Assistant Secretary of Defense for manpower, identified civil defense as the primary role of the National Guard in the atomic age. If Hanna was enunciating the true administration policy, it would reverse the direction the Guard had been trying to take since 1879. General Walsh said, "If they want war, let it begin here!," and picked up the political weapons, which he wielded with great skill. Hanna, on his last day in office, had to recant and say that the Guard was the most reliable segment of the reserve component. Secretary of Defense Charles E. Wilson, who personified the president's confidence in the managers of big business and who seemed to have little feel for states' rights, found it necessary to say that future military plans included added strength for the Guard.[3]

In spite of Wilson's statement, a proposal emerged to enlarge the Army Reserve by 300,000 men and to cut the Army Guard by 40,000. An amount of $13,509,000 was appropriated to build armories for the Reserves, but the Guard, which was 1,300 armories short of minimum need in 1956, received only $3,000,000. An additional irritation to the Guard was the proliferation of Reserve units, some of them placed in communities where there were already flourishing Guard outfits. Two units could not prosper in some of these places. Representative Albin Norblad of Oregon said his home town, Astoria, was one such place. Why not allow the small reserve unit to train with the full-sized Guard unit? Secretary of the Army Wilbur Brucker replied to this that the units would fight to keep separate.[4]

After the Korean War, rebuilding manpower was difficult for all reserve components. Major General Lewis B. Hershey, always a favorite with the Guard, suggested that the active services could release men before their assigned two years were up, and these men could serve the balance of their obligated time in the reserves.[5] But President Eisenhower did not want to load reserve time on war veterans and looked instead to UMT for the men needed. The 1951 law authorizing

UMT was still on the books, and the president reconstituted the National Security Training Commission, created in the law, and appointed Julius Ochs Adler, himself a major general in the reserves as well as publisher of the *New York Times*, as chairman.[6]

Adler pushed the commission to complete its report by year's end as the president had ordered. The report stressed the need for trained citizen soldiers to deter a "terrible third world war" which could easily be sparked into flame by the "vicious and slow-burning hatred" the Soviet Union felt for the United States. All men, upon reaching 18, would be required to draw lots to see who would enter active service and who would enter the training program. All, however, must go through six months of military training. Those men whose lot had placed them in the training program must enter the Ready Reserve. When that reserve contained 300,000 persons, the active services would be able to release 100,000 men and achieve savings of millions of dollars.[7] The president presented these findings to Congress, which now had to weigh the economic advantages of the program against the political hazards of UMT. They once more rejected UMT, whereupon Eisenhower dissolved the commission on June 30, 1957.[8]

Congressmen knew that they must upgrade the reserve components. The first move to do so originated with Carl Vinson, who had been a representative from Georgia since 1914, was presently chairman of the House Armed Services Committee, and probably exerted more clout in military matters than a pride of officers of star rank. Vinson's bill might have slid through had not Adam Clayton Powell, black congressman from New York City, attached a rider to it, saying that funds would be cut for all states that segregated blacks in their National Guards. Vinson, a southerner from crown to sole, withdrew his bill and substituted one which did not even mention the National Guard. Although General Walsh stated that the Guard did not mind being left out since it was doing well under existing legislation, the president was annoyed by the change. In any event, Vinson's bill set off lively committee hearings. Tensions between the Guard and the regulars appeared again in these hearings through the legislators themselves. In the earlier hearings on reserves in 1951, Representative Clyde Doyle of California had asked why the Guard and the regulars found it necessary to air their disagreements before congressional committees; could they not resolve problems between them? In the hearings concerning the Armed Forces Reserve Act in 1952, Congressman Landsdale Sasscer of Maryland had not expected the two components to be able to reach an agreement. To him the proposed law was an attempt to use Guardsmen as replacements for regular units to build up one big regular army. Now Representative E. Keith Thomson of Wyoming accused the "West Point Protective Association," of blocking the advancement of reserve officers, and Congressman William A. Winstead of Mississippi cited the treatment of National Guard troops in the Korean conflict as showing bad faith on the part of the regulars. The part of the 31st Infantry Division that came from Mississippi had been trained to enter national service intact, but it was ordered in, broken up, and used as fillers. Galen Marten, speaking for Students for Democratic Action, told the House Committee what it knew but did not want to hear, namely, that the National Guard was not mentioned in Vinson's bill in order to keep the Guard racially segregated.[9]

When the hearings were concluded and the bill put before House and Senate, Carl Vinson, allied with other powerful legislators, turned the proposal into what was entitled the Reserve Forces Act (RFA), signed into the statute books on August 9, 1955. Sweeping though the title was, the National Guard was not mentioned in the statute. The following are its vital provisions:

1. It extended the draft to 1 July 1959.

2. It authorized the army and air force reserves to enlist men 17-18½ years old and exempt them from the draft if they agreed to remain active in the reserves to age 28. Only the National Guard had enjoyed this recruiting perquisite in the past.

3. It reduced the maximum military obligation from eight years to six. (The army, exercising legal discretion, cut the term to five years if preceded by six months' basic training under regular army direction).

4. It stipulated that only 250,000 persons could take basic training in any given year.

5. It directed that recruits who joined after the passage of the act must fulfill their entire training obligation or be subject to the draft.

6. It raised the ceiling of the Ready Reserve from 1,500,000 to 2,900.000.[10]

Stimulated by this act, in which the Eisenhower administration endorsed stronger and more ready reserves, the Reserves for the first time began to put viable units together. As for the Guard, though not mentioned, most of the provisions clearly applied to it. It at once became embroiled with the regular establishment over interpretation of the length of basic training. The regulars said that the act required six months of basic training before entering service, active or reserve. The NGA said that if six months of prior training was enforced, its units would lose 50,000 potential recruits every year. General Walsh insisted that much of the six months was wasted, that three months in the summer, efficiently operated, would provide the same training.[11] Foiled there, the next tactic was to get the required six months split into two three-month periods which a Guard recruit could fulfill in two summers without losing his civilian job. This too failed.

Confusion reigned. NGB urged the states to require at least one-fifth of their recruits who had no prior service to agree to six months of basic training at the start of their tours. In fiscal year 1956, the Army Guard recruited 133,362 people from the 17-18½ age group, of whom 6,983 agreed to six months' basic before further service. The next fiscal year, only 3,463 opted for this route, while 4,598 entered an eight-week basic program. The Air Guard stuck to eleven weeks. Amid these variations, there were 126,000 Guardsmen without any basic training at all and with no legal obligation to take any beyond what was offered in the unit to which they belonged.[12]

The issue required special hearings, in preparation for which General Walsh called an emergency meeting of the adjutants general. If six months of prior basic was enforced, the Guard might wither away, he told the adjutants. Congressman William G. Bray of Indiana, a strong Guard supporter, censured the army for making the six months a requirement for federal recognition when that provision had been purposely stricken from the RFA. Congressman F. Edward Hébert, another champion of the Guard, said that his state, Louisiana, was adamantly opposed to six months' basic training as a prerequisite for federal recognition. If the governor rejected this ruling, which he had the power to do, could the Department of Defense withdraw federal recognition from the entire Guard of the State? After some waffling, the answer from one of the undersecretaries appeared to be "yes."[13]

The army now threw in its heavyweights. General Maxwell D. Taylor, Army Chief of Staff, testified that six months was the absolute minimum to qualify a person for the Ready Reserve. If every member of a reserve unit had six months of basic, the unit would be ready for combat seventeen months after call, half the time otherwise required. To Taylor, two years of Guard training was equal to no more than two weeks in the regular service. Next Wilbur Brucker, Secretary of the Army, spoke in favor of six months, and the president himself sent over a note to the same effect. The army even found a National Guard general who testified that less than six months was, in his experience, not enough. This was Major General Roy Green, Commanding General of the 49th Division, California National Guard, who had commanded at the division level both in war and in peace. General Walsh considered it dirty play for the army to have ferreted out a Guardsman of standing willing to contradict the NGA position.[14]

The army for security reasons now demanded closed hearings,

excluding even the NGA. This so offended General Walsh that when he was once again permitted to testify, he made no attempt to be tactful. He appeared flanked by eight major generals, four brigadier generals, and nine other Guard dignitaries. Army testimony, he said, had consisted of "flowery phrases, half-truths, self-serving statements, and a smoke screen of figures, graphs and charts."[15] Although the six-month program was already a failure, the high command was determined to foist it on the Guard. One of Walsh's flankers, the adjutant general of Colorado, spoke as bluntly as Walsh himself. "We know what we can do," he said, "and the Pentagon does not know. . . . [T]he offices of the Secretary of Defense and the Secretary of the Army are either bullheaded or trying to destroy the National Guard."[16] Representative Leroy Johnson from California accused the regulars of attempting to "massacre" the reserve system, while Thomas E. Curtis of Missouri said that "the Nation's highest military leaders are sabotaging Congressional efforts to develop a working reserve program in favor of a large standing army."[17]

The fracas over the length and timing of basic training seemed to be ending in an impasse. But then Carl Vinson stepped in and pooled his political power with that of Representative Overton Brooks of Louisiana, who had achieved authority in military affairs through twenty years of service in the House of Representatives. They worked out a compromise containing the following provisions.

1. The National Guard could get away with a shorter basic training period during the balance of 1957, but after January 1, 1958, it would have to accept six months.

2. National Guard strength would be guaranteed at no less than 400,000.

3. Recruits in the 17-18½ age bracket, if they started with six months' basic, could complete their military obligation with five and one-half years in the Ready Reserve.

4. Older recruits, starting with six months of basic, could serve three years in the Ready Reserve, then transfer to the Standby Reserve for the balance of their obligation, that is four and one-half years. Note that total obligation for the seniors was two years longer than for the juniors.

5. Persons still in high school could be graduated before having to start basic training.

6. Only the Guard was permitted to try to recruit men who had a military obligation left during the first two months after they were discharged.

7. The Army was to direct its recruiters, 2,500 of them in 1,071 stations, to get recruits for the National Guard.[18]

Recruiting, right after the Eisenhower administration brought some sort of conclusion to the Korean conflict, started slowly. In 1954, six of the Guard Divisions that had been ordered into service were released: 28th, 31st, 37th, 40th, 43rd, and 45th. The NGA requested that these released men be assigned to Guard units to complete their military obligation, but it could not bring this about. Nor did the military establishment attempt to enforce completion of military obligations upon some 1.5 million men. Thus at first no more than 123 veterans per month were enrolling in the Guard. This obliged the recruiters to concentrate on the 17-18½ age bracket, with the result that 70 percent of the Guardsmen had had no basic training at all.[19]

The Guard now turned to large-scale advertising. Twenty thousand mail trucks carried the slogan, "Be a citizen soldier in the National Guard!" Fifty million books of matches carried a Guard message. For this and perhaps other reasons, enrollment rose. In 1954, there were 4,783 Guard units and 276,647 federally recognized persons. Eighty-six percent of the officers had had wartime experience. In 1956, 1,200 regular officers were attached as advisers, and 32,600 Guardsman technicians were employed full time. In March 1957, enrollment reached 434,000, an all-time high. Since the authorized ceiling was 400,000, recruiters had to slack off a bit until attrition cut numbers back to 400,000.[20]

Attrition could be counted on to reduce numbers too rapidly if not carefully controlled and combated. Resignations each year ran between 30 and 50 percent of total force. Some of this was due to employers who were not willing to release their workers for Guard duty, and some came from the mandatory six-month basic training requirement. By 1961, 214,000 Guard recruits had taken their six months, but 100,000 of them left the Guard during the same year as they completed the training. The basic training regulation, however, had at least one good feature; it freed the Guard for the first time from the responsibility of conducting basic training and enabled it to concentrate on unit development.[21]

Once reduced to authorized strength, the Guard had to work hard to stay there. To do so required 88,000 enlistments per year projected to come from the following sources: 18,000 from veterans; 14,000 from persons with reserve obligations; 32,000 new recruits with no prior service.[22]

Up to this point, the Guard had not found it necessary to draw in women. To be sure, there were women in the active armed forces, and thousands had served during World War II. *The National Guardsman* claimed that the Constitution restricted the militia to males, but the editors did not point out on what clauses in the document this interpretation rested. The NGB, disregarding that position, announced in September 1956 that for the first time women would be commissioned as nurses in the National Guard. By February 1957, there were one commissioned female nurse in the Army Guard and two in the Air Guard. There were no enlisted women in either service.[23]

Readiness more and more became the key word. To help achieve it Guard units were directed to substitute three weekend exercises per year for an equivalent number of hours of armory drill. As a result, in 1955, 94.3 percent of all Army Guardsmen took part in field exercises. Force balance required 60,000 Guardsmen to shift from infantry to armor. The 27th Division, New York National Guard, and the 44th Division—transferred from Illinois to Tennessee—as well as the 48th Division converted from infantry to armor. The Guard, in order to insure itself a supply of trained officers in all branches, established more state Officer's Candidate Schools (OCSs). Massachusetts had founded the first of these in 1913, graduating fifty-eight officers from it in 1953. By 1949, forty-two states operated their own OCSs, with 3,000 candidates training in them.[24]

The Department of Defense apparently felt the need to concentrate control of the National Guard as far as possible in the Pentagon. For the Army Guard alone there were seven civilian boards concerned with Guard matters. These reported to strongman Hugh Milton, Secretary of the Army for Manpower, Personnel, and Reserve Forces. Within the military command structure there were around ten staff agencies or committees that could affect the Guard. General Walsh openly spoke of a conspiracy headed by Hugh Milton, Carter Burgess, Assistant Secretary of Defense for Reserve Forces, and Major General P. G. Ginder, Deputy Army Chief of Staff for Reserves, to weaken the Guard.[25] Someone in this hierarchy, without consulting the Guard, decided to shift responsibility for Guard personnel from the Military Districts to the Continental Army. He, or they, created in the Continental Army a new slot, deputy commanding general for reserve forces, and selected Lieutenant General Ridgley Gaither as its first occupant. Gaither held the highest grade anywhere in the reserve system, and the Guard might have welcomed the higher rank as an overall benefit. No so; *The National Guardsman* said the position had been created just to make it more difficult for the Guard to gain access to the chief of staff himself.[26]

In 1958, the Eisenhower administration vastly increased the power of the secretary of defense and weakened the Army, Navy, and Air Force Departments. Command over unified forces all over the world was shifted from those departments to the Joint Chiefs of Staff. The Guard was perhaps less concerned with this than with the frightening power vested in the secretary of defense to "transfer, abolish, reassign, and consolidate." This was rendered somewhat less menacing by the stipulation that Congress had seventy days in which to countermand any use of it. Certainly some satisfaction could be drawn from the statutory standing at last given to the NGB.[27]

No doubt the centralizing process would have gone farther except for the support the Guard received from people who believed in states' rights, especially in Congress. To those people the National Guard was an integral part of the federal system. One congressman from North Carolina said, "Unless we have a Guard, we just don't have a country." Carl Vinson warned the secretary of defense, "You leave our National Guard alone because . . . it is a state organization." Vinson, joining with George Mahon of Texas, another civilian power in military affairs, accused the high command of flouting the will of Congress by failing to spend funds appropriated for the National Guard.[28] Jim Folsom, governor of Alabama, said that if the military power had not been dispersed from the beginning, the United States would have succumbed more than a century before to a military dictatorship.[29]

The executive branch of the United States was the source of the most publicized criticism of the Guard. Charles E. Wilson ("Engine Charley"), Secretary of Defense, made little effort to refine his own remarks and suggested that the National Guard was a refuge for draft dodgers. This brought down on him a gale of criticism from the states so strong that he felt it necessary to assert that he had not exactly meant what he said.[30] Next to give offense was General Curtis LeMay, a towering figure in the air force. LeMay informed the Air Force Association in the fall of 1959 that the weekend warriors were not much good to the air force. The NGA requested at once that the general be reevaluated. After an interval in which some sort of evaluation took place, the secretary of the air force said that the general "only intended to stimulate dynamic thinking which would insure vital and essential roles" for the reserve components.[31]

The Air National Guard fitted better into the Eisenhower pattern of smaller-but-more-ready than did the Army Guard. State officials acquiesced in the program as they came to realize that the Air Guard was primarily a part of the national reserve force, and at the national level the air force also began to view it as such. Charles J. Gross asserts that until the Korean conflict the Air National Guard was mostly a government-sponsored flying club.[32] Afterward, however, planners began to put it into the scheme of air power, less because of the Guard's Korean performance than because of politics and budgetary considerations. Generals Twining and White, when air force chiefs of staff, used the Air Guard to influence states' rights legislators in favor of the air force. Finally, there was a personality factor in the smart upgrading of the Air Guard. In 1952, Brigadier General Earl T. Ricks, Adjutant General of Arkansas, became chief of the Air Division of the NGB. He brought with him Lieutenant Colonel I. G. Brown and Major Winston P. Wilson, and the three of them, known as the Arkansas Connection, ran the Air Guard for the next twenty-three years.[33]

Strength and appropriations improved steadily. Air Guard manpower, which had stood at 26,272 before Korea, rose to 71,000 in 1959, and the number of full-time technicians was up from 5,814 to 13,200. Appropriations jumped from $114,690,000 to $233,440,000 in the same period. Turnover of personnel ran at 25 to 30 percent, considerably lower than in the Army Guard.[34]

Nevertheless, after Korea the Air Guard faced grave problems of rebuilding. Its units had been scattered and it had transferred $500,000,000 worth of equipment to the air force. It lacked trained pilots and most of its airfields would not accommodate jet craft. Forty percent of the Air Guardsmen had had no prior training; half of these 40 percent were between the ages of 17 and 18½. Although eminently teachable, they had yet to be taught. Up to 1958, basic training was only eleven weeks, with a postbasic program of two hours each during two nights per month and one eight-hour day. This training schedule gave way to one full strenuous weekend every month.[35]

During the Eisenhower administrations the Air Guard's mission grew more diversified. Now it included Tactical Air Command (TAC) fighters, fighter interceptors, reconnaissance units, troop carriers, heavy air lift, and aero-medical evacuation. By 1960, equipped with F-104 Starfighters, F-100 Supersabers, and F-102 Delta Daggers, the TAC units rated 68.8 percent ready in planes and 87.5 percent in crews. The main mission, however, remained air defense of the homeland. Guard capability here was enhanced in 1954 when some units received 7F-94AB all weather interceptors, the first craft specifically designed for air defense that they had ever received. By 1957, there were seventy-six squadrons of fighter interceptors in the Air Guard, twenty of them on around-the-clock alert. The Air Guard claimed that it handled a substantial portion of continental air defense at one-third of the cost of regulars, and in addition guarded Hawaii almost alone.[36]

The Army Guard also received a slice of homeland defense. By 1957, it had converted twenty-nine 90mm AAA batteries to air defense missiles. It manned its missile sites with seventy-six persons, whereas the air force used 111. The Guard units also had 111 members, but the thirty-five not on site continued to train. Control of the Guard's missiles resided with the professionals but had to be exercised through the adjutants general of the states.[37]

During the first Eisenhower administration, the Supreme Court in 1954 handed down one of its most influental decisions. Since separate schools for the races, even if equal, violated the Constitution; they must be integrated. Demonstrations took place at once and involved the National Guard. The first use of the Guard occurred in Clinton, Tennessee, in September 1956. The black population of Clinton was only 220, but John Kaspar of the Ku Klux Klan traveled there to whip up antagonism. Governor Frank Clement concluded that it was his duty to enforce the ruling of the Court. Accordingly, with reluctance, he sent one tank company to Clinton, and along with it Joe Henry, Adjutant General of Tennessee. At 35, Henry was the youngest adjutant general in the nation's Guard. He insisted that the entire company make the trip, whatever their outlook on desegregation, not to help the blacks attend a white school but to enforce the law and maintain order. The Guardsmen carried loaded weapons and stayed nine days but there were no casualties, and some black children did attend the desegregated school.[38]

Satisfied that Clinton would remain orderly, Henry next led a task force of two tanks, twelve jeeps, and seventy-five men to Oliver Springs where trouble seemed imminent. With his weaponry lined up behind him, Henry ordered the crowd to disperse. To his great relief it did melt away, and his task force was able to leave within twenty-four hours.[39]

North of Tennessee, Governor Happy Chandler of Kentucky had also decided that he must enforce the Court's mandate and that the best way to do it was to get his troopers in position before trouble flared up. The hot point was Sturgis, so when the first day of school came, Adjutant General Jacob Williams of Kentucky was on the spot himself with his men in a solid line along the entire length of the school block and a tank at each end of the block. Even though the crowd was mostly women, there was some scuffling and minor bloodshed. The *Sturgis News*, reporting the affair, said Guardsmen were behaving like Nazis, but black children did enter the white school. Major General Williams then moved his column to Clay, with similar results. About 900 Guardsmen were involved in Clay and Sturgis, and they were the total force used, since most of the schools in Kentucky integrated peacefully. The Tennessee and Kentucky experience demonstrated two facts about the Guard: that an adjutant general determined to carry out the orders of his governor could do it effectively, and that Guardsmen could be relied on to do their duty, even when it ran counter to their cultural background.[40]

Governor Orville Faubus of Arkansas chose the opposite course. When the school year opened in 1957, Faubus himself blocked the entrance of blacks into Central High School in Little Rock. On September 2, he called out some of the Arkansas Guard to keep the high school white, necessary, he said, in order to maintain law and order. Meanwhile, certain of the president's advisers had with some difficulty persuaded him that he must intervene in Arkansas. Eisenhower's first step was to federalize the Arkansas Guard. Because there was no precedent since the Civil War for using Guardsmen in federal service to control internal disorder, there were many high-level conferences. Out of these came the decision to order rather than call the Guard, since that way, although the orders must pass through the governor, he would lose control of the state troops. Against the possibility that Faubus might refuse to transmit the federal order, the president placed Major General Edwin A. Walker, a professional, in command and directed him to be sure that the order reached all Guardsmen. Thus, the order from the national commander-in-chief went out to the Arkansas National Guard, totaling 10,000 persons, on September 24, 1957.[41]

This order created a situation without precedent: it directed the Guardsmen to disregard their state commander-in-chief and obey the commands of the president at a time when they were on active state duty. Such a confrontation had always been possible because of the wording of the militia clauses of the Constitution. The Arkansas Guard, no doubt after some intense deliberation, followed their national commander-in-chief. After all, the United States paid roughly 95 percent of the Guard's bills; every man who ignored the president's order would be absent without leave and subject to the penalties pertaining to that offense.[42] Since no federal money had been budgeted for such a contingency as this, the army had to stretch its operating funds to meet costs of $79,000 a day.

President Eisenhower had ordered the entire Arkansas Guard into federal service to take it out of Faubus's hands. No more than 15 percent of the men served near the high school, but the rest had to report to their home stations once a day and to drill eight hours each week. For this they drew the same pay and rations as the 15 percent, and in addition they continued to work at their civilian jobs and draw that money. This inequitable arrangement ended when General Walker organized a task force of 1,800 Guardsmen and discharged the rest.[43]

The president sent a detachment from the 101st Airborne at Camp Campbell, Kentucky, to Little Rock, and for a time they became the key force. Their approach impressed at least one of the teachers as much more professional, much more crisp than the Guard's, but economy required them to return to Kentucky in November. The policy was to rely on school officials to maintain order inside Central High, but in time it became necessary to assign two Guardsmen to follow each of the nine black students everywhere except into classrooms. Governor Faubus claimed that the bodyguards even trailed into the girls' dressing room, but his charge was examined and disproved. Incidents were constant, and more than once some of the blacks insisted that they must have more protection or they would have to drop out. The lot of the principals and the teachers was more strenuous than that of the Guardsmen, for no day passed without the need for judgment on whether or not harassment had occurred. When Governor Faubus addressed the military at all, he referred to them as the "occupation forces," but notes so addressed were not accepted at headquarters. Guardsmen stayed on through graduation, taking place on May 27, 1958, when one of the nine, Ernest Green, received a degree without incident. Little Rock authorities closed the high schools for the 1958 and 1959 terms.[44]

Around the nation, the governors continued to employ their Guards for state uses. During the summer of 1954, Governor Gordon Persons of Alabama gave his Guard a unique assignment. For more than a century, Phenix City, Alabama, had been notorious for vice. Since it lay just across the Chattahoochee River from Ft. Benning, it had been a trouble spot to the army as long as the fort had existed. The murder of a reform candidate for state office brought a detachment of the Guard to town to clean it up. At first, the detachment was to join with local officials in raiding known centers of vice, but the local officials tipped off the proprietors. Once it became clear that the city officials were part of the vice ring, the governor declared martial law, freeing the Guardsmen to make raids on their own. The adjutant general himself governed the city under martial law for 200 days, a regime unprecedented in American history. When the Guard moved out some vice moved back in, but Phenix City never returned to the old days.[45]

An increasing number of states established their own police forces until by 1953 there were 22,000 such officers. The National Guard was delighted to turn law and order over to the state police because it freed them from an unpopular activity and enabled them to fit better into the national reserve. Moreover, the Guard was able to retain its most popular mission: rescue and relief. Year after year, that function was part of Guard duty; from 1947 to 1953 its percentages were: floods, 29.7 percent; wind, 15.2 percent; missing persons, 14.2; city fires, 6.2; forest fires, 5.9; mercy transport, 5.9; snow, 5.2; traffic and crowd control, 3.9; wrecks, 3.6; strikes, 2.1; all other missions 6.5 percent.[46]

For the NGA an era ended when Ellard Walsh stepped down from the presidency in 1957 after holding the office for fourteen years. The

NGA, building on what Walsh had done, continued forcefully to represent the Guard. Representation became more impressive when in 1959 NGA moved into imposing new headquarters at One Massachusetts Avenue, Washington, D.C., a giant stride from the hotel suite which Walsh had rented with his own money at the start of his presidency.[47]

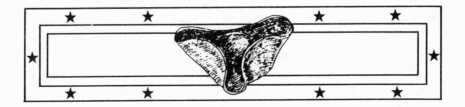

SIXTEEN

The Turbulent 1960s

The administration of John F. Kennedy had been in place only five months when in August 1961, the Soviets began to build a wall separating East from West Berlin. Premier Khrushchev informed the president that the United States must agree to make Berlin a free city or his forces would choke off all access to it from the West. Kennedy replied to this by alerting some of the military forces, among them parts of the National Guard.

Units of the Air National Guard went early. Eleven of twenty-five squadrons ordered out were in Europe within a month of induction. During the first two weeks of October 1961 they flew 216 jets across the Atlantic. Of the personnel on the rolls, 99 percent responded at once, taking an average cut in pay of 61 percent. In the end, a total of 21,067 Air Guardsmen were involved. The Guard was proud of its response, but the air force saw it as somewhat flawed. The main problem was that the tactical fighter units of the Air Guard had never been considered part of the M-Day force. Thus, they were prepared not for mobilization but for training.[1]

The first of the Army Guard to be ordered into federal service were the 32nd Infantry and the 49th Armored Divisions, as well as 264 separate units. Ninety-eight percent of the Guardsmen on the rolls answered the call promptly, but since Army Guard units contained only 60 percent of combat-level strength, they needed 39,000 new men to round them out. As in the Korean mobilization, these fillers came from the individual reserves. Most of them had served before, were not drawing pay as active reservists, and had not planned their lives to enter service a second time. They complained bitterly that it was not fair to reuse them when hordes of eligible men had never served a day for their nation. Accordingly, 18,000 of the individual reservists requested exemption as did 6,000 who were drawing pay but were in units not ordered into service.[2]

In the end, 45,118 Army Guardsmen entered federal service. Some of their units were ready in three months, but the slowest were not yet fully organized when demobilized ten months later. None of the Army Guard units went overseas.[3]

Partial mobilization for the Berlin crisis as for Korea worked hardship on many Guardsmen. Some lost homes they had just saved enough money to buy; others had to close down businesses that could not run without them. Many wives, outraged by the injustice of the order, took their bitterness out on their husbands, who had no choice but to go. A few firms cut off credit to families whose breadwinners had been ordered into the service. Senator Richard Russell of Georgia, responding to the complaints arising from the hardships, proposed that fillers in the future be drawn from the draft rather than from the individual reserves.[4]

After the Russians had cut off the emigration of people from East Berlin, they eased the pressure on the West. This made it possible for all Guard units to return to civil life by the end of August 1962. But another international crisis came to a head in October. High altitude surveillance revealed that the Soviets had placed missiles capable of inflicting heavy damage on the United States in Cuba. This time President Kennedy issued the ultimatum. If the missiles remained in Cuba, he said, the United States would use all its power, including nuclear weapons, to remove them. The Air Guard was required to transfer certain strategically placed air bases to the air force and put some units on twenty-four-hour alert, but no part of the Guard was ordered into federal service. When the Soviet Union removed the missiles, the crisis passed, and accelerated training was stopped.[5]

Partial mobilization had caused so much personal discomfort that the Air Guard and the Army Guard had trouble rebuilding. The Air Guard was handicapped because the air force did not return vital equipment. The retention rate throughout the Guard dropped to an average of 54.6 percent in 1964.[6]

The Berlin crisis was the first instance in which the Guard had been partially mobilized as a tool of foreign policy. The chief of the National Guard Bureau (NGB) and the president of the National Guard Association (NGA) insisted that the Guard had shown itself ready, but they worried about the strain caused by partial mobilization. The sharp decline in membership caused the editors of the *National Guardsman* to ask their readers how often a National Guard unit "could be used and wrung out in this manner?" The deeper, unarticulated question was whether or not the reserve components could fulfill the administration's expectations as pawns in the game of Cold War diplomacy.[7]

The office of secretary of defense had been progressively strengthened since unification in 1947, and John Kennedy appointed to it a unique person who was to exert considerable impact on the National Guard. Robert S. McNamara grew up in California obviously an achiever at all stages. In high school he always dressed neatly, never took to denim and sloppiness, fashionable as it was. At the University of California at Berkeley, he made Phi Beta Kappa and then went on to earn a graduate degree at the Harvard Business School. In the air corps during World War II, he rose to be a colonel with a specialty in statistical control. Afterward, he sold himself and several other statistics experts—the "Whiz Kids"—to the Ford Motor Company, and that company made McNamara its president at the same moment, almost, when Kennedy was elected president. His tenure as president of Ford was very short.[8]

McNamara thought that the Guard had not shown itself ready enough during the Berlin crisis and set out to shape a smaller, quicker responding reserve.[9] His first step was to eliminate four National Guard divisions: the 34th, Iowa and Nebraska; 35th, Kansas and Missouri; 43rd, Connecticut, Rhode Island, and Vermont; and the 51st, Florida and South Carolina. These divisions were to be replaced by separate infantry brigades, containing four to six battalions each. He also marked three reserve divisions for termination.[10]

The NGA, bitterly opposed to this reduction, turned to Carl Vinson, now 80 years old but powerful as ever, and his House Committee on Military Affairs to block it. The state governors, too, were asked to refuse to approve the slaughter. None of the obstacles stopped McNamara; he trimmed 802 units from the Guard effective May 1, 1963, but he added a brigade in each of the following states: Nebraska, Connecticut, Vermont, and Florida, cutting the net unit loss to 416.[11]

Thereafter, the National Guard contained twenty-three divisions, six of them armored, and seven separate brigades and 1,743 smaller units. The Army Reserve, too, dropped from ten to six combat divisions. Four of the Guard divisions were placed in what was designated the Immediate Reserve: the 26th Infantry, Massachusetts, the 28th, Pennsylvania; 30th, North Carolina; and 50th Armored, New Jersey; all one-state divisions. Counting nondivisional elements, 58 percent of the Guard was in the Immediate Reserve, compared to 77 percent of the Reserves, but the latter were in support roles. Congress funded the Immediate Reserve to maintain itself at 80 percent of combat strength and to be ready to enter action ten months after M-Day.[12]

The streamlining of the Guard was part of the Kennedy administration's turning away from the New Look reliance on nuclear weapons and toward conventional forces that were more efficient and more ready. In 1956 the Eisenhower administration had adopted what it called the pentomic configuration for divisions, deemed to be more survivable than the old triangular formation on a nuclear battlefield. The pentomic division had five battle groups instead of the three regiments of the triangular division, each of the battle groups being smaller than a regiment and without a fixed table of organization. Kennedy planners, shifting away from reliance on atomics, replaced the pentomic division with the Reorganized Army Objective Division, called ROAD. The idea of the ROAD structure was to have three brigade headquarters to which any sort of variation of units could be attached, depending on the mission.

The Guard leadership protested that at each reorganization it lost units. More such rearrangements, they added, might cripple the effectiveness of the Guard for years to come. Still, each time the secretary or other agents of the high command mandated changes, the Guard loyally proceeded to transform itself. In spite of everything the chief of the NGB said in 1963, "step by step the Guard has moved across the hazy boundaries that separate the near amateur from the near professional to the full professional."[13]

Lyndon Johnson, who became president after Kennedy was assassinated, retained McNamara as secretary of defense and supported fully in the matter of ready reserves. The secretary's next move was remarkable because it reversed the trend of reserve matters since the end of World War II. At a press conference on December 12, 1964, he announced a plan to merge the units of the Army Reserve into the Army National Guard. The Army Reserve thereafter would consist entirely of invividuals not units. In addition, he proposed to reduce the authorized size of all reserves from 700,000 to 550,000 and the number of units from 8,100 to 6,000. He intended to inactivate fifteen Army Guard divisions and six divisions from the Army Reserve. This would leave the Guard with eight divisions and sixteen separate brigades.[14]

Opposition to his project was fierce and immediate. Why, some opponents asked, reverse the stand for ever larger reserves which the department had been taking since 1948? The secretary had clear responses to this. First, the divisions to be terminated were 50 percent short of combat manpower and 65 percent short of equipment. To make them militarily useful would require at least a year and a half and $10,000,000,000. Second, none of them were in the nation's contingency plans. In contrast, the department would maintain the surviving units at 75 percent of combat strength and program them to be ready as soon as the regulars had completed their mobilization (two months at the most). Finally, the secretary pointed out that times had changed, and currently did not call for large numbers of untrained men but for highly efficient, quick-response units.[15]

The Senate Committee on the Armed Forces began its hearings on this radical proposal in March 1965, parading before it the entire high command of the army, both civil and military. The Air Guard, not being included in the merger, was not involved. Secretary McNamara was not at his best as a witness before congressmen. He offended them at the start by claiming that he had the power to make the changes without congressional approval. Often, too, he appeared to be concentrating on paper work he had brought with him and paid no attention to the lectures being directed at him. At this time, he announced that military transportation for junketing legislators would be sharply cut.[16]

Why select the Guard rather than the Reserve to receive merged units and persons? The Gray Board had recommended just the opposite in 1948; the Armed Forces Reserve Act of 1952 and the Reserve Forces Act of 1955 had favored the Reserve over the Guard. Proponents found no difficulty in responding. The states, they said, had to have their National Guards and could defeat any plan that weakened the state-Guard relationship. Besides, all the combat divisions in the military contingency plans were already in the National Guard. In addition, 24 percent of the Guardsmen were careerists as opposed to only 12 percent of the Reservists; there were five times as many full-time technicians in the Guard as in the Reserves. Finally, the long tradition of the militia could not be ignored.[17]

From the viewpoint of management theory and practice, the dual reserve system was cumbersome and expensive. But some people who sought a single system argued that the state connection of the National Guard made it unsuitable as a national reserve force in the era of the Cold War. The line of control of the Reserve did not have to run through a state chain of command as it did in the Guard. In only eight states did the adjutant general have command power and in many he was not even a federally recognized officer.[18] These people said that it was impossible to make an efficient national instrument out of fifty-two state-oriented military establishments which already had the important mission of helping to preserve internal order and mitigating human suffering caused by fire, flood, drought, snow, and wind. The rebuttal to this last argument was that the control line from the army to the Guard had worked in the past and that the Guard was well managed and could make it work in the future.[19]

The top command of the Guard and the NGA supported the proposal. Even with the reduction in total reserve strength the Guard stood to gain 2,000 units. There was no doubt that the change would cause great turbulence, but no more than had the shift to ROAD. The NGB chief asserted that the Guard could handle the task if given the chance. Secretary McNamara sweetened the plan by estimating that it would save $150,000.000.[20]

Major General J. W. Kaine, chairman of the army General Staff's Committee on the Reserves, dared oppose the merger. Unemotionally, he presented fifteen reasons why the change was not in the national interest.[21] Colonel John T. Carleton, the Executive Director of the Reserve Officer's Association, did not try to keep his emotions out of his testimony. McNamara, Lieutenant General E. H. S. Wright, Chief of Reserve Components, and Wright's deputy, Brigadier General Thomas Kenan, Carleton said, "like Israel of old came forth with a coat of many colors to wrap around their produce. . . . It was soaked in the blood of the Army Reserve."[22] By this time the Reserve had supporters as loyal as the Guard had; the Reserve had obtained a vested interest.[23]

Controversy did not center so much on the merits or demerits of the proposed merger as on the question of who had the power to make so radical a change. Congressmen charged the secretary with having ignored the agencies that by statute had to be considered in reserve policy. They grilled him on whether or not he had really consulted the Army Reserve Forces Policy Board, called the Section 5 Committee, and the Reserve Forces Policy Board of the Secretary of Defense's Office. They took exception to a booklet called *Why Merge*, issued by the Defense Department even before Congress had been notified of the proposal. *Why Merge*, they said, attempted illegally to take the issue out of Congress to the people.[24] They charged the secretary with holding reserve levels below those mandated by Congress. McNamara rejoined angrily, "When the Congress says 'You shall program 700,000 men' even though I think it is a terrible waste, as I do, we program them. We wasted the money, but by God we did it, and we did it exactly as Congress authorized."[25] The senators and congressmen did not like to be told that they had wasted taxpayers' money, especially by a man whom many considered to be far too high-handed. Congressman F. Edward Hébert suggested the following diplomatic formula for the secretary to use: "Gentlemen, we have this plan and we want it to work. We believe . . . that it is the best plan for our country but we need your help under the law, we need your cooperation."[26] McNamara either could not or would not take such an approach, and Congress killed his merger plan in the Appropriations Act for fiscal year 1966.

Apart from the vindication of congressional authority and the dislike of the secretary, another development doomed the merger plan. The war in Vietnam was requiring a higher level of combat readiness in American conventional forces than ever before, and the legislators feared that so radical a change in the reserves would diminish rather than increase readiness.[27]

Secretary McNamara, foiled in the merger route, tried a different way to heighten reserve readiness. Deputy Secretary Cyrus Vance outlined it to a House committee on September 30, 1965. The department was creating a Selected Reserve Force (SRF) of units which would be funded to recruit and equip up to 100 percent of combat strength. The ground portion of SRF was to consist of three divisions with three brigades each, the first one drawn from active Guard brigades in Pennsylvania, Maryland, and Ohio; the second from Indiana, Illinois, and Michigan; and the third from Minnesota and Wisconsin, with a third brigade drawn from far off Oklahoma. In addition, SRF would contain six separate infantry brigades, a separate mechanized cavalry regiment, and 822 company and detachment-size units. The total drawn from the National Guard was 744 units with 118,700 persons, and that from the army reserve amounted to 232 support-type units and 31,300 people. Unfortunately, there was no place from which to find the supplemental strength of the SRF units except from the other 70 percent of the Army Guard, which would suffer in order to build up the elite 30 percent.[28]

The Air Guard contributed nine tactical fighter groups and four tactical reconnaissance groups to the SRF which, like the Army units, were funded for 100 percent strength in men and equipment.[29]

To stimulate enrollment, the authorities authorized a 50 percent increase in paid drill time to members of the SRF. Numbers by the end of fiscal year 1966 stood at 115,251 Guardsmen and 28,779 reservists. Perhaps these figures were high enough, but the level of readiness was not, hence the secretary commenced in a surprisingly short time to cut back the new elite corps. By June 1967, only 720 units remained in the SRF, and the allowance for 50 percent extra paid drill time was gone. Funding at 100 percent strength ceased when 1967 ended, and the residue of SRF was designated SRF 1a. The reasons for the swift demise of this project are not clear, but insufficient readiness is the key.[30]

Early in 1968, the department replaced SRF 1a with SRF II. This new configuration contained the same Air Guard elements as before, while its Army Guard members were the 26th Infantry Division, Massachusetts and Connecticut; 42nd Infantry Division, New York; 39th Infantry Brigade, Arkansas; 40th Infantry Brigade, California; 116th Armored Cavalry Regiment, Idaho; plus thirty-four separate battalions, ten headquarters units, three evacuation hospitals, and 107 miscellaneous companies. The Guard's contribution totaled 89,000 people in 622 units, drawn from 798 communities in forty-nine states. Pentagon planners programmed SRF II to be ready in seven days after call with 93 percent of combat strength. SRF II lasted only until September 30, 1969, by which time the perennial search for reserve forces able to respond almost instantly had taken a different direction.[31]

The Department of Defense, continuing to stress a high state of readiness rather than large numbers, announced through Deputy Secretary Vance that the reduction of the Army Reserves proposed in 1965 would be carried out in 1967. This meant the deactivation of six understrength divisions not in the contingency plans, involving 751 units and 55,200 persons. Vance denied that this cut violated the 1966 law, stating categorically not only that the reduction was legal but also that defense had the power to carry it out without specific approval from Congress. There was, after all, no trace of merger left in the program. Following his announcement, various witnesses pleaded for the doomed divisions because of their fine war records, but the reduction took place anyway.[32]

The 1965 proposal had included steep cuts in the Army National Guard also, and the department now prepared to carry them out. It did, however, offer the Guard something in return: the transfer of all combat units from the Army Reserve to the Army Guard. McNamara, speaking on June 2, 1967, set September 1 as the date when the changes must be completed. Between June and September, though, Congress intervened to forbid the transfer of the combat units. The inactivation of the fifteen Army Guard divisions took place on schedule: of infantry, the 27th, 29th, 31st, 32nd, 33rd, 36th, 37th, 39th, 41st, 45th, 46th, and 49th; and of armored, the 40th, 48th, and 49th. This left the following divisions in the Army Guard:

26th	Massachusetts with one brigade from Connecticut
28th	Pennsylvania with brigades from Maryland and Virginia
30th Mechanized	North Carolina with brigades from Georgia and South Carolina
38th	Indiana with brigades from Pennsylvania
42nd	New York with a brigade from Michigan and Ohio.
47th	Minnesota with brigades in Iowa and Illinois
30th Armored	Alabama and Mississippi
50th Armored	New Jersey with brigades from New York and Vermont.[33]

Major General James Cantwell, president of NGA, contended that the high command had broken faith with the Guard. The Army Guard, expecting the transfer to it of reserve combat units, had submitted to a reduction of its units from 5,493 to 4,001 and later to 2,883. Then the Pentagon reneged and handed back to the Reserve much more than Congress had mandated, "and took it out of the National Guard hide—the all important combat units needed to do the state mission."[34] Actually what the Department of Defense did was to add three brigades to the Army Reserve, take twelve battalions from the Guard, and transfer thirty-eight combat and combat support battalions from Guard to Reserve, giving the Guard service-type units to replace them.[35]

The high command continued to impose changes on the Guard and the Reserves at a dizzying pace. In 1968, it phased out the fourteen corps, created in 1958 and 1959 to facilitate control of reserves, releasing thereby 2,900 military personnel and 1,400 civilian employees from routine work to move them into more direct aid for the enlarging action in Vietnam. The office of deputy secretary of defense for reserve matters came into being, as did a new assistant secretary for the purpose of coordinating reserves in each of the three services.[36]

McNamara had failed in his attempt to develop but one reserve component instead of two. He had made the effort for efficiency's sake, but he had learned that there were vested interests in the military establishment, which were concerned with military attributes other than efficiency. Even the attempt to place all combat units in the National Guard and all support units in the Reserve had failed. What had resulted was a substantial reduction in the size of the reserve component and a great deal of experimentation. The cuts and constant changes presented staggering problems to the Guard leadership, for the officers and men could not be moved like pawns. A captain in a unit in his home town might not be able or willing to accept a majority in some distant city. It was possible, of course, to pick up the number of a unit and move it, leaving the men who had made it up where they were, but it is obvious that this would require constant retraining and bring on many resignations.[37]

Deep cuts in the reserve components were possible because of the Johnson administration's decision to rely on the draft for manpower to go to Vietnam. This reliance and the existence of the draft brought large numbers of volunteers into the Guard. There were 420,924 Guardsmen in the spring of 1966, and 79,000 of them had to wait for spaces to open up in training camps before they could take their basic.[38]

Because race relations occupied the United States during the 1960s, the National Guard became increasingly involved in riot control. It was common to speak of progress in racial integration in the system; in 1965, McNamara denied that segregation existed in the armed forces, but the statistics continued to look lean. In 1965, of 370,269 blacks eligible and qualified, only 5,356 were in the Guard. Three years later, at the end of fiscal year 1968, there were only 4,944 blacks among 390,874 Guardsmen.[39]

With little delay, the Kennedy administration decided to support James Meredith, a black, when he sought admission into the University of Mississippi, but it chose to follow a use of force somewhat different from Eisenhower's at Little Rock. Prime dependence was to be upon federal marshals, and before the incident was over, it had assembled 400 marshals from far and wide. The marshals did not prove to be enough, whereupon the president sent regulars and ordered the entire Mississippi National Guard into federal service to keep it out of Governor Ross Barnett's hands. At its peak, the force available for use at Ole Miss totaled 30,656 men, 10,393 of them Mississippi National Guard. About 14,700 of this small army was in Oxford itself, 12,000 of them regulars, most of the balance Mississippi Guardsmen. The latter had scant training in riot control, and probably hated the duty, but 92 percent had turned out, facing hostile mobs with their rifles unloaded.[40]

During the last day of September and the first of October, 1962, a virtual battle went on in Oxford. Of the 400 federal marshals, 166 were injured, along with 48 men in uniform and 31 civilians. Major General Creighton Abrams, Jr., a general officer of high competence, personally represented the army chief of staff. By October 9, the worst was past; most of the Mississippi Guardsmen were released except for 2,600 who remained on duty with the same number of regulars. A small detachment of marshals was responsible for the personal safety of Meredith until he was graduated on August 18, 1963. Total costs for enforcing the Supreme Court ruling in this case came to $5,000,000.[41]

During the summer of 1963, when blacks applied to enroll at the University of Alabama, the integration controversy shifted to that state. Governor George Wallace ordered out 700 Guardsmen to preserve order, that is, to keep the black applicants from attending. To offset this, the Kennedy administration—which had become sensitive on racial issues through Attorney General Robert Kennedy—on June 11, 1963, ordered the entire Alabama Guard into federal service. As in Mississippi, the Guardsmen obeyed the orders of their national commander-in-chief. By June 16, the number in active service was down to 4,000, only 100 of whom were around the campus. They were sufficient to maintain a few blacks at the University, but in the fall the president once more federalized the entire state Guard to foil Governor Wallace's attempt to keep the schools white in Birmingham, Mobile, and Tuskegee.[42]

In 1961, Martin Luther King, Jr., had organized a freedom ride from Selma to Birmingham. Menacing crowds of whites surrounded the church from which the ride was to start. Since the governor would offer no protection, one hundred U. S. marshals formed a cordon and withstood two assaults. Just as the marshals were about to be overcome, the governor changed his stance and sent 800 Guardsmen to accompany the freedom-ride buses. Four years later, King believed it was possible to risk a march on foot. On March 7 and again on March 9, 1965, state troopers turned back the freedom march covering the same terrain as the ride of 1961. On March 9, hostiles savagely beat three white marchers, killing one of them. Governor Wallace refused to interfere. When on March 17, a federal district judge ruled that the march, being orderly, must be permitted, Wallace still refused to intervene on the grounds that the state could not afford the expense. After reasoning in vain with Wallace, President Johnson federalized part of the Guard, placing them in a task force with 1,000 regulars. Marchers were limited to 300, but these were guarded on land by the task force, and overhead by the Air Guard. Before all troops were released on March 25, 1965, 1,938 Guardsmen had been involved.[43]

Racial warfare was not confined to the South. In its severest form it flared up beginning on the night of August 11, 1965, in Watts, a black suburb of Los Angeles. Although not the worst ghetto, Watts was a place where resentment against white exploitation of blacks festered. Gangs were an intrinsic part of life there, hatred of the white police was intense, and some 60 percent of the population were on relief. When a white highway patrolman arrested a young black for driving while intoxicated, there began a scuffle which turned into six days of pitiless rioting. The police tried to cope, but on the third day the police chief asked that the Guard be sent to help. Because of a mixup of orders, it was twelve hours before the first troops were deployed. Their arrival made a difference, and by Saturday night the worst was over. Law and order forces the size of a small army had had to be summoned to quell this insurrection. Part of these forces consisted of 13,400 Guardsmen drawn from the 40th and 49th Infantry Divisions, not yet eliminated in the reserve cuts. Whole blocks of Watts were burned to the ground, and stores not burned were wrecked and gutted by looters. Property damage was estimated at $200,000,000. Thirty-five people died, most of them black; 1,000 more were wounded. By August 18, the battle was considered sufficiently at an end that the Guardsmen could leave it. Seven months later, Watts flared up again, and 500 Guardsmen returned. All in all, during the two periods of rioting, 60 percent of the California Guard was in service. Its performance was creditable; it deterred violence, and most of the destruction cannot be charged to the intervention of the Guard.[44]

A prolonged heatwave in the Midwest during the summer of 1966 ignited latent racial hatred there. As the temperature soared over 100 degrees, residents of one of the black slums in Chicago turned on a fire hydrant to play in the cool water. When police came to shut it off, rioting commenced. Anarchy reigned for seven hours, two people died, and at least fifty were injured. At the start of the second day, Mayor Daley appealed to Governor Otto Kerner who responded so rapidly that by evening 4,000 men from the 33rd Infantry Division, well trained in riot control, were in the trouble zone. Their orders were, "if fired on, shoot to kill."[45]

Police and National Guard established an effective liaison. The Guard, for its part, stationed a squadron at each intersection while a second squadron, divided into two columns, worked both sides of the street. When it was necessary to clear a passage, Guardsmen formed the tested wedge. Because of the effectiveness of these methods and police cooperation, the Guard was able to go home on July 24, after nine days. Martin Luther King, Jr., praised their conduct.[46]

Heat and hatred set off rioting in the Hough District of Cleveland, Ohio, triggered by a perfectly trivial incident in July 1966. In Hough, black leaders persuaded the mayor to request Guard help. Governor Rhodes ordered 1,000 Guardsmen to leave Camp Pickett, where they were engaged in summer training, to go. Since the military vehicles were needed at camp, the detachment, now swelled to 2,034, rode to the scene in chartered buses. Once there they ate food bought at the local markets and slept in the armories of the local Reserve. Each man lost the $6 difference between the federal pay for summer training and the state rate for riot duty. After eleven days, with thirty-two injured Guardsmen and a cost of $200,000, the Guardsmen were allowed to withdraw.[47]

It was hot in Milwaukee, Wisconsin, too, and when a group of blacks were picketing the home of a judge, a white crowd, in an ugly mood, started to gather around them. At this point, Guardsmen began to appear, until 3,000 were there, interposing themselves between the crowd and the blacks. The Guard sealed off traffic to the area. By the third night it took no more than 195 Guardsmen, officers and men, to preserve order, and the following day, August 31, 1966, all were able to return home.[48]

The same day that the Guardsmen were relieved in Milwaukee, a pressing need for the Michigan Guard arose in Benton Harbor. Although one person died and several were injured, the Guard remained aloof, assembled in an armory twenty-two miles away, training in riot duty. For five days, disorder continued and all that time the Guard remained detached. Local law enforcement officers finally closed the incident without Guard aid.[49]

During the first week of September 1966, someone shot a black from a passing auto in Dayton, Ohio, and set off a riot. Mobsters looted fifty or more stores before local officials could stop them. Mayor Hall read the riot act over radio and TV and called out 1,198 Guardsmen. Since Guard units were not drawn together in summer camp as they had been in Hough two months earlier, response was slower; not until the third day did 1,000 Guardsmen reach the scene, and lacking any advanced planning, they were at first ineffective. In collaboration with the local police, they began to develop a system. One policeman and three Guardsmen rode in each police cruiser, while Guardsmen controlled all intersections. Given a section of the city to handle by itself, the Guard leaders posted two men in every liquor store and enforced a curfew. After disorder waned, all but a few Guardsmen were relieved on September 4, the rest three days later.

In California, the next violence requiring Guard intervention, took place in San Francisco in September 1966. It resulted from the death of a black youth at the hands of a white officer. The 49th Infantry Division was required to put 3,163 Guardsmen into state service. Some of these men, having served the year before in Watts, were better trained and able to clear the streets rapidly. Cooperation with the governor's office, the state disaster agency, and the local enforcement people was good enough to conclude the need for the Guardsmen in four days.[51]

The balance of the year 1966 was relatively quiet, but the following summer again brought racial hatred to the surface. A policeman in Newark, New Jersey, arrested a black cab driver, but the black community believed that he had beaten the cabby to death. Rioting commenced on July 12, 1967, and continued unabated for the next two days. The disorder was so appalling that Mayor Hugh J. Addonizio roused Governor Richard J. Hughes at 2:20 A.M. to ask for the aid of the Guard. Responding swiftly, Hughes placed Major General James Cantwell in command of a composite force of 3,000 Guardsmen, 375 state troopers, and 1,400 policemen. By the afternoon of July 14, Cantwell's column had established an effective cordon around the riot area, making it possible for the governor to assure President Johnson that no federal intervention was needed. Pickets stood guard behind barbed wire, while mobile squadrons in an armored personnel carrier closed in on snipers. By the time the Guard could be released on July 17, twenty-six persons had lost their lives and 1,500 suffered injuries. Thirty-one percent of the 14,733 members of the Jersey Army Guard had been committed.[52]

Of these 14,733 Army Guardsmen only 251 were black or Puerto Rican, and only 50 of the 2,500 in the Air Guard were nonwhite. What went on in Newark looked like a lily-white Guard battering a suppressed black and Puerto Rican population. To alter this image, the governor announced a drive to enlist 700 persons from the state's two largest minorities.[53]

One week after rioting had died down in Newark, it flared up in Detroit, Michigan. This riot, too, was ignited by a petty incident, but before it was quelled 85 percent of the Michigan Guard entered state service. When they could not stop the disorder, President Johnson sent General John Throckmorton to take command of what became a small army which at its peak included 10,399 Guardsmen and 5,547 regulars. Throckmorton banned the use of live ammunition, but the Guard either did not receive the order or, because the state commander disagreed, did not obey it. What followed was a great deal of unnecessary gunplay, killing 40 persons and wounding an astonishing number of 2,000. All of July passed before the Guardsmen could be released.[54]

In the use of the National Guard by state authorities to preserve order, there had never been a quarter-century equal to the twenty-two years from 1945 to 1967. Officials in 28 states had called Guardsmen out 72 times, involving 197,579 citizen soldiers. Before the Detroit riots, the Department of the Army had done little to direct the National Guard toward riot training, but the excessive use of the rifle by the Guardsmen in Detroit and their lack of less lethal weapons called attention to the need for change. Accordingly, the army issued a directive requiring all Guard units to complete thirty-two hours of training in riot control and to follow this up with sixteen hours each year. FM 19-15 went out to all adjutants general in August 1967, followed by a revised version in 1968. In addition, the Chief of Staff sent federal teams to state headquarters to inspect and to spread the word.[55]

It was apparent that the weapons of the National Guard were not suited to riot control. In 1967 the army began to distribute more appropriate instruments: tear gas grenades, mace, super sound makers, barbed and barbless tape, foam, face masks, riot helmets, vests, shields, and shotguns.[56] In addition it conducted schools to show senior Guard officers how to use the new equipment and a school in each state for junior officers who were then assigned to conduct four-day sessions in their states. During August and September, 1967, 9,000 junior officers received some instruction in riot control. These officers learned that they need not concern themselves with the right or wrong of societal conflicts, only with the means to restore order in as short a time as possible with a minimum loss of life and property. By October 1, 1967,

403,000 Army and 26,000 Air Guardsmen had received the thirty-two hours of basic training in riot control.[57]

Training notwithstanding, racial hatred continued to spawn violence. With the murder of Martin Luther King, Jr., on April 4, 1968, the number of incidents multiplied to 107 during the balance of 1968, involving 150,000 Guardsmen.[58] The army found it necessary to establish a directorate for civil disturbances in the office of the Chief of Staff, with a lieutenant general as director. But after 1968, the race issue began to yield to the war in Southeast Asia as a cause of riots, and the locale of civil commotions shifted from cities to campuses.

Early in United States involvement in Vietnam, President Johnson decided not to mobilize the reserves and to rely on draftees to fight in Asia. In making this decision he overruled both Secretary McNamara and the Joint Chiefs of Staff who wanted to order at least 200,000 reservists into federal service. There seem to have been three major reasons for President Johnson's decision:

1. To conceal from the American people the high level of military commitment that the nation was making in a distant land.

2. To avoid sending belligerent vibrations to the North Vietnamese, the Soviets, and the Chinese. Major General James Cantwell, by this time president of the NGA, agreed with this idea in these words: "When America mobilizes its reserves, a shock wave goes around the nation and around the world."

3. Secretary McNamara gave expression to the third reason: to preserve the reserve component as untapped power "available to meet further contingencies for fulfilling our treaty commitments." In those words he voiced the administration's fear that Vietnam was no more than a diversion to distract attention from a greater effort elsewhere.[59]

In spite of the policy, portions of the Air Guard began in January 1966 to fly cargo to Southeast Asia. In the first six months of their involvement, they flew 687 round-trip missions. The crews, however, were not mustered into the active air force but were paid as trainees, carrying out exercises required by federal regulations.[60] Once the air force was heavily committed in the war, the Air Guard took over many of its duties, both stateside and in Europe. It handled an average of 110 flights per month, carrying men and cargoes wherever they were needed. At that time, it constituted the main strategic reserve.[61] The Air Guard units that were ordered into federal service at first seemed threatened with dismemberment because they lacked pilots, but in the end this lack was filled and they were allowed the rare privilege of continuing to operate as units.

Two events in 1968 induced President Johnson to order a limited number of Guardsmen into federal service. The first was the Tet offensive which the North Vietnamese began in January and continued far into the spring. Under other circumstances, this attack would have produced total mobilization of the reserves, but not in this case.[62]

The second event was the capture of U. S. *Pueblo*, loaded with electronic equipment, by North Korean naval forces. In another era the seizure of a ship which the United States government claimed was in international waters, would have brought military reprisal, but in 1968, with American forces heavily engaged in Vietnam, all the United States did was bring a few reserves into federal service. The president ordered up some units of the Air Guard on January 25, and more on April 11. The Air Guardsmen had thirty-six hours to reach their assembly points, which they accomplished, and within four months four tactical squadrons were in the danger zone. In all, the Air Guard deployment included eight tactical fighter groups, three tactical reconnaissance groups, and three brigade headquarters, consisting of 10,511 Air Guardsmen drawn from twelve states and the District of Columbia. The rest of the Air Guardsmen served as trainees.[63]

Concurrent with the second call for the Air Guard, the president ordered thirty-four major units of the Army Guard into federal service. The final total came to 12,234 Army Guardsmen from seventeen states, but only 7,000 of them ever reached Southeast Asia. Of these 7,000, 4,000 were detached from their units and sent as fillers. The war in Vietnam was over for Guardsmen by mid-June 1969, four years before the last American troops left the area. No Guard unit, air or army, had served more than one year.[64]

Because the National Guard was scarcely used in Vietnam, it became a refuge for men who sought to escape being drafted into that war. During the conflict, there were always more Guard recruits than the training centers could accommodate. In 1969, for example, 28,000 more college-trained men entered the reserves than volunteered for active service. Ten of the Dallas Cowboys' most powerful players enrolled in the same Guard unit. This, and similar obvious evasions, prompted Senator Edward Kennedy to say, "We have a system which allows professional athletes to join National Guard units which neither train nor guard." Although the senator later disavowed this statement, it hurt the image of the Guard and brought strong rebuttals from the Guard leaders.[65] They had urged the president, they said, from the start to mobilize the National Guard. Their units, they insisted, were at the highest peak of readiness and resented being sidelined when they had earned the right to participate. Their men, far from trying to dodge the draft, knew perfectly well that their units might be ordered in at the convenience of the government.[66] Whatever the leaders said, the rank and file of the Guard was probably glad to be left at home, and the many applicants to enter the Guard did so to keep out of Vietnam.

Thousands of Guardsmen were obliged to take part in that portion of the war that occurred in the United States. During May 1970, for example, Guard detachments served twenty-four times at twenty-one different universities in sixteen states to control the rioting students induced by President Nixon's decision to bomb in Cambodia. The climax came at Kent State University, Ohio. After the students there had set fire to the ROTC building and pelted with stones the firemen who tried to put out the fire, the mayor of Kent asked the governor for help, but he did not bother to inform the president of Kent State that he had done so. Thus the president learned of it first when advanced detachments of the 145th Infantry and the 107th Armored Cavalry began to arrive on the campus on May 2, 1970.

The adjutant general of Ohio, Major General Sylvester Del Corso, traveled with them and assumed personal command of the task force on the campus. Del Corso formed his men in a skirmish line near the gutted ROTC building, ordered his men to fix bayonets, and laid down a tear gas barrage to clear the area. The students hurled rocks, bottles, and foul epithets at the Guardsmen. One student received a bayonet wound.[67]

FM 19-15 prescribed the following sequence of actions against rioters:

1. A show of force accompanied by a proclamation to disperse.

2. If the crowd did not scatter, enter riot control formations and move against the resisters.

3. If resistance persisted, use tear gas or high pressure water, or both.

4. Use rifles, but unloaded.

5. Only as a last resort use gunfire.

Many of the men in the Guard ranks had had only fourteen of the thirty-two hours of riot-control instruction, and their commanders did not follow the FM 19-15 sequence. Moreover, Ohio was the only state in the Union that required Guardsmen to keep a live round in their weapons.[68]

On May 3, the second day of Guard duty, control passed from the local police to General Del Corso. That day the students injured ten

Guardsmen with rocks or bottles. The next day, May 4, 1970, as the Guardsmen marched down Main Street to their positions, student demonstrators again pelted them. They also burned the American flag and displayed in its place the red flag of North Vietnam. All the while they chanted:

One, two, three, four, we don't want your fucking war
Ho, Ho, Ho Chi Minh, the NLF is gonna win
Two, four, six, eight, we don't want your fascist state.

News reporters from every big city recognized that if this sort of provocation continued there would be gunfire. It is evidence of how little the students understood the culture in which they had been brought up that the same truth was not apparent to them. The officers of the Guard, through poor maneuvering, had managed to get their troops surrounded. Students threw rocks and obscenities, and yelled "Shoot!" at a few Guardsmen who had leveled their rifles. What they did not expect to happen, happened; at 12:22 P.M. on May 4, twenty-six of the Guardsmen did shoot. They fired fifty-nine shots in thirteen seconds, killing four students, some of them not even rioters, and wounding nine others.[69]

This fusillade set off a nationwide emotional outburst. It obliged President Nixon to appoint a commission to investigate campus unrest; the commission condemned students who bombed and otherwise destroyed property, and at the same time condemned citizen soldiers who were needlessly quick on the trigger. In Kent, however, prominent citizens thanked the Guard for restoring order, and alumni doubled their donations to the university. The Governor of Ohio, Frank J. Lausche, for his part, said that he would not hesitate to call out the Guard again under similar provocation and to order that their rifles be loaded. Still, there lingered a general belief that the Ohio National Guard had lacked adequate training in riot duty and that it could have restored order less brutally.[70]

The American Civil Liberties Union filed suit on behalf of the riot victims. As the case proceeded, the ACLU lawyers found that there was no well-developed body of law by which to restrain the National Guard. The lawsuit dragged on for nine years until in January 1979 Ohio agreed to pay $675,000 to aggrieved parties. The governor and twenty-seven Guard officers signed a statement expressing deep regret over the bloodshed, acknowledging that they ought to have found a better way to restore order. The plaintiffs accepted this as an apology.[71]

Through all the troubled 1960s the Guard was able to keep its ranks full. Whereas the Army Guard had reached a low of 276,647 in

1954, it attained a high of 466,000 in the spring of 1966. The draft and the war were responsible. Even though the press to enter the Guard was such that recruits had to wait to enter training centers, in the decade 1957-1967 a total of 572,619 completed their basic; 55 percent through regular army centers, 22 percent through prior service, and 18 percent through the Guard program. In the mid-1960s, only 5 percent had received no basic training at all.[72]

The reserve obligation for recruits with no prior service was six years. Most of the men who joined the Guard frankly stated that it seemed the easiest route by which they could serve out their six years, even though the Guard was intensifying its training. The traditional two-hour weekly evening drill in the armory was giving way to an entire weekend once each month in the field. Using movies, radio, brochures, outdoor advertising, and hundreds of thousands of comic books, the Guard sought to develop its image as a vehicle toward a healthy and useful life.[73]

In 1965, Senator Margaret Chase Smith attacked the Guard for its lack of blacks and especially its lack of women. Nevertheless, not until 1968 was a law enacted that permitted women, in addition to nurses, in the National Guard. The Air Guard quickly let it be known that it would employ women more widely than the Army Guard, which stopped their use in any position below corps headquarters. The first three WAFs in the Air Guard completed basic training in 1969.[74]

As always, the state governments used their Guardsmen. The high point of state use to preserve law and order came from 1970-1973, when 233,000 Guardsmen served on 201 occasions.[75] Relief and rescue missions were more numerous, the foes being snow, floodwaters, drought, fire, and earthquake. In the winter of 1961, the New York Guard helped dig the city out of its heaviest snowfall on record. Guardsmen in the Southwest rescued travelers stranded by severe snowstorms. Guard helicopters dropped fuel to the Eskimos in Alaska; they dropped necessities to animals as well as people in other parts of the nation. A California artillery battery fired its guns to start an avalanche under controlled conditions. There were rescue missions due to trainwrecks releasing deadly chemicals. The Guard loaned its ambulances where none were available to local populations and it airlifted desperately sick people to hospitals. It freed birds caught in an oil spill, then helped to clean up the spill. A quarter of a million Guardsmen donated their blood to bloodbanks. In November 1961, the Guards along the east coast had to cope with Hurricane Carla.[76]

In spite of the high frequency of use by the states, the states paid a smaller and smaller proportion of total Guard costs. In 1933, the states' share was 33 percent; by 1963, it had dropped to 6 percent. This meant that the Guard was more secure as part of the first-line military reserve than ever before, but it also meant that the Guard would obey the national commander-in-chief rather than the governor. Guard leaders pointed out that their portion of the component was a good federal investment, for the 94 percent of Guard costs was no more than 4 percent of the military budget for 1963. The share of the defense burden borne by the Guard far exceeded 4 percent.[77]

How was the health of the National Guard after a turbulent decade? In spite of the fact that the Guard had been a constant actor in the violence of the 1960s, the Guard thrived. Guardsmen had been employed on both sides of the issue of civil rights for blacks, doing on both sides what they had been ordered to do. Did this make of the Guard a plastic institution with no conscience? Not necessarily. The basic question is, "To what extent is an individual obliged to follow his own conscience when duly constituted authorities have spoken?" Many dissenters of the right of the United States to be in Vietnam elected to follow their own lights, but the average Guardsman went with the institution in which he was embedded.

In the rioting on the campuses, the Guard was uniformly on the side of law and order. From some points of view, they committed atrocities, the most conspicuous one at Kent State. What would have been the fate of the nation if maintenance of law on campuses had rested with local police forces or the regular military? What if the most radical of the rioters had achieved their objectives, namely, to destroy the universities and beyond them the other institutions of the nation in order to clear the ground for a new society not as rotten as the one they thought they were living in?

Although there are no certain answers to these questions, they have to be asked. What is clear is that the National Guard survived with relatively minor scars despite its central role as a force arm. The Guard survived the taint of being a refuge for draft dodgers. One advantage of its exclusion was that it came through without the lingering scent of napalm and Agent Orange upon it. The National Guard had advanced under adverse conditions. It had shown itself to be a reliable constabulary at the same time that it became an effective part of the national military reserve.

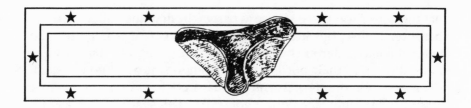

SEVENTEEN

The Guard in the 1970s

Two events dominated the history of the National Guard in the decade of the 1970s. The first one was the end of United States involvement in the war in Vietnam. The second one was the end of the draft. Well before its finish, however, the draft had lost much of its dread due to the reduction by the Nixon administration, as the war wound down, in draft calls. Whereas the requirement per month in the summer of 1971 had been 10,000 draftees, by the end of 1972 it was zero.

A blue ribbon committee, headed by Thomas S. Gates, Jr., Secretary of Defense under President Eisenhower, had found that the draft was no longer needed. It voiced the public mood, turned antidraft by the Vietnam experience. Diverse public persons accepted the conclusions of the Gates Committee. One was Dr. Curtis Tarr, Director of Selective Service; another was Senator Barry Goldwater—always in favor of a muscular America—because he believed that when the nation needed soldiers, there would be more than enough young men who would volunteer. Morris Janowitz, distinguished student of military sociology, disagreed with Goldwater's expectations, since he believed that the military spirit had waned in America; but even he approved of the end of the draft. His reason was a conviction that the era of mass armies was over everywhere in the world.[1]

There was also opposition to the lapse of the draft. The president of the NGA doubted the will of the nation to maintain adequate reserves without conscription. The National Guard could not keep up its strength without the draft in the background. Senator John Stennis of Mississippi, powerful in military affairs, opposed the move, as did Mendel Rivers of South Carolina, Chairman of the House Armed Services Committee.[2]

An amendment to the Selective Service Act of 1967 became law on September 28, 1971. This provided for a draft of specified numbers of men up to June 30, 1973, but, in fact, Secretary of Defense Melvin Laird announced the end of actual drafting on January 27, 1973. The basic law is the Act of 1967 which provides that the selective service system be maintained on a standby basis. In addition, it provides that the president have the power to select men and induct them. To exercise that power, however, he must have a substantial appropriation from Congress.

Early in 1980 President Carter announced his intention to commence again to register men and women in order to have the needed roster if selective service was ever again put into operation. The first batch to be registered were those born in 1960 and 1961; after that men and women would be registered upon reaching age 18. Congress voted $13,300,000 to fund registration of men, but nothing for women; on June 25, 1981, the Supreme Court of the United States ruled that it was legal to register men without registering women. Since that time, different agencies offer different figures on the number of men, required to register, who have done so. The law enforcement agencies have commenced to press cases against selected young men refusing to register. These are defended by the Civil Liberties Union on the grounds that they are being discriminated against, selected as they are from among thousands of others at random.[3]

It was obvious that the National Guard would have trouble maintaining its strength. The number of men waiting to enter the Guard had dwindled from above 100,000 late in the 1960s to 15,000 in October 1971. At the same time, the strength of all the regular forces was also declining; late in 1973, the active army stood at 800,000, but by the fall of 1975, it was 600,000. The navy had slipped below 500 ships, and the air force retained only two-thirds of its earlier peak strength. To professional military people, the sinister part of this trend was that the Soviet Union and the Warsaw Pact nations were steadily enlarging their armed might.[4]

It seemed unlikely that the reserve component would enlarge as the regular component shrank. Polls showed that 75 percent of all Guardsmen would not have enrolled if it had not been for the draft. It was obvious that few young men in the early years of the decade had the slightest interest in a military career. Of the large numbers of Guardsmen completing their obligatory tour, only three out of a hundred were willing to reenlist. As for people with prior service in the active forces, only one out of 200 joined the National Guard. Worse yet, one-fifth of all recruits dropped out before a berth opened for them to take their basic training and of those who entered basic, one-quarter failed to finish.[5]

Nevertheless, some time passed before the Guard began to reflect the lapse of conscription. The Army Guard strength at the end of fiscal year 1974 stood at 410,682 persons; in 1976, it was 375,706; in 1978, it was 350,000 and dropping. Congress funded the Army Guard at 400,000 strength, but the Guard could not climb up to that figure. Strength for the Air Guard was 95,000, which it maintained for a time, but at the end of fiscal year 1977 it had declined to 92,000.[6] Army Guard leaders began to state publicly that their branch could not keep up essential strength under the All-Volunteer Force (AVF). Whereas the Gates Committee had anticipated that 265,000 recruits each year would be enough, actual requirements were closer to 470,000 due to turnover of personnel. The solution, certain leaders said, was to adopt some sort of national service under which every male, and perhaps female, upon reaching eighteen, would be required to serve the nation either in a civil or in a military capacity.[7]

In the absence of a compulsory incentive, the Guard had to launch an intensive recruiting campaign. It trained 7,000 recruiters and received permission to place some of them at army separation points where they could at least approach the men leaving active service. These recruiters were able to offer several inducements: for example, men with long hair could keep it provided they were willing to wear a wig when on duty. More important, they could offer prior service people the opportunity to sign up for a one-year trial period—"Try one" was the slogan—and get out at the end of the year if not satisfied. They could give men with an uncompleted military obligation the chance to cut their active service by as much as eighteen months if they would agree to serve out their contracted term in the Guard. In addition, during the year beginning April 1, 1974, they could place one out of every five prospects in a six-year program, half in the active army and half in the reserves. Army Guard and Army Reserve could even enroll high school seniors who were sure to be graduated within ninety days.[8]

As a recruiting device the Guard publicized its role as an indispensable part of state and local life. It aimed this effort especially at employers who were reluctant to give their workers time off for military duty. But it aimed also at the larger community. The 875th Engineer Battalion in Arkansas, distressed by the plight of boys who dropped out of school, established a trade school for dropouts so that such boys could find useful work. The 102nd Engineer Battalion created a park at the northern tip of Manhattan Island for underprivileged children. The West Virginia Guard dragged in more than

100,000 derelict automobiles defacing the landscape, and junked them. The Guard in Newark, New Jersey, and a company of engineers in Tennessee did the same thing on a smaller scale. In California, a Guard unit provided tents and camping gear for underprivileged children to use at Yosemite.[9]

Guard leaders began to press Congress to appropriate money to pay bonuses both for enlistment and for reenlistment. Even with a bonus, they argued, a reenlistee was much cheaper than a raw recruit. But Congress used a different arithmetic. Its members knew that the reserve component would need 60,000 recruits each month and that a bonus for each one, original or reenlisted, would require millions of dollars. If recruiting costs became exorbitant, the entire volunteer army might be priced out of existence, and they did not act until 1977. At that time the decline in numbers in the reserves and the contrasting increase in Soviet bloc forces stimulated Congress to appropriate $3,000,000 for the Army Guard to use in ten states on a trial basis. But since there was a shortfall in recruiting, half of this appropriation was held back. The active army also fell short and lost the use of $64,100,000. Nevertheless, in 1978 Congress made another appropriation for bonuses, this time for $25,000,000; $10,700,000 of it for the Army Guard, $1,600,000 for the Air Guard, and the balance for the other reserve forces. Beginning in December 1978, recruiters could offer two sorts of inducement: cash and educational benefits. To quality for a bonus for original enlistment, a recruit had to have no prior service, be a high school graduate, and be in the top three categories of aptitude tests.[10]

There was another financial reform for which leaders strove that had at least an indirect bearing on recruiting and a great deal on retention of personnel. The law stipulated that a Guardsman might serve twenty years or more in which he accrued retirement, but that he could draw no retirement pay, even if he retired early, until aged 60. There was scant complaint about this; rather, the flaw was that if he died before reaching 60 his dependents received nothing at all for his years of service. The NGA, along with other interested parties, urged that this be corrected, and in time it was.[11]

Guard recruits with no prior service were required to start their tour with six months' training under regular army control. What hurt recruiting was that those volunteers could not begin to draw pay until enrolled for basic training and often had to wait extended periods for a berth to open up in a replacement training center. In 1974, the secretary of defense ruled that high school graduates might train with their units until ordered to report for basic training and might draw pay for the training time. Even so, too many recruits were not willing to wait and did not appear when at last a berth was opened for them. The waiting list at the end of fiscal year 1977 stood at 15,567.[12]

Throughout the decade Congress raised military pay, and Guardsmen shared the raises for training. From 1967 to 1975, civil service pay rose 55 percent, military pay 87 percent. If an E-3, for example, had three or more years of service, his pay for a day of duty in 1969 was $7.71, and in 1976, $15.85.[13]

Since about 6,000 officers left the Guard each year, Guard units welcomed those who had been forced out of the regular service due to reduction in force. Unfortunately, although there were 2,138 riffed officers in fiscal year 1976, few of them became Guardsmen. The states attempted to fill the need by operating office candidate schools (OCSs), and they supplied most of the second lieutenants who came in as replacements. This source was flawed because the OCS graduates had no prior active service as officers and less than six months in most cases as enlisted men. There were many experienced officers in the Individual Ready Reserve (IRR), but they sought to keep out of service rather than return to it. This obliged the Guard to look to ROTC for additional second lieutenants. To aid here, the Department of the Army ruled that an ROTC person could escape two years of active service if he affiliated with a Guard unit. Moreover, he could obtain his commission as second lieutenant before graduation and receive pay in that grade. In spite of these inducements, the reserve components received less than the 2,000 officers they had expected to draw from ROTC each year.[14]

So hard pressed was the Guard to keep its numbers up that it turned to sources not heavily tapped before. One of them was the black population. Since the civil rights movement of the 1960s it was good for the image of the Guard to seek them out. The results of the quest were remarkable: at the end of 1969 no more than 5,541 blacks were in the Army Guard, 1.18 percent of total strength; by the end of June 1977 there were 54,595, or 15.2 percent of total strength. When other racial minorities were added in, the total came to 85,304, or 23.4 percent. About one thousand blacks had made their way into the officer corps.[15]

The Guard also turned to women, but not counting nurses it started very slowly. In 1971, recruiters could accept no woman unless she had had prior experience at the E-5 level or above. That rule had to be relaxed, so by the fall of 1972 there were 338 women in the Guard, excluding nurses. By June 30, 1973, 518 had joined the Army Guard and 604 the Air Guard with a total in both branches of twenty-four officers. Forty-eight military specialties were closed to women, including all combat roles. But in other ways the services were relaxing restrictions on women. In 1973, the Supreme Court hurried the process along by ruling that women in the services must be allowed full benefits for their dependents. In 1974, recruiters were permitted to enlist married women. The Guard's female soldiers could share the same buildings with men if in separate sections from the men and provided with separate latrines. One way or another, by the end of fiscal year 1977 the Army Guard contained 12,908 women, the Air Guard 9,709, including nurses in both of the services. The Air Guard passed a new milestone when in 1978 it produced its first certified female pilot. She could not fly combat aircraft, but could and did pilot one of the enormous KC-135 tankers. These aircraft, just coming into the Guard, refueled combat aircraft in flight. For all of this, discrimination due to sex had not disappeared. A woman could not enter the Guard unless she was a high school graduate, but a man could.[16]

Secretary of Defense Melvin Laird spoke in August 1970 in terms of a total force. The National Guard was part of it, and with the Reserve, it would in the future replace the draft in filling out the combat army when there was need to expand on a grand scale. The Guard, in short, ceased to be part of the strategic reserve and became a component of the force in being. Reserve forces now made up roughly 50 percent of the ground combat troops and 66 percent of all support elements. The National Guard accounted for 30 percent of the army's strength, 50 percent of the army's infantry battalions, and the same proportion of its artillery.[17]

The army made arrangements to draw Guard and regular units closer together. To this end, by the conclusion of fiscal year 1976, eighty-one Army Guard battalions were affiliated with regular divisions and brigades, to train with them as much as possible and become organic parts of them during crises. In addition, the high command designated four brigades and nine separate combat battalions of the Army Guard to round out active divisions. It also rearranged Guard units in order to shift maximum numbers from support into combat roles when a need arose. At the same time, the army scrapped previous arrangements for controlling and training the Guard and the reserves, replacing them with nine regional directorates. Inclusion of the Guard in the total force called for added rank at the top, which in the summer of 1979 elevated the chief of the NGB to the rank of lieutenant general, with a major general as his deputy for the Army Guard, and a major general for the Air Guard. The assistant to both of the deputy chiefs was a brigadier general.[18]

Through all the changes and pressures, the leaders of the Army Guard remained aware that Guard units had been broken up in past conflicts and the individuals in them used as fillers for unrelated units.

With the IRR eroding away, these leaders foresaw the strong likelihood that their units might be raided once more in a new crisis and become mere manpower pools for strengthening the emergency force. Even the total force concept and the consequent intermingling of reserve and regular units—which appeared to point to the use of units rather than individuals—and the assurances of the high command did not exorcise their lingering fear.[19]

This fear was not shared by the Air Guard, which fitted more easily into the force in being than the Army Guard. One reason was that its strength hovered quite close to upper authorized limits. High school graduates, if they volunteered at all, usually chose the Air Guard because of the glamor of flying. Thus, 85.5 percent of the Air Guard recruits were high school graduates, contrasting with 44.4 percent for the army. These statistics and some other factors caused General Lew Allen, Air Force Chief of Staff, to say in August 1978 that the AVF and the total force concept were both working well for the air force. He made this statement even though a cut in 1974 had wiped out 5,314 Air Guard spaces, 1,257 of which were full-time technicians. The fact is that beginning in the 1950s the Air National Guard had proved itself to be an efficient part of the American air arm. Recognizing this, the air force, as frequently as it could, transferred up-to-date planes to the Guard. Also, it allotted to the Air Guard and to the Air Reserve a substantial role in support of the active force in Latin America. The two reserves shared this responsibility by assuming it alternately every six months. Within the Air Guard, units rotated to Latin America every two weeks. In a similar way, the Air Guard shared in the defense of Panama.[20]

That the Air Guard was an effective part of the total air force is illustrated by the following figures of the various assignments which it fulfilled: fighter-intercepters, 60 percent; tactical fighters, 40 percent; tactical reconnaissance, 50 percent; tactical air support, 60 percent; and tactical airlift and air refueling, 33 percent.[21]

Readiness was critical to the Army Guard in its role as part of the total force. Estimates of its readiness ranged from M-Day plus sixty to M-Day plus six months or more, but the Department of the Army set M-Day plus seventy as the level to be achieved. Unfortunately, a joint exercise in 1976 demonstrated that the Army Guard could not do it. It lacked both manpower and equipment to meet such a requirement. Accordingly, the NGA resolved in 1977 that "if the National Guard . . . is indeed to be effective as the means of filling the gap between the federal force in being and the combat objective force, then a serious and significant commitment must be undertaken by the Department of Defense . . . on a scale unprecedented in American history."[22]

The NGA was quick to point out that if the Guard was not ready enough, it was due to no lack of spirit. The Guard had only 58 percent of the equipment it needed to be combat ready, and much of that was not up to date. It was necessary to cannibalize some units to supply others with enough to make them effective. Guard leaders pointed out, too, that the Marine Corps Reserve system permitted eleven times more persons fully employed than the Army Guard had, and that the Guard needed to come closer to equaling the Marine model. The full-time people, they added, ought to be members of the Guard rather than technicians, who were really civil servants.[23]

The low quality of recruits the Army Guard could attract under the AVF handicapped readiness. The percentage of those recruits who had high school diplomas dropped from 98 percent in 1976 to 44.4 percent in 1977. Nearly 60 percent of the male volunteers scored in the lower half on aptitude tests, while one-third of them read at or below the fifth grade level. These statistics caused the president of the NGA quite early to announce that the AVF was a failure.[24]

Readiness not only of the Guard but of the entire military establishment was jeopardized by the falling numbers in the IRR. All elements of the establishment had to look to the IRR for fillers with needed skills. Really, this reserve had never been much more than a list of names—General Reckord had called it a list of names with wrong addresses. In any case, within sixty days after M-Day, the best estimates said that the army would be half a million men short of the number needed to hold the Soviets if they invaded western Europe, and the IRR would be entirely drained.[25]

Should the draft be reestablished, it would be three months before the first draftee would be available. By this time, according to the short-war hypothesis, the conflict would be all over. But NGA spokesmen vigorously attacked that hypothesis. It sprang, they said, not from strategic analysis, but from the desire to save money. They denied that the next war would be short and stressed the need to prepare the nation to survive a long conflict. This view contained, no doubt, an ingredient of self-interest. If the short-war hypothesis was accepted, the role of the National Guard was perforce downgraded. A short war would be over before any of the reserves could affect the outcome.[26]

During the 1970s, as in every other decade of American history, there were those who believed that the National Guard would never be ready enough to be an effective part of the total force, especially in the nuclear age. They pointed out that Guard training was often unrealistic and boring. It contained too much of the old army system of hurry up and wait, too much make work to fill in time that ought to have gone into realism in combat training. One Guardsman said that all he learned from two weeks at summer camp—the central segment of a year's training—was new places to hide forbidden beer cans. Far more condemnatory was the report by the General Accounting Office that in 1974 the reserve components had wasted 15,000,000 man-days, valued at $1,200,000,000, in useless training.[27]

Criticism of the Guard rose too from the fact that it had been left on the sidelines in Vietnam. Why maintain 1,000,000 persons in drill status and pay them only to leave them idle and turn instead to draftees? To this criticism as to that of failure to be ready enough, Major General LaVern Weber, Chief of the NGB, gave the following rebuttal: "The Total Force Policy is rational, logical and workable. There is really no alternative to a military strategy based on realistic interface of the active, the National Guard and the Reserve forces. If there is an alternative, it is a huge standing Army and Air Force, which would fail the affordability test by all standards."[28] In addition, he could have, but did not choose, to point out that the decision not to activate the reserves, including the National Guard, was not up to the Guard to make, and had, indeed, been made by the commander-in-chief himself.

With the war in Vietnam ended, President Ford in 1975 urged a cut in military expenses of $503,000,000, of which $161,000,000 would come out of Guard funds. When the in-fighting in Congress was over, the Guard lost only $950,000. Guard leaders joined the fight to curb the cut, arguing that the National Guard was the most reasonably priced of all parts of the military establishment. Although reserves made up 30 percent of the total force, they received only 2½ to 5 percent of the military budget. One regular soldier cost as much as 13 Guardsmen. Partly due to figures such as these, Congress pushed up its appropriations for the reserves from $2,600,000,000 in 1970 to $4,400,000,000 in 1974, but because of inflation Guard purchasing power remained about the same. President Carter did not alter very much his Republican predecessors' posture toward the reserves. The higher appropriation of $6,700,000,000 made by his administration had at least $400,000,000 less purchasing power than in 1946.[29]

After World War II, the reconstituted Army Guard consisted of twenty-five infantry and two armored divisions, plus many separate units. At the start of the 1970s, only eight combat divisions and miscellaneous separate units remained. During the decade, those eight were rearranged geographically. Four existed within the boundaries of one state each and the others within no more than three states each. Many of the divisions that had been phased out were replaced by separate brigades, designed to expand into divisions if necessary.[30]

If such streamlining worked hardship on the Guard, the up-or-out promotion system of the regulars hurt more. Promotion for a Guardsman often meant serving as an officer in some community other than his own. If the community was distant, the change was difficult for him. True, he could refuse the promotion, but the regulars frowned on this because he then stood in the way of promotion for other officers in his home unit. From the Guard point of view it was all right for an efficient captain to remain a captain. Through long service he might become a model company commander. Why should he not remain in a role he played so well?[31]

On December 28, 1970, the Guard lost one of its old friends in Congress: Lucius Mendel Rivers of South Carolina, who had served in the House of Representatives from 1941 until his death and had been a member of the committees controlling the fate of the armed forces. Throughout, he had been a supporter of the Guard and a foe of the Uptonian concentration of military power in the hands of the regulars. Fortunately for the Guard, he was succeeded as chairman of the House Committee on Military Services by F. Edward Hébert of Louisiana. Before entering Congress Hébert had been part of a courageous group opposing the near dictatorship of Huey Long. In Congress, he had shown himself a skillful dramatizer of National Guard needs.

The next powerful friend of the Guard to die was Harry S Truman. He had entered the Missouri National Guard in 1905 and supported the system throughout the balance of his eighty-eight years. He died on December 26, 1972.

The two men who virtually personified the Guard in the post-World War II era died less than a month apart. Ellard Walsh died at the age of 88 on August 31, 1975, and Milton Reckord followed him on September 8, having reached the age of 91.[32]

In spite of these losses, the NGA continued to let the public know its positions on national security. It lobbied for a fleet of 244 B-1 bombers, whatever the cost, to replace the aging B-52s. Where national survival was at stake, the legislators must not be squeamish concerning the humanity or inhumanity of new weapons. It agreed that the United States should be prepared to fight one major war and, at the same time, a minor war (rated as half a war). In 1977, the NGA resolved that a merger with the reserves was no longer in the public interest. Early in the decade it began to view the AVF as a failure. F. Edward Hebert told the convention delegates, "The only way you can have a volunteer army is to draft it."[33] At all conventions the members spoke out strongly against unionization of the armed forces.

Leaders implored the Defense Department to refrain from additional drastic reorganization. From 1945 to 1971, there were only four years free of racking realignments that hampered recruiting and retention. Leaders also implored the high command to stop commandeering Guard equipment for prepositioning in Europe. The more of their essentials the Guard lost that way, the less able it was to function as an efficient part of the total force.[34]

The units of the National Guard continued, as they always had, to provide the states with a force arm to supplement police, sheriffs, and highway patrolmen in maintaining law and order. In 1970, detachments involving 60,316 Guardsmen carried out ninety-two law-and-order missions. In 1972, 3,000 Florida Guardsmen protected the Democratic National Convention meeting in Miami. Their presence eliminated unpleasant incidents, but at the same time it hurt two images: that of the Democratic Party and that of the National Guard. There were only seven constabulary calls on Guardsmen in 1973, but the next year, largely due to a trucker's strike, there were twenty-five in eighteen states, employing 21,139 Guardsmen. Thereafter, law-and-order use became less frequent. In 1977, for example, there were only nine calls using 5,605 men.[35]

Noteworthy was the performance of the Wisconsin National Guard in 1978 when state employees in eighteen correctional institutions struck. A red-light alert brought out 6,000 Guardsmen, already trained for such duty. The prisoners said that their new wardens treated them like men, not things. Wisconsin commended its citizen soldiers for doing a difficult job well.[36] Elsewhere, strikes by public servants became more frequent. Both firemen and policemen walked out in Memphis in 1978; 2,000 Guardsmen walked in. Since some of the striking firemen were in the Guard, they continued in the old job, wearing different uniforms. When firemen struck in Louisville, Kentucky, 300 Guardsmen replaced them.[37]

Whereas Guard constabulary work load declined, its role in relief and rescue mounted. In 1972, South Dakota experienced the worst flood in its history, bringing into the field 3,000 Guardsmen, three of whom died attempting to save other people. Some 200 persons could not be saved. During 1973, 137 Guard detachments took part in relief and rescue work in thirty-six states. The next year, the figure rose to 181 detachments in thirty-seven states. Sometimes, it was nature that created the crises through tornadoes, heavy snow, bitter cold, forest fires, drought, and flood; at other times, the disasters were man-made spills of toxic substances, explosions, and roaring fires. The long, harsh winter of 1979 illustrated the diversity. Storms striking the east coast paralyzed traffic. Using its tracked and four-wheel drive vehicles, the Guard rescued stranded motorists and cleared roads. Blizzards in Utah and Wyoming made similar work, with the added task of hauling feed to starving cattle. In Missouri and in Maryland, the Guard loaned generators to keep certain vital activities in operation until power lines could be restored. In parts of Ohio and West Virginia, Guard trucks brought potable water to dry areas, as it did in New Mexico. A tornado crippled northwest Louisiana, requiring Guard aid to clear the streets and help with the injured. The storm strewed debris which took 7,000 truckloads to remove. At the peak of the annual camp exercise in the summer of 1978, 3,659 Guardsmen had to turn from training for one of their basic functions—serving as part of the total force—to the second function, the relief of their fellow citizens.[38]

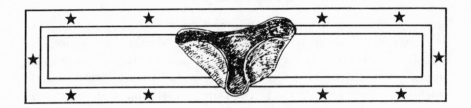

EIGHTEEN

Conclusion

There has never been a moment in the history of the United States when responsible leaders assumed that the professional military forces, existing in peacetime, would be able to wage war unassisted. Until the era of the Cold War, beginning in 1947, the number of professional soldiers retained in peacetime was ridiculously low compared to other nations. Certain reasons for so low a regular establishment were: (1) geographical isolation from possible enemies; (2) fear of standing armies; (3) unwillingness to bear the cost of peacetime standing forces; and (4) the widely held convinction that male citizens would always turn out in sufficient numbers and in time to wage any sort of war successfully.

The militia, part of the American scene from the earliest settlement of the British colonies, rested on the principle that every able-bodied male of suitable age owed military service to the society. Ideally, each man would accept his obligation and volunteer when his state or his nation called him; but if the ideal was not realized the colonies/states possessed the power to draft. It was easy for them to pick men up from the bottom of the social structure by drafting. Before the Civil War, the power to draft resided solely with the states, but in that, the nation's first mass war, both the Union and the Confederate armies used conscription, thereby establishing an important and enduring precedent. Since the Civil War also made it clear that large-scale modern war cannot be manned by volunteers alone, conscription was used in both world wars.

The National Guard grew out of the volunteer portion of the militia, but when the United States government decided to use it during World War I, it drafted the individual Guardsmen into federal service, thus lifting them out of the Guard. After World War II, the draft continued until 1973 except for a fifteen-month gap beginning in March 1947. In the Cold War era, issues were not as clear-cut as they used to be. Americans had always thought that a nation was either at war or in peacetime, but the post-World War II era was a hybrid of those two conditions which it had been assumed could not be cross-bred. Patriotism had trouble finding points of focus. Consequently, volunteers did not come forward in the numbers needed to give the Soviets the conviction that the United States was strong enough to resist aggression; and the National Guard was obliged to use the draft to fill its ranks. When the All-Volunteer Force was adopted in 1973, the Guard's enrollment began to fall, but by effective advertising and for other reasons recruiters were able to stem the tide. Thus, at the end of fiscal year 1981, the Army Guard stood at 89.5 percent of authorized strength, with fifteen states at 100 percent. The Air Guard showed better figures than the army. In spite of this improved enrollment, the Guard leadership feared the future and favored a return to some sort of draft, at least enough to secure full manning of the Selected Reserve.

There was not one militia in the English colonies but several, with units and tables of organization that were not interchangeable. During the American Revolution, the militias provided part of a counterforce to the British regulars and their mercenary associates from Germany. Behind them the Continental Army developed as a semiprofessional body. Therefore, out of the Revolution emerged a prototype for a future professional force, side by side with one made up of civilians, serving in the crisis as soldiers.

Since every colony grew up with a culture peculiar to it, the succeeding states carried into the United States several different cultures. The framers of the Constitution, of course, had to accept this background but at the same time create a workable policy. They did this by employing federalism, in which the central government received certain powers and duties from a pool of authority possessed by the people, while the states retained other powers and duties. In this division, the provisions for the militia system were more explicit than any others. States' rights appeared early in political talk, and, as they became based more and more upon slavery, created a second nationalism within United States boundaries. In the Civil War, the military power of the center defeated that of states' rights but did not succeed in killing the concept. The militia system ever since has seemed a bulwark for states' rights, without which they might wither away. Later, the National Guard performed the same function, and even late in the twentieth century states' rights legislators continued to warn the mighty Pentagon not to tamper too much with the Guard.

Even though the national government had by this time taken over 95 percent of Guard costs, the states continued to be possessive of the Guard and prepared to defend it against the professional military establishment.

Ever since the Constitution set up the federal system, the National Guard has had two commanders-in-chief: the governor of a state and the president of the United States. During the War of 1812 and again during the Civil War, the governors in some states had the final word. In later wars, however, such confrontations did not occur; they shifted instead to domestic disturbances. Apparently, the framers of the Constitution intended the militia to be used only to suppress insurrections and enforce the laws. Accordingly, a column of federalized militia subdued the Whiskey Rebels in 1794, and President Jefferson thought he had to ask Congress for permission to use regulars to enforce the Embargo. There were other cases in the pre-Civil War years, but none from 1867 to 1957. In the latter year, President Eisenhower ordered the Arkansas National Guard into federal service to take it out of the hands of the governor, who was obstructing carrying out the mandate of the Supreme Court to integrate the races in the schools. Throughout the 1960s, the federal commander-in-chief used the National Guard to support desegregation, and the state commanders were powerless to stop him. Why so powerless? Federal money for the Guard was one reason; another was that Guardsmen who failed to answer a federal summons were considered absent without leave.

Beginning during the Revolution, a tension between professional soldiers and amateur soldiers has run through American history. The pressures of mass war, starting with the Civil War and persisting through the two world wars, exacerbated it. In these, the officers trained in the military academies and others who had entered the professional caste by different means, laid claim to the top commands, pushing militia and Guard leaders out of the command of divisions, corps, and armies, but not without creating resentment among the displaced.

The militia system was built on units. These were supposed to train together and fight together. Their traditions and peacetime training gave them cohesion and heightened fighting power. At all times in American history, leaders of citizen soldiers advocated the use of these units in wartime, but hardly in any war was what they advocated carried out. In early wars, the standing militia was used largely as a place from which detachments could be secured, to be formed with other detachments into new units that had no peacetime history together. Troops raised outside the militia system and in some cases small state armies became alternatives to the organized militia companies and battalions. Some volunteer units, it is true, entered federal service and remained intact, but they made up only a small percentage of the manpower employed.

During the two world wars, the professional high command, confronted with the need to react rapidly to the demands of mass war, was not able to pay close attention to history and lineages. They cranked pedigreed old units through a mathematical system for designating units that wrung out of them their lineages and honors. This detraditionalization combined with the ruthless displacement of officers in favor of regulars led Guard leaders to believe that the Army General Staff used the mass wars purposely to weaken and eventually destroy the National Guard system. Whether this belief was true or false is not as important as the fact that it existed and influenced the people who held it.

Curiously enough, the Cold War era, full of sophisticated weaponry as it is, seems more likely to give peacetime Guard units a chance to fight together in wartime than ever before. Since 1952, the shapers of the active force have variously designated segments of the Guard as Ready Reserves, Immediate Reserves, and the Selected Reserve. These elite portions of the Guard and the reserves are supposed to maintain themselves close to war strength and to have equipment nearly adequate for wartime needs. Moreover, they are presumed to be well enough trained to deploy anywhere in the world within a very short time after M-Day. There is a running dispute as to how ready they really are, but the mobilization plans are built on their availability.

Some of the professional/amateur tension has centered on the character of the reserves. The professionals have traditionally felt that the Guard system was too cumbersome, because it involved two chains of command, to be useful as an efficient part of the ever ready national reserves. Therefore, they have always striven for a reserve which they could control directly, free of state interference. But they could never push aside the powerful influence of the militia/National Guard/states' rights interests. However, in the National Defense Act of 1916 they secured the creation of the sort of reserve they sought. Over the years, this, the Organized Reserve, gathered members and strength and developed its own constituency. The Reserve Officers Association grew to do for the reserves what the NGA had for so many years done for the National Guard.

The Gray Board in 1948 recommended that the Guard be merged into the Organized Reserves, a proposal which the NGA fought with all the political instruments at its command and which it and the Guard defeated. That left two reserve systems intact, which from the viewpoint of management theory seemed inefficient. So it appeared to Robert S. McNamara, a high priest of efficiency, who, as secretary of defense in 1964 reversed the historical pattern by announcing that he intended to merge the Organized Reserve into the National Guard. This was acceptable to the Guard, highly offensive to the Reserve, and unacceptable to the professionals; and it too was defeated. The dual system, although much modified, continues, and the Guard has acquiesced in it. At the annual convention of the National Guard in 1977, the delegates resolved that it was no longer in the national interest even to consider merging the two systems.

Nothing about the militia/National Guard system is more important than its continuous and extensive use by the states. Few agencies exceed the Guard in alleviating the impact of disasters. The states have also used their Guards extensively to maintain law and order. Figures on these uses are scattered chronologically throughout the text. It was law-and-order use that brought the National Guard out of the doldrums after the Civil War. The last thirty years of the nineteenth century were a period of increasing industrial warfare. Most of the time in that conflict the states maintained law and order by using the Guard to protect the property of entrepreneurs from employees organized into unions and striking for higher wages and better working conditions. The concept of a living wage had not yet entered the thinking of enterprisers and government officials. There were other reasons for the revival of the Guard following the Civil War, but none of them could have worked without the occurrence of industrial warfare.

Until the 1960s, blacks, if in the system at all, were second-class Guardsmen. Except for Reconstruction there was never a time when they tilted the Guard away from support of white supremacy; yet Guard detachments were frequently used to prevent the lynchings of black men. Not until the racial conflict of the 1950s and 1960s—the bitterness of which the white society had not anticipated—did the Guard really begin to welcome blacks. Its welcome grew warmer when the draft ended in 1973 and the need for soldiers to fill the ranks became critical. The need for manpower exceeded concern over its color, and it also overcame concern over its sex. Finally, in 1968, Guard regulations permitted women other than nurses to join, and Guard leaders looked forward to larger numbers of women to fill empty spaces.

At least as early as the founding of the NGA in 1879, Guard leadership began to work toward establishing the National Guard as the reserve of first resort in national emergencies. Their determination raised this question: can a military organization made up of people who spend most of their time being citizens ever be sufficiently trained and flexible to fill out the nation's military forces rapidly? This problem became more acute in the atomic age when the time to react to aggressions was very much shortened and when those aggressions might take place in the far corners of the earth.

The Guard has always insisted that it can be the reserve of first resort if given adequate support. This argument, backed by political clout, brought more and more federal money to sustain the Guard, until the federal government paid about 95 percent of costs. The Dick Bill of 1903 started the United States toward increased involvement in the day-by-day activity of the Guard. Thirty years later, the 1933 amendment to the National Defense Act of 1916 created the National Guard of the United States, which made most of the Guard part of the effective national military force in peacetime as well as war. The Guard had arrived where it wanted to be, but in so doing had become at least as much a servant of the federal government as of the states. To states' rightsmen, who had always sustained the Guard, this was not all good. What had happened showed clearly during the racial troubles of the 1960s. The president of the United States several times federalized certain state Guards that had already been called out by their state commanders-in-chief. He took control away from them at times when the national interest opposed that of the states. Certainly then some of the governors regretted the power they had lost in order to obtain federal funds.

The National Guard, together with the other reserves and the regular services, has become part of the total force, a term first used in 1970. The Total Force Policy is based on the certainty that the nation will never support enough professionals in peacetime to wage war unassisted. Backup forces, therefore, must be available and sufficiently ready to enter combat shortly after M-Day anywhere in the world. The Guard supplies a substantial part of these supplementary forces and is more and more intertwined with the regular force by training as part of regular units and being programmed to become organic parts of regular divisions in case of emergency. If the chances of future war are as great as predicted, the Total Force Policy must succeed. National survival depends upon it. Readiness, then, is a key word, and both the Guard and the regulars in the 1980s are trying as hard as they can to achieve it.

The centralization of the National Guard, which began in 1903, is one aspect of a broad trend in the United States. In the private sector, centralization has taken the form of ever larger corporations, big ones acquiring smaller ones. States' rights people have not opposed economic centralization to any great extent; nor in government have they been able to resist the appeal of larger and larger federal funds which brought with them more central control. President Reagan asserts that his administration intends to transfer power back to the states, which will have to mean transferring heavier financial burdens as well. It is notable that the military establishment remains firmly under the control of the federal government; indeed, the sole exception to this is such military power as the National Guard has.

The National Guard of the United States, keyed to mobilization, found it difficult to adjust to the partial mobilization applied during Korea and Vietnam. Guard leaders resented the manpower policy that slighted the reserve of first resort and used draftees instead. Of course, if Guard units had been ordered into service in full mobilization, they would have had to use selectees to fill out but far fewer than reliance on the draft required, and they could have brought in morale at a time when soldiers seemed more than ever devoid of any commitment to the fight they were in. Rotation of individuals after a year in the combat zone further diluted loyalty to units which in the past had stiffened the will of fighting men. All in all, the manpower policy used in Vietnam made the American soldier a lonely person, not much convinced that he was fighting for a national interest significant enough for him to be willing to lay down his life.

Originally, the militia was a form of UMT. It required every male of military age to turn out at intervals prescribed by colonial/state law and train, using his own weapons. Following the War of 1812, the United States was relatively free of foreign dangers while at the same time the people were presented with unprecedented opportunities to exploit seemingly unlimited natural resources. These conditions resulted in decline of the militia. In time, therefore, the system abandoned UMT and came to rest upon volunteering as its source of manpower. Even national conscription in the Civil War did not utilize UMT, for a man could always try to find a substitute. In the two world wars, it was universal registration that was used, but not UMT, for the choice of who should enter the service and who should be exempted was done by selective service.

World War I was so traumatic that when it was over the issue of readiness in peacetime once more arose in the United States. There was a sharp debate about UMT in 1919, another following World War II in 1948, and still another in 1951. Congress rejected UMT in all these cases. The National Guard leadership had helped to revive the issue and was sorry when it failed, for it seemed to them virtuous to go back to the principle on which the early militia had been operated, applying it in the twentieth century at the national rather than the state level.

A strain of fear of standing military forces runs through most of the history of the United States. It rests on historical evidence, ancient and modern, that the military is more likely than any other institution to overthrow representative government. But dislike of a standing army rested, too, on another, and perhaps a more potent factor, its cost. The militia/National Guard prided itself on its ability to provide military force at low cost. Professionals, however, believed that the low price bought an inefficient product, one that could not really defend the United States.

With the Reagan administration, it seems that the nation has entered an era in which the high cost of the military establishment is no longer a retardant to large standing forces. Fear of the power of the Soviet Union is widespread and seems to be allayed by a massive buildup of the military system, whatever the cost. The Cold War has gone far to accustom the American people to large standing military forces. Ever larger and more expensive armies over a long period of time may obliterate the historical American aversion to them. Should this be the case, the National Guard will become more important than ever before. It will help to keep alive the citizen soldier tradition and the division of military power between the center and the parts. Its existence may prevent the United States from becoming militaristic. Ever since World War II, the nation has been military, but never, then or before, militaristic. There is a life and death difference.

Appendix: Chiefs of the National Guard Bureau and Predecessor Organizations

CHIEF OF
NATIONAL GUARD BUREAU 1933-PRESENT
MILITIA BUREAU 1916-1933
DIVISION OF MILITIA AFFAIRS 1908-1916

Colonel Erasmus M. Weaver	1908-1911
Brigadier General Robert K. Evans	1911-1912
Major General Albert L. Mills	1912-1916
Major General William A. Mann	1916-1917
Major General Jessie McI. Carter	1917-1918
Brigadier General John W. Heavey (Acting)	1918-1919
Major General Jessie McI. Carter	1919-1921
Major General George C. Rickards	1921-1925
Major General Creed C. Hammond	1925-1929
Colonel Ernest R. Redmond (Acting)	1929-1929
Major General William G. Everson	1929-1931
Major General George E. Leach	1931-1935
Colonel Herold J. Weiler (Acting)	1935-1936
Colonel John F. Williams (Acting)	1936-1936
Major General Albert H. Blanding	1936-1940
Major General John F. Williams	1940-1944
Major General John F. Williams (Acting)	1944-1946
Major General Butler B. Miltonberger	1946-1947
Major General Kenneth F. Cramer	1947-1950

Major General Raymond H. Fleming (Acting)	1950-1951
Major General Raymond H. Fleming	1951-1953
Major General Earl T. Ricks (Acting)	1953-1953
Major General Edgar C. Erickson	1953-1959
Major General Winston P. Wilson (Acting)	1959-1959
Major General Donald W. McGowan	1959-1963
Major General Winston P. Wilson	1963-1971
Major General Francis S. Greenlief	1971-1974
Lieutenant General LaVern E. Weber	1974-1982
Lieutenant General Emmett H. Walker, Jr.	1982-Present

Abbreviations

AEF	American Expeditionary Force, World War I
AFPLC	Air Force Policy Letter for Commanders
AFRA	Armed Forces Reserve Act, 1952
AR	Annual Report
ARASDRF	Annual Report, Assistant Secretary of Defense for Reserve Forces
ARCDMA	Annual Report, Chief Division of Militia Affairs
ARCMB	Annual Report, Chief Militia Bureau
ARCNGB	Annual Report, Chief National Guard Bureau
ARNGA	Annual Report, National Guard Association
ARRF	Annual Report, Reserve Forces
ARSW	Annual Report, Secretary of War
ASPMA	American State Papers Military Affairs
AVF	All-Volunteer Force
CMTC	Citizens Military Training Camp
diss.	dissertation
ETO	European Theater of Operations
FY	Fiscal Year
GHQ	General Headquarters
GO	General Orders
HQ	Headquarters

HR	House of Representatives
HRRC 1951	Hearing, House of Representatives Committee on Armed Services, 1951
IRR	Individual Ready Reserve
MS	Manuscript
NA	National Archives
NGA	National Guard Association
NGB	National Guard Bureau
OCMH	Office, Chief of Military History, Department of the Army
OR	Organized Reserves
Q	Quarterly
RC	Reserve Components
RCT	Regimental Combat Team
RFA	Reserve Forces Act, 1955
ROAD	Reorganized Objective Army Division
ROTC	Reserve Officer's Training Corps
SRF	Selected Reserve Force
UMT	Universal Military Training
USAMHI	United States Army Military History Institute, Carlisle Barracks, Penna.
USSL	United States Statutes at Large
WD	War Department

Notes

INTRODUCTION

1. According to 10 United States Code, sec. 311 (a), 1970: "The militia of the United States consists of all able-bodied males at least 17 years of age and . . . under 45 years of age who are, or have made a declaration of intention to become, citizens of the United States. . . ."

CHAPTER 1. THE ENGLISH BACKGROUND

1. C. Warren Hollister, *Anglo-Saxon Military Institutions on the Eve of the Norman Conquest* (Oxford Univ. Press, 1962). As one reads about this period, one encounters contradictions about the fyrd. Hollister considers these and takes a position which I have followed. As an example of the problem, Samuel T. Ansell in an article in 1917 stated that the fyrd obligation rested on the ownership of land. If this was so it could not rest on a universal military obligation owed by all able-bodied men, yet Ansell says, "No American institution bears a closer resemblance to its ancient English ancestor than our militia." There is no basis to say this if the militia obligation rested on the ownership of land because that was never the case in the United States. Ansell, "Legal and Historical Aspects of Militia," *Yale Law Review*, XXVI (April 1917), pp. 471-480.
2. A hide varied, as far as is known, from about 40 acres to 120 acres. The several counties set the measurement. See Hollister, *Anglo-Saxon*, pp. 41, 48.
3. Ibid., p. 57; David W. Cole, "Organization and Administration of the South Carolina Militia System, 1670-1783" (unpublished Ph.D. diss., Univ. of South Carolina, 1948), pp. 4, 5.
4. Douglas E. Leach, "The Military System of Plymouth Colony," *New England Quarterly*, XXIV (Sep. 1951), p. 343.
5. Cole, "South Carolina Militia," p. 6; Charles G. Cruickshank, *Elizabeth's Army* (Oxford Univ. Press, 1966), p. 4.

6. Alfred H. Burne, *The Crecy War* (Oxford Univ. Press, 1955), p. 30.

7. Ibid., pp. 30ff.; Lois G. Schwoerer, *No Standing Armies: The Antiarmy Ideology in Seventeenth Century England* (Johns Hopkins Press, 1974), p. 12.

8. Lindsay Boynton, *The Elizabethan Militia, 1558-1638* (London, 1967), p. 108.

9. Cruickshank, *Elizabeth's Army*, p. 2.

10. Schwoerer, *No Standing Armies*, p. 12; Cruickshank, *Elizabeth's Army*, pp. 4, 6.

11. Cole, "South Carolina Militia," p. 6; Boynton, *Elizabethan Militia*, pp. 16, 62.

12. Ibid., pp. 11, 13, 17, 18, 27, 91.

13. Ibid., p. 29.

14. Cruickshank, *Elizabeth's Army*, p. 16.

15. Boynton, *Elizabethan Militia*, p. 199.

16. Ibid., pp. 117, 118.

17. Cruickshank, *Elizabeth's Army*, p. 24.

18. Boynton, *Elizabethan Militia*, pp. 91, 105, 121, 148; Stewart L. Gates, "The Militia in Connecticut Public Life, 1660-1860" (unpublished Ph.D. diss., Univ. of Connecticut, 1975), p. 9; Darrett B. Rutman, "A Militant New World, 1607-1640" (Ph.D. diss., Univ. of Virginia, 1959), p. 26; published in 1979 by Arno Press in photocopy form as part of Richard H. Kohn, ed., *The American Military Experience.*

19. The truth of this is seen in the evidence already presented of placing the burden of recruitment, supply, and pay for soldiers on the owners of land during Anglo-Saxon times. Impressment was a cheap way to obtain manpower; see Rutman, "Militant New World," p. 40; Boynton, *Elizabethan Militia*, pp. 108, 118.

20. Quoted in ibid., p. 195.

21. Correlli Barnett, *Britain and Her Army, 1509-1970* (Morrow, 1967), p. 36.

22. Schwoerer, *No Standing Armies*, pp. 20, 49; Cole, "South Carolina Militia," pp. 8, 9.

23. Schwoerer, *No Standing Armies*, pp. 52, 53.

24. Ibid., pp. 62, 76, 83, 87; Archibald Hanna, "New England Military Institutions, 1683-1750" (unpublished Ph.D. diss., Yale, 1951), pp. 9, 12, 14.

25. John Toland, *The Oceana and Other Works of James Harrington, Esquire with an Exact Account of his Life* (London, 1727), cited in Schwoerer, *No Standing Armies*, pp. 62, 89; and Lawrence D. Cress, "The Standing Army, the Militia and the New Republic: Changing Attitudes Toward the Military in American Society (Ph.D., diss., Univ. of Virginia, 1976), pp. 39, 43, 48, 49; published as *Citizens in Arms: The Army and Militia in American Society to the War of 1812* (Univ. of North Carolina Press, 1981); Cole, "South Carolina Militia," p. 10.

26. Schwoerer, *No Standing Armies* pp. 76, 107, 146, 174.

27. Ibid., pp. 17, 110, 130, 132, 136; Cole, "South Carolina Militia," pp. 63, 65.

28. Schwoerer, *No Standing Armies*, pp. 137, 151.
29. Trenchard, as cited in the text; see also *A Letter from the Author of the Argument Against a Standing Army to the Author of the Balancing Letter* (London, 1697); Cole, "South Carolina Militia," pp. 63, 65.
30. Blackstone, Sir William. *Commentaries on the Laws of England*, 4 vols. (Garland Publishing, 1978); facsimile copy of the edition printed in London in 1783.

CHAPTER 2. MILITIA IN THE COLONIES

1. Richard Henry Marcus, "The Militia of Colonial Connecticut, 1639-1775" (unpublished Ph.D. diss., Univ. of Colorado, 1965), p. 65; Douglas Edward Leach, *Arms for Empire: A Military History of the British Colonies in North America* (Macmillan, 1973), p. 11.
2. Ibid., p. 187.
3. When Pennsylvania first adopted militia law.
4. *The Exercise of the Militia of the Province of Massachusetts Bay* (Boston, 1758), p. 3, quoted in Leach, *Arms for Empire*, p. 8.
5. David W. Cole, "Organization and Administration of the South Carolina Militia System, 1670-1783" (unpublished Ph.D. diss., Univ. of South Carolina, 1948), p. 27; W. J. Eccles, "Social, Economic, and Political Significance of the Military Establishment of New France," *Canadian Historical Review*, LII (March 1971), pp. 4, 5, 7; William Lee Shea, "To Defend Virginia: The Evolution of the first Colonial Militia, 1607-1677" (unpublished Ph.D. diss., Rice Univ., 1975); Emmons Clark, *History of Seventh Regiment of New York, 1806-1889*, 2 vols. (New York, 1890), I, pp. 2, 3.
6. Marcus, "Connecticut Militia," pp. 7, 241; Jack S. Radabaugh, "The Militia of Colonial Massachusetts," *Military Affairs*, XVIII (Spring 1954), pp. 2, 5; Darrett B. Rutman, "A Militant New World, 1607-1640" (unpublished Ph.D. diss., Univ. of Virginia, 1959), pp. 496, 524; Shea, "To Defend Virginia," pp. 18, 33.
7. Cole, "South Carolina Militia," pp. 15, 30; Marcus, "Connecticut Militia," pp. 231, 233; Rutman, "Militant New World," p. 751; Shea, "To Defend Virginia," p. 218; Louis Dow Scisco, "Evolution of the Colonial Militia in Maryland," *Maryland Historical Magazine*, XXXV (June 1940), pp. 176, 177.
8. Archibald Hanna, "New England Military Institutions, 1693-1750" (unpublished Ph.D. diss., Yale Univ., 1951), p. 282; Marcus, "Connecticut Militia," pp. 7, 8.
9. Cole, "South Carolina Militia," p. 40; Lawrence Delbert Cress, "The Standing Army, the Militia and the New Republic: Changing Attitudes Toward the Military in American Society" (unpublished Ph.D. diss., Univ. of Virginia, 1976), p. 133; Marcus, "Connecticut Militia," pp. 219, 232, 250; Rutman, "Militant New World," pp. 674, 732.

10. Cole, "South Carolina Militia," p. 36; Hanna, "New England," pp. 294, 295; Marcus, "Connecticut Militia," p. 77; Shea, "To Defend Virginia," p. 81.

11. Cole, "South Carolina Militia," p. 30; Theodore Harry Jabbs, "The South Carolina Colonial Militia, 1633-1733" (unpublished Ph.D. diss., Univ. of North Carolina, 1973), p. 71; Scisco, "Evolution," p. 168; Shea, "To Defend Virginia," pp. 140, 206, 223.

12. Ibid., p. 72; Jabbs, "South Carolina Militia," p. 97; Marcus, "Connecticut Militia," p. 220; Earl Milton Wheeler, "Development and Organization on the North Carolina Militia," *North Carolina Historical Review*, XLI (July 1964), p. 318.

13. Radabaugh, "The Militia," pp. 3, 4.

14. Ibid., p. 18.

15. Frederick Porter Todd, "Our National Guard: An Introduction to Its History," *Military Affairs*, V (Summer 1941), pp. 73-86; (Fall 1941), pp. 152-170.

16. Radabaugh, "The Militia," pp. 4, 16; Rutman, "Militant New World," p. 729; Shea, "To Defend Virginia," p. 18.

17. Frederick S. Aldridge, "Organization and Administration of the Militia System of Colonial Virginia" (unpublished Ph.D. diss., American Univ., 1964), pp. 117, 152; Cole, "South Carolina Militia," p. 37; Jabbs, "South Carolina Militia," p. 205; Marcus "Connecticut Militia," p. 70; Wheeler, "Development," p. 317; Earl Milton Wheeler, "The Role of the North Carolina Militia in the Beginning of the American Revolution" (unpublished Ph.D. diss., Tulane Univ., 1969), p. 25.

18. Hanna, "New England," pp. 230-240; Leach, *Arms for Empire*, p. 21; Luther L. Gobbel, "Militia in North Carolina in Colonial and Revolutionary Times," *Historical Papers*, Trinity College Hist'l Society, Series 13 (1919), p. 36.

19. Aldridge, "Virginia Militia," p. 89; Jabbs, "South Carolina Militia," pp. 43, 167; Radabaugh, "The Militia," pp. 4, 10; Wheeler, "Role of the N.C. Militia," p. 23.

20. Leach, *Arms for Empire*, p. 331.

21. Ibid., p. 22; Aldridge, "Virginia Militia," p. 142; Cole, "South Carolina Militia," p. 30; Hanna, "New England," pp. 59, 72, 301; Jabbs "South Carolina Militia," p. 307; Marcus, "Connecticut Militia," pp. 216-218; Rutman, "Militant New World," p. 685; Shea, "To Defend Virginia," p. 102.

22. Ibid., p. 169.

23. Ibid., p. 107; Hanna, "New England," pp. 256-259, 262, 275; Marcus, "Connecticut Militia," p. 227; Rutman, "Militant New World," p. 329; Wheeler, "Development," p. 310.

24. Hanna, "New England," p. 111; Jabbs, "South Carolina Militia," p. 102.

25. Hanna, "New England," pp. 83, 85, 126; Shea, "To Defend Virginia," pp. 173, 184; Stephen S. Webb, "The Strange Career of Francis Nicholson," *William and Mary Q.*, XXIII (October 1966), p. 539.

26. Aldridge, "Virginia Militia," pp. 79-82, 158; Cole, "South Carolina Militia," pp. 47, 49, 55; Cress, "Standing Army," p. 7; Jabbs, "South Carolina Militia," pp. 98, 303, 310, 311, 409; Wheeler, "Development," p. 316.

27. Shea, "To Defend Virginia," p. 204.

28. Ibid., p. 85; Hanna, "New England," pp. 100, 104; Marcus, "Connecticut Militia," p. 290; Wheeler, "Development," pp. 316, 317.

29. Shea, "To Defend Virginia," p. 174; Cress, "Standing Army," p. 9; Hanna, "New England," p. 134; Marcus, "Connecticut Militia," pp. 325, 326; John W. Shy, "A New Look at the Colonial Militia," *A People Numerous and Armed* (Oxford Univ. Press, 1976), pp. 29, 30.

30. Aldridge, "Virginia Militia," p. 117; Cole, "South Carolina Militia," pp. 34, 68, 87; Jabbs, "South Carolina Militia," pp. 120, 270, 304, 361, 414, 418; Charles J. Johnson, "Black Soldiers in the National Guard, 1877-1949" (unpublished Ph.D. diss., Howard Univ., 1976), pp. 2-13; Shea, "To Defend Virginia," p. 255; Shy, "A New Look," p. 29.

31. Rutman, "Militant New World," p. 688; Marcus, "Connecticut Militia," pp. 9, 90, 101.

32. Ibid., pp. 90, 93; Douglas E. Leach, "The Military System of Plymouth Colony," *New England Q.,* XXIV (Spring 1951), p. 351.

33. Ibid.; Marcus, "Connecticut Militia," pp. 164, 165, 205; David S. Lovejoy, *The Glorious Revolution in America* (Harper and Row, 1972), pp. 8-31.

34. Ibid., passim; Marcus, "Connecticut Militia," p. 188.

35. Dallas Irvine, "The First British Regulars in North America," *Military Affairs* IX (Winter 1945), pp. 337-353.

36. Cole, "South Carolina Militia," p. 55; Jabbs, "South Carolina Militia," pp. 359, 397; Marcus, "Connecticut Militia," p. 304; Brian Connell, *The Savage Years* (Harper, 1959), pp. 45, 47, 260, 267; Webb, "Francis Nicholson," p. 544; J. A. Leo Lemay, "The American Origins of Yankee Doodle," *William and Mary Q.,* XXXIII (July 1976), p. 444; Cress, "Standing Army," p. 114.

37. Ibid., p. 119; Webb, "Francis Nicholson," p. 539.

38. Ibid., p. 541; Jabbs, "South Carolina Militia," pp. 356, 358, 365, 366; Marcus, "Connecticut Militia," p. 304; Leach, *Arms for Empire,* p. 505.

39. Howard H. Peckham, *The Colonial Wars, 1689-1762* (Univ. of Chicago Press, 1962), chap. 2, pp. 25-56.

40. Leach, *Arms for Empire,* pp. 82, 91, 101, 105, 276; Marcus, "Connecticut Militia," pp. 115, 116, 118, 120, 126, 135, 192.

41. Ibid., p. 142; Peckham, *Colonial Wars,* chap. 3, pp. 57-76; Leach, *Arms for Empire,* chap. 4, pp. 116-158.

42. See notes 23, 24, 25.

43. Peckham, *Colonial Wars,* p. 63; Marcus, "Connecticut Militia," p. 139.

44. Ibid., p. 152.

45. Jabbs, "South Carolina Militia," pp. 301-303.

46. Shy, "A New Look," p. 30; Marcus, "Connecticut Militia," pp. 263-265; Leach, *Arms for Empire,* p. 219; Peckham, *Colonial Wars,* p. 91.

47. Ibid., p. 89; Marcus, "Connecticut Militia," pp. 150-152.

48. Ibid., p. 267; Hanna, "New England," pp. 134-138; Leach, *Arms for Empire*, pp. 231, 242; Connell, *Savage Years*, p. 28.

49. Ibid., pp. 29-39.

50. Ibid., p. 66; Aldridge, "Virginia Militia," p. 140; Leach, *Arms for Empire*, p. 368; Marcus, "Connecticut Militia," p. 300.

51. Ibid. p. 326.

52. Aldridge, "Virginia Militia," p. 166.

53. Connell, *Savage Years*, p. 117.

54. Ibid., p. 150; also pp. 72, 114, 116, 121, 166, 167.

55. Ibid., passim; Marcus, "Connecticut Militia," pp. 307, 309.

56. Connell, *Savage Years*, p. 190; Leach, *Arms for Empire*, pp. 435-445.

57. Lemay, "Yankee Doodle," p. 444.

58. Connell, *Savage Years*, p. 276.

59. Leach, "Plymouth," p. 350; Marcus, "Connecticut Militia," pp. 48, 49; Shea, "To Defend Virginia," p. 288n.

60. Cress, "Standing Army," p. 5; Shy, "A New Look," pp. 26, 27.

61. Hanna, "New England," p. 25; Rutman, "Militant New World," pp. 487, 523; Marcus, "Connecticut Militia," p. 299; Radabaugh, "The Militia," p. 16; Arthur H. Buffington, "The Puritan View of War," *Publications*, Colonial Society of Massachusetts, XXVIII (1930-1931), pp. 71, 74, 79.

62. Cress, "Standing Army," p. 5; Shea, "To Defend Virginia," pp. 10, 53, 67, 137-139; Scisco, "Evolution," p. 168; Cole, "South Carolina Militia," p. 17; Gobbel, "North Carolina Militia," p. 36; Leach, *Arms for Empire*, p. 187; Wheeler, "Role of the North Carolina Militia," p. 10.

63. Aldridge, "Virginia Militia," pp. 195, 196; Cole, "South Carolina Militia," p. 44; Leach, *Arms for Empire*, p. 368; Shea, "To Defend Virginia," p. 220; Marcus, "Connecticut Militia," p. 300.

64. Quoted in ibid., p. 329.

65. Ibid., p. 305; Hanna, "New England," p. 306.

66. Cress, "Standing Army," p. 29; Shea, "To Defend Virginia," p. 164.

67. Donald L. Boucher, "The Colonial Militia as a Social Institution . . . Salem, Mass., 1764-1775," *Military Affairs*, XXXVII (Dec. 1973), pp. 125, 126.

68. Hanna, "New England," p. 305; Eccles, "New France," pp. 4, 5, 7.

69. Shea, "To Defend Virginia," p. 255; Hanna, "New England," pp. 303, 308.

70. Leach, *Arms for Empire*, p. 69.

71. Ibid., p. 407; Hanna, "New England," pp. 48, 116; Marcus, "Connecticut Militia," pp. 327-330.

CHAPTER 3. THE AMERICAN REVOLUTION

1. Christopher Ward, *The War of the Revolution*, 2 vols. (Macmillan, 1952), pp. 3, 4.

2. Ibid., p. 30; Don Higginbotham, *The War of American Independence* (Macmillan, 1971), p. 273; Earl M. Wheeler, "The Role of the North Carolina Militia in the Beginning of the American Revolution" (unpub-

lished Ph.D. diss., Tulane Univ., 1969); John Shy, "Mobilizing Armed Forces in the American Revolution," in *The American Revolution: A Heritage of Change*, John Parker and Carol Urness, eds. (Univ. of Minnesota, 1973), pp. 96-106.

3. Wheeler, "North Carolina Militia," p. 118; Luther L. Gobbel, "Militia in North Carolina in Colonial and Revolutionary Times," *Historical Papers*, Trinity College Historical Society (Series 13, Durham, 1919), p. 51; David W. Cole, "Organization and Administration of the South Carolina Militia System, 1670-1763" (unpublished Ph.D. diss., Univ. of South Carolina, 1948), pp. 94, 103, 105; James B. Deerin, "Our Militia in the Revolutionary War," *National Guardsman*, XXX (Aug.-Sept. 1976), p. 3.

4. Ibid.; Higginbotham, *Independence*, pp. 22, 46; Wheeler, "North Carolina Militia," p. 50; Ward, *Revolution*, p. 20; Richard Henry Marcus, "The Militia of Colonial Connecticut, 1639-1775" (unpublished Ph.D. diss., Univ. of Colorado, 1965), p. 352.

5. "From Boston, 8 Dec. 1774," Margaret Wheeler Willard, ed., *Letters on the American Revolution, 1774-1776* (first published in 1925, reissued by Kennikat Press, 1968), p. 26.

6. "Private gentleman in Phila. to a London Merchant, 6 May 1775," ibid., p. 101.

7. Deerin, "Our Militia," p. 3; Wheeler, "North Carolina Militia," pp. 115, 120; Cole, "South Carolina Militia," p. 94; Ward, *Revolution*, pp. 30, 36, 38.

8. Ibid., pp. 40, 41, 46; Higginbotham, *Independence*, p. 63.

9. Quoted in Deerin, "Our Militia," p. 7.

10. Ibid., p. 11.

11. Ward, *Revolution*, p. 130; Higginbotham, *Independence*, p. 58.

12. Ibid., pp. 77, 111, 356; Deerin, "Our Militia," pp. 30, 54, 55; Cole, "South Carolina Militia," p. 116; Trumbull, quoted in Emory Upton, *The Military Policy of the United States* (Washington, D.C., 1907), pp. 6, 7.

13. Ward, *Revolution*, p. 112; Higginbotham, *Independence*, pp. 85-88.

14. "To Joseph Reed, 28 Nov. 1775." *Writings of Washington*, 39 vols., John C. Fitzpatrick, ed., (Washington, D.C., 1931-1944), vol. 4, p. 124.

15. "To the President of Congress, 20 Dec. 1776," ibid., vol. 6, p. 403.

16. Arthur Alexander, Jr., "Service by Substitute in the Militia of Northampton and Lancaster Counties during the War of the Revolution," *Military Affairs*, IX (Fall 1945), pp. 278-282; and "How Maryland Tried to Raise Her Continental Quotas," *Maryland Historical Magazine*, XLII (Sep. 1947), pp. 186, 194; Wheeler, "North Carolina Militia," pp. 181, 185, 186; Cole, 'South Carolina Militia," pp. 116, 119, 120; Higginbotham, *Independence*, pp. 392, 394, 395.

17. Ibid., p. 393.

18. Ibid., pp. 275, 394, 395; Ward, *Revolution*, p. 798; Wheeler, "North Carolina Militia," p. 320.

19. "Letter from Phila., 15 May 1775," in Willard, *Letters*, p. 109.

20. Cole, "South Carolina Militia," p. 107; Ward, *Revolution*, chap. 58.

21. Ibid., pp. 125, 204; Higginbotham, *Independence*, p. 153.

22. Ibid., p. 159; Ward, *Revolution*, p. 237.

23. Ibid., pp. 285, 286; Higginbotham, *Independence*, p. 164; "Greene to Jacob Greene, 4 Dec. 1776," *The Papers of General Nathanael Greene* (Univ. of North Carolina Press, 1976), vol. 1, p. 362.

24. Higginbotham, *Independence*, p. 192; Ward, *Revolution*, pp. 424, 428, 484, 497; Benson J. Lossing, *Pictorial Field Book of the American Revolution*, 2 vols. (Harpers, 1860), pp. 48, 145, 147, 243.

25. Quoted in Ward, *Revolution*, p. 535.

26. Ibid., p. 538; for the end at Saratoga, see chaps. 42 and 43; Lossing, *Field Book*, vol. 1, pp. 50, 59, 81, 83; George A. Billias, "Horatio Gates," in Billias, *George Washington's Generals* (Morrow, 1964), pp. 90-97.

27. Higginbotham, *Independence*, pp. 186, 187; Ward, *Revolution*, chaps. 33, 37.

28. Ibid., pp. 679, 683, 690, 697, 698, 703, 706; Higginbotham, *Independence*, pp. 355, 357; Cole, "South Carolina Militia," pp. 122-125; Clifton K. Shipton, "Benjamin Lincoln," in Billias, *Generals*, p. 203.

29. Ward, *Revolution*, chap. 67; Gobbel, "North Carolina Militia," p. 30; Cole, "South Carolina Militia," pp. 96, 102, 115; Wheeler, "North Carolina Militia," p. 91.

30. Don Higginbotham, *Daniel Morgan: Revolutionary Rifleman* (Univ. of North Carolina Press, 1961).

31. Higginbotham, *Independence*, p. 382.

32. Richard G. Stone, *A Brittle Sword: The Kentucky Militia, 1776-1912* (Univ. Press of Kentucky), pp. 4-6; John K. Mahon, "Anglo-American Methods of Indian Warfare, 1676-1764," *Miss. Valley Historical Review*, XLV (Sep. 1968), pp. 265ff.

33. Wheeler, "North Carolina Militia," pp. 202, 209; Stone, *Kentucky Militia*, pp. 8, 9; Ward, *Revolution*, pp. 630, 631; Lossing, *Field Book*, p. 241; Charles P. Whittemore, *A General of the Revolution: John Sullivan of New Hampshire* (Columbia Univ. Press, 1961), chaps. 8 and 9.

34. Mahon, "Anglo-American Methods," pp. 273ff.; Temple Bodley, *George Rogers Clark* (Houghton Mifflin, 1926), pp. 199-205.

35. "Adams to Joseph Warren, 7 Jan. 1776," Warren-Adams Letters, Mass. Historical Society *Collections*, LXXII, LXXIII (Boston, 1917-1925), LXXII, pp. 197, 198.

36. Higginbotham, *Independence*, pp. 16, 354; Ward, *Revolution*, p. 203.

37. Ibid., pp. 424, 672, 826, 868, 883; Deering, "Our Militia," p. 3; Cole, "South Carolina Militia," pp. 107-109, 125-129, 131-133; Stone, *Kentucky Militia*, p. 10.

38. Ward, *Revolution*, pp. 118, 147, 158, 159, 714, 723; Higginbotham, *Independence*, p. 211; Gobbel, "North Carolina Militia," p. 53; Cole, "South Carolina Militia," p. 115; Wheeler, "North Carolina Militia," p. 196; Billias, *Generals*, pp. 100, 138, 165, 193, 200.

39. "To John Augustine Washington, 22 Sep. 1776," *Writings*, vol. 6, p. 96.

40. "To Jacob Greene, 28 Sep. 1776," *Greene Papers*, vol. 1, p. 303.

41. Higginbotham, *Independence*, pp. 182, 369; Upton, *Military Policy*, p. 58; Billias, *Generals*, p. 27; Lawrence D. Cress, "The Standing Army, the Militia and the New Republic: Changing Attitudes Toward the Military in American Society" (Ph.D. diss. Univ. of Virginia, 1976), pp. 132-134; published as *Citizens in Arms: The Army and the Militia in American Society to the War of 1812* (Univ. of North Carolina Press, 1982).
42. Billias, *Generals*, pp. 92, 93, 100.
43. Louis Gottschalk, *LaFayette and the Close of the American Revolution* (Univ. of Chicago Press, 1942), pp. 108, 109.
44. Shy, "Mobilizing," pp. 96-106.
45. Higginbotham, *Independence*. pp. 10, 93, 395, 414.
46. Douglas Southall Freeman, *George Washington: A Biography,* 7 vols. (New York, 1948-1957), vol. 1, p. xiv; vol. 3, p. 86; Higginbotham, *Independence*, pp. 85-88.

CHAPTER 4. MILITIA IN THE EARLY NATIONAL PERIOD

1. Don Higginbotham, *The War of American Independence* (Macmillan, 1971), pp. 206, 438.
2. The Articles of Confederation are printed in most anthologies of documents on United States history. See, for example, *Documents of American History to 1898*, Henry Steele Commager, ed. (8th ed., Appleton-Century-Crofts, 1968), pp. 111-116.
3. John K. Mahon, "Pennsylvania and the Beginnings of the Regular Army," *Pennsylvania History* (Jan. 1954), pp. 33-43; James Ripley Jacobs, *The Beginnings of the U. S. Army, 1783-1812* (Princeton, 1947), chap. 2, pp. 13-39.
4. Richard G. Stone, Jr., *The Brittle Sword: The Kentucky Militia, 1776-1912* (Univ. Press of Kentucky, 1977), p. 21.
5. John Bakeless, *Background to Glory: The Life of George Rogers Clark* (Lippincott, 1957), pp. 319-321; Temple Bodley, *George Rogers Clark* (Houghton-Mifflin, 1926), pp. 199-206, 282-286.
6. For detail on Shays' Rebellion, see Marion L. Starkey, *A Little Rebellion* (Knopf, 1955); see also Richard H. Kohn, *Eagle and Sword; The Federalists and the Creation of the Military Establishment in America, 1783-1802* (Free Press, 1975), pp. 74, 75.
7. For general information on the division of opinion, see Merrill Jensen, *The New Nation* (Knopf, 1950).
8. Kohn, *Eagle*, p. 83.
9. Higginbotham, *Independence*, pp. 455-456; Charles A. Lofgren, "Compulsory Military Service under the Constitution: The Original Understanding," *William and Mary Q.*, XXXIII (Jan. 1976), pp. 61-88.
10. Arthur A. Ekirch, *The Civilian and the Military* (Oxford Univ. Press, 1956), p. 2.
11. Max Farrand, ed., *The Records of the Federal Convention*, 3 vols. (Yale Univ. Press, 1911), vol. 3, pp. 207-209.

12. Jonathan Elliot, ed., *Debates in the Several State Conventions on the Adoption of the Federal Constitution . . .*, 5 vols. (reprint, New York, 1901), vol. 2, p. 136.

13. Edmund C. Burnett, ed., *Letters of Members of the Continental Congress*, 8 vols. (Carnegie Inst. of Wash., D.C., 1921-1938), vol. 7, p. 604.

14. Farrand, *Records*, vol. 3, p. 318.

15. *American State Papers, Indian Affairs*, 2 vols. (Wash., D.C., 1832), vol. 1, p. 23; for the detailed story of Harmer's campaign, see Jacobs, *Beginnings*, chaps. 4 and 5.

16. John K. Mahon, "The Citizen Soldier in National Defense, 1789-1815" (unpublished Ph.D. diss., UCLA, 1950), pp. 37, 38.

17. Arthur St. Clair, *A Narrative of the Campaign Against the Indians in the Year 1791* (Philadelphia, 1812), p. 183. For an account of the battle, see Jacobs, *Beginnings*, chaps. 4 and 5.

18. John McA. Palmer, *Washington, Lincoln, Wilson* (Doubleday, Doran, 1930), part I, "Washington's Legacy."

19. Ibid., chaps. 8, 9, 10.

20. I *USSL*, 8 May 1792, p. 271.

21. Ibid.

22. John K. Mahon, *The American Militia: Decade of Decision, 1789-1800* (Univ. of Florida Press, 1960), chap. 2.

23. Ibid.

24. I *USSL*, 2 May 1792, p. 264.

25. Mahon, *Decade*, chaps. 3 and 4.

26. Ibid.

27. Ibid.

28. Leland D. Baldwin, *Whiskey Rebels . . .* (Univ. of Pittsburgh Press, 1939). For briefer treatment with emphasis on the use of militia, see Mahon, "Citizen Soldier," chap. 7.

29. William Watts H. Davis, *The Fries Rebellion, 1798-1799* (Doylestown, Penna., 1899).

30. John Bach McMaster, *History of the People of the United States*, 8 vols. (Appleton, 1902-1913), vol. 2, pp. 435-438.

31. Kohn, *Eagle*, pp. 12, 193, 212, 219, 279.

32. See chart in *The Army Lineage Book* Infantry (GPO, 1953), pp. 58, 59.

33. Kohn, *Eagle*, pp. 260, 263.

34. *Diary and Autobiography of John Adams*, Lyman H. Butterfield, ed., 4 vols. (Belknap Press, Harvard, 1961), vol. 3, p. 195.

35. Kohn, *Eagle*, pp. 260, 263.

36. *Annals of Congress*, 6 Cong., 1 sess., 1799-1801, p. 306.

37. For data to prove this thesis, see John K. Mahon, "Anglo-American Methods of Indian Warfare, 1676-1794," *Mississippi Valley Historical Review*, XLV (Sep. 1958), pp. 254-275; see also Stone, *Brittle Sword*, p. 38.

38. For example, a news item announced a new major general in North Carolina because the previous one was elected governor, *North Carolina Minerva and Fayetteville Gazette*, 15 Dec. 1798. The rise of Andrew

Jackson through his position as major general of the Tennessee militia is the most conspicuous case; see Marquis James, *Andrew Jackson. The Border Captain* (Bobbs-Merrill, 1933).

39. The New Hampshire legislature voted sums, not fixed, periodically; Virginia, $200 per year; Massachusetts, sums at the discretion of the legislature; North Carolina, 25 shillings a day when on active service; Georgia, $1.75 per day when on active militia duty.

40. Brigade Inspector, Philadelphia County, to AG, 16 Feb. 1797, MS, *Harmar Papers*, Clements Library, University of Michigan.

41. Court martial of Capt. Joab Blackwell, 22 Oct. 1802, MS, *Military File*, South Carolina Historical Commission.

42. For an example, see Davis, *Fries Rebellion*, p. 45.

43. The account of training days, given here and in the next two paragraphs, is a composite drawn from the following accounts: H. Telfer Mook, "Training Day in New England," *New England Q.*, XI (Dec. 1936), pp. 675-697; "Extracts from the Diary of the Reverend William Bentley of Salem. . . ," Danvers Historical Society, *Historical Collections*, I (1913), pp. 72, 73; Guion G. Johnson, *Ante-Bellum North Carolina* (Univ. of North Carolina Press, 1937), pp. 102-104; Andrew D. Mellick Jr., *The Story of an Old Farm or Life in New Hampshire in the Eighteenth Century* (Somerville, New Jersey, 1889), pp. 577-580; Mary H. Northend, *Memories of Old Salem* (New York, 1912), pp. 278-289; J. W. Dearborn, ed., *A History of the First Century of Parsonsfield Maine* (Portland, 1888), pp. 228-230; John J. Dearborn, ed., *History of Salisbury, New Hampshire* (Manchester, New Hampshire, 1890), pp. 280ff.; George Mays, "Battalion or Training Day at Schaefferstown in the Olden Time," *Historical Papers and Addresses of the Lebanon County Historical Society, I (1899), pp. 148-168;* William H. Zierdt, *Narrative History of the 109th Field Artillery, Pennsylvania National Guard* (Wilkes-Barre, 1932), p. 43.

44. Brigade Inspector of Huntington County to Adjutant General of Penna., 24 Oct. 1795, MS, *Harmar Papers*.

45. Act of 28 May 1798, Sections 11 and 12; Act of 22 June and Act of 6 July 1798, I *USSL*, pp. 563, 569, 576.

46. Adjutant General to Governor, 10 Dec. 1788, MS, Letterbook of the Adjutant General of Massachusetts, No. 1, Military Archives, AGO, Mass.

47. Act of 22 June 1798, *Acts and Laws of the Commonwealth of Massachusetts*; Samuel Shepherd, *The Statutes at Large of Virginia, 1792-1806* (Richmond, 1835), p. 365.

48. Adjutant General to Governor, 12 June 1789, MS, Letterbook of the Adjutant General of Massachusetts, No. 1.

49. Act of 22 June 1793 and Resolve of 24 Feb. 1792, *Acts and Laws of the Commonwealth of Massachusetts.*

50. For examples of chiseling, see *Georgia Military Affairs*, 9 vols. covering 1789-1842 (typed from the original manuscripts and bound in 1940 under the direction of Mrs. J. E. Hays, State Historian), vol. 1, pp. 248, 249, 251, 280, 281, 283, 285.

51. Receipt signed by Peter Grey, Captain, Goose Creek Company, 2 May 1793, MS, *Military File*, South Carolina Historical Commission.

52. Data on militia fines drawn from: Act of 1794, chaps. 2, 5; Act of 1796, chap. 8; Act of 1798, chap. 5, Act of 1800, chap. 28, Laws of North Carolina; George and Robert Watkins, *Digest of the Laws of the State of Georgia* (Philadelphia, 1800), p. 458; Act of 10 May, 1794; Benjamin Elliott, *The Militia System of South Carolina* (Charleston, 1835); Act of 22 June 1793, *Acts and Laws of the Commonwealth of Massachusetts*; Act of 25 July 1788, Theodore C. Pease, *Laws of the Northwest Territory* (Illinois State Historical Library Collections, XVII, Springfield, 1925), p. 1; Act of 2 Dec. 1793, Shepherd, *Virginia Statutes*, p. 203; Act of 28 Dec. 1792, *Constitution and Laws of the State of New Hampshire* (Dover, N. H., 1805). See also Lena London, "The Militia Fine, 1830-1860," *Military Affairs*, XV (Fall 1951), pp. 133-144.

53. Memorial of Officers of 28th and 29th Regiments, South Carolina Militia to the S. C. Senate, 11 Dec. 1798, MS, *Military File*, South Carolina Historical Commission.

54. Returns of the Militia of the United States transmitted to Congress, 5 Jan. 1803, ASPMA, vol. 1, p. 159.

55. The operation of the mechanism described in this and the next four paragraphs has to be reconstructed from many, many specific instances or laws. Examples can be found in: Act of 22 Dec. 1792, William W. Hening, *The Statutes at Large of Pennsylvania, Being a Collection of all the Laws of Virginia ... from 1619,* 13 vols. (Philadelphia, 1823), vol. 13; Act of 20 March 1780, James T. Mitchell & Henry Flanders, compilers, *Statutes At Large of Pennsylvania, 1682-1801,* 16 vols. (Harrisburg, 1896-1911), vol. 10; Mifflin to Harmar, 25 Aug. 1798, MS, Mifflin Papers, Pennsylvania Historical Commission, vol. 52; Col. Campbell to Governor Mifflin, 15 Jan. 1792, *Pennsylvania Archives,* series 2, vol. 4, p. 580.

56. Act of 9 May 1794 and Act of 24 June 1797, I *USSL*, pp. 367, 522.

57. General Order, 28 Feb. 1795, General Orders, vol. 1, MS, *Military Archives*, AGO Mass., p. 119; Items 37, 39, 782, MSS, *Military File*, South Carolina Historical Commission.

58. An example is Georgia's claim pressed year after year for defense carried out in 1794 which was finally settled in 1827, HR *Report Number* 77, 10 Feb. 1827, 19 Cong., 2 sess.

59. John K. Mahon, "The Defense of Georgia, 1794," *Georgia Historical Q.,* XLIII (June 1959), pp. 138-155.

60. Henry Adams, *The Life of Albert Gallatin* (Philadelphia, 1879), p. 211; McMaster, *History*, vol. 2, p. 494.

CHAPTER 5. JEFFERSONIAN MILITIA AND THE WAR OF 1812

1. "Jefferson to (recipient unknown)," in *The Writings of Thomas Jefferson,* 20 vols. (Thomas Jefferson Memorial Assn., Washington, D.C., 1905), vol. 10, p. 365.

2. Acts of 2 March 1801 and 3 March 1803, II USSL, pp. 108, 227.

3. "Jefferson to Congress, 8 Dec. 1801," in James D. Richardson, *Messages and Papers of the Presidents*, 10 vols. (GPO, 1899), vol. 1, p. 329.

4. Returns of the Militia of the U. S. transmitted to Congress 5 Jan. 1803, ASPMA, vol. I, p. 159.

5. John K. Mahon, *The American Militia: Decade of Decision, 1789-1800* (Univ. of Florida Press, 1960), p. 63n; and "The Citizen Soldier in National Defense, 1789-1815 (unpublished Ph.D. diss., UCLA, 1950), p. 229.

6. James Ripley Jacobs, *The Beginnings of the United States Army, 1783-1812* (Princeton Univ. Press, 1947), chaps. 10 and 11; Theodore Joseph Crackel, "The Founding of West Point: Jefferson and the Politics of Security," *Armed Forces and Society*, VII (Summer 1981), pp. 529-543.

7. Act of 24 Feb. 1807, II USSL, p. 236.

8. Circular, Jefferson to the Governors of Territories Adjacent to Spain, 21 March 1807, MS, NA, Old War Records.

9. Act of 3 March 1807, II USSL, p. 443; "Use of the Militia and the National Guard by the Federal Government in Civil Disturbances" (typescript, Center for Military History, Dep't. of the Army, Wash., D.C. n.d.), p. 10, printed, Robert W. Coakley, same title, in *Bayonets in the Streets*, ed. Robin Higham, (Univ. Press of Kansas, 1969).

10. Secretary of war to governors, 18 Jan. 1809, MS, NA, Old War Records.

11. Coakley, "Use of Militia," p. 10.

12. *Annals of Congress*, 10 Cong., 1 sess. (26 Oct. 1807-25 April 1808), pp. 1903-1911.

13. Ibid., 12 Cong., 1 sess. (4 Nov. 1811-6 July 1812), p. 731.

14. Ibid., 11 Cong., 1 & 2 sess. (22 May 1809-1 May 1810), p. 1589.

15. Ibid., 12 Cong., 1 sess. (4 Nov. 1811-6 July 1812), p. 35.

16. Act of 23 April 1808, II USSL, p. 490.

17. Mahon, "Citizen Soldier," pp. 213-232.

18. *Annals of Congress*, 12 Cong., 1 sess., pp. 45, 737, 782.

19. Ibid., p. 58.

20. "J. H. Campbell to Thomas Worthington, 17 June 1812." *Thomas Worthington and the War of 1812*, ed. Richard C. Knopf (Columbus, Ohio, 1957), p. 96.

21. John K. Mahon, *The War of 1812* (Univ. of Florida Press, 1972), p. 4.

22. Smith to secretary of war, 2 July 1812; Roger Griswold to secretary of war, 13 Aug. 1812; Gov. of Connecticut to secretary of war, 25 Aug. 1814; ASPMA, vol. I, pp. 325, 326, 618.

23. Strong to secretary of war, 5 Aug. 1812, ibid., p. 323; General Order to Mass. Militia, 3 July 1812, MS, Orderly Book 4, Archives of the Adjutant General of Mass.

24. "Proclamation of the Gov. of Vermont, 10 Nov. 1813." *Official Letters of the Military and Naval Officers of the United States during the War with Great Britain in the Years 1812, 1813, 1814, & 1815,* Comp. John Brannan (Washington, D.C., 1823), pp. 261, 262; *Niles Register*, Vol. 7, p. 65.

25. For the narrative of Hull's campaign, see Mahon, *War of 1812*, pp. 43-54; William Hull, *Memoirs of the Campaign of the Northwest Army* (Boston, 1824).

26. Mahon, *War of 1812*, pp. 75-81; Solomon Van Rensselaer, *A Narrative of the Affair at Queenstown in the War of 1812* (New York, 1836), pp. 10, 24, 67; John K. Mahon, "Principal Causes for the Failure of the United States Militia System during the War of 1812," *Indiana Military History Journal*, IV (May 1979), pp. 15-21.

27. Mahon, *War of 1812*, pp. 81-85.

28. Ibid., p. 94.

29. Ibid., pp. 94, 95, 210.

30. John Gano to Gov. Meigs, 10 Dec. 1813, "Selections from the Gano Papers," *Quarterly Publication of the Historical and Philosophical Society of Ohio*, vols. 15-18 (Columbus, 1920), vol. 18, p. 11; Mahon, *War of 1812*, pp. 63, 162, 178, 186.

31. Samuel R. Brown, *Views of the Campaigns of the Northwestern Army* (Burlington, Vt., 1814), p. 109.

32. Harrison to secretary of war, 5 & 9 May, 1813, Microcopy 221, Reel 53, H156, NA; see also Mahon, *War of 1812*, pp. 159-165.

33. Ibid., p. 185; "Shelby to Harrison, 8 Aug. 1813," *Messages and Letters of William Henry Harrison*, ed. Logan Esarey, 2 vols. (Indiana Historical Collections, Indianapolis, 1922), vol. 2, pp. 518, 519.

34. McClure to Tompkins, 21 Dec. 1813, Letters to Daniel D. Tompkins, Gov. of New York, 1812-1814, MS, NA, p. 70; same to secretary of war, 25 Feb. 1813, ASPMA, vol. I, p. 487.

35. Secretary of war to Gen. James Wilkinson, 1 Jan. 1814, Microcopy 6, Reel 7, p. 97; Hall to Tompkins, 6 Jan. 1814, Letters to Tompkins, p. 12; Mahon, *War of 1812*, pp. 190, 191.

36. Ibid., p. 147.

37. "Porter to Tompkins, 29 July 1814," *Documentary History of the Campaigns upon the Niagara Frontier in 1813 and 1814*, ed. Ernest A. Cruikshank, 9 vols. (Welland, Ontario, Lundy's Lane Historical Society, n.d.), vol. 1, p. 101.

38. Jacob Brown to Tompkins, 20 Sep. 1814, ibid., p. 207; Mahon, *War of 1812*, p. 280.

39. Izard to secretary of war, 20 Nov. 1814, George Izard, *Official Correspondence . . .* (Philadelphia, 1816), p. 120.

40. For Cockburn's riverine actions in the Chesapeake area, see Mahon, *War of 1812*, pp. 111, 112, 115-117, 222, 289.

41. Secretary of Penna. to secretary of war, 25 July 1814, ASPMA, I, p. 551.

42. Gen. Winder to secretary of war, 27 Aug. 1814, Brannan, *Official Letters*, p. 400.

43. (George Robert Gleig), *A Narrative of the Campaigns of the British Army at Washington, Baltimore, and New Orleans. . . .* (Philadelphia, 1821), p. 125.

44. Mahon, *War of 1812*, pp. 305-316.

45. Mooers to Tompkins, 4 Sep. 1814. Letters to Tompkins, p. 18; for a general account of the Battle of Plattsburgh, see Mahon, *War of 1812*, pp. 317-328.
46. Ibid., p. 316.
47. Ibid., p. 221; *Charleston Courier*, 30 Aug. 1813.
48. Mahon, *War of 1812*, p. 315.
49. "Report of the Hartford Convention," 4 Jan. 1815, *Niles Register*, vol. 7, pp. 305-313.
50. Lillian Schlissel, ed. *Conscience in America: A Documentary History of Conscientious Objection in America* (E. P. Dutton, 1968), p. 69.
51. Robert V. Remini, *Andrew Jackson and the Course of American Empire, 1767-1812* (Harper and Row, 1977), pp. 15, 31, 100, 118, 119, 127, 160.
52. Jackson to President, 15 March 1813, *Correspondence of Andrew Jackson*, ed. John Spencer Bassett, 7 vols. (Carnegie Inst., Washington, D.C., 1926-1935), vol. 1, p. 292.
53. Quoted in Marquis James, *Andrew Jackson: The Border Captain* (Bobbs-Merrill, 1933), p. 176.
54. Mahon, *War of 1812*, pp. 354-372.
55. Bicentennial Edition, *Historical Statistics of the United States*, 2 vols. (Dept. of Commerce, Bureau of the Census, Washington, D.C., 1975), vol. 2, pp. 1140, 1146.

CHAPTER 6. DECLINE OF THE MILITIA; RISE OF THE VOLUNTEERS

1. Report of the Committee on Militia, 27 Feb. 1827, *HR Reports 92*, 19 Cong., 1 sess.; also printed in ASPMA, vol. III, pp. 599-602.
2. Dudley Knox, *History of the United States Navy* (Putnam, 1936), pp. 143-147.
3. GO 4 July 1833, copy in James Miller Papers, MS, Library, U.S. Military Academy; Report, Adjutant General of Mass., 9 Jan. 1823, from Annual Reports, Adjutant General of Mass., 1789-1840, MS, Military Archives, Adjutant General of Mass., Boston.
4. Tomlinson quote, *Annals of Congress*, 16 Cong., 2 sess., p. 922; Black quote, *Congressional Globe*, 24 May 1842, 27 Cong., 2 sess., p. 418.
5. Report, Comm. on Militia, 27 Feb. 1827; Report on the Militia, 5 Jan. 1832. *Speeches and Occasional Addresses by John A. Dix*, 2 vols. (Appleton, 1864), vol. 2, pp. 117, 178, 179; Petition, 23 Feb. 1831, ASPMA, vol. IV, p. 701.
6. As an extreme example of an attack on the regulars and the Military Academy, see "Memorial of Alden Partridge and Edmund Burke . . .", 9 Feb. 1839, *Sen. Doc. 197*, 25 Cong., 3 sess.
7. Gov. Eustis of Mass., 1823, ASPMA, vol. 3, p. 59; Memorial of a Military Convention at Norwich, Vermont, 28 Feb. 1840, printed in the *Citizen Soldier*, vol. 1, 29 July 1840.

8. Dix, Report on Militia, p. 179.

9. Defense of the United States, 5 April 1836, *Sen. Doc. 293*, 24 Cong., 1 sess., p. 71.

10. Dix, Report on Militia, pp. 117, 178.

11. Militia Plan submitted by the sec. of war to HR, 13 Dec. 1816, War Office Reports to Congress, Book 1, MS, NA, Old War Records; Report, sec. of war, 28 Nov. 1826, *Sen. Doc. 1*, 19 Cong., 2 sess.; Report on Militia, 4 Feb. 1829, *HR Doc. 68*, 20 Cong., 2 sess.; *HR Report 875*, 11 May 1838, 25 Cong., 2 sess.; Militia of the United States, 20 March 1940, *Sen. Docs. 531 and 560*, 26 Cong., 1 sess.

12. John K. Mahon, "A Board of Officers Considers the Condition of the Militia in 1826," *Military Affairs*, XV (Summer 1951), pp. 90-93.

13. *The Papers of John C. Calhoun*, ed. Robert L. Meriwether, 5 vols. (Univ. of South Carolina Press, 1959), vol. 3, pp. xxv, xxvi; New York Statute, 11 May 1835.

14. Cyril B. Upsham, "Historical Survey of the Militia of Iowa," *Iowa Journal of History and Politics*, XVII (July 1919), p. 330; Jerry M. Cooper, "To Be a Soldier: History of the Wisconsin National Guard in the Nineteenth Century" (unpublished typescript, 1976), pp. 78-82; Dello G. Dayton, "The California Militia, 1850-1866" (unpublished Ph.D. diss., Univ. of California, Berkeley, 1951), pp. 235-253.

15. William Jay, *War and Peace* . . . (Wiley and Putnam, NY, 1842).

16. Report of the Secretary of War, 28 Nov. 1826, *Sen. Doc. 1*, 19 Cong., 1 sess.

17. Secretary of War to HR, 11 Dec. 1818, ASPMA, vol. 3, p. 377; Report of the Secretary of War, 1837, ASPMA, vol. VII, p. 574; Russell F. Weigley, *Towards an American Army* (Columbia Univ. Press, 1962), pp. 31-33.

18. Constitution of the State of Mississippi, 1817; Dayton, "California Militia," p. 155; George C. Bittle, "The Organized Florida Militia from 1821 to 1920" (unpublished Ph.D. diss., Florida State Univ., 1965), p. 222; Report, Adjutant General of Mass., 28 Dec. 1837, MS, Archives of the Adjutant General of Mass.; Arming the Militia, *HR Doc. 72*, 3 March 1830, 21 Cong., 1 sess.

19. Message of the Gov. of Mass., 19 Jan. 1835, *Mass Acts and Resolves* (Boston, 1836); Lena London, "The Militia Fine, 1830-1860," *Military Affairs*, XV (Fall 1951), pp. 138-144; Stewart L. Gates, "The Militia in Connecticut Public Life, 1660-1860" (unpublished Ph.D. diss., Univ. of Connecticut, 1975), p. 137; Frederick R. Todd, "The Militia and Volunteers of the District of Columbia, 1783-1820," *Records of the Columbia Historical Society*, vol. 50, p. 4.

20. Ibid.; Marcus Cunliffe, *Soldiers and Civilians* . . . (Little, Brown, 1968), p. 8; Letterbook of James Adger, MS, South Caroliniana Library, Columbia, S. C.; George M. Whipple, *History of the Salem Light Infantry* (Salem, Mass., 1890), pp. 30ff; Report, Adjutant General of Mass., 31 Dec. 1824, MS, Archives of the Adjutant General of Mass.; John Glendower Westover, "Evolution of the Missouri Militia, 1804-1919" (unpublished Ph.D. diss.,

Univ. of Missouri, 1948), p. 105; Dayton, "California National Guard," pp. 45, 50.

21. Ibid., pp. 45, 72, 117, 300; Todd, "D.C. Militia," p. 17.

22. Dayton, "California National Guard," see note 21; An Act Relating to the Militia of the State of New York, 16 April 1851; Mass. Act of 29 March 1834, *Mass. Acts and Resolves* (Boston, 1835); Pennsylvania Act of 19 March 1838; Gates, "Connecticut Militia," p. 217.

23. Uniform file, USAMHI.

24. Dayton, "California National Guard," p. 285; Whipple, *History*, p. 22.

25. Ibid.; Theo G. Gronert, "The First National Pastime in the Middle West," *Indiana Magazine of History*, XXIX (Sep. 1933), pp. 171-186; Emmons Clark, *History of the Second Company Seventh New York State Militia* (New York, 1864), pp. 117, 270ff; Westover, "Missouri Militia," p. 100; General Orders, State of New Hampshire, 4 July 1833, Miller Papers.

26. William Packer Clarke, *Official History of the Militia and National Guard of the State of Pennsylvania*, 3 vols., (Phila., 1909), pp. 36-39; Cooper, "To Be a Soldier," pp. 143ff.; Todd, "D.C. Militia," pp. 2, 43; Gates, "Connecticut Militia," p. 258; R. Ernest Dupuy, *The National Guard: A Compact History* (Hawthorne, 1971), p. 54.

27. Clark, *Second Company*, pp. 111, 123, 125, 129.

28. Dupuy, *National Guard*, p. 54.

29. Patrick D. O'Flaherty, "History of the 69th Regiment, New York State Militia, 1852-1861" (unpublished Ph.D. diss. Fordham Univ., 1963), pp. 1-224.

30. Ibid., pp. 126, 137.

31. Cecil D. Eby, *That "Disgraceful Affair": The Black Hawk War* (Norton, 1973), p. 264.

32. Quoted in Roger L. Nichols, *General Henry Atkinson: A Western Military Career* (Univ. of Oklahoma Press, 1965), p. 168.

33. Eby, *Black Hawk War*, pp. 100, 140.

34. Ibid., pp. 174, 254.

35. Ibid., pp. 199, 228, 239, 244.

36. For the general history of this conflict, see John K. Mahon, *History of the Second Seminole War* (Univ. of Florida Press, 1965).

37. Ibid., pp. 110-112.

38. Ibid., chap. 8; see especially pp. 161, 163.

39. Ibid., pp. 219-230; William R. Gentry, *Full Justice: The Story of William R. Gentry and his Missouri Volunteers in the Seminole War* (St. Louis, 1937); J. Floyd Monk, "Christmas Day in Florida, 1837," *Tequesta*, XXXVIII (1978), pp. 5-38.

40. V USSL, 19 March 1836; Mahon, *Seminole War*, p. 290.

41. Ibid., p. 225.

42. Ibid., p. 136.

43. Frank F. White, Jr., ed. "Macomb's Mission to the Seminoles: John T. Sprague's Journal. . . ," *Florida Historical Q.*, XXXV (Oct. 1956), p. 173.

44. Mahon, *Seminole War*, pp. 208, 222.

45. Ibid., p. 276; Poinsett to HR, 21 March 1838, War Office Reports to Congress, Book 4, MS, NA, Old War Records.

46. Bittle, "Florida Militia," pp. 126, 132, 163, 170, 172.

47. For a brief treatment of the Buckshot and Aroostook Wars, see *Dictionary of American History*, 7 vols. and index volume (Scribners, 1976).

48. K. Jack Bauer, *The Mexican War, 1846-1848* (Macmillan, 1974), pp. 20, 87; Justin Smith, *The War with Mexico*, 2 vols. (Macmillan, 1919), vol. 1, p. 205.

49. Emory Upton, *Military Policy of the United States* (Washington, D.C., 1907), p. 221.

50. Statistics drawn from the following sources: ibid., pp. 229-221; Bauer, *Mexican War*, pp. 71, 72; Smith, *War*, vol. 1, p. 192; vol. 2, p. 511; "Resources of the United States . . . Men," Army War College Study number 20, June 1906 (Typescript, USAMHI), p. 26.

51. Bauer, *Mexican War*, pp. 71, 318.

52. Smith, *War*, vol. 2, pp. 64ff, 319.

53. Quoted in ibid., pp. 512, 513.

54. Ibid., vol. 2, pp. 208, 475; Bauer, *Mexican War*, pp. 83, 204; Samuel Chamberlain, *Recollections of a Rogue* (Museum Press, London, 1957), p. 31.

55. Bauer, *Mexican War*, p. 83.

56. Raphael Semmes, *Service Afloat and Ashore during the War with Mexico* (Cincinnati, 1851), p. 165; W. A. Croffut, ed., *Fifty Years in Camp and Field: The Diary of Ethan Allen Hitchcock* (New York, 1909), p. 321.

57. Smith, *War*, vol. II, pp. 211-216, 450; Chamberlain, *Recollections*, pp. 64, 83.

58. J. Jacob Oswandel, *Notes on the Mexican War* (Philadelphia, 1885), p. 121.

59. Smith, *War*, vol. I, p. 195.

60. Upton, *Military Policy* pp. 204, 206; James K. Holland, "The Diary of a Texan Volunteer in the Mexican War," *Southwestern Historical Q.*, XXX (July 1926), pp. 3, 17, 19.

61. Bauer, *Mexican War*, pp. 214, 360; Charles W. Elliott, *Winfield Scott: The Soldier and the Man* (Macmillan, 1937), p. 487.

62. Upton, *Military Policy*, p. 220; Smith, *War*, vol. 1, p. 195.

63. *Congressional Globe*, 35 Cong., 1 sess., p. 867.

64. See table of strength in *The Army Lineage Book: Infantry* (Washington, D.C., 1953). This table was not reprinted in the hardback edition, 1972; Russell F. Weigley, *History of the United States Army* (Macmillan, 1967), strength tables, pp. 566-569.

65. Westover, "Missouri Militia," p. 75.

66. Detail on the Mormon War, Charles P. Roland, *Albert Sidney Johnston* (Univ. of Texas Press, 1964), pp. 185-237.

67. Patrick H. McLatchy, "The Development of the National Guard of Washington as an Instrument of Social Control, 1854-1916" (unpublished Ph.D. diss., Univ. of Washington, 1973), pp. 39-50.

68. James W. Covington, *The Billy Bowlegs War, 1855-1858: The Final Stand of the Seminole Indians against the Whites* (Mickler House Publishers, 1982).

CHAPTER 7. CIVIL WAR

1. "Resources of the United States . . . Men," Army War College Study #20, June 1906, USAMHI, p. 26; Marvin A. Kreidberg and Merton G. Henry, *History of Military Mobilization in the United States Army, 1775-1945* (DA Pamphlet 20-212, Washington, D.C., 1955), p. 89; Thomas L. Livermore, *Number and Losses in the Civil War* . . . (Indiana Univ., Civil War Centennial Series, a reissue, 1957), pp. v, 1.

2. Kreidberg and Henry, *History*, pp. 90, 91, 93.

3. John J. Pullen, *The Twentieth Maine* . . . (Philadelphia, 1954), pp. 3, 4; John Robertson, *Michigan in the War* (Lansing, 1882), p. 10; Otis F. R. Waite, *New Hampshire in the Great Rebellion* (Claremont, N.H., 1870), p. 49; Whitelaw Reid, *Ohio on the War*, 2 vols. (Cincinnati 1868), vol. 1; Report of the Adjutant General of Vermont, 1862, p. 42.

4. *Congressional Globe*, LVIII, 37 Cong., 1 sess., p. 42.

5. John G. Barrett, *The Civil War in North Carolina* (Univ. of North Carolina Press, 1963), p. 100; George C. Bittle, "The Organized Florida Militia from 1821 to 1920" (unpublished Ph.D. diss., Florida State Univ., 1965), pp. 227ff.; John E. Johns, *Florida during the Civil War* (Univ. of Florida Press, 1963), p. 33; Michael B. Dougan, *Confederate Arkansas* (Univ. of Alabama Press, 1976), p. 69.

6. For Scott's estimate, see Kreidberg and Henry, *History*, p. 90; see also the table on p. 92 of quotas apportioned to the states and their responses, and p. 116; Leonard L. Lerwill, *The Personnel Replacement System of the United States Army* (DA Pamphlet 20-211, Washington, D.C., 1954), p. 72.

7. Alfred S. Roe, *The Fifth Regiment, Massachusetts Volunteer Infantry* (Boston, 1911), pp. 7, 12, 33, 41; Patrick D. O'Flaherty, "History of the 69th Regiment, New York Militia, 1852-1861" (unpublished Ph.D. diss., Fordham Univ., 1963), pp. 225ff., 243; R. Ernest Dupuy, *The National Guard: A Compact History* (Hawthorne, 1971), p. 61; Frederick P. Todd, "Our National Guard: An Introduction to Its History," *Military Affairs*, V (Fall 1941), p. 154.

8. Reid, *Ohio*, vol. 1, pp. 25, 27; W. A. Newman Dorland, "The Second Troop of Philadelphia City Cavalry," *Pennsylvania Magazine of History and Biography* (scattered in vols. XLV-LIV, 1921-1930).

9. Edain B. Quiner, *The Military History of Wisconsin* . . . *in the War for the Union* (Chicago, 1866), pp. 70ff.; Jerry M. Cooper, "To Be a Soldier: History of the Wisconsin National Guard in the Nineteenth Century" (unpublished book-length typescript, 1976), p. 182.

10. Dello G. Dayton, "The California Militia, 1850-1866" (unpublished

Ph.D. diss., Univ. of California, Berkeley, 1951), pp. 330-361; Patrick R. McLatchy, "The Development of the National Guard of Washington (State) as an Instrument of Social Control, 1854-1916" (unpublished Ph.D. diss., Univ. of Washington, 1973), pp. 58-65.

11. *Organization and Status of Missouri Troops (Union and Confederate) in Service during the Civil War* (War Department Records and Pensions Office, 1902), pp. 16ff.; Richard G. Stone, Jr., *A Brittle Sword: The Kentucky Militia, 1776-1912* (Univ. Press of Kentucky, 1977), pp. 62ff.

12. The percentage used here is derived from a count made through the brief unit histories included in vol. III, Frederick B. Dyer, *A Compendium of the War of the Rebellion* (reprint in 3 vols. by Thomas Yoseloff, 1959); Roe, *Fifth*, pp. 121-176.

13. Emmons Clark, *History of the Seventh Regiment of New York, 1806-1889*, 2 vols. (New York, 1890); Todd, "National Guard," p. 156; James M. Rice, "The Defense of Our Frontier," *Journal of the Military Service Institution*, VIII (March 1896), p. 306.

14. Kreidberg and Henry, *History*, pp. 100ff.; Lerwill, *Replacement*, p. 89; Roe, *Fifth*, p. 119; Cooper, "To Be a Soldier," p. 11.

15. Ibid., pp. 149, 161; Kreidberg and Henry, *History*, p. 90.

16. Reid, *Ohio*, vol. 1, pp. 46-49, 69, 93.

17. Ibid., pp. 139-150; Francis A. Lord, *They Fought for the Union* (Stackpole, 1960), p. 9.

18. *Missouri Troops*, pp. 18, 20, 21, 38, 48, 246, 277, 282; John G. Westover, "Evolution of the Missouri Militia, 1804-1919" (unpublished Ph.D. diss., Univ. of Missouri, 1948), pp. 121-171, especially pp. 121, 139, 146, 154.

19. Stone, *Brittle Sword*, pp. 62-74.

20. Russell F. Weigley, *History of the United States Army* (Macmillan, 1967), p. 199.

21. Kreidberg and Henry, *History*, pp. 134, 136, 137, Louise B. Hill, *Joseph E. Brown and the Confederacy* (Greenwood Press, 1939, reprint 1972), p. 79.

22. Kreidberg and Henry, *History*, pp. 104-112; Lerwill, *Replacement*, p. 92.

23. For general coverage of the draft, see Jack F. Leach, *Conscription in the United States . . .* (Rutland, Vt., 1952), and Eugene C. Murdoch, *One Million Men: The Civil War Draft* (State Historical Society of Wisconsin, 1971).

24. James McCague, *The Second Rebellion: The New York Draft Riots* (Dial, 1968), especially pp. 45, 49, 139, 151; Roe, *Fifth*, p. 246; Adrienne Cook, *Armies of the Streets: The Civil War Draft Riots* (Univ. Press of Kentucky, 1974).

25. Lovell D. Black, "The Negro Volunteer Militia Units of the Ohio National Guard" (unpublished Ph.D. diss., Ohio State Univ., 1976), pp. 64, 82, 91, 92, 101, 113, 117; Charles J. Johnson, "Black Soldiers in the National Guard, 1877-1949" (unpublished Ph.D. diss., Howard Univ. 1976), pp. 46, 49, 53.

26. Henry I. Smith, *History of the Seventh Iowa Veteran Volunteer Infantry*

during the Civil War (Mason City, Ia, 1903), pp. 88, 112,

27. Kreidberg and Henry, *History*, pp. 99-102; Lerwill, *Personnel*, pp. 88, 93, 94.

28. Roe, *Fifth*, p. 270; Reid, *Ohio*, vol. 1, p. 181; Thomas M. Eddy, *Patriotism of Illinois*, 2 vols. (Chicago, 1865), vol. 1, p. 148; Frederick Phisterer, *Statistical Record of the Armies of the United States* (Scribners, 1884), p. 7.

29. "Papers of James G. Blunt," *Kansas State Historical Collections*, 17 vols. (Topeka, 1875-1928), vol. 1, pp. 218, 220, 227, 228, 240, 241, 248, 249.

30. John A. Logan, *The Volunteer Soldier of America* (Chicago, 1887), pp. 399, 417, 418.

31. Dougan, *Arkansas*, pp. 90, 91; Johns, *Florida*, p. 113, cites Governor Milton of Florida complaining that Confederate troops were raised in Florida in disrespect of state authority and disregard of states' rights.

32. Hill, *Brown*, pp. 48, 52, 54, 55, 165, 183, 185, 192.

33. Cooper, "To Be a Soldier," p. 204.

34. Lerwill, *Replacement*, p. 85.

35. Todd, "National Guard," p. 74.

36. Pullen, *Twentieth Maine*.

37. Logan, *Volunteer Soldier*, pp. 78, 105.

CHAPTER 8. RECONSTRUCTION;
BIRTH OF THE NATIONAL GUARD

1. Charles J. Johnson, "Black Soldiers in the National Guard, 1877-1949" (unpublished Ph.D. diss., Howard Univ., 1976), p. 60. Most of the material in the next six paragraphs on the black militia is drawn from Otis A. Singletary, *Negro Militia and Reconstruction* (Univ. of Texas Press, 1957), pp. vii, 5, 8, 9, 29, 34, 37, 81-93.

2. Lovell D. Black, "The Negro Volunteer Units of the Ohio National Guard" (unpublished Ph.D. diss., Ohio State Univ., 1976), p. 15.

3. Singletary, *Negro Militia*, pp. 50-65, 122.

4. Ibid., pp. 124-128, 136, 144.

5. Ibid., pp. 146-148.

6. Johnson, "Black Soldiers," pp. 84ff., 90ff.; Martin K. Gordon, "The Black Militia in the District of Columbia, 1867-1898," *Records of the Columbia Historical Society*, 1971-1972 (Washington, D.C., 1972), pp. 413, 414.

7. Black, "Negro Ohio National Guard," pp. ii, iii, 41, 182, 198, 200.

8. *Encyclopaedia Britannica*, 1952 ed.

9. Winthrop Alexander, "Ten Years of Riot Duty: A Record of the Active Service performed by the National Guard, 1886-1895," *Journal of the Military Service Institution of the United States*, XIX (July 1896), pp. 1-62.

10. George C. Bittle, "The Organized Florida Militia from 1821 to 1920" (unpublished Ph.D. diss., Florida State Univ., 1965), pp. 321, 327-330, 335, 341, 344, 347, 352.

11. Ibid.

12. Act of 16 May 1865, *Mass. Acts and Resolves for 1865* (Boston, 1865), pp. 55, 56.

13. John G. Westover, "Evolution of the Missouri Militia, 1804-1919" (unpublished Ph.D. diss., Univ. of Missouri, 1945), pp. 169-233.

14. Charles A. Peckham, "The Ohio National Guard and Its Police Duties, 1894," *Ohio History*, LXXXIII (Winter 1974), pp. 52, 54, 56, 59; John Waksmundski, "Governor McKinley and the Working Man," *Historian*, XXXVIII (Aug. 1976), pp. 638-642.

15. Robert V. Bruce, *1877: Year of Violence* (Bobbs-Merill, 1959), pp. 135, 138, 143.

16. Ibid., pp. 18, 77-80, 101-103, 138-190, 199, 238, 239, 249.

17. Joseph J. Holmes, "The National Guard of Pennsylvania: Policeman of Industry, 1895-1905" (unpublished Ph.D. diss., Univ. of Connecticut, 1971), pp. 77, 78, 81.

18. William H. Riker, *Soldiers of the States: The Role of the National Guard in American Democracy* (Washington, D.C., 1958), p. 47.

19. Holmes, "National Guard of Pennsylvania," pp. 93, 158, 253; Alexander "Riot Duty," p. 33; Richard G. Stone, Jr., *A Brittle Sword: The Kentucky Militia, 1776-1912* (Univ. Press of Kentucky, 1977), p. 80; Jim Dan Hill, *The Minute Man in War and Peace* (Stackpole, 1964) indignantly denies the connection between the growth of the Guard and industrial conflict, pp. 128-131. In contrast, this connection is a major theme in Riker, *Soldiers of the States*.

20. Holmes, "National Guard of Pennsylvania," pp. 189, 190, 192, 217.

21. Kenneth R. Bailey, "A Search for Identity: The West Virginia National Guard, 1877-1921" (unpublished Ph.D. diss., Ohio State Univ., 1976), pp. 4, 39, 47, 50-52, 67, 90.

22. Jerry M. Cooper, "To Be A Soldier: History of the Wisconsin National Guard in the Nineteenth Century" (unpublished typescript, 1976), pp. 236, 238, 248, 252, 257, 351; portions relating to the theory of the Guard in Wisconsin, pp. 244, 249-251, 406, 407, 354-356; Martin K. Gordon, "The Milwaukee Infantry Militia, 1865-1892," *Historical Messenger of the Milwaukee County Historical Society*, XXIV (March 1968), pp. 2-15; Ralph J. Olson, "The Wisconsin National Guard," *Wisconsin Magazine of History*, XXXIX (Summer 1956), p. 233.

23. For this and the next paragraph, see Charles King, *Trials of a Staff Officer* (Philadelphia, 1891), pp. 147, 148, 150-152, 155, 161, 164, 169-173, 176, 178.

24. Source for this and the next two paragraphs is Patrick H. McLatchy, "The Development of the National Guard of Washington (State) as an Instrument of Social Control, 1854-1916 (unpublished Ph.D. diss., Univ. of Washington, 1973), pp. 100-106, 114, 128, 147, 153, 165, 303, 306, 311.

25. Ibid., p. 174, see also p. 268.

26. Richard C. Roberts, "History of the Utah National Guard, 1894-1954" (unpublished Ph.D. diss., Univ. of Utah, 1973), pp. 2, 3, 5, 6, 12, 13, 35, 40.

27. King, *Trials*, pp. 113-146; Holmes, "National Guard of Pennsylvania,"

pp. 104, 106, 123, 146, 248, 249, 313, 318; Bruce, *1877*, pp. 104, 135, 225-228, 312.

28. Holmes, "National Guard of Pennsylvania," p. 104; McLatchy, "Washington National Guard," pp. 194, 268; King, *Trials*, pp. 113ff.; *The National Guard*, 30 May 1891, p. 167.

29. Cooper, "To Be a Soldier," pp. 346-350.

30. Holmes, "National Guard of Pennsylvania," pp. 266-274.

31. Samuel Yellen, *American Labor Struggles* (Harcourt Brace, 1936), pp. 118-122; John P. Altgeld, *Live Questions* (Chicago, 1899), pp. 650-679.

32. Source for this and the next paragraph is Colston E. Warne, *The Pullman Boycott of 1894: The Problem of Federal Intervention* (D.C. Heath, 1955).

33. James J. Hudson, "The California National Guard, 1903-1940" (unpublished Ph.D. diss., Univ. of California, Berkeley, 1953), p. 38.

34. Warne, *Pullman Boycott*.

35. Hill, *Minute Man*, pp. 322-327; Riker, *Soldiers of the States*, p. 65; Louis Cantor, "Creation of the Modern National Guard: The Dick Militia Act of 1903" (unpublished Ph.D. diss., Duke Univ., 1963), pp. 81-85, 90, 93.

36. Ibid.

37. Cantor, "Creation," p. 166; Hill, *Minute Man*, p. 327.

38. Paul I. Wellman, *Indian Wars of the West* (Doubleday, 1947), pp. 20-36, 70-74, 81, 309, 311, 316.

39. Cantor, "Creation," p. 93.

40. *Reports of the Chief of Ordnance* for 1895, 1897, 1898; Carl Bakal, *The Right to Bear Arms*, (McGraw-Hill, 1966), p. 130.

41. "The Militia and the Army," *Harpers New Monthly Magazine*, LXXII (1886), pp. 294-313, in part reprinted or paraphrased in *The National Guard*, 28 March 1891, pp. 61, 62.

42. "The Militia," *Journal of the Military Service Institution*, VI (1885), pp. 1-26; for comments of other officers on the same subject, see adjutant general to secretary of war, 18 Jan. 1878; quartermaster general to secretary of war, 31 Jan. 1878, printed with *Annual Report of the Secretary of War* for 1878; Theo F. Rodenbough, "Militia Reform without Legislation," *Journal of the Military Service Institution*, II (1882), pp. 388-391.

43. Stephen E. Ambrose, *Upton and the Army* (Louisiana State Univ. Press, 1964), pp. 101, 102, 105, 108-113, 135.

44. Ibid.; Richard C. Brown, "General Emory Upton: The Army's Mahan," *Military Affairs*, XVII (1953), pp. 125-131; Upton, *The Military Policy of the United States* (Washington, D.C., 1907), pp. 66, 67, 90.

45. James M. Rice, "The Defense of Our Frontier," *Journal of the Military Service Institution*, XVIII (March 1896), pp. 298-320.

46. *Congressional Record*, 52 Cong., 2 sess., 1892, vol. XXIV, part I, p. 445; *The National Guard*, 29 Aug. 1891, p. 320.

47. Hill, *Minute Man*, pp. 135, 136; Cohen, "Creation," p. 51; Cooper, "To Be a Soldier," p. 242.

CHAPTER 9. THE WAR WITH SPAIN

1. *The Statistical History of the United States from Colonial Times to the Present* (Fairfield Publishers, Stamford, Conn., 1965), p. 718; Graham A. Cosmas, *An Army for Empire: The United States Army in the Spanish American War* (Univ. of Missouri Press, 1971), p. 50.
2. Ibid., p. 11.
3. Ibid., pp. 30-33; Report of the Adjutant General to the Major General Commanding the Army, Oct. 22, 1898, ARSW for FY ended June 30, 1898, *HR Doc. 2*, 55 Cong., 3 sess. (Washington, D.C., 1898), vol. 1, part 2, p. 489.
4. Cosmas, *Army for Empire,* p. 51.
5. Ibid., pp. 89-97; General Orders 30, HQ of the Army, 30 April 1898.
6. Gerald F. Linderman, *The Mirror of War: American Society and the Spanish American War* (Univ. of Michigan Press, 1974), p. 34; Jim Dan Hill, *The Minute Man in War and Peace* (Stackpole, 1964), p. 161; *Report of the Adjutant General of Massachusetts, 1898,* p. 143; Louis Cantor, "Creation of the Modern National Guard: the Dick Act of 1903" (unpublished Ph.D. diss., Duke Univ., 1963), p. 126; Jerry M. Cooper, "To be a Soldier: History of the Wisconsin National Guard in the Nineteenth Century" (unpublished typescript), p. 372.
7. Linderman, *Mirror,* p. 34.
8. Cosmas, *Army for Empire,* p. 109; Senator Hoar quoted in Linderman, *Mirror,* pp. 6, 7; Cannon quoted in Robert C. Roberts, "History of the Utah National Guard, 1894-1954" (unpublished Ph.D. diss., Univ. of Utah, 1973), p. 75.
9. Russell A. Alger, *The Spanish American War* (New York, 1901), p. 27.
10. David F. Trask, *The War with Spain in 1898* (Macmillan, 1981), p. 157.
11. Alger, *War,* p. 136; Lowell D. Black, "The Negro Volunteer Units of the Ohio National Guard (unpublished Ph.D. diss., Ohio State Univ., 1976), p. 213; Charles J. Johnson, "Black Soldiers in the National Guard, 1877-1949" (unpublished Ph.D. diss. Howard Univ., 1976) pp. 310-316; Trask, *War with Spain,* p. 158.
12. Linderman, *Mirror,* p. 76; Report, Adjutant General to Commanding General, 22 Oct. 1898, pp. 489, 490; AG to SW, 1 Nov. 1898 in ARSW, 1898, vol. 1, part 1, pp. 258, 259; Cosmas, *Army for Empire,* p. 135.
13. Report, Adjutant General to Commanding General, 22 Oct. 1898, p. 486; Cosmas, *Army for Empire,* pp. 148, 149; Alger, *War,* p. 33; for criticism of the appointments, see *New York Times,* 21 May 1898.
14. Linderman, *Mirror,* pp. 60, 72-74.
15. IG to Commanding General, 4 June 1898, p. 573; Report, Quartermaster General, p. 448, both in ARSW, 1898, vol. 1, part 2; Trask, *War with Spain,* pp. 159-161.
16. Report, Chief of Ordnance, 19 Oct. 1898, in ARSW, 1898, pp. 206, 207; Report of a Tour of Duty with the Army of Invasion of Cuba by IG, 5 June-25 July 1898, in ibid., vol. 1, part 2, p. 600.

17. IG to Commanding General, 4 June 1898, p. 573, ARSW, 1898, vol. 1, part 2.
18. *Webster's American Military Biographies* (Merriam Publishers, 1978), p. 376.
19. Trask, *War with Spain*, pp. 185, 186, 188.
20. Ibid., p. 240; Reports of Officers of 71st New York, pp. 306-315; Report, Capt. James B. Goe, 13th Infantry, 4 Sep. 1898, p. 421; Report, Lt. John H. Parker, 23 July 1898, p. 458, all included in ARSW, 1898, vol. 1, part 2.
21. Chart entitled "Casualties in Action by Organizations between May 1, 1898 and June 30, 1899," Report, Major General Commanding the Army in ARSW, 1899, vol. 1, pp. 386, 387, part 3, pp. 386, 387; Trask, *War with Spain*, p. 288.
22. Linderman, *Mirror*, pp. 79, 90; William T. Sexton, *Soldiers in the Philippines* (Infantry Journal Press, 1944), p. 52.
23. Report, Surgeon General, 10 Nov. 1898, ARSW, pp. 688, 691; GO 94, 12 July 1898 printed in ibid., p. 541; Cosmas, *Army for Empire*, pp. 175, 264; Trask, *War with Spain*, pp. 328, 334.
24. With Miles in Puerto Rico: 1st Kentucky, 2nd & 3rd Wisconsin, 3rd Illinois, 4th Ohio, 4th Pennsylvania, 6th Massachusetts & 16th, and 6th Illinois. Pennsylvania sent two troops of cavalry with ancient lineages, the First Troop of Philadelphia City Cavalry and the Sheridan Troop; Ohio provided one regiment of cavalry, New York, two; from Pennsylvania came artillery units, also from Indiana, Illinois, and Missouri, ARSW, 1898, vol. 1, part 2, 137ff; Report of the Adjutant General, 22 Oct. 1898, p. 501.
25. Report of the Major General, in ARSW, 1899, vol. 1, part 3, p. 386.
26. Wilson to Adjutant General, 23 Aug. 1898, included in ARSW, 1898, vol. 1, part 2, p. 234; see also French E. Chadwick, *The Relations of the United States with Spain*, 2 vols. (Scribners, 1911; reprint Russell & Russell, New York, 1968) vol. 2, pp. 266-268.
27. Cosmas, *Arms for Empire*, p. 119; Sexton, *Soldiers*, pp. 6, 7, 19.
28. Ibid., pp. 22, 34, 61, 68, 78, 79; James J. Hudson, "The California National Guard, 1903-1940" (unpublished Ph.D. diss., Univ. of California, Berkeley, 1953), pp. 42, 43; Cooper, "To Be a Soldier," p. 99.
29. Roberts, "Utah National Guard," p. 99; Trask, *War with Spain*, p. 210.
30. Sexton, *Soldiers*, pp. 99ff.
31. Casualties, from *Report of Secretary of War, 1899*; Report of the Major General, p. 387.
32. Statement showing monthly strength, *Report of the Secretary of War, 1899*, pp. 13, 384; Alger, *War*, p. 412.
33. Report of the Major General, ARSW, 1899, pp. 367-369; Roberts, "Utah National Guard," pp. 109, 110; Sexton, *Soldiers*, p. 117.
34. Ibid., p. 131.
35. See note 21.
36. Cosmas, *Arms for Empire*, pp. 115, 126; Cooper, "To Be a Soldier," p. 373; Cantor, "Modern National Guard," p. 116.
37. Report of the Major General, ARSW, 1899, vol. 1, part 3, pp. 367-369.

38. R. Ernest Dupuy, *The National Guard: A Compact History* (Hawthorne, 1971), pp. 77-79; George C. Bittle, "The Organized Florida Militia from 1821 to 1920" (unpublished Ph.D. diss., Florida State Univ., 1965), p. 367.

CHAPTER 10. REORGANIZATION, 1900-1916

1. For reorganization of the command structure of the army, see Russell F. Weigley, *History of the United States Army* (Macmillan, 1967), pp. 313-341; for greater detail; see Otto L. Nelson, *National Security and the General Staff* (Washington, D.C., 1946), pp. 1-72; see also Elbridge Colby, "Elihu Root and the National Guard," *Military Affairs*, XXIII (Spring 1959), pp. 28-34.

2. William C. Sanger, *Report on the Reserve and Auxiliary Forces of England and the Militia of Switzerland: Prepared for President McKinley and Secretary of War Root* (GPO, 1903), p. 9.

3. Louis Cantor, "Creation of the Modern National Guard: The Dick Militia Act of 1903" (unpublished Ph.D. diss., Duke Univ., 1963), pp. 188, 191; Edward K. Eckert, "Conservative Opposition to Federal Control of the Militia" (unpublished M. A. thesis, Univ. of Florida, 1966), pp. 47, 50.

4. Ibid., pp. 54-57; Cantor, "Creation," pp. 199, 222, 231, 234, 245.

5. Eldridge Colby, *The National Guard of the United States: A Half Century of Progress* (photocopy of unfinished typescript, published by the American Military Institute, 1977; since all chapters begin with a page 1, it is necessary to cite chapter and page), chap. 2, p. 14.

6. An Act to Promote the Efficiency of the Militia . . . , 21 Jan. 1903 (hereafter cited as the Dick Act), 32 USSL, pp. 775ff.

7. Ibid., section 14; John M. Gould & George F. Tucker, *Second Supplement to Notes on the Revised Statutes*, 1 Jan. 1898-1 March 1904 (Little, Brown, 1904), section 1625; Cantor, "Creation," pp. 209, 211; Louis Cantor, "Elihu Root and the National Guard," *Military Affairs*, XXXIII (Dec. 1969), p. 371.

8. Dick Act, p. 775.

9. An Act Further to Amend the Act, entitled "An Act to Promote the Efficiency of the Militia . . . , passed 21 Jan. 1903," 27 May 1908, 35 USSL, part 1, chap. 204, pp. 399-403; An Act to Provide for Raising the Volunteer Forces of the United States in Time of Actual or Threatened War, 25 April 1914, 38 USSL, part 1, chap. 71, pp. 347-351.

10. GO, HQ of the Army, No. 3, 7 Jan. 1907, USAMHI.

11. Russell F. Weigley, *Towards an American Army* (Greenwood, 1974), p. 211.

12. Cantor, "Elihu Root," pp. 364, 366; Cantor, "Creation," pp. 155, 160; Robert Bacon and James Brown Scott, *The Military and Colonial Policy of the United States: Addresses and Reports by Elihu Root* (Harvard Univ. Press, 1916), pp. 135, 136, 147, 150.

13. Cantor, "Creation," pp. 211, 265; Eckert, "Conservative Opposition," p. 75; John Dickinson, *The Building of an Army* (Century, 1922), p. 21.
14. A Study of the Methods to Be Adopted in Feeding and Caring for the Organized Militia When Called into the Service of the United States Army (unpublished Army War College Study No. 11, 1905, 1906; typescript in USAMHI), p. 3; "13,000,000 Men to Draw From," *National Guard Magazine*, I, p. 104; ARCDMA. 1906; ibid., 15 Oct. 1908, p. 329, gives the 40 percent figure enrolled less than one year.
15. Ibid., 16 Oct. 1911, p. 5; *National Guard Magazine*, I, p. 18.
16. Martha Derthick, *The National Guard in Politics* (Harvard Univ. Press, 1965), p. 24; Walter M. Pratt, *Tin Soldiers: The Organized Militia and What It Really Is* (Boston, 1912), p. 24.
17. An Act Further to Amend the Act entitled "An Act to Promote the Efficiency of the Militia . . . , passed 21 Jan. 1903," 27 May 1908, 35 USSL, part 1, chap. 204, pp. 399-403; ARCDMA, 15 Oct. 1908; General Orders, War Department, 11 June 1908, USAMHI.
18. Wickersham's opinion is reprinted, in *U.S. Army Bulletin No. 12*, 8 Aug. 1912 (USAMHI), pp. 83-86; *Organization of the Land Forces of the United States*, (Washington, D.C., 1912), p. 19; Jim Dan Hill, *The Minute Man in War and Peace*, (Stackpole, 1964), p. 213.
19. *Organization of the Land Forces*, p. 19. It is not clear why Wood used 50 as the number of allies.
20. Ibid., pp. 12, 13, 55.
21. Dickinson, *Building*, p. 12.
22. John G. Clifford, *The Citizen Soldiers: The Plattsburg Training Camp Movement* (Univ. Press of Kentucky, 1972), p. 130, see also pp. 80, 131, 181.
23. ARCDMA, 3 Oct. 1910, p. 11.
24. Ibid., 16 Oct. 1911, pp. 155, 156, 163-165; ibid., 1 Oct. 1914, pp. 7, 10; Colby, *National Guard*, chap. 3, p. 17; *Preparedness for National Defense*, Hearings by the Senate Committee on Military Affairs, 64 Cong., 1 sess. (Washington, D.C., 1916), pp. 137-198.
25. *National Guardsman and Volunteer*, June and August 1904; *The National Guard Magazine*, I, p. 147. For a brief history of Guard periodicals, see Bruce Jacobs, "The National Guard's Magazine," in *The First One Hundred Years* (NGA, Washington, D.C., 1978). Printed histories do not agree on this period; Hill, *Minute Man*, entitled his chapter, "The Guard Fights for Its Life," chap. 9; pp. 207-224; Colby, *National Guard*, shows the Guard as improving its status, chap. 3, p. 29; while R. Ernest Dupuy, *The National Guard: A Compact History* (Hawthorne, 1971), p. 95, calls 1903-1916 a heyday for the Guard; most of the units had access to comfortable armories, were socially accepted in their communities, and were enthusiastically received when they performed in public.
26. Frederick M. Stern, *The Citizen Army* (St. Martin's Press, 1957), pp. 147, 148; William H. Riker, *Soldiers of the States: The Role of the National*

Guard in American Democracy (Washington, D.C., 1958), p. 74; Derthick, *National Guard,* p. 30; Martha Derthick, "The Militia Lobby in the Missile Age: The Politics of the National Guard," in Samuel P. Huntington, *Changing Patterns in Military Politics* (Free Press, 1962), p. 201; Hill, *Minute Man,* pp. 213, 216.

27. Wilson quoted in Dickinson, *Building,* p. 33.
28. John McAuley Palmer, *An Army of the People* (Putnam, 1916).
29. John H. Parker, *Trained Citizen Soldiers: A Solution to General Upton's Problem* (Menasha, Wisc., 1916).
30. Pratt, *Tin Soldiers,* pp. 88, 140; Cantor, "Creation," p. 152; ARCDMA, 25 Oct. 1908, ibid., 3 Oct. 1910, p. 46; Colby, *National Guard,* chap. 1, p. 13; ARCDMA, 1 Oct. 1916, p. 21; *National Guard Magazine,* I, p. 220.
31. ARCDMA, 1907, p. 149; ibid., 15 Oct. 1908, p. 164; ibid., 1901, pp. 234, 238, 241; ibid., 3 Oct. 1910, pp. 253; ibid., 13 Jan. 1911, p. 35.
32. *Hearing Before the Committee on Military Affairs, House of Representatives* on HR 29496, A Bill to Increase the Efficiency of the Organized Militia and for Other Purposes (GPO, 1911), pp. 7-10; Weigley, *Towards,* p. 200; Stern, *Citizen Army,* p. 160.
33. Hill, *Minute Man,* p. 201; Colby, *National Guard,* chap. 1, p. 18, chap. 3, p. 12; ARCDMA, 1905, p. 9.
34. Ibid., 1909, pp. 124, 125, 244.
35. Ibid., 27 Oct. 1913; Colby, *National Guard,* chap. 1, p. 17; Hill, *Minute Man,* p 213.
36. Russell Gilmore, "Rifles and Soldier Individualism, 1876-1918," *Military Affairs,* XL (Oct. 1976), pp. 97-102.
37. An Act Making Appropriation for the Support of the Army . . . 2 March 1907, 34 USSL, part 1, chap. 2511, pp. 1174, 1175; ARCDMA, 1 Oct. 1914, pp. 7, 10; Colby, *National Guard,* chap. 3, p. 17.
38. Charles J. Gross, "The Origins and Development of the Air National Guard, 1943-1969" (unpublished Ph.D. diss., Ohio State Univ., 1979), pp. 1, 2; AR, Acting Chief, Militia Bureau, 1 Oct. 1916, p. 27; *The National Guardsman,* VII (Jan. 1953) p. 3; ibid., XII (Dec. 1968), "Golden Anniversary of the Air National Guard," pp. 12-14; Hill, *Minute Man,* p. 521; James C. Elliott, *The Modern Army and Air National Guard* (Van Nostrand, 1965), pp. 108-110.
39. *A Proper Military Policy for the United States,* (Washington, D.C., 1915), p. 22; Colby, *National Guard,* chap. 1, p. 8.
40. Derthick, *National Guard,* p. 34; Hill, *Minute Man,* p. 220; George C. Herring, Jr., "James Hay and the Preparedness Controversy, 1915-1916," *Jr. of Southern History,* XXX (Nov. 1964), pp. 383-404.
41. Quoted in Eckert, "Conservative," p. 102.
42. *Preparedness for National Defense,* Hearings by the Senate Committee on Military Affairs, 64 Cong., 1 sess., (Washington, D.C., 1916), Garrison testimony, pp. 6-64; Wood, pp. 65-93.
43. Hill, *Minute Man,* pp. 215-222; Derthick, *National Guard,* pp. 37, 38, 50.
44. An Act for Making Further and More Effectual Provision for the National

Defense and for Other Purposes, 3 June 1916, 39 USSL, part 1, chap. 134, Officer's Reserve Corps, pp. 188-191; Enlisted Reserve Corps, pp. 195, 196.

45. Ibid., pp. 191-193.

46. Ibid., pp. 198-212, especially 198, 200, 202; see also p. 166.

47. Ibid., pp. 200, 201, 206, 210.

48. Ibid., p. 203; AR, Acting Chief, Militia Bureau, 1 Oct. 1916, pp. 53, 54.

49. ARCDMA, 3 Oct. 1910, p. 260; Clifford, *Citizen Soldiers,* pp. 200, 222; Lovell D. Black, "The Negro Volunteer Militia Units of the Ohio National Guard" (unpublished Ph.D., diss., Ohio State Univ., 1976), p. 260.

50. James J. Hudson, "The Calfiornia National Guard, 1903-1940" (unpublished Ph.D. diss., Univ. of California, Berkeley, 1953), pp. 82-105.

51. George C. Brittle, "The Organized Florida Militia from 1821 to 1920" (unpublished Ph.D. diss., Florida State Univ., 1965), pp. 378, 395, 400; Richard G. Stone Jr., *A Brittle Sword: The Kentucky Militia, 1776-1912* (Univ. Press of Kentucky, 1977), p. 100; David A. Lockmiller, *Enoch H. Crowder* (Univ. of Missouri Press, 1955), pp. 42, 43; Kenneth R. Bailey, "A Search for Identity: The West Virginia National Guard, 1877-1921." (unpublished Ph.D. diss., Ohio State Univ., 1976), p. 98.

52. Ibid., pp. 94, 96, 112, 116, 127.

53. Robert J. Cornell, *The Anthracite Coal Strike of 1902* (Catholic Univ. Press, 1957), pp. 139, 144, 153, 185.

54. Richard C. Roberts, "History of the Utah National Guard, 1894-1954" (unpublished Ph.D. diss., Univ. of Utah, 1973), pp. 58, 66, 68, 71; Richard M. Brown, *Strain of Violence* (Oxford Univ. Press, 1975), p. 75; Patrick H. McLatchy, "The Development of the National Guard of Washington State as an Instrument of Social Control" (unpublished Ph.D., diss., Univ. of Washington, 1973), p. 371.

55. ARCDMA, 3 Oct. 1910, pp. 124, 125.

56. *The National Guardsman*, 15 Aug. and 15 Oct. 1902.

57. Hill, *Minute Man*, pp. 231-239; AR, Acting Chief, Militia Bureau, 1 Oct. 1916, p. 6; ARSW, 1916, pp. 11, 13, 14; Hudson, "California National Guard," p. 156.

58. Ibid., p. 169; Hill, *Minute Man*, pp. 241, 243; *Annual Report of the Chief of Staff*, 1916, p. 156; Roberts, "Utah National Guard," pp. 131, 132.

59. Ibid., pp. 116, 121, 131; Hudson, "California National Guard," p. 159.

60. Roberts, "Utah National Guard," pp. 114, 115, 119.

61. Hudson, "California National Guard," p. 160; AR, Acting Chief, Militia Bureau, 1 Oct. 1916, p. 6; Donald E. Houston, "The Oklahoma National Guard on the Mexican Border, 1916." *Chronicles of Oklahoma*, LIII (Winter 1975-1976), pp. 452, 453, 456.

62. Riker, *Soldiers*, p. 74; Hill, *Minute Man*, pp. 212-217; Colby, *National Guard*, pp. 7, 8, 16.

63. Weigley, "Leonard Wood," in *Towards*, pp. 199-222.

64. Ibid.

CHAPTER 11. THE NATIONAL GUARD IN WORLD WAR I

1. Wilson's address to the Senate on 22 Jan. 1917 and his war message, 2 April 1917, in Henry Steele Commager, ed., *Documents in American History to 1898*, 8th ed. (Appleton-Century-Crofts, 1968), pp. 125-128, 132.

2. Richard J. Beamish, *America's Part in the World War* (Philadelphia, 1919), p. 57.

3. Hermann Hagedorn, *Leonard Wood*, 2 vols. (Harpers, 1931), vol. II, pp. 191ff; ARCMB 1 Oct. 1917, p. 13.

4. Benedict Crowell and Robert F. Wilson, *The Road to France*, 2 vols. (Yale University Press, 1921), p. 37; James J. Hudson, "The California National Guard, 1903-1940" (unpublished Ph.D. diss., Univ. of California, Berkeley, 1953), p. 74.

5. Jim Dan Hill, *The Minute Man in War and Peace* (Stackpole, 1964), pp. 250, 254; David A. Lockmiller, *Enoch H. Crowder* (Univ. of Missouri Press, 1955), p. 158; AR, Acting CMB, 25 Sep. 1918, p. 5.

6. 40 USSL, part 1, chap. 15, pp. 76-83.

7. "Conscription," *Encyclopaedia Britannica*, 1960 ed., vol. VI, p. 286; Enoch H. Crowder, *The Spirit of Selective Service* (Century, 1970).

8. Hill, *Minute Man*, p. 261; Elbridge Colby, *The National Guard of the United States* (American Military Institute, 1977), chap. 6, p. 13; chap. 8, pp. 1, 2; Beamish, *America's Part*, pp. 54, 55.

9. AR, Acting CMB, 25 Sep. 1918, p. 8.

10. Ibid.; ARCMB, 1 Oct. 1917, pp. 5, 10, 19; ARCMB, 1918, p. 1102.

11. Hill, *Minute Man*, pp. 257, 294; Frederick L. Paxson, *America at War, 1917-1918,* vol. II in a three-volume series, *American Democracy and the World War* (Boston, 1939), p. 104.

12. ARSW, 1919, p. 84; ARCMB, 1 Oct. 1917, p. 23; ARCMB, 1918, p. 1162; AR, Acting CMB, 25 Sep. 1918, pp. 53, 61, 64.

13. *Order of Battle of the United States Land Forces: American Expeditionary Forces, Divisions* (prepared by Historical Section, Army War College, 1931), pp. 446, 447.

14. Hill, *Minute Man*, p. 268.

15. Emerson G. Taylor, *New England in France, 1917-1919: History of the 26th Division* (Houghton-Mifflin, 1920), p. 13.

16. Colby, *National Guard*, chap. 6, p. 12; H. G. Proctor, *The Iron Division: National Guard of Pennsylvania in the World War* (Philadelphia, 1919), p. 20; Frederick L. Huidekoper, *Story of the 33rd Division* (Chicago, 1919), p. 11; John A. Cutchins and George Scott Stewart, Jr., *History of the 29th Blue and Gray Division, 1917-1919* (Philadelphia, 1921), pp. 12, 60; Elmer A. Murphy and Robert S. Thomas, *The 30th Division in the World War* (Lepanto, Arkansas, 1936), p. 20.

    Other units with ancient lineages which were obscured by reorganization are: 26th Division: parts of the 101st Infantry had Massachusetts components dating back to 1600s; 102nd Infantry contained Connecticut components as old as 1672; 103rd Infantry with Maine components from the Civil War; 27th Division: its oldest unit traced to 1806, others to the War with Spain; 28th Division: 111th Infantry, part of it dating to 1747; 30th Division: 118th Infantry, components traced from Mexican War, and two regiments to the Civil War; 32rd Division: two regiments with Civil War lineages; 33rd Division: 130th Infantry traced to early nineteenth century, and two regiments with Civil War lineages; 34th Division: four regiments with Civil War lineages; 35th Division: 138th Infantry to 1832; 37th Division: four regiments with Civil War lineages; 38th Division: 105th Infantry to 1778 and three regiments from the Mexican War; 39th Division: 155th Infantry to 1798; 42nd Division: besides the Irish 69th, the 166th Infantry to the Mexican War, the 167th to 1836, and the 168th to the Civil War. For official lineages, see *The Army Lineage Book,* vol. II, *Infantry* (GPO, Washington, D.C., 1953).

17. Colby, *National Guard*, chap. 6, p. 16; Cutchins, *29th Division*, p. 34; Hill, *Minute Man*, p. 280.

18. John F. O'Ryan, *The Story of the 27th Division*, 2 vols. (New York, 1920), vol. I, pp. 117, 118; Proctor, *Iron Division*, pp. 17, 239.

19. Colby, *National Guard*, chap. 6, p. 18; Richard C. Roberts, "History of the Utah National Guard" (unpublished Ph.D. diss., Univ. of Utah, 1973), pp. 137, 144, 145, 153; R. Ernest Dupuy, *The National Guard: A Compact History* (Hawthorne, 1971); p. 106; *The Nation's National Guard: Addresses Delivered by Major General Ellard A. Walsh and Major General Edgar Erickson* (National Guard Assn., 1954), p. 33; O'Ryan, *27th Division*, vol. I, p. 443.

20. ARCMB, 1918, p. 1105; James C. Elliott, *Modern Army and Air National Guard* (Van Nostrand, 1965), p. 33.

21. AR, Acting CMB, 25 Sep. 1918, p. 11.

22. "Reorganization of the Army," testimony before Senate Subcommittee on Military Affairs, 66 Cong., 1 sess., p. 1509.

23. John Dickinson, *The Building of an Army* (Century, 1922), p. 123; AR, Acting CMB, 25 Sept. 1918, pp. 77-82, 126; *Nation's National Guard*, p. 33; Cutchins, *29th Division*, p. 11.

24. Taylor, *26th Division*, pp. 19, 21, 249-269; Paxson, *America at War*, vol. II, p. 314.

25. Charles B. Hoyt, *Heroes of the Argonne: An Authentic History of the 35th Division* (Kansas City, 1919), pp. 34, 66, 128-133; Ben B. Chastaine, *The Story of the 36th* (Oklahoma City, 1920), p. 10.

26. Proctor, *Iron Division*, p. 161; Taylor, *26th Division*, p. 135.

27. Roberts, "Utah National Guard," pp. 143, 152.

28. Hill, *Minute Man*, pp. 265n, 269, 275, 296; Chastaine, *36th Division*, p. 10; *History of the 26th, Yankee Division, 1917-1919, 1941-1945* (YD Veterans Assn., Salem, Mass., 1955), p. 17; *The 32nd Division in the World War, 1917-1919* (Madison, 1920), p. 29.

29. *Register of Graduates and Former Cadets, 1802-1965, United States*

Military Academy (Civil War Centennial Edition, vol. II, West Point Alumni Foundation, 1965). The method was to locate the division commanders whose names can be found in *Order of Battle*.

30. *32nd Division*, p. 151; Chastaine, *36th Division*, p. 55. Figures on initial fillers are drawn from division histories and from *Order of Battle*.

31. Taylor, *26th Division*, pp. 120, 155, 246.

32. Cutchins, *29th Division*, p. 16; Huidekoper, *33rd Division*, p. 17; Proctor, *Iron Division*, p. 53; *32nd Division*, p. 7.

33. *Order of Battle*, pp. 436-442; Hill, *Minute Man*, pp. 273, 277, 278; Lovell D. Black, "Negro Militia Units of the Ohio National Guard" (unpublished Ph.D. diss., Ohio State Univ., 1976), pp. 269, 280, 283, 294; Charles J. Johnson, "Black Soldiers in the National Guard, 1877-1949" (unpublished Ph.D. diss., Harvard Univ., 1976), p. 137.

34. Ibid.

35. Chastaine, *36th Division*, pp. 17ff.

36. *Final Report of General John J. Pershing, Commander in Chief, AEF* GPO, Washington, D.C., p. 15; Colby, *National Guard*, chap. 6; p. 20; Hoyt, *35th Division*, pp. 30-35.

37. Pershing, *Final Report*, p. 269; Colby, *National Guard*, chap. 6, p. 12.

38. *American Armies and Battlefields in Europe* (prepared by the American Battle Monuments Commission, GPO, Washington, D.C., 1938), p. 33; Paxson, *America at War*, vol. II, p. 105.

39. Bruce Jacobs, "July 4, 1918: A National Guard 'Model Company' from Chicago Goes to War—over General Pershing's Protest—and Fireworks Follow," *National Guardsman*, July 1978, pp. 16-18, 38, 39.

40. Ernest and Trevor N. Dupuy, *Military Heritage of America* (McGraw-Hill, 1956), p. 359.

41. Hoyt, *35th Division*, p. 35.

42. Cutchins, *29th Division*, p. 204.

43. O'Ryan, *27th Division*, p. 663.

44. Proctor, *28th Division*, pp. 51-53.

45. Huidekoper, *33rd Division*, p. 17.

46. John H. Parker to Gen. Harbord, 16 March 1918, printed in *National Guardsman* (Feb. 1953), pp. 2-4, 29.

CHAPTER 12. THE NATIONAL GUARD BETWEEN WORLD WARS

1. The Kahn-Chamberlain Bill was based on the Swiss citizen-army system. At 18, a man must enter six months of military training, then remain subject to call during the next five years. It included 300,000 men for the regular army. Colonel John McAuley Palmer drew up a bill which Senator Wadsworth of New York introduced and championed. It also required six months' training for every able-bodied male, plus a five-year reserve obligation. The reservist would be required to take part in two annual mobilizations during his five years. This bill recommended a much smaller

regular army; in Palmer's view, a large regular army was alien to the American system. Russell F. Weigley, *Towards an American Army* (Greenwood Press, 1974), pp. 225, 227; John Garry Clifford, *The Citizen Soldiers: The Plattsburg Training Camp Movement, 1913-1920* (Univ. Press of Kentucky, 1972), pp. 274, 301; Chase C. Mooney and Martha E. Layman, "Some Phases of the Compulsory Military Training Movement, 1914-1920," *Mississippi Valley Hist. Review*, XXXVII (March 1952), p. 650; *Hearing before the HR, Committee on Military Affairs*, 1919, 66 Cong., 1 sess., pp. 1187-1190, 1195, 1196, 1198.

2. Ibid., pp. 698, 707, 1436; Weigley, *Towards*, p. 233.

3. Mauritz Hallgren, *The Tragic Fallacy* (Knopf, 1937), p. 13.

4. Pershing quoted in Clifford, *Citizen Soldiers*, p. 32; *HR Hearing, 1919*, pp. 1273, 1514, 1522; *Reorganization of the Army: Hearings before the Subcommittee of the Senate on Military Affairs*, 66 Cong., 1 sess., pp. 523, 663.

5. *HR Hearing, 1919*. Carter testimony, pp. 1883-1889; Clifford, *Citizen Soldiers*, p. 274; Jim Dan Hill, *The Minute Man in War and Peace* (Stackpole, 1964), pp. 293, 294.

6. *HR Hearing*, 1919, pp. 398, 804.

7. Ibid., pp. 398, 399, 1194, 1892, 1904-1908, 1915, 1928, 1931; *Senate Hearing, 1919*, pp. 467, 513, 537; Mooney and Layman, "Phases," p. 650; Robert David Ward, "The Movement for Universal Military Training, 1942-1953" (unpublished Ph.D. diss., Univ. of North Carolina, 1957), p. 19.

8. *The First One Hundred Years* (Washington, D.C.; NGA, 1978), p. 15.

9. Hill, *Minute Man*, p. 294; HR *Hearing, 1919*, pp. 163, 191.

10. Edward M. Coffman, *The Hilt of the Sword: The Career of Peyton C. March* (Univ. of Wisconsin Press, 1965), p. 45.

11. Hill, *Minute Man*, p. 296; *Report, Chief, National Guard Bureau*, 2 March 1942, p. 60; ibid., 30 June 1925, pp. 51, 52; *Senate Hearing; 1919*, pp. 1874-1878.

12. Amendment to the Act of 1916, 4 June 1920, 41 USSL, pp. 759, 760, 763, 764, 782; Elbridge Colby, *National Guard of the United States* (Amer. Military Inst., 1977), chap, 8, pp. 8, 32; Charles Dale Story, "The Formulation of Army Reserve Forces Policy" (unpublished Ph.D., diss., Univ. of Oklahoma, 1958), pp. 48, 49; Hill, *Minute Man*, pp. 311, 312.

13. Amendment of 4 June 1920, pp. 763, 776, 781, 782; *Chronological History of the U.S. Army Reserve Components*, Lt. Col. John P. Barker, ed., 1965 (xerox copy in my possession).

14. Amendment of 4 June 1920, pp. 775, 780.

15. Colby, *National Guard*, chap. 8, p. 8; Factors Operating to Influence Recruitment, Retention, Dedication and Professionalism of the Army (prepared by the Histories Division, OCMH, Dept. of the Army, 1970), pp. 24, 25.

16. ARCMB, 30 June 1920, pp. 5, 7.

17. Ibid., 1919, p. 5.

18. Robert Lee Daugherty, "The Ohio National Guard, 1919-1940" (unpublished Ph.D. diss., Ohio State Univ., 1974), pp. 4ff, 27.

19. ARCMB, 20 June 1920, p. 8; ibid., 1921, p. 6; ibid., 1922, p. 6.

20. ARCMB, 30 June 1922, p. 8; ibid., 1921, p. 10, ARSW, 30 June 1921, p. 24; Hill, *Minute Man*, pp. 362, 365.

21. Ibid., p. 360.

22. ARCMB, 30 June 1922, p. 57; Story, "Formulation," p. 221.

23. ARCMB, 30 June 1924, p. 7; ibid., 1927, p. 10; ibid., 1932, p. 7; William H. Riker, *Soldiers of the States: The Role of the National Guard in American Democracy* (Washington, D.C., 1958), p. 84.

24. ARCMB, 30 June 1926, p. 33; ARCNGB, 30 June 1935, p. 16; ARSW, 30 June 1922, p. 138; Daugherty, "Ohio National Guard," pp. 41, 121.

25. Testimony of MG Milton Reckord, *Hearing, Senate Military Affairs Committee*, July 1941, pp. 51, 56; Act of 15 June 1933, 48 USSL, p. 155.

26. Frederick B. Wiener, "The Militia Clause of the Constitution," *Harvard Law Review*, LIV (Dec. 1940), pp. 208-210; James J. Hudson, "The California National Guard, 1903-1940" (unpublished Ph.D. diss., Univ. of California, Berkeley, 1935), p. 30.

27. Act of 15 June 1933, pp. 155, 157; *The Nation's National Guard: Addresses Delivered by Major General Ellard Walsh and Major General Edgar Erickson* (NGA, Washington, D.C.), p. 3; John W. Gulick, "National Guard as a Federal Force," *War Department, Militia Bureau Doc. #992* (Washington, D.C., 1930), pp. 1, 3.

28. Act of 15 June 1933, p. 153.

29. Ibid., p. 156.

30. School of Instruction for State Adjutants General, 1924, USAMHI, pp. 9, 11, 15, 21; ibid., 1925, pp. 21, 85, 133, 134.

31. ARCMB, 30 June 1921, p. 26; ibid., 1932, p. 1; ARCNGB, 30 June 1933, p. 37; ibid., 1934, p. 1; *HR Hearing*, 1919, p. 1867; ARSW, 1922, p. 138; George C. Bittle, "The Organized Militia of Florida from 1821-1920" (unpublished Ph.D. diss., Florida State Univ., 1965), p. 430; Kenneth Bailey, "A Search for Identity: The West Virginia National Guard, 1877-1921" (unpublished Ph.D. diss., Ohio State Univ., 1976), p. 147; Daugherty, "Ohio National Guard," pp. 436, 437; Derthick, *National Guard*, p. 51.

32. ARCMB, 30 June 1921, p. 27; ibid., 1926, p. 3; ibid., 1927, p. 3; ARCNGB, 30 June 1936, p. 15.

33. Bailey, *Search*, pp. 152-162.

34. Richard C. Roberts, "History of the Utah National Guard, 1894-1954" (unpublished Ph.D. diss., Univ. of Utah, 1973), pp. 220, 231, 233, 236-239. Total calls for state use in selected years ran as follows:

1922	11	1928	16
1925	15	1934	35
1926	11	1935	32
1927	17	1936	28

35. School of Instruction for State Adjutants General, 1925, pp. 167-170; Hudson, "California National Guard," pp. 268-293; James J. Hudson, "The Role of the California National Guard during the San Francisco General Strike in 1934," *Military Affairs*, XLVI (April 1982), pp. 76-83.

36. Daugherty, "Ohio National Guard," pp. 315-403.

37. Wiener, "Militia Clause," p. 219; *Sterling* v. *Constantin*, 1932, 287 U.S. Reports, p. 378; *Russell Petroleum Co.* v. *Walker*, 162 Oklahoma, 1933, p. 216.

38. Sterling A. Wood, *Riot Control by the National Guard* (Harrisburg, 1940), pp. 16, 32ff, 39, 43, 48, 86.

39. ARCNGB, 30 June 1935, p. 22; ibid., 1941, p. 11.

40. Roberts, "Utah National Guard," p. 291; Hudson, "California National Guard," p. 223.

41. *National Guard Armories*, Joint Hearing, House and Senate Military Affairs Committees, 17 April 1935, 74 Cong.; 1 sess.; Daugherty, "Ohio National Guard," p. 439; Roberts, "Utah National Guard," p. 274; ARCNGB, 30 June 1940, p. 3.

42. ARCNGB, 30 June 1933, p. 1; ibid., 1934, pp. 1, 34.

43. Derthick, *National Guard*, p. 46.

44. ARCNGB, 30 June 1940, p 14; Colby, *National Guard*, chap. 9, pp. 24, 26.

45. Hill, *Minute Man*, pp. 354, 368.

46. ARCNGB, 30 June 1941, p. 14; W. D. McGlasson, "Mobilization 1940: The Big One," *National Guard* (September 1980), p. 14; Mark S. Watson, *Chief of Staff: Prewar Plans and Preparations* (a volume in *United States Army in World War II*, Washington, D.C., 1950), pp. 192, 194.

47. *Compulsory Military Training and Service*, House Committee on Military Affairs, 10, 11 July 1940, 76 Cong., 3rd sess., pp. 27, 28, 59.

48. *An Act to Provide for the Common Defense by Increasing Personnel of the Armed Forces of the United States and Providing for its Training* (Known as the Selective Service Act), 16 September 1940, 54 USSL, p. 885; Watson, *Chief of Staff*, pp. 192, 194.

49. Hill, *Minute Man*, p. 371.

50. Ibid., pp. 373-380; McGlasson, "Mobilization," p. 12.

51. Ibid., pp. 14, 15; ARCNGB 30 June 1941, pp. 19, 20, 27 and tables pp. 83-91; Hill, *Minute Man*, p. 373; *Report of the Army Chief of Staff, 1939-1941*, p. 29.

52. ARCNGB, 30 June 1941, p. 79.

53. Ibid., pp. 1, 2, 14, 15; Hill, *Minute Man*, pp. 366, 367; McGlasson, "Mobilization," pp. 10, 12.

54. ARCMB, 30 June 1920, p. 9; *House Hearing, 1919*; Ulysses G. Lee, *Employment of Negro Troops* (A volume in *United States Army in World War II*, Washington, D.C., 1955), pp. 5, 29-32, 37, 38, 192, 198; Charles I. Johnson, "Black Soldiers in the National Guard, 1877-1949" (unpublished PhD. diss., Howard Univ., 1976), pp. 403, 417, 432, 460, 482.

55. Riker, *Soldiers of the States*, p. 95.

56. Hill, *Minute Man*, pp. 372, 407-409; McGlasson, "Mobilization," pp. 14, 16.

57. Hill, *Minute Man*, p. 412.
58. Ibid., p. 391. Hill uses the 30th Division to make his point; pp. 411-415.
59. Ibid., pp. 434-437; Riker, *Soldiers of the States*, p. 95.
60. Ibid., pp. 382, 421, 440.
61. Robert R. Palmer, Bell I. Wiley, and William R. Keast, *The Procurement and Training of Ground Combat Troops*, (a volume in *United States Army in World War II*, Washington, D.C., 1948), pp 433, 434.

CHAPTER 13. WORLD WAR II

1. *Retention of Reserve Components and Selectees beyond Twelve Months*, Senate Military Affairs Committee, July 1941, 77 Cong., 1 sess., pp. 3, 5; ARCNGB, 2 March 1942, pp. 32, 33; Mark S. Watson, *Chief of Staff: Prewar Plans and Preparations* (a volume in *United States Army in World War II*, Washington, D.C., 1950), pp. 216, 366.
2. *Retention*, pp. 74, 123, 131, 145, 163-165; ARCNGB, 30 June 1942, p. 3.
3. ARCNGB, 30 June 1946, p. 9; Charles Dale Story, "The Formulation of Army Reserve Forces Policy" (unpublished Ph.D. diss., Univ. of Oklahoma, 1958), p. 158.
4. Watson, *Chief of Staff*, pp. 231, 232, 244-246.
5. ARCNGB, 30 June 1941, p. 51; *Army Lineage Book, Infantry*, vol. II, (Washington, D.C.), pp. 301, 349, 375.
6. Jim Dan Hill, *The Minute Man in War and Peace* (Stackpole, 1964), p. 469.
7. Ibid., pp. 468, 469; ARCNGB, 30 June 1935, p. 23; Ralph E. Jones et al., *Fighting Tanks Since 1916* (Harrisburg, Pa., 1933), p. 276.
8. Charles J. Gross, "The Origins and Development of the Air National Guard, 1943-1969" (unpublished Ph.D. diss., Ohio State Univ., 1979), pp. 2, 3; James J. Hudson, "The California National Guard, 1903-1940." (unpublished Ph.D. diss., Univ. of California, Berkeley, 1953), pp. 220, 221; Robert Lee Daugherty, "The Ohio National Guard, 1919-1940" (unpublished Ph.D. diss., Ohio State Univ., 1974), p. 134; ARCMB, 30 June, 1934, p. 12; ARCMB, 30 June 1940, p. 37; W. D. McGlasson, "Mobilization 1940: The Big One," *National Guard*, XXXIV (Sep. 1980), p. 10.
9. Hill, *Minute Man*, pp. 436, 458.
10. ARCNGB, 30 June 1941, pp. 36-40; Elbridge Colby, *The National Guard of the United States* (American Military Institute, 1977), chap. 10, pp. 4, 27; Elbridge Colby and James F. Glass, "Legal Status of the National Guard," *Virginia Law Review*, XXIX (May 1943), pp. 839-856; Stetson Conn and Byron Fairchild, *The Framework of Hemisphere Defense* (a volume in *United States Army in World War II*, Washington, D.C., 1960), pp. 76, 77. John David Millett, *The Organization and Role of the Army Service Forces* (a volume in *United States Army in World War II*, Washington, D.C., 1954), p. 351; Richard C. Roberts, "History of the Utah National Guard, 1894-1954" (unpublished Ph.D. diss., Univ. of Utah, 1973), p. 428.

11. ARCNGB, 30 June 1942, pp. 2, 3, 83.
12. Robert R. Palmer, Bell I. Wiley, and William R. Keast, *Procurement and Training of Ground Combat Troops* (a volume in *United States Army in World War II*, Washington, D.C.), pp. 91, 96.
13. Hill, *Minute Man*, p. 478.
14. Ibid., pp. 475, 476.
15. Palmer, et al., *Procurement*, p. 459; Story, "Reserve Forces Policy," p. 157; McGlasson, *"Mobilization,"* p. 14.
16. Data for chart drawn largely from the *Army Almanac* (Washington, D.C., 1950), pp. 528-545; Ely J. Kahn and Henry McLemore, *Fighting Divisions* (Infantry Journal Press, 1945).
17. Robert C. Erickson, Reserve Components in 1965 (unpublished typescript, USAMHI, prepared in 1957), p. 14.
18. *Army Almanac*, pp. 532, 534, 536, 544, 572; Kahn, *Fighting Divisions*, by division number; Bruce Jacobs, "D-Day," *National Guardsman*, XXIII (June 1969).
19. Drawn from *Army Almanac* and Kahn, *Fighting Divisions*.
20. *History of the 26th YD, 1917-1919, 1941-1945*, (YD Vets. Ass'n, Salem, Mass., 1955), pp. 24, 33, 45, 133.
21. Edmund G. Love, *The 27th Infantry Division in World War II* (Infantry Journal Press, 1949), pp. 1, 121, 137, 184, 246, 247.
22. Ibid., pp. 264, 289, 427-430, 485, 522, 523; Holland M. Smith, *Coral and Brass* (Scribner's, 1949), pp. 118, 125-127, 171-175.
23. Jack Colbaugh, *The Bloody Patch: 28th Division* (Vantage, 1973), pp. xii, 99; the theme of Colbaugh's book is the withholding of deserved credit by the regulars.
24. Joseph H. Ewing, *29 Let's Go! A History of the 29th Infantry Division in World War II* (Infantry Journal Press, 1948), pp. 8, 16, 34-59; *Retention*, p. 50; Hill, *Minute Man*, pp. 451, 459, 462, 463; Kahn, *Fighting Divisions*, p. 39.
25. Ibid., pp. 41, 42; Hill, *Minute Man*, pp. 461, 464; Robert L. Hewitt, *Work Horse of the Western Front: The Story of the 30th Infantry Division* (Infantry Journal Press, 1946), pp. 1, 5, 17.
26. Ibid., pp. 37, 40.
27. *The Red Arrow: 32nd Division Wisconsin National Guard, 1955* (prepared by the division staff, 1955, NP); Hill, *Minute Man*, pp. 445-452; Kahn, *Fighting Divisions*, p. 45.
28. Ibid., p. 48; Hill, *Minute Man*, pp. 448-463; *The Golden Cross: A History of the 33rd Infantry Division in World War II*, prepared by the 33rd Infantry Division Historical Commission (Infantry Journal Press, 1948), pp. 249, 253, 255, 256, 267.
29. John H. Hougen, *The Story of the Famous 34th Infantry Division* (San Angelo, Tx., 1949), n. p.
30. Hill, *Minute Man*, pp. 460, 463; Fred L. Walker, *From Texas to Rome* (Taylor Pub. Co., Dallas, 1969), pp. 4, 11, 14, 67, 84, 96, 134, 232, 264, 300, 310, 325, 336, 382, 393; Kahn, *Fighting Divisions*, pp. 53, 54.

31. Ibid., pp. 52, 70, 71; *Army Almanac*, pp. 544, 545; Hill, *Minute Man*, 463.
32. Ibid., pp. 451, 452, 454; ARCNGB, 30 June 1941, p. 51.
33. Hill, *Minute Man*, p. 440.
34. Ibid., pp. 453, 470; Chronological Survey of U.S. Army Reserve Components, John P. Barker, ed. (xerox copy CMH, 1965), p. 9.
35. Martha Derthick, *The National Guard in Politics* (Harvard Univ. Press, 1965), pp. 60, 70.
36. Ibid., pp. 70, 75, 76; Martha Derthick, "The Militia Lobby in the Missile Age," in Samuel P. Huntington, ed. *Changing Patterns in Military Politics* (Free Press, 1962), pp. 207, 212.
37. Hearing before the Select Committee on Post-war Military Policy, 24 April 1944, *HR Report*, 78 Cong., 2nd sess., pp. 9-12; 286-291; Derthick, *National Guard*, pp. 61, 62, 66, 68.
38. Ibid., p. 66; *WD Circular 347*, 25 Aug. 1944.
39. Derthick, *National Guard*, pp. 67, 68.
40. Ibid., pp. 67, 69.

CHAPTER 14. THE IMMEDIATE POSTWAR PERIOD

1. For the story of the National Security Act and added bibliography related to it, see Demetrios Caraley, *The Politics of Military Unification* (Columbia Univ. Press, 1966).
2. Charles Dale Story, "The Formation of Army Reserve Forces Policy" (unpublished Ph.D. diss., Univ. of Oklahoma, 1958), p. 10; Elbridge Colby, *National Guard of the United States* (American Military Institute, 1977), chap. 11, p. 11; *The Nation's National Guard: Addresses Delivered by Major General Ellard Walsh and Major General Edgar Erickson* (NGA, 1954), p. 3.
3. Same sources as in note 2; ARCNGB, 30 June 1947, p. 9.
4. Ibid., 30 June 1948, p. 2; *Nation's National Guard*, p. 48; Jim Dan Hill, *The Minute Man in War and Peace* (Stackpole, 1964), pp. 45, 500; Theodore Celmer, "The Post-World War II National Guard of the United States" (unpublished M. A. thesis, Univ. of Maryland, 1955), p. 18.
5. Memo on Army Policies on the Training of Civilian Reserves, 16 Jan. 1945, (typed copy, USAMHI); Chester Morrill, "Mission and Organization of the Army National Guard of the United States; With Emphasis on the Period Since 1952," (unpublished Ph.D. diss., American Univ., 1958), p. 109.
6. ARCNGB, 30 June 1947, pp. 5, 6, 130.
7. Ibid., p. 113; ARCNGB, 30 June 1948, p. 14; ARCNGB, 30 June 1949, p. 7; ARCNGB, 30 June 1950, pp. 3, 4; ARCNGB, 30 June 1954, p. 5.
8. William F. Levantrosser, *Congress and the Citizen Soldier: Legislative Policymaking for the Federal Armed Forces Reserve* (Ohio State Univ. Press, 1967), pp. 41, 43.
9. Selective Service Act, 24 June 1948, 64 USSL; ARCNGB, 30 June 1948,

p. 23; ibid., 30 June 1950, p. 22; Robert David Ward, "The Movement for Universal Military Training, 1942-1952," (unpublished Ph.D. diss., Univ. of North Carolina, 1957), pp. 331, 456; Martha Derthick, *The National Guard in Politics* (Harvard Univ. Press, 1965), p. 72.

10. Ward, UMT, pp. 330, 346, 351; Hill, *Minute Man*, p. 500; ARCNGB, 30 June 1950, p. 4.

11. Derthick, *National Guard*, pp. 60, 70, 75, 76; Martha Derthick, "The Militia Lobby in the Nuclear Age," in Samuel P. Huntington, ed. *Changing Patterns in Military Politics* (Free Press, 1962), pp. 207, 212; Story, "Formation," pp. 208-214.

12. *National Guardsman*, XX (Feb. 1966), pp. 22-25; Interview by Lt. Col. Bernie Callahan with Lt. Gen. Reckord, Senior Officers Debriefing Program, 1974 (typescript. USAMHI).

13. Raymond S. McLain, Comments on Certain Aspects of the National Guard Considered Worthy of National War College Committee Study, 8 Aug. 1951 USAMHI, p. 19.

14. Morrill, "Mission," p. 134; Levantrosser, *Congress*, p. 38.

15. James Forrestal, Report Covering the Present State of Readiness of the Several Reserve Components, 14 Dec. 1958 (stencilled copy, USAMHI); Colby, *National Guard*, chap. II, p. 29.

16. *The National Guardsman*, II (Sep. 1948), pp. 2-4; ibid., Dec. 1948, editorial.

17. McLain, "Comments."

18. See note 16.

19. Colby, *National Guard*, chap. II, p. 26; Levantrosser, *Congress*, p. 38; Memo for War Department Agencies on Combat Units for the Organized Reserves, 26 Dec. 1946 (USAMHI); ARCNGB, 30 June 1946, p. 106; Story, "Formation," p. 150.

20. ARCNGB, 30 June 1947, pp. 33, 124; Story "Formation," p. 216.

21. ARCNGB, 30 June 1946, pp. 5, 8; ibid., 30 June 1950, p. 2; Morrill, "Mission," p. 84.

22. ARCNGB, 30 June 1947, p. 109; Celmer, "Post World War II," pp. 61, 63.

23. Story, "Formation," pp. 22, 39, 234-241; *Hearing before the Committee on Armed Services*, HR, Jan.-Aug. 1951, 82 Cong., 1 sess., pp. 438-440.

24. Charles J. Gross, "The Origins and Development of the Air National Guard, 1943-1969," (unpublished Ph.D. diss., Ohio State Univ., 1979), pp. 4, 10.

25. Ibid., pp. 12, 13, 26, 40-42, 74, 76.

26. Ibid., pp. 64, 67, 72, 81; *National Guardsman*, IV (Jan. 1950), p. 5.

27. Gross, "Origins," pp. 37, 46, 82-86.

28. Ibid., pp. 9, 28; Celmer, "Post World War II," pp. 17, 25; ARCNGB, 30 June 1947, p. 8.

29. *National Guardsman* (June 1951), editorial; Levantrosser, *Congress*, p. 41; Summary of Army Reserves Since 1792 (typescript prepared in Center for Military History, Department of the Army, 1964), pp. 29, 30.

30. ARCNGB, 30 June 1948, p. 27; ibid., 30 June 1949, p. 32; Story, "Forma-

tion," p. 23; Staff Memo, Civilian Components Policy Board (typed copy, USAMHI), pp. 3, 9.

31. ARCNGB, 30 June 1948, pp. 3, 13; *House Hearing*, 1951, pp. 134, 136, 137; *Nation's National Guard*, p. 19.

32. Hill, *Minute Man*, pp. 498, 499.

33. *National Guardsman*, I (Oct. 1947), p. 32; *Hearings before the House Select Committee on Postwar Military Policy, UMT,* 4-19 June 1945, 79 Cong., 1 sess., p. 53; Ward, UMT, pp. 66, 88, 93, 95, 102, 114, 128; John M. Swomley, Jr., "The Universal Military Training Campaign, 1944-1952" (unpublished Ph.D. diss., Univ. of Colorado, 1959), pp. 45-50.

34. Ibid., pp. 66-69, 85-95; Ward, UMT, pp. 203, 245, 253, 277, 278, 313, 321; *House UMT Hearings*, June 1945, pp. 77, 83, 91-97, 111.

35. Ward, UMT, pp. 100, 120, 125, 151, 152, 157, 291; Swomley, UMT, p. 99.

36. Ward, UMT, pp. 283, 286.

37. Ibid., pp. 377, 385, 392, 407, 409; *House Hearing*, 1951, pp. 99, 166, 187.

38. The Selective Service Act 1948, redesignated Universal Military Service and Training Act, 19 June 1951, 65 USSL, pp. 75-87; Ward, UMT, pp. 408, 409.

39. Ibid., pp. 412, 425, 433, 442, 447.

40. Lt. Col. Charles S. D'Orsa, speaking to a National Guard Training Conference, 14 Aug. 1950 (typescript, USAMHI).

41. John D. Bruen, "Repercussions from the Vietnam Mobilization Decision," *Parameters,* II (Spring-Summer 1972), p. 38; Robert Coakley, Paul Scheips et al., Anti-war and Anti-military Activities in the United States, 1846-1954 (typescript, USAMHI, 1970), p. 123; *House Hearing,* 1951, p. 1969; *Subcommittee Hearing on HR 5462 to Amend the UMT and Service Act*, House Committee on the Armed Services, 2 May 1952, p. 3856.

42. *National Guardsman*, VI (Nov. 1952), p. 31; Hill, *Minute Man*, pp. 506-514; *Twentieth Century Minuteman*, a Report to the President on a Reserve Forces Training Program by the National Security Training Commission, Washington, D.C., 1 Dec. 1953.

43. *House Hearing*, 1951, pp. 78-80, 1966, 1972, 1973.

44. Ibid., pp. 81, 97; ARCNGB, 30 June 1951, p. 7; William H. Riker, *Soldiers of the States* (Public Affairs Press, 1957), p. 68; *National Guardsman*, V (Dec. 1951), p 30.

45. *Hearing on HR 5462*, pp. 3856, 3857; ARCNGB, 30 June 1951, pp. 1, 2, 12, 27, 31; 30 June 1952, p. 9; 30 June 1954, p. 10; Hill, *Minute Man*, pp. 506, 507, 510; Colby, *National Guard*, chap. 12, p. 2; *National Guardsman*, VI (Nov. 1952), p. 31; Celmer, "Post World War II," pp. 75, 116; *House Hearing*, 1951, pp. 144, 234.

46. Richard C. Roberts, "History of the Utah National Guard, 1894-1954" (unpublished Ph.D. diss., Univ. of Utah, 1973), p. 495; R. Ernest Dupuy, *The National Guard: A Compact History* (Hawthorne, 1971), p. 137; *Nation's National Guard*, p. 50; Hill, *Minute Man*, p. 507; *House Hearing*, 1951, pp. 338, 340.

47. ARCNGB, 30 June 1951, pp. 1, 31; Gross, "Air National Guard," pp. 107, 116, 117, 123, 124, 125, 127.

48. *House Hearing*, 1951, pp. 89, 1969; *Hearing on HR 5472*, pp. 3859, 3863.

49. See note 48.

50. ARCNGB, 30 June 1954, p. 10; *National Guardsman*, VI (Nov. 1952), p. 31; Hill, *Minute Man*, p. 510; Celmer, "Post World War II," pp. 75, 116; *House Hearing*, 1951, pp. 144, 234.

51. Ibid, pp. 326, 482, 483, 1968; *Hearing before a Subcommittee of the Senate Armed Services Committee on the Armed Forces Reserve Act*, 26-29 May 1952, 82 Cong., 1 sess., p. 2.

52. Ibid., pp. 115-118; *National Guardsman*, VI (Sep. 1952), editorial.

53. Ibid., *Senate Hearing AFRA*, pp. 173-177.

54. Armed Forces Reserve Act (AFRA), Public Law 476, 9 July 1952, 66 USSL, pp. 482-498; Levantrosser, *Congress*, pp. 57ff.

55. Lovell D. Black, "The Negro Volunteer Militia Units of the Ohio National Guard" (unpublished Ph.D. diss., Ohio State Univ., 1976), pp. 333, 338, 340-342, 347; Charles J. Johnson, "Black Soldiers in the National Guard, 1877-1949" (unpublished Ph.D. diss., Howard Univ., 1976), p. 572.

56. ARCNGB, 30 June 1950.

57. Robert W. Coakley, Paul J. Scheips, and Vincent Demma, "Use of Troops in Civil Disturbances since World War II, 1945-1965," (photo offset, OCMH Study No. 75, revised 1971), p. 27.

58. William Ronald Wachs, "The National Guard and Race-related Civil Disturbances in the 1950s" (unpublished Ph.D. diss., Univ. of North Carolina, 1977), pp. 8-60.

CHAPTER 15. THE EISENHOWER ADMINISTRATIONS

1. "We live in an age of peril from Soviet aggression . . . we know that we cannot afford fully to mobilize the best army, the best navy, the best air force in the world. Our economy will not stand such luxury." *Status of Reserve and National Guard Forces* . . . Report of the Interim Sub-committee on Preparedness of the Senate Committee on Armed Services, 83 Cong., 2 sess., 1954, p. 1.

2. *Review of the Reserve Program*, Hearing, HR Armed Services Committee, 1957, 85 Cong., 1 sess., p. 693; James M. Gerhardt, *The Draft and Public Policy* . . . , (Columbus, Ohio, 1971), pp. 196ff.

3. Charles G. Stevenson, "Reason for Being," *National Guardsman*, IX (Jan. 1955), p. 13; Charles Dale Story, "The Formation of Army Reserve Forces Policy" (unpublished Ph.D. diss., Univ. of Oklahoma, 1958), p. 226.

4. *Review, Reserve Program, 1957*, pp. 685, 704; George W. Carter, "The Army Reserve Components Effectiveness for Limited War" (unpublished M.A. thesis, Univ. of Vermont, 1972), pp. 58-60; *National Guardsman*, VII (April, 1953), pp. 8, 9; ibid., June 1953, cover editorial; William V.

Kennedy, "The Citizen Soldier," ibid., XII (March 1958), pp. 4-7.

5. Ibid., VII (April 1953), p. 5.

6. Ibid., VII (Sep. 1953), p. 12; John M. Swomley, Jr., "The Universal Military Training Campaign, 1944-1952" (unpublished Ph.D. diss., Univ. of Colorado, 1959), pp. 160, 170.

7. *Twentieth Century Minutemen*, a report to the President on a Reserve Forces Training Program by the National Security Training Commission, 1 Dec. 1953, pp. 1, 2, 6, 38-40, 70-72, 129.

8. *National Guardsman*, IX (Nov. 1955), p. 62; Swomley, UMT, p. 170.

9. *National Guardsman*, VIII (Nov. 1954), p. 12; ibid., IX (July 1955), p. 10; ibid., IX (Oct. 1955), p. 9; Story, "Formation," pp. 78, 99, 103, 200; William F. Levantrosser, *Congress and the Citizen Soldier* (Ohio State Univ. Press, 1967), pp. 66, 67; *National Reserve Plan*, Hearing by the Senate Armed Services Committee, July 1955, 84 Cong., 1 sess., pp. 7, 83, 111, 113, 160, 161; Eileen Galloway, *A Legislative History of the Reserve Forces Act of 1955*, Washington, D.C., p. 7567; *Review, Reserve Program, 1957*, pp. 673, 701, 702; *Hearing before the Committee on Armed Services, HR*, Jan.-Aug. 1951, 82 Cong., 1 sess., p. 168; *Hearing before a Subcommittee of the Senate Armed Services Committee*, 26-29 May 1952, 82 Cong., 2 sess., p. 1969.

10. *Review Reserve Program*, 1957, p. 741; Reserve Forces Act, 9 Aug. 1955, 69 USSL; Story, "Formation," p. 105; Galloway, *1955 Act*, pp. 7574-7579; Richard J. Stillman, "An Analysis of Six Months Active Duty Training Program in Accordance with the Reserve Forces Act of 1955" (Typescript, U.S. Army War College, 25 Sep. 1960), p. 6.

11. Robert C. Erickson, Reserve Components in 1965 (typescript, U.S. Army War College, 1957), p. 1; Levantrosser, *Congress*, p. 67; *National Reserve Plan*, 1955, p. 94; *National Guardsman*, X (Feb. 1956), extra edition, p. 6; *Factors Operating to Influence Recruitment, Retention, Dedication and Professionalism: An Historical Perspective* (OCMH, 1970), p. 27; *Review, Reserve Program, 1957*, pp. 949, 950, 952.

12. Ibid., pp. 58, 649, 650, 741, 825; Martha Derthick, *The National Guard in Politics* (Harvard Univ. Press, 1965), pp. 118, 138; ARASDRF, FY 1957, pp. 14, 15; *National Guardsman*, X (Jan. 1956), pp. 4, 7.

13. *National Guardsman*, X (Oct. 1956), editorial & p. 6; ibid., XI (Feb. 1957), p. 10; ibid. (March 1957), p. 27; ibid., May 1957, editorial; *Review, Reserve Program*, 1957, pp. 676-681.

14. Ibid., pp. 689, 692, 706, 971-985.

15. Ibid., p. 928.

16. Ibid., pp. 921-923.

17. Story, "Formation," pp. 162-164; *National Guardsman*, XI (March 1957), pp. 10, 11.

18. Ibid., April 1957, editorial and pp. 4-8; ibid., May 1957, p. 33; *Review, Reserve Program*, 1957, p. 700; Eileen Galloway, *History of United States Military Policy on Reserve Forces, 1775-1957* (Paper No. 17, Legislative Reference Branch, Lib. of Congress, 85 Cong., 1 sess., 1957), pp. 487-491.

19. Ibid., p. 479; *Status of Reserve*, pp. 3, 5; *Hearing on HR 5472 to Amend the UMT Service Act as Amended* 2 May 1952, p. 3898; ARCNGB, 30 June 1956, p. 11; *Presentation of a National Reserve Plan by Carter L. Burgess, Asst. Secretary of Defense*, Hearing before HR Armed Forces Subcommittee No. 1, 15 Feb. 1955, pp. 22, 310; ARASDRF, FY 1957, p. 10; *National Guardsman*, VIII (May 1954), p. 8; ibid., IX (Jan. 1955), p. 10; see also note 39.

20. Chester Morrill, "Mission and Organization of the Army National Guard of the United States with Emphasis on the Period Since 1952" (unpublished Ph.D. diss., American Univ., 1958), pp. 165, 166; *Nation's National Guard*, (Washington, D.C.; NGA, 1954), pp. 65, 68; ARASDRF, FY 1957, pp. 50, 441, 798; *National Guardsman*, VIII (April 1954), p. 6; ibid., XI (March 1957), p. 4; ibid., XIV (Feb. 1960), p. 9; *National Guard Presentation*, 27 Jan. 1958, p. 71.

21. *Status of Reserve*, pp. 5, 8; *National Guardsman*, XII (Nov. 1958), p. 56; ibid., XV (Feb. 1961), pp. 3, 5; ARASDRF, FY 1960, p. 33.

22. *National Guardsman*, XI (Dec. 1957), p. 30.

23. Ibid., X (May 1956), p. 32; ibid., Sep. 1956, p. 10; ibid., Nov. 1956, p. 20; ibid., XI (Feb. 1957), p. 25; Morrill, "Mission," p. 165.

24. *National Guardsman*, VII (March 1953), p. 17; ibid., Sep. 1953, p. 30; ibid., Oct. 1953, p 15; ibid., IX (Jan 1955), p. 20; ibid., July 1955, p. 5; ARCNGB, 30 June 1955, p. 15; ibid., 30 June 1956, p. 15; ARASDRF, FY 1957, p. 11; ibid., FY 1958, p. 10; ibid., FY 1959, p. 6; Richard C. Roberts, "History of the Utah National Guard, 1894-1954" (unpublished Ph.D. diss., Univ. of Utah, 1973), p. 449.

25. Story, "Formation," pp. 35, 40, 44, 45.

26. Ibid., p. 71; William H. Riker, *Soldiers of the States* (Washington, D.C., 1958), p. 99; *Review, Reserve Program, 1957*, p. 731; ARASDRF, FY 1957, pp. 8, 9; *National Guardsman*, XI (March 1957), pp. 10, 11.

27. Ibid., XII (Aug. 1958), p. 6.

28. Ibid., IX (Jan. 1955), p. 9; ibid., X (July 1958), p. 14; Levantrosser, *Congress*, pp. 98, 105; Carter, "Reserve Components," p. 19; Derthick, *National Guard*, p. 148.

29. *Review, Reserve Program*, 1957, p. 877; *National Guardsman*, XIII (Sep. 1959), p. 8.

30. Ibid., XI (March 1957), pp. 12-16; Riker, *Soldiers*, p. 99.

31. *National Guardsman*, XIII (Nov. 1959), pp. 10, 13, 14, 43; ARCNGB, 30 June 1954, p. 28.

32. Charles J. Gross, "The Origins and Development of the Air National Guard, 1943-1969" (unpublished Ph.D. diss., Ohio State Univ., 1979), pp. 10, 109.

33. Ibid., pp. 129, 136.

34. Ibid., p. 168; *Review Reserve Status*, 1957, pp. 649, 894, 914, 915, 918; *Status of Reserve*, 1954, p. 7; Roberts, "Utah National Guard," pp. 449, 450; ARASD, FY 1958, p. 17; ibid., FY 1959, p. 14; ARCNGB, 30 June 1956, pp. 21, 22.

35. Gross, "Air National Guard," pp. 127, 172, 176, 189.

36. Ibid., pp. 168, 190, 192, 202, 214.

37. ARASD, FY 1958, p. 8; ibid., FY 1960, p. 5; Warren K. Wells, "Air Defense and the Army National Guard," *Military Review*, XLI (Sep. 1961), pp. 86, 87, 90.

38. William R. Wachs, "Off Guard," The National Guard and Race-related Disturbances in the 1950s" (unpublished Ph.D. diss., Univ. of North Carolina, 1977), pp. 72-149.

39. Ibid., pp. 149-206.

40. Ibid., pp. 212-278, 312, 313, 319.

41. Robert Coakley, *Operation Arkansas* (OCMH, Dept of the Army Monograph 158M, Washington, D.C., 1957); ARCNGB, 30 June 1958, pp. 24-28.

42. Ibid.; Roberts, "Utah National Guard," p. 451; *Report of the Adjutant General of Florida*, 1957, 1958, p. 57.

43. See note 40.

44. Elizabeth Huckaby, *Crisis at Central High: Little Rock, 1957* (Louisiana State Univ. Press, 1980), pp. 51, 55, 56, 62, 63, 118, 207, 221.

45. *National Guardsman*, IX (Feb. 1955), p. 21; ibid., April 1955, pp. 2, 3, 20; ibid., May 1955, pp. 2, 4; Gene Wortsman and Edwin Strickland, *Phenix City* (Birmingham, Ala., 1955).

46. Bennett M. Rich and Philip Birch, "The Changing Role of the National Guard," *American Political Science Review*, L (Sep. 1956), pp. 702-706.

47. *National Guardsman*, XI (Nov. 1957), editorial and p. 2; ibid., Aug. 1957, editorial; ibid., XIII (May 1959).

CHAPTER 16. THE TURBULENT 1960s

1. Charles J. Gross, "The Origins and Development of the Air National Guard, 1943-1969" (unpublished Ph.D. diss., Ohio State Univ., 1979), pp. 226, 235, 237, 247, 254; *National Guardsman*, XVI (Jan. 1962), p. 2; Sep. 1952, pp. 15-19, 35, 36; James C. Elliott, *The Modern Army and Air National Guard* (Van Nostrand, 1965), p. 14.

2. Ibid., pp. 2-13; Jim Dan Hill, *The Minute Man in War and Peace* (Stackpole, 1964), pp. 548, 549; George W. Carter, "The Army Reserve Components Effectiveness for Limited War" (unpublished M.A. thesis, Univ. of Vermont, 1972), p. 67; ARCNGB, 31 Oct. 1962, pp. 10-12; *National Guardsman*, XVI (April 1962), p. 9.

3. Ibid., Sep. 1962, pp. 9-13, 32-34; Carter, "Army Reserve," p. 68.

4. Ibid., p. 67; John D. Bruen, "Repercussions from the Vietnam Mobilization Decision," *Parameters*, II (Spring/Summer 1972), p. 31; *National Guardsman*, XV (Nov. 1961). pp. 5, 6.

5. Ibid., Jan. 1963, p. 10; Elliott, *National Guard*, p. 26; ARCNGB, 30 June 1963, pp. 27, 40, 63.

6. Ibid., p. 52; *National Guardsman*, XV (Nov. 1961), pp. 4, 5; ibid., XVII

(Feb. 1963), editorial; ibid., (March 1963), pp. 2, 3; ibid., May 1963, editorial and p. 12; ibid., XVIII (Feb. 1964), p. 9; ibid., Sep. 1964, p. 16.

7. Ibid., XVII (March 1963), pp. 2, 3; Elliott, *National Guard*, pp. 4, 19; William V. Kennedy, "Should State Adjutants Be Civilians," *Military Review*, XLVIII (March 1968), p. 67; ARCNGB, 31 Oct. 1962, p. 12; *National Guardsman*, XVIII (Sep. 1964), p. 16.

8. Jack Raymond, "The 'McNamara Monarchy,'" in Stephen E. Ambrose and James A. Barber, eds., *The Military and American Society* (Free Press, 1972), pp. 19-32.

9. Bruen, "Repercussions," p. 31.

10. *National Guardsman*, XVI (May 1962), p. 6.

11. Ibid., and Aug. 1962, p. 5.

12. Ibid., XVII (Jan. 1963), p. 3; ibid., July 1963, p. 9; ibid., Aug. 1963, p. 29; OCMH, Chronicle (mimeograph, 1965), p. 11.

13. *National Guardsman*, XV (June 1961), p. 6; ibid., Aug. 1961, p. 11; ibid., XVIII (Feb. 1963), p. 3; ibid., XIX (Jan. 1965), editorial; Hill, *Minute Man*, pp. 544, 545.

14. *National Guardsman*, XIX (Jan. 1965), editorial and p. 16; Elliott, *National Guard*, p. 151; William F. Levantrosser, *Congress and the Citizen Soldier* (Ohio State Univ. Press, 1967), pp. 106-168; *Why Merge?* (Chief of Information, Army, 1965), pp. 4, 6, 9, 11; *Proposal to Realign the Army National Guard and the Army Reserve Forces*, Hearing before the Preparedness Investigating Subcommittee of the Senate Committee on Armed Services (*Proposal to Realign*), 1 March 1965, pp. 2, 5; *Merger of the Army Reserve Components*, Hearings before Subcommittee No. 2, HR Comm. on the Armed Services (Paper no. 39, 89 Cong., 1 sess.), pp. 3573-3578.

15. Ibid., pp. 3623, 3957, 3958.

16. Ibid., pp. 3578, 3593, 3594, 3624, 3739, 3740, 3933, 3959; *National Guardsman*, XVI (March 1962), editorial; *Why Merge*, p. 12; ARCNGB, 31 Oct. 1962, p. 39; Levantrosser, *Congress*, pp. 99-120; *Proposal to Realign*, pp. 6, 37.

17. *Merger*, pp. 3740, 3919, 4693.

18. *Proposal to Realign*, pp. 6, 449; Kennedy, "Adjutants General," pp. 67-74; ARCNGB, 31 Oct. 1962, p. 20; Elliott, *National Guard*, p. 97.

19. *Proposal to Realign*, pp. 27, 65; *Merger*, p. 3663.

20. Ibid., pp. 4118, 4137, 4138; *National Guardsman*, XIX (June 1965), editorial.

21. *Proposal to Realign*, p. 585.

22. Ibid., p. 536.

23. Levantrosser, *Congress*, p. 174.

24. *Merger*, pp. 3705, 3983.

25. Ibid., p. 3584.

26. Ibid., p. 4157; ibid., supplemental hearing on 30 Sep. 1965, pp. xli, xcviii, cii, ciii, civ.

27. *National Guardsman*, XIX (Sep. 1965), pp. 10, 11; Levantrosser, *Congress*, p. 169.

28. ARCNGB, 30 June 1966, pp. 10, 20, 30; Carter, "Army Reserve," p. 82; *Merger*, supplemental hearing, pp. v-ix, xxix; Annual Report, Reserve Forces (ARRF), FY 1966, pp. 5, 6; ARRF, FY 1967, p. 7; *National Guardsman*, XIX (Nov. 1965), p. 8; ibid., May 1966, pp. 8-11; ibid., XX (Sep. 1966), pp. 3-11.

29. Gross, "Air National Guard," pp. 262-264.

30. *National Guardsman*, XIX (Jan. 1965), p. 17; ibid., XXI (Sep. 1967), p. 15; ibid., XXII (Jan. 1968), p. 8.

31. Ibid., June 1968, p. 31; ibid., XXIII (Sep. 1969), pp. 12, 15, 16; ARCNGB, 30 June 1968, pp. 27, 30, 34, 35; ARCNGB, 30 June 1969, p. 31; ARRF, FY 1968, pp. 13, 14.

32. ARRF, FY 1966, pp. 8-11; ARCNGB, 30 June 1966, p. 20; ARCNGB, 30 June 1968, p. 34; Levantrosser, *Congress*, p. 170; *Merger*, supplemental hearing, pp. x, xiii, xx; *National Guardsman*, XIX (Dec. 1965), p. 24.

33. Ibid., XXI (June 1967), editorial; ibid., July 1967, pp. 2, 5, 6; ibid., XXII (Jan. 1968), p. 8; ibid., Feb. 1968, editorial and p. 14; *Statement of Stanley Resor* before the Armed Services Committee, 26 June 1967, pp. 2-5.

34. *National Guardsman*, XXI (Oct. 1967), p. 36.

35. Ibid.; ARRF, FY 1968, pp. 5-8.

36. *Merger*, pp. 3643, 3963, 3993; ARRF, FY 1967, p. 6; ARRF, FY 1968, p. 9; *Resor Statement*, p. 1.

37. ARCNGB, 31 Oct. 1962, p. 5; ibid., 30 June 1963, pp. 1-4.

38. Ibid., 30 June 1966, p. 7; ARRF FY 1966, p. 10.

39. *Merger*, p. 4430; *Proposal to Realign*, pp. 27, 28; ARCNGB, 30 June 1968, p. 24; *National Guardsman*, XXI (Oct. 1967), p. 38; ibid., XXII (Feb. 1968), p. 37; ibid., Aug. 1968, p. 37; ibid., XXIII (March 1969), p. 22; ibid., May 1969, p. 26.

40. Paul J. Scheips, *The Role of the Army in the Oxford, Mississippi, Incident, 1962, 1963* (OCMH, Monograph 73M, 24 June 1965); Scheips, "Enforcement of the Federal Judicial Process by Federal Marshals: A Comparison of Little Rock and Oxford," in Robin Higham, *Bayonets in the Streets* (Univ. Press of Kansas, 1969), pp. 35-60.

41. See note 40; *National Guardsman*, XVI (Nov. 1962), pp. 4-9, 48.

42. Robert W. Coakley, Paul J. Scheips, and Vincent Demma, *Use of Troops in Civil Disturbances since World War II, 1945-1965* (OCMH, Study No. 75, revised 1971), pp. 91-93, 98; *National Guardsman*, XVII (Aug. 1963), pp. 9, 13, 24.

43. Ibid., XIX (May 1965), p. 10; Coakley et al., *Use of Troops*, pp. 104-110.

44. Ibid., pp. 66-69; Milton Viorst, *Fire in the Streets* (Simon & Schuster, 1979), pp. 311, 313, 319.

45. *National Guardsman*, XIX (Oct. 1965), pp. 9-13; ibid., XXII (April 1968), p. 13; Clarence C. Clendenen, "Super Police: The National Guard as a Law Enforcement Agency in the Twentieth Century," in Higham, *Bayonets*, pp. 101-109.

46. Paul J. Scheips, *Use of Troops in Civil Disturbances Since World War II*, (OCMH Study no. 75, supplement No. 1, 1966), pp. 28-41.
47. Ibid.
48. Ibid., pp. 44-63.
49. Ibid., revision of 1973, pp. 75-85; *National Guardsman*, XXII, April 1968, p. 13.
50. Ibid., p. 31.
51. Ibid., pp. 87-94.
52. Ibid., pp. 122-127.
53. *National Guardsman*, XXII (April 1968), p. 13; *Facts on File*, week of 20-26 July 1967, pp. 283-285.
54. ARCNGB, 30 June 1968, pp. 13, 14; Martin Blumenson, "On the Function of the Military in Civil Disorders," Ambrose and Barber, *Military and Society*, pp. 252, 256.
55. *The National Guard and the Constitution* (Legal study by the American Civil Liberties Union, 1971), p. 82; James R. Gardner, "The Military and Domestic Disturbances, 1967-1969" (paper presented at the annual meeting of the Interuniversity Seminar on the Armed Forces and Society, 1972), pp. 12-16; *National Guardsman*, XXII (April 1968), pp. 12-14; ARRF, FY 1968, pp. 15-20; ARCNGB, 30 June 1968, p. 13.
56. *National Guardsman*, XXIII (Nov. 1969), pp. 10ff.
57. Ibid., XXI (Aug. 1967), p. 34; ibid., Sep. 1967, editorial; ARCNGB, 30 June 1968, pp. 13-16; ARRF, FY 1968, pp. 15-20.
58. *National Guardsman*, XXIV (Sep. 1970).
59. Ibid., XX (April 1966), editorial and p. 9; Bruen, "Repercussions," pp. 30, 32-34; Carter, "Army Reserve," p. 146; David Halberstam, *The Best and the Brightest* (Random House, 1972), pp. 593, 594, 598; Lawrence M. Baskir and William Strauss, *Chance and Circumstance: The Draft, the War, and the Vietnam Generation* (Knopf, 1978), p. 50; *National Guardsman*, XXI (March 1967), p. 14; ARCNGB, 31 Oct. 1962, p. 10.
60. Ibid., XX (30 June 1966), pp. 6, 40.
61. Gross, "Air National Guard," p. 274; ARCNGB, 30 June 1968, p. 52; *National Guardsman* XVII (March 1963), pp. 10, 11; ibid., XXI (Aug. 1967), p. 20; ibid., XXII (April 1968), p. 28; ibid., XXIII (Jan. 1969), editorial; ARRF, FY 1967, p. 81.
62. ARRF, FY 1968, pp. 101, 105; ARCNGB, 30 June 1968, p. 10; ibid., 30 June 1969, p. 2; *National Guardsman*, XXII (March 1968), p. 3.
63. Ibid., March 1968, p. 3; ibid., May 1968, p. 18; Carter, "Army Reserve," p. 87; ARCNGB, 30 June 1968, p. 10; ibid., 30 June 1969, pp. 2, 8, 9; Gross, "Air National Guard," p. 285.
64. See note 62; ARRF, FY 1968, pp. 101, 105.
65. *National Guardsman*, XXI (Feb. 1967), editorial and p. 14; Baskir, *Chance*, pp. 49, 51.
66. ARRF, FY 1965, p. 49.
67. *National Guardsman*, XXIV (Sep. 1970); ACLU Legal Study, p. i; Joe Eszterhaus and Michael D. Roberts, *Confrontation at Kent State: Thirteen Seconds* (College Press, 1970).

68. Ibid., p. 283; Albert Brien, "The Case for Uniform Regulation of the National Guard," *Boston University Law Review* (Special issue, Spring 1970), p. 171.

69. Eszterhaus and Roberts, *Thirteen Seconds*, pp. 8, 82, 152, 157, 162.

70. Ibid., pp. 5, 26, 296, 299, 303; *National Guardsman*, XXIV (Sep. 1970), pp. 31-33.

71. ACLU Legal Study, p. 11; *Civil Liberties* (American Civil Liberties Union, New York, periodically), Feb. 1979, p. 1.

72. ARCNGB, 30 June 1963, pp. 8, 40; ARRF, FY 1965, p. 8.

73. ARRF, FY 1965, p. 13; ARCNGB, 31 Oct. 1962, p. 24; Adam Yarmolinsky, *The Military Establishment* (Harpers, 1971), p. 203; ARRF, FY 1966, p. 13; *National Guardsman*, XVII (Sep. 1963), p. 19; ibid., Nov. 1963, p. 3.

74. Ibid., XXII (March 1968), p. 13; ibid., XXIII (April 1969), p. 36; ARCNGB, 30 June 1968, p. 21; ARCNGB, 30 June 1969, p. 36; *Proposal to Realign*, p. 18.

75. Scheips, *Use of Troops*, p. vi; ACLU Legal Study; *National Guardsman*, XXIV (June 1970).

76. Derived from going through *National Guardsman*, 1961-1965; ARCNGB, 31 Oct. 1962, p. 33; Scheips, *Use of Troops*, p. vii.

77. Martha Derthick, *The National Guard in Politics* (Harvard Univ. Press, 1965), p. 110; Elliott, *National Guard*, p. 75; *Twentieth Century Minuteman*, A Report to the President on the Reserve Forces Training Program by the National Security Training Commission (Washington, D.C., 1 Dec. 1953), p. 70.

CHAPTER 17. THE GUARD IN THE 1970s

1. *The Report of the President's Committee on an All-Volunteer Armed Force* (Collier Books, 1970); Jerald G. Bachman, John D. Blair, and David R. Segal, *The All-Volunteer Force* (Univ. of Michigan Press, 1977); Bruce Bliven, Jr., *Volunteers One and All* (Reader's Digest Press, 1976), p. 26; *National Guardsman*, XXIV (Nov. 1970), p. 20, on Dr. Tarr; see ibid., XXVI (March 1972), for Goldwater's statement; ibid., XXXI (Jan. 1977), p. 15; ibid., June 1977.

2. Ibid., Jan. 1970, editorial and p. 10; ibid., March 1970, p. 4, on Rivers view; ibid., XXV (Dec. 1971), on Stennis view.

3. An Act to amend the Military Selective Service Act of 1967, Sep. 28, 1971, 85 USSL pp. 348-355; *Facts on File*, 1971, pp. 515, 753; ibid., 1980, pp. 110, 349, 478, 493, 597, 683; Ibid., 1981, pp. 439, 951.

4. *National Guardsman*, XXIV (April 1970), editorial; Testimony of Sec. of Defense, 17 Feb. 1972, *Hearings on Military Posture*, House Comm. on Armed Service, 92 Cong., 2 sess., part 1, p. 9426; George W. Carter, "The Army Reserve Components Effectiveness for Limited War" (unpublished M.A. thesis, Univ. of Vermont, 1972), p. 98; *Annual Report, National*

Guard Assn, 13 Sep. 1977, pp. 58, 59 (ARNGA); *Air Force Policy Letter for Commanders* (AFPLC), 15 Oct. 1975.

5. Lowndes F. Stephens, "Citizen Soldiers: Why They Enlist and Reenlist," *Military Review,* LVII (Dec. 1977), pp. 37-39; Stephens, "Recruiting and Retaining the Citizen Soldier," *Armed Forces and Society,* IV (Fall 1977), pp. 29-39; Robert S. McGowan, "The Army National Guard in the 1970s" (Army War College Research Report, Library AWC), p. 10; John T. Fishel, "The National Guard Strength: The Wisconsin Example," *Military Review,* LV (Sep. 1975), pp. 59, 63.

6. ARCNGB, 30 June 1970, p. 7; ibid., 30 June 1973, p. 46; ibid., 30 June 1974, p. 127; *National Guardsman,* XXIX, March 1975, p. 12; ibid., Feb. 1977, p. 22; ibid., April 1977, p. 4; ibid., Feb. 1978, table on p. 9.

7. *National Guardsman,* XXXI (April 1977, editorial.

8. Ibid., XXIV (May 1970), p. 21; ibid., July 1970, p. 16; ibid., XXV (Dec. 1971), p. 9; ibid., XXVI (Jan. 1972), p. 17; ibid., XXVII (April 1973), p. 12; ibid., XXVIII (April 1974), p. 10; ibid., XXXII (March 1978), p. 16; ibid., July 1978, p. 7; ibid., June 1978, President's page; ARCNGB, 30 June 1970, pp. 2, 29, 30; ibid., FY 1971, p. 3; ibid., 30 June 1973, p. 28; Raymond E. Bell, Jr., "National Guardsmen: Those Behind You," *Recruiting and Career Counseling Journal,* Feb. 1976, pp. 19-21; Asst. Sec. of Def. Hadlai Hull to HR Committee, 7 Feb. 1972, *Hearings on Military Posture and HR 12604,* House Armed Services Committee 92 Cong., 1 sess.

9. *National Guardsman,* XXV (Jan. 1971), p. 32; ibid., Feb. 1971, p. 28; ibid., XXVI (Jan. 1972), editorial and p. 12.

10. *National Guardsman,* XXXI (Sep. 1977), p. 23; ibid., Oct./Nov. 1977, editorial; ibid., XXXII (Jan. 1978), p. 19; ibid., April 1978, p. 20; *National Guard* (*National Guardsman* redesignated in Nov. 1978), XXXIII (Jan. 1979). President's page and pp. 11, 12; Martin Binkin, *United States Reserve Forces: The Problems of the Weekend Warrior* (Brookings Institution, 1974), p. 52.

11. McGowan, "Guard in the 1970s," pp. 16, 24, 32, 33; Resolution of the NGA 1977, *National Guardsman* (Nov. 1977).

12. Ibid., XXXII (April 1978), p. 26; ARCNGB, 30 June 1974, p. 130; 30 June 1970, p. 28.

13. Pay increases drawn from tables in the following issues of *National Guardsman:* Sep. 1964, p. 32; Aug. 1969, p. 13; Nov. 1973, p. 15; Dec. 1974, p. 32; Nov. 1976, pp. 4, 10; Bachman et al., *All Volunteer Force,* p. 20.

14. Arseny A. Melnick, "Are We Achieving Maximum Use of the Reserve Components Officer?" (Army War College Study, 8 Jan. 1973, AWC Library), pp. 2, 8, 12; *National Guardsman,* XXV (May 1971), pp. 8, 11; ibid., XXIX (Nov. 1975), p. 38; ibid., XXXII (Feb. 1978), p. 24; ibid., June 1978, pp. 12, 15.

15. Ibid., XXIV (March 1970), p. 28; ibid., XXV (Nov. 1971), President's page; ibid., XXVI (Aug./Sep. 1972), p. 16; ibid., XXXII (March 1978),

p. 16; ARCNGB, 30 June 1970, p. 91; ibid., FY 1971, p. 91; ibid., 30 June 1973, p. 14; Greenlief to HR Committee, 7 Feb. 1972, *Hearings on Military Posture*, p. 11635.

16. *National Guardsman*, XXV (Feb. 1971), p. 33; ibid., Oct. 1971, p. 32; ibid., XXVI (Nov. 1972), p. 40; ibid., XXVII (May 1973), p. 48; ibid., Nov. 1973, p. 16; ibid., XXV (July 1974), pp. 2ff; ibid., Dec. 1974, p. 15; ibid., XXXI (April 1977), p. 19; ibid., XXXII (March 1978), p. 35; ARCNGB, 30 June 1973, p. 29; ibid., FY 1975, p. 30.

17. Binkin, *Reserve Forces*, p. 10; ARNGA, 13 Sep. 1977, p. 58.

18. Fishel, "National Guard Strength," p. 59; Benjamin L. Abramowitz, "Can the Reserve Components Make it?" *Military Review*, LVI (May 1976), pp. 62, 63; Sec. of Defense Laird to HR Armed Services Committee, *Hearings on Military Posture*, p. 9429.

19. *National Guardsman*, XXIV (Dec. 1970), p. 27; ibid., Aug./Sep. 1971, pp. 5ff.; *National Guard*, Jan. 1979, p. 38; *Reserve Call-up*, Hearings, Senate Armed Services Committee's Subcommittee on Manpower, 30 July 1975, 94 Cong., 1 sess., p. 29.

20. AFPLC, 1 Sep. 1975; ibid., 1 Sep. 1978; ARCNGB, 30 June 1973, pp. 43, 44; ibid., 30 June 1974, p. 155; *National Guardsman*, March 1974, p. 15; ibid., March 1978, p. 17; *National Guard*, XXXIII (Jan. 1979), p. 5.

21. Ibid., p. 38; *National Guardsman*, XXV (May 1971), p. 14; ibid., XXXI (May 1977), p. 2; ARCNGB, FY 1976, p. 86; AFPLC, 1 March 1977; ibid., 15 Oct. 1978; Binkin, *Reserve Forces*, p. 10; *Reserve Call-up*, p. 14; Gross, "Air National Guard," p. 5.

22. ARNGA, 13 Sep. 1977, p. 10; *National Guardsman*, XXIV (Oct. 1970), p. 8; ibid., XXIX (Nov. 1975), p. 17.

23. William V. Kennedy, "New Initiatives in the Reserve Forces," *Military Review*, L, (May 1970), pp. 74-81.

24. Bliven, *Volunteers All*, p. 11.

25. *National Guardsman*, XXXI (June 1977), p. 3; ibid., XXXII (July 1978), p. 7; *National Guard*, XXXIII (Feb. 1979), p. 40.

26. *National Guardsman*, XXIX (Dec. 1975), editorial; ibid., XXXI (Sep. 1977), President's page; ARNGA, 13 Sep. 1977, pp. 58, 59.

27. Ibid., p. 60; Roy A. Werner, "The Other Military: Are Reserve Forces Viable?" *Military Review*, LVII (April 1977), pp. 21-23; *National Guardsman*, XXXI (Jan. 1977), p. 14; Stephens, "Citizen Soldiers," pp. 38, 39.

28. Edward L. King to HR Committee, 24 March 1972, *Hearings on Military Posture*, part 2, pp. 10376-10381; Binkin, *Reserve Forces*, p. 40; George H. Gray, "What Are the Reserve Forces Really For," *Military Review*, LV (June 1975), p. 90; *National Guardsman*, XXXI (Nov. 77), p. 2.

29. *National Guardsman*, XXIV (Oct. 1970), p. 8; ibid., XXIX (Jan. 1975), editorial; ibid., Oct. 1975, editorial; ibid., XXX (March 1976), p. 13; ibid., XXXI (June 1977), p. 4; ibid., XXXII (March 1978), p. 4; Fishel, "National Guard Strength," p. 59; Marr to HR Committee on Armed Services, 7 Feb. 1972, *Hearings on Military Posture*, p. 11586.

30. *National Guardsman*, XXXII (Aug. 1978), p. 40; ARCNGB, FY 1975, p. 2; ARCNGB, 30 June 1970, p. 74. The eight divisions that survived were 26th, 28th, 38th, 42nd, and 47th Infantry, 30th Mechanized and 30th and 50th Armored.

31. *National Guardsman*, XXIV (June 1970), p. 24; ibid., June 1976, p. 11; Robert H. Brigham, "A Career Development Program for Reserve Officers," *Military Review*, LIII (Sep. 1973), p. 41; Melnick, "Are We Achieving," p. 8.

32. *National Guardsman*, XV (Feb. 1971), p. 21, on Rivers's death; ibid., XXVII (Jan. 1973), p. 10, on Truman; ibid., XXIX (Oct. 1975), pp. 24, 25, on Walsh, p. 88 on Reckord; ibid., XXXI (July/Aug. 1977) on Hershey.

33. Ibid., XXX (March 1976), p. 47; ibid., May 1976, President's page; Resolutions NGA, ibid., XXXI (Nov. 1977), p. 27; ARCNGB, FY 1977, p. 7; Bachman, *All-Volunteer Force*, p. 151.

34. *National Guardsman*, XXV (May 1971), p. 8; ibid., XXXI (April 1977), p. 22; ibid., XXXII (Sep./Oct. 1978), President's page.

35. Ibid., XXV (May 1971), pp. 5-7; ibid., XXVI (May 1972), p. 32; ibid., July 1972, p. 22; ibid., Aug./Sep. 1972, p. 21; ARCNGB, 30 June 1973, p. 21; ibid., 30 June 1974, pp. 127, 130; ibid., FY 1975, p. 2; ARCNGB, FY 1977, p. 22.

36. *National Guardsman*, XXXII (June 1978), p. 24; *Changing the Guard: Citizen Soldiers in Wisconsin Correctional Institutions* (League of Women Voters of Wisconsin, July 1978).

37. *National Guardsman*, XXXII (Sep./Oct. 1978), p. 9; ARCNGB, 30 June 1970, p. 26.

38. *National Guardsman*, XXVI (March 1972), p. 32; ibid., July 1972, pp. 8, 11, 22; ibid., XXVII (June 1973), p. 28; ibid., XXIX (March 1975), pp. 5ff.; ibid., XXXI (Sep. 1977), p. 8; "The Long Harsh Winter of 1979," *National Guard*, XXXIII (March/April 1979), pp. 8-12, 38, 39.

Bibliography

Sources, Published and Unpublished That Appear in the Notes

ABRAMOWITZ, BENJAMIN L. "Can the Reserve Components Make it?", *Military Review*, LVI (May 1976), 58-64.

ADAMS, HENRY. *The Life of Albert Gallatin*. Philadelphia: J. B. Lippincott, 1879.

ADAMS, JOHN. *Diary and Autobiography*, Lyman H. Butterfield (ed.), 4 vols. Cambridge, Mass.: Belknap Press, 1961.

Air Force Policy Letters for Commanders. Director of Information, AF, Washington, D.C. Letters of 1 Sep. & 15 Oct. 1975 (abbreviation, AFPLC).

ALDRIDGE, FREDERICK S. Organization and Administration of the Militia System of Colonial Virginia. Unpublished Ph.D. diss., American Univ., 1964.

ALEXANDER, ARTHUR J. "How Maryland Tried to Raise Her Continental Quotas," *Maryland Historical Magazine*, XLII (Sep. 1947), 184-196.

ALEXANDER, ARTHUR J. "Service by Substitute in the Militia of Northampton and Lancaster Counties during the War of the Revolution," *Military Affairs*, IX (Fall, 1945), 278-282.

ALEXANDER, WINTHROP, "Ten Years of Riot Duty: A Record of Active Service Performed by the National Guard, 1886-1895," *Journal of the Military Service Institution of the United States*, XIX (July 1896), 1-62.

ALGER, RUSSELL A. *The Spanish American War*. New York: Harper and Bros., 1901.

ALTGELD, JOHN P. *Live Questions*. Chicago: G. S. Barren, 1899.

AMBROSE, STEPHEN E. *Upton and the Army*. Baton Rouge: Louisiana State Univ. Press, 1964.

AMBROSE, STEPHEN E. and JAMES A. BARBER (eds.). *The Military and American Society*. New York: Free Press, 1972.

American Armies and Battlefields in Europe. Prepared by the American Battle Monuments Commission. Washington, D.C.: GPO, 1938.

American State Papers: Indian Affairs, 2 vols. Washington, D.C. 1832.

American State Papers: Military Affairs, 7 vols. Washington, D.C.: Gales and Seaton, 1832-1860.

ANSELL, SAMUEL T., "Legal and Historical Aspects of Militia," *Yale Law Review*, XXVI (April 1917), 471-480.

Archives of Pennsylvania, series 2.

Army Almanac, Washington, D.C. 1950.

Army Chief of Staff Report, 1939-1941. Washington, D.C., 1941.

Army Lineage Book: Infantry. OCMH, Department of the Army. Washington, D.C., 1953.

Army and Navy Chronicle, W. B. Homans (ed.), 13 vols. Washington, D.C. 1835-1842.

Army War College Studies

ERICKSON, COL. ROBERT C. Reserve Components in 1965. Typescript, 42 pp., 1957.

McGOWAN, ROBERT S. LTC. The Army National Guard in the 1970s. Typescript, 69 pp., 5 March 1971.

MELNICK, ARSENY A. Are We Achieving Maximum Use of the Reserve Component Officer? 39 pp., typescript, 8 Jan. 1973.

A Study of the Methods to Be Adopted in the Feeding and Caring for the Organized Militia When Called into the Service of the United States. Typescripts, 1905-1906.

Resources of the United States . . . Men. Useful figures on the size of force from the Revolution to 1906. Typescript, June 1906.

STILLMAN, RICHARD I. An Analysis of Six Months Active Duty Training Program in Accordance with the Reserve Forces Act of 1955. Typescript, 54 pp., 25 Sep. 1960.

BACHMAN, JERALD G., JOHN D. BLAIR, and DAVID A. SEGAL. *The All-Volunteer Force*. Ann Arbor: Univ. of Michigan Press, 1977.

BAILEY, KENNETH R. A Search for Identity: The West Virginia National Guard, 1877-1921. Unpublished Ph.D. diss., Ohio State Univ., 1976.

BAKAL, CARL. *The Right to Bear Arms*. New York: McGraw-Hill, 1966.

BAKELESS, JOHN. *Background to Glory: The Life of George Rogers Clark*. Philadelphia: Lippincott, 1957.

BALDWIN, LELAND D. *Whiskey Rebels* . . . Univ. of Pittsburgh Press, 1939.

BARNETT, CORELLI. *Britain and Her Army, 1509-1970*. New York: Morrow, 1970

BARRETT, JOHN G. *The Civil War in North Carolina*. Chapel Hill: Univ. of North Carolina Press, 1963.

BASKIR, LAWRENCE M. and WILLIAM A. STRAUSS. *Chance and Circumstance: The Draft, the War and the Vietnam Generation*, New York: Knopf, 1978.

BAUER, K. JACK. *The Mexican War. 1846-1848*. New York: Macmillan, 1974.

BEAMISH, RICHARD J. *America's Part in the World War*. Philadelphia, John C. Winston, 1919.

BELL, RAYMOND E., "National Guardsman: Those Behind You," *Recruiting and Career Counseling Journal*, Feb. 1976, 19-21.

"Extracts from the Diary of the Reverend William Bentley of Salem . . .," *Historical Collections of the Danvers Historical Society*, I (1913), 72-73.

BILLIAS, GEORGE A. *George Washington's Generals*. New York: Morrow, 1964.

BINKIN, MARTIN, *U.S. Reserve Forces: The Problem of the Weekend Warrior*. Washington, D.C.: Brookings Institution, 1974.

BITTLE, GEORGE C. The Organized Florida Militia from 1821 to 1920. Unpublished Ph.D. diss., Florida State Univ., 1965.

BLACK, LOVELL D. The Negro Volunteer Units of the Ohio National Guard. Unpublished Ph.D. diss., Ohio State Univ., 1976.

BLACKSTONE, SIR WILLIAM. *Commentaries on the Laws of England*, 4 vols. New York: Garland Publishing, 1978 facsimile of the original edition of 1783.

BLIVEN, BRUCE, JR. *Volunteers One and All*. Pleasantville, N.Y.: Reader's Digest Press, 1976.

BLUMENSON, MARTIN. "On the Function of the Military in Civil Disorders," in *The Military and American Society*, Stephen E. Ambrose and James A. Barber, eds. New York: Free Press, 1972.

Blunt, James G. Papers of . . . , 17 vols. Kansas State Historical Collections, Topeka, 1875-1928.

BODLEY, TEMPLE. *George Rogers Clark*. Boston: Houghton-Mifflin, 1926.

BOUCHER, RONALD L. "The Colonial Militia as a Social Institution . . . Salem, Massachusetts," *Military Affairs*, XXXVII (Dec. 1973), 125-129.

BOYNTON, LINDSAY, *The Elizabethan Militia, 1558-1638*. London, 1967.

JOHN BRANNAN (comp.). *Official Letters of the Military and Naval Officers of the United States during the War with Great Britain in the Years 1812, 1813, 1814, & 1815*. Washington, D.C., 1823.

BRIEN, ALBERT. "The Case for Uniform Regulation of the National Guard," *Boston Univ. Law Review* (Special issue, Spring 1970), 169-177.

BRIGHAM, ROBERT H. "A Career Development Program for Reserve Officers," *Military Review*, LIII (Sep. 1973), 41-48.

BROWN, RICHARD C. "Emory Upton: The Army's Mahan," *Military Affairs*, XVII (1953), 125-131.

BROWN, RICHARD M. *Strain of Violence*. New York: Oxford Univ. Press, 1975.

BROWN, SAMUEL R. *Views of the Campaigns of the Northwest Army*. Burlington, Vt.: Samuel Mills, 1814.

BRUCE, ROBERT V. 1877: *Year of Violence*. Indianapolis: Bobbs-Merrill, 1959.

BRUEN, JOHN D. "Repercussions from the Vietnam Mobilization Decision," *Parameters*, II (Spring-Summer 1972), 30-39.

BUFFINGTON, ARTHUR H. "The Puritan View of War," Colonial Society of Massachusetts, *Publications*, XXVIII (1930-1933), 67-86.

BURNE, ALFRED H. *The Crecy War*, New York: Oxford Univ. Press,1955.

BURNETT, EDMUND CODY (Ed.). *Letters of Members of the Continental Congress*, 8 vols. Carnegie Institution of D.C., 1921-1938.

CANTOR, LOUIS. Creation of the Modern National Guard: The Dick Militia Act of 1903. Unpublished Ph.D. diss., Duke Univ., 1963.

CANTOR, LOUIS. "Elihu Root and the National Guard," *Military Affairs*, XXXIII (Dec. 1969), 361-373.

CARALAY, DEMETRIOS. *The Politics of Military Unification*. New York: Columbia Univ. Press, 1966.

CARTER, GEORGE W. The Army Reserve Components Effectiveness for Limited War. Unpublished M.A. thesis, Univ. of Vermont, 1972.

CELMER, THEO BERNARD. The Post-World War II National Guard of the United States: Development and Organization. Unpublished M.A. thesis, Univ. of Maryland, 1955.

Center of Military History, Department of the Army

Chronological History of the Army Reserve Components. Mimeograph, Washington, D.C., 1965.

COAKLEY, ROBERT W. *Operation Arkansas.* Photocopy, Washington, D.C., 1967.

_____. Use of the Militia and the National Guard by the Federal Government in Civil Disturbances. Typescript, 1966.

COAKLEY, ROBERT W., PAUL J. SCHEIPS, and VINCENT DEMMA. *Use of Troops in Civil Disturbances since World War II, 1945-1965.* Photocopy, 1965, revised 1971.

COAKLEY, ROBERT W., PAUL J. SCHEIPS, et al. Anti-war and Anti-military Activities in the United States, 1846-1954. Typescript, 1970, 148 pp.

Factors Operating to Influence Recruitment, Retention, Dedication, and Professionalism of the Army: An Historical Perspective. Washington, D.C., 1970.

SCHEIPS, PAUL J. *The Role of the Army in the Oxford, Mississippi Incident, 1962, 1963.* Monograph 73M, Photocopy, 24 June 1965.

SCHEIPS, PAUL J. *Use of Troops in Civil Disturbances since World War II.* Supplement I, 1966. Study 75 is a revision of Supplement I. Photocopy, 1973.

SCHEIPS, PAUL J. and M. WARNER STARK. *Use of Troops in Civil Disturbances Since World War II.* Study 75 (II), 1974.

Summary of Army Reserves since 1792. Mimeographed, no date, but contains material through 1964. 31 pp.

CHADWICK, FRENCH E. *The Relations of the United States with Spain,* 2 vols. New York: Scribner's, 1911; reprinted by Russell and Russell, 1968.

CHAMBERLAIN, SAMUEL EMERY. *Recollections of a Rogue.* London: Museum Press, 1957.

Changing of the Guard: Citizen Soldiers in Wisconsin Correctional Institutions. League of Women Voters of Wisconsin, July 1978.

Charleston Courier, 30 Aug. 1813.

CHASTAINE, BEN H. *The Story of the 36th.* Oklahoma City: Harlow Publishers, 1920.

The Citizen Soldier. Published weekly at Norwich, then Winsor, Vt., July 1840-July 1841.

Civil Liberties. Published Feb., April, June, Sep., and Dec. by ACLU, New York.

CLARK, EMMONS. *History of the Second Company, 7th New York State Militia.* New York: J. G. Gregory, 1854.

CLARK, EMMONS. *History of the Seventh Regiment of New York, 1806-1889,* 2 Vols. New York, 1890.

CLARK, WILLIAM PACKER. *Official History of the Militia and National Guard of the State of Pennsylvania,* 3 vols. Philadelphia: J. C. Handler, 1909.

CLENDENEN, CLARENCE C. "Super Police: The National Guard as a Law Enforcement Agency in the Twentieth Century," in Robin Higham (ed.), *Bayonets in the Streets*, Lawrence: Univ. Press of Kansas, 1969.

CLIFFORD, JOHN GARRY. *The Citizen Soldiers: The Plattsburg Training Camp Movement, 1913-1920*. Lexington: Univ. Press of Kentucky, 1972.

COFFMAN, EDWARD. *The Hilt of the Sword: The Career of Peyton C. March*. Madison: Univ. of Wisconsin Press, 1966.

COLBAUGH, JACK. *The Bloody Patch: 28th Division*. New York: Vantage Press, 1973.

COLBY, ELBRIDGE. "Elihu Root and the National Guard," *Military Affairs*, XXIII (Spring 1959), 28-34.

COLBY, ELBRIDGE and JAMES F. GLASS. "Legal Status of the National Guard," *Virginia Law Review*, XXIX (May 1943), 839-856.

COLBY, ELBRIDGE. *National Guard of the United States: A Half Century of Progress*. Photocopied from double-spaced typed draft, uncorrected, and distributed by the American Military Institute, Univ. of Kansas, 1977.

COLE, DAVID W. Organization and Administration of the South Carolina Militia System, 1670-1783. Unpublished Ph.D. diss., Univ. of South Carolina, 1948.

COMMAGER, HENRY STEELE (ed.) *Documents in American History*, to 1898. New York: Appleton-Century-Crofts, 8th edition, 1968.

CONN, SETSON, and BYRON FAIRCHILD. *The Framework of Hemisphere Defense*. Washington, D.C., 1960. A volume in *The United States Army in World War II*.

CONNELL, BRIAN. *The Savage Years*. New York: Harper's, 1959.

COOK, ADRIENNE. *Armies of the Streets: Civil War Draft Riots*. Lexington: Univ. Press of Kentucky, 1974.

COOPER, JERRY M. To Be a Soldier: History of the Wisconsin National Guard in the Nineteenth Century. Unpublished booklength typescript, 1976.

CORNELL, ROBERT J. *Anthracite Coal Strike of 1902*. Washington, D.C.: Catholic Univ. Press, 1957.

COSMAS, GRAHAM, *An Army for Empire*. Columbia: Univ. of Missouri Press, 1971.

COVINGTON, JAMES W. *The Billy Bowlegs War, 1855-1858: The Final Stand of the Seminole Indians against the Whites*. Chuluota, Fla.: Mickler Publishers, 1982.

CRACKEL, THEODORE JOSEPH, "Founding of West Point: Jefferson and the Politics of Security," *Armed Forces and Society*, VII (Summer 1981), 529-543.

CRESS, LAWRENCE DELBERT. The Standing Army, the Militia and the New Republic: Changing Attitudes toward the Military in American Society. Ph.D. diss., Univ. of Virginia, 1976. Published as: *Citizens in Arms: The Army and Militia in American Society to the War of 1812*. Chapel Hill: Univ. of North Carolina Press, 1981.

CROWDER, ENOCH J. *The Spirit of Selective Service*. New York: Century, 1970.

CROWELL, BENEDICT and ROBERT F. WILSON. *The Road to France*, 2 vols. New Haven: Yale Univ. Press, 1921.

CRUICKSHANK, CHARLES G. *Elizabeth's Army*. New York: Oxford Univ. Press, 2nd edition, 1966.

CRUIKSHANK, ERNEST A. (ed.). *Documentary History of the Campaigns upon the Niagara Frontier in 1813 and 1814*, 9 vols. Welland, Ontario: Lundy's Lane Historical Society, no date.

CUNLIFFE, MARCUS. *Soldiers and Civilians.* Boston: Little, Brown, 1968.

CUTCHINS JOHN A. and GEORGE SCOTT STEWART, JR. *History of the 29th Blue and Gray Division, 1917-1919.* Philadelphia: MacCalla Co., 1921.

DAUGHERTY, ROBERT LEE. The Ohio National Guard, 1919-1940. Unpublished Ph.D. diss., Ohio State Univ., 1974.

DAVIS, WILLIAM WATTS H. *The Fries Rebellion, 1798-1799.* Doylestown, Pa.: Doylestown Printers, 1899.

DAYTON, DELLO G. The California Militia, 1850-1866. Unpublished Ph.D. diss., Univ. of California, Berkeley, 1951.

DEARBORN, JOHN J. (ed.). *History of Salisbury, New Hampshire*, Manchester, N.H., 1890.

DEARBORN, JEREMIAH W. *A History of the First Century of Parsonsfield, Maine.* Portland, Me.: B. Thurston, 1888.

DEERIN, JAMES B. "The Militia in the Revolutionary War." Separate section of 32 pages in *The National Guardsman*, XXX (Aug.-Sep. 1976).

DERTHICK, MARTHA, "The Militia Lobby in the Missile Age: The Politics of the National Guard," in Samuel P. Huntington (ed.), *Changing Patterns of Military Politics.* New York: Free Press, 1962.

DERTHICK, MARTHA. *The National Guard in Politics.* Cambridge, Mass.: Belknap Press, 1965.

DEWEY, DAVIS RICH. *Financial History of the United States.* New York: Longmans, Green, 1907.

DICKINSON, JOHN. *The Building of an Army.* New York: Century Press, 1922.

DIX, JOHN A. "Report on the Militia System, 5 Jan. 1832," in *Speeches and Addresses* ..., vol. II. New York: Appleton, 1864.

DORLAND, W. A. NEWMAN. "The Second Troop of Philadelphia City Cavalry," serialized in *Pennsylvania Magazine of History and Biography*, vols. XLV (1921)-LIV (1930).

DOUGAN, MICHAEL B. *Confederate Arkansas.* Univ. of Alabama Press, 1976.

DUNCAN, JAMES. Papers, 1811-1849, MSS, Archives of the U.S. Military Academy.

DUPUY, R. ERNEST. *The National Guard: A Compact History.* New York: Hawthorn, 1971.

DUPUY, R. ERNEST and TREVOR N. DUPUY. *The Military Heritage of America.* New York: McGraw-Hill, 1956.

DYER, FREDERICK B. *A Compendium of the War of the Rebellion*, 3 vols. New York: Thomas Yoseloff, reprint 1959.

EBY, CECIL D. *"That Disgraceful Affair": The Black Hawk War.* New York: Norton, 1973.

ECCLES, W. J. "Social, Economic and Political Significance of the Military Establishment of New France," *Canadian Historical Review*, LII (March 1971), 1-22.

ECKERT, EDWARD K. Conservative Opposition to Federal Control of the Militia. Unpublished M.A. thesis, Univ. of Florida, 1966.

EDDY, THOMAS MEARS. *Patriotism of Illinois*, 2 vols. Chicago: Clark & Co., 1865.

EKIRCH, ARTHUR A., JR. *The Civilian and the Military*. New York: Oxford Univ. Press, 1956.

ELLIOT, JONATHAN (ed.). *Debates in the Several State Conventions on the Adoption of the Federal Constitution*, 5 vols. New York, 1901 reprint; Lippincott, 1937.

ELLIOTT, BENJAMIN. *The Militia System of South Carolina*. Charleston: A. E. Miller, 1835.

ELLIOTT, JAMES C. *The Modern Army and Air National Guard*. Florence, Ky.: Van Nostrand, 1965.

ESZTERHAS, JOSEPH and MICHAEL D. ROBERTS. *Confrontation at Kent State: 13 Seconds*. New York: College Press, 1970.

EWING, JOSEPH H. *29 Let's Go! A History of the 29th Infantry Division in World War II*. Washington, D.C.: Infantry Journal Press, 1948.

FARRAND, MAX (ed.). *The Records of the Federal Convention*, 3 vols. New Haven: Yale Univ. Press, 1911.

The First One Hundred Years: National Guard of the United States. Washington, D.C.: National Guard Association, 1978.

FISHEL, JOHN T. "The National Guard Strength: The Wisconsin Example," *Military Review*, LV (Sep. 1975), 58-68.

Florida, *Report of the Adjutant General*, 1957, 1958.

FOX, DIXON RYAN. *The Decline of the Aristocracy in the Politics of New York*. New York: Columbia Univ. Press, 1919.

GALLOWAY, EILEEN. *History of U. S. Military Policy on Reserve Forces, 1775-1957*. Prepared in the Legislative Reference Branch, Library of Congress, as Paper No. 17 for the House of Representatives Committee on Armed Services, 85 Cong., 1 sess., 1957.

GALLOWAY, EILEEN. *A Legislative History of the Reserve Forces Act of 1955*. Prepared in the Legislative Reference Branch, Library of Congress, for the House of Representatives Committee on the Armed Services. Washington, D.C., 1956.

Gano Papers, "Selections from . . .," *Quarterly Publications of the Historical and Philosophical Society of Ohio*, vols. XV-XVIII. Columbus, Ohio, 1920.

GARDNER, JAMES R. The Military and Domestic Disturbances, 1967-1969. Unpublished paper read before a session of the Interuniversity Seminar on Armed Forces and Society, 15 Sep. 1975.

GATES, STEWART L. The Militia in Connecticut Public Life, 1660-1860. Unpublished Ph.D. diss., Univ. of Connecticut, 1975.

GENTRY, WILLIAM R. *Full Justice: The Story of William R. Gentry and His Missouri Volunteers in the Seminole War*. St. Louis, 1937.

Georgia Military Affairs, 1789-1842, 9 vols., typed from the original MSS and bound in 1940 under the direction of Mrs. J. E. Hays, state historian. Georgia Department of History and Archives, Atlanta, Georgia.

GERHARDT, JAMES M. *The Draft and Public Policy*. Columbus, Ohio, 1971.

GILMORE, RUSSELL. "The New Courage: Rifles and Soldier Individualism, 1876-1918," *Military Affairs*, XL (Oct. 1976), 97-102.

(Gleig, George R.). *A Narrative of the Campaigns of the British Army at Washington, Baltimore, and New Orleans* . . . Philadelphia: M. Carey, 1821.

GOBBEL, LUTHER L. "Militia in North Carolina in Colonial and Revolutionary Times," *Historical Papers: Trinity College Historical Society*, series 13, 1919, 35-61.

GORDON, MARTIN K. "The Black Militia in the District of Columbia, 1867-1898," *Records of the Columbia Historical Society*, 1971-1972, 411-420.

GORDON, MARTIN K. "The Milwaukee Infantry Militia, 1865-1892," *Historical Messenger of the Milwaukee County Historical Society*, XXIV (March 1968), 2-15.

GOTTSCHALK, LOUIS R. *Lafayette and the Close of the American Revolution.* Univ. of Chicago Press, 1942.

GOULD, JOHN M. and GEORGE F. TUCKER. *Second Supplement to Notes on the Revised Statutes, 1 Jan. 1898-1 March 1904.* Boston: Little, Brown, 1904.

GREENE, NATHANAEL. *The Papers of* . . . , Richard K. Showman (ed.). Chapel Hill: Univ. of North Carolina Press, 1976, vol. I, Dec. 1766-Dec. 1776.

GREENFIELD, KENT ROBERTS, ROBERT R. PALMER, and BELL I. WILEY. *The Organization of Ground Combat Troops.* Washington, D.C.: 1947. A volume in the series: *The United States Army in World War II.*

GRONERT, THEO G. "The First National Pastime in the Middle West," *Indiana Magazine of History*, XXIX (1933), 171-186.

GROSS, CHARLES J. The Origins and Development of the Air National Guard, 1943-1969. Unpublished Ph.D. diss., Columbus: Ohio State Univ., 1979.

GULICK, JOHN W. "National Guard as Federal Force," Militia Bureau, War Dept. Doc. 922, 1930, 15 pp.

HAGEDORN, HERMANN. *Leonard Wood*, 2 vols. New York: Harper's, 1931.

HALBERSTAM, DAVID. *The Best and the Brightest.* New York: Random House, 1972.

HALLGREN, MAURITZ. *The Tragic Fallacy.* New York: Knopf, 1937.

HANNA, ARCHIBALD. New England Military Institutions, 1693-1750. Unpublished Ph.D. diss., Yale Univ., 1951.

Josiah Harmar Papers. MSS, William L. Clements Library, Univ. of Michigan.

HARRISON, WILLIAM HENRY. *Messages and Letters of* . . . , Logan Esarey (ed.), 2 vols. Vols. VIII and IX, *Indiana Historical Collections.* Indianapolis, 1922.

HENING, WILLIAM W. (ed.). *The Statutes at Large: Being a Collection of all the Laws of Virginia* . . . *from 1619*, 13 vols. Philadelphia, 1823.

HERRING, GEORGE C., JR. "James Hay and the Preparedness Controversy, 1915-1916," *Journal of Southern History*, XXX (Nov. 1964), 383-404.

HEWITT, ROBERT L. *Work Horse of the Western Front: The Story of the 30th Infantry Division.* Washington, D.C.: Infantry Journal Press, 1946.

HIGGINBOTHAM, DON. *The War of American Independence.* New York: Macmillan, 1971.

HIGGINBOTHAM, DON. *Daniel Morgan: Revolutionary Rifleman.* Chapel Hill: Univ. of North Carolina Press, 1961.

HIGHAM, ROBIN. *Bayonets in the Streets*. Lawrence: Univ. Press of Kansas, 1969.

HILL, JIM DAN. *The Minute Man in Peace and War*. Harrisburg, Pa.: Stackpole, 1964.

HILL, LOUISE B. *Joseph E. Brown and the Confederacy*. Westport, Conn.: Greenwood, 1939; reprint, 1972.

Historical Statistics of the United States: Colonial Times to 1957. Department of Commerce, Bureau of the Census, Washington, D.C., 1960.

History of the 26th YD, 1917-1919; 1941-1945. Produced by the YD Veterans Association, Salem, Mass., 1955.

HITCHCOCK, ETHAN ALLEN. *Fifty Years in Camp and Field: The Diary of Major General . . .* W. A. Croffut (ed.). New York: G. P. Putnam's Sons, 1909.

HOLLAND, JAMES K. "The Diary of a Texan Volunteer in the Mexican War," *The Southwestern Historical Quarterly*, XXX (July 1926), 1-33.

HOLLISTER, C. WARREN. *Anglo-Saxon Military Institutions on the Eve of the Norman Conquest*. New York: Oxford Univ. Press, 1962.

HOLMES, JOSEPH J. The National Guard of Pennsylvania: Policeman of Industry, 1865-1905. Unpublished Ph.D. diss., Univ. of Connecticut, 1971.

HOUSTON, DONALD E., "The Oklahoma National Guard on the Mexican Border, 1916," *Chronicles of Oklahoma*, LIII (Winter 1975-1976), 447-462.

HOYT, CHARLES B. *Heroes of the Argonne: An Authentic History of the 35th Division*. Kansas City: Franklin Hudson, 1919.

HUCKABY, ELIZABETH, *Crisis at Central High: Little Rock, 1957*. Baton Rouge: Louisiana State Univ., 1980.

HUDSON, JAMES J. The California National Guard, 1903-1940. Unpublished Ph.D. diss., Univ. of California, Berkeley, 1953.

HUDSON, JAMES J. "The Role of the California National Guard during the San Francisco General Strike of 1904," *Military Affairs*, XLVI (April 1982), 76-83.

HUIDEKOPER, FREDERICK L. *The Story of the 33rd Division*, reprinted from the *Chicago Daily News*, 1919.

HULL, WILLIAM. *Memoirs of the Campaign of the Northwest Army*. Boston: True and Greene, 1824.

IRVINE, DALLAS. "The First British Regulars in North America," *Military Affairs*, IX (1945), 337-353.

IZARD, GEORGE. *Official Correspondence . . .*, Philadelphia: Thomas Dobson, 1816.

JABBS, THEODORE HARRY. The South Carolina Colonial Militia, 1633-1733. Unpublished Ph.D. diss., Univ. of North Carolina, 1973.

JACKSON, ANDREW. *Correspondence of . . .*, John Spencer Bassett (ed.), 7 vols. Washington, D.C.: Carnegie Institution, 1925-1936.

JACOBS, BRUCE. "July 4, 1918: A National Guard 'Model Company' from Chicago Goes to War—over General Pershing's Protest—and Fireworks Follow." *Guardsman*, XXXII (July 1978), 16-18, 38, 39.

JACOBS, BRUCE. "The National Guard Magazine," *The First One Hundred Years*. Washington, D.C.: NGA, 1978.

JACOBS, BRUCE. "D-Day," *National Guardsman*, XXIII (June 1969).

JACOBS, JAMES RIPLEY. *Beginning of the United States Army*. Princeton Univ. Press, 1947.

JAMES, MARQUIS. *Andrew Jackson: The Border Captain*. New York: Bobbs-Merrill, 1933.

JAY, WILLIAM. *War and Peace: The Evils of the First and the Plan for Preserving the Last*. New York: Wiley and Putnam, 1842.

JEFFERSON, THOMAS. *Writings of. . . .* 20 vols. Washington, D.C.: Thomas Jefferson Memorial Association, 1905.

JENSEN, MERRILL. *The New Nation*. New York: Knopf, 1950.

JOHNS, JOHN E. *Florida during the Civil War*. Gainesville: Univ. of Florida Press, 1963.

JOHNSON, CHARLES J. Black Soldiers in the National Guard, 1877-1949. Unpublished Ph.D. diss., Howard Univ., 1976.

JOHNSON, GUION G. *Ante-Bellum North Carolina*. Chapel Hill: Univ. of North Carolina Press, 1937.

JONES, RALPH E. et al. *Fighting Tanks since 1916*. Washington, D.C.: National Service Pub., 1933.

KAHN, ELY JACQUES and HENRY MCLEMORE. *Fighting Divisions*. Washington, D.C.: Infantry Journal Press, 1945.

KENNEDY, WILLIAM V. "The Citizen Soldier," *National Guardsman*, XII (March 1958), 4-7.

KENNEDY, WILLIAM V. "Should State Adjutants General Be Civilians?" *Military Review*, XLVIII (March 1968), 67-74.

KING, CHARLES. *Trials of a Staff Officer*. Philadelphia: J. B. Lippincott, 1891.

KNOPF, RICHARD C. (ed.). *Thomas Worthington and the War of 1812*. Columbus, Ohio, 1957.

KNOX, DUDLEY. *History of the United States Navy*. New York: Putnam, 1936.

KOHN, RICHARD H. *Eagle and Sword: The Federalists and the Creation of the Military Establishment in America, 1783-1802*. New York: Free Press, 1975.

KREIDBERG, MARVIN R. and MERTON G. HENRY. *History of Military Mobilization in the U.S. Army*. Washington, D.C.: DA Pamphlet 20-212, 1956.

LAFAYETTE, MARQUIS DE. *Letters of. .. to George Washington, 1777-1799*, Louis Gottschalk (ed.). New York, 1944.

LEACH, DOUGLAS E. *Arms for Empire: A Military History of the British Colonies in North America*. New York: Macmillan, 1973.

LEACH, DOUGLAS E. "The Military System of Plymouth Colony," *New England Quarterly*, XXIV (Sep. 1951), 342-364.

LEACH, JACK F. *Conscription in the United States: Historical Background*. Rutland, Vt.: Tuttle Pub., 1952.

LEE, ULYSSES GRANT. *Employment of Negro Troops*. Washington, D.C., 1955. A volume in the series: *The United States Army in World War II*.

LEMAY, J. A. LEO. "The American Origins of 'Yankee Doodle.'" *William and Mary Quarterly*, XXXIII (July 1976), 435-464.

LERWILL, LEONARD. *History of the United States Replacement System*. Washington, D.C.: DA Pamphlet 20-211, 1954.

Levantrosser, William F. *Congress and the Citizen Soldier: Legislative Policy Making for the Federal Armed Forces Reserve.* Columbus: Ohio State Univ., 1967.

Lillie Papers. MSS, Archives of the U.S. Military Academy.

Linderman, Gerald F. *The Mirror of War: American Society and the Spanish American War.* Ann Arbor: Univ. of Michigan Press, 1974.

Livermore, Thomas L. *Numbers and Losses in the Civil War in America.* Civil War Centennial Series. Bloomington: Univ. of Indiana, reprinted, 1957.

Lockmiller, David A. *Enoch H. Crowder.* Columbia: Univ. of Missouri Press, 1955.

Lofgren, Charles A. "Compulsory Military Service under the Constitution: The Original Understanding," *William and Mary Quarterly,* XXXIII (Jan. 1976), 61-88.

Logan, John A. *The Volunteer Soldier of America.* Chicago: R. S. Peale, 1887.

London, Lena. "The Militia Fine, 1830-1860," *Military Affairs,* XV (Fall 1951), 133-144.

Lord, Francis A. *They Fought for the Union.* Harrisburg, Pa.: Stackpole, 1960.

Lossing, Benson J. *The Pictorial Field Book of the American Revolution,* 2 vols. New York: Harper's, 1960.

Love, Edmund G. *The 27th Infantry Division in World War II.* Washington, D.C.: Infantry Journal Press, 1949.

Lovejoy, David S. *The Glorious Revolution in America.* New York: Harper and Row, 1972.

McCague, James. *The Second Rebellion: New York Draft Riots.* New York: Dial Press, 1968.

McClellan, George B. "The Militia and the Army," *Harpers New Monthly Magazine,* LXXII (1886), 294-303.

McDugal, Lelia. *Up Hill and Down: A History of the Texas National Guard.* Waco, Texas: Texian Press, 1966.

McGlasson, W. D., "Mobilization 1940: The Big One," *National Guard,* XXXIV (Sep. 1980), 10-23.

McLain, Raymond S. Comments on Certain Aspects of the National Guard Considered Worthy of National War College Committee Study, 8 August 1951. Unpublished ditto machine pamphlet.

McLatchy, Patrick H. The Development of the National Guard of Washington (State) as an Instrument of Social Control, 1854-1916. Unpublished Ph.D. diss., Univ. of Washington, 1973.

McMaster, John Bach. *History of the People of the United States,* 8 vols. New York: Appleton, 1902-1912.

Mahon, John K. *The American Militia: Decade of Decision, 1789-1800.* Gainesville: Univ. of Florida Press, 1960.

Mahon, John K. "Anglo-American Methods of Indian Warfare, 1676-1764." *Mississippi Valley Historical Review,* XLV (Sep. 1958), 254-275.

Mahon, John K. "A Board of Officers Considers the Condition of the Militia in 1826," *Military Affairs,* XV (Summer 1951), 85-94.

Mahon, John K. The Citizen Soldier in National Defense, 1789-1815. Unpublished Ph.D. diss., UCLA, 1950.

MAHON, JOHN K., "The Defense of Georgia, 1794," *Georgia Historical Quarterly*, XLIII (June 1959), 138-155.

MAHON, JOHN K. *History of the Second Seminole War*. Gainesville: Univ. of Florida Press, 1965.

MAHON, JOHN K. "Pennsylvania and the Beginnings of the Regular Army," *Pennsylvania History* (Jan. 1954), 33-43.

MAHON, JOHN K., "Principal Causes for the Failure of the United States Militia System during the War of 1812," *Indiana Military History Journal*, IV (May 1979), pp 15-21.

MAHON, JOHN K. *The War of 1812*. Gainesville: Univ. of Florida Press, 1972.

MARCUS, RICHARD HENRY. The Militia of Colonial Connecticut, 1639-1775. Unpublished Ph.D. diss., Univ. of Colorado, 1965.

MARINE, WILLIAM M. *The British Invasion of Maryland, 1812-1815*. Baltimore, 1913.

Acts and Laws of the Commonwealth of Massachusetts, 1788-1805. Boston, reprinted by the state printer, 1895.

Laws of the Commonwealth of Massachusetts, 1806-1814. Laws of each session printed separately at Boston.

Military Archives of Massachusetts, MSS, State House, Boston.
  Letterbook Number 1 of the Adjutant General.
  Report of the Adjutant General for 1898.

MAYS, GEORGE, "Battalion or Training Day at Schaefferstown in the Olden Time," *Historical Papers and Addresses of the Lebanon County Historical Society*, Lebanon, Pa., I (1899), 148-168.

Mechanic's Free Press. Philadelphia, 1820s-1830.

MELLICK, ANDREW D., JR. *The Story of an Old Farm or Life in New Hampshire in the 18th Century*. Somerville, New Jersey, 1889.

Thomas Mifflin Papers. MSS, Pennsylvania Historical Commission, Harrisburg.

MERIWETHER, ROBERT L. (ed.). *The Papers of . . . John C. Calhoun*, vol I. Columbia: Univ. of South Carolina Press, 1959.

Military File, 1789-1815. MSS, South Carolina Historical Commission, Columbia.

"The Militia and the Army," *Harpers New Monthly Magazine*, LXXII (1886), 294-303.

JAMES MILLER PAPERS. MSS, Archives of the U.S. Military Academy.

MILLETT, JOHN DAVID. *The Organization and Role of the Army Service Forces*. Washington, D.C., 1954. A volume in the series: *The United States Army in World War II*.

MITCHELL, JAMES T. and HENRY FLANDERS (comps.). *Statutes at Large of Pennsylvania, 1682-1801*, 16 vols. Harrisburg, 1896-1911.

MOOK, H. TELFER, "Training Day in New England," *New England Quarterly*, XI (Dec. 1938), 675-697.

MOONEY, CHASE C. and MARTHA E. LAYMAN, "Some Phases of the Compulsory Military Training Movement," *Mississippi Valley Historical Review*, XXXVIII (March 1952), 633-656.

MORRILL, CHESTER. Mission and Organization of the Army National Guard of the United States with Emphasis on the Period since 1952. Unpublished Ph.D. diss., American Univ., 1958.

MURDOCH, EUGENE C. *One Million Men: The Civil War Draft*. Madison: State Historical Society of Wisconsin, 1971.

MURPHY, ELMER A. and ROBERT S. THOMAS. *The 30th Division in the World War*. Lepanto, Ark.: Old Hickory Pub., 1936.

National Archives, Old War Records Branch

Circular, Thomas Jefferson to Governors of the Territories Adjacent to Spain, 21 March 1807, MS.

Secretary of War to Governors, 18 Jan. 1809, MS.

Letters to Daniel D. Tompkins, Governor of New York, MSS.

William Henry Harrison to Secretary of War, 5 & 9 May 1813, MSS.

Secretary of War to James Wilkinson, 1 Jan. 1814, MS.

War Office Reports to Congress, MSS.

National Cyclopaedia of American Biography, vol. A. New York: James A. White Co., 1926.

National Guard. Washington, D.C., 1891-1892. Published by J. Polkinhorn for the National Guard of the District of Columbia.

National Guard Gazette. Columbia, Ohio, 1897.

The National Guardsman and Volunteer. Minneapolis, 1896-April 1902. Thereafter published in Chicago by E. W. Peckham and F. W. Barber through 1905.

National Guard Magazine. Columbus, Ohio. Col. Edward T. Miller, publisher, 1907-1917. Recognized by the NGA.

The National Guardsman. Washington, D.C. 1947, Redesignated in November 1978 as the *National Guard*. Official publication of the NGA.

National Guard Association, *Annual Reports*.

The National Guard and the Constitution. An American Civil Liberties Union Legal Study, prepared by Melvin L. Wulf and issued in photocopy, July 1971.

The Nation's National Guard. Addresses delivered by Major Generals Ellard Walsh and Edgar Erickson. Washington, D.C.: NGA, 1954.

NELSON, OTTO L. *National Security and the General Staff*. Washington, D.C.: Infantry Journal Press, 1946.

New Hampshire. *Constitution and Laws of . . . .* Dover, New Hampshire, 1805.

NICHOLS, ROGER L. *General Henry Atkinson: A Western Military Career*. Norman: Univ. of Oklahoma Press, 1965.

New York Times, 21 May 1898.

Niles Weekly Register, Hezekiah Niles (ed.), 76 vols. Baltimore, 1811-1849.

North Carolina Minerva and Fayetteville Gazette, 15 Dec. 1798.

NORTHEND, MARY H. *Memories of Old Salem*. New York: Moffet, Yard Co., 1917.

O'FLAHERTY, PATRICK D. History of the Sixty-ninth Regiment, New York State Militia, 1852-1861. Unpublished Ph.D. diss., Fordham Univ., 1963.

OLSON, RALPH J. "The Wisconsin National Guard," *Wisconsin Magazine of History*, XXXIX (Summer 1956), 231-233; 267-271.

Order of Battle of the United States Land Forces in the World War: AEF Divisions. Washington, D.C.: Historical Section, Army War College, 1931.

Ordnance. *Reports of the Chief of. . . .* Washington, D.C., 1895, 1897, 1898.

Organization and Status of Missouri Troops (Union and Confederate) in Service during the Civil War. War Dept. Record and Pension Office, 1902.

Organization of the Land Forces of the United States. 10 Aug. 1912. Washington, D.C., 1915.

O'RYAN, JOHN F. *The Story of the 27th Division,* 2 vols. New York: Wynkoop Pub., 1921.

OSWANDEL, J. JACOB. *Notes on the Mexican War, 1846, 1847, 1848.* Philadelphia, 1885.

PALMER, JOHN MCAULEY. *America in Arms.* New York: Oxford Univ. Press, 1941.

PALMER, JOHN MCAULEY. *An Army of the People.* New York: Putnam, 1916.

PALMER, JOHN MCAULEY. *Washington, Lincoln, Wilson.* New York: Doubleday, 1930.

PALMER, ROBERT R., BELL I. WILEY, and WILLIAM R. KEAST. *Procurement and Training of Ground Troops.* Washington, D.C., 1948. A volume in the series: *U.S. Army in World War II.*

PARKER, JOHN H. *Trained Citizen Soldiers: A Solution to General Upton's Problem.* Menasha, Wisconsin, 1916.

PAXON, FREDERICK LOGAN. *America at War, 1917-1918.* Boston, 1939. This is vol. II of *American Democracy and the World War,* 3 vols.

PEASE, THEODORE CALVIN (ed.). *Laws of the Northwest Territory.* Springfield, Ill.: *Illinois State Historical Library Collections,* vol. VIII, 1925.

PECKHAM, CHARLES A. "The Ohio National Guard and Its Police Duties," *Ohio History,* LXXXIII (Winter 1974), 51-67.

PECKHAM, HOWARD H. *The Colonial Wars, 1689-1762.* Univ. of Chicago Press, 1962.

PERSHING, GENERAL JOHN J. *Final Report of. . .: Commander in Chief, American Expeditionary Force.* Washington, D.C., 1920.

PHISTERER, FREDERICK. *Statistical Record of the Armies of the United States.* New York: Scribner's, 1884.

PRATT, WALTER M. *Tin Soldiers: The Organized Militia and What It Really Is.* Boston: R. G. Badger, 1912.

PROCTOR, HARRY G. *The Iron Division: National Guard of Pennsylvania in the World War.* Philadelphia: John C. Winston Co., 1919.

A Proper Military Policy for the United States. Washington, D.C., 1915.

PULLEN, JOHN J. *The Twentieth Maine.* Philadelphia, 1954.

QUINER, EDAIN B. *The Military History of Wisconsin . . . in the War for the Union.* Chicago: Clark Co., 1866.

RADABAUGH, JACK S. "The Militia of Colonial Massachusetts." *Military Affairs,* XVIII (Spring 1954), 1-18.

The Red Arrow: 32nd Division, Wisconsin National Guard, 1955. Prepared by Division staff, no place or date shown.

Register of the Graduates and Former Cadets of the United States Military Academy, 1802-1965. Civil War Centennial Edition, West Point Alumni Fund, 1965.

REID, WHITELAW. *Ohio in the War*, 2 vols. Cincinnati: Moore, Willstock, 1868.

REMINI, ROBERT V. *Andrew Jackson and the Course of American Empire, 1767-1812*. New York: Harper and Row, 1977.

Reports

    Report of the Military Secretary of the Army on the Militia for the Fiscal Year Ended 30 June 1905. Washington, D.C., 1906.

    Report of the Military Secretary of the Army on the Militia for the Fiscal Year Ended 30 June 1906. Washington, D.C., 1907.

    Report of the Adjutant General of the Army Relative to the Militia . . . for the Fiscal Year Ended 30 June 1907. Washington, D.C., 1908.

    Report of the Division of Militia Affairs, 15 Oct. 1908. Washington, D.C., 1908.

    Reports of the Chief, Division of Militia Affairs. All reports from 1909 through 1932. In 1933, the Division was redesignated the National Guard Bureau.

    Annual Reports, Chief of the National Guard Bureau. All reports from 1933-1975 except: 1938-1939, 1943-1945, 1953, 1959-1961, 1964-1965.

    Annual Review, Fiscal Year 1976 and Terminal Quarter, Chief, National Guard Bureau. Washington, D.C., 1977.

    Annual Review, Fiscal Year 1977, Chief National Guard Bureau. Washington, 1978.

    The Report of the President's Committee on an All-Volunteer Force. New York: Collier Books/Macmillan, 1970.

RICE, JAMES M. "The Defense of Our Frontier," *Journal of the Military Service Institution*, XVIII (March 1896), 298-320.

RICH, BENNET M. and PHILIP BURCH, "The Changing Role of the National Guard," *American Political Science Review*, L (Sep. 1956), 702-706.

RICHARDSON, JAMES D. (ed.). *Messages and Papers of the Presidents*, 10 vols. Washington, D.C., 1899.

RIKER, WILLIAM H. *Soldiers of the States: The Role of the National Guard in American Democracy*. Washington, D.C.: Public Affairs Press, 1958.

ROBERTS, RICHARD C. History of the Utah National Guard, 1894-1954. Ph.D. diss., Univ. of Utah, 1973.

ROBERTSON, JOHN, *Michigan in the War*. Lansing: W. S. George Co., 1882.

RODENBOUGH, THEO F. "Militia Reform without Legislation," *Journal of the Military Service Institution*, II (1882), 388-420.

ROE, ALFRED S. *The Fifth Regiment, Massachusetts Volunteer Infantry*. Boston, 1911.

ROLAND, CHARLES P. *Albert Sidney Johnston*. Austin: Univ. of Texas Press, 1964.

ROOT, ELIHU. *The Military and Colonial Policy of the United States: Addresses and Reports by . . .*, Robert Bacon and James Brown Scott (eds.). Cambridge, Mass., 1916.

Russell Petroleum Co. v. Walker. *162 Oklahoma Reports*, 216.

RUTMAN, DARRETT B. A Militant New World, 1607-1640. Ph.D. diss., Univ. of Virginia, 1959. Photocopy by Arno Press as part of Richard H. Kohn, ed. *The American Military Experience*, New York, 1979.

ST. CLAIR, ARTHUR. *A Narrative of the Manner in which the Campaign against the Indians in the Year 1791 was Conducted.* Philadelphia: J. Aitken, 1812.

SANGER, WILLIAM C. *Report on Reserve and Auxiliary Forces of England and the Militia of Switzerland.* Prepared for President McKinley and Secretary Root. Washington, 1903.

SCHEIPS, PAUL J. "Enforcement of the Federal Judicial Process by Federal Marshals," in Robin Higham, ed., *Bayonets in the Streets.* Lawrence: Univ. of Press of Kansas, 1969.

SCHLISSEL, LILLIAN (ed.). *Conscience in America: A Documentary History of Conscientious Objection in America.* New York: Dutton, 1968.

SCHWOERER, LOIS G. *No Standing Armies.* Baltimore: John Hopkins Univ. Press, 1974.

SCISCO, LOUIS DOW. "Evolution of the Colonial Militia in Maryland," *Maryland Historical Magazine,* XXXV (June 1940), 166-177.

Secretary of Defense. Annual Reports on Reserve Forces for Fiscal Years 1957-1960, 1965-1968. Washington, D.C.

SEMMES, RAPHAEL S. *Service Afloat and Ashore during the War with Mexico.* Cincinnati: W. H. Moore, 1851.

SEXTON, WILLIAM THADDEUS. *Soldiers in the Philippines.* First published in 1939; reprint, Washington, D.C.: Infantry Journal Press, 1944.

SHEA, WILLIAM LEE. To Defend Virginia: The Evolution of the First Colonial Militia, 1607-1677. Unpublished Ph.D. diss., Rice Univ., 1975.

SHEPHERD, SAMUEL (ed.). *The Statutes at Large of Virginia, 1792-1806.* Richmond, 1835.

SHERMAN, WILLIAM TECUMSEH. "The Militia . . .," *Journal of the Military Service Institution,* VI (March 1885), 1-26.

SHY, JOHN. "Mobilizing Armed Force in the American Revolution," in *The American Revolution: A Heritage of Change,* John Parker and Carol Urness (eds.). Minneapolis: Univ. of Minnesota Press, 1973.

SHY, JOHN. "A New Look at the Colonial Militia," *William and Mary Quarterly,* XX (April 1963), 175-185. Reprinted in *A People Numerous and Armed.* New York: Oxford Univ. Press. 1976.

SINGLETARY, OTIS A. *Negro Militia and Reconstruction.* Austin: Univ. of Texas Press, 1957.

SMITH, HENRY I. *History of the Seventh Iowa Veteran Volunteer Infantry during the Civil War.* Mason City, Iowa, 1903.

SMITH, HOLLAND M. *Coral and Brass.* New York: Scribner's, 1949.

SMITH, JUSTIN H. *The War with Mexico,* 2 vols. New York: Macmillan 1919.

South Carolina Historical Commission, Columbia, Military File, MS.

STARKEY, MARION L. *A Little Rebellion* (Shays' Rebellion). New York: Knopf, 1955.

Statistical History of the United States from Colonial Times to the Present. Stamford, Conn.: Fairfield Publishers, 1965.

STEPHENS, LOWNDES F., "Citizen Soldiers: Why They Enlist and Reenlist," *Military Review,* LVII (Sec. 1977), 35-40.

STEPHENS, LOWNDES F., "Recruiting and Retaining the Citizen Soldier," *Armed Forces and Society*, IV (Fall 1977), 29-39.

Sterling v. Constantin, *287 U.S. Reports*, 378 (1932).

STERN, FREDERICK MARTIN. *The Citizen Army*. New York: St. Martin's Press, 1957.

STEVENSON, CHARLES G. "Reason for Being," *National Guardsman*, IX (Jan. 1955).

STONE, RICHARD G., JR. *A Brittle Sword: The Kentucky Militia, 1776-1912*. Lexington: Univ. Press of Kentucky, 1977.

STORY, CHARLES DALE. The Formulation of Army Reserve Forces Policy. Ph.D. diss., Univ. of Oklahoma, 1959.

STRICKLAND, EDWIN and GENE WORTSMAN. *Phenix City*. Birmingham, Ala.: Vulcan Press, 1955.

SWOMLEY, JOHN M., JR. The Universal Military Training Campaign, 1944-1952. Ph.D. diss., University of Colorado, 1959.

Tallahassee *Floridian*. 1835-1842.

TAYLOR, EMERSON G. *New England in France, 1917-1919: History of the 26th Division*. Boston: Houghton Mifflin, 1920.

The 32nd Division in the World War, 1917-1919. By a committee headed by Charles King. Madison, Wisconsin, 1920.

The 35th Infantry Division in World War II. Produced by Albert Love Enterprises, Atlanta, 1946.

TODD, FREDERICK PORTER. "The Militia and Volunteers of the District of Columbia," *Records of the Columbia Historical Society*, L.

TODD, FREDERICK PORTER, "Our National Guard: An Introduction to Its History," *Military Affairs*, V (Summer 1941), 73-86; (Fall 1941), 152-170.

TRASK, DAVID F. *The War with Spain in 1898*. New York: Macmillan, 1981.

TRENCHARD, JOHN. *Argument Showing that a Standing Army is Inconsistent with a Free Government*. London, 1697.

TRENCHARD, JOHN. *A Letter from the Author of the Argument against a Standing Army to the Author of the Balancing Letter*. London, 1697.

Twentieth Century Minutemen. A Report to the President on a Reserve Forces Training Program by the National Security Training Commission. Washington, D.C., 1 Dec. 1953.

United States Army Military History Institute, Carlisle Barracks, Pa.

Bulletin 12, Headquarters, U.S. Army, 8 Aug. 1919.

Civilian Components Policy Board. Minutes of meetings beginning in January 1950.

Civilian Components Policy Board. Progress Report of the Research and Planning Staff of . . ., 1 Jan. 1950. Stencilled.

Civilian Components Policy Board. Staff Memo. No date.

Department of Defense Policies Relating to the Reserve Forces, approved by Gen. G. C. Marshall, 6 April 1951.

FORRESTAL, JAMES. Report Covering the Present State of Readiness of the Several Reserve Components, 14 Dec. 1948. Stencilled copy attached to an 18-page letter to the president. 39 pp.

General Orders No. 3, Headquarters of the Army, 7 Jan. 1907.

General Orders No. 99, Headquarters of the Army, 11 June 1908.

History of the National Guard and National Guard Bureau. Army adviser orientation presented by Army Division NGB, 27 Jan. 1958. Photocopy, 73 pp. plus charts.

Interview Transcript: General Reckord interviewed by LTC Bernie Callahan. Senior Officer Debriefing Program, 1974.

LTC. Charles S. D'Orsa to a National Guard Training conference, 14 Aug. 1950.

Memo on Army Policies on the Training of Civilian Reserves, 16 Jan. 1946. Typed.

Memo for War Department Agencies on Combat Units for the Organized Reserves, 26 Dec. 1946.

National Guard Bureau, Office of the Assistant Chief of the . . . Army Area Conference, 1961. Stencilled.

Rose, William B. Training the National Guard. Stencil, 17 April 1954.

School of Instructions for State Adjutants General, 1924. Washington, 1925.

School of Instructions for State Adjutants General, 5-10 March 1925. Washington, 1925.

United States Statutes at Large

To provide for calling forth the Militia to execute the laws of the Union, suppress insurrections and repel invasions, 2 May 1792, I.

More effectually to provide for the National Defense by Establishing a Uniform Militia throughout the United States, 8 May 1792, I.

Directing a Detachment from the Militia of the United States, 9 May 1794, I.

Authorizing a detachment from the Militia of the United States, 24 June 1797, I.

Authorizing the President of the United States to Raise a Provisional Army, 28 May 1798, I.

Making appropriation for the Military establishment for the Year 1798; and for other purposes, 12 June 1798, I.

To amend an act entitled "An act authorizing the President of the United States to raise a provisional army, 22 June 1798, I.

Providing Arms for the Militia throughout the United States, 6 July 1798, I.

Making appropriation for the Military establishment of the United States for the year 1801, 2 March 1801, II.

Making appropriation for the Military establishment of the United States in the year 1803, 3 March 1803, II.

Authorizing the President of the United States to accept the service of a number of volunteer companies, not exceeding 30,000 men, 24 Feb. 1807, II.

Authorizing the employment of the land and naval forces of the United States in cases of insurrections, 3 March 1807, II.

Making provision for arming and equipping the whole body of the Militia of the United States, 23 April 1808, II.

To Promote the Efficiency of the Militia . . ., 21 Jan. 1903, XXXII.

Making an Appropriation for the Support of the Army, 2 March 1907, XXXIV, part 1.

Further to Amend an Act entitled "An Act to Promote the Efficiency of the Militia . . ." passed 21 Jan. 1903, 27 May 1908, XXXV, part 1.

To Provide for Raising the Volunteer Forces of the United States in Time of Actual or Threatened war, 25 April 1914, XXXVIII, part 1.

Making Further and more Effectual Provision for the National Defense and for Other Purposes, 3 June 1916, XXXIX, part 1.

Authorizing the President to Increase temporarily the Military Establishment of the United States (Selective Service Act), 18 May 1917, XL, part 1.

To Amend an Act Entitled "An Act for making further and more effective provision for the National Defense, 4 June 1920, XLI, part 1.

To Amend the National Defense Act of 1916 as amended, 15 June 1933, XLVIII, part 1.

To Provide for the common defense by increasing the personnel of the armed forces of the United States and providing for its training, 16 Sep. 1940, LIV, part 1.

Selective Service Act, 24 June 1948, LXIV. This Act was redesignated as the Universal Military Service and Training Act on 19 June 1951, LXV.

Armed Forces Reserve Act, 9 July 1952, LXVI.

Reserve Forces Act, 9 Aug. 1955, LXIX.

UPSHAM, CYRIL B. "Historical Survey of the Militia in Iowa," *Iowa Journal of History and Politics*, XVII (July 1919), 299-405.

UPTON, EMORY. *Military Policy of the United States*. Washington, D.C., 1907.

VAN RENSSELAER, SOLOMON. *A Narrative of the Affair at Queenstown in the War of 1812*. New York, 1836.

Vermont, *Report of the Adjutant and Inspector General*, 1 Nov. 1862. Montpelier.

VIORST, MILTON. *Fire in the Streets*. New York: Simon & Schuster, 1979.

WACHS, WILLIAM RONALD. "Off Guard": The National Guard and Race-related Disturbances in the 1950's. Unpublished Ph.D. diss., Univ. of North Carolina, 1977.

WAITE, OTIS F. R. *New Hampshire in the Great Rebellion*. Claremont, N.H.: N. H. Tracy, 1870.

WAKSMUNDSKI, JOHN, "Governor McKinley and the Working Man," *Historian*, XXXVIII (Aug. 1976), 629-647.

WALKER, FRED L. *From Texas to Rome*. Dallas, Texas: Taylor Publishing Co., 1969.

WARD, CHRISTOPHER. *The War of the Revolution*, 2 vols. New York: Macmillan, 1952.

WARD, ROBERT DAVID. The Movement for Universal Military Training, 1942-1952. Unpublished Ph.D. diss., Univ. of North Carolina, 1957.

WARNE, COLSTON E. *The Pullman Boycott of 1894*. Boston: D. C. Heath, 1955.

Warren-Adams Letters. Massachusetts Historical Society, Collections, LXXII-LXXIII. Boston, 1917-1925.

WASHINGTON, GEORGE. *Writings of . . .*, John C. Fitzpatrick (ed.), 39 vols. Washington, D.C., 1931-1944.

WATKINS, GEORGE and ROBERT. *Digest of the Laws of the State of Georgia.* Philadelphia, 1800.

WATSON, MARK S. *Chief of Staff: Prewar Plans and Preparations.* Washington, 1950. A volume in *United States Army in World War II.*

WEBB, STEPHENS S. "The Strange Career of Francis Nicholson," *William and Mary Quarterly,* XXIII (1966), 513-546.

Webster's American Military Biographies. Springfield, Mass.: G. & C. Merriam Co., 1978.

WEIGLEY, RUSSELL. *History of the United States Army.* New York: Macmillan, 1967.

WEIGLEY, RUSSELL. *Towards an American Army.* Westport, Conn.: Greenwood, 1974.

WELLMAN, PAUL I. *Indian Wars of the West.* Garden City, N.Y.: Doubleday, 1947.

WELLS, WARREN K. "Air Defense and the Air National Guard," *Military Review,* XLI (Sep. 1961), 85-90.

WERNER, ROY A. "The Other Military: Are Reserve Forces Viable?" *Military Review,* LVII (April 1977), 20-36.

WESTOVER, JOHN GLENDOWER. Evolution of the Missouri Militia, 1804-1919. Unpublished Ph.D. diss., Univ. of Missouri, 1948.

WHEELER, EARL MILTON, "Development and Organization of the North Carolina Militia," *North Carolina Historical Review,* XLI (July 1964), 307-323.

WHEELER, EARL MILTON. The Role of the North Carolina Militia in the Beginning of the American Revolution. Unpublished Ph.D. diss., Tulane Univ., 1969.

WHIPPLE, GEORGE M. *History of Salem Light Infantry, 1805-1890.* Salem, Mass.: Essex Institute, 1890.

WHITE, FRANK F. JR. (ed.). "Macomb's Mission to the Seminoles: John T. Sprague's Journal . . .," *Florida Historical Quarterly.* XXXV (Oct. 1956), 130-193.

WHITTEMORE, CHARLES P. *A General of the Revolution: John Sullivan of New Hampshire.* New York: Columbia Univ. Press, 1961.

Why Merge? Chief of Information, Department of the Army, Washington, D.C., March, 1965.

WIENER, FREDERICK BERNAYS. "The Militia Clause of the Constitution," *Harvard Law Review,* LIV (Dec. 1940), 181-220.

WILLARD, MARGARET WHEELER (ed.). *Letters on the American Revolution, 1774-1776.* First published 1925; reissued by Kennikat Press, 1968.

WOOD, STERLING A. *Riot Control by the National Guard.* Harrisburg, Pa.: Military Service Pub., 1942.

Working Man's Advocate. New York, 31 Oct. 1829-5 Jan. 1830.

YARMOLINSKY, ADAM. *The Military Establishment.* New York: Harper, 1971.

YELLEN, SAMUEL. *American Labor Struggles.* New York: Harcourt, 1936.

ZIERDT, WILLIAM H. *Narrative History of the 109th Field Artillery, Pennsylvania National Guard.* Wilkes-Barre, Pa.: E. P. Yordy, 1932.

Sources Created by the United States Congress and Cited in the Footnotes

Annals of Congress, 42 vols. Washington, D.C.: Gales and Seaton, 1832-1856.

Congressional Globe, 109 vols. Washington, D.C., 1834-1873.

Congressional Record. Washington, D.C., 1873-

Report of the Secretary of War, 28 Nov. 1826. *Sen. Doc. 1*, 19 Cong., 2 sess.

Report of the Committee on Militia, 27 Feb. 1827. *HR Report 92*, 19 Cong., 1 sess.

Report of a Committee on Militia, 4 Feb. 1829. *HR Doc. 68*, 20 Cong., 2 sess.

Arming the Militia, 3 March 1830. *HR Doc. 72*, 20 Cong., 1 sess.

Memorial of the Officers of Massachusetts Militia to Improve the Militia System, 23 Feb. 1831. *Sen Doc. 62*, 21 Cong., 2 sess.

Defense of the United States, 5 April 1836. *Sen. Doc. 293*, 24 Cong., 1 sess.

Report of a Militia Committee, 4 May 1838. *HR Report 875*, 25 Cong., 2 sess.

Memorial of Alden Partridge and Edmund Burke . . . Praying Adoption of a Plan Proposed by them for Reorganizing the Militia, 9 Feb. 1839. *Sen. Doc. 197*, 25 Cong., 3 sess.

Militia of the United States, 20 March 1840. *Sen. Docs. 531 & 560*, 26 Cong., 1 sess.

Annual Report of the Secretary of War, 30 June 1898, *HR Doc. 2*, 55 Cong., 3 sess.

Increase of the Efficiency of the Army. Hearing by the Senate Military Affairs Committee, 5 May 1910, 61 Cong., 2 sess.

Hearing before the HR Committee on Military Affairs on HR 29496: A Bill to increase the Efficiency of the Organized Militia, and for other purposes. Washington, D.C., 1911.

Preparedness for National Defense. Hearings, Sen. Committee on Military Affairs, 64 Cong., 1 sess. Washington, D.C., 1916.

Hearings before HR Committee on Military Affairs, 3 Sep.-12 Nov. 1919. 66 Cong., 1 sess.

Reorganization of the Army. Hearings before the Senate Subcommittee on Military Affairs, 1919. 66 Cong., 1 sess.

National Guard Bill. HR Report 141, 16 May 1933, 73 Cong., 1 sess.

National Guard Armories. Joint Hearings Senate and House Committees on Military Affairs, 17 April 1935, 74 Cong., 1 sess.

Disbursement of Funds for Care of National Guard Material . . ., Senate Military Affairs Committee, 7 April 1938, 75 Cong., 3 sess.

Compulsory Military Training and Service. Hearings before HR Committee on Military Affairs, 10, 11 July, 24, 26 July, 30, 31 July, 1 & 2 & 12-14 Aug. 1940, 76 Cong., 3 sess.

Retention of Reserve Components and Selectees Beyond Twelve Months. Hearings before Senate Committee on Military Affairs, July 1941, 77 Cong., 1 sess.

Hearings before the House Select Committee on Post-war Military Policy, 24 April 1944, 78 Cong., 2 sess.

Universal Military Training. Hearings before the House Select Committee on Post-war Military Policy, June 1945, 79 Cong., 1 sess.

Reserve Components. Hearings before the House Committee on Armed Services, 8-15 Jan., 18-30 April, 3 July & 1-22 Aug. 1951, 82 Cong., 1 sess.

Full Armed Services Committee of the House on the Armed Forces Reserve Bill. 27-29 Sep. 1951. *HR Report 1066*, 82 Cong., 1 sess.

Hearings before Subcommittee No. 1 of House Committee on Armed Forces on HR 5472 to Amend the Universal Military Training and Service Act as amended, 2 May 1952.

Armed Forces Reserve Act. Hearings before a Subcommittee of the Senate Committee on Armed Services, 26-29 May 1952, 82 Cong., 2 sess. The Appendix contains "A Brief History of U.S. Military Policy on Reserve Forces, 1775-1951," pp. 317-344.

Armed Forces Reserve Act. Sen. Report 1795, 19 June 1952. 82 Cong., 2 sess.

Status of Reserve and National Guard Forces of the Armed Services. Report of the Interim Subcommittee on Preparedness of the Senate Committee on Armed Services. There is a second report dated 28 Dec. 1954, 83 Cong., 2 sess.

Providing for Strengthening of the Reserve Forces. HR Report 987, 28 June 1955, 84 Cong., 1 sess.

A National Reserve Plan. Hearings before the Senate Armed Services Committee, July 1955, 84 Cong., 1 sess.

Presentation of a National Reserve Plan by Carter L. Burgess, assistant secretary of defense for manpower and personnel, before the House Armed Forces Subcommittee No. 1, 15 Feb. 1955. Separately printed, Washington, D.C., 1955.

Review of the Reserve Program. Hearings before the House Armed Services Committee 1957, 85 Cong., 1 sess.

Proposal to Realign the Army National Guard and the Army Reserve Forces. Hearings before the Preparedness Investigating Subcommittee of the Senate Committee on the Armed Services, March 1965.

Merger of the Army Reserve Components. Hearings before Subcommittee Number 2 of the House Committee on the Armed Services, 25, 26, 29-31 March; 5-9, 12, 14, 29 April; 2-4 Aug., 30 Sep. 1965, 89 Cong., 1 sess.

Statement of General Harold K. Johnson, Chief of Staff, U. S. Army, before the Preparedness Investigating Subcommittee of the Senate Committee on the Armed Services, 1 March 1965. Stencilled copy, 1965, U.S. Army Military History Institute.

Statement of Stanley R. Resor, secretary of the army, before the Senate Armed Services Committee, 26 June 1967. Included is Resor's statement of 11 Sep. 1967. Stencilled copy, 1967, U. S. Army Military History Institute.

A Volunteer Armed and Selective Service. Hearings before Subcommittee on a Volunteer Armed Force of the Senate Armed Services Committee, March 1972, 92 Cong., 2 sess.

Hearings on Military Posture and on HR 12604, Feb.-April 1972. House Committee on Armed Services, 92 Cong., 2 sess.

Military Manpower Issues of Past and Future. Subcommittee on Manpower of Senate Armed Services Committee, Aug. 1974, 93 Cong., 2 sess.

Reserve Call-up. Hearings before Subcommittee on Manpower of Senate Armed Services Committee, July 30, 1975, 94 Cong., 1 sess.

Materials, Published and Unpublished, Consulted Profitably But Not Cited in the Notes

ADAMS, JOHN QUINCY. *The Diary of. . ., 1794-1845*. New York: Scribner's, 1951.

ADAMS, MARY P. Jefferson's Military Policy. Ph.D. diss., Univ. of Virginia, 1958.

AMBROSE, STEPHEN E. *Halleck: Lincoln's Chief of Staff*. Baton Rouge: Louisiana State Univ. Press, 1962.

_____. *Duty, Honor, Country: A History of West Point*. Baltimore: Johns Hopkins Univ. Press, 1966.

ANDERSON, T. M., "Militia, Past and Present." *Journal of the Military Service Institution*. LIX (July-Aug. 1916), 75-79.

ARIELI, YEHOSHUA, *Individualism and Nationalism in American Ideology*, Cambridge, Mass.: Harvard Univ. Press, 1964.

The Army National Guard, 30 June 1950-8 Sep. 1951. Typescript marked *Restricted*, U. S. Army Military History Institute.

Army Study of the Guard and Reserve Forces: Alternatives for Improved Army Forces Capabilities, 4 vols. 15 May 1972. U. S. Army Combat Development Commands: Strategic Studies Institute. *Secret*.

Army War College Studies

Study of the Laws Relating to the Organization of the Militia and Volunteer Forces with a History of the Operations and Efficiency of these Forces in our Several Wars. Study Number 13, 1905-1906, in four parts. Typescript.

United States Planning for Past Wars. Typescript, 1927-1928.

A Study of Volunteer Enlistments, Army of the United States, 1775-1945. Typescript compiled under the direction of Col. C. C. Benson by the Historical Section, AWC, 23 pp., Sep. 1945.

KALLMAN, HOWARD J. Reserve Forces Preparedness. Unpublished study, March 15, 1955. Marked Confidential.

Reinforcing United States Forces in Europe: Implications for the Reserve components. Prepared by five members of the Class of 1977-1978. Secret.

Authority of the President to Send Militia into a Foreign Country. In *Official Opinions of the Attorney Generals of the U. S. Advising the President and*

Heads of Departments in Relation to Their Official Duties. Kearney, George (ed.). Washington, D.C., 1913.

AVINS, ALFRED, "State Court Review of National Guard Courts Martial," *Cornell Law Quarterly*, XLI (Spring 1956), 457-471.

AXTELL, GEORGE C. J. and ROBERT S. STUBBS II. "Universal Military Training: A Study," *George Washington Law Review*, XX (March 1952), 450-488.

AYRES, GEORGE B. "Old Time Militia Training," *Transactions of the Historical Society of Dauphin County, Pennsylvania*, I (1903), 156-158.

Backgrounds of Selective Service System. Special Monograph No. 1 has 14 vols; 13 of them are devoted, one each, to the original 13 colonies. Special Monograph No. 2 has 5 vols. and related to the draft beginning with 1940. There are 17 additional special monographs, some with several volumes each. Washington, D.C., 1949.

BEAUMONT, ROGER A. "Constabulary or Fire Brigade? The Army National Guard," *Parameters*, XII (March 1982), pp. 62-69.

BELL, RAYMOND E. "They Did the Air Guard Proud." *National Guardsman*, XIX (May 1965), 17-19.

_____. "Newburgh National Guardsmen Take Pride in History Going Back to 1738," *Cornwall Local*, New York, 15 March 1972, 4, 5.

_____. "Army Reserve Schools," *Army* (June 1972), 53, 54.

_____, "National Guard Post Planning," *The Military Engineer.* (May-June 1972), 186, 187.

_____, "Guard Tanks," *Armor* (Jan.-Feb. 1975), 32-36.

_____, "The National Guard-Army Partnership: The Key Is Mutual Respect," *Army* (Jan. 1976), 24-26.

_____, "Affiliation Is the Key to National Guard Recruiting," *Army* (Nov. 1976), 57-59.

_____, "Die Nationalgarde der USA," *Oster Militär Zeitschrift* (March 1977), 201-212.

BELLOWS, HENRY A. *A Treatise on Riot Duty for the National Guard.* Washington, D.C.: GPO, 1920.

BERNARDO, C. JOSEPH and EUGENE H. BACON. *American Military Policy.* Harrisburg, Pa.: Military Science Pub., 1955.

BOIES, H. M. "Our National Guard," *Harper's Magazine*, IX (May 1880), 915-923.

BRAYTON, ABBOTT A. "American Reserve Policies since World War II," *Military Affairs*, XXXVI (Dec. 1972), 139-144.

BROOKS, ELBRIDGE STREETER. *The Story of the American Soldier in War and Peace.* Boston: Lothrop, 1889.

BRUNDAGE, LYLE D. The Organization, Administration and Training of the United States Ordinary and Volunteer Militia, 1792-1861, Unpublished Ph.D. diss., Univ. of Michigan, 1959.

BUSH, HAROLD M. *The Diary of an Enlisted Man.* Columbus, Ohio: E. T. Miller, 1908.

CARTER, WILLIAM H. "The Militia Not a National Force," *North American Review*, CLXLVI (July 1912), 130-135.

Casey, Powell A. "Early History of the Washington Artillery of New Orleans," *Louisiana Historical Quarterly*, XXIII (1940), 471-484.

Casso, Evans J. *Louisiana Legacy: A History of the State National Guard.* Gretna, La.: Pelican Press, 1976.

Chester, James. "Organization of Militia Defense for the United States," *Journal of the Military Service Institution*, XIII (Sep. 1892), 907-936.

Clark George. *War and Society in the 17th Century.* Cambridge: At the Univ. Press, 1958.

Cloudman, S. B. "Recollections of the Old Time Militia and the Annual General Muster," *Collections of the Maine Historical Society*, series 3, vol. II, 1906, 331-341.

Coakley, Robert W. "Federal Use of Militia and the National Guard in Civil Disturbances: the Whiskey Rebellion to Little Rock," in Robin Higham, *Bayonets in the Streets*. Lawrence: Univ. Press of Kansas, 1969.

Cole, David W. "A Brief Outline of South Carolina's Colonial Militia System," *Proceedings, South Carolina Historical Association*, 1954, 14-23.

A Comparison of Mr. Poinsett's Plan for the Reorganization of the Militia with That of General Harrison, and Both with the Old Law. Washington, D.C.: Globe Printing, 1840.

Compulsory Military Training and Service. Hearings before the Senate Committee on Military Affairs, July 1940. 76 Cong., 3 sess.

Cooper, Mildred Jo. The Virginia Militia, 1700-1763. Unpublished M.A. thesis, Duke Univ., 1951

Cooper, Richard V. L. *Military Manpower and the All-volunteer Force.* Santa Monica, Calif.: Rand Corp., 1978.

Covington, Harry F. (ed.). "The Worcester County Militia of 1794," *Maryland Historical Magazine*, XXI (June 1926), 149-169.

Cramer, Kenneth F. "The National Guard: Our Modern Minutemen, 1795-1948," *Armored Cavalry Journal*, LVII (1948), 40-42.

———. "The National Guard in the Post-war Military Establishment," *Military Review*, XXVIII (June 1948), 3-9.

Crist, Allan G. and W. D. McGlasson, "A Century of Service," *National Guard*, XXXII (Nov. 1978), 6-9, 40-47.

Cunliffe, Marcus. "The American Military Tradition," in *British Essays in American History*, H. C. Allen and C. P. Hill (eds.). New York: St. Martin's Press, 1957.

Cunningham, Frank Dale. The Army and Universal Military Training, 1942-1948. Unpublished Ph.D. diss., Univ. of Texas, 1976.

Damon, Frank C., "Danvers Light Infantry, 1818-1851," *Collections of the Danvers Historical Society* (Mass.), XIV (1926), 1-24; XV (1927), 49-64.

Davies, Godfrey, "The Militia in 1685," *English Historical Review*, XLIII (1928), 604, 605.

Davis, T. Frederick. "The First Militia Organization," *Florida Historical Quarterly*, XXIV (April 1946), 290-292.

Dayton, Dello G., "Polished Boot and Brand New Suit: California Militia in

Community Affairs, 1849-1866," *California Historical Society Quarterly*, XXXVII (Dec. 1958), 359-368; XXXVIII (1959), 17-23.

Debow's Review, 34 vols. New Orleans, 1846-1864.

Department of Defense Policies Relating to the Reserve Forces. Approved by G. C. Marshall, 6 April 1951.

DIFFENDERFFER, F. R., "The Militia Muster," *Historical Papers and Addresses of the Lancaster County Historical Society*, IV (1899-1900), Lancaster Pennsylvania, 33-43.

DUNN, EDWARD C. "U. S. Army Command and General Staff School Role in Reserve Component Affairs," *Military Review*, XXXVIII (Nov. 1958), 57-67.

DUTCHER, L. L. "June Training in Vermont," *Vermont Historical Gazetteer*, II (1871), 347-355.

EBEL, WILFRED L. "Guard and Reserve Forces," *Military Review*, LIV (March 1974), 21-24.

EKIRCH, ARTHUR A. JR. "The Idea of a Citizen Army," *Military Affairs*, XVIII (Spring 1953), 30-36.

ELIOT, GEORGE FIELDING. *Reserve Forces and the Kennedy Strategy*. Harrisburg, Pa.: Stackpole, 1962.

ESCH, JOHN J. "Our Second Line—The National Guard," *North American Review*, CLXXVII (Aug. 1903), 288-296.

EVANS, BILL. "The Greening of Spec 4 William O. Evans," *Gainesville Sun* (Florida), 5 June 1977.

EVERETT, DONALD E. "Emigres and Militiamen: Free Persons of Color in New Orleans, 1803-1815," *Journal of Negro History*, XXXVIII (Oct. 1953), 377-402.

FISHEL, JOHN T. "Effective Use of Reserve Components," *Military Review*, LVII (May 1977), 58-62.

FLEMING, V. KEITH. "Mobilizing of a Rifle Company," *National Guard*, XXXIV (Sep. 1980).

FRASER, RICHARD H. Foundations of American Military Policy, 1783-1800. Unpublished Ph.D. diss., Univ. of Oklahoma, 1959.

FRENCH, ALLEN. "The Arms and Military Training of Our Colonial Ancestors," *Proceedings of the Massachusetts Historical Society*, LXVII (1945), 3-22.

(FRENCH, W. C.). *Reform of the Militia*. Boston: William C. Brown, 1855.

FULLER, EZRA B. "The Relationship of the National Guard to the United States and to the Regular Army," *National Guard Magazine*, I (Nov. 1907), 567-569.

FURBER, GEORGE C. *The 12-month Volunteer: A Journal of a Private in the Tennessee Regiment of Cavalry in the Campaign in Mexico, 1846-1847*. Cincinnati: V. P. James, 1857.

GABRIEL, RICHARD A. and PAUL L. SAVAGE. *Crisis in Command: Mismanagement in the Army*. New York: Hil and Wang, 1978.

GANOE, WILLIAM ADDLEMAN. *History of the United States Army*. New York: D. Appleton-Century, 1924.

GANS, DANIEL. "Active Army Support of the Reserve Components," *Military Review*, LIV (July 1974), 78-89.

GEORGE, ALBERT E. and EDWIN H. COOPER. *Pictorial History of the 26th.* Boston, Ball Park, 1920.

GIFIN, WILLIAM W. "Mobilization of Black Militiamen in World War I: Ohio's 9th Battalion," *The historian, XL (Aug. 1978), 686-703.*

GOEBEL, DOROTHY B. and JULIUS J. *Generals in the White House.* Garden City, N.Y. Doubleday, 1952.

The Golden Cross: A History of the 33rd Infantry Division in World War II. 33rd Infantry Division Historical Committee. Infantry Journal Press, 1948.

GOLDICH, ROBERT L, "Historical Continuity in the United States Military Reserve System," *Armed Forces and Society,"* VII (Fall 1980), 88-112.

GORDON, MARTIN, K. "The Congress' Own Militia: The District of Columbia Militia, Then and Now," Unpublished paper presented at Ohio State Univ. October 1976.

GRAHAM, JOHN R. *A Constitutional History of Military Draft.* Minneapolis: Ross & Haines, 1971.

GRAY, GEORGE H. "What Are the Reserve Forces Really For?" *Military Review,* LV (June 1975), 82-91.

GRIFFITH, ROBERT K., JR. "Conscription and the All-Volunteer Army in Historical Perspective," *Parameters,* X (Sep. 1980), 61-69.

The Guard and Reserve in the Total Force. Dep't of Defense, 1975.

HAGAN, WILLIAM THOMAS. "General Henry Atkinson and the Militia," *Military Affairs,* XXIII (Winter 1959), 194-197.

HALLECK, HENRY WAGER. *Elements of Military Art and Science.* Westport, Conn.: Greenwood, 1971 reprint of 1846 original.

HARMELING, HENRY JR. "The Future Employment of Reserves," *Military Review,* XXXIII (Aug. 1953), 6-9.

HEYMONT, IRVING and MELVIN H. ROSEN, "Five Foreign Army Reserve Systems," *Military Review,* LIII (March 1973), 83-93.

HICKEN, VICTOR. *The American Fighting Man.* New York: Macmillan, 1969.

HILL, JIM DAN. "The National Guard in Civil Disorders: Historical Precedents," in Robin Higham, ed., *Bayonets in the Streets.* Lawrence: Univ. Press of Kansas, 1969.

Historical Sketch of the Ancient and Honorable Artillery Company of Massachusetts and Catalogue of the Museum of the Company. Boston, 1914.

History of the National Guard and National Guard Bureau. Presented by the Army Division of the National Guard Bureau for Army Advisor Orientation, 27 Jan. 1958. Washington, D.C., 1958. Photo offset.

HITZ, ALEXANDER M., "Georgia Militia Districts, 1755-1899." *Georgia Bar Journal,* XVIII (Feb. 1956), 283-291.

HOLMES, JACK D. L. *Honor and Fidelity: The Louisiana Infantry Regiment and the Louisiana Militia Companies, 1766-1821.* Birmingham, Ala., 1965.

HONE, PHILIP. *The Diary of . . . ,* Allan Nevins (ed.)., 2 vols. New York: Dodd, Mead, 1936.

HOWARD, JAMES L. *Origin and Fortunes of Troop B.* Hartford, Conn.: Lockwood and Brainard, 1921.

HUIDEKOPER, FREDERICK L. *The Military Unpreparedness of the United States.* New York: Macmillan, 1916.

_____. *The U. S. Army and the Organized Militia Today*. New York, 1911.

HUNT, I. L. "Federal Relations of the Organized Militia," *Journal, U.S. Infantry Association*, V (Jan. 1909), 528-544.

HUNTINGTON, SAMUEL P. *The Soldier and the State*. Cambridge, Mass.: Belknap Press, 1957.

HUZAR, ELIAS, "Prewar Conscription," *Southwestern Social Science Quarterly*, XXIII (Sep. 1942), 8 pp.

IKEDA, MOSS M. "Reserve Component Strength in the Face of Zero Draft," *Military Review*, LIII (May 1973), 58-66.

INGERSOLL, L. D. *History of the War Department of the United States with Biographical Sketches of the Secretaries*. Washington, D.C.: F. B. Mohun, 1879.

JACOBS, BRUCE. "The National Guard . . . Its Armor," *Armor*, LXVI (Sep.-Oct. 1957, 10-23, 36-41.

_____. "The National Guard Policy Makers and Policy Problems," *Army*, VII (Sep. 1956), 49-55.

_____. "Three Centuries of Service: The National Guard in War and Peace: *National Guardsman*, XIII (June 1959), 20-23, 36, 37.

JAMESON, HUGH. "Equipment for the Militia of the United States, 1775-1781," *Journal of the American Military Institute*, III (1939), 26-38.

JOHNSRUD, GARY. National Guard, Ready or Not. Unpublished typescript, Univ. of Florida.

KAMMEN, MICHAEL. *People of Paradox* . . . . New York: Knopf, 1972.

KARSTEN, PETER. "Armed Progressives: The Military Reorganizes for the American Century," in Peter Karsten, ed., *The Military in America*. New York: The Free Press, 1980.

KELLEY, JAMES M. An Analysis of the Relationship between the Defense Institution and the Community. Unpublished M.A. thesis, University of Florida, 1972.

KEMBLE, CHARLES ROBERT. *The Image of the Army Officer in America*. Westport, Conn.: Greenwood, 1973.

KENNEDY, WILLIAM V. "Mobilization: 1861 Model," *National Guardsman*, VII (Feb. 1973), 13-15.

_____. "Why Should There be a National Guard?" *National Guardsman*, VIII (May 1954), 4-7.

_____. "The Citizen Soldier," *National Guardsman*, XII (March 1958), 4-7.

_____. "Continuity Through the Regiment," *National Guardsman*, XIII (Feb. 1959), 2, 3, 31.

_____. "Moment of Truth: Bull Run and the Modern National Guard," *National Guardsman*, XV (July 1961), 2-4, 26.

_____. "Ready or Not," *National Guardsman*, XVIII (July 1964), 10-14, 40.

_____. "Is ROTC Important to the National Guard?" *National Guardsman*, XVIII (Aug. 1964), 14-17, 40.

_____. "The National Guard Plugs a Gap," *National Guardsman*, XIX, (Jan. 1965), 8-15, 40.

_____. "Turn out the National Guard: Riot Duty in Chicago," *National Guardsman*, XX (Sep. 1966), 12-17.

KUENZLI, FREDERICK A. *Right and Duty, or Citizen and Soldier.* New York: National Defense Institute, 1916.

KURTZ, H. IRA. "A Character Sketch of the Militia of the United States, 1800-1860," *King's Crown Essays*, 5-15. New York: Columbia Univ. Press, 1959.

LANARD, THOMAS S. *One Hundred Years with State Fencibles, 1813-1913.* Philadelphia: Nields Co., 1913.

LAURENT, FRANCIS W. *Organization for Military Defense of the United States, 1789-1959.* National Security Studies Group, Univ. of Wisconsin, Madison, 1959.

LEE, E. BROOKE, JR. "The Politics of Our National Military Defense: *Sen Doc. 274.* 76 Cong., 3rd sess. 1940.

(LEE, HENRY). *The Militia of the United States. What It Has Been, What It Should Be.* Boston, 1864.

LEE, JOHN, "National Guard and National Security" *Military Review,* LII (Jan. 1972), 9-16.

LEVANTROSSER, WILLIAM F. "The Army Reserve Merger Proposal," *Military Affairs*, XXX (Fall, 1966), 135-147.

LEWIS, ARNOLD M. *A Brief History of the 176th Infantry.* Ft. Benning, Georgia, 1943.

MCALLISTER, MARY C. "Some Account of the Second Troop of Philadelphia Horse," *Pennsylvania Magazine of History,* XX (1896), 552-561.

MCGLASSON, W. D. "Phenix City 1954: Putting out the Flames of Corruption," *National Guard* (June 1981), 8-13, 29.

MCMASTER, FITZHUGH. *Soldiers and Uniforms: South Carolina Military Affairs, 1670-1775.* Columbia, S. C., 1972.

MCWILLIAMS, KEITH E. "Divisions or Brigades for the Army National Guard?" *Military Review*, LI (Jan. 1971), 35-42.

MADISON, EDWARD T. *32d Division in World War II.* 32d Div. Veterans Assn, 1957.

MARSHALL, S. L. A. "McNamara's Latest Reform: Why His National Guard Scheme Won't Work," *New Republic*, CLII (23 Jan. 1965), 13-15.

——. *Island Victory.* Washington, D.C.: Infantry Journal/Penguin Books, 1944.

MEADE, GEORGE. *Life and Letters of General George Gordon Meade*, 2 vols. New York: Scribner's, 1913.

MIDDLETON, DREW. *Can America Win the Next War?* New York: Scribner's, 1975.

Military and Naval Magazine of the United States, Benjamin Homans (ed.), 5 vols. Washington, D.C., 1833-1835.

Military Laws of the United States, 1915. Washington, D.C., 1915.

"The Militia and the Army," *Outlook*, CI (3 Aug. 1912), 742.

The Militia as Organized under the Constitution and Its Value to the Nation as a Military Asset. War Department Document No. 516, Nov. 1915. Washington, D.C., 1916.

"Militia of the United States," *Military and Naval Magazine of the United States*, I (1833), 235-243, 269-280, 352-362.

"The Militia of the United States," *North American Review*, XIX (Oct. 1824), 275-297.

MILLER, E. ARNOLD. "Some Arguments Used by English Pamphleteers, 1697-1700. Concerning a Standing Army," *Journal of Modern History*, XVIII (1946), 306-313.

MILLIS, WALTER. *Arms and Men*. New York: Putnam, 1956.

___ (ed.). *American Military Thought*. Indianapolis: Bobbs-Merrill, 1966.

MONTEFIORE, CECIL SEBAG. *A History of the Volunteer Forces from the Earliest Times to the Year 1860*. London: A. Constable Co., 1908.

MORTON, LOUIS, "The Origins of American Military Policy," *Military Affairs*, XXII (Summer 1958), 75-82.

MOSS, JAMES A. and MARCH B. STEWART. *Self-helps for the Citizen Soldier*. Menasha, Wisc.: Banta Printing Co., 1915.

MURPHY, ORVILLE T. "The American Revolutionary Army and the Concept of Levee en Masse," *Military Affairs*, XXIII (Spring 1959), 13-20.

National Guard Commanders Training Conference, 14 Aug. 1950. Unpublished stencil of the program. U. S. Army Military History Institute.

NEBLETT, WILLIAM H. *No Peace with the Regulars*. New York: Pageant Press, 1957.

___. *Pentagon Politics*. New York: Pageant Press, 1953.

NEIMANIS, GEORGE J. Militia versus the Standing Army in the History of Economic Thought from Adam Smith to Friedrich Engels. Unpublished typescript, 1978.

NELSON, PAUL DAVID. "Citizen Soldiers or Regulars: The Views of American General Officers on the Military Establishment, 1775-1781," *Military Affairs*, XLIII (Oct. 1979), 126-132.

NIEBAUM, JOHN H. "The Pittsburgh Blues," *Western Pennsylvania Historical Magazine*, IV (1921), 110-122, 175-185, 259-270; V (1922), 244-250.

NIHART, BRUCE (ed.). "A Humorous Account of a Militia Muster Circa 1807," *Military Collector and Historian*, X (Spring 1958), 11-14.

"No Authority to Send Militia into a Foreign Country," *National Guard Magazine*, IX (May 1912), 196-200.

ORDWAY, ALBERT. "A National Militia for the United States," *North American Review*, CXXXIV (1882), 395-400.

Origins, History and Accomplishments of the U. S. Army Reserve. Historical Evaluation and Research Organization, P.O. Box 157, Dun Loring, Va., 7 April 1965.

O'SULLIVAN, JOHN J. From Volunteerism to Conscription: Congress and Selective Service. Unpublished Ph.D. diss., Columbia Univ., 1971.

OSUR, ALAN M. "The Role of the Colorado National Guard in Civil Disturbances," *Military Affairs*, XLVI (Feb. 1982), 19-24.

"Outline of Reserve Realignment," *Army* (Jan. 1965), 14-20, 60.

PARKER, JAMES, "The Militia Act of 1903," *North American Review*, CLXXVII (Aug. 1903), 278-287.

The Peaceable Militia, or the Cause and Cure of the Late and Present War. London, 1648.

PECK, ESTHER ALICE. "A Conservative Generation's Amusements . . .," *University of Maine Studies*, Number 44, Series 2 (1938), 17-22.

POORE, BEN POORLY. "The Ancient and Honorable Artillery Company of Massachusetts, 1638-1884," *The United Service*, XII (Feb. 1885), 156-168.

POWELL, JAMES W. *Customs of the Service: National Guard and Volunteers.* Kansas City, Mo.: Hudson-Kimberly, 1902.

PUGH, ROBERT C. "The Revolutionary Militia in the Southern Campaign, 1780-1781," *William and Mary Quarterly*, XIV (April 1957), 154-175.

"Regulars and Militia," *The Nation*, XCIII (5 Oct. 1911), 306, 307.

REINDERS, ROBERT. "Militia and Public Order in Nineteenth Century America," *Journal of American Studies* (April 1977), 81-101.

Report of the Adjutant and Inspector General of the State of Vermont. Montpelier, 1862. Shows the mechanics of raising troops in Vermont.

Reserve Forces Act. *Army Information Digest*, XI (Feb, 1956). This issue is entirely taken up with opinions about this statute.

Reserve Forces for National Security. Report of the Gray Board. Washington, D.C., 1948.

The Reserves of the Armed Forces. *Military Affairs,* XVIII (Spring 1953). Most of this issue is taken with this topic.

RICHARDS, JOHN J. *Rhode Island's Early Defenders and Their Successors.* East Greenwich, R.I.: Rhode Island Pendulum, 1937.

ROBERTS, OLIVER A. *History of the Military Company of Massachusetts Now Called The Ancient and Honorable Artillery Company of Massachusetts, 1637-1888,* 4 vols. Boston, 1895-1899.

Romance and Reality, or an Examination of the Advantages and Disadvantages . . . of Joining Independent Militia Companies. Boston, 1835.

ROSE, WILLIAM B. Training the National Guard. Unpublished stencilled study of answers given by governors of states to a questionnaire, 17 April 1954. U. S. Army Military History Institute.

SCHIFFMAN, MAURICE K. "Reserve Component Duty," *Military Review*, XXXV (March 1956), 15-21.

SCHOLIN, ALLEN R. "The Guard Needs ROTC," *National Guardsman*, XXXIX (April 1963).

SCOTT, JAMES B. "The Militia," *Sen. Doc. 695*, 64 Cong., 2 sess., 1917.

SHARP, MORRISON. "The New England Trainbands in the Seventeenth Century." Unpublished Ph.D. diss., Harvard Univ., 1938.

SHEA, WILLIAM L. "The First American Militia," *Military Affairs*, XLVI (Feb. 1982), 15-18.

SINGLETARY, OTIS A. "Militia Disturbances in Arkansas during Reconstruction," *Arkansas Historical Quarterly*, XV (Summer 1956), 140-150.

———. "Negro Militia during Radical Reconstruction," *Military Affairs*, XIX (Winter 1955), 177-186.

SKELTON, WILLIAM B. The United States Army, 1821-1837: An Institutional History. Unpublished Ph.D. diss., Northwestern Univ., 1968.

SLOTKIN, RICHARD. *Regeneration through Violence: The Mythology of the American Frontier.* Middletown, Conn.: Wesleyan Univ. Press, 1974.

SMITH, LOUIS. *American Democracy and Military Power.* Univ. of Chicago Press, 1951.

SMITH, PAUL T. "Militia of the United States, 1846-1860," *Indiana Magazine of History*, XV (1919), 20-47.

SMITH, ROBERT ATWATER. *History of the Colony of New Haven*. Meriden, Conn.: Journal Pub., 1902.

SMITH, W. H. B. "Lining Em Up: On required military training, 1630-1775." *American Legion Magazine*, XLIV (Jan. 1948), 34, 36, 37.

SPARROW, JOHN C. *History of Personnel Demobilization in the United States Army*. Department of the Army Pamphlet 2-210. Washington, D.C., 1952.

SPAULDING, CHARLES S. "An Old-Time Muster," *The Granite Monthly*, XL (1908), 403-406.

SPAULDING, OLIVER LYMAN. *The United States Army in War and Peace*. New York: Putnam, 1937.

SPENCER, SAMUEL R., JR. History of the Selective Service and Training Act of 1940, 2 vols. Unpublished Ph.D. diss., Harvard Univ., 1951.

STERN, FREDERICK M. "Disarmament and a Citizen Army," *Army* (Oct. 1960), 41-43.

STEUBEN, BARON FRIEDRICH W. *Letter on the Subject of an Established Militia*. . . . New York, 1784.

STEVENS, FRANK E. *The Black Hawk War*. Chicago, 1903.

STRONG, GEORGE TEMPLETON. *The Diary of*. . ., Allan Nevins and Milton Halsey (eds.), 4 vols., New York: Macmillan 1952.

Summary of Operations in the World War. American Battle Monuments Commission, 28 vols. Washington, D.C., 1944.

SUMNER, WILLIAM H. *An Inquiry into the Importance of the Militia to a Free Commonwealth*. Boston: Cummings and Hilliard, 1823.

Sumner's Address to the Charlestown Artillery Company upon Delivering Their Field Pieces. Charlestown, Mass.: William W. Wheildon, Publisher, 1832.

SWAIN, MARTHA, "It Was Fun to Be a Soldier—Until the Shooting Started," *American Heritage*, VII (Aug. 1956), 12-23.

TOWER, C. C. "The Weymouth Cavalry Company, 1798-1811," in *History of Weymouth, Massachusetts*, 4 vols. Boston, 1923.

"The State's Regiments of the American Revolution," *Tyler's Quarterly*, VIIII (1926-1927), 247-252.

VALINGER, LEON DE. *Colonial Military Organization in Delaware, 1638-1776*. Wilmington, 1938.

VIGMAN, FRED K. "A 1745 Plan for . . . A National Militia in Great Britain and . . . America," *Military Affairs*, IX (Winter 1945), 355-360.

WALSH, ELLARD A. "The National Guard: Guardian of Liberty," *National Guardsman*, VII (Oct. 1953), 2-6; (Nov. 1953), 2-5; (Dec. 1953), 2-4, 35.

WARD, HARRY M. *The War Department*. Univ. of Pittsburgh Press, 1962.

WASHBURN, HAROLD C. *The American Blind Spot: The Failure of the Volunteer System* . . . . *New York: Doubleday, 1917*.

Washington Light Infantry of Charlestown, South Carolina. Charleston: Walker, Evans & Cogswell, 1873.

WATT, WILLIAM J. and JAMES R. H. SPEARS. *Indiana's Citizen Soldiers: The Militia and National Guard in Indiana's History.* Indiana State Armory Board, 1980.

WEIGLEY, RUSSELL. *The American Way of War.* New York: Macmillan, 1973.

WEILER, HAROLD J. "Development of the National Guard: *Quartermaster Review,* XIV (March-April 1935), 25-35.

WESTERN J. R. *English Militia in the Eighteenth Century.* London, 1965.

WHELPLEY, J. D. "The Militia Force of the United States," *North American Review,* CIXXIV (Feb. 1902), 275-280.

WILLIAMS, T. HARRY. *Americans At War.* Baton Rouge: Louisiana State Univ. Press, 1960.

WOOD, WALTER S. "The 130th Infantry, Illinois National Guard . . . 1778-1919," *Journal of the Illinois State Historical Society,* XXX (July 1937), 193-255.

ZECCA, MARIO J., "Career Management for the Reserve Component Officer," *Military Review,* XXXVIII, 47-59.

Sources Created by the United States Congress But Not Cited in the Notes

Universal Military Training. Hearings before House Committee on Military Affairs, Nov., Dec. 1945. 79 Cong., 1 sess.

Universal Military Training. Hearings before the Senate Committee on Armed Services, March, April 1948. 80 Cong., 2 sess.

Review of Administration and Operation of the Draft Law. Hearings before the Special Subcommittee on the Draft of the House Committee on the Armed Services, July, Aug., Sep. 1970. 91 Cong., 2 sess.

Hearings before the Special Subcommittee on Recruiting and Retention of Military Personnel of the House Armed Services Committee, 92 Cong., sessions 1 and 2, 1971, 1972.

A Few Useful Bibliographies

List of References on the Militia. Division of Bibliography, Library of Congress. Washington, D.C., 1916.

CONOVER, HELEN F. *List of References on Militia and National Guard: A Supplement to the 1916 list.* Division of Bibliography, Library of Congress, Washington, D.C., 1940.

Compulsory Military Training: A Selected List. Division of Bibliography, Library of Congress, Washington, D.C., 1940.

Universal Military Training: A Selected and Annotated List of References, Frances Cheney, comp. General Reference and Bibliography Division, Library of Congress, Washington, D.C., 1945.

Military Manpower Policy: A Bibliographical Survey. Prepared by Harry Moskowitz & Jack Roberts for the Adjutant General, Department of the Army, 1 June 1965.

Civilian in Peace, Soldier in War: A Bibliographical Survey of the Army and Air National Guard. Department of the Army Pamphlet 130-2, Washington, D.C., 1967.

Strength in Reserve. A Bibliography Survey of the U. S. Army Reserve. Department of the Army Pamphlet 140-3. Washington, D.C., April 1968.

The Guard and Reserve in the Total Force: A Bibliographical Survey. Office of the Assistant Secretary of Defense (Manpower and Reserve Affairs). Washington, D.C., March 1974.

National Security, Military Power, & the Role of Force in International Relations: A Bibliography, Harry Moskowitz and Jack Roberts, comps. Department of the Army Pamphlet 550-19. Washington, D.C. Sep. 1976.

The Role of the Reserve in the Total Army: A Bibliographical Survey of the United States Army Reserve. Department of the Army Pamphlet 140-7. Washington, D.C., Aug. 1977.

Index

Abrams, Creighton, Jr., Maj. Gen., 237
Adams, John, Pres. US, 55, 56, 66
Adams, John Quincy, Pres. US, 81
adjutant general, AG's Ass'n., 170
  military information division, 170
  state, 52, 57, 59, 60, 63, 79, 97, 109, 111, 113,
    115, 151, 156, 176, 195, 199, 200, 203, 218,
    219, 223, 224, 226, 232, 241, 244
  United States, 83, 143, 147, 186
Ainsworth, Fred C., Maj. Gen., AG, 147, 153
air
  cargo, 242
  power, 206, 222
  travel, 192, 193
Air Force, US, 198, 203, 204, 223, 228, 229, 249,
  254
  chiefs of staff, 203
  commands, 209
  department, 221
  secretary, 222
airplanes, 146, 195, 209
  B-1, 257
  B-52, 257
  fighter, 223
  interceptors, national guard, 223
  jets, 223
  KC-135, 253
  reconnaissance, national guard, 223
Alabama, 122, 127, 164, 205, 235
  Birmingham, 238
  Civil War, 101
  Mobile, 238
  Phenix City, 226
  Selma, 238
  Tuskegee, 238
  volunteers, 89
Alaska, 246
Alien and Sedition Acts, 55, 62
Allen, Lew, Gen., AF Chief of Staff, 254

all-volunteer force (AVF), 2, 250, 251, 254, 255,
  257, 261
Altgeld, John Peter, Gov. Ill., 117
America, Americans, 3, 15, 19, 24-29, 32, 33, 36-
  38, 41, 44, 49, 51, 64, 65, 71-74, 77, 86, 94,
  107, 116, 121, 126, 127, 144, 154, 155, 161,
  167, 168, 174, 176, 182, 194, 195, 204, 206,
  242, 245, 248, 260, 261, 267, 272, 304
  Legion, 207
  North, 8, 30, 35
  Panama, 254
American Civil Liberties Union, 245, 249
American Revolution, 13, 30, 33, 46, 47, 56, 58,
  64, 68, 70, 75, 77, 79, 91, 261, 262
  American army, 38, 39, 40, 44, 46: continental
    regiments, 37, 38, 40-45, 47, 55, 261
  American commanders: Benedict Arnold, 43;
    George Rogers Clark, 43, 47; Horatio Gates,
    43; Nathanael Greene, 36, 38, 39, 41, 43;
    Moses Hazen, 30; Henry Knox, 36; Lafayette,
    44, 85, 166; Charles Lee, 38, 43; Benjamin
    Lincoln, 43; Francis Marion, 41; Daniel
    Morgan, 40, 44, 45; William Moultrie, 41;
    Capt. John Parker, 36; Andrew Pickens, 41;
    Seth Pomeroy, 30; Israel Putnam, 30, 36, 37;
    Philip John Schuyler, 30; John Stark, 42; Adam
    Stephen, 30; Baron Steuben, 40; John Stuart,
    30; John Sullivan, 42, 43; Thomas Sumter, 41,
    42; Artemas Ward, 37; David Wooster, 30
  battles: Bennington, 79; Bunker Hill, 36, 79;
    Camden, 44; Concord, 36, 79; Cowpens, 40;
    Germantown, 39; Guilford CH, 41; King's
    Mountain, 40, 79; Lexington, 36, 37, 79; Long
    Island, 38; Princeton, 39; Saratoga, 43;
    Savannah, 40; Trenton, 39; Valley Forge, 40;
    Yorktown, 41, 42
  British commanders: John Burgoyne, 39, 40, 41,
    43; Earl Cornwallis, 41; Thomas Gage, 35, 36;
    William Howe, 39; Lord Percy, 36

American Revolution *(cont.)*
  civic leaders: Samuel Adams, 42; Benjamin
    Franklin, 34
  government, 35, 36
  Minutemen, 36
  Tories, 35, 40
ammunition, 77, 90, 92, 106, 146
  black powder, 120, 128
  live, 241
  M-1, 192
Andros, Edmund, Gov. N.Y. colony, 23
appropriations, 63, 66, 78, 83, 95, 108, 111, 119,
    122, 124-126, 141, 152, 172, 175, 185, 199,
    200, 204, 215, 222, 223, 247, 249, 250, 251,
    256
  Act of 1867, 108
  Act of 1912, 142
  Act of 1966, 233
Arizona, 173, 180, 212; gov., 177
Arkansas, 122, 164, 173, 205, 223, 234
  Central High School, Little Rock, 225: Ernest
    Green, graduate, 226
  Civil War, 98, 105
  Little Rock, 226, 237
Armed Forces Reserve Act, 1952, 210-212, 216,
    232
  Magna Carta of Reserves, 210
armories, militia and NG, 84, 111, 113, 114, 145,
    172, 175, 177, 178, 204, 205, 215, 239, 246,
    296
Army, US
  Air Corps, 186, 203, 230
  Air Force, 186, 192
  Chief of Staff, 138, 143, 144, 149, 221, 237, 241
  Civil War, 97, 98
  command structure, 138, 139, 147, 183, 195,
    222, 232, 235: Chief, Adm. Services, 186;
    Directorate for Civil Disturbances, 242;
    Organization of Land Forces of the US, 142
  dark ages of, 121
  Department of, 203, 221, 241, 252
  general staff, 143, 158, 162, 170, 171, 173, 174,
    178, 195, 196, 221, 263
  ground forces, 157, 174, 181, 183, 186, 209,
    253
  Legion of the US, 51
  Regulars, 50, 51, 53-57, 62, 64-68, 70-73, 78-
    80, 82, 85, 87-92, 94, 96, 102, 105, 108, 112,
    114, 115, 117-121, 126-130, 132, 133, 136,
    138-141, 143-151, 154-157, 169-172, 175-
    177, 180, 182, 194, 196, 198-200, 202-204,
    207, 210, 211, 215-219, 225, 226, 232, 237,
    238, 241, 247, 249, 251, 252, 255-257, 260,
    262, 265, 303, 304, 312
  secretary of dept.: Wilbur Brucker, 215, 218;
    Hugh Milton, 221
  service forces, 186
  tables of organization, 142, 145, 164, 180, 231,
    261
Army, US, officers, 4, 64, 67, 69, 71, 73, 74, 82,
    87, 88, 90, 91, 93, 113, 114, 143-146, 148-
    150, 152, 153, 161, 163, 164, 174, 186, 187,
    195, 201, 202, 207, 220, 252, 263
  commanding general, 91, 131, 138
  commanding irregulars, 69, 74, 128, 152
  generals, 162, 187, 192, 195; IG, 129; JAG, 142,
    156
Army, US, units, 157, 216, 231, 245, 253, 265
  armies, continental (20th century), 173, 174,

    221: First, WWI, 165; National (draftees),
    155, 157, 163, 167, 262; provisional, 55
  battalions, 158, 253: areas, 173; brigades, 158,
    231, 253; company, 144; corps, 185, 193,
    236, 262; V Corps, 129; hqs., 246; II Corps,
    167; WWI, 165
  divisions, 52, 60, 167, 173, 178, 183, 253, 262:
    mixed, 145; pentomic, 231; ROAD, 231, 233;
    1st Div., 166; 2nd Div., 166; 6th Depot Div.,
    161, 163; 8th Div., 185; 101st Airborne, 225;
    WWI, 187, 194
  regiments, 3, 4, 92, 158, 231; Civil War, 104;
    First American, 50; 15th Inf., 117
  schools, 138, 140, 146, 171, 174, 194, 204
Army of the US, 126, 136, 141, 148, 158, 161,
    163, 166, 171, 172, 174, 175, 183, 186, 187,
    198, 199
Articles of Confederation, 46, 47, 50, 280
Asia, 121, 243
  Cambodia, 244
  Far East, 242
  Southeast, 242
  Turkey, 204
Atlantic Ocean, 8, 13, 25, 80, 136, 228
atrocities,
  Black Hawk War, 87
  William Crawford, 42
  cruelty, 88
  Gnadenhutten, 42
  Mexico, 93, 94
  Philippines, 132
  Sand Creek, 119
  scalp bounty, 22
  student protest, 247
  Washington Terr., 95
  WWI, alleged, 168
Barnett, Ross, Gov. Miss., 237
battle, 139, 141, 166, 194, 238
  battlefields, 146, 173, 231
  groups, 231
  Crecy, 8
  Oxford, Miss., 237
  sham, 9, 58, 85, 111, 114
Beightler, Robert S., MG, CG 37th Inf. Div. Ohio
    NG, 187
Benton, Thomas Hart, Sen. Mo., 89
Black, Edward, Cong. Ga., 79
Blacks, Negroes: *see also* Black soldiers; National
    Guard, Blacks; slaves: 18, 54, 77, 103, 110,
    111, 115, 116, 149, 237-240
  free, 18
  insurrections, 22, 54
  mulattoes, 110
  segregation, 212, 224, 226, 237, 247, 262
Black soldiers, 104, 109
  American Revolution, 44
  Civil War, 103
  desegregation, 212, 237
  Spanish-American War, 127
  US colored, 103, 105
Blackstone, Sir William, 13
Blount, Willie, Gov. Tenn., 76
boycott, 35, 117, 118
Bray, William G., Cong. Ind., 218
brevet rank, 98, 100, 121, 129
Brooks, Overton, Cong. La., 219
Brown, Albert Gallatin, Sen. Miss., 94
Brown, I.G., LTC, Air NG, 223; Arkansas
    connection, 223

Brown, Joseph, Gov. Ga., 105
Buchanan, James, Pres. US, 96
Burgess, Carter, Deputy Sec. Def., 221
business, businessmen; *see also* economy: 111,
    113, 114, 157, 182, 199, 214, 215, 220, 229,
    232, 239, 250, 264, 265
  auto, 177
  building, 178
  Ford, 230
  Genl. Mgrs. Assn., 118
  management theory, 264
  military-industrial complex, 214
  and National Guard, 145
  oil, 177
  steel, 177
Byrd, William II, 29
Calhoun, John C., Sec. of War, expandable army
    concept, 82, 120, 201
California, 82-84, 99, 118, 122, 131, 132, 136,
    146, 154, 155, 161, 185, 205, 206, 230, 234,
    246, 251
  gov., 110, 149
  Los Angeles, 238
  San Diego, 146
  San Francisco, 82, 149
  strike, 176
  Watts, 238, 240
  Yosemite, 251
camps
  Campbell, Ky., 225
  Pickett, Ohio, 229
Canada, 33, 39, 63, 65, 68, 69, 71-74, 90, 91
  border, 126
  Halifax, 38
  militia, 33
  Montreal, 26
  Ontario penin., 68
  Quebec, 25, 26, 30, 41
  Queenstown, 68
  upper, 20
Cannon, Frank J., Sen. Utah, 127
Caribbean Sea, 129, 131, 136
Carter, James Earl, Pres. US, 249, 256
Carter, Jessie McI., MG, CNB, 170, 268
casualties
  Blue Licks, 42
  Chesapeake-Leopard, 65
  Cowpens, 40
  Detroit, 241
  1st Minn., 193
  45th Div., 194
  Guilford CH, 41
  Illinois, 117
  Kent State, 245
  Mexico, 92
  Newark, 240
  New Orleans, 77, 109
  Ohio, 112
  Ole Miss, 237
  Penna., 112
  Philippines, 132
  riots, 85, 86
  Sand Creek, 119
  San Francisco, 176
  Sioux, 119
  Spanish-American War, 130, 134, 135
  Wash. Terr., 114
  Watts, 238
  West Virginia, 41

WWI, 159, 160, 167
WWII, 194
cavalry, 161
  dragoons, 75
  English, 12
  1st US dragoons, 93
  horsemen, 17, 76
  Philippines, 133, 136
  scouts, 17
centuries
  14th, 7
  15th, 8
  17th, 22, 32, 33
  18th, 24, 31, 44, 47, 57, 58, 62
  19th, 62, 83, 136
  20th, 32, 49, 50, 138, 151, 176, 261, 264, 266
ceremonies, parades, festivals, reviews, 56-58, 60,
    82, 83, 85-87, 110, 114, 131, 133, 177
chain of command, 5, 9, 16, 19, 60, 172, 203
  dual, 3, 141, 232, 263
Chamberlain, George E., Sen. Ore., 147, 153
Chandler, Happy, Gov. Ky., 224
Chesapeake Bay, 31, 32, 72, 73
Chesapeake v. *Leopard,* June 22, 1807, 65, 84
  Capt. Salisbury Humphreys, 65
  Capt. James Barron, 65
China, Chinese, 114, 121, 242
Chittenden, Martin, Gov. Vt., 67
citizens, civilians, 76, 79, 83, 98, 99, 107, 114, 144, 145,
    149, 151, 164, 174, 178, 199, 202, 207, 218,
    225, 233, 236, 237, 245, 259-261, 265, 272
  citizen army, 44, 152, 153, 169, 201, 206
    reserve, 82, 196
    Swiss, 303
  citizen soldiers, 3, 4, 6, 8, 10, 14, 15, 19, 20, 24,
    25, 28-32, 34, 37, 38, 40-43, 47, 49-51, 54,
    56, 62, 66, 69-71, 73, 77, 79, 80, 86, 87, 89,
    90, 92-96, 98, 100, 105, 111, 114, 116, 119,
    121, 127, 130, 133, 139, 144, 146, 154, 161,
    168, 182, 199, 206, 216, 220, 241, 245, 258,
    261, 262, 267
Civil War, 97, 106, 108, 110, 111, 113, 116, 118-
    121, 127, 131, 136, 137, 140, 142, 148, 155,
    156, 169, 185, 194, 225, 261, 262, 266, 302
  guerrillas, 102
  post-, 264
  pre-, 260
Civil War, armies
  Confederate, 97, 99, 101, 102, 104, 105, 108,
    260, 292
  Union, 97, 99, 103, 104, 260
Civil War battles
  Atlanta, 105
  Bull Run, 1st, 99
  Bull Run, 2nd, 144
  Corinth, 101, 104
  Gettysburg, 99, 100, 103, 106, 193
  Shenandoah Valley, 101
  Shiloh, 104
  Wilson's Creek, 101
Civil War commanders
  Confederate: Gen. P.G.T. Beauregard, 118; LTG
    Simon Buckner, 102; Jefferson Davis, C-in-C,
    105; MG T.C. Hindman, 105; Gen. John B.
    Hood, 105; Gen. T. J. Jackson, 101; Gen.
    Robert E. Lee, 100, 101; Gen. James B.
    Longstreet, 109; MG Dabney Maury, 118; BG
    John Hunt Morgan, 101
  Union: MG James G. Blunt, 104; Col. Joshua

Civil War commanders *(cont.)*
    Chamberlain, 106; MG John C. Fremont, 104;
    LTG U.S. Grant, 104, 108, 128; MG Henry
    Wager Halleck, 101, 104; MG Winfield Scott
    Hancock, 193; MG Oliver O. Howard, 105;
    MG John A. Logan, 104, 105, 107, 128; MG
    George B. McClellan, 101, 104, 120, 121; MG
    James B. McPherson, 105; MG John McA.
    Schofield, 104; MG William T. Sherman, 105,
    121; Daniel Sickles, 193
Civil War units: Arkansas State Army 105; Army of
    the Tennessee, 105
    brigades, 98, 105
    Georgia State Army, 105
    Invalid Corps, 105
    old volunteer units, 98
    regiments: 15th Alabama, 106; 47th Alabama,
        106; 7th Iowa, 104; 20th Maine, 106; Mass.,
        100; 5th Mass., 98, 100, 103; 1st Minn., 193;
        Missouri, 99; New Jersey, 100; 7th New York,
        98, 100, 103; 69th, 98; 74th, 103; Ohio,
        99, 103; 83rd Penna., 106; Rhode Island, 101;
        volunteer, 100, 104, 105; Wisconsin, 99
    US Sharpshooters, 105
Clement, Frank, Gov. Tenn., 224
Cleveland, Grover, Pres. US, 117, 118
Coast Guard Reserve, 3
coasts, 64, 65, 67, 120, 126, 136
    artillery, 180
    cities, 85
    east, 246, 258
    forts, 6, 125, 144
    west, 99
Cold War, 2, 204, 206, 208, 215, 230, 232, 260,
    261, 263, 267
colleges, universities, 116, 148, 244, 247
    Univ. of Alabama, 237
    Bowdoin, 106
    Univ. of Cal. Berkeley, 230
    campuses, 242, 244
    Harvard Business, 230
    Kent State, 244, 245
    Univ. of Miss., 237
    Univ. of Missouri, 150
    Phi Beta Kappa, 230
    training, 243
    Yale Univ., 22
Collins, J. Lawton, Gen., army CS, 208
colonial era, 2, 36, 37, 54
Colorado, 122, 131, 132, 150, 173, 180, 212
    AG, 219
    Sand Creek, 119
combat, 40, 42, 81, 92, 94, 132, 152, 154, 155,
    158, 161-163, 167, 168, 170, 187-189, 192-
    195, 201, 202, 204, 209, 218, 231, 234, 253,
    255, 256, 265, 266
    divisions, 232
    strength, 228, 230
    units, 235, 236
    women excluded, 252
commander-in-chief, 35, 38, 49, 51, 60, 75, 88,
    142, 237, 247, 256, 262
    gov. as, 53
    pres. as, 49
    two commanders in chief, 68, 99, 141, 201,
        225, 262, 265
Communism, Communists, 116, 176, 212
    containment of, 214
Confederacy, Confederates, 102, 104, 105, 108,
    109, 127

congress, 102
    governors, 105
    states, 8, 9, 99
    war dept., 105
Congress, US, 49, 51-53, 55, 56, 58, 62, 64-67, 75,
    78, 79, 81, 89, 94, 95, 98, 100, 106, 108, 109,
    113, 124-127, 131, 133, 138-142, 144, 147,
    148, 154-156, 169, 171, 172, 174, 178, 179,
    184-186, 196, 198-203, 205-208, 211, 212,
    216, 222, 230, 233, 235, 236, 249-252, 256,
    257, 262, 266
Congress, Continental, 35-38, 41, 43, 45
    confederation, 46, 47
Congressmen, 119, 139, 147, 170, 207, 216, 222,
    232, 233
Connally, Tom, Sen. Tex., 193
Connecticut, 47, 59, 68, 79, 83, 84, 86, 122, 136,
    164, 173, 205, 212, 230, 234, 235
    colony, 14-16, 21-23, 25-27
    governor, 29, 67
    Hartford, 74
    New Haven, 23
    officers, 67
    revolution, 37, 38, 43
conscription, *see* draft
Constitution, US, 13, 48-50, 53, 61, 62, 65-68, 75,
    77, 140, 142, 144, 175, 202, 210, 220, 261,
    262
    army clauses, 49, 103, 143, 156, 170, 175
    convention, 47, 48
    militia clauses, 4, 49, 143, 151, 156, 170, 175,
        225
    Second Amend., 49
    state conventions, 48, 49
    unconstitutional, 74, 108, 224
Cooke, Philip St. George, Lt., 87
court martial, 57, 68
courts, 49, 177, 212
    courthouse, 57
    grand jury, 115
    injunction, 118
    judges US, 53, 238, 239
    US supreme court, 74, 224, 237, 249, 253, 262
Coxey's army, Jacob Coxey, 113, 115
Cramer, Kenneth F., MG, CNGB, 199, 202, 203,
    268
Crowder, Enoch H., MG, JAG, 142, 150, 156
Cuba, 120, 125-127, 129, 131
    El Caney, 130
    Havana, 127
    missiles in, 229
    San Juan Hill, 130
    Santiago, 130
Curtis, Thomas E., Cong. Mo., 219
Davis, Benjamin O., first Black general in US army,
    181
Davy, Martin Luther, Gov. Ohio, 177
declaration of war, 46, 66, 90, 94, 121, 155, 156
    on Germany, 154
    on Spain, 127
    War of 1812, 67
Defense, Department of, 201, 207, 218, 221, 235,
    236, 254, 257
Defense, Secretary of, 198, 199, 202, 204, 219,
    221, 222, 230-233, 251, 264
    undersecretary, 218
Delaware, 29, 83, 122
    Civil War, 97
    regiment, 98
    Revolution, 38

Del Corso, Sylvester, MG, AG Ohio NG Kent State, 244
democracy, 154, 155, 169, 267
Democratic Party, Jeffersonian Republicans, 65, 109, 131, 139, 206
  brigades, 66
  national convention, 258
  southern, 126, 208
desertion, 39, 43, 100
  British, 65
  Union army, 104
Dick Act, Charles Dick, 6, 139-141, 143, 153, 265
Dinwiddie, Gov. colony of Virginia, 28
disease, 24, 26, 27, 61, 75, 85, 128, 131, 132
  diarrhea, 132
  dysentery, 76
  malaria, 131, 132
  measles, 132
  quarantine, 111
  typhoid, 128, 131, 132
  yellow fever, 131, 132
District of Columbia, 73, 84, 89, 110, 133, 181, 243
Doniphan, Alexander, BG, Mo. militia, 95
Doyle, Clyde, Cong. Calif., 216
draft, conscription, 1, 2, 4, 17, 19-21, 26-30, 32, 33, 37, 38, 47, 53, 54, 60, 71, 75, 127, 136, 148, 154, 164, 180, 184, 192, 198-200, 209, 229, 236, 242, 246, 249, 250, 253, 255, 256, 260, 261, 264, 266, 273
  Blacks, 212
  Civil War, 6, 100-106
  dodgers, 208, 222, 243, 247
  end of, 199, 248
  peacetime, 6, 179, 184, 207, 217
  WWI, 155-158, 164
drill, 12, 17, 18, 57-59, 61, 82, 84, 110, 111, 128, 140, 145, 150, 171, 175, 178, 200, 221, 225, 234, 246, 256
Dulles, John Foster, Sec. of State, 214
economy, economic conditions, 64, 82, 120, 121, 141, 180, 185, 214-216, 265, 312
  business cycle, 175
  great depression, 175, 177, 178
  GNP, 214
  Panic of 1837, 85
  resources, 266
Eisenhower, Dwight D., Pres. US, 199, 214-217, 220-225, 231, 237, 248, 262
embargo, 1807, 65, 66, 262
embarkation, 164, 165
  ports of, 162
engineers, 111, 148, NG, 141, 161
England, Britain, 3, 6, 8, 16, 19, 26-30, 33, 35, 36, 40-43, 46, 54, 65, 67, 68, 70-73, 76, 77, 86, 89, 120, 210
  channel, 8, 166, 188, 192
  civil war, 23
  Danish invasion, 6
  Glorious Revolution, 13, 23
  history, 9
  London, 10
  repel invasion, 12
  threatened invasion, 10
England, government, 6, 9, 10, 12, 25, 26, 29, 72
  civil leaders: Oliver Cromwell, 111; Earl of Dartmouth, 36; William Pitt, 29
  Constitution, 13
  Crown, monarchs, 9, 10, 12, 15, 24, 25, 28, 35
  kings and queens, 8, 11: Charles I, 11; Charles

II, 12, 14, 23; Edward I, 7; Edward III, 8; Edward, Prince of Wales, 86; Elizabeth I, 8-10; Harold, 7; Henry II, 7; James II, 12, 23, 24; Saxon, 7; Stuart Restoration, 11; Tudors, 8, 10, 11; William I, 7; William III and Mary, 13
  local officials, 9; lords lieutenant, 9, 11, 12
  Parliament, 7, 11-13; political parties, 12
England, military policy, 10, 12; James Harrington on, 12; John Trenchard on, 13
  army, regulars, in American Revolution, 39, 40: discipline, 13, 32; houseguards, 7; independent companies, 32; Sgt. Lamb, 39; New Model, 11, 12; officers and militia, 25, 28; redcoats, 24, 32, 36, 261; standing, 12, 13; in WWI, 166, 167; in WWII, 183, 192
  citizen soldiers, militia, 9, 10-12, 13, 15, 139, 272; Anglo-Saxon, 7, 273; Earl of Essex, 10; numbers, 10; training, 10
  Navy, 11, 26, 27, 41, 55, 64; lake squadron, 74; officers, 66; sailors, 27; ships, 71, 73
  statutes, Assize of Arms, 7; Winchester 1572, 10; 1573, 8-10
England, North American colonies, 1, 5, 7-11, 13-18, 20-22, 24-26, 28-30, 32, 33, 38, 46, 260, 261
  charters, 14, 19
  cooperation, 23-27, 30
  government, 20, 22
  infantry equip., 16
  Plymouth, 16, 23, 30, 31
  proprietary, 16
  royal, 16, 23, 24
enlisted men, 78, 82, 104, 110, 129, 130, 141, 142, 144, 146, 149, 157, 171, 174, 184, 186, 194, 210, 236, 252, 266
  cooks, 131, 182
  NCOs, 59, 148
esprit de corps, morale, 1, 61, 126, 158, 170, 266
Europe, 6, 8, 21, 25, 26, 28, 30, 44, 64, 72, 82, 116, 139, 143, 146, 147, 153, 154, 158, 166-168, 179, 192, 208, 209, 215, 228, 242, 255, 258
  fortress, 188
  Greece, 204
  Italy, 165, 193
  Poland, 178
  Sweden, 165
  the West, 228, 229
Evans, Robert K., BG, CMB, 143, 268
expeditionary force, 8, 26, 27, 56, 91, 129, 179
  AEF, WWI, 157, 166, 167
farms, farmers, 19, 39, 111
Faubus, Orville, Gov. Ark., 224-226
Federalist party, 55, 56, 63-65
  brigades, 66
  George Cabot, 56
  Alexander Hamilton, 55
  high, 55, 64
  Timothy Pickering, 33
Federal system, 124, 261, 262, 267
  aid, 149, 222
  intervention, 240
  investment, 247
  regulations, 242
feudal array, 7, 8, 11
firearms, guns, 31, 49, 50, 52, 57, 58, 62, 64, 66, 76, 81, 109, 151, 177
  gunpowder, 17, 59
  gunsmiths, 17
firearms, shoulder type, 82, 120, 128, 146

firearms, shoulder type *(cont.)*
  loaded, 224, 244
  marksmen with, 36, 73, 85, 119, 120, 129, 146,
    177
  muskets, 27, 38, 81, 97
  rifles, 41, 89, 107, 112, 118, 128, 241, 245:
    Krag-Jorgensen, 120, 129, 146; Spanish
    mauser, 130; Springfield 1873, 120, 128-130,
    132; Springfield '03, 146
  shotgun, 58, 186, 241
  simulated, 182
  unloaded, 237, 244
Florida, 40, 88, 89, 96, 122, 136, 149, 164, 206,
   212, 230
  aborigines, 25
  Castillo, 27
  Civil War, 98, 102
  constitution, 111
  Miami, 258
  St. Augustine, 27
  Spanish, 25
  Tampa, 90, 128, 129
  territory, 87, 90
Folsom, Jim, Gov. Ala., 222
Ford, Gerald, Pres. US, 256
Forrestal, James, first SD, 201, 203
Forts
  Benning, 226
  Duquesne, 20
  Erie, 71
  Frontenac, 29
  George, 71
  Meigs, 70
  Necessity, 28
  Pitt, 29
  Sumter, 98
  Washington, 50
  William Henry, 29
France, 14, 15, 17, 24, 26, 28, 29, 40, 43, 54, 55,
   58, 61, 64, 89, 173, 181
  army, 8, 41
  Deiskau, 28
  directorate, 56
  Louis XIV, 12, 25
  Marshall Foch, 166-168
  New, 23, 24
  Port Royal, 25
  revolution, 55, 79
  Rochambeau, 44
  WWI, 165, 166
frontier, frontiersmen, 47, 50, 51, 56, 75
  Carolina, 24
  forts, 24
  New York, 71
  Niagara, 71
  northwest, 50
Fry, James, B., MG provost marshal, 120, 121
Fyrd, 6, 7, 272

Garfield, James A., Pres. US, 113
Gates, Thomas S., SD, 248
  committee, 248, 250
Geesen, Edward S., Col., acting CNGB, 202
GHQ, general headquarters, 181, 182, 184, 186,
   193
general orders, 73, 140, 157, 161, 162
Georgia, 62, 66, 79, 89, 108, 122, 136, 146, 164,
   173, 180, 206, 235, 282
  Civil War, 105
  colony, 14, 19, 27

Revolution, 40, 42
Savannah, 80
troops, 92
Germany, Prussia, 6, 8, 28, 120, 261
  Angles, Saxons, 6
  Berlin, 204, 206
  crisis, 229, 230
  general staff, 138
  Hitler, 179
  Nazis, 178, 192, 224
  wall, 228
  WWI, 165, 166, 168
  WWII, 185, 189
Giles, William Branch, Sen. Va., 67
Ginder, P.G., MG, dep. CS, 221
Goldwater, Barry, Sen. Ariz., 248
government, centralized, national, US, 3, 24, 42, 43,
   46-50, 79, 102, 199, 214, 261
  Federalists favored, 55
government, decentralized, US, 3, 46, 48, 49, 50,
   266
  anti-Federalist, 53, 55
  v. center, 105
  Patrick Henry proponent, 48
government, local, US, 35, 177, 196, 250; city, 15,
   18, 57, 66, 85, 86, 91, 104, 111, 114, 116,
   117, 242, 245
  community, 205, 215, 235, 250, 257, 296
  country, 15, 29, 31, 101, 110
  firemen, 244, 258
  mayor, 149
  sheriff, 118, 258
  town, township, 15, 17, 20, 31, 56, 59, 111,
   114, 172, 212, 226, 236
governors, colonial, 15, 16, 19, 20, 23, 25, 29, 35
  state, 35, 36, 52-54, 56, 58, 59-60, 63, 64, 68,
   90, 98, 99, 101, 104, 108-112, 114, 115, 117,
   126, 131, 133, 139, 140, 142, 147, 148, 150,
   151, 157, 176, 185, 202, 203, 212, 218, 225,
   226, 230, 238, 240, 241, 244, 247, 262, 265,
   281
Gray board, Gordon Gray, Asst. Sec. Army, 201-
   203, 232, 263
Great War for Empire, 1754-1763
  English commanders: Abercrombie, James, Gen.,
   29; Braddock, Edward, Gen., 28; Bradstreet,
   John, Col., 29; Forbes, John, Gen., 29; Earl of
   Loudoun, 28; Wolfe, James, Gen., 30
  French and Indian War, Seven Years' War, 14,
   15, 19, 20, 24, 28, 30, 32, 33, 37, 41, 45
Green, Roy, MG, CG 49th Inf. Div., 218
Gulf of Mexico, 80, 136; states, 90

Hanna, John D., dr., asst. SD, 215
Harmar, Josiah, BG, 47, 50
Harrison, William Henry, MG, 69, 70, 75
Hawaii, 141, 223
Hay, James, Cong. Va., 147, 153
Hebert, F. Edward, Cong. La., 218, 233
Hill, Jim Dan, MG, NG historian, 163, 174, 182,
   194
history, 79, 83, 127, 147, 152, 173, 185, 196, 248
  United States, 10, 11, 102, 179, 192, 207, 226,
   254, 255, 260, 262, 267
Hitchcock, Ethan Allen, LTC, 92
Hoar, George F., Sen. Mass., 127
honor and glory, 69, 71, 79, 151, 152, 168
  national, 94
horses, 9, 12, 17, 20, 32, 37, 41, 58, 70, 89, 90,
   114, 168, 173, 178, 181, 193

House of Representatives, US, 78, 147, 153, 210,
    217, 219, 257
    military committees, 139, 145, 147, 169, 196,
        209, 210, 217, 230, 234, 248
Houstoun, John, Gov. Ga., 42
Hughes, Richard J., Gov. N.J., 240
Hull, John A. T., Cong. Iowa, 126
Idaho, 122, 131, 132, 180, 234
Illinois, 86, 87, 93, 95, 122, 127, 136, 164, 185,
    205, 212, 221, 234, 235
    Chicago, 110, 117, 158, 168, 239
    Cicero, 212
    Civil War, 104
    Mayor Daley, 239
    militia, 87
    Peoria, 100
immigrants, immigration, 116, 170
impressment, see draft
Indians, 14-17, 19-22, 25-27, 31, 34, 39, 41, 47,
    50, 56, 62, 64, 71, 86-90, 93, 95, 96, 114,
    116, 120, 165, 195
    Apache, 119
    Choctaw, 165
    Creek, 76
    Eskimo, 246
    fighting style, 33
    Florida, 88, 95
    Iroquois, 42
    Sauk and Fox, 86, 87
    Seminole, 88
    Sioux, 119
Indian wars
    Blackhawk, 86, 87
    Chief Black Hawk, King Philip's, 23
    Kussoe, 21
    Pequot, 16, 23, 31
    Second Seminole, 87, 90, 95, 96
    Third Seminole, 95, 96
    Yamassee, 21, 22, 27
    Battles: Bad Axe River, 87; Beecher's Island,
        119; Blue Licks, Daniel Boone, 42; Horseshoe
        Bend, 76; Little Big Horn, 51: Okeechobee,
        88; Stillman's run, 87
    US commanders: Walker K. Armistead, BG, 90;
        Atkinson, Henry, BG, 87; Call, R.K., gov., 88;
        Carson, Kit, BG, 119; Clinch, Duncan L., 88;
        Dodge, Henry, col., 87; Henry, James D., BG,
        87; Sprague, John T., col., 89; St. Clair, Arthur,
        MG, 50, 51; Wayne, Anthony, MG, 51
Indiana, 104, 122, 127, 136, 141, 205, 212, 234,
    235
industrial strife, 117, 118, 120, 150, 151, 176, 264
    Carbon County, Utah, 150, 176
    Carnegie steel, 121
    coal and iron police, 112, 150
    general strike, 176
    Haymarket, 117
    Homestead, 117
    mine guards, 150
    Ohio, 177
    Pullman, 117, 118
    strikers, 113, 116, 118
    Washington state, 115
        1877, 112, 113
insurrection, see rebellion
Iowa, 83, 86, 94, 118, 122, 132, 177, 195, 205,
    212, 230, 235
    Civil War, 97
    1st Regt. Territorial Militia, 81,
    7th Vol. Inf. Regt., 104

Irish, Ireland, 21, 98, 165
    Roman Catholic, 85
    St. Patrick's Day, 86
irregulars (soldiers), 28, 30, 39-41, 43, 69, 71, 72,
    77, 80, 87-90, 98, 105, 119, 146
Jackson, Andrew, 75, 77, 79, 88, 282
    Aaron Burr, MG US army, 76
    removal policy, 86
    duel with John Sevier, 75
Japan, Japanese, 186, 187
    emperor, 189
    WWII, 189
Jay, John, and William, 82
Jefferson, Jeffersonians, 63-66, 144, 262
Jesup, Thomas S., MG, QMG, 88, 89
Johnson, Andrew, Pres. US, 108
Johnson, LeRoy, Cong. Calif., 219
Johnson, Louis, second SD, 199, 202, 203
Johnson, Lyndon, Pres. US, 231, 236, 238, 240-243
Johnston, Albert Sidney, Col., 95
Joint Chiefs of Staff (JCS), 198, 208, 221, 242

Kaine, J.W., MG, chm. AGS comm. on reserves, 233
Kansas, 96, 122, 127, 132, 133, 205, 230
    Civil War, 104
Kennedy, Edward, Sen. Mass., 243
Kennedy, John F., Pres. US, 228-231, 237
Kennedy, Robert, US Atty Gen., 237
Kent State Univ., 244, 245, 247
Kentucky, 42, 50, 69, 70, 76, 122, 185, 225
    Civil War, 98, 99, 101, 102, 104
    Clay, 224
    Home Guards, 102
    Louisville, 258
    Louisville legion, 91
    Sturgis, 224
    Jacob Williams, AG, 224
Kerner, Otto, Gov. Ill., 239
King, Martin Luther, 238, 239, 242
King George's War (War of Austrian Succession),
    1740-1748, 27
    Jamaica, 27
    Louisbourg, 21, 27
    James Oglethorpe, MG, 27
    Sir William Pepperrell, 27
    Edward Vernon, adm., 27
King William's War, 1689-1702, 25, 26
    Sir William Phips, 25
Kitchin, Claude, Cong. N.C., 153, 165
Korea, 2, 208-212, 215, 217, 222, 223, 228, 243,
    266

labor unions, 82, 116, 139, 150, 151, 176, 206,
    257, 264; AFL, 199; anti-NG, 117, 150, 172;
    CIO, 177, 199
    Knights of Labor, 115
    railroad, 117
    strike, public employees, 258
LaFollette, Robert, Sen. Wisc., 155
Laird, Melvin, SD, 249, 253
Lakes
    Champlain, 26, 69, 70
    Erie, 69, 70
    George, 28
    Great, 24, 136
    Ontario, 71
land, 67
    bounty, 20, 93
    foreclosure on, 47
    hide (measure), 272
    ownership, 7, 10, 16, 28, 272, 273

Lausche, Frank J., Gov. Ohio, 245
law, 38, 49, 52, 53, 83, 210, 216, 233, 235, 245, 262
  enforcement, 249
  lawyers, 13
  martial, 115, 226
  state, 5, 53, 54, 57, 60, 80, 110, 266
  supreme, 202
  US, 54, 55, 57, 64, 65, 67, 75, 126, 140, 151, 171
law and order, 7, 82, 85, 115-117, 157, 169, 212, 224-226, 232, 238, 241, 246, 247, 258, 264
Leach, George E., MG, CNGB, 195, 268
legislators, 53, 100, 138, 170, 216, 222, 232, 234, 257, 261
legislatures, 58, 90
  Civil War, 101, 102
  colonial, 16, 19, 20, 28
  Massachusetts, 282
  Missouri, 89, 111
  New Hampshire, 282
  New York, 97
  Ohio, 112
  Revolution, 35-37
  Utah, 115
  West Virginia, 113
  Wisconsin, 113, 117
LeMay, Curtis, Gen. AFCS, 222
liberty, freedom, 48, 64, 79, 80, 151, 163, 214
Lincoln, Abraham, Pres. US, 86, 97, 99-101, 103
liquor, whiskey, 57, 59, 82, 116, 238, 240
logistics, supply, 56, 58, 59, 70, 76, 128, 131, 182
  contractors, 59
Louisiana, 65, 89, 122, 136, 164, 173, 205, 212, 218, 259
  Civil War, 101
  Huey Long, 257
  New Orleans, 80, 109
  Purchase, 66
  Washington Artillery, 181
loyalty, 148, 158, 187, 210, 231, 266
lynching, 85, 110, 112, 149, 264
MacArthur, Douglas, Gen., 166, 178, 207
McIver, G.W., acting CMB, 149
McKinley, William, Pres. US, 110, 126, 127, 138; Gov. Ohio, 111
McLain, Raymond S., LTG, 187, 201
McNair, Lesly J., Gen., 181, 182, 185, 192
McNamara, Robert S., SD, 230-237, 242, 264
machine guns, 120, 146, 161, 167, 176
  bandoleers, 192
  Gatling guns, 112, 120, 130
  simulated, 182
M-day, 228, 230, 254, 255, 263, 265
Madison, James, Pres. US, 67, 68, 74-76
Mahon, George, Cong. Tex., chm. HR Armed Ser. Comm., 222
Maine, 83, 90, 122, 173, 212
  Civil War, 97, 106
  Colonial, 23, 27
major general, 35, 75, 76, 128, 171, 202, 216, 219, 281
maneuvers, joint RA-NG, 139, 144, 145
manifest destiny, 94
manpower, 2, 20, 22, 23, 28-30, 33, 74, 90, 91, 97, 100, 102-104, 106, 126, 141, 147, 155, 158, 180, 207-209, 215, 223, 231, 236, 254, 263, 264, 266, 273
manuals, 15, 81
  riot control, 177

March, Peyton C., LTG, ACS, 161, 169, 170
Marines, 85, 88, 112, 189, 194
  reserves, 3, 4, 202, 255
Marshall, George C., Gen., 179, 181, 184, 187, 189, 195, 196, 200, 203, 207
marshals, US, 55, 90, 124, 237, 238
martial spirit, 12, 36, 72, 80, 83, 94, 141, 168, 193, 208, 248
Maryland, 54, 72, 122, 136, 234, 235, 258
  Baltimore, 72-74, 91
  Benedict, 72, 80
  Civil War, 98, 100, 101
  colonial, 15, 17, 29, 31
  division, 205
  governor, 73
  militia, 73
  Revolution, 38
Massachusetts, 15-21, 23-26, 27, 29, 31, 36-38, 43, 47, 58, 59, 61, 64, 66-68, 79, 83, 86, 122, 164, 181, 221, 234, 282
  Boston, 15, 18, 31, 35-37, 41, 80, 85, 103
  Civil War, 98, 104, 111, 136
  Deerfield, 26
  division, 205, 230, 235
  governor, 83
  military academy, 163
  Salem, 85
mass war, 114
  Civil War, 97, 98, 102, 103
  20th century, 127, 140, 161, 248, 260, 262
Medal of Honor, Congressional
  Joshua Chamberlain, BG, 107
  Tom Pope, corp.; also British distinguished conduct medal and French Croix de Guerre, 167
Meigs, Return Jonathan, Gov. Ohio, 69
merchant shipping, 64, 65
  impressment of sailors, 66
Meredith, James, Black at Ole Miss, 237
Merger, AR & NG, 201-203, 231, 234, 235, 263, 264
  Why Merge, 233
Mexican War, 93, 94, 96, 302
  Buena Vista, 94
  enlisted men: Samuel Chamberlain, 93; Jacob Oswandel, 93
  Mormons, 95
  US officers: W.W.S. Bliss, 94; Gideon Pillow, 92; Raphael Semmes, 92; John E. Wool, 95;
Mexico, 90-93, 120, 165
  border war, 151, 152, 154, 162
  land cession, 95
  Mexico City, 92
  officers, 91
  Pancho Villa, 151
  peasants, 93
  Santa Anna, 91
  soldiers, 91
Michigan, 83, 118, 122, 129, 136, 205, 234, 235
  Civil War, 97
Middle Ages, 6, 33; Renaissance, 12
Middle West, Mid-West, US, 119, 132, 164, 171, 206, 239
Miles, Nelson A., LTG, 117, 296
militarism, militaristic, 139, 140, 144, 169, 178, 267
  mil. dictator, 222
military capability, 207
  career, 249
  cohesion, 56

courtesy, 130, 132
districts, 221
doctrine, 166
duty, 80, 250
elite, 105
equipment, 82
experience, 172, 198
future, 153
instrument, 198
intelligence, 76
music, 83, 111
necessity, 184
personnel, 236
power, 222
pros, 249
reprisal, 243
sociology, 248
specialities, 252
transport, 232
military affairs, 48, 50, 52, 173, 203, 216, 219, 222, 248
military caste, 3, 130, 196, 262
military costs, 55, 62, 64, 66, 77, 78, 80-85, 101, 104, 111, 117, 119, 122-126, 141, 152, 157, 175, 178, 202, 207, 214, 216, 225, 233, 237, 247, 249, 251, 256, 260, 267
military equipment, 32, 46, 82, 131, 151, 254, 255, 258, 263
    National Guard, 179, 182
military establishment, 63, 94, 118, 119, 138, 139, 147, 163, 169, 170, 178, 198, 209, 217, 220, 232, 236, 255, 264, 266, 267
military force, fighting force, 38, 39, 66, 77, 81, 82, 87, 89-92, 94-96, 98, 115, 116, 119, 121, 126, 131, 132, 136, 140, 144, 148, 150, 151, 165-168, 172, 174, 178, 179, 185, 189, 194, 208, 212, 228, 234, 243, 247, 249, 257, 260, 261, 263, 265
    conventional, 215, 231
    ground forces, 157, 174
    in being, 253
    reduction, 252
    unified, 221
    women excluded, 220
military, medical, 131, 148, 152, 153, 202, 234, 246
    National Guard, 141
    surgeons, 128, 131
military obligation, 211, 217, 219, 220, 246, 249, 250, 260, 303
    in colonies, 14, 15, 18-20, 31, 52, 202, 207
    universal, 7, 111, 126, 145, 149, 272
military policy, US, 10, 77, 78, 196, 214, 256
    A Proper Military Policy for the US, 146
military posture, 144, 147, 179, 195, 196
    committee on, 195, 196, 200
military services, 172, 179, 209, 211, 212, 216, 236, 237, 252, 253, 262
    contingency plans, 231, 235
    departments, 5, 212
    high command, 179, 201, 208, 209, 211, 219, 236, 253, 254, 257, 262-264
    Pentagon, 201, 209, 219, 221, 235, 236, 261
    secretaries, 211
    strenuous conditions, 133: desert, 132; jungle, 132, 193; partial mobilization, 229; street fights, 132; WWI trenches, 168

militia, 1-5, 7, 11, 12, 15, 18, 21-24, 26, 28, 29, 31-33, 35-46, 48-88, 90, 91, 94-103, 106,
108-111, 113-115, 121, 133, 139-145, 149, 168, 175, 220, 260, 262, 263, 266, 272
    acts: regulations, 4, 7, 14, 18, 274; Act of May 2, 1892, To Call Forth the Militia, 53; Act of May 8, 1792, Uniform Militia, 52-54, 56, 58, 63, 64, 138; repealed, 139; Act of 1908, 140; Act of April 25, 1914, 140
    alternatives to: 21, 22, 24, 26, 29, 30, 33, 38, 43, 46, 61, 66; levies, 51
    ancient: Carthage, 79; Greece, 13; defeated Xerxes, 79; Xenophon, 89; Rome, 13, 79, 89
    arms, armament: 7, 14, 17, 31, 36, 46, 52, 53, 58, 59, 66, 76, 80, 83, 109, 141, 144
    artillery: 2, 4, 17, 31, 46, 52, 58, 64; Civil War, 101, 111
    Blacks, 108-111, 149
    as bulwark: 11, 14, 31-33, 79; National Guard, 114, 179
    cavalry: 2, 4, 31, 52, 58, 83, 111
    classify: 51, 60, 75, 80, 82, 83
    colonial: 6, 22, 32, 34, 57, 261; cooperation, 21, 22, 25, 27, 30, 31; Dominion of New England, 23; United Colonies of New England, 23
    defense only: 19, 22, 38, 68, 69, 90, 142
    detachments: 55, 60, 61
    discipline: 15, 34, 46, 49, 63, 68, 78, 87; punishment, 18
    economical: 3, 10, 33, 80
    elite corps: 2, 5, 17, 32, 35, 48, 52, 53, 82, 83; grenadiers, 4, 18, 52, 83; Minute Men, 10; light infantry, 4, 18, 52, 83; Riflemen, 4, 18, 52
    en masse: 32, 39, 60, 61, 70, 71, 73, 101, 105
    exemptions from service: 52, 53, 60, 100, 103
    in federal service: 2, 4, 49, 50, 53, 58-60, 67, 73, 91, 98, 99, 140, 262, 263
    fines: 10, 18, 19, 33, 37, 38, 59, 60, 66, 81-83
    geographical limits: 8, 19, 32, 38, 66, 121, 156, 170; will not cross borders, 68, 69
    infantry: 16, 52, 58, 63, 111
    Militia Bureau: 149, 156; chief, 154, 157, 171, 268
    musters, drill: 5, 9, 18, 57, 60, 82, 84
    as national reserve: 51-53, 64, 67
    naval: 4, 64, 136, 149
    officers: 2, 7, 16, 18, 25, 28, 30, 35, 36, 46, 49, 50, 55-57, 59, 61, 65, 67, 68, 72, 75, 79, 81, 87, 88, 98, 99, 115, 143, 145, 262; generals, 58, 71; LTCs, 60; major, 60; prestige, 15, 16; QM, 16, 59
    organized: 110, 111, 113, 140-145, 148-150, 175, 263; N.Y., 86
    pay: 9, 20, 84, 111, 382
    standing: 4, 5, 18, 31-33, 35, 57, 61, 262
    state use of: 61, 65, 85, 110, 111, 264
    system: 6, 16, 20-22, 24, 25, 27-35, 38, 43, 44, 60, 62, 64, 66, 67, 72, 75, 77, 79-84, 86, 91, 101, 102, 106, 110, 114, 144, 261, 262; Swiss, 8
    time limitation: 1, 8, 19, 32, 37, 38, 53, 70, 76, 99, 140, 156
    tradition: 7, 31, 136, 232, 262, 263
    training: 5, 9, 14, 15, 18, 31, 34, 49, 51, 52, 57, 59-61, 63, 66, 80-82, 84, 91, 111, 144, 266
militia units, 31, 36, 40, 52, 61, 64, 73, 81, 109, 111, 261-263
    battalion, 1, 52, 57, 61, 84, 89, 263
    brigade, 57, 60, 67, 87, 98; general, 57; major, 57; Irish, 86
    company, 1, 5, 15, 18, 30-32, 35, 57, 58, 60, 61,

militia units *(cont.)*
   67, 70, 85, 99, 263; officers, 15, 19, 36, 54, 60
  integrity broken, 1, 2, 30, 61, 262, 263
  interchangeability, 31, 52, 54, 64, 81, 261
  regiment, 1, 15, 16, 18, 35, 57, 58, 60, 64, 66, 84, 98, 99, 101; colonels, 16, 19, 35, 43, 46, 57, 60, 81, 86
Mills, Albert L., MG, CMB, 143, 268
Milton, John, Gov. Fla., 292
Miltonberger, Butler, B., MG, CNGB, 202, 268
Minnesota, 119, 122, 131, 181, 185, 205, 212, 235, 243
  Bonus Review Board, 195
Mississippi, 83, 108, 122, 164, 173, 205, 217, 235, 237
  Civil War, 101
  Oxford, 237
  Vicksburg, 110
Missouri, 83, 89, 94, 111, 114, 115, 123, 145, 146, 149, 170, 212, 230, 258
  Francis Preston Blair, 99
  Civil War, 99, 101, 102, 104
  BG Alexander Doniphan, 95
  53rd Infantry Regt., 95
  1st Mtd. Vols., 89
  St. Louis Legion, 91
mobilization, 152, 154, 172, 180-182, 187, 204, 205, 208, 209, 228, 229, 232, 242, 243, 263, 266, 303, 312
  plans, 125, 177
Monroe, James, Pres. US, 74, 75, 82
Montana, 123, 132, 180, 212
Mormons, 94
  battalion, 95
  legion, 95, 115
  Joseph Smith, 95
  LTG Daniel Wells, 115
  Brigham Young, 95
mortars, 161
  simulated, 182
motor vehicles, motorization, 177, 186, 195, 209, 258
  ambulance, 246
  armored personnel carrier, 240
  mechanized cav., 181
  tanks, 185, 189
  trucks, 176, 259
  vehicles, 239, 251
Myers, Dillon S., Col., Acting CNGB, 202

Napoleon, 64, 72, 77, 116
National Defense Act, 1916, 147-149, 151, 155, 156, 263
  1920 amendment, 171, 172
  1933 amendment, 174, 175, 265
national emergency, 173, 174, 179, 180, 202, 211, 212, 253, 254, 264, 265
National Guard, 1-4, 18, 50, 110-113, 116-120, 125-127, 129, 133, 136, 139-149, 151-156, 163, 164, 167, 170-172, 174, 177, 178, 181, 182, 192, 194, 196-204, 206-212, 215-222, 224, 226, 228, 230-236, 238, 239, 241, 243, 245-253, 255-258, 260-267
  acts (statutes): 119, 128; vitalization, 199; volunteer, 127; March 2, 1907, 146; May 27, 1908, 142
  air: 186, 202, 203, 204-211, 218, 221-223, 229, 232, 238, 240, 242, 243, 250, 251, 254, 261; aircraft, aeromedical evac., 223; F-100

Supersaber, 223; F-102 Delta dagger, 223; F-104, Starfighter, 223; fighters, 223, 234, 243, 254; heavy airlift, 223, 254; interceptors, 223, 254; helicopters, 228; jets, 228; KC-135, 253, 254; recon, 223, 234, 243, 254; 7F-94AB, 223
  airfields, 209, 223, 229: history, Aero Club, 146; Beckwith Havens, 146; Buffalo, N.Y., 146; Curtiss Aviation, 146; Eugene Ely, 146; Ohio 177, 1st Aero Co. N.Y., 146; 7th Co. Cal. CA, 146; observation sqs., 105, 116, 119, 180, 185, 254; pilots, 186, 204, 223, 242; women, 253; SRF, 234; squadrons, 185, 186, 223, 228; WAF, 243, 246—anti-air, 204, 209, 223
  armor: 186, 195, 204, 209, 221, 224, 230; company, 185; divisions, 256; WWII, 189
  army: 200, 202-205, 209, 211, 215, 218, 221-223, 228, 229, 231, 235, 243, 245, 246, 250-252, 254-256, 261
  artillery: 113, 125, 140, 141, 145, 152, 161, 181, 209; corps, 185; Spanish-American War, 127; 159th Bn., 176
  Blacks: 113, 151, 164, 165, 237, 241, 246, 252, 264; segregated, 207, 212, 216, 217; regiments—6th Mass., 127; 8th Ill., 127, 164, 165, 181; 9th Ohio, 164; 15th N.Y., 165; 369th Inf., 165, 181; 370th Inf., 165, 181, 184; 371st Inf. 165, 181; 372nd Inf., 165, 181; smaller units, 165; 93rd Inf. Div., 165, 167
  bureau: 149, 175, 186, 196, 200, 203, 218, 221, 222; chiefs, 178, 199, 203, 229, 231, 233, 253, 268, 269
  camps: WWI, 157; WWII, 182
  cavalry: 125, 140, 141, 152, 161; armored, 204; 107th Armored, 244; conversion, 181; divisions, 173; mechanized, 181, 234; Spanish-American War, 127
  as constabulary: 65, 115, 118, 143, 151, 170, 247, 258
  as part of effective force: 139, 143, 144, 147, 149, 151, 171, 175, 176, 178-180, 196, 201, 203, 204, 211, 231, 232, 247, 253, 254, 258, 263-266
  federal funds: 141, 152, 175, 178, 199, 204, 205, 223, 247, 262, 266
  federal inspectors: 139-141, 182
  federalization: 139, 140, 165, 196, 246, 266
  federal recognition: 172, 174, 175, 204, 205, 218, 220, 232
  in federal service: 126, 136, 140, 142, 146, 148, 151, 152, 156, 157, 166, 167, 171, 174, 179, 180, 185-188, 192-194, 200, 202, 204, 208, 209, 211, 217, 225, 228, 229, 237, 238, 242, 243, 256, 260, 262, 265; order or call, 175, 225
  general officers: 113, 139, 150, 152, 162, 182, 184, 186, 187, 193, 218, 219, 253
  infantry: 125, 127, 140, 141, 152, 161, 176, 192, 221, 256
  leaders: 116, 150, 151, 179, 181, 187, 209, 211, 215, 231, 232, 243, 247, 250, 251, 253-257, 261, 263, 264, 266
  lineages and honors: 171, 185, 263
  monies, costs: 141, 154, 157, 175, 202, 204, 205, 223, 233, 246, 247, 256, 265, 266
  as national reserve: 119-121, 124, 143, 147, 222, 226, 232, 247, 263
  officers: 111, 112, 114, 126, 130, 140-143, 149-152, 155, 161, 163, 171, 174, 175, 177, 179, 180, 182, 184-186, 195, 202, 205, 208-210,

215, 220, 231, 232, 236, 241, 243, 245, 257, 262, 263; age in grade, 182; election of, 145; lts., 252; OCS, 221, 252; reclassify, 184, 186; up or out, 256; resign, 252; warrant, 180

opponents: 222; John C. Calhoun, 82, 120; Granville Clark, 143; Peyton C. March, 170; Lesley J. McNair, 181; Emory Upton, 120, 121, 152, 153, 170, 181; Leonard Wood, 142, 153

pay: 150, 171, 175, 200, 204, 225, 228, 239, 251, 252, 256; for drill, 145; retirement, 199

public relations: 199, 296; advertising, 172, 181, 220, 246, 261

reorganization, reconstitution: 145, 172, 173, 178, 185, 198, 203, 204, 209, 223, 229, 231, 236, 256, 257

state use: 112, 117, 118, 149, 175, 176, 178, 212, 226, 236, 240, 241, 246, 258, 259, 264, 305; rescue and relief, 226, 232, 246, 258; by state: Ala., 226, 237, 238; Ariz., 151; Ark., 225, 262; Calif., 176, 218, 238, 240; Fla., 258; Ill., 139, 213; Iowa, 177; Kan., 149, 162; La., 212, 218; Md., 192, 200; Mich., 241; Minn., 195; Miss., 237; Mo., 257; N.J., 240; N.Y., 161, 246; Ohio, 239, 240, 244, 245; Pa., 112, 113, 121, 150; Tex., 151; Utah, 150, 152, 176; Wash., 115; W.Va., 150, 176, 250; Wisc., 114, 239, 258; Puerto Rico, 212

strength: 140, 141, 156, 172, 173, 175, 179, 196, 199, 200, 204-206, 215, 219, 220, 234, 246, 249, 250, 252, 261, 263; air, 223; attrition, 220, war, 151, 164

technicians: 208, 220, 223, 232, 254, 255

training: 113, 114, 118, 120, 124, 136, 140, 145, 147, 148, 152, 167, 175, 178, 179, 187, 195, 196, 200-204, 221, 223, 228, 229, 240, 252, 255, 256, 259, 265; basic, 220, 223, 236, 246, 250, 251

turnover: 141, 175, 223, 250

National Guard units, 126, 128, 140, 142, 145, 153, 155, 156, 158, 159, 165-167, 170-172, 174, 178, 180, 182, 184, 185, 188, 192, 193, 194, 196, 200, 203, 205, 208, 209

battalions: 103, 108, 158, 159-161, 181, 185, 230, 234, 236, 250, 253

brigades: 113, 125, 130, 148, 157, 159, 160, 163, 230, 231, 235, 253, 256; Black, 165; 39th Inf., 234; 40th Inf., 234; 51st Depot, 158; 52nd Inf., 162; 70th Inf., 162, 163; 73rd FA, 256; 92nd, converted to CA, 181

companies: 113, 144, 155, 167, 172, 193, 234; captain, 142, 236, 257; Indians, 165; machine gun, 146; tank, 185; Tenn., 251

divisions: 125, 146, 148, 156, 163, 164, 166, 167, 173, 179, 180, 183-185, 187, 199, 204, 210, 212, 230, 231, 233, 256, 262; CG, 163; div. arty., 161, 163, 164, 168, 187; histories, 158, 161, 164, 166, 168; mixed, 145; pentomic and ROAD, 231; square, 157; triangular, 158; tri. to square, 161

divisions by number in peacetime: 26th Inf., 205, 230, 234, 235, 322; 27th Inf., 185, 205, 221, 235; 28th Inf., 185, 205, 209, 220, 230, 235, 322; 29th Inf., 173, 185, 203, 235; 30th Armored, 235, 322; 30th Inf., 173, 180, 185, 205, 230; 30th Mechanized, 235, 322; 31st, 173, 180, 185, 205, 209, 217, 220, 235; 32nd, 180, 205, 228, 235; 33rd, 181, 185, 205, 235, 239; 34th, 173, 185, 205, 230; 35th, 173, 185, 205, 230; 36th, 173, 185, 205, 230;

37th Inf., 173, 185, 187, 205, 209, 212, 220, 235; 38th, 185, 205, 235, 322; 39th, 173, 205, 235; 40th, 173, 185, 205, 209, 220, 238; 40th Armored, 235; 41st, 173, 180, 185, 205, 235; 42nd, 205, 234, 235, 322; 43rd, 173, 185, 205, 209, 220, 230; 44th, 173, 180, 181, 185, 205, 209, 221; 45th, 173, 180, 185, 205, 209, 210, 220, 235; 46th, 205, 235; 47th, 205, 209, 235, 322; 48th, 206, 221; 48th Armored, 235; 49th, 206, 218, 235, 238, 240; 49th Armored, 206, 228, 235; 50th Armored, 206, 230, 235, 322; 51st, 206, 230

integrity impaired: 2, 140, 145, 151, 153, 156, 158, 170, 171, 174, 175, 181, 185, 189, 209, 217, 253, 260, 262

regiments: 125, 126, 128, 129, 146, 157, 159, 160, 192; Chicago, 117; colonel, 112, 162, 163, 168, 174, 187, 193; West Va., 113; Wisc., 114; 2nd Ill., 117; 7th N.Y., 126; 69th N.Y., 302; 101st Inf. Mass., 301; 102nd Inf. Conn., 168, 302; 103rd Inf. Maine; 302; 105th Inf., 302; 108th Inf. N.Y., 185; 109th Inf., 163; 111th Inf., 302; 118th Inf., 302; 121st Inf., Ga., 185; 129th Inf. Ill., 185; 130th Inf., 302; 131st Inf., 158, 167; 138th Inf., 302; 145th Inf., 244; 155th Inf., 302; 165th Inf., 158; 166th Inf., 302; 167th Inf., 302; 168th Inf., 302

women: 220, 246, 252, 253, 264; air, 252, 253; army, 252, 253; high school, 253; nurses, 221, 252, 253, 264

National Guardsmen, air: 204, 223, 228, 242, 243; army: 2-4, 113, 115-120, 130, 139, 142, 146, 148, 150-152, 154, 157, 158, 161, 163, 164, 168, 170-172, 174, 176-182, 184, 186, 194, 195, 198-202, 205, 208, 209, 212, 213, 216, 218, 220, 221, 224-226, 228, 229, 232, 234, 237-247, 249, 251, 252, 255, 256, 258, 259, 262, 264; physical condition, 126, 152, 162, 180

National Guardsman (periodical), 143, 151, 201, 202, 211, 220, 221, 229

National Guard of the United States, 174, 175, 202, 265, 266

air, 211, 212

army, 211, 212

National Guard Association (NGA), 118, 119, 124, 140, 143, 147, 170, 171, 174, 175, 185, 195, 196, 199-201, 203, 204, 206, 207, 210, 211, 217-220, 222, 226, 227, 229, 230, 232, 248, 251, 254, 255, 257, 263, 264

founders: William L. Alexander, Iowa, 118; P.G.T. Beauregard, La., 118; A.H. Berry, Mass., 118; John W. Denver, Ohio, 118; Dabney Maury, Va., 118; George W. Wingate, 118

interstate NGA, 119

presidents: James Cantwell, 235, 242; Bennett Champ Clark, 170; Charles Dick, 139

National Guard Magazine, 116, 143

National Rifle Association, 119, 146

national security, national defense, 124, 138, 141, 143, 184, 194, 198, 201, 206, 214, 233, 247, 257, 267

cheap, 120

National Security Act, 198, 230, 309

Navy, US, 55, 64, 70, 71, 74, 78, 129, 136, 198, 249, 312

citizen sailors, 136

department, 221

high command WWII, 189

Navy, US *(cont.)*
  Frank Knox, SN, 206
  reserve, 3, 4, 136, 202
  sailors, crews, 65, 85, 88, 127
  sea power, 206
  ships, 74, 78, 92, 136, 146: destroyer, 192; gunboats, 64, 74; *Harvard,* 130; *Maine,* 127; *Pueblo,* 243; transports, 129
Nebraska, 123, 131, 132, 173, 205, 212, 230
Netherlands (Holland), 12, 15, 17
  colonial wars, 24, 32
Nevada, 123, 133, 141, 145, 154, 173
New England, 15-17, 20, 23, 26, 30, 31, 33, 35, 37, 39, 54, 56, 58, 74, 79, 91, 164, 188
New Hampshire, 79, 83, 123
  Civil War, 97
  colonial, 20, 23, 25, 26, 27
  Revolution, 37, 43
New Jersey, 47, 54, 83, 123, 136, 173, 180, 181, 206, 212, 230, 235
  Civil War, 98, 100, 104
  colonial, 23, 26, 29
  governor, Newark, 241, 251
  Hugh J. Addonizio, mayor, 240
  Revolution, 38-40
New Mexico, 99, 119, 154, 173, 180, 259
  Columbus, 151
  territory, 133
news media, 57, 65, 116, 127, 128, 199, 206, 245
  periodicals: *Chicago Daily News,* 164; *Chicago Tribune,* Floyd Gibbons, 151; *Salt Lake Tribune,* 163; *Sturgis News* (Ky.), 224; *New York Times,* Hanson Baldwin, 206, 216; *Time,* 189
New York, 47, 58, 65, 67-72, 74, 80-83, 85, 86, 89, 94, 110, 119, 123, 136, 141, 163, 164, 173, 180, 212
  Black Rock, 71
  Buffalo, 71
  Cherry Valley, 40
  City, 85, 246
  Civil War, 97, 101, 103, 104
  colonial, 23
  divisions, 145, 189, 205, 212, 234, 235
  Erie Canal, 85
  governor, 74
  Manhattan, 250
  opera house, 85
  regiments: 7th, 85, 103; 9th, 86; 69th, 86; 74th, 103
Nixon, Richard M., Pres. US, 244, 245, 248
Norblad, Albert, Cong. Ore., 215
North Carolina, 75, 92, 123, 127, 136, 180, 205, 222, 230, 235, 281, 282
  Civil War, 98
  colonial, 18-21, 24, 27-29
  Pamlico Sound, 100
  Revolution, 44
North Dakota, 123, 132, 194, 195, 205, 212
Ohio, 67, 110, 123, 127, 136, 172, 181, 212, 234, 259
  air NG, 177, 185
  Civil War, 97, 99, 101, 103, 104
  Dayton, Mayor Hall, 246
  historical units, 99
  Kent, 244, 245
Oklahoma, 165, 173, 177, 180, 205, 210, 212, 234
  territory, 133
ordnance, 148
  chief, 120, 128, 129

Oregon, 123, 131, 180, 205
  Astoria, 215
O'Ryan, John F., MG, CG 27th N.Y. Div., 161, 162, 170
Pacific Ocean, 129, 136, 186, 194
pacifism, conscientious objectors, 177
Palmer, John McAuley, BG, 144, 169, 195, 196, 303, 304
Parker, John H. (Gatling gun), 130, 144
patriotism, 170, 179, 204, 261
  Nat'l. Assn. Patriotic Soc., 169
  Rev. Daniel Poling, 206
pay, 29, 33, 82, 84, 90, 93, 95, 103, 108, 111, 112, 145, 148, 178, 228, 229, 234, 273
  for AGs, 57
  living wage, 116, 264
  volunteers, 89
peace, 50, 96, 141, 150, 154, 206, 218
  American Peace Society, 82
  mission, 55
  peacekeeping, 55
peacetime, 10, 25, 31, 44, 59, 61, 82, 136, 140, 142, 153, 164, 171, 175, 179, 184, 196, 199, 203, 207, 260-263, 265, 266
peace treaties
  Amiens, 1802, 64
  Ghent, 1814, 77, 78
  Mexican-American, 94
  Ryswick, 1697, 25
  Utrecht, 1713, 26
Pennsylvania, 84, 89, 90, 117, 123, 131, 136, 150, 164, 234, 235
  Bethlehem, 55
  Bucks County, 54, 55
  Civil War, 99, 101
  colonial, 14, 15, 26, 27, 31, 274
  divisions, 113, 145, 146, 192, 205, 230; MG Robert M. Brinton, 112; MG Alfred Pearson, 112
  historical units, 99
  HR, 90
  militia, 47, 70
  Northampton County, 37
  Philadelphia, 39, 54, 66, 72, 73, 80, 85, 112
  Pittsburgh, 112
  Pottstown, 99
  Revolution, 38
  western, 54
  Wyoming, 41
pensions, 77, 80
Pershing, John J., Gen., 146, 151, 157, 158, 161, 163, 165-167, 169-171
Persons, Gordon, Gov. Ala., 226
Philippines, 131-133, 136
  battle, Manila Bay, 129
  Filipinos, 132
  harsh conditions, 132
  independence 132
  Manila, 132
  regiments: 10th Penna., 132; 20th Kansas, 132; new regiments, 133, 136
  WWII, 185, 193
Plattsburg idea, 143; CMTC, 143, 149
plunder, loot, pillage, 21, 22, 25, 28, 54, 71, 85, 149, 238, 240
police, 112, 118, 213, 238-240, 244, 247, 258
  Ala. troopers, 238
  Calif. patrol, 238
  N.J. troopers, 240
  state, 176, 226

policy, US, 64, 82, 142, 229, 242
  massive retaliation, 214
  new look, 123, 215
  reserve, 233
political parties, minor, 66, 75
  disputes, 110
  North American (Know Nothing), 86
  Populist, 126
Polk, James K., Pres. US, 90, 92, 94
population, 83, 84, 88, 91, 94, 107, 110, 126, 141,
  170, 238, 246, 252
  discipline in, 107, 170
Porter, Peter B., BG, N.Y. militia, 65, 68, 69, 71,
  72, 75
Powell, Adam Clayton, Cong. N.Y., 216
President, US, 49, 50, 52, 53, 55, 58, 68, 98, 100,
  126, 128, 131, 139, 140, 142, 147, 148, 150,
  151, 154-156, 171, 174, 178-180, 184, 194,
  198, 200, 202, 207, 208, 211, 214, 215, 218,
  222, 225, 228, 237, 243, 249, 262, 265
presidential elections
  1800, 63
  1834, 85
  1940, 179
  1944, FDR v. Thomas E. Dewey, 206
  1948, 200
prices, 16, 22, 27, 58, 59, 66, 82-84, 166, 202,
  267
prisoners, 40, 83, 85, 110, 130
professionals, see regulars and Army, US
promotion (of officers), 182, 187, 256, 257
property, homesteads, wealth, 79, 80, 82, 112,
  113, 116, 141, 177, 241, 245, 264
public affairs, 109, 112, 114, 257
  debt, 94
  opinion, 199
  persons, 199
  sanitation, 128
Puerto Rico, 131, 212, 241
quartermaster, 15, 148, 168, 182
  state, 59, 111, 125
quasi-standing armies, see militia, alternatives to
Queen Anne's War (War of the Spanish
  Succession), 1702-1713, 25-27
  Sir Hovenden Walker, 26
racial strife, hatred, 109, 110, 115, 149, 165, 236,
  238-240, 242, 264, 265
  KKK, John Kasar, 224
railroads, railroad system, 78, 111, 118, 129, 157,
  176, 192, 203
  Pa. railroad, 113
  strikes, 246
  wrecks, 246
Randolph, Edmund, Gov. Va., 48
Randolph, John, Cong. Va., 56, 65
rangers, 21, 27
  Revolution, 42
rations, 92, 182, 225
  commissary, 16, 125
  Spanish-American War, 131
  WWII, 189, 192
readiness, 55, 61, 153, 154, 155, 169, 173, 174,
  178, 187, 196, 207, 209, 215, 217, 221-223,
  231, 234, 235, 243, 265, 266
  National Guard: 201, 203, 230; preparedness
    movement, 153; quick response, 232
Reagan, Ronald, Pres. US, 266, 267
rebellion, insurrection, 49, 53, 63, 64, 67, 118,
  140, 238, 262
  Cuban, 125

William Duane, 55
Fries, 54
  mob, 176
Puerto Rico, 212
Shays, 47, 54
  slaves, 22, 54
Stono, 22
Whiskey, 54, 262
Reckord, Milton A., LTG, 192, 196, 200, 201, 209-
  211, 255, 257
Reconstruction, 108, 264
  Brooks-Baxter War, Ark., 109
  Dunning School, 109
  racial hatred, 109
  Carl Schurz, 108
recruiting, recruits, 104, 105, 126, 133, 172, 175,
  180, 217, 220, 243, 249-253, 257, 261, 273
  army National Guard, 255
  bonus, 251
  bounties, 93, 104, 155
  educational benefits, 251
  women, 253
  17-18½ age group, 217-220, 223, 257
regimental combat team (RTC), 192, 199, 204,
  209
regions of US, 208
  East, 126, 132
  North, 109; in Civil War, 97-100
  see Middle West
  Northwest, 186
  Old NW, 50
  see South
  West, 102, 206
Regulars other than US, 10, 12, 15, 88, 92
  British, 24, 27-30, 32, 40, 42, 43
  Europe, 82
  Roman, 13
religions, sects, 32, 38, 116
  Anglican 23, 31
  Henry Ward Beecher, 116
  church, churchmen, 17, 56
  Congregational, 23
  Cotton Mather, 17
  Mormon, 94, 115
  see also Mormon
  Protestant, 12
  Puritan, 31
  Quaker (Friends), 14, 18, 31, 38
  Roman Catholic, 12, 21, 31, 93
repel invasion, 49, 53, 66-68, 72-74, 124, 140
replacements, fillers, 104, 159, 160, 164, 166, 192,
  194, 216, 228, 243, 253, 255
  second lieutenants, 252,
  training centers, 81, 236, 243, 246, 251
Republican Party, 55, 56, 63-66, 110, 127 139,
  206, 208, 256
  radicals, Civil War, 108, 109
Reserve
  air force: 3, 4, 202, 203, 217, 254
  army: 3, 4, 196, 215, 217, 230, 231, 233-235,
    250
  components: 174, 179, 185, 196, 211, 214-216,
    230, 236, 242, 249, 251-253; specific officers:
    deputy SD for reserves, 236; LTG Ridgely
    Gaither, dep. CG for, 221; BG Thomas Kenan,
    deputy, 233; LTG E.D.S. Wright, chief RC, 233
  enlisted: 148, 172, 175, 201
  Reserve Forces Act (RFA), Aug. 9, 1955, 217,
    218, 232

Reserve Forces Policy Board: Sec. 5 Committee,
203, 204, 207, 233; began as Civilian
Components Policy Board, 202
individual: 228, 229, 231
national: 75, 126, 139, 141-144, 147, 148, 169,
170; Continental Army (20th century), 147,
153
National Guard reserve: 156
officers: 172, 174, 177, 202, 211, 214-217, 230,
236, 242
Officers Reserve Corps: 148, 171, 172, 174, 175,
186, 187
Reserve Officers Training Corps (ROTC): 148,
244, 252
organized, 171-173, 175, 201, 202, 263, 264
ready: 211, 216-219, 231, 263; immediate, 230,
263; individual ready (IRR), 252, 254, 255
retired: 212
selected (SRF): 234, 235, 261, 263; SRF 1a, 234;
SRF II, 234
standby: 211, 212, 219
system: 138, 141, 147-149, 153, 171, 219, 221,
253; dual, 232, 263, 264; English and Swiss,
139; state connected, 170, 232
units: 4, 142, 148, 172, 196, 198, 200, 202, 215,
217, 218, 229, 231, 234, 236; army brigades,
236; divisions, 187, 230, 231, 234, 235—with
regulars, 254
reservists, reserves, 195, 197, 200-202, 207, 208,
210, 211, 215, 216, 228, 230, 232, 243, 248,
250, 251, 253, 255, 256, 263, 265, 303
Reserve Officer's Association, 207, 263
Col. John T. Carlson, ex. dir., 233
BG E.A. Evans, ex. dir., 211
BG Melvin Maas, marine ROA, 211
Reynolds, John, Gov. Ill., 87
Rhode Island, 64, 123, 136, 145, 173, 205, 230
Civil War, 98, 101
colonial, 23, 26, 29, 31
Newport, 39, 80
Revolution, 37
Rhodes, James, Gov. Ohio, 239
Rickards, George C., MG, CMB, 174, 268
Ricks, Earl T., BG, AG Ark., chief air division
National Guard, 223
riots, 47, 54, 81, 85, 116, 242
cities: Alexandria, 55; anti-Chinese, 110; Benton
Harbor, 239; Chicago, 239; Cicero, 213; CW
draft, 103; Dayton, 240; Detroit, 241;
Georgetown, 85; Haymarket, 117; Hough,
Cleveland, 239, 240; Milwaukee, 239; Newark,
240; New Orleans, 1874, 109; N.Y. anti-
abolition, 85; Philadelphia, 85; San Francisco,
176, 240; Watts, 238
control, tools of, 213: mace, 241; other, 241;
night stick, 177; tear gas, 177; training, 2,
157, 177, 213, 236, 237, 239, 241, 242, 245
duty, 85, 239; FM 19-15, 241, 244
university students: 244, 247
rivers
Arkansas, 119
Aroostook, 90
Chattahoochee, 226
Elbe, 192
French Broad, 40
Hudson, 26
Maumee, 70
Mississippi, 25, 76, 77, 86; valley, 43
Niagara, 68, 71-73
Ohio, 28

Potomac, 73
Richelieu, 72
Tallapoosa, 76
Wabash, 47
Withlacoochee, 88
Rivers, L. Mendel, chm. HR Armed Services
Committee, 257
roads, 60, 78, 130
romanticism, 89, 93
Roosevelt, Franklin D. (FDR), 174, 178, 180, 185,
206
boondoggles, 182, 183
Civilian Conservation Corps (CCC), 177
National Labor Relations Board (NLRB), 177
New Deal, 175, 177
v. Wendell Willkie, 179
Roosevelt, Theodore, 110, 131, 143, 144, 150,
153, 155
Rough Riders, 129
Root, Elihu, SW, 121, 138-41, 147, 152, 153
Rosenberg, Anna, asst. SD, 207
rotation of individuals, 2, 209, 210, 266
Rusk, Jeremiah, Gov. Wisc., 116
Russell, Richard, Sen. Ga., 229
Sasscer, Lansdale, Cong. Md., 216
scholars cited in text
Douglas S. Freeman, 45
Charles J. Gross, 222
Don Higginbotham, 39
Jim Dan Hill, see entry
C. Warren Hollister, 6
Morris Janowitz, 248
Douglas E. Leach, 133
Gerald Linderman, 130
William Riker, 3
John Shy, 35, 44
Frederick P. Todd, 106
Russell F. Weigley, 102
schools, 56
Central, Little Rock, 225, 226
high, 219, 230, 250, 251, 253, 254, 255
integration of, 224, 262
officials, 226
white, 224, 238
Scotland, Scotsmen, 8, 21, 27
Scott, Hugh L., MG, ACS, 152
Scott, Winfield, LTG, CG army, 68, 74, 88, 91-94,
98
Sanger, William, IGNYNG, 138, 139
Selective Service, 174, 208, 210, 266
acts: 1940—179, 180, 198, 206; 1948—200,
207;1967—249
draft boards, 156, 179; exemptions, 155; Lewis
B. Hershey, 215
lottery, 154, 179; registration, 155, 179, 249,
266
Dr. Curtis Tarr, dir., 248
Senate, US, 139, 148, 154, 184, 202, 210, 217
Comm. on Armed Forces, 232
Comm. on Mil. Affairs, 147
Senators, 89, 119, 136, 170, 207, 233
Sewell, William J., Sen. N.J., 128
Shelby, Isaac, Gov. Ky., 70
Shirley, William, Gov. Mass. colony, 27
signal corps, 148; NG, 141, 146, 161
size of force
Cartagena, 27
civil rights, 241
Civil War, 97, 98, 102, 103
federal era, 55

Florida, 89
Great War, 29
Jefferson era, 63
with William Johnson, 28
Korea, 209
Mexican border, 151
Mexican War, 91, 92
after Mexican war, 94
Mormon, 95
NW Indians, 50
Puerto Rico, 131
Revolution, 37, 38, 40
SRF, 234
Spanish-American, 133-135
US guards, 157
Univ. of Miss., 237
War of 1812, 67, 72, 74
Whiskey Rebellion, 54
WWI, 167
WWII, eve of, 180
Yorktown, 41
1821, 78
1877, 112
1970s, 249
slaves, slavery, 18, 20-22, 27, 37, 73, 76, 96
Abolitionists, 85
fugitive law, 85
patrol, 22
states, 18, 22, 54, 61
Smith, John Cotton, Gov. Conn., 67
Smith, Margaret Chase, Sen. Maine, 246
social status, 118
anarchist, 117, 151, 170
aristocracy, 12
discipline, 96
elite, 16, 32, 33, 59, 60
gentry, 12
low, 10, 11, 21, 22, 26, 28, 31, 38, 44, 60, 116, 151, 260
poor, 60, 66, 82, 85
servants, 37, 149
societal strife, 241, 247
well-to-do, 18, 60, 66, 82, 83, 103, 112, 114, 115-117, 143
working class, 127
South, 16, 76, 109, 110, 129, 165, 206, 238
South Carolina, 64, 83, 89, 109, 123, 136, 180, 206, 212, 230, 235
John Barnwell, SC commander, 21, 22
Charleston, 31, 32, 38, 40, 57, 61, 74, 80, 89, 91
colonial, 15, 16, 18, 19-21, 24, 25, 27
Revolution, 38
South Dakota, 123, 132, 195, 212, 258
sovereignty, state, 42, 43, 46, 48, 102, 202
national, 64, 65
popular, 96
Spain, 15, 17, 24, 32, 64, 120, 125, 127, 129, 130
Armada, 11
New, 63
Spanish-American War, and Philippine Islands, 2, 136, 138, 152, 302
BGs, 128
commanders, US: John Jacob Astor, 128, 132; William Jennings Bryan, 131; George Dewey, 129; Fitzhugh Lee, 128, Nelson Miles, see entry; Elwell Otis, 133; John H. Parker, see entry; William H. Shafter, 129-131; Joseph Wheeler, 128; James H. Wilson, 131
fervor for, 127, 136

non-regimental units in Puerto Rico, 296
regiments in Cuba and Philippines, 129-131, 133
regiments in Puerto Rico, 296
V Corps, 129, 131
sports, 83, 177
Dallas Cowboys, 243
prize fights, 110
standing forces, 3, 11, 24, 33, 42, 48, 50, 51, 63, 64, 79, 80, 83, 114, 121, 152, 196, 219, 256, 260, 266, 267
air force, 256
discipline, 42
monarchy, 79
opponents of: Elbridge Gerry, 48; Luther Martin, 48; Samuel Nason, 48; Edmund Randolph, 48
state armies, 143, 262, 263; see also militia, alternatives
state or home guards, 172
US guard, 163, 186
Utah, 186
WWI, 157
WWII, 186
states, 36, 37, 46, 50-54, 57-60, 66, 75, 79, 81, 83, 84, 86, 91, 100, 104, 105, 108-113, 119, 120, 124-126, 131, 133, 136, 139, 141, 142, 148, 149, 156, 161, 165, 166, 170-173, 176, 177, 185, 186, 194, 200, 202, 203, 205, 210, 212, 215, 216, 218, 221, 222, 226, 232, 235, 241, 243, 244, 246, 250-252, 256, 258, 260-262, 264-266
border, 99, 101, 103, 104
Middle Atlantic, 72
rights, 3, 121, 124, 143, 144, 147, 201, 215, 222, 261, 263, 265, 292
seceded, 103
southern, 110
v. US 62
western, 99
Stennis, John, Sen. Miss., 248
Stevens, Isaac, Gov. Wash. Terr., 95
Stevenson, Adlai, Gov. Ill., 212, 213
Stevenson, Coke, Gov. Texas, 198
Strong, Caleb, Gov. Mass., 67
substitutes for military service, 18, 19, 29, 30, 37, 38, 53, 60, 103, 155, 266
subversives, subversion, 49, 176, 177
un-American, 206
summer camp, 111, 113, 114, 124, 139, 140, 144, 145, 147-150, 175, 178, 239, 240, 256, 259
Symington, Stuart, sec. AF, 204

tactics, 41, 92, 121, 244
Japan, 189
for riot control, 112
Taft, Robert A., Sen. Ohio, 206
taxes, 84, 115
direct, 54
taxpayers, 149, 233
whiskey, 54
Taylor, Maxwell D., Gen. ACS, 218
Taylor, Zachary, Pres. US, 87-91, 93, 94
telephone, 165, 167
Tennessee, 75, 89, 93, 123, 132, 141, 180, 205, 221, 251
Civil War, 98, 99
Clinton, 224
gov., 75, 76
Joe Henry, AG, 224
Memphis, 110, 258

Tennessee *(cont.)*
  militia, 282
  Oliver Springs, 224
  John Sevier, 75
  troops, 76
tensions, international, 204, 229, 243
tensions, irregulars and regulars, 69, 74, 92, 93,
    104, 158, 161-163, 170, 171, 182, 194, 195,
    201, 203, 209, 216, 217, 219, 222, 228, 262,
    263, 308
territories, US, 66, 83
Texas, 108, 123, 165, 173, 177, 193, 194, 205,
    206, 212
  border, 90
  Lone Star flag, 193
  mounted Texans, 93
Thomson, E. Keith, Cong. N.Y., 216
Throckmorton, John, Gen., 241
tobacco, 16, 116
Todd, David, CW, Gov. Ohio, 101
Tomlinson, Gideon, Cong. Conn., 79
Tompkins, Daniel D., Gov. N.Y., 74
total force, 243-256, 258, 259, 265
training, 128, 140, 142, 153, 158, 166, 198, 203,
    216, 218, 253, 263, 265, 303
  basic, 217-220, 251
  combat, 255
  regional directorate, 253
  trained bands, 30
treason, traitor, 36, 55
Truman, Harry S., Pres. US, 203, 206-208, 212,
    257
Trumbull, Jonathan, Gov. Conn., 37
Twining, Nathan, Gen. AFCS, 222
uniforms, 4, 9, 18, 32, 39, 57, 59, 83, 84, 86, 93,
    105, 108, 111, 113, 130, 182, 204, 258
Union of Soviet Socialist Republics (USSR), 203,
    204, 216, 229, 242, 249, 251, 255, 261, 267,
    312
  army, 206, 208
  Berlin wall, 228
  Czechoslovakia invaded, 206
  Hungary invaded, 214
  Khrushchev, 228
  Sputnik, 214
United Nations, 208
United States (the republic, the nation), 6, 13, 34,
    40, 46, 49, 50, 52, 54-56, 61-63, 65-69, 72,
    75-80, 83, 85-87, 90-92, 95, 97, 99-105, 110,
    116, 118, 120, 121, 125, 127, 129-133, 136,
    138, 139, 141-143, 147-149, 152-154, 157,
    161, 166-169, 174, 176-179, 182, 183, 192-
    194, 199, 200, 202-206, 209, 214, 216, 222,
    226, 228, 229, 233, 236, 242-244, 247, 248,
    250, 255, 257, 260, 261, 265-267, 272
United States government, 3, 4, 48, 50, 52-56, 58,
    61, 65, 66, 68, 72, 73, 76, 80, 81, 87, 88, 102,
    103, 109, 111, 113, 114, 120, 121, 125, 128,
    141, 148, 175, 177, 178, 209, 211, 243, 244,
    260, 262, 265, 266
US Military Academy, West Point, 64, 79, 105, 118,
    121, 128, 140, 162, 163, 174, 193, 262, 286
  protective association, 217
universal military training (UMT), 1, 5, 6, 33, 83,
    90, 111, 120, 121, 144, 147, 149, 153, 169,
    171, 173, 196, 197, 203, 206, 207, 210, 211,
    215, 216, 266
  Baker-March Bill, 169, 170
  Kahn-Chamberlain Bill, 303

National Security Training Commission, 207,
    208; Julius Ochs Adler, chm., 216
National Security Training Corps, 207, 209, 216
UMT and Service Act, 207
Upton, Emory, MG, 120, 138, 152, 153, 170, 181,
    257
  Military Policy of the US, 201
Utah, 95, 115, 131, 132, 141, 161, 163, 258
  Carbon County, 150, 176
  gov., 133
  Mormons, 115
  Nauvoo legion, 115
  LTG Daniel Wells, comdg., 115
Vance, Cyrus, dep. SD, 234, 235
Vermont, 65, 67, 83, 123, 136, 173, 205, 230, 235
veterans, 131, 139, 170, 211, 215, 220
  Black, 212
  Civil War, 20, 36, 74, 77, 104, 114
  reserve, 119
  WWII, 208, 212
Vietnam, 2, 234, 236, 242, 243, 244, 246-248, 266
  Ho Chi Minh, 245
  NLF, 245
  North Vietnam, 242
  red flag of, 245
  TET, 243
vigilante groups, 82, 109
Vinson, Carl, 216, 217, 219, 222, 230
Virginia (Old Dominion), 47, 48, 54, 58, 59, 64,
    66, 123, 127, 136, 235, 282
  William Byrd II, 29
  Civil War, 101
  colonial, 15, 16, 18, 19, 21, 27-29, 31
  division, 205
  Jamestown, 16, 22, 30, 31; militia, 19, 20, 28,
    33, 45, 62, 70, 73, 108
  Norfolk, 80,
  Ohio County, 19
  Revolution, 37, 41, 43, 44; Lord Fairfax, 28
volunteers, 2, 8, 17-19, 21, 25-30, 33, 52, 55, 60,
    64, 67, 68, 71, 76, 77, 83-85, 89, 92-96, 111,
    120, 121, 126-133, 136, 140, 141, 144, 155,
    156, 175, 179, 199, 236, 243, 248, 254, 255,
    260, 261, 266
  army, 257
  Civil War, 100-103, 106, 119, 137
  discipline, 107
  individual, 126, 136, 196
  officers, 127, 128, 132, 148
  state, 131-133
  war, 5, 31, 90, 91, 93, 94, 98, 106, 107
volunteer units, 18, 37, 58, 61, 83, 84, 86, 96,
    100, 110, 113, 128, 155, 263
  with ancient lineages, 18, 43, 57, 66, 83, 84, 86,
    91, 98, 100, 103, 158, 189
  militia, 2, 5, 31, 85, 97, 108, 111
  old, 98, 99, 110
  regiments, 104, 128, 132, 133, 137
Wadsworth, James W., Jr., Sen. N.Y., 303
Walker, Edwin A., MG, 275
Wallace, George, Gov. Ala., 237, 238
Walsh, Ellard A. MG, NGA, 195, 196, 200, 201,
    206, 208-210, 215-219, 221, 226, 227, 257
war, 64, 82, 91, 138, 141, 142, 154, 155, 164,
    169, 172-174, 182, 184, 186, 195, 196, 204,
    208, 214, 218, 244, 245, 248, 257, 260-263,
    265
  American, 2, 50, 132, 140
  deterrent to, 206

short war, 255
WWIII, 216
War, Department, of (US), 81, 83, 91, 95, 103,
    104, 106, 109, 112, 126, 128, 131, 139, 140,
    142-146, 148, 149, 151, 152, 156, 157, 162,
    165, 166, 169, 171, 172, 174, 181, 184
  Circular 347, 196, 199
  Division of Militia Affairs, 143, 149: BG Robert
    K. Evans, chf., 143; MG Albert L. Mills, 143;
    Col. Erasmus M. Weaver, chf., 143
War, Secretary of the Department of, 63, 66, 71,
    82, 83, 103, 149
  assistant, 143, 171; Russell Alger, 129; John
    Armstrong, 72-74; Newton D. Baker, 152,
    157, 169; James Barbour, 81; John C.
    Calhoun, 82; Lindley, Garrison, 147, 152;
    Henry Knox, 51-53; James Monroe, 74; Joel R.
    Poinsett, 82; Elihu Root, see entry; Henry
    Stimson, 206
War of 1812, 66, 69, 75-77, 81, 86, 88, 91, 94,
    142, 262, 266
  battles: Bladensburg, 73; Detroit, 68; Ft. Erie, 71;
    Horseshoe Bend, 76; New Orleans, 76, 77, 79;
    Plattsburg, 70, 74, 79; Queenstown, 68;
    Thames, 79
  Black units, 77
  commanders, US: James Barron, 65; Jacob
    Brown, 71, 72, 75; John Coffee, 76; Henry
    Dearborn, 69; Amos Hall, 71; Wade Hampton,
    69; William Hull, 68, 69; George Izard, 72;
    Andrew Jackson, see entry; Richard Mentor
    Johnson, 75; George McClure, 71; Thomas
    Macdonough, 74; Alexander Macomb, 74;
    Benjamin Mooers, 70, 74; Zebulon M. Pike,
    69; Peter Buel Porter, see entry; Samuel Smith,
    73-75; Alexander Smyth, 69; John Stricker, 74;
    Stephen Van Rensselaer, 68, 69; William
    Winder, 73; John E. Wool, 95
  commanders, British: George Cockburn, 72, 73;
    LTG Sir George Prevost, 72, 74; Robert Ross,
    72, 73
wars, minor, US
  Aroostook, 90
  Brooks-Baxter, 109
  Buckshot, 90
  Mormon, 95
  Walker, 95
Washington, 115, 123, 132, 180, 205, 212
  Seattle, 114, 150
  territory, 95, 99, 114
  Washington, D.C., 72, 74, 91, 98, 99, 101, 155,
    195, 200, 227
Washington, George, 19, 28-30, 37-39, 42-45, 50-
    52, 54, 55
weapons, 7, 9, 16, 17, 34, 63, 83, 92, 99, 105,
    108, 109, 113, 118, 139, 150, 176, 182, 186,
    224, 241, 257, 263, 266; air, 179, 192, 203,
    214, 244; artillery, cannon, 16, 17, 58, 70, 71,
    76-78, 91, 116, 128, 133, 136, 158—coast,
    144; TDs, 185; WWI, 161, 168
  missiles: 22, 223, 229; nuclear, 204, 229, 231,
    255; atomic age, 215, 265; H-bomb, 214;
    Soviet, 219
  other than firearms: Agent Orange, 247; armor,
    16; bayonet, 44, 106, 116, 167, 177, 244;
    grenade, 192; longbow, 8; machete, 132;
    napalm, 247; polearms, 8, 16; sword, 65, 68,
    94
Weaver, Erasmus M., Col. CMB, 143, 268

Webb, Francis, Gov. Va. colony, 21
Weber, LaVern, LTG, CNGB, 253, 256, 269
Webster, Daniel, Sen. N.H., 75
western hemisphere, 179
West Virginia, 101, 112, 113, 115, 123, 150, 175,
    212, 259
White people, 14, 44, 52, 83, 88, 89, 103, 104,
    108, 110, 114, 116, 127, 149, 238-240, 264;
    divisions, 165; National Guard, 241; officers,
    22; supremacy, 109
White, Thomas D., Gen. AFCS, 222
Wickersham, George W., US Atty. Gen., 142
Wilson, Charles E. (Engine Charley), SD, 215, 222
Wilson, Winston P., maj. air div., NGB MG, CNGB,
    Arkansas connection, 223, 268
Wilson, Woodrow, Pres. US, 143, 144, 147, 148,
    151, 154-157
Winstead, William A., Cong. Miss., 217
Wisconsin, 86, 113, 123, 185, 205, 234
  Civil War, 99, 100, 104, 106
  gov., 85
  Milwaukee, 85, 114, 116, 239
  strike, state workers, 258
women, wives, 77, 79, 106, 150, 193, 221, 226,
    229, 246, 249, 250, 253, 264
  Indian, 87, 88
  widow, 89
Wood, Leonard, MG, ACS, 142-144, 146, 147, 152-
    154, 170
Wool, John E., MG, 95
world, 55, 154, 178, 196, 207, 221, 242, 248, 263,
    265
  history, 173
  new, 8, 15, 34, 125
  old, 34, 116
  post-WWII, 195
World War I (WWI), the Great War, 2, 6, 50, 141,
    146, 149, 152, 168-173, 177, 181, 182, 185-
    187, 189, 192, 195, 196, 206, 209, 260, 262,
    263, 266
  Allies, 166-168
  armistice, 164
  Australia in, 167
  battles: Cantigny, 166; Hamel, 167; Marne, 167,
    168; Meuse, Argonne, 162, 163; Seicheprey,
    166
  cooties, 168; divisions: 26th, 158, 159, 162, 164,
    166, 168, 301; 27th, 159, 161, 162, 164, 170,
    302; 28th, 159, 161, 163, 164, 166, 168, 302;
    29th, 160, 168; 30th, 159, 164, 302; 31st,
    158, 159; 32nd, 129, 164, 168, "Les
    Terribles," 192, 302; 33rd, 159, 164, 167,
    302; 34th, 158, 159, 164, 302; 35th, 159,
    162, 164, 166, 168, 302; 36th, 160, 162, 164,
    165; 37th, 160, 164; 38th, 158, 160, 164,
    302; 39th, 158, 160, 164, 168, 302; 40th,
    158, 160, 161, 163, 164; 41st, 158, 160, 164;
    42nd (Rainbow), 158, 160, 164, 166, 189,
    302
  commanders, US: BG Frank E. Bamford, 162; MG
    Clarence E. Edwards, 162; BG John A. Hulen,
    162; Gen. Peyton C. March, see entry; BG
    Charles I. Martin, 162, 163; MG John F.
    O'Ryan, see entry; Gen. John J. Pershing, see
    entry; MG George W. Read, 167; MG F.S.
    Strong, 163; MG Peter E. Traub, 162, 263
  First Army: 165; Marshal Ferdinand Foch,
    166-168

World War I *(cont.)*
  national army: 155, 157, 163, 167
  no-man's-land: 168
World War II, 2, 6, 50, 171, 172, 194, 197, 200,
    201, 203, 204, 206, 208, 209, 220, 230, 256,
    260, 262, 263, 266, 267

  battles: Bulge, 189; cross-channel, 192;
    Guadalcanal, 187; Omaha Beach, 192; Pearl
    Harbor, 194; Rapido River, 193; Saipan, Sicily,
    188

  commanders, US: Gen. H.H. Arnold, 186; Gen.
    Mark Clark, 193, 194; BG Paul Cota, 192; MG
    Willard S. Paul, 188; LTG Robert C.
    Richardson, 189; LTG Holland M. Smith, MG
    Ralph C. Smith, 189; MG Fred L. Walker, 193,
    194

  D Day, 188, 192; ETO, 187, 188, 192, 194-196,
    200; Stanley Range, 193; New Guinea, 192;
    North Africa, 188, 193; Pacific Theater, 187-
    189, 192, 194; post-war, 257, 261; sec. of
    war, 231

  units: arty. battalions, 190, 191; National Guard
    divisions: Americal, 187, 188, 190, 194; 26th,
    188, 190, 192; 27th, 188, 189, 190; 28th,
    188, 189; "bloody bucket," 190, 192; 29th,
    188, 190, 192; 30th, 188, 190, 192; 31st, 188,
    190; 32nd, 187, 188, 190, 192, 193; 33rd,
    188, 190, 193; 34th, 187, 188, 190, 193;
    35th, 188, 190; 36th, 188, 190, 193, 194;
    37th, 188, 190; 38th, 188, 190; 40th, 188,
    190; 41st, 188, 191; 42nd, 188, 191; 43rd,
    188, 191; 44th, 188, 191; 45th, 188, 191,
    194. National Guard regiments: 190, 191,
    193; 69th, 189; 105th, 189; 116th, 192;
    126th, 193; 132nd, 194; 135th, 193; 164th,
    187, 194; 182nd, 188, 194; TF 6814, 194
VE Day, 187; 101st Airborne Div., 189
Wyoming, 123, 131, 132, 180, 217, 258
Yankees, 91